MW00592866

Reviewing
Global History
and
Geography

SECOND EDITION

HENRY BRUN
Principal (Ret.), John Jay High School
New York City

LILLIAN FORMAN
Social Studies Writer and Researcher

HERBERT BRODSKY
District Coordinator for Social Studies
Freeport School District, N.Y.

AMSCO SCHOOL PUBLICATIONS, INC.,
a division of Perfection Learning®

Reviewers and Consultants

Vincent Asaro
Teacher, Social Studies
Franklin Delano Roosevelt High School
New York City

Edward W. Berg
Assistant Principal, Social Studies
Murry Bergtraum High School
New York City

Cornelius Cahill
Social Studies Department Chairperson
Highland High School
Highland, N.Y.

Sheila Kavovit
Assistant Principal, Social Studies
John F. Kennedy High School
New York City

Ann-Jean Paci
Assistant Principal, Social Studies
Sheepshead Bay High School
Brooklyn, N.Y.

Mary Ann Pluchino
Global Studies Teacher
Kings Park High School
Kings Park, N.Y.

Mark D. Rothman
Social Studies Department Chairperson
Paul D. Schreiber High School
Port Washington, N.Y.

Stephen A. Shultz
Social Studies Coordinator
Rocky Point Public Schools
Rocky Point, N.Y.

Cover and Text Design: Wanda Kossak
Maps, Charts, Graphs: Tech-Graphics
Compositor: Northeastern Graphic, Inc.

Please visit our Web sites at:

www.amscopub.com and *www.perfectionlearning.com*

When ordering this book, please specify:
14789 *or*
REVIEWING GLOBAL HISTORY AND GEOGRAPHY, SECOND EDITION

ISBN 978-1-56765-679-4

Copyright © 2008 by Amsco School Publications, Inc.,
a division of Perfection Learning®

No part of this book may be reproduced in any form without written permission from the publisher.

Printed in the United States of America

5 6 7 8 9 10   20 19 18 17 16 15 14

PREFACE

Reviewing Global History and Geography is designed to help students in grades nine and ten review this wide-ranging subject and prepare for the New York State Regents examination.

Historical topics are in outline form—numbered main topics and lettered subtopics. The basic facts and ideas are illustrated and enlivened by maps, time-lines, photos, prints, cartoons, charts, and graphs. As much as possible, general ideas are presented in the context of specific events.

Our goal is to lead students as easily as possible through this complex two-year course. The reading level is carefully coordinated with student abilities. Mid-chapter info checks provide step-by-step reinforcement, while chapter and unit reviews familiarize students with Regents-level exercises: multiple choice, traditional and skill-oriented; thematic essays; document-based questions and essays. Both forms of review build knowledge while bolstering test-taking confidence.

The eight units comprise an overview and 30 chapters. The overview discusses methods and tools used by historians and geographers and the major concepts they formulate. The chapters cover the major historical themes and issues set forth in the New York State curriculum. The focus is on global connections and linkages: cultural diffusion, migrations, multiregional empires, belief systems, trade, and conflict. The experiences of women and ethnic minorities are intrinsic to the coverage throughout.

Four important features conclude the presentation. The student's study guide acquaints students with basic study techniques and test-taking strategies. The glossary defines all vocabulary terms that appear in bold type in the text. The index facilitates searching for key names, ideas, and terms. Finally, three Regents examinations reinforce the review and give students realistic test-taking experience.

Henry Brun
Lillian Forman
Herbert Brodsky

PHOTO CREDITS

1 AKG **2** Borromeo/Art Resource, NY **5** Library of Congress **11** Giraudon/Art Resource, NY **13** British Museum, London, UK/Bridgeman Art Library **19** Yat Min Chan/Image Bank **22** IFA Bilderteam/eStock **35** Adam Woolfitt/Woodfin Camp **37** Louvre, Paris, France/Bridgeman Art Library **47** Werner Forman/Art Resource, NY **49** Oronoz, Madrid **54** Alexander Low/Woodfin Camp **56** Bibliothèque Nationale, Paris **61** Corbis **62** Scala/Art Resource, NY **65** New York Public Library **75** *top and bottom*: Laurie Platt Winfrey, Inc. **83** Science Museum, London, UK/Bridgeman Art Library **85** Bibliothèque Royale Albert Iᵉʳ Brussels **94** *top*: The Granger Collection, New York; *bottom:* Corbis **96** North Wind Pictures Archives **101** Giraudon/Art Resource, NY **103** Marteen II Mytens or Meytens (1695–1770), Schloss Schöenbrunn, Vienna, Austria/Bridgeman Art Library **116** Vidler/eStock **118** Fritz Henle/Photo Researchers **120** A. Ramey/Woodfin Camp **125** Marc and Evelyn Bernheim/Woodfin Camp **128** The Granger Collection, New York, **134** AMNH neg. #4051(2) (photo by Chesek/Beckett) courtesy Department of Library Services, American Museum of Natural History **143** *left*: Corbis; *right*: The Granger Collection, New York **144** Corbis **146** The Granger Collection, New York **152** Courtesy of John Carter Brown Library at Brown University **153** Giraudon/Art Resource, NY **162** Brown Brothers **164** Museum of Modern Art, New York. Abby Aldrich Rockefeller Fund © 2000 The Museum of Modern Art, New York **172** UPI/Corbis-Bettmann **177** White House **180** Mary Evans Picture Library **183** Corbis **184** *top*: Alinari/Art Resource, NY; *bottom*: Metropolitan Museum of Art, Bequest of Mrs. H.O. Havemeyer, 1929 **186** Mary Evans Picture Library **196** Stock Montage **197** Theodore Roosevelt Collection, Harvard University Library **206** The Granger Collection, New York **207** UPI/Corbis-Bettmann **208** UPI/Corbis-Bettmann **215** Mary Evans Picture Library **218** © 2000 Artists Rights Society (ARS), New York/ADAGP, Paris Estate of Marcel Duchamp, Philadelphia Museum of Art/Bridgeman Art Library **224** Mary Evans Picture Library **225** Corbis-Bettmann **227** Bildarchiv Preussicher Kulturbesitz **235** Holland, Nashville Banner, 1940 **240** Library of Congress **245** The Granger Collection, New York **250** Corbis-Bettmann **256** Robert Nickelsburg/Gamma Liaison **258** J. Langevin/Sygma **269** Ulli Michel/Reuters **271** A. Johannes/Sygma **275** © Shanks, *Buffalo News* **276** © 1962 *Herblock: A Cartoonist's Life*, Times Books, 1998 **277** D. Aubert/Sygma **279** Stringer Russia/Reuters **281** Petr Josek Snr/Reuters **285** © 1989 by Herblock in *The Washington Post* **287** STR New/Reuters **290** Str Old/Reuters **291** Aventurier-Buu-Hires/Gamma Liaison **297** Jerome Delay/AP/Wide World **303** © 1979 Herblock **310** Luc Delahaye/Sipa Press **313** AUTH © 1998 **321** left: Corbis; *right*: Gamma Liaison **326** Jagadeesh N.V/Reuters

CONTENTS

Methods of the Social Sciences: An Overview

I. HISTORY: THE HUMAN STORY

History is the chronological story of the human race and its many civilizations. Historians examine the ideas, actions, and words of earlier peoples as well as the political, geographic, economic, military, and cultural forces that shaped their lives. These patterns help us understand the impact that the past has had on us.

A. Historical Evidence

The historian combines logical thinking with a careful search for evidence of the past, such as:

- **Documents:** written records of a people—books, reports, letters, and government papers
- **Epigraphs:** inscriptions on monuments and buildings
- **Artifacts:** physical remains of a people—tools, weapons, clothes, money, household goods, and food, mummies, and skeletons
- **Literature:** poetry, stories, myths, and legends revealing a people's thoughts, beliefs, religion, and values
- **Graphics:** a people's art, architecture, sculpture, jewelry, and interior decoration

Historians must research, analyze, and interpret such evidence objectively and without bias. They must willingly accept conclusions arising from the evidence that contradict their previously held theories.

B. Early Historians

Some people in every society have been knowledgeable about the past. Early historians usually relied on memory rather than written records. In some preliterate societies, poet-historians called **skalds** created historical poems called **sagas**. They recounted genealogies of royal families, important events, and stories of how deities interacted with mortals. Sagas were passed down through the generations by word of mouth as **oral histories**. So were **epics**, long poems about legendary or historical heroes.

As societies developed writing, it became more common to preserve sagas and epics as written history.

C. Periodization

Periodization is the method by which historians study how cultures and civilizations of the

Fierce animal carved in wood decorates the prow of a Norse ship.

Ancient Egyptian model in stucco and painted wood showing granary workers

same period differed and interacted. Usually, great patterns of political, cultural, and economic development and change occur during a particular period. These patterns make the period distinct.

D. Critical-Thinking Skills

To reach conclusions based on evidence, historians must develop **critical-thinking skills**, which enable them to obtain and process information and use it to arrive at conclusions. They are:

- **Analysis:** separating basic facts and ideas to better understand an issue or problem

- **Inference:** noting facts or ideas to reach a conclusion

- **Judgment:** weighing evidence to form an opinion

- **Hypothesizing:** stating an idea or theory and testing whether it is a fact

- **Generalization:** making a statement of opinion that is not particular or specific

- **Prediction:** using observation, experience, or reasoning to describe a future event or result

Sites of the Earliest Agricultural Communities

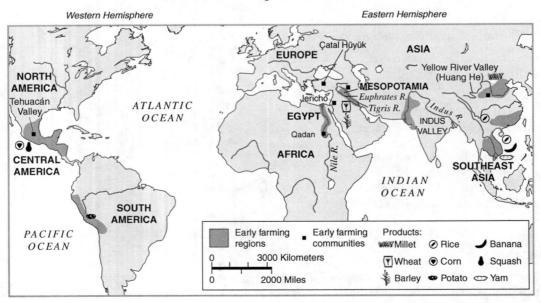

II. GEOGRAPHY: A PHYSICAL VIEW OF THE WORLD

Geography is the scientific study of Earth and its place in the universe. Geographers identify the distribution of people, animals, plants, resources, and industry around the world.

A. The Spatial World

Geographers must study Earth and its components in terms of the space they occupy. Globes and maps help us understand this spatial world by showing how it is put together physically and where its people and places are in relation to one another. Since globes are round, they are the most accurate models of Earth. They let us see where on Earth its continents and oceans are and how they are shaped. Location also provides information about climate, time zones, and distance.

Maps also convey such information and are easier to transport and store. However, since Earth's surface is curved rather than flat, maps must distort the shapes of some parts of the planet.

Maps depict as accurately as possible the sizes, shapes, and locations of Earth's landforms and bodies of water. These include mountains, plateaus, canyons, plains, valleys, lakes, rivers, and oceans. Landforms and bodies of water influence how people live and work.

PLACES AND REGIONS. To better study the physical and human characteristics of places, geographers have divided the world into regions. Each region has physical features, resources, lifestyles, and cultural, economic, political, and historical patterns that set it apart from other regions.

B. Interpretation of the Past

Historical developments such as agriculture, trade, cities, and government often arise as a result of geographical features. Examples include fertile soil, abundant water, and great rivers such as the Nile, Tigris, Euphrates, Indus, and Huang He, which deposit arable floodplains and serve as transportation and communication routes. The Egyptian, Mesopotamian, Indus, and Chinese civilizations arose near these rivers.

Geography also plays a role in the decline of civilizations. Climate changes, volcanic activity, and earthquakes have destroyed great civilizations. Profiting from knowledge of natural disasters in the past, geographers help governments understand contemporary problems and plan for the future. They use maps, charts, and land and climate graphs to help them predict the impact of environmental changes on present-day civilizations.

Statistical studies, field research, and computer technology compile and analyze the data needed for effective interpretation and planning. For example, geographers use these tools to analyze volcanic eruptions and hurricanes, assess their impact on people and places, and determine how effective government preparations will be.

III. ECONOMICS: SEARCH FOR SECURITY AND PROSPERITY

Economics is the study of the production and consumption of goods and services. It is also concerned with other matters—taxation, business organization and operation, banking, money, and insurance. Economic forces determine whether people obtain the necessities of life and how comfortably they live.

A. Major Economic Concepts

Before money was invented, people used **barter** (trading goods and services one has for those one wants). Later, people assigned value to desirable goods such as salt, cacao, beans, shells, or furs, and they became a type of **currency** (money). People then exchanged these prevalued goods for whatever they needed or wanted. Decisions had to be made about what goods were essential and how to obtain them. Making decisions about buying and selling is the very basis of economics.

ECONOMIC VOCABULARY. All people are **consumers**; they buy goods and services. Goods are items of value that can be seen or touched—a computer, automobile, or book. Services are intangible things of value—health care, education, and legal advice. Societies have **limited resources** (natural sources of wealth), which cause **scarcity**. Very scarce resources, such as gold or diamonds, are very valuable.

The laws of supply and demand determine how resources are distributed. **Supply** is the quantity of available goods and services at whatever prices are placed on them. **Demand** is the quantity of goods and services that consumers want to buy at fair prices. **Price** is the deciding factor. If prices are too low, sellers make no profits even if they sell a lot of goods. If prices are too high, consumers will not buy. The price of a good or service, therefore, is determined by supply and demand.

B. Economic Systems

There are three types of economic systems in the world today. In the **traditional economy**, families and their community produce basic necessities. People in such an economy survive by farming, herding, fishing, or a combination of all three. In a **command economy**, by contrast, government controls industry and agriculture by deciding on producers, products, quantities, and prices. In a **market economy** (capitalist system), people and businesses decide what to produce, sell, and purchase; means of production are privately owned, and businesses compete for profits. The market economy is most responsive to the laws of supply and demand. Businesses produce what they think consumers want and sell at prices that consumers are willing to pay.

Today, countries far distant from one another have become trading partners. Thus, regional economies are globally **interdependent**. An economic crisis in one region can spread rapidly to other regions.

Regional economic associations have strengthened interdependence. By joining together to establish a regional market, neighboring countries have removed barriers to the free movement of goods and services across their borders. International organizations now try to deal with widespread economic crises.

In the 21st century, political and economic leaders in pursuit of national prosperity have shown a preference for cooperation rather than unlimited competition.

IV. POLITICAL SCIENCE: GOVERNING NATIONS AND PEOPLES

A government is a nation's system of keeping order and making decisions. Government springs from customs and laws that allow people to live with one another and with other groups.

Politics is the science of government. Political scientists study the ideas and beliefs behind different forms of government and how citizens relate to these systems. They also consider how laws are created and enforced, leaders chosen, and group decisions made.

A. Purposes of Government

The earliest governments mainly controlled land, resources, and people. Rulers imposed taxes; with the proceeds, they paid soldiers to enforce royal authority, built royal palaces, and bought luxuries and slaves for their own comfort.

NATURAL RIGHTS. In time, governments became responsible for the people's well-being. In the 17th and 18th centuries, British and French political scientists developed the theory of **natural rights**: people were born with rights to liberty and the possession of property, and governments were formed to protect these rights. Some thinkers went further: if governments did not fulfill this basic purpose, citizens had a right to overthrow them by force.

DEMOCRACY VERSUS TOTALITARIANISM. Citizens of the United States and many other nations benefit from the **rule of law** and the rights and freedoms guaranteed to individuals in democratic societies.

Democracies are expected to guarantee basic freedoms—speech, press, religion, assembly—and to act in their people's best interests. Democratic leaders are elected to promote and protect the common good. Citizens, therefore, have a responsibility to be educated about political, economic, and legal matters in order to make informed decisions about issues and candidates for public office.

A **totalitarian state** imposes total control over its citizens, who have few rights. The needs of government are placed before the needs of people. Totalitarian governments enact laws designed to keep one political party and its leaders in power. The party chooses the lawmakers. Criticism of government policies is not tolerated.

A democracy enacts laws to reflect its citizens' concerns, problems, and needs. Eligible voters elect lawmakers. A system of checks and balances makes sure that lawmakers and law enforcers share power.

In a totalitarian state, the police and the military exist to control the population and prevent its opposition to the government and the ruling party. In a democracy, police and security services maintain public law and order and defend the population against military threats. Law enforcers are responsible to elected local and national officials, who have a duty to see that they function as servants of the people.

V. CULTURE AND CIVILIZATION

The wide range of ideas, feelings, beliefs, and habits that members of a society share is a major part of their **culture**. Understanding any culture lies in examining its many elements—language, dress, religion, art, architecture, family structure, education, economic organization, government, and technology.

Artist's rendering of fabled West African city of Timbuktu

A. Significance of Civilization

Throughout history, cultures have united to form civilizations. A **civilization** is a large group of cultures with a high degree of social and technological development.

Social scientists use the term **Western civilization** to designate the inclusive cultures of the Americas and Europe. Asia's cultures— China, Japan, the Indian subcontinent, and the island chains of the vast Pacific region—make up **Eastern civilization**.

B. Importance of Cities, Literacy, and Technology

Some historians have defined civilization as the **culture of cities**. They believe that cities as political, social, and cultural centers are marks of civilized societies. The art, architecture, religion, commerce, and government that distinguish each civilization were developed in its cities. Then, by land and sea, these cultural features were carried out from the cities to influence the rest of the world. One culture's borrowing of another culture's useful and attractive elements is known as **cultural diffusion**.

WRITTEN LANGUAGES AND CIVILIZATION. Literacy is a key element in any civilization. Writing systems were developed by civilized societies to keep records and to pass on to future generations the cumulative ideas—literature, history, science, religion, and so on—that reflect their way of life.

TECHNOLOGICAL DEVELOPMENT. The development of technology is another important characteristic of civilizations. Civilized societies learn to understand the uses of metals and power sources to produce tools, weapons, and other products, whether for efficient production or for luxury and amusement.

UNIT I

Ancient World (4000 B.C.–A.D. 500)

Year	Dates and Events

B.C.

4000 — **4000 B.C.:** Rise of Sumer civilization in Fertile Crescent (Mesopotamia)

3000 B.C.: Unification of Upper and Lower Egypt
Peak of Yellow River (Huang He) civilization in China

2500–1500 B.C.: Rise and decline of Indus Valley civilization

3001

1750–1122 B.C.: Shang Dynasty in China

1650 B.C.: Rise of Minoan (Crete) and Mycenaean (Greece) civilizations

3000

1122–221 B.C.: Zhou Dynasty in China

587–538 B.C.: Babylonian Captivity of Jews

550 B.C.: Spread of Persian rule from India to Aegean Sea

509–508 B.C.: Romans overthrow Etruscans, set up first democratic republic

2001

480–479 B.C.: Persians defeat Spartans at Thermopylae; Athenians defeat Persians at Salamis

2000

431–404 B.C.: Three Peloponnesian wars between Athens and Sparta

343 B.C.: End of 30th (last) Dynasty in Egypt
Rome begins conquest of Italy, makes Latin official language

1001

334 B.C.: Alexander the Great begins 11-year conquest from Greece to Indus River Valley

1000

321–185 B.C.: Maurya Dynasty in India; rise and spread of Buddhism

200s B.C.: Rise of Silk Road trade between China and India, Middle East, and Mediterranean

264–146 B.C.: Punic Wars; Carthage destroyed, Rome controls Mediterranean

1

206–A.D. 220: Han Dynasty in China

A.D.

27 B.C.–A.D. 180: Golden Age of Roman civilization (Pax Romana)

1

A.D. 33: Crucifixion of Jesus; rise of Christianity

A.D. 232: Spread of Buddhism to Southeast Asia, China, Korea, Japan

A.D. 320–567: Gupta Empire, India's golden age

A.D. 324: Emperor Constantine reunites Roman Empire, moves capital to Constantinople

1000

A.D. 622: Muhammad's Hegira to Medina; rise of Islam

CHAPTER
1

Rise of Societies and Civilization

I. THE STONE AGE (BEFORE 4000 B.C.)

The term **hominid** refers to prehumans, early humans, and modern humans. Human beings originated in the savannas (grasslands) of central and southern Africa. *Homo sapiens* (wise humans) were hominids that were fully human but lacked some features of modern humans. Modern humans are known as *Homo sapiens sapiens* (wise, wise humans).

During the Stone Age, hominids began to make tools and weapons from stone, wood, and bone and developed from prehumans into *Homo sapiens sapiens*. The Stone Age had three divisions:

- Old Stone Age (500,000 to 10,000 years ago)

- Middle Stone Age (10,000 to 8000 years ago)

- New Stone Age, or Neolithic period (8000 to 5000 years ago)

A. Human Life During the Old and Middle Stone Ages

The earliest humans did not farm; they gathered wild plants and hunted small animals. They traveled on set routes through wide-ranging territories. When the animal and plant resources in one place were temporarily used up, the hunter-gatherers moved to another.

These hunter-gatherer groups multiplied and spread northward in Africa. Between 300,000 and 100,000 years ago, North Africa became warmer and wetter, and the climate changed. The North African area now known as the Sahara became wetter, and grassland replaced desert. This change made it possible for early humans to branch out into the Middle East and Europe.

NEANDERTHALS. **Neanderthals** were humans who belonged to the group *Homo sapiens*. They lived between 100,000 and 30,000 years ago and migrated from Africa to Europe and the Middle East.

Survival Techniques. Neanderthals lived during the last Ice Age, which lasted from 2 million to about 10,000 years ago. Harsh conditions in Europe and the Middle East forced them to develop important survival techniques. They invented new weapons and tools. They built hearths, which helped them control fire. They made clothing out of animal skins.

Cultural Developments. Neanderthals also showed advances in culture. They buried their dead in ways that suggest belief in an afterlife. They made objects that resembled flutes and ornamental jewelry.

Disappearance. **Cro-Magnons**, who belonged to the group *Homo sapiens sapiens,* also migrated to Europe and Asia from Africa. For a while, Neanderthals and Cro-Magnons coexisted. Then, for unknown reasons, the Neanderthals disappeared.

CRO-MAGNON PEOPLE

Technology. Cro-Magnons developed a greater variety of tools and weapons and more advanced skills than the Neanderthals.

Culture. Cro-Magnon burial sites show good evidence of a belief in an afterlife. Cro-Magnons produced art—painted images on cave walls and carved figures of people and animals. Such art was probably linked to magical or religious ceremonies.

INFO CHECK

1. Explain how environmental change affected the ability of hunter-gatherers to expand outward.

2. Define the following terms: hominids, Homo sapiens, Homo sapiens sapiens, Neanderthals, Cro-Magnons.

3. State two ways in which Neanderthals and Cro-Magnons differed.

Sites of Prehistoric Peoples and Spread of Modern Humans

B. Human Life During the New Stone Age

During the late Middle Stone Age and early New Stone Age, technology advanced so rapidly that scientists call the period the **Neolithic Revolution** (a revolution is a sudden or complete change in the state of things).

RISE OF FARMING. The greatest change of the Neolithic period was in how people obtained food. About 8000 B.C., people in the Middle East began to grow grain. **Agriculture**, or farming, became more important than hunting and gathering.

Impact. People began to make specialized farm tools and pottery to store food. They domesticated animals and learned to weave.

Since farming led to food **surpluses** (more than was needed), trading increased.

SOCIAL CLASS AND CONFLICT. In the competition for fertile land, some people became very rich and others very poor. Poor people borrowed from the rich and then worked for them to pay off their debts. Some wealthy landowners began to rule large numbers of people who worked and pledged their loyalty for food, shelter, and protection. Competition also led to war over the ownership of large tracts of land.

FARMING COMMUNITIES

Towns. Farming communities flourished and grew into towns. Scholars have learned what they were like from such ruins as those in Çatal Hüyük,

a farming town in present-day Turkey. The ruins date from 9000 years ago.

Pastoral Societies. Pastoral societies consisted of people who herded animals. They moved from place to place to find grazing areas. Herding people had close family ties, shared resources with one another and other groups, and enjoyed more equality than people in farming communities. Pastoral women and men shared tasks.

AGE OF METALS. About 5000 years ago, people in the Middle East began to use metals, such as copper and bronze, to make tools and weapons.

INFO CHECK

1. Complete each sentence:
   • During the Middle Stone Age, human technology advanced because _____.
   • Among the great changes brought by the Neolithic Revolution were _____.
2. Explain how the Neolithic Revolution brought competition and conflict to human society.
3. State the significance of Çatal Hüyük.

II. BEGINNING OF CIVILIZATIONS (AFTER 4000 B.C.)

A **civilization** is a large group of people with a high degree of social and technological development. Civilization resulted from the development of agriculture, the population increase that agriculture brought about, and the need to solve problems posed by the environment.

Because human survival depended on agriculture, early civilizations took root in fertile areas around rivers. Besides fertile soil and water, the rivers provided fish for food and a means of transporting people and goods. The first civilizations began to form when people in river areas built canals to irrigate their crops and dikes (walls of earth) to protect their fields and cities from floods.

A. Early Civilizations and Their Characteristics

MESOPOTAMIA

First City-States. Beginning about 4000 B.C., the Sumerians of the Middle East settled part of an area between the Tigris and Euphrates rivers, which is known as the **Fertile Crescent**. Swampy areas separated settlements, causing them to develop into isolated **city-states**. A city-state included a city and the farms and villages around it.

Beginnings of Empire. After a period of unity under a leader named Sargon, the city-states of Mesopotamia fought among themselves. Weakened by war, they fell under the control of a foreign ruler named Hammurabi (1792–1750 B.C.). The city-states became part of the many lands and cultures he ruled as an **empire**.

EGYPT

Two Early Kingdoms. Beginning about 4000 B.C., the Egyptians established cities beside the Nile River in northern Africa. The cities were grouped into two kingdoms—Upper Egypt in the south and Lower Egypt in the north.

Dynastic Rule. The rulers of the two Egyptian kingdoms were called **pharaohs**. About 3000 B.C., the pharaoh Menes united Upper and Lower Egypt. He established Egypt's first **dynasty** (a succession of rulers from the same family).

INDUS VALLEY. An early Indian people in South Asia built a civilization near the Indus River in what is now Pakistan. Two cities, Harappa and Mohenjo-Daro, flourished from around 2500 to 1500 B.C.

HUANG HE CIVILIZATION. Chinese farmers in East Asia developed a civilization beside the Huang He between 3000 and 2500 B.C. When this river flooded, it brought a rich yellow soil called **loess** to the area.

TRADITIONAL ECONOMIES. The economies of these early civilizations were based mainly on agriculture. Farm surpluses led the way to **specialization**; people became full-time craftsworkers or merchants. Eventually, craftwork and trade became as important as agriculture.

GOVERNMENT AND LAW. A strong central authority was necessary to organize the building and maintenance of canal and flood control systems. This power was given to governments, which also controlled roads and city walls and raised taxes to pay for them. Rulers made laws to keep order and raised armies to defend their people. Kings often shared these powers and responsibilities with priests.

An Early Law Code. Hammurabi, ruler of the Babylonian Empire, developed one of the first written law codes. Written law codes made the laws of the land clear to the population. The 300 laws of Hammurabi's Code strengthened the central government by identifying crimes, setting punishments for criminals, regulating business practices, and establishing the legal rights of citizens.

BUREAUCRACIES. Civil-service bodies called **bureaucracies** were made up of ministers, priests, nobles, and governors working directly for the government. In Egypt and China, bureaucracies made

Stone shaft showing Hammurabi and, inscribed below, a portion of his law code for governing Babylonia

Earliest Civilizations

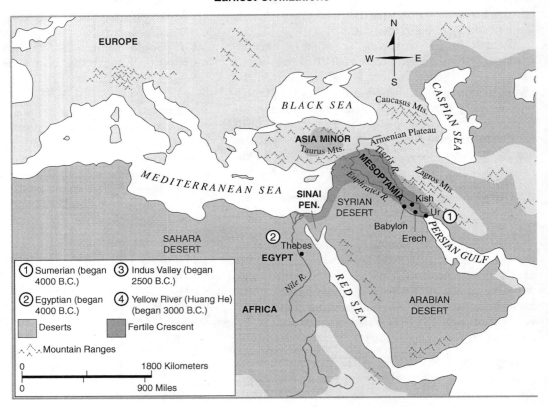

decisions about land ownership, collected taxes, and determined how tax money should be spent.

SOCIAL STRUCTURE OF EARLY CIVILIZATIONS

Fixed Class Systems. In nearly all the early civilizations, kings and priests made up the highest class. Just below them were members of the nobility, who held large tracts of land. Next came commoners, who owned small pieces of land. They had a voice in government and were protected by laws, but they had less power than the nobles. Below the commoners were tenant farmers, who did not own land but worked a noble's land in exchange for using part of it for their own crops. The lowest class included criminals, debtors, and prisoners of war who had been enslaved. In most civilizations, women seldom had political power or owned businesses.

Patriarchies. Early societies were **patriarchies**. The father ruled the household. The family was known by the father's last name and traced its descent from male ancestors.

Indus Valley—A Possible Exception. The ruins of the Indus Valley cities give little evidence of social class. Some scholars believe that Indus Valley societies were **matriarchies**. That is, families traced their descent from female ancestors.

INFO CHECK

1. Identify the similarities between the economies of the early civilizations.

2. List an important fact about government in Mesopotamia, Egypt, and China.

3. Determine which statements are correct:
   - The women of most early civilizations did not have equality with men.
   - Priests had little power in Mesopotamian society.
   - Egyptian workers paid no taxes.
   - There is little evidence of social classes in Indus Valley civilization.

RELIGIONS. Religions of early civilizations were strongly influenced by their environments. The peoples of Mesopotamia, Egypt, the Indus Valley, and China all believed that their gods controlled the forces of nature.

Mesopotamia. Mesopotamians believed that their gods were responsible for the floods that ruined their crops, so they viewed these gods as harsh and unpredictable. Only the gods, they thought, enjoyed true immortality (eternal life). When humans died, they entered a realm of shadows.

Earliest Civilizations (*Continued*)

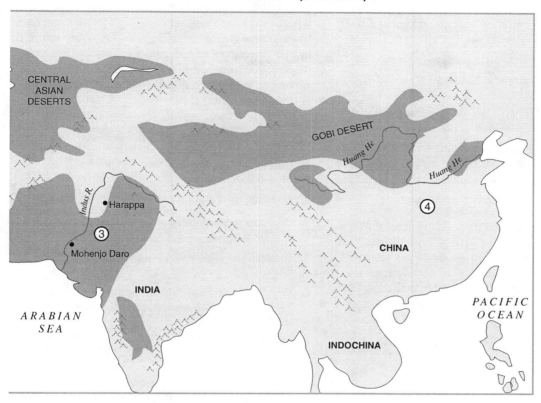

Egypt. Egypt's environment was less harsh than Mesopotamia's. Egyptians believed in kinder gods that gave the souls of humans eternal life. When a person died, the god Osiris judged whether that person had led a just life. If so, that soul could enter Osiris's kingdom.

Egyptians also believed that each person had a special life force that could return to the body after death. This belief led to the **mummification** (preservation) of corpses.

Indus Valley. Scholars believe that the people of the Indus Valley worshiped a nature goddess. Carvings of female figures have been uncovered, as well as the remains of a great public bathing pool, possibly used for religious ceremonies.

China. The Chinese believed in an afterlife and felt that dead ancestors could persuade the nature gods to give them good crops. This belief may have developed into the ancestor worship common in China's later periods.

WRITING SYSTEMS. Scholars do not know when writing was invented. As civilizations developed, it became necessary to keep business records, write down law codes, and document property ownership.

Mesopotamia. Specimens of writing dating back to about 3300 B.C. have been found in Mesopotamia. This writing is in the form of wedge-shaped marks called **cuneiform**. The system contains 700 symbols, each of which stands for a name of an object, idea, or sound.

Gilgamesh is an early example of written Mesopotamian poetry.

Egypt. Specimens of Egyptian writing date from about 3000 B.C. This system of writing is called **hieroglyphics**. It uses pictures to represent sounds, words, and ideas and contains about 600 symbols.

Chinese-script-engraved animal bone of the Shang Dynasty, used for prophecy

Egyptians made the first paper, using papyrus plants. An important example of hieroglyphic writing is the Book of the Dead, a famous collection of ancient Egyptian literature.

Indus Valley. The writing system of the people of the Indus Valley was similar to those of Egyptians and Mesopotamians. It consisted of at least 400 different symbols. To date, scholars have not learned how to read this writing.

China. Early Chinese writing was a complex system containing at least 2000 characters (picture symbols). Only the ruling classes were permitted to learn how to read and write.

CITIES AND ARCHITECTURE. The cities of Mesopotamia, Egypt, the Indus Valley, and China were important religious centers, seats of government, and marketplaces. Buildings were used as temples, palaces, and dwellings. Massive walls kept enemies out of the cities. Building materials varied according to the natural resources and technological skills of each civilization.

SCIENCE AND TECHNOLOGY

Mesopotamia. Sumerians originated the manufacture of bronze and the use of wheels.

Babylonian astronomers used their knowledge of the stars and planets to develop a 12-month **lunar calendar** based on the phases of the moon. Babylonian mathematicians created an arithmetic system based on the number 60. From this, they developed the 60-minute hour and the 360-degree circle. Babylonians also made accurate maps, as had earlier Mesopotamians.

Egypt. Egyptians invented the formula for mummifying corpses; their method has never been learned. Egyptian doctors performed complicated surgery and developed prescriptions for painkilling medications.

Like the Babylonians, Egyptians had a 12-month calendar. In addition, they invented a number system based on 10 and developed a system of geometry.

Indus Valley. The people of the Indus Valley constructed advanced drainage systems for their cities, used wheels, and manufactured bronze artifacts.

China. The ancient Chinese learned to cast bronze that was superior to that found in other early civilizations.

Chinese potters used a fine white clay called *kaolin* to make dishes and ornaments. Chinese clothmakers wove the fibers produced by silkworms into silk.

DEMOGRAPHIC PATTERNS. Cities of early civilizations had very diverse populations. The people who moved into walled cities for protection came from many different villages and from nomadic herding groups. Indeed, many cities contained people from a number of villages that had been absorbed into one great population. Differing social classes also made for diversity.

INFO CHECK

1. Contrast religious beliefs in Egypt and Mesopotamia.
2. Describe the origins of ancestor worship in China.
3. Why are writing systems important characteristics of civilizations?
4. Explain the relationship between architecture, natural resources, and technology in early cities.
5. What technological achievements of the Indus Valley civilization made their cities somewhat like modern cities?

B. Interactions of Early Civilizations

Scholars have found significant similarities between Sumerian and Egyptian cultures and between the Indus Valley civilization and those of Mesopotamia and Egypt.

Early Chinese civilizations, on the other hand, seem to have developed with little or no contact with cultures to the west.

TRADE. Traders used water routes because boats were a cheap and efficient way to transport goods. Some popular trade items were metals, precious stones, incense, razors, and mirrors.

The Indus Valley people traded with civilizations to the west. Mesopotamian pottery, for example, has been found in the ruins of Indus Valley cities.

ASSYRIAN AGGRESSION. The Assyrians were a warlike group that first took over many established city-states in Mesopotamia. They were a powerful force in the Middle East from about 1813 to 612 B.C. This group eventually conquered an empire that extended from Egypt to Turkey and Iran.

In spite of their militaristic tendencies, Assyrians valued the culture of their time. Their last great king, Ashurbanipal, built a library in the Assyrian capital of Nineveh. This library preserved the literature of the Sumerians and the Babylonians.

EGYPT AND NUBIA. The Nubians were a conquered people that played an important role in the history of early civilization. In 1522 B.C., Egypt

Africa: Nubia and Kush

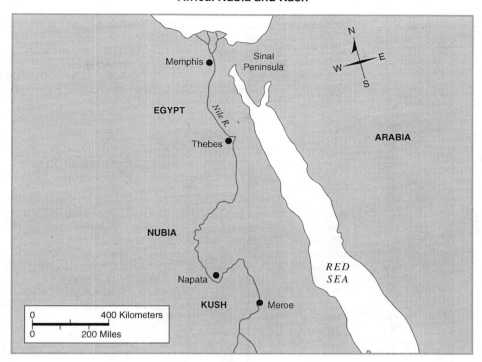

conquered Kush, a part of Nubia. The people of Kush adopted Egyptian culture and preserved it. Later, when Egypt's culture had been destroyed by foreign invaders, it still flourished in Kush.

INFLUENCES WITHIN CHINA. The Shang kingdom was influenced by neighbors with whom it fought border wars. One of these groups, the Zhou, took over the Shang empire. The Zhou created the first legal documents in China. They improved roads and canals, expanded trade, introduced iron, and originated Chinese philosophy.

MIGRATIONS OF INDO-EUROPEANS. Pastoral groups moved into already settled areas when harsh seasons destroyed their own pastures. Sometimes, they joined the existing community peacefully; sometimes they took the communities by force.

The Indo-Europeans were several different groups of herding people from the plains of **Eurasia**, a term describing Europe and Asia as one landmass. Between 2500 and 1000 B.C., waves of these people swept into Europe, the Middle East, and South Asia.

Migrations of Indo-European Peoples

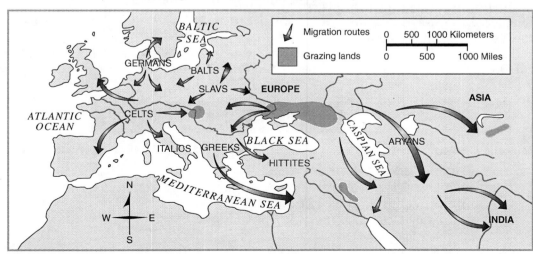

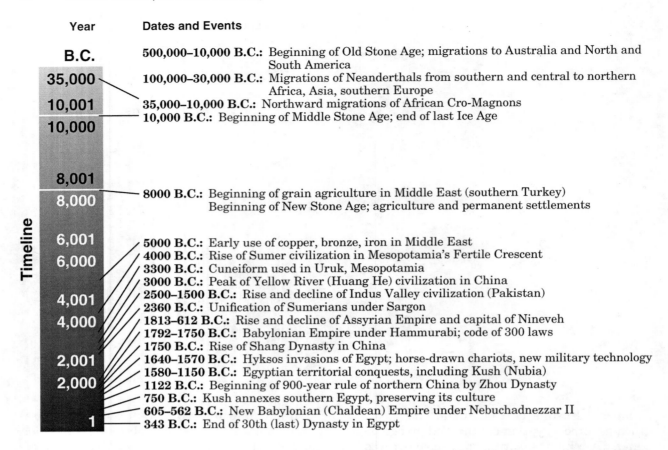

Year	Dates and Events
B.C.	**500,000–10,000 B.C.:** Beginning of Old Stone Age; migrations to Australia and North and South America
35,000	**100,000–30,000 B.C.:** Migrations of Neanderthals from southern and central to northern Africa, Asia, southern Europe
10,001	**35,000–10,000 B.C.:** Northward migrations of African Cro-Magnons
10,000	**10,000 B.C.:** Beginning of Middle Stone Age; end of last Ice Age
8,001	
8,000	**8000 B.C.:** Beginning of grain agriculture in Middle East (southern Turkey) Beginning of New Stone Age; agriculture and permanent settlements
6,001	**5000 B.C.:** Early use of copper, bronze, iron in Middle East
6,000	**4000 B.C.:** Rise of Sumer civilization in Mesopotamia's Fertile Crescent
	3300 B.C.: Cuneiform used in Uruk, Mesopotamia
	3000 B.C.: Peak of Yellow River (Huang He) civilization in China
4,001	**2500–1500 B.C.:** Rise and decline of Indus Valley civilization (Pakistan)
4,000	**2360 B.C.:** Unification of Sumerians under Sargon
	1813–612 B.C.: Rise and decline of Assyrian Empire and capital of Nineveh
	1792–1750 B.C.: Babylonian Empire under Hammurabi; code of 300 laws
	1750 B.C.: Rise of Shang Dynasty in China
2,001	**1640–1570 B.C.:** Hyksos invasions of Egypt; horse-drawn chariots, new military technology
2,000	**1580–1150 B.C.:** Egyptian territorial conquests, including Kush (Nubia)
	1122 B.C.: Beginning of 900-year rule of northern China by Zhou Dynasty
	750 B.C.: Kush annexes southern Egypt, preserving its culture
	605–562 B.C.: New Babylonian (Chaldean) Empire under Nebuchadnezzar II
1	**343 B.C.:** End of 30th (last) Dynasty in Egypt

Timeline

The different Indo-European groups spoke closely related languages. These languages form the basis for most modern European languages and an early Indian language called Sanskrit.

SEMITIC NOMADS

The Hyksos. These nomads from Arabia invaded Egypt between 1640 and 1570 B.C. They contributed advanced military technology to the Egyptians.

Chaldeans. These nomads, also from Arabia, conquered the Assyrian Empire and established the New Babylonian Empire.

The greatest Chaldean emperor, Nebuchadnezzar II (ruled from 605 to 562 B.C.), beautified the city of Babylon and ordered the building of the Hanging Gardens.

Chaldean astrologers tried to foretell the future by observing stars and planets. They also contributed accurate knowledge about the movements of heavenly bodies, predicted solar and lunar eclipses, and calculated the length of a year.

INFO CHECK

1. What evidence is there that early civilizations influenced one another?

2. Why was China influenced more by the Zhou than by Egypt or Mesopotamia?

3. Briefly identify each of the following: Assyrians, Indo-Europeans, Hyksos, Chaldeans.

CHAPTER REVIEW

Multiple Choice

1. Humans who originated in south and central Africa moved from place to place because

   1. weather became too hot or too cold
   2. they ate up all the plants in the area
   3. animals they hunted had moved away
   4. all of the above.

2. People without permanent homes who move from place to place are

   1. farmers
   2. laborers
   3. peasants
   4. nomads.

3. The Neanderthals were able to survive the last Ice Age of Europe and the Middle East because

1. climates were warmer and food plentiful
2. they grew their own food supply
3. they invented weapons and controlled fire
4. the Ice Age ended quickly.

4. Select the group that has the correct title and lifestyle:

1. Neanderthals—Homo sapiens, nomads—hunter-gatherers
2. Cro-Magnon—Homo sapiens, nomads—huntergatherers
3. Neanderthals—Homo sapiens sapiens, nomads—farmers
4. Cro-Magnon—Homo sapiens sapiens, nomads—farmers.

5. Hunter-gatherers survived by

1. working long hours
2. fighting wars
3. spending long hours tilling soil
4. living near rivers and seacoasts.

6. A turning point for human society during the Stone Age was

1. the end of the Ice Age and flooding of dry land
2. metal and iron tools in place of stone ones
3. conquering land in Europe, Asia, Australia, and South America
4. agriculture in place of hunting-gathering as the main food source.

7. The society that required men and women to share the same tasks was

1. pastoral
2. hunting-gathering
3. agricultural
4. warlike.

8. Dynasty means a succession of rulers

1. from the same tribe
2. from the same country
3. from the same religion
4. from the same family.

9. The first city states arose in

1. China
2. Mesopotamia
3. Egypt
4. Pakistan

10. Use the map on pages 12–13 and your knowledge of Global History and Geography to identify three of the earliest centers of civilization.

1. Sahara, Arabian Desert, Gobi Desert
2. Nile River Valley, Tigris-Euphrates River Valley, Indus River Valley
3. Black Sea, Caspian Sea, Red Sea
4. Taurus Mountains, Caucasus Mountains, Zagros Mountains

11. Refer to the timeline on page 16 and identify the empire that existed from 1792 to 1750 B.C.

1. Assyria
2. Babylonia
3. Kush
4. Chaldea

Thematic Essays

1. Select one of the civilizations introduced in the chapter. *Task:* Discuss how political and economic developments were affected by geographic location.

2. *Task:* Describe how the Neolithic Revolution affected the governmental structure of Indus Valley or Mesopotamian civilization.

Document-Based Questions

For each document or illustration, explain the message or intent of the speaker.

1. ". . . Furthermore, due reverence shall be shown to the gods, but to the Storm-god special reverence shall be shown. If some temple has a leaking roof, the commander of the border guards and the town commandant shall put it right, or . . . if the Storm-god or any implement of any other god is in disrepair, the priests, the 'anointed' [and] the mother-of-god shall restore it."

2. "When they perform the ritual at the boundary of the enemy country they sacrifice one sheep to the Sun-goddess of Arena and the Storm-god, the Patron-god [and] all the gods . . . the gods and goddesses of Turmitta . . . to all the mountains [and] rivers."

3. "Hail to thee, O Nile! Who manifest thyself over this land and come to give life to Egypt. . . . Watering the orchards created by Ra to cause all the cattle to live, thou givest the earth to drink, inexhaustible one!"

Document-Based Essay

Task: Use your answers to the previous questions to develop an essay explaining why people of ancient civilizations believed in many gods.

CHAPTER
2

Brilliance of the Classical Age

I. GENERALIZATIONS ABOUT CLASSICAL CIVILIZATIONS

A classical civilization is a society in which intellectual and artistic works achieve enduring value and political thinking identifies government as a system to serve the people it governs.

A. Characteristics of Classical Civilizations

Classical civilizations shared not only the idea that a government should serve its people but also that people had the right to make political decisions.

Once people began to share in government, they asked what constitutes the good life. This concern led to an interest in art, science, and philosophy.

II. CHINA

A. Zhou Dynasty (1027–256 B.C.)

China's classical age began when the Zhou Dynasty replaced the Shang Dynasty. The Zhou kings expanded the kingdom they had won from the Shang. (For the extent of the Zhou Dynasty, see the map on page 19.)

GOVERNMENT. The Zhou kings appointed administrators to run the new states. The administrators recruited poor but well-educated people to responsible positions in a civil service. Thus, China's class structure was relaxed to some extent.

The Zhou justified their rebellion by claiming that the Shang king had been unfit to rule. Thus arose the idea of the *Mandate of Heaven* (a **mandate** is the authority to rule.) According to the Mandate of Heaven, heaven would favor the rule of a king who worked for the people's welfare and cause a bad king to lose the throne. While this suggested that kings had divine support, the man-

date also empowered people to overthrow a king who did not serve them well.

ECONOMY. Under the Zhou, cities and towns grew, and the number of craftspeople and merchants increased. After metalworkers learned how to make iron, iron plows made farmland more productive. Money was coined and used to pay for goods. Coined money replaced barter (the exchange of one item for another), and trade expanded.

CULTURE

Writing. Zhou scholars improved the Shang system of writing. Today, the Chinese use almost the same characters as those developed by the Zhou.

Art. Chinese artists carved beautiful objects from precious materials.

Literature. During the Zhou Dynasty, some important literature was written. The *Book of Songs* is a collection of poems about love, heroic deeds, and farming. The *I Ching* (Book of Changes) contains many beliefs of the time. It was used to foretell the future.

Philosophy. Two famous philosophers of the time were Confucius and Lao-tzu. Their teachings will be discussed in Chapter 3.

B. Qin Dynasty (221–206 B.C.)

The Qin overthrew the Zhou in 221 B.C. There was only one Qin king, Shi Huangdi. He extended the kingdom southward to the South China Sea.

GOVERNMENT BY REPRESSION. Under Shi Huangdi, the power of the king became more important than serving the will of the people. A strong central government was set up and ruled by the priciples of Legalism. That is, human beings are too selfish to act in the best interests of the community; therefore, the ruler should make all decisions and be backed up by strict laws.

China: Zhou and Qin Dynasties

[Map showing China during the Zhou and Qin Dynasties with labels: GOBI DESERT, MONGOLIA, MANCHURIA, Great Wall, Huang He, KOREA, YELLOW SEA, Loyang, Hao, Wei R., CHINA, ZHOU, Yangtze R., Hsi R., SOUTH CHINA SEA. Legend: Qin Dynasty, Zhou Dynasty. Scale: 400 Kilometers, 300 Miles. Compass rose.]

Shi Huangdi discouraged cultural advancement. He jailed philosophers critical of his regime and tried to destroy all of the writings of Confucius.

ACHIEVEMENTS. Shi Huangdi ordered the building of the Great Wall of China to keep nomadic tribes from invading.

END OF THE QIN DYNASTY. Shi Huangdi died in 210 B.C. An army general then took over the kingdom and established the Han Dynasty.

Great Wall of China crossing the Bada Range near Beijing

INFO CHECK

1. What is a classical civilization?

2. How did religion influence the Zhou kingdom?

3. Why is the Zhou Dynasty regarded as the beginning of China's classical age?

4. How did Shi Huangdi create a strong central government?

III. GREECE

A. Early History

ROOTS. Greek civilization had its roots in the Minoan and Mycenaean civilizations (1650–1100 B.C.). The Minoans lived on the island of Crete, and the Mycenaeans in southern Greece. Long-distance trade made both civilizations wealthy. The Mycenaeans conquered the Minoans and adopted their advanced culture. Waves of other peoples invaded the area, and their cultures mingled with those of the Minoans and Mycenaeans. People of the area began to speak a common language and became known as Greeks.

Ancient Greece

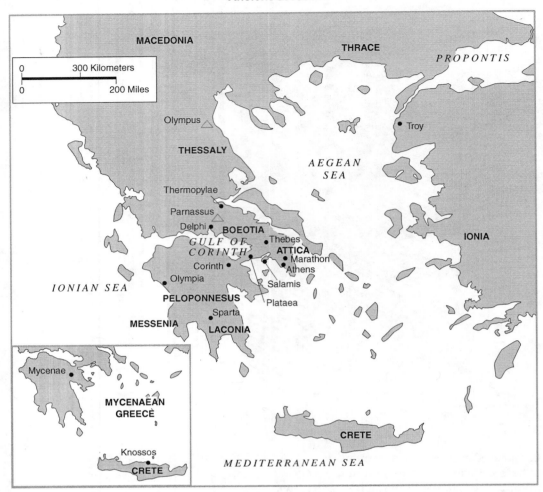

THE DARK AGE. The period of Minoan-Mycenaean decline is known as the Dark Age. Trade diminished; bronze making and writing were lost.

The Greeks began to form their own culture about 1200 B.C. They learned how to make iron and developed new styles in art. About 800 B.C., the early Greek poet Homer composed and recited two great epics, the *Iliad* and the *Odyssey*.

About 700 B.C., farming expanded, the population increased, and cities grew. Greek civilization began to take shape.

THE POLIS. Rugged hills, uneven distribution of good farmland, and an irregular coastline separated Greek communities. Therefore, each of them developed into a city-state called a **polis** (plural, **poleis**). The two most important were Sparta and Athens.

Types of Government

- **Monarchy**—rule by a king
- **Oligarchy**—rule by wealthy businesspeople
- **Aristocracy**—rule by nobles
- **Tyranny**—rule by a leader who persuades followers to overthrow the government and put him in power
- **Democracy**—rule by the people

Because each polis had a small population, all citizens had some influence on how they were ruled. Women, slaves, and foreigners were not citizens and had no influence.

WRITING SYSTEM. As Greek trade increased, foreigners were a source of new ideas and skills. The Greeks adapted and improved the writing system of the Phoenicians.

B. Classical Period

Classical Greek civilization arose in Athens, which developed from a monarchy to an aristocracy and then to a democracy. Under its democratic government, Athens became a center of art, science, literature, and philosophy

DEVELOPMENT OF ATHENIAN DEMOCRACY

Solon. Around 594 B.C., aristocratic leaders elected Solon to calm social unrest and reform the government. He outlawed the enslaving of debtors and set limits to the size of landholdings. He weakened the power of the aristocracy by giving political power to other groups. The poor gained new rights but little political power.

Cleisthenes. In 508 B.C., the Athenians elected another aristocrat to make further reforms. Cleisthenes wrote laws guaranteeing citizens freedom of speech and equality before the law. No longer did a citizen have to own land to take part in political decision making. The assembly was given power to pass laws, elect military leaders, and act as the supreme court of Athens. In effect, Cleisthenes created the world's first democracy.

Athens had a **direct democracy**—all citizens voted on an issue. (In a **representative democracy**, such as the United States government, citizens elect officials to make decisions for them.) Athenian women, slaves, and foreigners were not citizens and, therefore, did not enjoy the benefits of democracy.

THE PERSIAN WARS (490–479 B.C.). By 529 B.C., the Persian Empire controlled the Middle East. In Ionia, a Greek colony on the eastern Aegean coast, the Persians restricted political freedom. In 499 B.C., the Athenians helped the angry Ionians rebel. A series of wars broke out when the Persians invaded the Greek mainland. By 479 B.C., the Greek city-states of Sparta and Athens had defeated the Persians and forced them to withdraw.

C. The Age of Pericles: The Height of Classical Greek Culture

From 460 to 429 B.C., Athens achieved the height of classical Greek culture under an outstanding leader called Pericles.

GOVERNMENT. Athenian democracy increased. Citizens who did not own property gained the right to hold office. Jurists were paid for their services, so poor people now participated in law trials.

ARCHITECTURE AND ART. Architects designed the Parthenon, a temple to the patron goddess Athena and a supreme example of Greek architecture. Sculptors produced beautiful friezes and representations of the human body. Artists decorated vases and pottery.

DRAMA. Dramatists wrote enduring plays. Typical tragedies depict flawed heroes who are undone: the *Oresteia* trilogy by Aeschylus (525–456 B.C.) and *Medea* by Euripides (484–406 B.C.). Comedies made fun of politicians, artists, and philosophers of the day: *The Birds* by Aristophanes (450–388 B.C.).

MATHEMATICS AND SCIENCE. A mathematician named Pythagoras (580–500 B.C.) developed the

Persian Empire and Sites of Battles With Greeks

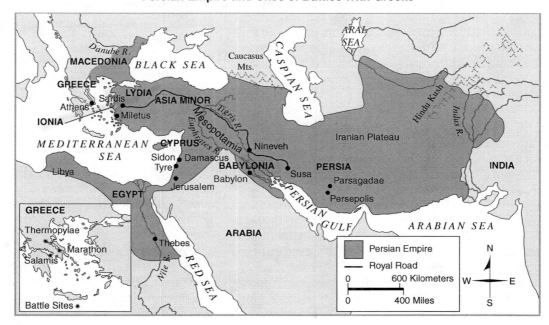

The Parthenon atop the Acropolis, dedicated to Athena, patron goddess of Athens

Pythagorean theorem used in geometry. A scientist, Democritus (460–370 B.C.), proposed that all matter is composed of tiny, invisible atoms. The early medical doctor Hippocrates (460–377 B.C.) showed that diseases had natural rather than magical or religious causes.

PHILOSOPHY. Socrates (470–399 B.C.) originated the Socratic method. By asking questions, he led people to reason out correct conclusions about values and behavior. Plato (427–347 B.C.) wrote the *Republic,* in which an ideal government is run by highly intelligent aristocrats trained to rule. Aristotle (384–322 B.C.) believed that people should observe the "golden mean" by practicing moderation in all things.

D. Sparta, the Military State

The Spartans acquired territory by conquering other city-states. In the early 700s B.C., they conquered their neighbor Messenia after 20 years of war and made its people state slaves, or **helots**. The Messenians rebelled so often that Sparta was in an almost constant state of war, which deeply affected its way of life.

GOVERNMENT. Sparta elected two kings every nine years. A council of elders (men over 60) and an assembly of freemen over 30 advised the kings. The most powerful group was the committee of five **ephors**, who kept close watch on the kings, controlled education, supervised helots, and saw that citizens lived up to government standards.

Although elected, the Spartan government did not serve its citizens; it fulfilled the needs of the state. Education mainly trained boys for warfare and girls for strong physical endurance. Women ran the farms while their husbands were at war. Women were also allowed to own businesses.

E. The Peloponnesian War

During the Persian wars, Athens and other city-states formed an alliance, the Delian League. It continued to exist after the Persian retreat. Under Pericles, Athens tried to use the league to build an empire, but the other city-states, led by Sparta, rebelled. Sparta and Athens fought for control of the Peloponnesian peninsula from 431 to 404 B.C. Sparta defeated Athens, became the leader of Greece, and ended Athenian democracy.

INFO CHECK

1. Why was the period from 1200 to 700 B.C. known as the Dark Age?

2. Define each of the following: polis, aristocracy, oligarchy, democracy, tyranny.

3. How was Athenian democracy more limited than modern American democracy?

4. State the importance of the Age of Pericles. When did it occur?

5. List major differences between Athens and Sparta.

6. State the cause and two results of the Peloponnesian War.

F. Macedonia and the Hellenistic Period

Philip II (382–336 B.C.), king of Macedonia, conquered and united all of the Greek city-states except Sparta. He preserved and perpetuated Greek culture.

ALEXANDER'S EMPIRE. Philip's son Alexander the Great set out to conquer the Persian Empire in 334 B.C. Greek became the major language in the eastern Mediterranean region. The combination of Middle East cultures and the Greek culture

Alexander the Great's Empire, 323 B.C.

carried east by Alexander became the basis of **Hellenistic civilization**.

When Alexander died in 323 B.C., his empire fell apart, but Hellenistic civilization continued to develop.

PHILOSOPHIC SCHOOLS

Cynics. Diogenes (412–323 B.C.) argued that humans should ignore social conventions and avoid luxuries since nature provides for every need. The Cynics wanted to regard themselves as citizens not of a country but of the world.

Epicureans. Epicurus (340–270 B.C.) taught that people should avoid pain and seek pleasure. He defined true pleasure, however, as leading a life of moderation and self-discipline.

Stoics. Zeno (335–265 B.C.) believed that nature is the expression of divine will. There is a **natural law**, he said, which stems from using nature as a model for human behavior. Under natural law, humans share the same nature and have the same needs and rights.

SCIENCE AND MATHEMATICS

Astronomy. About 270 B.C., Aristarchus concluded that Earth revolves around the Sun.

Mathematics. About 300 B.C., Euclid organized the study of geometry into a textbook called *Elements*.

Physics. Archimedes (287–212 B.C.) invented the catapult, grappling devices to pull ships out of the water, and a pulley that could move heavy objects with a minimum of effort. He also developed the principle of **specific gravity** (the relative density of an object).

Medicine. Herophilus (335–280 B.C.) discovered the nervous system.

Art and Literature. Hellenistic art emphasized human individuality and emotions rather than the ideal depictions in classical Greek art. Plays and poetry dealt less with heroic actions than with everyday lives and feelings.

INFO CHECK

1. Identify each of the following: Macedonia, Philip II, Hellenistic civilization, Alexander.

2. Which of the Hellenistic philosophers do you find most interesting? Explain.

3. Match each scientists with an achievement: Aristarchus, Euclid, Archimedes, Herophilus.

IV. ROME

A. Early History

LATINS. In about 1200 B.C., a group of Indo-Europeans invaded Italy and settled in its central plains, an area called Latium. By the early 7th century B.C., Latin villages had united to form the city of Rome.

Society and Government. Latin society was based on the family and was strongly patriarchal. Latins elected their kings.

Italy: Early Settlement and the Roman Republic

ETRUSCANS. The Etruscans conquered the Latins in the 600s B.C. and imposed their own forms of government and culture. Etruscans had adopted many aspects of Greek and Middle Eastern culture and brought these influences to the Latins.

B. Roman Republic

In 509 B.C., the Romans successfully rebelled against the Etruscans and set up a **republic** (form of government in which elected officials make the laws).

SOCIETY. Roman society had two classes: **patricians**, or wealthy landowners, and **plebeians**, or small farmers, tradespeople, craftsworkers, and debtors.

GOVERNMENTAL ORGANIZATION (509–133 B.C.). The **consuls** were the highest Roman officials. The assembly elected two consuls each year. They enforced the laws, ensured proper administration of the city, and commanded the army in time of war. Lesser officials counted population, kept order, and supervised upkeep of public buildings.

In times of emergency, the consuls chose a **dictator** to rule for no more than six months. The government followed the dictator's decisions without question.

Senate. The senate was the most powerful government body. Its members served for life. They proposed laws, handled foreign affairs, and controlled public finances.

Tribunes. Tribunes protected the rights of the plebeians. They could **veto**, or reject, decisions of the consuls and the Senate.

C. Roman Empire

CONQUESTS. Between 343 and 290 B.C., Rome fought several wars with its neighbors and acquired more and more territory. By alliance and

The Roman Empire at Its Greatest Extent, A.D. 150

conquest, they gained control of all of Italy. They then began foreign conquests:

- There were three Punic Wars (264–146 B.C.) waged by Rome against Carthage, a city-state founded by the Phoenicians in North Africa. (*Punic* means "Phoenician.") Rome defeated and destroyed Carthage.

- By 64 B.C., Rome had conquered almost all of the Mediterranean region. Pompey, a general and powerful political leader from 78 to 48 B.C., was mainly responsible for eastern Mediterranean conquests.

- Another general, Julius Caesar, conquered the peoples north of Italy.

- The emperor Claudius conquered much of Britain.

ACHIEVEMENTS

Roman Law. Roman law was designed to protect the lives and well-being of citizens and aid the victims of crime or injustice. Eventually, lawmakers were guided by the Stoic idea of natural law, which benefited all humanity, not just the powerful.

As Roman conquest spread, the laws and customs of conquered peoples became part of Roman law.

Trade. Trade routes through southern Asia linked the Roman Empire to the East. The most famous route was the Silk Road used by merchants to and from China. Sea routes also connected Rome to the East.

Architecture and Engineering. Romans built roads, dams, drainage systems, and aqueducts (bridgelike structures supporting water pipes to supply city populations). They developed the rounded arch and the dome. They built buildings with plumbing and ventilation systems. They mastered the use of concrete as a building material.

Spread of Roman Culture. The influence of Greek and Hellenistic culture on the Romans is called the **Greco-Roman civilization**. The Romans, in turn, spread this cultural blend far and wide. Roman architectural styles took hold throughout Europe, northern Africa, and the Middle East. Latin gave rise to Italian, French, and Spanish and indirectly influenced English. Eventually, legal codes in southern Europe, Latin America, and the United States reflected Roman law: all citizens are equal under the law; accused persons are innocent until proven guilty; they have the right to know who their accusers are; no one should be punished for private thoughts.

V. INDIA

Prior to its classical age, India had gone through a period of social upheaval, which left it open to invaders. Alexander the Great conquered a large

India: The Maurya Empire, 250 B.C.

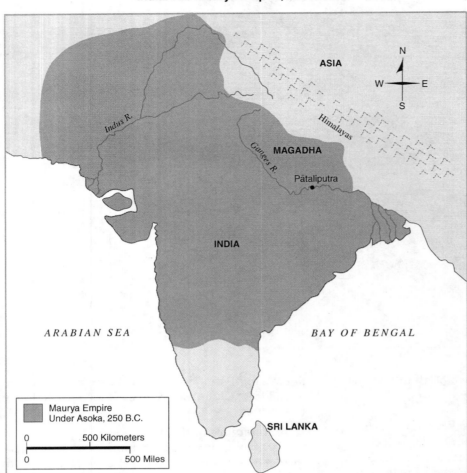

Maurya Empire
Under Asoka, 250 B.C.

0   500 Kilometers

0   500 Miles

part of western India but died before he could organize it under Macedonian rule.

A. Chandragupta, First King of the Maurya Dynasty (321–184 B.C.)

Without strong leadership, the states of western India fell into the hands of Chandragupta Maurya, the ruler of a small state in the Ganges Valley. Chandragupta, who ruled all of northern India from 321 to 298 B.C., initiated its classical period.

GOVERNMENT. Chandragupta organized his large empire into small provinces, with family members governing each one. Agents traveled from the capital at Pataliputra to oversee the governors and keep Chandragupta informed of prevailing conditions. A large bureaucracy helped run the state smoothly. These officials were mainly responsible for the tax system that supported public services. Although Chandragupta was repressive and sometimes brutal, his efficiency brought stability to India.

B. Asoka

Chandragupta's grandson Asoka expanded the Maurya Empire to include almost all of India. He ruled from 272 to 232 B.C.

In about 261 B.C., Asoka was stricken by remorse after killing an enormous number of people in battle. He converted to Buddhism and tried to rule by its humane principles. Asoka sent out monks to spread Buddhism throughout Asia, the Middle East, and North Africa. Asoka ordered that rules of conduct for his people be carved on stone pillars. They were set up throughout the empire for everyone to see.

After Asoka's death in 232 B.C., foreigners repeatedly invaded India, and the Maurya Empire declined.

INFO CHECK

1. How did early Romans benefit from Etruscan rule?

2. Describe the government of the Roman republic. Identify its democratic features.

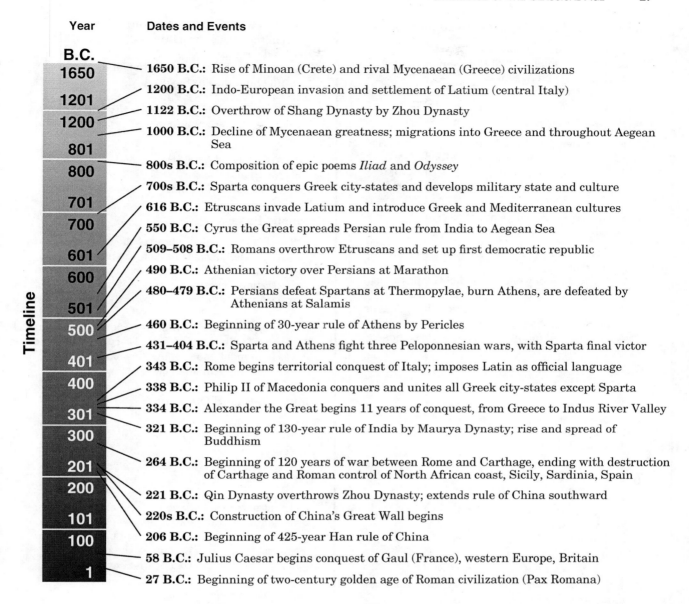

Year	Dates and Events

B.C.

1650 B.C.: Rise of Minoan (Crete) and rival Mycenaean (Greece) civilizations

1200 B.C.: Indo-European invasion and settlement of Latium (central Italy)

1122 B.C.: Overthrow of Shang Dynasty by Zhou Dynasty

1000 B.C.: Decline of Mycenaean greatness; migrations into Greece and throughout Aegean Sea

800s B.C.: Composition of epic poems *Iliad* and *Odyssey*

700s B.C.: Sparta conquers Greek city-states and develops military state and culture

616 B.C.: Etruscans invade Latium and introduce Greek and Mediterranean cultures

550 B.C.: Cyrus the Great spreads Persian rule from India to Aegean Sea

509–508 B.C.: Romans overthrow Etruscans and set up first democratic republic

490 B.C.: Athenian victory over Persians at Marathon

480–479 B.C.: Persians defeat Spartans at Thermopylae, burn Athens, are defeated by Athenians at Salamis

460 B.C.: Beginning of 30-year rule of Athens by Pericles

431–404 B.C.: Sparta and Athens fight three Peloponnesian wars, with Sparta final victor

343 B.C.: Rome begins territorial conquest of Italy; imposes Latin as official language

338 B.C.: Philip II of Macedonia conquers and unites all Greek city-states except Sparta

334 B.C.: Alexander the Great begins 11 years of conquest, from Greece to Indus River Valley

321 B.C.: Beginning of 130-year rule of India by Maurya Dynasty; rise and spread of Buddhism

264 B.C.: Beginning of 120 years of war between Rome and Carthage, ending with destruction of Carthage and Roman control of North African coast, Sicily, Sardinia, Spain

221 B.C.: Qin Dynasty overthrows Zhou Dynasty; extends rule of China southward

220s B.C.: Construction of China's Great Wall begins

206 B.C.: Beginning of 425-year Han rule of China

58 B.C.: Julius Caesar begins conquest of Gaul (France), western Europe, Britain

27 B.C.: Beginning of two-century golden age of Roman civilization (Pax Romana)

Timeline years (top to bottom): 1650, 1201, 1200, 801, 800, 701, 700, 601, 600, 501, 500, 401, 400, 301, 300, 201, 200, 101, 100, 1

3. What did Rome gain as a result of the Punic Wars?

4. What did each of the following contribute to the growth of the Roman Empire: Pompey, Julius Caesar, Claudius.

5. How did the spread of the Roman Empire affect Roman law?

6. Explain why you AGREE or DISAGREE with the following statement: The Romans had little knowledge of engineering or architecture.

CHAPTER REVIEW

Multiple Choice

1. The Chinese Mandate of Heaven was used

1. every time a new ruler was born
2. when soldiers were sent to fight invaders
3. to explain Chinese superiority to the West
4. to justify rebellion and replacement of one ruler by another.

2. The creation of civil servants in China became necessary because

1. the ruler had no family to assist in governing provinces
2. as the empire expanded, administrators were needed to govern provinces
3. the ruler distrusted the nobility
4. only civil servants could read and write.

3. The earliest recorded Greek civilizations were

   1. Minoan and Roman
   2. Mesopotamian and Mycenaean
   3. Assyrian and Athenian
   4. Mycenaean and Minoan.

4. The *Iliad* and the *Odyssey* were

   1. love poems written during the Periclean Age
   2. written by Homer during the Dark Age
   3. epic poetry describing Greece's Dark Age
   4. religious folktales written by Euripides.

5. In Greece, small independent city-states developed because

   1. Greek families did not get along with their neighbors
   2. the topography encouraged development of widely scattered settlements
   3. foreign invaders divided Greece into smaller settlements for ease of control
   4. Greeks had many languages and religions.

6. The only type of leadership that did not arise in Greece was

   1. tyranny
   2. aristocracy
   3. oligarchy
   4. communism.

7. During the Roman republic, the most powerful government officials were

   1. plebeians
   2. patricians
   3. consuls
   4. magistrates.

8. A philosopher whose method was to encourage students to reason for themselves was

   1. Confucius
   2. Archimedes
   3. Socrates
   4. Ptolemy.

9. The ruler who converted to Buddhism and spread it throughout his empire was

   1. Pericles
   2. Alexander
   3. Shi Huangdi
   4. Asoka.

10. Refer to the photographs on pages 19 and 22 and select the correct statement.

    1. Imperial Romans knew little about engineering.
    2. The Athenians relied heavily on border fortifications.

3. A high degree of architectural skill characterized the cultures of ancient China and Greece.
4. There was little construction of monuments and buildings in Egypt.

11. Use the map on page 25 to identify two European rivers fortified by the Romans.

    1. Rhine and Danube
    2. Atlantic and Mediterranean
    3. North and Black
    4. Corsica and Sardinia

Thematic Essays

1. "The Romans, unlike many of the other classical civilizations, concentrated on the practical sciences." *Task:* Identify two examples of Roman civilization that support this statement and explain your choices.

2. "If Greece was the birthplace of democracy, then Athens was its center." *Task:* Discuss the truth of this statement as it applies to women and men who were not Athenian citizens.

Document-Based Questions

Use your knowledge of Global History and Geography and the source documents to answer these questions about governments.

1. From a description of Sparta by Xenophon:

   "I first noted the unique position of Sparta among the states . . . the relative sparse population . . . at the same time . . . the power and prestige. . . . In Sparta, the stronger a man is the more readily does he bow before constituted authority."

   What, according to Xenophon, makes Sparta different from other city-states?

2. From Pericles' funeral oration:

   "We are called a democracy, for the administration is in the hands of the many and not the few. If few of us are originators [creators] we are all sound judges of policy. The great impediment [block] to action is . . . not discussion but the want of knowledge . . . gained by discussion."

   According to Pericles, how are decisions and policies made in a democracy?

3. From the Roman historian Polybius:

   "As for the Roman Constitution . . . it has three elements, each of them possessing sovereign power . . . and their respective share of power in the whole state has been regulated with such a . . .

regard to equality and equilibrium [balance] that no one can say for certain . . . whether the constitution is an aristocracy, or democracy or despotism."

Why does Polybius admire the government established by the Roman Constitution?

Document-Based Essay

Task: Identify and discuss three Greek or Roman political practices that influenced future Western political systems.

C H A P T E R
3

Trade, Empire, and Religion in the Classical Age

I. GLOBAL TRADE ROUTES

Early civilizations influenced each other predominantly by trade. The Phoenicians were especially active in carrying goods, skills, and ideas to distant peoples.

A. Phoenicians (3000–64 B.C.)

CITIES AND TRADE. The Phoenicians established trading centers along the Mediterranean region that is now Lebanon. These cities manufactured and traded in dyes, jewelry, blown glass, and ivory and gold objects.

World Trade Routes in Classical Age

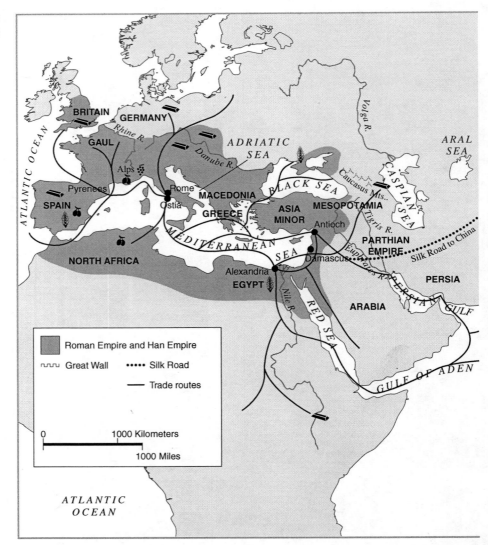

ATLANTIC OCEAN

BRITAIN
GERMANY
Rhine R.
GAUL
Alps
Pyrenees
Rome
Ostia
SPAIN
MACEDONIA
GREECE
NORTH AFRICA
MEDITERRANEAN SEA
ADRIATIC SEA
Danube R.
BLACK SEA
ASIA MINOR
Antioch
Damascus
Alexandria
EGYPT
Nile R.
RED SEA
Volga R.
Caucasus Mts.
CASPIAN SEA
ARAL SEA
MESOPOTAMIA
Tigris R.
Euphrates R.
PARTHIAN EMPIRE
Silk Road to China
PERSIA
ARABIA
PERSIAN GULF
GULF OF ADEN

Roman Empire and Han Empire
Great Wall
Silk Road
Trade routes

0   1000 Kilometers
        1000 Miles

ATLANTIC OCEAN

EXPLORATION AND COLONIZATION. Phoenician colonies sprang up along the coasts of Europe, North Africa, Sardinia, and Corsica. The Phoenicians adopted many ideas, skills, and customs from the people who settled nearby and then spread this culture to other nations.

LITERACY. The Phoenician writing system was more efficient than earlier ones. It had only 22 letters, each of which represented a sound rather than an idea or word. The letters could be combined in various ways to form many words. The Phoenicians introduced this system to the Greeks.

B. Greeks and Romans

By 500 B.C., some Greek *poleis* had also established trading colonies around the coasts of the Aegean, Mediterranean, and northern Black seas.

They traded grain and timber for luxury goods such as pottery and jewelry.

The Roman trading network comprised both land and sea routes covering all of Europe and parts of India, China, Africa, and the Middle East. (See map on pages 30–31.)

The peoples of Europe especially prized silk from China. Great quantities of silk, as well as tea and spices, traveled west along a 5000-mile route called the Silk Road.

INFO CHECK

1. Explain the importance of global trade to the spread of ideas and knowledge.

2. Why did the Phoenician alphabet mean so much to the development of trade and culture in the Classical Age?

3. How extensive was the Roman trading network?

World Trade Routes in Classical Age (*Continued*)

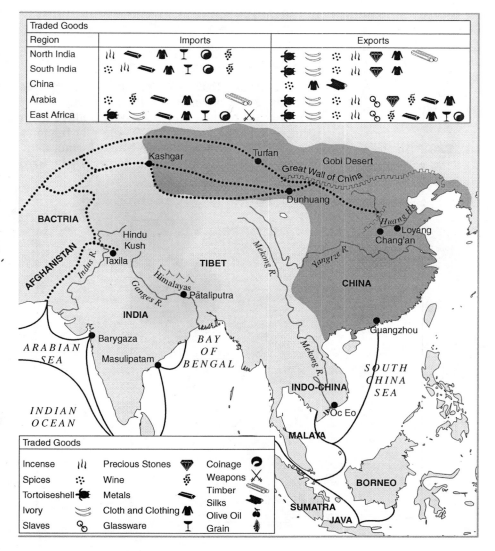

Traded Goods									
Region	Imports					Exports			
North India									
South India									
China									
Arabia									
East Africa									

Traded Goods

Incense · Spices · Tortoiseshell · Ivory · Slaves · Precious Stones · Wine · Metals · Cloth and Clothing · Glassware · Coinage · Weapons · Timber · Silks · Olive Oil · Grain

II. HAN DYNASTY AND THE ROMAN EMPIRE

A. Han Dynasty (206 B.C.–A.D. 220)

The Han Dynasty and the Roman Empire existed at the same time. After the death of the Qin emperor, Liu Bang, a peasant who had risen in the bureaucracy, became the first emperor of the Han Dynasty. Under the Hans, the empire acquired new lands. (See the map on page 32.)

Han emperors needed a competent bureaucracy to rule new provinces efficiently. Civil-service candidates took tests on law, mathematics, and **Confucianism**. Thus, poor men were able to take active parts in government.

TRADE AND TECHNOLOGY. As the empire expanded, there was more contact between China and other cultures. The Silk Road trade began during the early 200s B.C.

Chinese technology advanced. Craftspeople made lacquerware (wooden objects covered with highly polished varnish). In A.D. 105, Cai Lun invented paper from cloth, rope, and bark fibers. Metalworkers improved the manufacture of iron tools and weapons, and produced crossbows, carpenters' rules, adjustable wrenches, and machine gears and cogwheels. A scholar wrote the world's first dictionary. Han scientists developed **cartography** (mapmaking).

FALL OF HAN EMPIRE (A.D. 220). In the last years of the Han Dynasty, only a few powerful people enjoyed China's great wealth. Peasants who served as farmers and soldiers were poorly paid and heavily taxed. While they fought off invaders, their farms were neglected. Without income from crops, many peasants were forced to sell their farms to large landholders.

Peasant revolts broke out. Generals sent to crush the uprisings seized the farms instead and set up their own kingdoms. During a peasant uprising in the reign of Hsien Ti (A.D. 189–221), members of the emperor's court dethroned him while his armies were away fighting.

China was eventually divided into three kingdoms. Nomadic tribes from the north set up their own dynasties. These groups, however, preserved China's culture by adopting language, religion, agricultural techniques, and political systems of their conquered subjects.

INFO CHECK

1.   Trace the rise and fall of the Han Dynasty.

2.   List the two important accomplishments of Han China.

B. Roman Empire

COLLAPSE OF ROMAN REPUBLIC. As the Roman Empire grew large and powerful, more slaves were introduced into the economic system. Slave labor resulted in fewer jobs and lower wages for freemen. The plebeians became poorer. Small farmers, unable to compete with large landowners who used

China: Han Empire

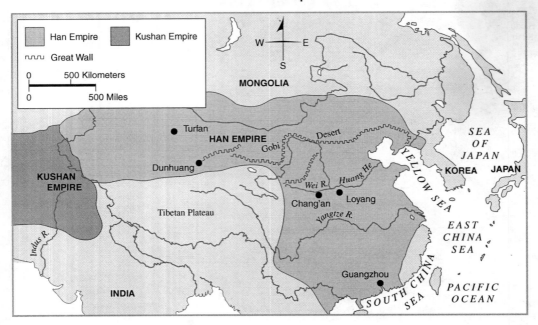

Roman Empire and Invaders, A.D. 400

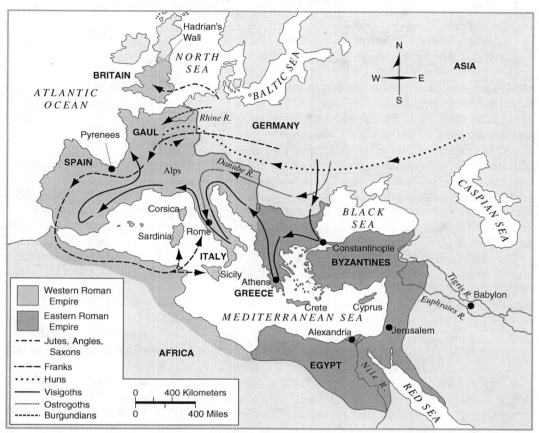

slaves, were forced to sell their land. Many plebeians without jobs or land moved to the cities and lived on government handouts. The gap between rich and poor widened.

The plebeians' poverty and loss of political power led to a long period of civil wars. Dictators made use of the disorder to increase their power.

JULIUS CAESAR. One of the most famous of the dictators was Julius Caesar (100–44 B.C.) He won the plebeians' support by championing their rights. Caesar believed that a republican government would be unable to rule the vast Roman Empire.

Caesar, the wealthy Marcus Licinius Crassus, and the popular general Gaius Magnus Pompey formed a triumvirate (three-person government) that ruled the Roman Empire from 60 to 53 B.C., when Crassus died. Caesar then fought a series of civil wars with Pompey and won control of the government in 46 B.C.

Caesar proved to be a capable dictator. He made the army and government more efficient. He enlarged the Senate so that it could better represent the provinces. He extended citizenship, improved

the tax system, introduced a more accurate calendar, and created new jobs for the poor.

A group of politicians, led by Marcus Brutus and resentful of Caesar's growing power, murdered him in 44 B.C. The outraged Romans forced the murderers into exile, where they plotted to gain power. Caesar's friend and chief general, Marc Antony, took control of Rome.

AUGUSTUS, FIRST ROMAN EMPEROR. Antony joined forces with Octavian, Julius Caesar's adopted son. They defeated Brutus and his allies and ruled the Roman world together. When Antony formed an alliance with Cleopatra, queen of Egypt, Octavian waged and won a war against his former co-ruler.

Octavian ruled Rome as emperor from 27 B.C. to A.D. 14. The Senate gave him the title of Caesar Augustus. Under his wise rule, the Roman Empire began a 200-year period of peace, the **Pax Romana**.

Several of the next emperors were corrupt and cruel—in particular, Caligula and Nero, both criminally insane. The wiser emperors who followed tried to appoint capable men to succeed them.

DECLINE. Marcus Aurelius, who ruled from A.D. 161 to 180, was one of the best of the later emperors. He did not, however, groom a capable successor. Instead, his son, Commodus, inherited the empire, and during his reign (A.D. 180–192) the empire declined. After his death, civil war, unstable leadership, and economic problems exposed Rome to foreign invaders. Emperor Diocletian, who ruled from 284 to 305, tried to strengthen the empire by dividing it into eastern and western sections. Diocletian ruled from Nicomedia in Asia Minor, while a co-emperor ruled from Milan in northern Italy. In 324, Constantine reunited the empire and ruled alone from Byzantium, which he renamed Constantinople. After 395, the empire was permanently divided. The western part declined while the eastern part grew strong and wealthy.

For most of Europe, the Classical Age had ended. In the Hellenistic cities of Asia Minor and the Middle East, however, it persisted as the Byzantine Empire (the former eastern Roman Empire), which lasted until 1453.

III. BORDER PEOPLES

Small agricultural and herding societies made some important cultural contributions. They invented the sail, the weaving loom, and the pottery wheel, and developed such farming techniques as crop rotation and the use of manure as fertilizer.

A. Celts

From 700 B.C. to A.D. 100, Celtic civilization existed in present-day Britain, Ireland, Spain, France, Germany, Switzerland, Austria, Hungary, the Czech Republic, and Slovakia.

WAY OF LIFE. The Celts had related languages and ways of life. Their tribes were ruled by kings and, sometimes, queens. They tended to be warlike, and their leaders were warriors. Towns and villages were built on hilltops and protected by deep ditches and high walls.

ACHIEVEMENTS. Celtic mastery in ironwork spread throughout Europe. There were iron plows to till the soil for planting, iron scythes to cut grain, and four-wheeled carts and two-wheeled chariots to travel over surfaced roads.

There was no Celtic writing system, although priests and scholars called **Druids** could read and write Latin and Greek. The Celts preserved their history and myths in long poems. Specially trained men called **bards** memorized and recited these poems. This oral literature influenced the development of written literature in Europe.

ROMAN INFLUENCE. By A.D. 100, the Romans ruled the Celts and gave them Roman law, the Latin language, and opportunities for long-distance trade. The blend of Roman and Celtic cultures was the basis for later European civilization.

B. Germans

HISTORY AND WAY OF LIFE. Germanic tribes migrated into present-day Germany from the northern parts of Europe between 1000 and 100 B.C. They were farmers and herders living in villages surrounded by farmland held in common.

A freemen's assembly governed each tribe. In times of crisis, the tribe elected a king, who ruled during the crisis.

ROMAN INFLUENCE. The Romans conquered only a few Germanic tribes, which reaped the benefits of foreign trade. Men from these tribes served in the Roman army and distinguished themselves. Until the early 5th century, Roman legions containing German soldiers prevented invasion by hostile German tribes. In 476, however, a German general named Odovacar forced the last western Roman emperor to give up his throne. The area then became dotted with German kingdoms.

C. Huns

The Huns were warlike herders from north of China. They did no farming. In the 3rd century B.C., the Chinese occupied Hun pastureland. In retaliation, the Huns raided Chinese towns and farms and set up a small empire in northern China. (Shi Huangdi's Great Wall was meant to stop deeper invasions by the Huns.) During the Han Dynasty, the Huns invaded China's northern border again. Emperor Han Wo Ti drove them away in 147 B.C.

In about A.D. 370, the Huns pushed the Goths from their lands in eastern Europe. The Goths fled west into Roman territory. In A.D. 378, rebellious Goths defeated a Roman army at Adrianople. From 434 to 453, the Huns threatened the western Roman Empire. After their leader Attila died, the Germans regained control in the west.

<hr>

INFO CHECK

1. Explain why you AGREE or DISAGREE with this statement: The Roman Empire and the Han Dynasty had nothing in common.

2. How did each of the following change, or attempt to change, the Roman world: Julius Caesar, Augustus, Diocletian, Constantine?

3. Complete the following sentences:
    *   Marcus Aurelius allowed his son _____.

    *   After the death of Commodus, there were many foreign invasions because _____.

    *   After Rome's decline, the culture of the Classical Age continued in Asia Minor as _____.

4. Explain why the Celts were important to the development of European civilization.

5. Describe the interaction between Romans and Germans.

6. What roles did the Germans and the Huns play in the fall of the western Roman Empire? Why were the Romans unable to prevent the loss of their empire?

IV. EMERGENCE AND SPREAD OF BELIEF SYSTEMS

A. Animism

Most early belief systems were based on **animism** (*anima* means "spirit"). Early peoples believed that objects and natural forces contained spirits. By controlling them, the people hoped to prevent disasters and reap benefits. Animism often led to ancestor worship, in which humans made offerings to the spirits of their dead ancestors; these spirits, in turn, could induce nature spirits to bring good crops and other rewards.

B. Indian Religions

After the fall of the Indus Valley civilization, Indo-Europeans called Aryans conquered the Dravidians, the likely descendants of Indus Valley peoples. Nomadic herders, the Aryans worshiped powerful forces—fire, war, storms. The Dravidians were farmers who worshiped nature gods.

The Dravidians taught the Aryans how to farm and write. At the same time, Dravidians adopted the Aryan social structure, gods, and language, called Sanskrit.

Aryan cities, built along the Ganges River, were ruled by powerful kings. Priests, called **Brahmins**, shared power with the kings.

HINDUISM. Some Brahmins searched for the meaning of life and developed the concept of **reincarnation**, the belief that a person's spirit is reborn after death—sometimes as a different person, sometimes as a different form of life. People who live good lives are reborn as superior people. Those who live bad lives are reborn as inferior people or lower animals.

To escape the cycle of death and rebirth, a person must atone for wrongdoing, study the Vedas (Hindu religious teachings), and meditate. Whoever reaches the highest moral and spiritual state is no longer reborn but, after death, becomes part of Brahma, the world soul.

Caste System. Hindu tradition teaches that each person is born into a **caste** (rank in society). From highest to lowest, they are:

*   Brahmins—priests
*   Kshatriyas—rulers and warriors
*   Vaisyas—merchants and professionals
*   Sudras—workers and servants

People in the higher castes could escape the reincarnation cycle more easily than others. Untouchables were people outside the caste system. They did work that caste members were forbidden to do and associated only with their own kind. (Classification as an untouchable is illegal in modern India.)

Hindu steplike temple at Shrirangam, India

Spread of Buddhism and Hinduism

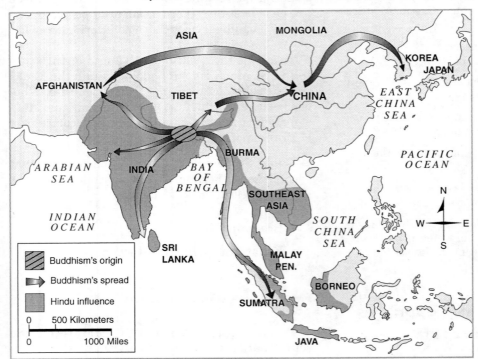

BUDDHISM. Buddhism grew out of Hinduism and the teachings of Siddhartha Gautama (563–483 B.C.), a prince who gave up power and luxury to meditate on why human misery exists. When he believed that he had the answer, he became known as "Buddha" (enlightened one).

Buddha believed in reincarnation but felt that, at any time, a person could escape the cycle by following the Middle Way and the Noble Eightfold Path. The Middle Way meant avoiding uncontrolled satisfaction of desires and extreme self-punishment. The Eightfold Path called for more:

- Knowledge of truth
- Intention to resist evil
- Saying nothing to hurt others
- Respect for life, morality, and property
- Doing work that injures no one
- Working to rid one's mind of evil
- Controlling feelings and thoughts
- Practicing proper forms of meditation

Observing these rules could help a person enter **nirvana**, a state in which the soul merges with the universe.

Spread of Buddhism. When King Asoka of the Maurya Dynasty converted to Buddhism, Buddhism spread through India and then throughout Asia (269–232 B.C.).

C. Chinese Philosophies

CONFUCIANISM. Confucius lived in China between 551 and 479 B.C. His students gathered his ideas into a book called *The Analects.*

Confucianism is not about the worship of gods or life after death. It deals mainly with living an ideal life. People achieve this through proper conduct—respect for parents, ancestors, teachers, and rulers. Rulers achieve it by respecting their subjects. Confucius advised people to do nothing that they would not want others to do to them.

While teaching respect for authority and tradition, Confucius also helped to relax the rigid Chinese class structure by pointing out that human worth depends on conduct rather than rank or wealth.

TAOSIM. Lao-tzu, the founder of Taoism, lived at the same time as Confucius. **Taoism** comes from the word "tao" and refers to the right way to live. Lao-tzu taught that people found inner peace by living simply and in harmony with nature. It was also important not to try to change the course of events.

According to Lao-tzu, people were better off with as little government as possible. (Confucius thought that good government was important.)

D. Judaism

The Hebrews, or Jews, belonged to ancient tribes in the Middle East. They were the first people to practice **monotheism** (belief in one god). This kind of belief eventually replaced most forms of **polytheism** (belief in many gods) in the ancient world.

HISTORY. An early Jewish leader, Abraham, led the Jews from Mesopotamia to Canaan, renamed Israel. During a famine, some Jews moved to Egypt and were enslaved. After a long captivity, Moses freed them and led them back to Israel. The Bible states that during the journey, God gave Moses the Ten Commandments, a code of moral behavior.

Around 1025 B.C., the Jews were united under Saul, their first king, and won control of Israel from the neighboring Philistines. Under King David, the Jews built their capital city of Jerusalem. The kingdom reached its peak of strength and wealth under David's son, Solomon.

In A.D. 135, the Romans destroyed Jerusalem, and renamed Israel as Syria Palestina.

CHOSEN PEOPLE. Even earlier than the Roman era, other groups, such as the Babylonians in 587 B.C., had captured Israel. Their religion, however, always kept the Jews united in spirit. As long as they followed God's commandments and worshiped no other gods, He would watch over them because they were his chosen people. One day, God would send a **messiah** (savior) to begin a new era of justice and righteousness.

INFLUENCE. As Jews moved to different places, Judaism was spread throughout the Middle East and Mediterranean regions. The Jews' God was just and merciful, while other people's gods were sometimes cruel and demanded flattery and gifts. The caring and just God of the Jews attracted many people. Eventually, Judaism became the foundation of Christianity and was a strong influence on Islam.

E. Christianity

Some Asian and Hellenistic mystery cults, popular during the Roman Empire, featured a god or goddess who had arisen from death and become immortal. Such cults influenced Christianity.

THE ESSENES. The Romans persecuted the Jews for resisting Roman rule on religious grounds. One group of Jews, the Essenes (150 B.C.–A.D. 68), looked for the coming of a prophet who would reform and strengthen Judaism. Thus, many Jews began to feel that a savior would soon appear.

JESUS. The teachings of a religious leader named Jesus had a wide appeal—to people seeking a meaning in life, to oppressed people in need of a champion, to lonely people longing for the warmth of a religious community.

Jesus was a Jew born during the rule of Augustus, probably in Bethlehem, Israel. When he was about 30, he began to teach his ideas to anyone who would listen, including the poor and unlearned.

Teachings. Jesus preached that God loved all people and wanted them to love one another. He stressed the Golden Rule: behave toward others as you want them to behave toward you. He promised the faithful that they would enter the Kingdom of Heaven. Jesus' teachings are recorded in the New Testament of the Bible. Twelve men became his **apostles**, or companions, and helped him spread his teachings.

Death and Resurrection. Jesus angered some Jewish leaders, who wondered why this self-acclaimed messiah did nothing to regain Israel for the Jews. Roman leaders believed that he was inciting the Jews to rebellion.

In A.D. 33, Jesus entered Jerusalem to celebrate the Jewish Passover. Threatened by the large crowds he attracted, Roman officials arrested him, tried him, found him guilty of treason against Rome, and sentenced him to die by crucifixion (being nailed to a wooden cross).

A few days later, the apostles claimed that they had seen and talked with Jesus. Belief in his

Christ surrounded by the Apostles, on a marble coffin from 4th-century France

Spread of Christianity

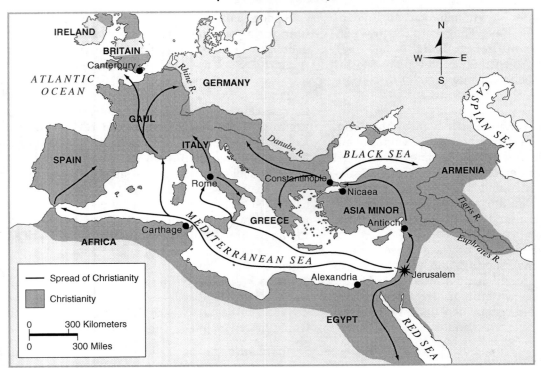

resurrection (return from the dead) strengthened the conviction that he was the messiah. (*Christos,* the Greek word for "messiah," gave Christianity its name.)

SPREAD OF CHRISTIANITY. After Jesus' death, the apostles taught his ideas to the peoples of the Mediterranean region. One of the most important of the apostles was Peter. He felt, in essence, that Jesus had fulfilled the prophecies of Judaism.

Paul, a later convert to Christianity, thought that Jesus had founded a new religion instead. According to Paul, people were to obey the Jewish moral code, but they did not have to practice Jewish rituals. Jesus had come to save everyone, he said, not just the Jews. Paul established the Christian church.

At first, Roman leaders persecuted Christians, mainly because they refused to obey such laws as army service, which contradicted their beliefs. In A.D. 313, Emperor Constantine ended such persecutions by issuing the Edict of Milan, which made Christianity the equal of all other religions. Constantine became the first Christian Roman emperor. By 395, Christianity had become the state religion and spread to non-Roman Europe. The most influential Christian community was the Catholic (universal) Church in Rome, headed by the pope.

F. Islam

Muhammad is the prophet who converted Arabians to monotheism. He belonged to the Quraysh tribe, whose members had served for generations as priests of a sacred black rock, the *Ka'ba,* in the city of Mecca.

ORIGIN. Muhammad spent much of his time praying and meditating. In A.D. 610, an angel told him that he was God's chosen messenger. He was to persuade people to give up their idols and believe in Allah (the Arabic name for God). Muhammad began teaching ideas similar to those of Jews and Christians. He did not claim that he had founded a new religion, but rather updated and clarified Jewish and Christian concepts.

Muhammad's teachings angered the Quraysh priests. They feared that he would attract worshipers away from the Ka'ba, the shrine that made them powerful and rich. In 622, they tried to kill Muhammad, who fled from Mecca to Medina. This escape is called the **Hegira** (departure). Muhammad formed an army in Medina, returned to Mecca, and overcame his opponents. To ensure lasting peace, he proclaimed Mecca sacred to Allah.

ISLAMIC TEACHINGS. Muhammad's teachings became known as Islam (Arabic for "surrender to

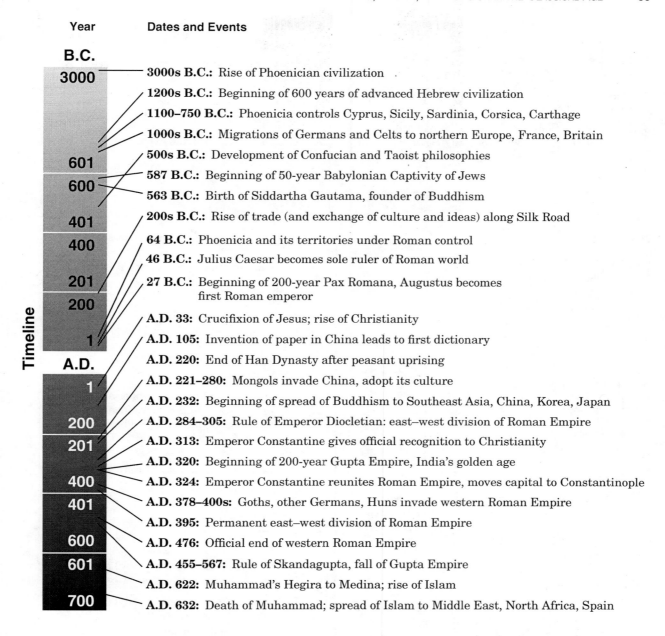

Year   Dates and Events

B.C.

3000s B.C.: Rise of Phoenician civilization

1200s B.C.: Beginning of 600 years of advanced Hebrew civilization

1100–750 B.C.: Phoenicia controls Cyprus, Sicily, Sardinia, Corsica, Carthage

1000s B.C.: Migrations of Germans and Celts to northern Europe, France, Britain

500s B.C.: Development of Confucian and Taoist philosophies

587 B.C.: Beginning of 50-year Babylonian Captivity of Jews

563 B.C.: Birth of Siddartha Gautama, founder of Buddhism

200s B.C.: Rise of trade (and exchange of culture and ideas) along Silk Road

64 B.C.: Phoenicia and its territories under Roman control

46 B.C.: Julius Caesar becomes sole ruler of Roman world

27 B.C.: Beginning of 200-year Pax Romana, Augustus becomes first Roman emperor

A.D. 33: Crucifixion of Jesus; rise of Christianity

A.D. 105: Invention of paper in China leads to first dictionary

A.D. 220: End of Han Dynasty after peasant uprising

A.D. 221–280: Mongols invade China, adopt its culture

A.D. 232: Beginning of spread of Buddhism to Southeast Asia, China, Korea, Japan

A.D. 284–305: Rule of Emperor Diocletian: east–west division of Roman Empire

A.D. 313: Emperor Constantine gives official recognition to Christianity

A.D. 320: Beginning of 200-year Gupta Empire, India's golden age

A.D. 324: Emperor Constantine reunites Roman Empire, moves capital to Constantinople

A.D. 378–400s: Goths, other Germans, Huns invade western Roman Empire

A.D. 395: Permanent east–west division of Roman Empire

A.D. 476: Official end of western Roman Empire

A.D. 455–567: Rule of Skandagupta, fall of Gupta Empire

A.D. 622: Muhammad's Hegira to Medina; rise of Islam

A.D. 632: Death of Muhammad; spread of Islam to Middle East, North Africa, Spain

Timeline years (B.C.): 3000, 601, 600, 401, 400, 201, 200, 1

Timeline years (A.D.): 1, 200, 201, 400, 401, 600, 601, 700

the will of Allah") and his followers as Muslims ("those who surrender to God").

The Quran is the holy book of Islam. It tells Muslims to follow the Five Pillars of Faith:

- Accept Allah as the one true god and Muhammad as his prophet.

- Pray five times a day.

- Fast during the daylight hours in the holy month of Ramadan.

- Give money to the poor.

- Make at least one **pilgrimage** (holy journey) to the holy city of Mecca.

Other duties include eating no pork, drinking no alcoholic beverages, treating all Muslims equally, respecting parents, and protecting the weak. The Quran also teaches that after death the soul is rewarded in heaven or punished in hell. Courage and religious devotion are important Islamic virtues.

SPREAD OF ISLAM. Muslims felt a religious duty to conquer and convert non-Muslim people. Led by Muhammad, they converted and unified all the Bedouin tribes of Arabia by 632. After Muhammad's death, Muslims set out to conquer Syria, North Africa, Spain, Persia, and India. Although they forced no one to convert to Islam, they gave special privileges to those who did so.

1. Identify or define: animism, reincarnation, the Noble Eightfold Path, Quran, Five Pillars of Faith.

2. Describe the role of the caste system in Hindu religion and society.

3. Explain why Confucianism and Taoism are philosophies rather than religions. State a central idea of each.

4. Define and explain the importance to Judaism of monotheism, Ten Commandments, messiah.

5. How was the rise of Christianity affected by mystery cults and Judaism?

6. Describe the roles of Peter and Paul in the spread of Christianity.

7. What factor explains the expansion of Islam beyond Arabia?

CHAPTER REVIEW

Multiple Choice

1. The advantage of the Phoenician system of writing was that it

   1. used fewer sounds
   2. used fewer pictures
   3. used fewer symbols
   4. none of the above.

2. The empire that relied on a highly educated, paid civil-service bureaucracy was the

   1. Persian
   2. Chinese
   3. Roman
   4. Dravidian.

3. The Roman and the Han empires declined because

   1. they attempted to conquer too many peoples
   2. natural disasters destroyed their economies
   3. the rise of new religions divided their peoples
   4. corrupt officials and weakened economies sapped their rulers' powers.

4. The First Triumvirate of Rome was

   1. popularly elected
   2. the union of Caesar, Crassus, and Pompey
   3. a dictatorship under Crassus
   4. a plebeian democracy.

5. Diocletian divided the empire into two parts because

   1. he had two sons
   2. he was granting his nobles part of it
   3. his wife's family were to rule the other half
   4. he wanted to strengthen it.

6. Plebeians in Rome and peasants in China were similar in that

   1. both were heavily taxed and served as soldiers
   2. both voted in all elections and influenced governmental decisions
   3. both owned most of the farmland and grew the majority of crops

   4. both were travelers and traders.

7. Celts influenced the development in Europe of

   1. nomadic living
   2. oral literature
   3. iron farm implements
   4. Christian religious doctrines.

8. The empires of Alexander and Attila did not last for long because

   1. more powerful nomadic tribes appeared
   2. technology created new weapons
   3. natural disasters destroyed both economies
   4. their deaths ended the unity of their followers.

9. The New Testament is to Christianity as the

   1. Quran is to Islam
   2. Analects is to Confucianism
   3. Old Testament is to Judaism
   4. all of the above.

10. The greatest difference between Lao-tzu and Confucius was their views on

    1. how to treat and respect people
    2. the need for self-control
    3. the need to live modestly
    4. the individual's relationship to government.

11. Use the maps on pages 30–31 to locate the only empire in the ancient world that exported, but did not import, goods.

    1. Rome
    2. Parthian Empire
    3. Kush
    4. China

12. With what religion is the temple in the photograph on page 35 associated?

    1. Hinduism
    2. Buddhism
    3. Christianity
    4. Islam

Thematic Essays

1. "Hinduism and Buddhism are linked together, but Buddhism became the religion of the masses." *Task:* Explain and comment on the correctness of this statement.

2. *Task:* Describe the effects on the individual and on society of the Five Pillars of Islam and the Eightfold Path of Buddhism.

Document-Based Questions

Use your knowledge of Global History and Geography and the illustrations and maps to answer the questions.

1. From the photo on page 35, what assumptions can you make about the Aryan culture in India?

2. According to the map on page 38, Christianity began in the Middle East and spread in what directions? What are these areas now named?

3. From the information on the map on page 36, describe the spread of Buddhism.

Document-Based Essay

Task: Discuss the social, economic, or political factors that caused so many people to accept the major religions.

UNIT REVIEW

Thematic Essays

1. Classical civilizations affected future societies. *Task:* Compare any two of the classical civilizations studied and discuss how they affected future societies in two of the following areas: philosophy, politics, economics, science, art, architecture, law.

2. Explain how the development of cartography (map making) has been important to our understanding of the politics and economics of great civilizations.

Document-Based Questions

Use your knowledge of Global History and Geography and the documents to answer the questions.

1. From a history of ancient civilizations:

"The ancients saw man . . . as part of society and society as imbedded in [part of] nature and dependent upon cosmic forces. The ancients told myths instead of presenting an analysis. . . . The Babylonians . . . say the gigantic bird Imdugud . . . covered the sky with black storm clouds and devoured the Bull of Heaven, whose hot breath had scorched the crops. . . . We would explain that certain atmospheric changes broke a drought and brought rain."

What did ancient people believe about their relationship with the forces of nature?

2. From a history of Judaism:

"Many of the most fundamental ideas of Hebrew religion go back to the days when the Hebrews were still nomads. . . . Thus God's commandments to Moses on Mount Sinai that 'Thou shall have no other gods before me,' 'Thou shall not make unto thee any graven image,' and 'Thou shall not take the name of the Lord thy God in vain' . . . determined three fundamental and permanent aspects of Judaism which were new among Near Eastern religions."

Describe what made the religion of the Hebrews unique in its time.

3. Look at the photo on page 37. Why did the sculptor organize the scene the way he did?

Document-Based Essay

Task: Compare and contrast the religions and religious beliefs that arose in the Middle East. In your discussion, include information about the number of deities and the concept and role(s) of God or gods.

UNIT II

Expanding Zones of Exchange and Encounter (A.D. 500–1200)

Year	Dates and Events
A.D.	**495:** Introduction of Buddhism into China
500	**527–565:** Byzantine Empire: west to Spain, south to North Africa, east to Asia; Emperor Justinian organizes Justinian Code
	610–641: Reign of Byzantine Emperor Heraclius, repulsion of Persian and Slav invaders
599	**618–907:** Tang Dynasty rules China
600	**622:** Muhammad's Hegira to Medina
	630: Muhammad and followers occupy Mecca; Meccans accept Islam and Muhammad as its prophet
699	**632–634:** Abu Bakr, Muhammad's successor, unites Arabia
700	**650s–750s:** Arabs carry Islam to North Africa, Spain, Persia, Iraq, Iran, southern Asia, borders of China and India
	700s–1000s: Vikings invade England, Scotland, Ireland, France, Italy, Sicily, Russia
	711–1212: Muslims (Moors) begin 500-year control of Spain
799	**717:** Byzantine Emperor Leo III defeats Arab invaders at Constantinople
800	**732:** Charles Martel defeats Arabs at Tours
	800: Pope Leo III crowns Charlemagne Holy Roman Emperor
899	**843:** Division of Charlemagne's empire into three kingdoms; end of political unity of western Europe
900	**878:** King Alfred of England and Viking invaders make peace
	900s–1000s: Christian kingdoms Navarre, Aragon, Castile begin to push Moors out of Spain
999	**900s–1171:** Descendants of Muhammad's daughter, Fatima, set up dynasty in North Africa
1000	**920–1270:** Sung Dynasty rules China
	1054: Great Schism divides Roman Catholic and Eastern Orthodox churches
1099	**1095:** Pope Urban II calls for crusade to drive Muslims from Holy Land
	1099–1187: Christians win Jerusalem, then lose it to Muslim leader Saladin
1100	**1122:** Concordat of Worms defines political and religious authority
	1207–1213: Pope Innocent III excommunicates King John of England; John accepts pope's candidate for Archbishop of Canterbury
1199	**1212:** Aragon, Navarre, Castile defeat Moors at Las Navas de Tolosa (al-Iqab)

CHAPTER
4

India, China, and Byzantium

I. GUPTA EMPIRE (A.D. 320–600)

A. History

In A.D. 320, a new ruler took over the northeastern Indian kingdom of Magadha. He had the same name as the founder of the Maurya Empire, Chandragupta. He added even more territory and became the first emperor of the Gupta Dynasty.

Two successors enlarged the empire by conquests and alliances. They also enriched it by gaining control of trade with the Middle East and China.

B. Cultural Achievements

SCHOLARSHIP, ART, AND LITERATURE. During the long peace following this period, fine universities were established. The upper classes supported art, science, and scholarship. Visiting scholars brought to India foreign ideas and customs and spread Indian culture throughout Asia.

Sculptors made beautiful statues of Buddha and the Hindu gods.

Literature flourished. A great poet named Kalidasa wrote dramas in verse. Two great epics, the *Ramayana* and the *Mahabharata,* which had begun as oral poems, were also completed and written down.

SCIENCE AND MATHEMATICS. Indian mathematicians developed the decimal system and the concept of zero. (These numbers are known as Arabic numerals because they came to the West through the Arab world.)

A mathematician and scientist named Ayabhata calculated the geometric concept of *pi,* which expresses the relationship between a circle's circumference and its diameter. He knew that Earth is a sphere and that lunar eclipses are caused by Earth's shadow falling on the moon. Other Indian scientists studied gravity.

C. Governmental Organization

Government under the Guptas was less centralized than during the Maurya Dynasty. Princes controlled outer provinces, sent the emperor **tribute** (taxes), and strove to please him because he was a relation of the Hindu gods. Alliances by marriages created another tie between the emperor and the princes.

Towns and villages were largely self-governing. The emperor exerted indirect control through Hinduism, the Guptas' favored religion. Local Hindu priests had strong influence because they kept public records and helped manage public works such as irrigation.

D. Hinduism and Buddhism

The rigid caste system that the Aryans brought to India divided people into four major groups and set up strict rules for living. Members of different castes could not intermarry or eat together.

The Hindu concept of reincarnation reinforced this system. People accepted their social status as the result of behavior in past lives. Only through acceptance could they be reincarnated in a higher form.

Hindu monks preserved Indian culture. Missionaries and religious pilgrims effected cultural exchanges throughout India and other lands. Architects designed beautiful Hindu and Buddhist monasteries.

While less popular than Hinduism, Buddhism influenced the culture through its excellent schools for young people.

E. Status of Women

Women of the Gupta period enjoyed new freedoms. Wealthy girls learned to read and write. Some women became philosophers. Many of them worked as **midwives** trained to deliver babies.

India: Gupta Empire

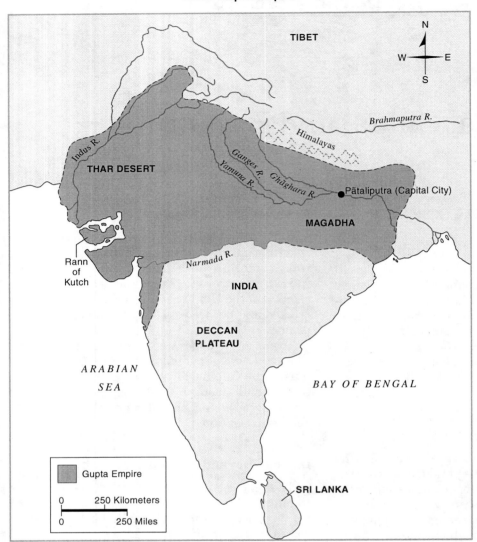

Men still ruled the family, however, and fathers arranged their daughters' marriages.

Widows could not remarry or inherit their husbands' property. Some women followed a tradition called **sati**—they committed suicide by throwing themselves on their husbands' funeral pyres.

F. Decline

During the 5th century A.D., political conflicts weakened the Gupta Empire. About 450, Central Asian warriors called the White Huns invaded India. They were driven off but continued to raid and weaken India economically. The Gupta Empire fell in the mid-6th century, and India again became a collection of small warring kingdoms.

INFO CHECK

1. How did oral history influence the literature of India during the Gupta period?

2. How did the scholars of Gupta India affect mathematics?

3. Explain how religion in Gupta India influenced social organization, education, and cultural life.

4. Indicate why you AGREE or DISAGREE with the following statement: Indian women enjoyed freedom and opportunity under Gupta rule.

II. TANG DYNASTY (618–907)

A line of emperors called the Sui preceded the Tang Dynasty in China. From 581 to 618, they

China: Tang Empire

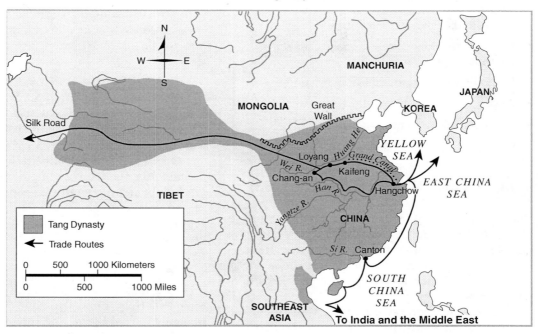

tried to stabilize and enrich the land, but expensive wars, extravagant public works, and harsh taxation frustrated this effort. The Chinese rebelled, the Sui emperor was assassinated, and a

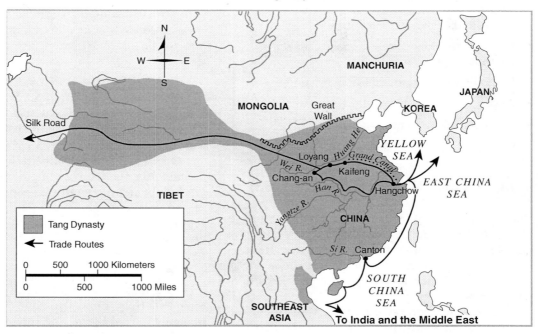

Pottery camel of the Tang Dynasty, artifact for a noble's tomb and token of the important Silk Road trade

general named Li Yuan became the first ruler in the Tang Dynasty.

A. Rule

The Tang emperors ruled more wisely. Under the Tang rulers, peasants regained the prosperity they had known during the Han Dynasty, the empire expanded, and trade was revived.

Tang government was efficient. Special departments supervised different kinds of government business—military matters, justice, finance, and education.

To staff these departments, the Tang emperors revived the Han system of civil-service testing. Successful candidates were known as **mandarins**. Once again, Confucian values became a strong influence on behavior.

B. Achievements

Scholarship and artistic expression flourished. One of China's greatest poets, Li Bo, wrote in the 700s. Dictionaries and encyclopedias were compiled. The invention of printing made books available to greater numbers of people.

C. End of the Dynasty

By 907, the emperor had lost power to provincial governors. As the empire broke up into independent states, foreign invaders conquered China.

INFO CHECK

Complete the following sentences:

1. Efforts of the Sui emperor to make China more stable failed because _____.

2. The Tang rulers improved China by _____.

3. Among the achievements of the Tang were _____.

4. The Tang Dynasty ended in A.D. 907 when _____.

III. BYZANTINE EMPIRE (395–1453)

The Byzantine Empire began as the eastern part of the Roman Empire. Greek was its official language and Christianity its official religion. Its capital, Constantinople, controlling the water route between the Black and Aegean seas, became a prosperous trading center.

Byzantine emperors ruled with the support of a well-trained secret police. They controlled the Eastern Christian Church as well as the government. Several Byzantine rulers were women.

A. Growth

The early emperors were not successful in increasing their territory. Emperor Justinian, however, conquered many lands around the Mediterranean Sea.

B. Invasion From All Sides

Justinian's conquests stirred up many new enemies. After his death, invaders reduced the empire to Asia Minor (Turkey), southern Italy, and Greece.

HERACLIUS. The rulers of Byzantium needed a reliable and inexpensive army. Emperor Heraclius (ruled 610–641) organized the empire into military districts governed by generals who recruited their armies from the local peasants. As payment for service, the general gave the peasants land. This arrangement was especially successful in the section of the Balkans (southeastern Europe) that remained part of Byzantium. There the peasants fought bravely to defend their farms from invaders.

THE ARABS. The Arabs conquered Persia and took the Holy Land (present-day Israel, Lebanon, and part of Syria) and Egypt from the Byzantines. Then they built a huge navy. They could now threaten Constantinople from both land and sea.

Emperor Leo III (ruled 717–741) won a decisive victory over the Arabs in 717. He used a new weapon called **Greek fire**. When pumped through a tube and ignited, this mixture of oil, resin, and sulfur became a jet of flame that could be aimed at enemy targets. By about 1000, Byzantium had gained new territory, and Constantinople became

Byzantine Empire

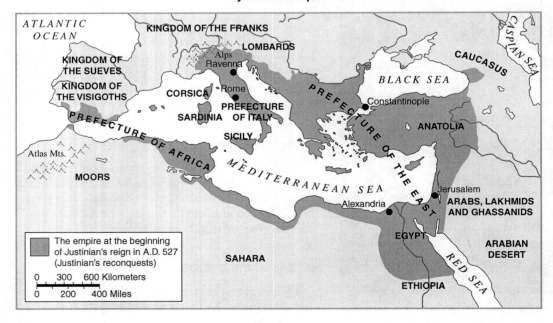

The empire at the beginning of Justinian's reign in A.D. 527 (Justinian's reconquests)

0   300   600 Kilometers

0   200   400 Miles

Illustrated history of Byzantium showing Greek fire used against enemy boat.

an important commercial center for Europe, Africa, Asia, and the Middle East.

C. End of the Byzantine Empire

In the 1070s, Muslims called the Seljuk Turks stepped up attacks on the Byzantines. The emperor asked the pope in Rome for help against such invaders. The pope then persuaded European rulers to send soldiers to the Holy Land. The ensuing wars, in which Europeans fought to regain the Holy Land from the Turks, became known as the **Crusades** (religious wars). They began in 1096 and lasted for 200 years. Meanwhile, the Italian city-state of Venice captured Constantinople and tried to control its trading routes to the Middle East.

The Byzantines won back their city in 1261, but they remained weak and unable to withstand attacks from a new group of Turks, the Ottomans. The Ottomans captured Constantinople in 1453 and put an end to the Byzantine Empire.

D. Orthodox Christian Church

The Greek Orthodox and Roman Catholic churches began to grow apart under the rule of Constantine. Because the emperor ruled from the eastern Roman Empire, the church leaders in the western section became more powerful than the local governors. Eventually, the pope and his bishops claimed that, as God's representatives, they had more authority than the emperor. The emperor firmly controlled Church leaders in the East and strongly opposed this position.

In the 4th century, a famous dispute took place between Bishop Ambrose and Emperor Theodosius over the issue of **primacy**. Ambrose argued that church leaders were responsible for saving everyone's soul and were, therefore, above even kings.

In 1054, territorial rivalry and a religious dispute finally split the Eastern and Western branches of the Christian Church in what is called the **Great Schism**. The Eastern branch became the Eastern Orthodox Church.

BYZANTINE MONASTICISM. The emperors and wealthy people of Byzantium supported **monasteries** and **nunneries** (religious communities where people serve God), which were free from taxes. Byzantine monks and nuns ran hospitals, provided refuges for victims of oppression and crime, and gave food and clothing to the poor. Some monks and nuns became missionaries.

E. Cultural Achievements

Religion strongly influenced Byzantine culture. The Church set rules for marriage and family relations and encouraged the possession of holy images.

ART. The domination of religious themes over everyday Byzantine life was especially exemplified by two kinds of religious artwork. **Mosaics** were wall or floor decorations made of colorful inlaid stones that formed meaningful pictures and patterns. **Icons** were religious images painted on wood and used in devotions.

ARCHITECTURE. Architects designed beautiful churches. One of the most famous was the Hagia Sophia in Constantinople. Its style blended Eastern and Western features.

SCHOLARSHIP. Byzantium produced many historians. Scholars wrote commentaries on classical Greek and Roman writers.

LAW. Emperor Justinian ordered scholars to collect and write down all the laws of Rome. The

Kievan Russia and Byzantine Empire

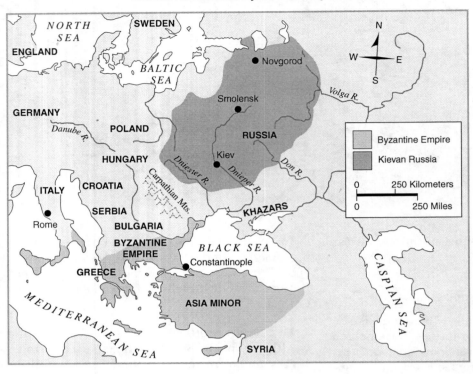

Year	Dates and Events

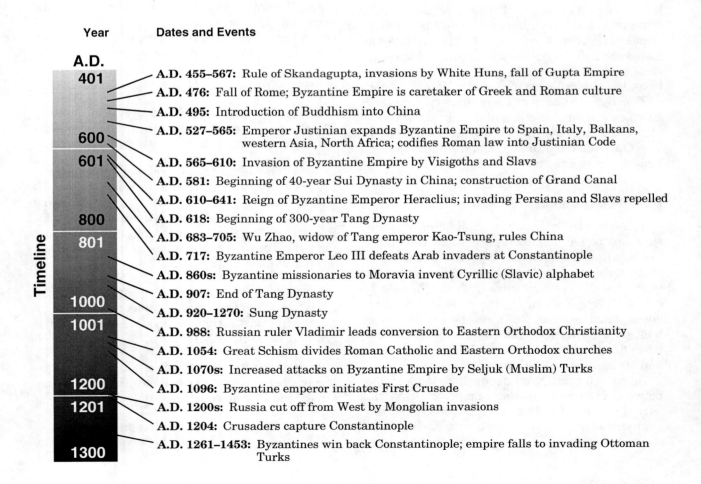

A.D.

401

600

601

800

801

1000

1001

1200

1201

1300

Timeline

A.D. 455–567: Rule of Skandagupta, invasions by White Huns, fall of Gupta Empire

A.D. 476: Fall of Rome; Byzantine Empire is caretaker of Greek and Roman culture

A.D. 495: Introduction of Buddhism into China

A.D. 527–565: Emperor Justinian expands Byzantine Empire to Spain, Italy, Balkans, western Asia, North Africa; codifies Roman law into Justinian Code

A.D. 565–610: Invasion of Byzantine Empire by Visigoths and Slavs

A.D. 581: Beginning of 40-year Sui Dynasty in China; construction of Grand Canal

A.D. 610–641: Reign of Byzantine Emperor Heraclius; invading Persians and Slavs repelled

A.D. 618: Beginning of 300-year Tang Dynasty

A.D. 683–705: Wu Zhao, widow of Tang emperor Kao-Tsung, rules China

A.D. 717: Byzantine Emperor Leo III defeats Arab invaders at Constantinople

A.D. 860s: Byzantine missionaries to Moravia invent Cyrillic (Slavic) alphabet

A.D. 907: End of Tang Dynasty

A.D. 920–1270: Sung Dynasty

A.D. 988: Russian ruler Vladimir leads conversion to Eastern Orthodox Christianity

A.D. 1054: Great Schism divides Roman Catholic and Eastern Orthodox churches

A.D. 1070s: Increased attacks on Byzantine Empire by Seljuk (Muslim) Turks

A.D. 1096: Byzantine emperor initiates First Crusade

A.D. 1200s: Russia cut off from West by Mongolian invasions

A.D. 1204: Crusaders capture Constantinople

A.D. 1261–1453: Byzantines win back Constantinople; empire falls to invading Ottoman Turks

resulting compilation was known as the Code of Justinian.

WEAPONS. The Byzantines invented many new weapons. In addition to Greek fire, they devised advanced siege machines such as accurate catapults and wheeled battering rams.

F. Influence on Russia and Eastern Europe

While trying to convert the Slavs of Eastern Europe to Orthodox Christianity, two Byzantine missionaries, Cyril and Methodius, invented the Cyrillic alphabet for them. Although the Slavs at first became Roman Catholics, they adopted the alphabet, which is still used by Russians, Bulgarians, and Serbs.

Byzantine relations with Russia were hostile at first. Gradually, however, the Byzantines and Russians became trading partners. In 988, the Russian king Vladimir and his subjects converted to Eastern Orthodox Christianity.

Russia was then known as Kievan Russia because of its capital, Kiev. The Kievan Russians made contact with several Western countries through trade, and Russian kings made alliances with the royalty of Sweden, France, and Germany.

Russian relations with the West were cut off during the 13th century when the Mongols conquered Kievan Russia. The Russians, however, remained Eastern Orthodox Christians, and their form of government continued to resemble that of Byzantium.

INFO CHECK

1. Identify a Byzantine achievement in each of the following areas: art and architecture, scholarship and literature, law, military technology.

2. Who were Cyril and Methodius? How did their work affect the cultures of Eastern Europe?

3. How did the Mongols affect Kievan Russia?

CHAPTER REVIEW

Multiple Choice

1. Methods of rule by leaders of the Byzantine, Gupta, and Tang empires included

   1. dividing the empire into military districts
   2. using religion to support authority
   3. encouraging acceptance of Confucian beliefs
   4. all of the above.

2. During the Gupta Empire, Indian customs and culture were spread throughout Southeast Asia and China by

   1. scholars who studied at Indian universities and took home new ideas and ways of living
   2. Indian workers who traveled in search of work
   3. traders who took new ideas and ways of living home to China and Southeast Asia
   4. military conquest of China and Southeast Asia by Gupta armies.

3. The mathematical concepts of pi, zero, and the decimal system originated under the

   1. Han Dynasty
   2. Gupta Dynasty
   3. Byzantine Empire
   4. Tang Dynasty.

4. To insure that government officials were honest and well-educated, Tang emperors relied on a civil-service examination based on

   1. Confucian values
   2. the Twelve Tables

   3. the principles of Legalism
   4. the Hippocratic Oath.

5. The Christian Church, though divided into Western and Eastern branches, remained unified until 1054, when

   1. Muslims conquered Rome
   2. Western Church leaders banned the use of icons and images
   3. a conflict arose over whether the pope or the emperor was head of the Church
   4. the Byzantine Church leaders introduced Latin prayers.

6. The Byzantines protected western Europe from most attacks by the

   1. Japanese
   2. Arabs
   3. Germanic tribes
   4. Indian nomads.

7. One of the early capitals of Russia was

   1. Kiev
   2. Constantinople
   3. Venice
   4. none of the above.

8. In the 13th century, the Mongols conquered Russia. Select the answer that correctly lists one activity that ended and one that continued in Russia under the Mongols.

   1. Eastern Orthodox Christianity was forbidden, but trade with the West continued.

2. Trade with the West was halted, but Eastern Orthodox Christianity continued.
3. Russian nobles no longer read Greek epic poetry, but they continued to study Hinduism.
4. Byzantine forms of culture and government were banned, but the Cyrillic alphabet continued to be used.

9. According to the timeline on page 50, the following periods were important to the growth of the Byzantine Empire.

   1. 527–565 A.D.
   2. 610–641 A.D.
   3. 860s A.D.
   4. all of the above

10. Compare the maps on pages 46 and 47 and select the most accurate statement.

    1. Both the Gupta and Tang empires were protected by defensive walls.
    2. Major river systems aided transportation and communication in both empires.
    3. Both empires were far from the sea.
    4. The Gupta and Tang empires were separated by the Ural Mountains.

Thematic Essays

1. The Gupta, Tang, and Byzantine cultures influenced future cultures. *Task:* Select two examples from Indian, Chinese, and Middle Eastern cultures and describe how they affected future cultures.

2. *Task:* Discuss the role that Byzantium played as protector and spreader of Greek and Roman culture.

Document-Based Questions

Use the documents and your knowledge of Global History and Geography to answer the questions.

1. From the Babylonian Code of Hammurabi:

   "If she [a wife] has not been a careful mistress, . . . [has] neglected her house and belittled her husband, they shall throw that woman into the water."

   According to this reading, what is expected of a woman in a household?

2. A description of the Greek family:

   " . . . Heaven so made their bodies, and set their lives, as to render man strong to endure cold and heat, journeying and warfare, so laying on him the works of the field; but to woman . . . so laying, I think, on her the works of the house. . . . Those who have work indoors will be under you; and you will take charge of everything that is brought into the house. . . . "

   What views are expressed in this reading about how tasks were divided between men and women and what these tasks are?

3. After viewing the picture on page 47, what can you say about the degree of artistic development during the Tang Dynasty?

Document-Based Essay

Task: Use information in the documents and your knowledge of Global History and Geography to compare and contrast the status of women in Mesopotamia, Rome, or Greece to those in India. Include in your answer the nature of the cultures in which women lived.

5

Rise of Islamic Civilization

I. MUSLIM EMPIRE

A. Geography and People

Most of Arabia is very dry. Its southwestern mountain valleys, however, receive enough rain to support farms. Early farmers produced substances used to make incense and perfumes. Arabian merchants grew wealthy trading these goods in India, China, Africa, and the Mediterranean region of Europe.

BEDOUINS. Nomadic herders called **Bedouins** occupied the barren Arabian desert. They grazed their flocks in **oases**—thinly scattered areas of fertile soil watered by underground streams.

Large oases became centers of trade where Bedouins bartered leather, milk, and cheese from their herds for oasis-grown produce. Bedouins also guided other traders to these centers.

TRIBES. Arabians lived in tribes based on common kinship through the male line. Tribal members were loyal to each other and to their elected leaders, called **sheiks**. Different tribes competed for control of the oases, their main source of water. A strong warrior tradition grew out of this rivalry.

LAW. Before Islam, Arab religions were polytheistic and forbade any killing near the gods' shrines. Therefore, warring tribes used the shrines as meeting places to discuss quarrels. Officiating priests often helped settle disputes. Thus, the priests came to have a strong influence on Arabic law.

B. Rise of the Muslim Empire

After Muhammad taught the Arabs to worship Allah, he became the political leader of his converts. When he died, the Muslims chose his father-in-law, Abu Bakr, as the new leader. He took the

Arabian Peninsula: Physical Map

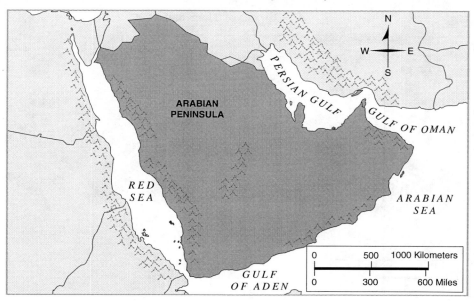

Temporary tent settlement
of nomads of the Sahara

title of **caliph** (successor). Under Abu Bakr's rule (632–634), Muslims began to attack neighboring states within Arabia. By the mid-600s, they had united Arabia under the rule of the caliph.

The Muslims then set out to conquer foreign lands. By 750, the Muslim Empire included all of southern Asia to the borders of India and China, most of Spain, and all of North Africa. The conquered peoples had various cultures and religions.

C. Arab Caliphate

The **caliphate** was the empire's central government. It consisted of the caliph and the officials directly under him.

REASONS FOR SUCCESS. The caliphate succeeded initially because the Muslims did not force

a new way of life on their subjects. They appointed Arabs as **emirs**, or governors, but assigned experienced local officials to work under them. Thus, the emirs learned to use methods of government that were familiar to their new subjects.

As the empire became more complex, new departments of government were set up to deal with new problems. Another adjustment to the empire's growth was creating a relay network by which members of the caliphate sent important reports.

MILITARY ORGANIZATION. The army that won the Muslim Empire consisted of Arab tribesmen. They had grown up in a warrior culture and were resourceful survivors, expert horsemen, and deeply loyal comrades.

As the empire grew larger, the caliphs formed units of soldiers from conquered cultures and

Spread of Islam, 634–1250

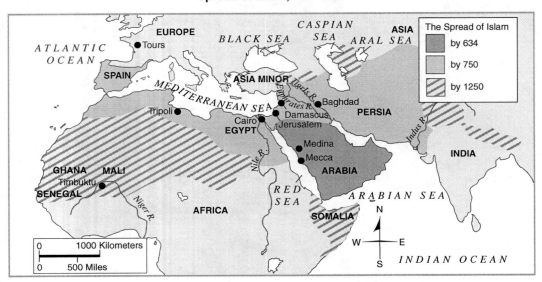

pared down some privileges that Arab troops had enjoyed. The intention was to instill in military units primary loyalty to the ruler rather than to a tribe. The new system, however, never entirely replaced the old one.

D. Umayyad Dynasty (661–750)

In time, the generals and governors of conquered lands became more powerful than the caliphs in Mecca. In 661, the Muslim governor of Syria rebelled, became the caliph, and established the Umayyad Dynasty. Damascus replaced Mecca as the capital.

The Umayyad caliphs added new territory to the empire. This expanded empire included an even greater variety of cultures.

Although the Umayyads did not force their subjects to convert to Islam, those who did were granted special privileges while the unconverted were heavily taxed. Taxes paid for the luxurious lifestyle of the Umayyads, which caused widespread unrest.

SHI'ITES. A group called the Shiah (supporters of Ali) contested Umayyad rule. Its members, called **Shi'ites**, believed that Muhammad's cousin Ali should have been caliph. They claimed that Muhammad's blood relatives had inherited his divine knowledge, which qualified them to be better political as well as religious leaders than others.

SUNNITES. The Umayyad rulers were **Sunnis**. Their name refers to the Sunna, a collection of Muhammad's teachings. For Sunnis, the caliph did not have to be descended from Muhammad. Many also felt that Islamic scholars, not the caliph, should interpret religious doctrine.

E. Abbassid Dynasty (750–1258)

The Abbassid family was descended from Muhammad. Therefore, the Shi'ites helped them overthrow the Umayyads in 750.

EASTERN RULE. The Abbassids moved the capital to a new city in present-day Iraq (still called Baghdad). The Abbassids, like the Umayyads, used tax money to pay for their indulgences. As opposition to Abbassid rule increased, law and order broke down, and the weakened empire could not defend itself from invaders. Seljuk Turks moved into the empire in the 1040s. In 1258, a Mongol invasion ended the Abbassid Dynasty.

WESTERN RULE. When the Abbassids overthrew the Umayyads, they took control of only the eastern part of the empire. An Umayyad prince who had fled to Spain ruled the western part.

FATIMID. In the 10th century, North Africa broke away from the Abbassids. A dynasty called the Fatamid, descendants of Muhammad's daughter Fatima, took control of what are now Tunisia, Morocco, Libya, and Egypt. The Fatamid's capital was Cairo, and the empire lasted until about 1171.

INFO CHECK

1. Explain the importance of Bedouins to the development of the economic and cultural life of the Arabian Peninsula.

2. What role did Arab military skill play in the rise of the Muslim Empire?

3. Trace the dynastic divisions of the Muslim Empire by creating a chart giving the name of the dynasty, dates, capital city, and territories ruled.

4. How do Shi'ites and Sunnis differ in origins and beliefs?

5. Define the following: sheik, caliphate, emir.

II. ISLAMIC SOCIETY

A. Islamic Law

During the Umayyad Dynasty, the caliph consulted officials about the use of Islamic principles, as set down in the Sunna and the Quran, in solving legal problems. Eventually, these legal interpretations became a collection of laws called the **shari'a**.

Some of the most important Islamic principles were:

- charity to the poor
- equality of all Muslims
- tolerance of other cultures
- respect for scholarship

B. Status of Women

Before Islam, Arabian women had no legal rights and could not own or inherit property. At first, the Islamic principle of equality improved women's lives. The Quran gave women the right to keep property they owned before marriage and to use it any way they wished. It allowed them to take part in politics, travel, and attend public religious ceremonies.

As the empire expanded, however, female slaves entered Muslim society as spoils of war. This inflow and the right under Islamic law for a man to have more than one wife encouraged the view that women were property. Scholars began to reinterpret passages in the Quran to show that women were less capable than men.

C. Social Class and Slavery

Muslim social classes, from highest to lowest, were as follows:

- Aristocrats—descendants of the Bedouins who first followed Muhammad

- Second class—non-Arabic converts to Islam, who served as doctors, teachers, artists, and lawyers

- Third class—so-called protected peoples, such as unconverted Jews, Christians, and Zoroastrians, who could enter the professions but had fewer privileges than the second class

- Fourth class—slaves, most of whom were soldiers and servants, while the educated ones held responsible business and professional positions. (The Quran recommended that masters treat their slaves humanely.)

D. Trade and Commerce

Islamic law encouraged trade as a means of making money, which, in turn, could be used for charity. During the height of the empire, Muslim traders had access to markets throughout the known world. Most of the goods traded were luxury items.

Muslim merchants developed business techniques still used today. They originated the **bill of exchange**, which enabled traders to stay at home and order foreign bankers to pay money to their business agents. Thus, people did not have to make long and dangerous trips carrying large sums of money. The Muslims may also have originated the **joint-stock company**. People who head a joint-stock company finance a business venture by selling shares in future profits. The investor, or buyer, receives a portion of the profits based on how much money was contributed.

E. Cultural Achievements

NAVIGATION. On trading voyages, Muslims gained knowledge about new navigational devices, which they then spread to other lands. From Chi-

Arab merchants beginning a long journey in search of profits

nese sailors, they learned about the **compass**. Its magnetic needle always points north and can help a traveler determine directions anywhere on Earth except at the North and South poles.

The Muslims perfected the Greek **astrolabe**. This instrument helps determine latitude and time of day. Muslims also became expert map-makers.

GEOGRAPHY. The Muslim historian Ibn-Khaldun (1332–1406) showed that a country's climate and natural features greatly effect its economy. The economy, in its turn, affects human behavior. Ibn-Khaldun is considered the first social scientist.

EDUCATION. Muslim scholarly tradition allowed men to move up in society. Muslim schools prepared young men to be preachers, judges, and professors. Muslim scholars helped preserve works from the Greco-Roman, Semitic, Indian, and Persian cultures.

Women did not attend school. Nonetheless, Muhammad had stated that every Muslim had a duty to seek knowledge. Therefore, many parents educated their daughters at home.

MATHEMATICS. Arab mathematicians used the zero and a Hindu number system and spread

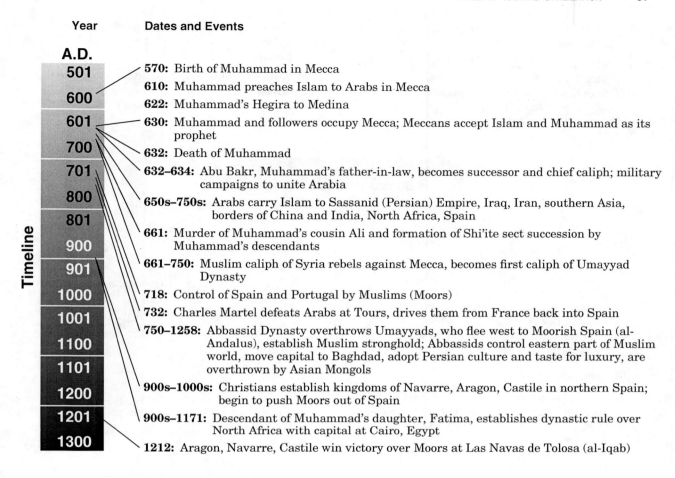

Year   Dates and Events

A.D.

501

600

601

700

701

800

801

900

901

1000

1001

1100

1101

1200

1201

1300

Timeline

570: Birth of Muhammad in Mecca

610: Muhammad preaches Islam to Arabs in Mecca

622: Muhammad's Hegira to Medina

630: Muhammad and followers occupy Mecca; Meccans accept Islam and Muhammad as its prophet

632: Death of Muhammad

632–634: Abu Bakr, Muhammad's father-in-law, becomes successor and chief caliph; military campaigns to unite Arabia

650s–750s: Arabs carry Islam to Sassanid (Persian) Empire, Iraq, Iran, southern Asia, borders of China and India, North Africa, Spain

661: Murder of Muhammad's cousin Ali and formation of Shi'ite sect succession by Muhammad's descendants

661–750: Muslim caliph of Syria rebels against Mecca, becomes first caliph of Umayyad Dynasty

718: Control of Spain and Portugal by Muslims (Moors)

732: Charles Martel defeats Arabs at Tours, drives them from France back into Spain

750–1258: Abbassid Dynasty overthrows Umayyads, who flee west to Moorish Spain (al-Andalus), establish Muslim stronghold; Abbassids control eastern part of Muslim world, move capital to Baghdad, adopt Persian culture and taste for luxury, are overthrown by Asian Mongols

900s–1000s: Christians establish kingdoms of Navarre, Aragon, Castile in northern Spain; begin to push Moors out of Spain

900s–1171: Descendant of Muhammad's daughter, Fatima, establishes dynastic rule over North Africa with capital at Cairo, Egypt

1212: Aragon, Navarre, Castile win victory over Moors at Las Navas de Tolosa (al-Iqab)

this knowledge to Europe. In the early 800s, Al-Kwarizmi improved the mathematical system called algebra. Another Muslim mathematician, Al-Hazan (965–1039), made important discoveries in optics, the study of light rays.

MEDICINE. The physicians Rhazes (865–932) and Ibn Sina (980–1037), who was also called Avecenna, wrote medical encyclopedias. Other Arab doctors learned to treat such diseases as measles and smallpox. Surgeons used animal gut to stitch up wounds and performed operations to remove cataracts from eyes.

LITERATURE. Omar Khayyam (1048–1123) wrote a book of poetry called the *Rubaiyat,* which has been widely translated and is still read today. *The Arabian Nights,* or *The Thousand and One Nights,* is a collection of folktales derived from the Middle East, North Africa, and India.

PHILOSOPHY. Ibn Rusd (1126–1198), also called Averroës, and Moses Maimonides (born 1135) commented on works by Aristotle and other Greek philosophers. These Muslim writings influenced later religious thinking in Europe.

III. ISLAMIC SPAIN

By 718, Muslims, or Moors, controlled almost all of the Iberian Peninsula (Portugal and Spain). Muslim Spain, known as al-Andalus, had a high culture and flourishing economy. Its capital, Cordoba, became a world-renowned center of learning.

As al-Andalus declined, the Christian kingdoms of Navarre, Aragon, and Castile in northern Spain began to push the Muslims out. The Castilian kings started a crusade against the Muslims called the **Reconquistá** (reconquest of the Iberian Peninsula). By 1492, Aragon, Navarre, and Castile had driven the Moors from Spain.

> ### INFO CHECK
>
> 1. Rewrite as correct statements the following statements that are incorrect:
>   - The shari'a was a Bedouin survival manual.
>   - Muslim women had no rights under Islamic law.
>   - Muslim society was divided into classes, with some groups enjoying more rights and privileges than others.

- Arab traders were restricted to Arabia and dealt only in the basic necessities of life.

2. Explain why you AGREE or DISAGREE with the following statements:
   - Life in the Muslim Empire was enriched by the acquisition of knowledge, the growth of new ideas, and inventions.

- There were few scholars, doctors, poets, or philosophers in the Islamic society of the Muslim Empire.

3. Why do you think many would have regarded Spain as more comfortable and enjoyable during the Middles Ages than other places in Europe?

CHAPTER REVIEW

Multiple Choice

1. The Arabian Peninsula was a center of agriculture, trade, and commerce because of its
   1. fertile soil
   2. production of incense and nearness to the Mediterranean Sea
   3. large crops of wheat and nearness to the Atlantic Ocean
   4. large amounts of rainfall and rapid transportation systems.

2. The Bedouins lived by
   1. serving as mercenaries in the emperor's armies
   2. growing large crops of palm and dates for sale
   3. their knowledge of the desert and raising animals
   4. helping to build vast cities for their Turkish rulers.

3. Arab tribes are joined together through
   1. kinship through a male line
   2. kinship through a female line
   3. arranged marriages
   4. agreements made by kings.

4. Because Arab tribes never fought near religious shrines,
   1. travelers in the Arabian Peninsula carried icons with them
   2. the priesthood became a safe life
   3. conflicts between Bedouin tribes were settled near shrines
   4. oases were always set up next to the shrines.

5. The term *caliph* was first given to
   1. Muhammad's father-in-law, as the successor and leader of the Muslims
   2. Muhammad's son, as the male successor and leader of the Muslims
   3. Muhammad as the successor to the throne
   4. none of the above.

6. The event that resulted in the expulsion of Moors from Spain was the
   1. Battle of Constantinople in 1492
   2. Battle of Paris in 1914
   3. Battle of the Atlantic in 1940
   4. Reconquistà.

7. The Muslims peacefully ruled a vast empire because they
   1. killed and tortured anyone who did not convert to Islam
   2. had a vast army of secret police and informers
   3. kept large armies in every town and city they ruled
   4. allowed other religions to exist and used native officials to assist in governing.

8. The first successful rebellion that led to a Muslim dynasty and shifted the base of political power was the
   1. Wahabi Dynasty of Mecca
   2. Umayyad Dynasty of Damascus
   3. Abbassid Dynasty of Baghdad
   4. Fatimid Dynasty of Cairo.

9. The Sunna, like the Quran, is
   1. a collection of Muhammad's teachings
   2. Islamic poetry
   3. a scientific journal
   4. none of the above.

10. Select the answer that correctly arranges the four classes of Muslim society from highest to lowest.
    1. Arab Muslims, protected peoples, non-Arab Muslims, and women
    2. Arab Muslims, protected peoples, non-Arab Muslims, and slaves
    3. Arab Muslims, non-Arab Muslims, protected peoples, and slaves
    4. Arab Muslims, Arab Muslim women, non-Arab Muslims, and non-Arab Muslim women.

11. What does the photograph on page 54 indicate about Bedouin life?
    1. Bedouins live in Asian cities.
    2. Bedouins wander the Sahara in search of grazing land.
    3. Bedouin farms are large and well irrigated.
    4. Bedouins work in heavy industries.

12. According to the timeline on page 57, which statement is correct?

1. Muhammad and his followers occupied Mecca in 1300 A.D.
2. The Umayyad Dynasty was established in 576 A.D.
3. Muslims took control of Spain and Portugal in 718 A.D.
4. The Abbassid Dynasty fell in 622 A.D.

Thematic Essays

1. Choose two of the following areas: the sciences, government, arts, literature. *Task:* Describe the contributions of the Muslims and how these contributions affected future civilizations.

2. *Task:* What use of tax money brought down the Abbassid Dynasty?

3. *Task:* How did the various Muslim dynasties treat non-Muslims?

Document-Based Questions

Use the documents presented and your knowledge of Global History and Geography to answer the questions.

1. Look at the map on page 54. Identify at least two areas where the Muslims and other empires previously studied would have come into conflict.

2. "I have been ordered to fight against people until they testify that there is no god but Allah and that Muhammad is the Messenger of Allah and . . . if they do so, they will have gained protection from me for their lives and property, unless [they do acts that are punishable] in accordance with Islam, and their reckoning will be with Allah the Almighty."

   Who would use this document and for what purpose?

3. Look at the illustration on page 56. What does it show about Muslim dealings with peoples outside the Muslim Empire?

Document-Based Essay

Using specific examples, AGREE or DISAGREE with the following statement: "The Muslim Empire was distinguished by its military conquests and cultural richness."

C H A P T E R
6

Medieval Europe (500–1200): Political, Social, and Cultural Changes

I. GEOGRAPHY

Europe is the western part of the great landmass comprising both Asia and Europe. The Ural Mountains in central Russia mark Europe's eastern boundary.

The nations in western and southern Europe have easy access to the Atlantic Ocean and the Mediterranean, North, and Baltic seas. Rivers such as the Seine in France and the Danube in Central Europe provide pathways to and from the interior.

A band of mountains runs from Spain in southern Europe to Russia. Although these ranges made early trade and travel in southern Europe difficult, they gave some protection against invasion.

Europe: Physical Map and Resources

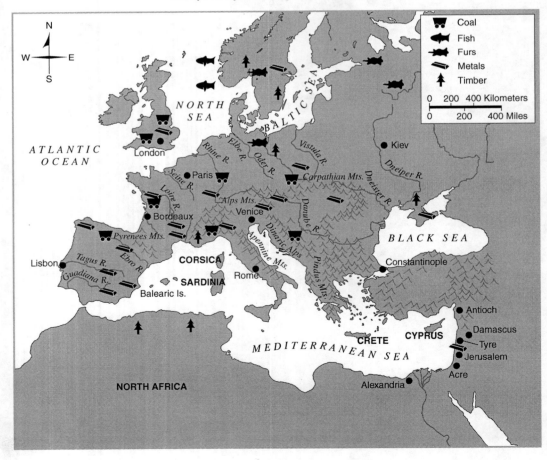

A vast plain stretches from France into Russia. It makes travel across the central part of Europe easy and supports productive farms.

INFO CHECK

1. Why might Europe be described as a peninsula of Asia?

2. Name one advantage and one disadvantage that the geography of southern Europe posed for its inhabitants.

II. WESTERN EUROPE AFTER THE FALL OF ROME

When German tribes invaded the western Roman Empire, they divided it into a collection of small kingdoms. No longer did a central government maintain public services such as water supply and sewage systems.

A. Breakdown of Law and Order

Roads crumbled. With no Roman soldiers to patrol remote districts, bandits robbed and killed travelers. Trade slowed down.

Communities were cut off from one another. People began to speak dialects (local forms) of Latin. The dialects developed into the French, Italian, Romanian, Portuguese, and Spanish languages.

CHANGE AND GROWTH. Although trade, learning, and the fine arts suffered during this period, farmers developed better farming methods and tools that made their land more productive.

Important political changes also took place. Instead of being representatives of a central government, German kings were independent rulers. They were, however, influenced by Roman law and institutions and adapted them to fit local needs. Thus, they developed new forms of government.

B. Leadership of the Christian Church

The Christian Church was a unifying force in Europe. In 380, Emperor Theodosius, hoping to bring order to a population of many different cultures, made Christianity the state religion of the Roman Empire. He gave Church leaders substantial political power; they could establish their own courts and laws for trying disobedient church officials.

Church leaders adopted the empire's political structure and set up bishops in the central cities of outlying areas. They represented the bishop of Rome as the governors represented the Roman emperor. Eventually, the bishop of Rome became known as the pope.

CONFLICTS. The Great Schism, the split between the eastern and western churches, occurred in 1054. By the 11th century, the Eastern Orthodox Church dominated eastern Europe. The patriarchs (church officials) recognized the authority of the Byzantine emperors over them.

By the 1200s, the Roman Catholic Church had become the strongest force in western Europe in both religious and secular matters.

MONASTERIES AND CONVENTS. Monasteries and convents had great influence on medieval society. Women who became nuns lived in convents ruled by abbesses. Monks and friars lived in monasteries ruled by abbots. Members of such religious orders took vows of poverty, chastity, and obedience.

Monks and nuns farmed, did housekeeping tasks, and sold surplus produce in the local markets. In many orders, they studied works in Greek and Latin. They copied and illustrated manuscripts. They also gave local people spiritual help, basic education, and medical care.

INFLUENCE ON LEARNING. The clergy were the main teachers and scholars of the Middle Ages. People asked their advice on medicine and law, as well as religious matters. Consequently, the clergy in medieval Europe had great control over culture and government. For example, the English scholar-priest Alcuin educated children of the nobility, wrote a book on how kings should rule, and sent letters of advice to the Holy Roman Emperor Charlemagne.

ART. Almost all medieval art was created as aids to worship. Monks illustrated the religious

Scholarly French monk of the 15th century scripting a manuscript copy

manuscripts they copied. Among the most beautiful is a decorated Bible, the Book of Kells, created by Irish monks.

The most impressive buildings were great churches. The two major styles of church architecture were **Romanesque** and **Gothic**. Romanesque churches, built from 1000 to 1150, had thick stone walls, very small windows, and rounded arches.

Gothic churches were built from about 1150 to 1300. They had thinner stone walls, high ceilings, large windows made of colored (stained) glass, pointed arches, and tall towers. Structures called **flying buttresses** supported the exterior walls.

INFO CHECK

1. Refute the argument that Europe was in a "dark age" after A.D. 476, during which nothing new or important developed.

2. List some ways in which the Church provided unity and leadership to medieval Europe.

3. Why did monasteries and convents attract so many Europeans during the Middle Ages?

4. Why were education and religion so closely connected in medieval Europe?

5. How was the art of medieval Europe influenced by the Church?

C. Frankish Empire

The Merovingian family belonged to a Germanic group called the Franks. Clovis, a Frankish king, conquered what is now Belgium, Luxembourg, and the Netherlands. To govern this large territory, he needed the support of local bishops. He therefore converted to Christianity.

After Clovis' death in 511, his kingdom was divided among his sons. They spent so much time fighting one another that much of their power fell to their chief officials, the "mayors of the palace."

CHARLES MARTEL AND PEPIN. The office of mayor of the palace became hereditary. One of these heirs was Charles Martel. He gained church support by helping Benedictine monks convert northern Europeans to Christianity. In 751, the pope approved the crowning of Martel's son, Pepin III, as king of the Franks.

Pepin strengthened his ties with the Church by defending an area in Italy against the invading Lombards. The Byzantine leaders, busy resisting Muslim invasions, could send no troops, so Pope Stephen II enlisted Pepin's help. He drove off the Lombards, took part of the territory for himself, and gave the rest to the pope as the Papal States. Pepin's close relationship with the Church gave him and his heirs even more authority. With the protection of Pepin's army, the Roman Church became less dependent on the Byzantine government.

CHARLEMAGNE. Pepin's son Charles ruled from 771 to 814. He became known as Charlemagne, or Charles the Great. Charlemagne expanded the Frankish Empire and forced conquered peoples to become Christians.

Charlemagne also put down an uprising against Pope Leo III. The grateful pope crowned Charlemagne Holy Roman Emperor in 800. The coronation outraged the Byzantine leaders because a Byzantine emperor already ruled the Roman Empire. Moreover, this coronation by a religious leader demonstrated that the Church was higher than the state. The kings who followed Charlemagne recognized the pope's right to crown them and increased his political power.

About 35 years after Charlemagne's death, the empire broke up when his grandsons waged war on one another. The Treaty of Verdun ended the war and divided the empire into three kingdoms.

CULTURE OF MEDIEVAL EUROPE. Charlemagne set up schools where his subjects could study clas-

Depiction of the coronation of Charlemagne by Pope Leo III

Charlemagne's Realm and Its Division

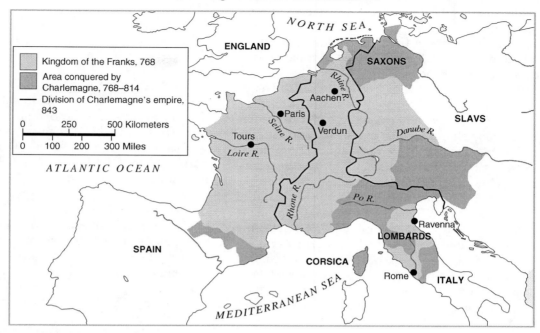

sical culture. The English scholar-priest Alcuin directed a school that Charlemagne had established for his nobles' children.

Because of these schools, educated people were able to speak and write Latin and Greek. Scholars, scientists, and professionals exchanged ideas with their peers in other cultural regions.

INFO CHECK

1. How did each of the following shape European history during the Middle Ages: Clovis, Charles Martel, Pepin III, Charlemagne?

2. Explain why you AGREE or DISAGREE with this statement: During the Middle Ages, the Byzantine Empire had more influence on events in western Europe than did the Frankish Empire.

3. Explain the importance of Latin and Greek to the spread of ideas throughout Europe.

III. GROWTH OF PAPAL POWER

A. Basis

St. Peter, the first head of the organized Christian Church, had been **martyred** (killed for his beliefs) in Rome. The popes of Rome considered themselves his successors.

The popes ruled the Papal States as kings. They also collected **tithes** (taxes) from people ruled by Christian kings.

Popes used Church law to pass judgment on kings, nobles, and commoners. Their two most important legal powers were **excommunication** and **interdiction**. Excommunication barred a person from church services, confession, and communion. People who died while excommunicated, it was believed, would go to hell. The subjects of an excommunicated ruler did not have to obey him.

Popes could place an interdiction on a king's entire realm. The churches in an interdicted land could perform no services except baptism and rites for the dying. No one could marry, take communion, confess, or be buried with a church service. People in interdicted lands often tried to force the king to give in to the pope.

The officials who managed Church business formed a **hierarchy** (system of ranking). Cardinals were the highest officials, with bishops next in rank, and priests lowest of all. Abbots and abbesses represented the pope's authority in their monasteries and also in surrounding areas.

B. Conflicts Between Church and State

Monarchs often expected the bishops in their domain to take on some of the duties of government. Therefore, they protected the Church lands. The bishops paid taxes to the monarchs and sent some of their own tenants and workers to serve in the army. This arrangement made for a stable government, so the popes did not, at first, object to the appointment of bishops by kings. Such an appointment was called **lay investiture**.

In the 11th century, however, Church reformers began to argue that lay investiture gave kings too much power over religious matters. A great controversy arose between the German king, Henry IV, and Pope Gregory VII, who ruled that only clergy could appoint bishops. Henry's appointed bishops defied the pope, who then excommunicated Henry. With his throne threatened by rival German nobles, Henry gave in and received Gregory's pardon. Once Henry had regained his throne and the support of his bishops, however, he put Rome under siege until it replaced Gregory. The new pope gave Henry the title of Holy Roman Emperor.

In 1122, the Concordat of Worms was held at Worms, Germany. Delegates resolved the problem of lay investiture by a compromise. A king could invest a bishop with land and the worldly symbols of office. Only the Church, however, could nominate and elect a bishop and invest him with spiritual powers. This decision made it harder for a king to place an ally in an important Church position.

INFO CHECK

1. Define excommunication and interdiction and explain how they increased papal power.

2. Describe the investiture controversy. How and when was it settled?

IV. INVADERS AND CONQUERORS

From the 8th to the 11th century, a series of invasions and migrations terrified established European settlements.

INVADERS FROM THE NORTH. The Vikings came from what is now Scandinavia and overran large parts of Europe and the British Isles. They could cover these long distances because they were expert sailors and shipbuilders. Other Europeans learned from them how to build ships that could sail the open seas.

By 1000, there were Viking settlements in England, Scotland, Ireland, France, Italy, Sicily, and Russia. A Frankish king gave a group of Vikings called Norsemen territory in the northwestern section of France—the area we know today as Normandy. In 1066, a Norman duke, William the Conqueror, invaded England and introduced the French language, laws, and government.

INVADERS FROM THE EAST. The Magyars migrated from central Asia to Hungary. In 890, they began to loot villages and monasteries in France, northern Italy, and southern Germany.

MUSLIM INVADERS. In the 9th and 10th centuries, Arabs raided Italy and other places on the Mediterranean coast. Like the Magyars, they were

---

Viking, Magyar, and Muslim Invasions of Europe

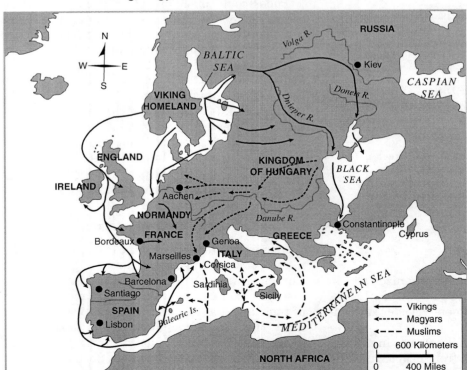

more interested in looting than in settling the places they attacked.

INFO CHECK

1. Complete the following sentences:
   * Medieval Europeans feared the Vikings and the Magyars because ＿＿＿.
   * An important Viking settlement in France came to be called ＿＿＿.
   * The most important Scandinavian contribution to Europe was ＿＿＿.
2. French culture, politics, and law became strong influences in England after ＿＿＿.

V. FEUDALISM AND MANORIALISM

Invasions by Vikings, Magyars, and Arabs caused European landowners to develop a system of government called **feudalism**. Feudalism is based on pledges of loyalty in return for land and protection. It developed from the political systems of German and Celtic tribes.

A. System of Feudalism

Charlemagne's successors were too weak to fight off the Vikings and other raiders. Instead, they relied on the military power of the great landowning nobles in their kingdoms. These lords raised armies to defend their king and themselves by giving land and protection to smaller landowners willing to fight for them. Those who accepted this arrangement were called **vassals**.

Vassals served as **knights** (soldiers on horseback) in a lord's army for about five weeks a year and paid for the privilege. In return, the lord provided money and soldiers for the common defense. He maintained roads and villages. He acted as a judge in disputes between vassals. Vassals often subdivided part of their land for men who promised loyal service in return.

When a lord or vassal died, the eldest son inherited his father's property and position in the feudal system. This practice, known as primogeniture, preserved large feudal landholdings intact.

Because the vassals were often nobles with connections to other noble families, they had considerable political power. As knights in the lord's army, they also had military power. Women, who could not own property, were under the protection of the men in their families.

B. Training for Knighthood

A boy of the nobility began training for knighthood when he was seven. He first served as a **page**, or general servant, in the household of a family friend. At 14, he became a **squire**, or the personal servant of a veteran knight, from whom he learned the code of **chivalry**. This code required a knight to be loyal, brave, courteous, merciful, generous, and charitable. The young squire also learned how to fight on horseback and handle weapons. He became a knight at the age of 21.

C. Manorial System

Agriculture was vital to the medieval economy. People of the time, therefore, measured wealth and power by ownership of land.

The economic relationship between a lord and the people who worked for him was called the **manorial system**. The lord's house, land, and workers made up his **manor**. Most of these workers were **serfs**; they belonged to the manor. Thus, if the ownership of the manor changed, the serfs stayed on the land. They could not marry without their lord's permission, and they could not rise to a higher social position. Workers who were free peasants, however, could move from place to place. Both serfs and peasants had to pay rent to raise their own crops on part of the lord's land.

In times of danger, peasants and serfs took refuge in the lord's castle. The castle's thick walls

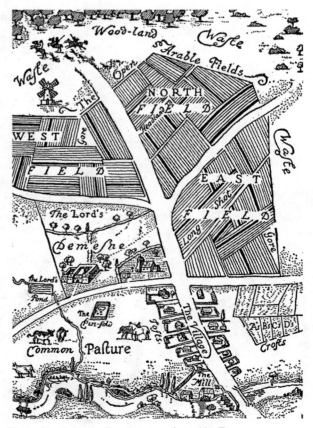

Plan of typical medieval manor found in Europe

and surrounding **moat** (water-filled ditch) protected them.

Manors were self-sufficient, producing food for everyone and all the tools, weapons, clothing, and furniture needed for daily living.

Many abbots and abbesses ran their monasteries and convents like manors. Owning land and serfs gave them significant political power.

INFO CHECK

1. PROVE or DISPROVE:
   • The purpose of feudalism was to provide Europeans with security in return for service.

   • Nobles could be lords and vassals at the same time.

2. Why did boys of the nobility want to become knights? What were the obligations of knighthood?

3. Why was the manorial system essential to feudalism?

D. The Crusades

The First Crusade to recapture Jerusalem and the Holy Land from the Seljuk Turks set off for the Holy Land in 1096. It ended when the Cru-

saders won back Jerusalem. They were unable to keep their conquest, however. During a period of 200 years, four major Crusades were launched to defend the Holy Land against renewed Muslim attacks. Saladin, a Muslim ruler of Syria and Egypt, retook Jerusalem in 1187. He granted Christians the right to visit their holy places there.

RESULTS. By their acts of cruelty and intolerance, the Crusaders aroused strong resentment in the Muslims. In the Holy Land, the Crusaders learned new ideas and developed a taste for Middle Eastern arts and luxuries. European merchants established a trade that proved profitable for themselves and Muslims alike. Several Italian city-states—particularly Venice and Genoa—controlled this trade.

INFO CHECK

1. List the major cause and results of the Crusades.

2. Explain why historians regard the Crusades as a military failure of the Christian kings that nevertheless brought economic and cultural benefits to western Europe.

Routes of the First Four Crusades

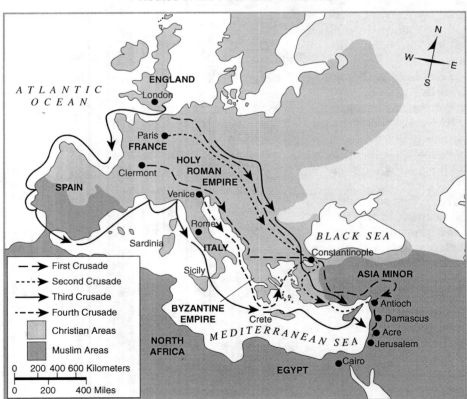

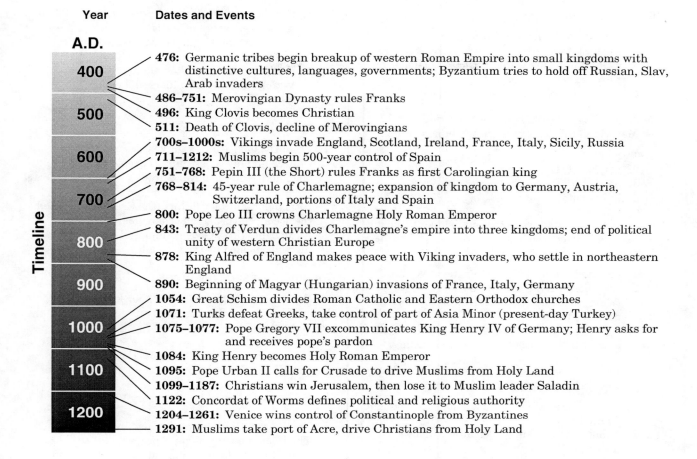

| Year | Dates and Events |

A.D.

400

500

600

700

800

900

1000

1100

1200

Timeline

476: Germanic tribes begin breakup of western Roman Empire into small kingdoms with distinctive cultures, languages, governments; Byzantium tries to hold off Russian, Slav, Arab invaders

486–751: Merovingian Dynasty rules Franks

496: King Clovis becomes Christian

511: Death of Clovis, decline of Merovingians

700s–1000s: Vikings invade England, Scotland, Ireland, France, Italy, Sicily, Russia

711–1212: Muslims begin 500-year control of Spain

751–768: Pepin III (the Short) rules Franks as first Carolingian king

768–814: 45-year rule of Charlemagne; expansion of kingdom to Germany, Austria, Switzerland, portions of Italy and Spain

800: Pope Leo III crowns Charlemagne Holy Roman Emperor

843: Treaty of Verdun divides Charlemagne's empire into three kingdoms; end of political unity of western Christian Europe

878: King Alfred of England makes peace with Viking invaders, who settle in northeastern England

890: Beginning of Magyar (Hungarian) invasions of France, Italy, Germany

1054: Great Schism divides Roman Catholic and Eastern Orthodox churches

1071: Turks defeat Greeks, take control of part of Asia Minor (present-day Turkey)

1075–1077: Pope Gregory VII excommunicates King Henry IV of Germany; Henry asks for and receives pope's pardon

1084: King Henry becomes Holy Roman Emperor

1095: Pope Urban II calls for Crusade to drive Muslims from Holy Land

1099–1187: Christians win Jerusalem, then lose it to Muslim leader Saladin

1122: Concordat of Worms defines political and religious authority

1204–1261: Venice wins control of Constantinople from Byzantines

1291: Muslims take port of Acre, drive Christians from Holy Land

CHAPTER REVIEW

Multiple Choice

1. During the European medieval period, there was no strong centralized government. However, advances were made in

   1. art, science, and communication
   2. agriculture and ship design
   3. medicine
   4. all of the above.

2. Germanic rule of Europe differed from Roman rule in that

   1. rulers used fortune-tellers to guide decision making
   2. the army had great influence in selection of the ruler
   3. women played a major role in political decision making
   4. no central political authority existed.

3. Select the pairs that correctly apply to Church leadership and responsibility.

   1. parish priest to his church as bishop to his diocese

   2. abbot to his nuns as the priest to his convent
   3. patriarch to his church as priests to missionaries
   4. none of the above.

4. A major difference between the Roman and Eastern Orthodox Church leadership was that

   1. Eastern Orthodox priests conducted services in Latin
   2. Roman priests allowed the use of pictures but not statues
   3. the authority of the pope was superior to that of kings
   4. in Byzantium, Church leaders made government policies.

5. The Great Schism of 1054 refers to

   1. the division of the Christian Church into two parts
   2. the major earthquake that destroyed Rome
   3. the division of the Roman Empire into two parts
   4. none of the above.

of the Merovingian Dynasty refers to

last of the Roman emperors
e first Asian hordes that conquered Europe
a Germanic king who conquered portions of
Europe
4. the Muslim dynasty that ruled Spain.

7. After Clovis's death, real power in the
Merovingian Dynasty was in the hands of the

1. nobles
2. mayors of the palace
3. parish priests
4. king's wife.

8. Charlemagne had many accomplishments during
his reign. Select the item that correctly identifies
one or more of them.

1. defeated the Arabs at the Battle of Verdun
2. established the Umayyad Dynasty
3. twice prevented the overthrow of the pope and
defeated the Mongols
4. expanded the Frankish empire in Europe and
established schools to encourage learning.

9. Match the architectural style that developed in
medieval Europe with its correct description.

1. Gothic—thin walls, large windows, towers, and
pointed arches
2. Romanesque—thin walls, large windows,
towers, and pointed arches
3. Romanesque—massive marble pillars, ornate
stone carvings, and walls having no images but
inlaid with multicolored stones
4. none of the above.

10. The importance of the Concordat of Worms was
that

1. the Church was recognized as having power
over all local rulers
2. local rulers continued to select and control
Church bishops
3. a ruler could provide someone with land and
title but the Church selected and gave religious
authority
4. the Holy Roman Emperor and the pope agreed
to end their quarrel.

11. What conclusion can be drawn from the manor
plan on page 65?

1. Manors were able to provide enough food for
all their inhabitants.
2. The families of lords and peasants shared the
same living quarters.
3. Manors were built near cities.
4. Manor-grown grains were shipped to cities for
grinding.

12. The map on page 64 and your knowledge of Global
History and Geography tell you that

1. the Magyar invaders of western Europe did not
cross large bodies of water
2. Muslims from North Africa invaded France
and Italy
3. the location of their homeland made the
Vikings great shipbuilders and sailors
4. all of the above are correct.

Thematic Essays

1. *Task:* Using specific examples, describe how
Church and lay (non-Church) people related to
one another in medieval Europe.

2. Although a military failure, the Crusades affected
the social, cultural, and economic lives of
Europeans. *Task:* Give examples of how European
life was affected by the Crusades.

Document-Based Questions

Use the documents provided and your knowledge of
Global History and Geography to answer the
questions that follow.

1. Look at the picture on page 62. How could Pope
Leo III use the act shown to claim political power?

2. From the letters of Pope Gregory VIII:

The Roman Church was founded by God alone.
The Roman bishop alone is properly called
universal. He alone may depose bishops and
reinstate them.
His legate, though of inferior grade, takes
precedence, in a council, of all bishops and may
render a decision of deposition against them.
He alone may use the insignia of empire.
The pope is the only person whose feet are kissed
by all princes. His title is unique in the world.
He may depose emperors.
No council may be regarded as a general one
without his consent.
No book or chapter may be regarded as canonical
without his authority.
A decree of his may be annulled by no one; he
alone may annul the decrees of all.
He may be judged by no one. No one shall dare to
condemn one who appeals to the papal see.
The Roman Church has never erred, nor ever, by
the witness of Scripture, shall err to all
eternity.

According to this document, what is the
relationship of the pope to the kings? Where does
the pope claim his authority comes from? When
can the Church ever be corrected?

Document-Based Essay

Task: Discuss how the conflict between Church and
state developed and give at least two specific examples
to illustrate the conflict.

UNIT REVIEW

Thematic Essays

1. *Task:* Use examples from Islam, Buddhism, and Christianity to discuss how traders and missionaries spread the beliefs and cultures of these societies.

2. *Task:* Select any two civilizations studied and write an essay explaining why you AGREE or DISAGREE with the following statement: Religion, philosophy, and government are essential to the development of all civilizations.

3. *Task:* Imagine you were a member of a minor noble family. Which of the societies studied would you have preferred to live in and why?

Document-Based Questions

Use the documents and your knowledge of Global History and Geogrpahy to answer the questions.

1. From the writings of a Syrian Arab:

   "I saw one of the Franks come to al-Amir . . . when he was in the Dome of the Rock and say to him, 'Dost thou want to see God as a child?' . . . The Frank walked ahead of us until he showed us the picture of Mary with Christ . . . as an infant in her lap. He then said, 'This is God as a child.' But Allah is exalted far above what the infidels say about him!"

   Describe how this passage shows different religious beliefs and attitudes.

2. Study the illustration on page 61. Why were the efforts of monks valuable for future societies?

3. From a history of Byzantium and Rome:

   "These three elements, then, Greco-Roman classicism (including the governmental traditions of Rome), the Byzantine brand of Christianity, and what we may call the oriental component were blended by the Byzantine . . . "

   What are the cultural elements that Byzantium preserved for future generations?

4. From a history of Byzantium:

   "It is not only in the Balkans that Byzantine influence survives. . . . It was preserved in that Russia of which, in the eleventh century, Byzantium had been the tutor, and in which Byzantine tradition remained the basis of state and national life."

   How did Byzantium influence Russian society?

Document-Based Essay

Culture can be transmitted by enemies as well as friends. *Task:* Using specific historical examples, discuss how cultural diffusion has occurred in the past and affected any two of the societies presented in this unit.

UNIT III

Global Interactions (1200–1650)

Year	Dates and Events
A.D.	
1200	**1200s:** First invasions of China by Mongols under Genghiz Khan Italian banks set up branches in Europe, North Africa, Middle East
	1237–1400s: Mongols invade and control Russia
	1260: Kublai Khan becomes first Mongol emperor of China
	1272–1292: Italian merchant Marco Polo reaches and explores China
	1295: Ghazan, Mongol ruler of Persia, converts to Islam, stimulates flow of Muslim and European culture to Asia
1299	
1300	**1337–1453:** Hundred Years' War bankrupts Europe; Hanseatic League controls more trading markets
	1347: Bubonic plague spreads from Asia to Europe; population loss, rebellions, decline in Church's influence
	1368–1644: Ming Dynasty in China; new cash crops increase trade with Asia, Philippines, Europe
	1394–1460: Advances in navigation by Prince Henry of Portugal spur trade by sea
1399	**1300s–1500s:** Renaissance—expansion of trade, exploration, technology, interest in classic culture
1400	**1405–1433:** Zheng He opens new markets throughout Asia for Chinese goods and culture
	1485–1509: Henry II of England centralizes power, expands trade and exploration
	1492: Columbus seeks westward sea route to Asia; opens up European contact with Americas
	1492–1500: Isabella and Ferdinand expel unconverted Jews and Muslims from Spain
1499	**1497–1499:** Vasco da Gama's expedition sparks Portuguese domination of spice trade with India
1500	**1500s:** Portuguese control of marine gold trade with Africa eliminates costly land routes Reformation changes Christianity as defined by Roman Catholic Church
	1526: India falls to Mogul (Islamic) invaders
	1534: Ignatius Loyola founds Jesuit Society (teachers and missionaries promoting Catholicism)
	1542: Portuguese traders arrive in Japan
1599	**1545–1563:** Council of Trent initiates Counter-Reformation to strengthen Roman Catholic Church
1600	**1549:** Jesuit Francis Xavier begins mission to Japan
	1550s: Jesuit and Franciscan missionaries arrive in Japan, begin conversions to Christianity
	1558–1603: Elizabeth I of England spurs trade, exploration, arts
	1600s: Japan forbids teaching of Christianity, expels missionaries, executes converts
	1610–1643: Louis XIII of France and Cardinal Richelieu expand industry, foreign trade
	1618–1648: Thirty Years' War involves most of Europe, devastates German economy and population
1699	**1641:** Shoguns initiate 200-year isolation of Japan from foreign trade and culture

CHAPTER
7

Asian Empires: Japan, China, and Mongolia

I. JAPANESE HISTORY AND FEUDALISM

A. Geography

Japan is an **archipelago**, or group of many islands. The largest are Kyushu, Shikoku, Honshu, and Hokkaido. These islands have little flat land suitable for farming. Nevertheless, plentiful rainfall and warm summers enable the Japanese to grow rice, vegetables, and fruits. The sea provides fish and other food.

Japan's mountains make land travel difficult. A water route through the Inland Sea, however, has facilitated contact among the people of Honshu, Shikoku, and Kyushu. During Japan's early history, the Korean Strait and the Sea of Japan discouraged invasions from the Asian mainland, and the Pacific Ocean kept away invaders from the east.

B. Cultural Development

Because the early Japanese had no written history, scholars do not know the origins of the people who settled Japan or what their society was like.

In A.D. 297, a Chinese historian, Wei Zhi, described the Japanese as farmers and warriors. Korean histories speak of warring Japanese **clans**—groups of families whose leaders have common ancestors.

Because rugged mountains separated these clans, the early Japanese had no central government. Clans competed for the scarce farmland. In the 300s, the Yamato clan defeated the others and set up an empire.

YAMATO YEARS (250–710). The Yamato state religion was Shinto ("the way of the gods"), a form of animism. Shintoists worshiped nature spirits. They believed that their emperor had descended from the sun goddess, the chief Shinto deity. Con-

sequently, the emperor controlled both religion and government.

KOREAN AND CHINESE INFLUENCES. During the 5th century, the Yamato emperors tried and failed to invade Korea. Nevertheless, this contact radically changed Japanese culture.

The Japanese learned many Chinese ways from the Koreans, and their architecture, clothing, and methods of preparing food began to show Chinese influence. They also adapted the Chinese writing system.

The Koreans also introduced Buddhism and Confucianism to Japan. A powerful group of Japanese nobles converted to Buddhism and made it the state religion.

In 604, Prince Shotoku wrote a new **constitution** (plan of government) called the Seventeen-Article Constitution. Based on Buddhist moral principles and Confucian political theory, it called for a bureaucracy similar to China's. After Prince Shotoku's death in 629, his supporters changed the government to conform to his constitution.

In about 710, the emperor ordered Nara, the Japanese capital city, to be built in the same style as the Tang imperial court of China.

MOVE TO KYOTO. About 180 years later, the emperor moved the capital to Kyoto, and a distinctive Japanese culture began to emerge. Noblemen and women wrote poems and stories and invented a new literary form—the novel. The most famous one, *The Tale of Genji,* was written in the early 1000s by a woman named Murasaki Shikibu. It recounted the romantic adventures of Prince Genji.

C. The Shogunate

Some clans became more powerful than the emperor and fought to gain control of the government. In 1185, the Minamoto clan defeated its rivals.

Japan: Physical Map

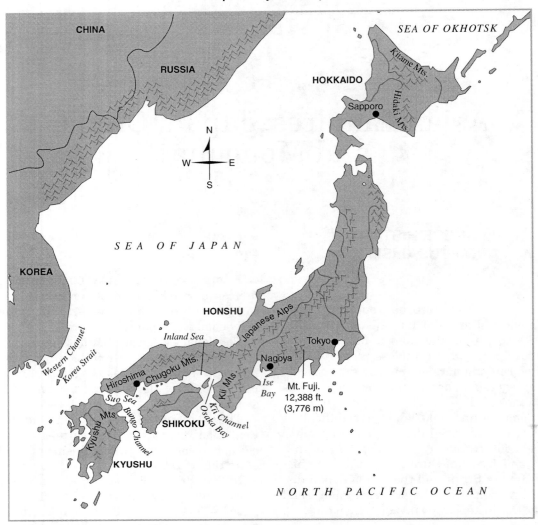

Its leader, Minamoto Yoritomo, became the first **shogun**.

Although the emperor still sat on the throne, the shogun ruled Japan. He was the country's chief military general and controlled its financial affairs, courts, and government appointments. Kamakura, the city where Yoritomo lived, outshone Kyoto in importance. The Kamakura Shogunate lasted from 1192 until 1333.

JAPANESE AND EUROPEAN FEUDALISM COMPARED. Under the shogunate, Japan had a feudal system similar to the one in medieval Europe. **Daimyos**, or landholders, controlled large parts of Japan. A daimyo gave part of his land to warriors known as **samurai**. They, in turn, fought for their lord and kept order in his territory, like the vassal knights of Europe.

In both feudal systems, land was the most important measurement of wealth, and landowners held greater political and military power than the kings or emperors.

Knights and samurai both swore loyalty to the lords who supported them. Both were skilled fighters on horseback. Just as knights lived by the code of chivalry, samurai followed the **Bushido**, or Way of the Warrior. It required samurai to live simply and be obedient, dutiful, kind, and honest. A dishonored samurai was supposed to commit suicide. Both knights and samurai began training when they were young boys.

The two systems also had differences. The daimyos' holdings were larger and more scattered than those of the European landlords. Moreover, the Japanese system did not include serfs. Japanese peasants could not own land, but they were free to leave a daimyo's service whenever they liked. European feudalism lasted from about 800 to 1400. In Japan, it lasted from about 1000 to 1871.

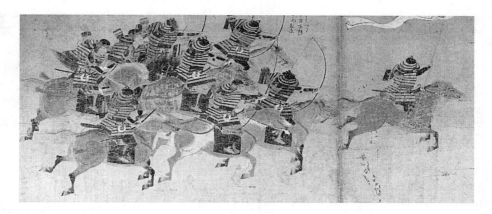

Vanguard force of samurai
warriors charging into battle

MONGOL THREAT. During the Kamakura Shogunate, the Mongol emperor of China, Kublai Khan, tried to conquer Japan. In 1274, the Japanese prevented his army from invading Kyushu. The Mongols tried again in 1281. This time, a typhoon forced them to withdraw. The Japanese felt that the gods had sent the typhoon and called it "Kamikaze" (Divine Wind).

D. Period of Disunity

Civil wars broke out during the rule of the Ashikaga family (1330–1568). In 1568, a daimyo named Oda Nobunaga captured Kyoto and began to unify Japan. When he died in 1582, his chief general Toyotomi Hideyoshi continued his work. In 1590, Hideyoshi became the ruler of all Japan. He died in 1598.

ARRIVAL OF EUROPEANS. During the civil wars, Japan had its first contact with people from the West. Portuguese traders arrived in 1542 and

Sixteenth-century Portuguese traders introduce the
Japanese to Western goods and ideas.

taught the Japanese to use muskets (long-barreled firearms). In 1549, Roman Catholic missionaries began converting the Japanese to Christianity.

ZEN CONCEPTS. In spite of political unrest, Japanese culture made many advances. Direct trade with China opened up. People began to practice a version of Buddhism called Zen. Buddhists, in general, believed that enlightenment was attained by meditation (clearing and focusing the mind) while concentrating on even breathing. Zen Buddhists, however, carried out other activities as well. For them, practicing the arts and the use of weapons could be kinds of meditation.

E. The Tokugawa Shogunate

In 1603, Tokugawa Ieyasu made the position of shogun hereditary. His descendants governed Japan until 1868.

Tokugawa Ieyasu moved the capital to Edo (present-day Tokyo), which could be more easily defended than Kyoto. He also developed the **bakuhan** form of government to limit the power of the daimyos. The strongest daimyos had to keep two households—one in their own territory and one in the capital. Every other year, they lived in the capital, and when they returned home, their families remained in Edo. If a daimyo rebelled, the shogun killed his family.

The bakuhan system also forced daimyos to spend most of their money maintaining two large households. Thus, they could not afford to finance a military uprising.

RIGID SOCIAL SYSTEM. Under the Tokugawa Shogunate, society was strictly divided into four classes. The highest class included the samurai. Next came peasants who produced food for the state. Artisans ranked third. Merchants were in the lowest class.

Although enjoying high status, the samurai lost some of their independence; they became dependent on the daimyos for their salaries and weapons. The peasants also lost many rights and had to pay crushingly heavy taxes.

ISOLATION. In the early 1600s, the Tokugawa shogun became hostile toward European missionaries and traders. He suspected that Japanese converts to Christianity would be more loyal to the Church than to him. Therefore, in 1612, he ordered missionaries to leave Japan.

The shogun also feared that trade with Europeans would make the daimyos wealthy and more powerful. In 1641, he closed all ports but Nagasaki to outsiders and limited the number of foreign ships that could dock there. As a result, Japan became isolated from the outside world for more than 200 years.

CULTURAL ACHIEVEMENTS. The Tokugawa rulers brought peace and prosperity to Japan. Culture flourished. Wood-block prints made during the Tokugawa Shogunate are still considered masterpieces. Japanese dramatists developed a form of theater called **kabuki**, which combines acting, dancing, and music.

The poets of this time perfected a poetic form called **haiku**. It contains exactly 17 syllables divided into three lines. Haiku are usually descriptions of nature suggesting intense emotions and deep ideas.

Many new schools opened in the cities. Elsewhere, Buddhist monks and Shinto priests ran schools for village children.

INFO CHECK

1. How did geography enable the ancient Japanese to develop their culture without outside interference?
2. List three ways China influenced Japan and one way Korea affected Japanese culture.
3. Define each of the following: shogun, daimyo, samurai, Bushido.
4. State similarities between Japanese and European feudalism. How did the Tokugawa shoguns weaken feudalism?
5. Why are students of Japanese culture attracted to *kabuki* and *haiku*?

II. SUNG DYNASTY (960–1279)

A. Two Empires

The Sung Dynasty of China began in 960. Early in the Sung period, nomads from Manchuria captured the Sung emperor and began the Chin Dynasty in the north. The son of the captured emperor set up a new Sung capital in the southern city of Hangzhou. By 1127, China consisted of the Chin Empire and the Sung Empire.

B. Science, Technology, and the Arts

Chinese advances in science, technology, and the arts continued under the Sung. Doctors developed an inoculation against smallpox. Mathemati-

China: Sung Empire

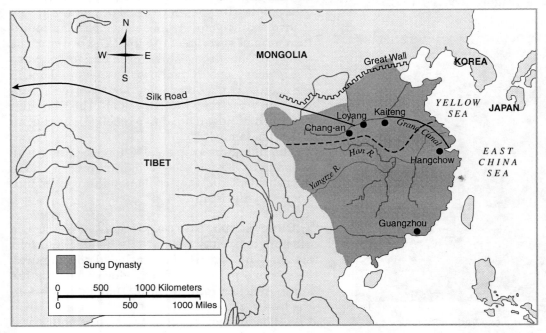

cians invented the **abacus**, the world's first adding machine. Soldiers began to use gunpowder. Printers developed movable wooden type, which speeded up the printing process.

Landscape painting reached its highest level during the Sung period. Potters invented beautifully colored glazes for their wares.

C. Trade and Prosperity

Chinese ships carried silk and porcelain to Korea, Japan, Southeast Asia, the Persian Gulf area, and Africa. Wealth from trade made China's cities centers of learning and art. Hangzhou was larger than most contemporary European cities and had paved streets and an efficient garbage collection system.

D. Social Conditions

Wealthy men in Sung China enjoyed the most advanced society of the 12th century. Peasants, however, lived poorly, paid heavy taxes, and were forced to labor on public works.

Women enjoyed few rights. When in public, wives walked ten steps behind their husbands to show subservience. Since tiny feet were consid-

ered marks of feminine beauty, the feet of little girls were bound to stunt growth. This practice crippled many women.

Corrupt and militarily weak, the Sung Dynasty fell in 1279, when the Mongols invaded China.

INFO CHECK

1. Why might you prefer to live in the Sung Empire rather than the Chin Empire?

2. In what ways were women at a disadvantage in medieval China?

III. MONGOL EMPIRE

The Mongols were nomadic herders from Central Asia. In the 13th century, their leader, Genghiz Khan, began a wave of conquest that lasted for 20 years. He died in 1227. In 1260, his grandson, Kublai Khan, became emperor of the Mongol Empire.

A. Mongol Conquests

Southwest Asia, Russia, and China became parts of the Mongol Empire. In victory, Mongol soldiers

Mongol Empire, 1300

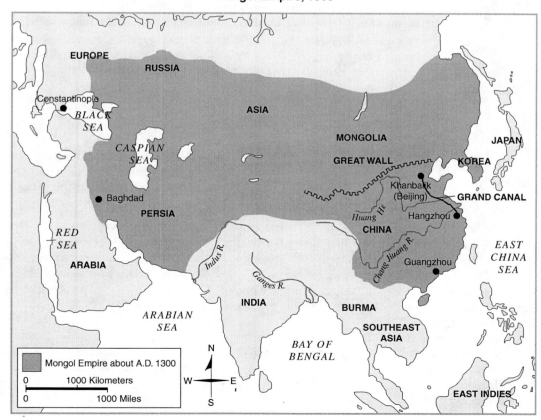

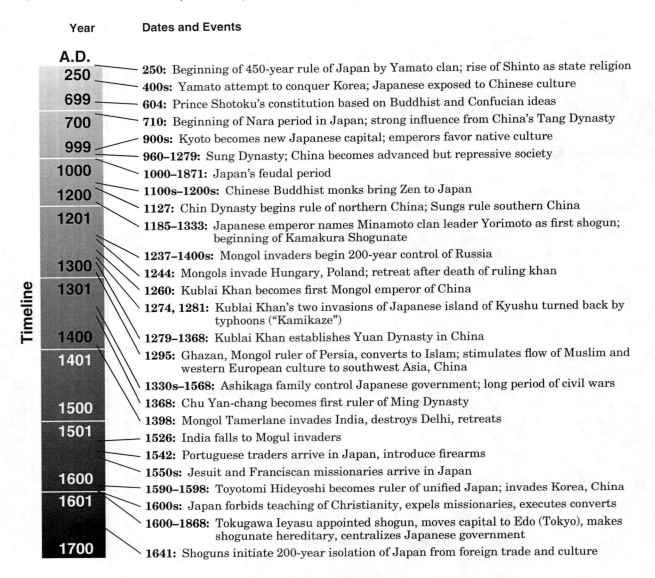

Year	Dates and Events
A.D.	
250	**250:** Beginning of 450-year rule of Japan by Yamato clan; rise of Shinto as state religion
	400s: Yamato attempt to conquer Korea; Japanese exposed to Chinese culture
699	**604:** Prince Shotoku's constitution based on Buddhist and Confucian ideas
700	**710:** Beginning of Nara period in Japan; strong influence from China's Tang Dynasty
999	**900s:** Kyoto becomes new Japanese capital; emperors favor native culture
	960–1279: Sung Dynasty; China becomes advanced but repressive society
1000	**1000–1871:** Japan's feudal period
1200	**1100s–1200s:** Chinese Buddhist monks bring Zen to Japan
1201	**1127:** Chin Dynasty begins rule of northern China; Sungs rule southern China
	1185–1333: Japanese emperor names Minamoto clan leader Yorimoto as first shogun; beginning of Kamakura Shogunate
1300	**1237–1400s:** Mongol invaders begin 200-year control of Russia
	1244: Mongols invade Hungary, Poland; retreat after death of ruling khan
1301	**1260:** Kublai Khan becomes first Mongol emperor of China
	1274, 1281: Kublai Khan's two invasions of Japanese island of Kyushu turned back by typhoons ("Kamikaze")
1400	**1279–1368:** Kublai Khan establishes Yuan Dynasty in China
1401	**1295:** Ghazan, Mongol ruler of Persia, converts to Islam; stimulates flow of Muslim and western European culture to southwest Asia, China
	1330s–1568: Ashikaga family control Japanese government; long period of civil wars
1500	**1368:** Chu Yan-chang becomes first ruler of Ming Dynasty
	1398: Mongol Tamerlane invades India, destroys Delhi, retreats
1501	**1526:** India falls to Mogul invaders
	1542: Portuguese traders arrive in Japan, introduce firearms
	1550s: Jesuit and Franciscan missionaries arrive in Japan
1600	**1590–1598:** Toyotomi Hideyoshi becomes ruler of unified Japan; invades Korea, China
1601	**1600s:** Japan forbids teaching of Christianity, expels missionaries, executes converts
	1600–1868: Tokugawa Ieyasu appointed shogun, moves capital to Edo (Tokyo), makes shogunate hereditary, centralizes Japanese government
1700	**1641:** Shoguns initiate 200-year isolation of Japan from foreign trade and culture

(Left margin label: Timeline)

were cruel, slaughtering civilians and destroying cities. In Southwest Asia, the early Mongol rulers almost erased Muslim culture. In 1295, however, a Mongol ruler of Persia, named Ghazan, converted to Islam. Under Ghazan and his successors, Muslim culture became stronger than ever.

The Mongols invaded Russia in 1237 and controlled it for about 200 years. The Mongol rulers showed tolerance by not interfering with Russian government, religion, language, or customs.

Mongol armies also swept through Hungary and Poland in 1241. However, they were unable to keep these territories.

In 1398, Tamurlane, a descendant of Genghiz Khan, led an army into India. Although the Mongols remained in India only a year, they weakened its military power. In 1526, India fell to a new Muslim group called the Moguls.

B. Yuan Dynasty (1279–1368)

It took more than 45 years for the Mongols to conquer China. Kublai Khan completed the conquest and established the Yuan Dynasty.

MONGOL GOVERNMENT IN CHINA. In order to prevent rebellion, Kublai Khan placed Mongols in the most important government positions and the Chinese in the lowest ones. It became illegal for Chinese to own weapons, meet in large groups, or travel at night.

Nevertheless, Kublai Khan brought many advantages to China. He constructed roads and canals and rebuilt the city of Beijing. He gave aid to orphans and old people and built hospitals. He stored food supplies in times of plenty for use during famines. He did not force the Mongolian form of Buddhism on the Chinese and even allowed Roman Catholic missionaries to settle in China. Since Kublai Khan and his successors did not force their culture on China, the Chinese way of life remained unchanged.

TRADE. Kublai Khan developed Chinese trade not only by constructing roads but also by showing tolerance and good will toward the cultures of foreign traders. This policy brought about great prosperity and a period of peace in Eurasia known as the **Pax Mongolia**.

During Kublai Khan's reign, the Italian merchant Marco Polo came to China, where he remained for 18 years, traveling throughout the empire. On his return, he wrote a book that encouraged other traders to visit China.

DECLINE OF MONGOL EMPIRE. After the death of Kublai Khan in 1298, the empire split into smaller realms. There were the Golden Horde in southern Russia and the Balkans, the Yuan Empire in China, and the Ilkhan Empire in western Asia.

In 1368, a rebel leader named Chu Yan-chang drove the Mongols out of Beijing. A new Chinese dynasty, the Ming, replaced Mongol rule.

INFO CHECK

1. Explain why you AGREE or DISAGREE with the following statement: Genghiz Khan was a great man and an admirable ruler.

2. List changes brought to China by Kublai Khan. Indicate which you regard as important or significant.

3. What kind of activity did Marco Polo's travel records inspire?

CHAPTER REVIEW

Multiple Choice

1. Before China influenced Japan, one could describe the Japanese as

   1. writers and scholars
   2. farmers and warriors
   3. industrialists
   4. none of the above.

2. Shinto is most similar to

   1. Buddhism
   2. Hinduism
   3. Islam
   4. animism.

3. China was influential in the Japanese adoption of

   1. a class of warriors and a code of honor
   2. religious and bureaucratic practices
   3. harmonious relations with their neighbors
   4. nomadic and pastoral lifestyles.

4. Match the terms that represent social or political similarities between Japan and Europe.

   1. A clan was to Japan as a dynasty was to Europe.
   2. A king was to Japan as a vassal was to Europe.
   3. A Zen master was to Japan as the patriarch was to Rome.
   4. *The Tale of Genji* was to Japan as Homer's epics were to Greece.

5. The Tokugawas established a rigid social structure. Select the answer that correctly ranks the highest to the lowest social classes.

   1. samurai, artisans, farmers, merchants
   2. merchants, artisans, farmers, samurai
   3. samurai, merchants, artisans, peasants
   4. samurai, peasants, artisans, merchants.

6. The Sung Empire became extremely wealthy because it . . .

   1. controlled all of the lands known as China
   2. conquered many nations.
   3. discovered gold and oil in the north
   4. exported silks, porcelain, and other trade goods.

7. Noblewomen in China

   1. participated in social and political activities
   2. were considered inferior to their husbands and suffered from foot-binding
   3. were often well educated and involved in trade
   4. none of the above.

8. The Mongols conquered other peoples and established several long-lasting dynasties because of their

   1. vast armies and heavy cannons
   2. use of secret police and repressive rule
   3. hardy warriors and tolerant rule
   4. hired mercenaries and religious beliefs.

9. The Yuan Dynasty is important because it

    1. united the Chinese and Mongolian peoples forever
    2. established foreign rule in China
    3. encouraged religious tolerance and economic development
    4. united the Chinese in rising up and rebelling against their ruler.

10. The decline of the Mongol Empire began with

    1. the death of Kublai Khan
    2. natural disasters that destroyed its economy
    3. new religions that sapped the army's spirit
    4. conflict over who was to rule.

11. The map on page 77 proves that

    1. the Great Wall prevented Mongols from conquering China.
    2. Korea was not part of the Mongol Empire in 1300 A.D.
    3. Mongols captured Constantinople in 1300 A.D.
    4. The Mongol Empire included Russia and Persia.

Thematic Essays

1. The cultures of Japan, China, and Mongolia affected one another. *Task:* Select *one* of these societies and give specific examples of the influence of cultural diffusion.

2. In East Asia, each society developed much that was unique. *Task:* From among the societies presented in this chapter, select one important contribution made by each that is still valued today.

Document-Based Questions

Use your knowledge of Global History and Geography and the documents to answer the following questions.

1. From a book about Asian civilizations:

"Tea is the most wonderful medicine for nourishing one's health; it is the secret of long life. India and China both value it highly. . . . I wonder why the Japanese do not care for bitter things. In the great country of China they drink tea, as a result of which there is no heart trouble and people live long lives. Our country is full of sickly looking, skinny persons, simply because we do not drink tea."

Do you think the writer is Japanese or Chinese? Give reasons for your answer. How does this reading selection illustrate cultural diffusion?

2. Look at the illustration on page 75. How does the artist convey the function of the samurai?

3. From the Japanese government's Act of Seclusion (1636):

"1. Japanese ships shall by no means be sent abroad.
2. No Japanese shall be sent abroad. Anyone violating this prohibition shall suffer the penalty of death, and the shipowner and the crew shall be held together with the ship.
3. All Japanese residing abroad shall be put to death when they return home. . . .
4. The samurai shall not purchase goods on board foreign ships directly from foreigners."

What steps did Japan take to isolate itself from foreign influences? Why do you think this was done?

4. From a study of Asian civilizations:

"Buddhist learning is broader in scope than Confucian, but Japanese learning is even more embracing. All the various types of learning . . . are embraced in Japanese learning. . . . [The] Japanese should study all the different kinds of learning— even though they are foreign—so that they can choose the good features of each and place them at the service of the nation. . . . [The] Japanese differ from and are superior to the peoples of China, India, Russia, Holland, Siam, Cambodia, and all other countries of the world."

Describe the writer's view of Japanese culture as compared to other cultures.

Document-Based Essay

It has been said that Japanese foreign relations are like young trees that bend but do not break in a windstorm. *Task:* Using specific examples, comment on the accuracy of this statement.

CHAPTER
8

Global Trade and Interactions

I. EXPANSION OF TRADE AND GROWTH OF EUROPEAN CITIES

A. Reasons for Growth

Medieval Europe began as a thinly settled, underdeveloped land with shabby port cities, difficult to defend. Gradually, it became a land of productive farms and bustling trade. Successful agriculture caused a rise in population. As Viking and Muslim raids ceased, merchants could safely live near the sea and ship their goods to faraway markets.

As trade picked up, so did the demand for manufactured products. Craftspeople now needed ready sources of raw materials and convenient transportation for their finished goods. Therefore, they moved to cities near rivers and seas. By the 13th century, Europe had many large cities, the largest of which were London, Paris, Venice, Florence, and Genoa.

The Crusades, which lasted from the 11th to the 13th century, stimulated long-distance trade. The spices, silks, sugar, and other luxuries from the Middle East brought home by Crusaders made other Europeans want these goods too. A brisk trade developed between Europe and the Middle East. (See the map on page 82.)

B. Italian City-States

During the early Middle Ages, Genoa, Pisa, and Venice built strong navies to protect their merchant ships from Viking and Muslim raids. Thus protected, these cities prospered while other port cities declined.

Before the Crusades, Venice—officially part of the Byzantine Empire—controlled trade with Constantinople. This commerce made other northern Italian cities wealthy as well. During the Crusades, merchants from these cities provided the Crusaders with funds and transportation to the Holy Land. In exchange, they received from the Crusaders economic and political rights in Middle Eastern port cites such as Acre and Tyre.

As banking developed, businesspeople, the nobility, and even royalty borrowed money and received investment services from Italian bankers. By the early 13th century, Italian banks had branches throughout Europe and the Middle East.

C. The Hanseatic League

In the 14th century, the French and English fought the Hundred Years' War. Their rulers borrowed vast amounts of money from the Italian banks to pay for armies and weapons. Many of the banks failed when these royal borrowers were unable to pay their debts.

As banks failed, Italian city-states lost their control of trade. A group of Scandinavian and German towns took over some northern markets. Such cities as Lübeck, Lüneburg, Visby, Bremen, and Cologne formed the Hanseatic League. (*Hansa* means "company" in German.) It remained strong from the 1100s to the 1400s.

INFO CHECK

1. Identify two causes of economic growth in Europe during the late Middle Ages.

2. Name the Italian city-states that prospered from trade in the Middle Ages. Explain how they lost power and wealth to the Hanseatic League.

II. EXPANSION OF CHINESE TRADE

During the 15th and 16th centuries, the first Ming emperor, T'ai Tsu, initiated a period of peace and prosperity. T'ai Tsu, who ruled from 1368 to 1398, diligently repaired war-damaged China. To revive

European Trade Routes, 1280–1500

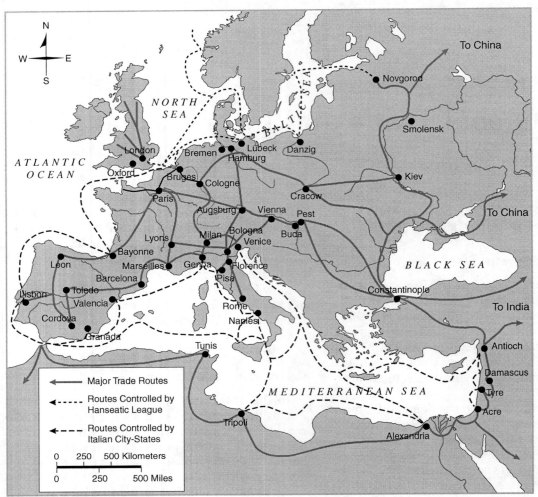

agriculture, he gave peasants who farmed on ruined land seeds, tools, and animals and promised to excuse them for three years from taxes and labor on public works.

A. Ming Achievements

The Ming Dynasty, which lasted from 1368 to 1644, made notable agricultural and technological advances:

- Scientists developed rice that could be harvested in 60 instead of 100 days, and China's supply of rice increased greatly.

- Inventors designed an irrigation pump worked by pedals.

- Farmers learned to stock rice paddies (fields covered by a few inches of water) with fish, thus producing both rice and food fish.

- Cotton and indigo (a plant yielding a blue dye) were grown commercially as raw materials for the textile industry.

- Overcut forests were replenished by new plantings of hardwood, fruit, and mulberry trees.

VOYAGES OF ZHENG HE. Between 1405 and 1433, one Ming emperor sent a Muslim admiral, Zheng He, on six expeditions. Voyaging to Sri Lanka, the coasts of the Persian Gulf, and the east coast of Africa, he opened up new markets for Chinese goods.

In spite of Zheng He's success, the government stopped all foreign voyages and confined trade to a few ports. Scholars believe that all China's resources were needed to keep out northern invaders. Nevertheless, by the late 16th century, Chinese merchants had trade relations with Japan, the Philippines, Portugal, and the Netherlands.

Chinese Trade and Exploration, 1400–1500

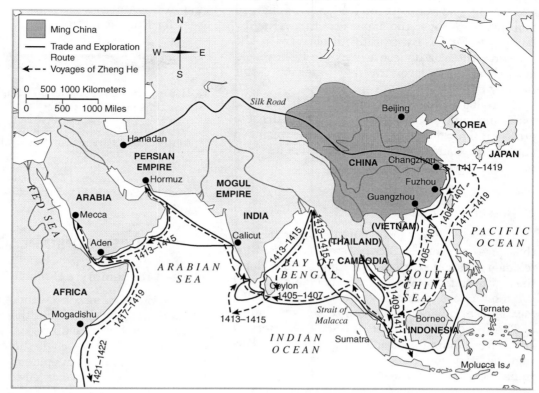

1. List improvements in China brought about by the Ming emperors.

2. What effect did the voyages of Zheng He have on China?

III. PORTUGUESE EXPLORATION

During the early 15th century, the Portuguese undertook voyages to find water routes to the African gold markets and Indian spice markets.

A. Prince Henry's Influence

Prince Henry of Portugal encouraged advances in seamanship. His scientists improved the astrolabe and magnetic compass and designed a ship called the **caravel.** The caravel was faster, sturdier, and easier to steer than other ships and, most important, could maintain a high speed against the wind. Its triangular sails could be turned more easily than the rectangular ones used on earlier ships.

B. The Gold Trade

The Portuguese first sailed along western Africa to the Songhai Empire, which contained the most

Model of Portuguese caravel with triangular sails furled

important gold markets. Traditionally, Europeans had bought gold from Muslim traders, who charged high prices to cover the expenses of traveling by land to Songhai. By trading directly with the Africans, the Portuguese were able to buy gold more cheaply. Moreover, travel by water was faster than by land.

By 1500, Portugal controlled the African gold trade and built up a military presence in Africa to protect it. Thus fortified, the Portuguese colonized parts of the continent and took control of its slave trade.

C. Rounding Africa

Portuguese explorers next sought a water route to the spice markets of South Asia. In 1488, Bartolomeu Dias sailed around the Cape of Good Hope, the southern tip of Africa. Vasco da Gama reached India on a voyage that lasted from 1497 to 1499. Portuguese traders now dealt directly with India.

The Muslims had been the chief carriers of spices from India to Europe and resented the Portuguese intrusion. Muslim forts were built along India's coast to drive the Portuguese away. The Portuguese, however, captured the forts and used them as trading posts and military bases, which allowed them to extend their influence deeper into Asia.

D. Race for Trade Routes

Other Europeans competed for sea routes to India. In 1492, King Ferdinand and Queen Isabella of Spain sent Christopher Columbus to find a west-ward sea route to Asia. When he landed on an island in the Americas, he opened up entirely new areas for Europeans to exploit.

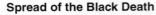

INFO CHECK

1. How did Prince Henry help Portugal become a maritime power?

2. What did Bartolomeu Dias and Vasco da Gama contribute to Portuguese control of the spice and gold trade?

3. How did the voyage of Christopher Columbus differ from the Portuguese voyages of exploration?

IV. BUBONIC PLAGUE

A. The 14th Century, a Difficult Time in Europe

As agriculture produced more crops, Europe's population expanded. In time, there was not enough food to meet the people's needs, so prices rose. A long period of severe cold, the "Little Ice Age," caused crop failures. An epidemic killed livestock. In many areas, people starved to death. Survivors were undernourished and susceptible to diseases.

B. A New Disease

In 1347, a trading ship from the Black Sea port of Caffa docked in Messina, Sicily. Many people aboard were infected with **bubonic plague**. Some had black swellings in their armpits and groins, as well as sores and dark bruises. Because of the

Spread of the Black Death

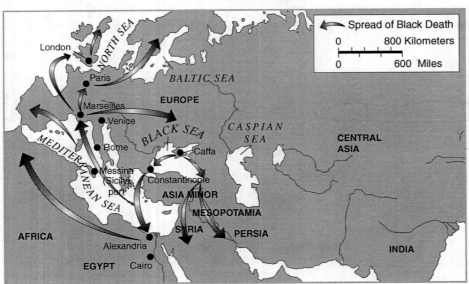

black swellings, the disease became known as the Black Death. Other victims had high fevers and coughs that made them spit up blood. These were signs of an even more deadly form of the disease.

Within a few days, all the sick people on the ship died. Some black rats scurried off the ship and ran into Messina. They carried fleas that spread the plague throughout the city.

A year earlier, travelers returning from Asia carried news of a terrible epidemic spreading from China to central Asia, India, Persia, Mesopotamia, Syria, Egypt, and Asia Minor. (Modern scholars think that the plague began not in China but in central Asia.) Pope Clement VI estimated the death toll in Asia at more than 23 million.

As more infected ships arrived from Asia, the Black Death spread to Venice, Genoa, and Marseilles, and then deeper inland. In time, it made its way west to the British Isles, north to Scandinavia, and east to Hungary. Modern historians think that the Black Death killed about one-third of Europe's population.

REACTION OF THE PEOPLE. Medieval doctors could not cure the disease or even identify its cause. Many blamed a sinister property of air for its spread. Bigoted people accused the Jews of a conspiracy to kill Christians by poisoning Europe's drinking water. Pope Clement VI tried to stop the resulting violence against Jews by pointing out that they, too, were dying of the plague. Nevertheless, mobs attacked Jews and burned their homes.

Some people thought that the disease was a punishment from heaven. A number of them were called **flagellants** (*flagellate* means "to whip"). They formed processions and publicly whipped themselves in an attempt to appease God.

Many people thought that Church leaders were not helping people enough. They also noted that some priests charged plague victims high prices for listening to deathbed confessions. Along with the flagellants, they took over such Church **sacraments** (rituals) as confession. The flagellants became so popular that Church leaders could not stop their processions, criticisms, and takeovers of religious ceremonies.

The Black Death struck Europe again in the 1360s and the 1370s, and as late as the 1700s. Not until the early 20th century did scientists develop a cure and methods of prevention.

SOCIAL IMPACT. After the plague, the reduction in population caused social unrest. When parents died, children came under the care of guardians who often kept their inheritances. Fewer men were available to defend farms and villages from looters. Since most medieval educators were members of the clergy, the death of monks and priests caused widespread illiteracy. Cities declined. As manufacturing and trade fell off, prices rose.

At first, working people benefited from the shortage of laborers. Peasants demanded lower rents. Artisans and craftspeople bargained for higher wages. Rulers then passed laws to fix wages at pre-plague rates and raise the taxes of workers with high incomes.

Throughout Europe, peasants began to rebel. In 1358, an uprising of French peasants had to be crushed by their lords' armies. In 1381, overtaxed English peasants marched on London, killed two royal officials, and threatened King Richard II. The king calmed them with false promises and later had their leaders executed. In 1378, wool workers in Florence took control of the city government for

Jews being burned alive by Christians, as fears of the Black Death spread

six weeks before an army put them down. Although none of these uprisings was successful, they were signs of a coming change in the social order.

IMPACT ON THE CATHOLIC CHURCH. Before the plague, conflicts between the Church and monarchs had already weakened religious authority. Medieval kings had always resented the Church's freedom from paying taxes on its property. In 1294, King Philip IV of France demanded the payment of such taxes. When Pope Boniface VIII refused, King Philip imprisoned him and elevated a new pope. The papacy then moved from Rome to Avignon, where it remained from 1309 to 1377.

In 1378, a religious conflict occurred when two popes were elected—one in Avignon and one in Rome. France, Scotland, and parts of Spain wanted the French pope. The remaining European countries supported the Roman pope. In 1417, Church officials elected a pope acceptable to all, and the papacy returned to Rome for good.

These power struggles had already weakened people's respect for the Church. The neglect and exploitation of plague victims by some clergy made matters worse. Public accusations of greed and corruption were directed against the Church. Its leaders tried to silence these critics by branding them heretics and burning them at the stake. By the 1500s, a group of religious reformers arose who defied the Roman Catholic Church by establishing other forms of Christianity.

INFO CHECK

1. Describe difficulties encountered by Europeans in the 14th century.

2. What arguments would you have made to those who blamed Jews and criticized the Church for the Black Death?

3. How did the plague lead to workers' revolts in France, England, and Italy?

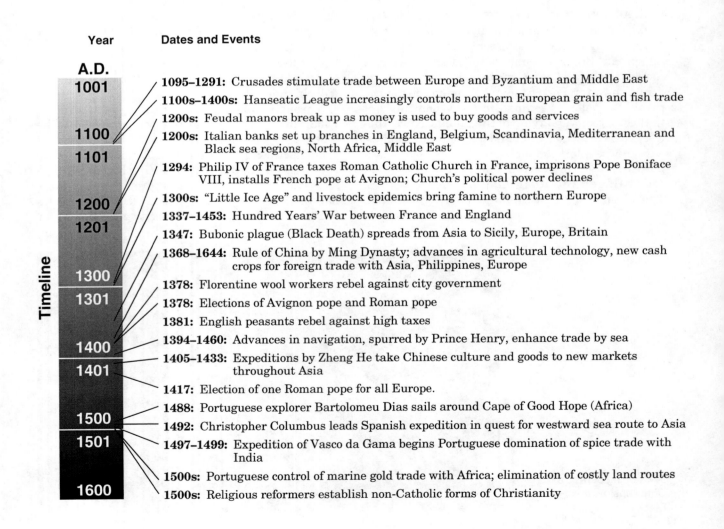

Year	Dates and Events
A.D.	
1001	**1095–1291:** Crusades stimulate trade between Europe and Byzantium and Middle East
	1100s–1400s: Hanseatic League increasingly controls northern European grain and fish trade
	1200s: Feudal manors break up as money is used to buy goods and services
1100	**1200s:** Italian banks set up branches in England, Belgium, Scandinavia, Mediterranean and Black sea regions, North Africa, Middle East
1101	**1294:** Philip IV of France taxes Roman Catholic Church in France, imprisons Pope Boniface VIII, installs French pope at Avignon; Church's political power declines
1200	**1300s:** "Little Ice Age" and livestock epidemics bring famine to northern Europe
1201	**1337–1453:** Hundred Years' War between France and England
	1347: Bubonic plague (Black Death) spreads from Asia to Sicily, Europe, Britain
	1368–1644: Rule of China by Ming Dynasty; advances in agricultural technology, new cash crops for foreign trade with Asia, Philippines, Europe
1300	**1378:** Florentine wool workers rebel against city government
1301	**1378:** Elections of Avignon pope and Roman pope
	1381: English peasants rebel against high taxes
1400	**1394–1460:** Advances in navigation, spurred by Prince Henry, enhance trade by sea
1401	**1405–1433:** Expeditions by Zheng He take Chinese culture and goods to new markets throughout Asia
	1417: Election of one Roman pope for all Europe.
1500	**1488:** Portuguese explorer Bartolomeu Dias sails around Cape of Good Hope (Africa)
	1492: Christopher Columbus leads Spanish expedition in quest for westward sea route to Asia
1501	**1497–1499:** Expedition of Vasco da Gama begins Portuguese domination of spice trade with India
	1500s: Portuguese control of marine gold trade with Africa; elimination of costly land routes
1600	**1500s:** Religious reformers establish non-Catholic forms of Christianity

Timeline

CHAPTER REVIEW

Multiple Choice

1. Select the reasons for the growth of European urban centers.

    1. Agriculture improved and population increased.
    2. Peace and order returned.
    3. The demand for manufactured products increased.
    4. All of the above.

2. Even before the Crusades, Italian bankers became wealthy because they controlled

    1. arms development in Italy
    2. loans to Arab merchants
    3. trade with Byzantium
    4. the treasury of the Holy Roman Emperor.

3. The name of the economic organization formed by German and Scandinavian cities to control trade was the

    1. Genoa League
    2. Portuguese League
    3. Marseilles League
    4. Hanseatic League.

4. The Ming Dynasty's expansion of Chinese influence and long-range trade resulted from

    1. the conquest of Japan
    2. the voyages of Zheng He
    3. the expulsion of foreigners
    4. all of the above.

5. The European desire for spices, silks, and gold encouraged the development or improvement of the

    1. magnetic compass
    2. astrolabe
    3. caravel
    4. all of the above.

6. As a result of the voyages of Bartolomeu Dias and Vasco da Gama

    1. Portugal gained control of the European spice and gold trade
    2. Italy gained control of the European spice trade
    3. trading posts were established in Canton
    4. trading posts were established in Kiev.

7. The bubonic plague came about because

    1. a famine forced people to eat unclean foods
    2. an earthquake destroyed water and sewer treatment plants

    3. trading ships carrying infected rats docked at several European ports
    4. infected cows were sold in European marketplaces.

8. The bubonic plague changed the economic relationship between the upper and lower classes of Europe because

    1. jobs were plentiful and peasants and craftspeople were in scarce supply
    2. there were fewer jobs because of the population decline
    3. nobles paid less because they needed less
    4. nobles raised wages because the plague was a warning from God.

9. The religious separation of 1378 refers to a

    1. power struggle between the emperors of Rome and Byzantium
    2. power struggle between the head of the Roman Catholic Church and the head of the Greek Orthodox Church
    3. power struggle between the French king and the pope
    4. debate over accepting icons and statues within Muslim hold places.

10. After the bubonic plague ended, the European ruling class attempted to regain economic control of the people by taxes and regulations. The immediate results of these actions were

    1. boycotts and peaceful picketing by workers
    2. demands that nobles pay fair wages for an eight-hour workday
    3. workers accepting lower wages
    4. attacks by peasants and workers against nobles and tax collectors.

11. Study the map on page 82 and decide which statement is correct.

    1. Antioch, Damascus, and Tyre were on the trade routes controlled by the Hanseatic League.
    2. Vienna and Kiev were not on major trade routes.
    3. The Italian city-states controlled the North Sea trade routes.
    4. Trade routes through the North and Baltic seas were controlled by the Hanseatic League.

12. The timeline on page 86 indicates that

    1. the Ming Dynasty ruled China from 1368 to 1644.
    2. feudal manors began to break up in the 1800s.

3. Portuguese and Spanish voyages of exploration began in 1294.
4. Europe experienced extreme cold and famine in the 1500s.

Thematic Essays

1. The development of global trade in the late Middle Ages increased contact between Europe and other lands. *Task:* Discuss the activities of the Italian city-states and the Hanseatic League.

2. Trade and banking made some peoples and nations wealthy and powerful. *Task:* Select one European and one Asian society or people. Describe the policies, actions, or practices that they used to become wealthy and powerful.

Document-Based Questions

1. Study the illustration on page 85. How did the townspeople justify their actions?

2. The following is from a book about the European economy after the Black Death:

"... men thought that, through the death of so many people, there would be an abundance of all produce of the land; yet, on the contrary ... most commodities were more costly,. . . . And the price of labor, and the products of every trade and craft rose in disorderly fashion. . . . "

Discuss the social and economic results of the Black Death.

3. The following is from a book about Florence and Siena after the Black Death:

"In both Florence and Siena the laws controlling immigration were relaxed, and special privileges, and a rapid grant of citizenship, or exemption from taxes were offered to badly needed artisans or professional men, such as physicians. . . . "

What caused Florence and Siena to alter their policies about immigration and skilled people?

Document-Based Essay

Task: Using specific examples, discuss positive and negative economic and social consequences related to the bubonic plague.

9

Beginning of Modern Times in Europe

I. EUROPE'S REVIVAL

A. Growth of Cities

The manors of the early Middle Ages were self-sufficient. In time, farmers learned new ways to produce more crops, and craftspeople turned out more goods than were needed locally. Landlords sold these surpluses and spent the money they received on goods made elsewhere. More people became traders, merchants, and manufacturers. Workshops, mills, and factories were built in and near cities. As long-distance trade increased, cities replaced manors as the hubs of the European economy.

EFFECT ON SERFS. After the plague, there was a labor shortage. Growth in industry created more jobs and an even greater demand for workers. City jobs drew peasants from the manors. (By avoiding capture for a year and a day, they became legally free.) Lords began to free serfs who remained on the land; they paid rent, which the landlords used to buy luxuries from the Middle East and eastern Asia.

INCREASED INFLUENCE OF CITIES. Cities grew rich and acquired more political influence. Wealthy urban businesspeople helped kings finance defense and public works, such as roads. In exchange, kings gave city dwellers special rights and privileges.

The **city charter** was an especially important new right. It made the city independent of the manorial system by allowing its leaders to set up law courts and make rules for conducting business. An elected mayor usually managed the city. As a result of these concessions by a king, townspeople usually supported him in disputes with his lords.

B. Guilds

Medieval **guilds** were organizations to protect businesspeople and regulate business practices.

Members of a town guild could trade in that town without a license. All guild members got a chance to sell an item in limited supply so that no one merchant could control the entire stock and charge high prices. Buyers as well as merchants thus benefited.

Craft guilds set quality standards for manufactured items and regulated the number of products that could be made and the prices that could be charged. The standards helped the manufacturer guarantee the quality of work done and protected customers from high prices and shoddy merchandise.

Apprentices worked for the craftspeople in exchange for training. By limiting the number of apprentices that a craftsperson could take on, guilds made sure that the young people got good training.

Guilds admitted women as members (more women were craftspeople than merchants). Often, however, master craftspeople were permitted to pay women less than men for the same work.

INFO CHECK

1. Describe the impact of the growth of trade on feudal life and the manorial system.
2. Explain how guilds benefited workers and consumers.

II. COMMERCIAL REVOLUTION

The change from feudalism and manorialism to business and trade is called the **Commercial Revolution**.

A. Rise of Capitalism

The new economic system was called **capitalism**. Merchants used their money to build

Trading Empires in the 1500s and 1600s

businesses. Money thus invested is called **capital**, and the investors are **capitalists**. Capitalists were not regulated by guilds and were not subject to sharing the supply of goods with other merchants or controlling their prices.

One of the biggest industries built by European capitalists was cloth manufacturing. Capitalists paid weavers to make woolen cloth in their homes (the **domestic system**). The capitalists paid for the raw materials and labor and sold the finished goods at a profit.

Capitalists began to form joint-stock companies. Merchants combined funds to raise large amounts of capital. Each partner received stock, or **shares**, in the company in proportion to the amount of money contributed. The money was then invested in a project. Such large investments often led to

huge profits. Losses, on the other hand, were spread among all stockholders, lessening individual risk.

B. Role of the Middle Class

Businesspeople became the new middle class of Europe. The nobles who believed that high birth determined human value, looked down on them. Church leaders, who thought that they valued money more than their souls, also disapproved of them.

Nonetheless, middle-class power increased. As manors lost economic importance, nobles borrowed from businesspeople and even invested in commercial enterprises. Monarchs relied on the high taxes that the middle class paid.

Trading Empires in the 1500s and 1600s (*Continued*)

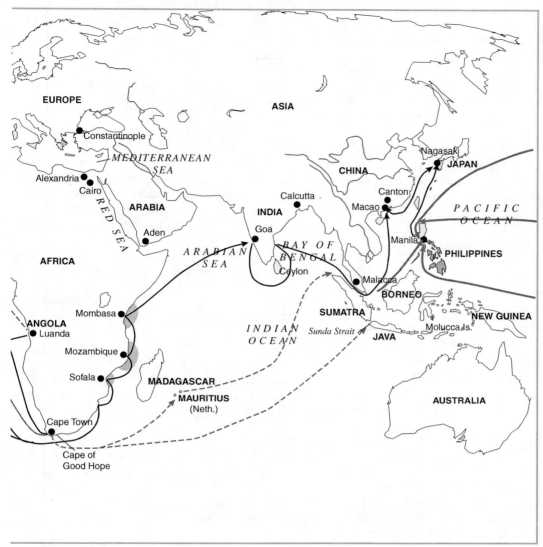

C. Rise of the Atlantic Powers

Voyages of exploration added to the influence and wealth of the middle classes in countries with ports on the Atlantic Ocean. At the same time, the economic and political power of the Italian city-states declined.

Spain, Portugal, England, the Netherlands, and France established American, Asian, and African colonies. They produced new products and rich resources for trade. Increased trade raised the European standard of living.

For non-European colonial peoples, life changed for the worse. Many were forced to labor long hours to provide riches for their new rulers.

European businesspeople invested in colonial plantations and mines, with varying success. A global economy began to develop.

Gold and silver from Spain's American colonies financed businesses in Europe. Europe's domestic markets grew as workers received higher wages and spent them on manufactured goods.

Rulers collected more taxes. With this new wealth, they created larger armies and navies. Central governments became stronger.

D. Mercantilism

A new economic theory based on global trade developed. It was called **mercantilism**. According to this theory, colonies existed to enrich the home country. Colonies sent out raw materials for use in Europe's industries. Products manufactured from the raw materials were sold back to the colonies at a profit. Colonies that manufactured products could sell them only to the home country.

A country's wealth was determined by how much gold or silver it had. Colonies were a controlled source of these precious metals.

Mercantilists believed in **tariffs** (taxes on imported goods) to protect home industries from competition. Tariffs raised the prices of imports and thus encouraged people to buy cheaper domestic products.

Mercantilism helped the industries of the Atlantic nations to grow. Through taxation, rulers gained better control of their countries' economies. Strong royal governments increased national unity.

INFO CHECK

1. Summarize the role of each of the following in the Commercial Revolution: capitalism, domestic system, joint-stock companies, the middle class.

2. List the Atlantic powers. How did they begin the development of a global economy?

3. Define mercantilism. How did it make the Atlantic powers economically and politically stronger?

III. RENAISSANCE AND HUMANISM

Renaissance means "rebirth." It refers to the renewed interest in classical Greek and Roman culture that occurred in Europe between the 14th and 16th centuries. It also refers to the remarkable surge of creativity that took place at that time.

A. Beginnings in Italy

The Renaissance began in the 14th century in northern Italy when it was a collection of independent city-states. A prominent family usually governed each city-state. Although not official rulers, the Medicis, a banking family, controlled the government of Florence from 1434 to 1737.

The Medicis and other ruling families were **patrons** of the arts. They hired the most creative painters, sculptors, musicians, and builders of the time and rewarded their efforts magnificently.

B. Shift in Thinking

Medieval artists had worked for the Church and produced religious art. Renaissance artists hired

by wealthy and powerful people were expected to deal with more worldly themes. This focus on the here-and-now is called **secularism**. It inspired realistic rather than spiritual art.

New information about the world, brought back by explorers, opened Renaissance people to new ideas. They also became comfortable in several different areas of learning and culture.

C. Art and Architecture

LEONARDO DA VINCI. Leonardo da Vinci (1452–1519) was an Italian painter, sculptor, architect, scientist, and engineer. His paintings include *Mona Lisa* and *The Last Supper.* He designed a flying machine, a bicycle, a machine gun, and a submarine. He laid plans for a canal system and several buildings for the city of Milan. Leonardo also studied botany, anatomy, and biology.

MICHELANGELO. Michelangelo Buonarroti (1475–1564) was another Italian painter, sculptor, and architect. (He was also a poet.) Pope Julius II hired him to paint biblical scenes on the ceiling of the Sistine Chapel in Rome. Michelangelo designed the dome that tops Saint Peter's Basilica (church) in the Vatican as well as a square of buildings forming Rome's civic center.

PALLADIO. Andrea Palladio (1508–1580) was a renowned Italian architect. He designed the Church of San Georgio Maggiore in Venice as well as palaces, public buildings, private homes, and a theater. His buildings were inspired by classical Roman architecture.

D. Literature

HUMANISM. **Humanism** was an important movement in Renaissance literature. Humanists believed that people could improve their lives through a combination of classical studies and new experiences. Humanists were interested in the individual and in the world around them.

DANTE. Although a medieval writer, Dante Alighieri (1266–1321) was a forerunner of Renaissance culture. His long poem *The Divine Comedy,* although religious in theme, refers to many classical heroes, poets, and philosophers. Moreover, Dante wrote in vernacular (native) Italian rather than in Latin.

PETRARCH. Francesco Petrarch (1304–1374) wrote sonnets (14-line poems) in Latin and Italian expressing his love for a woman named Laura. He also popularized the works of neglected Greek and Latin writers.

BOCCACCIO. The Italian Giovanni Boccaccio (1313–1375) wrote a book of short stories called *The Decameron*. These stories make fun of many medieval customs.

SHAKESPEARE. The plays of the English genius William Shakespeare, (1564–1616) are still performed. They include histories, such as *Richard III* and *Henry V*; tragedies, such as *Hamlet* and *Romeo and Juliet*; and comedies, such as *A Midsummer Night's Dream* and *The Taming of the Shrew*. Shakespeare also wrote sonnets and long, narrative poems.

CERVANTES. The Spaniard Miguel de Cervantes (1547–1616) wrote the great novel *Don Quixote,* in which the old man of the title believes that he is a knight in defense of noble causes. Although the deluded Quixote is often a figure of fun, his idealism also arouses affection and admiration.

MACHIAVELLI. The Italian Niccolò Machiavelli (1460–1527) wrote about political power. Medieval political thought was based on religious principles. In contrast, Machiavelli looked at how his contemporaries thought and acted. He urged rulers to grant only those rights that do not limit their power. He felt that leaders should be strong and ruthless when necessary, kind and generous when possible.

INFO CHECK

1. Why do you think the Renaissance began in Italy rather than in one of the other European countries?

2. Define secularism. How was Renaissance art influenced by both secularism and religion?

3. Why is Leonardo da Vinci regarded as a prime example of a Renaissance person?

E. Scientific and Technological Innovations

SCIENTIFIC METHOD. For many centuries, science was practiced according to ancient scholarship, religion, and philosophy. As the Middle Ages ended, scientists began to question old beliefs.

Scientists now made systematic observations of nature. They accepted statements as facts only after testing them. Tests and results were written down so that other scientists could repeat the procedures. Eventually, the **scientific method** (observation, experimentation, drawing conclusions) led to revolutionary advances in chemistry, physics, mathematics, astronomy, and medicine.

GALILEO. The Italian Galileo Galilei (1564–1642) built a telescope to study the planets. He then concluded that Earth and the other planets move around the sun. His theory conflicted with the beliefs of the Roman Catholic Church, which taught that Earth is the center of the universe. Church officials forced Galileo to deny his discovery. Eventually, however, his theory about the **solar system** was accepted as scientific fact.

NEWTON. The Englishman Isaac Newton (1642–1727) created a system of advanced mathematics called calculus. He also explained the force called gravity, which operates on every planet to pull objects toward the surface and keep them from flying off into space. Gravity also keeps planets in orbit around the sun. With this knowledge, Newton laid the foundation of modern astronomy.

ANATOMY AND CHEMISTRY. In 1543, a Belgian doctor named Andreas Vesalius published the first accurate book on human anatomy, knowledge he had learned from dissecting corpses.

In 1628, William Harvey, an English doctor, wrote a book explaining how the heart pumps blood through the body.

Modern chemistry began with the work of Robert Boyle, an Irish scientist. He proved that air is a mixture of gases. He also studied how animals breathe.

PRINTING. In the mid-1400s, Johannes Gutenberg, a German printer, invented movable metal type and the printing press. (Westerners did not know about the earlier Chinese invention of another type of printing press.) Gutenberg's new machine printed books quickly. As more people read more books, the ideas in them spread.

INFO CHECK

1. Why was the scientific method so important to the expansion of human knowledge?

2. Which Renaissance scientist do you think made the most important discovery or contribution? Explain your choice.

Book printing shop in the late 16th century

IV. REFORMATION AND COUNTER-REFORMATION

People's confidence in the Roman Catholic Church began to slip after bubonic plague spread to Europe. During the Renaissance, more people questioned traditional religious beliefs and practices. They came to be called **Protestants** (those who protest). Church leaders accused them of **heresy** (holding beliefs not approved by the Church) and burned them at the stake. Nevertheless, the dissat-

isfactions grew into a major movement for change in organized religion called the **Reformation**.

A. The First Protestants

In 1517, a German monk named Martin Luther posted a document called the Ninety-five Theses (articles for debate) on a church door in Wittenberg. They criticized the Church for selling **indulgences**. An indulgence was a promise bought from a Church official that limited a person's stay in

Papal officials selling indulgences at German country fair in the 1500s

purgatory (the place where souls of the dead who regret their sins are made worthy of heaven through suffering).

Luther's plea for reform was based on three ideas unacceptable to Catholic leaders:

- A person could be saved through "faith alone"; that is, neither good works nor indulgences guaranteed salvation.

- The Bible was the only guide to salvation.

- Christians could interpret the Bible without the help of a priest.

CHURCH REACTION. In 1521, the pope excommunicated Luther as a heretic. The next year, Charles V, the Holy Roman Emperor, outlawed him.

Luther, however, was not silenced. The printing press spread his ideas throughout Germany. Luther translated the Bible into German, and more people read it. Many German princes sided with Luther against the pope and established Protestantism as an alternate Christian faith. A series of wars between German Catholics and Protestants followed.

These civil wars ended in 1555, when the Peace of Augsburg allowed each German prince to choose between the two faiths. The prince's subjects had to practice whichever faith he chose.

SPREAD OF THE REFORMATION. In England, King Henry VIII wanted an **annulment** (making a marriage invalid) from his wife, Catherine of Aragon, who had not given him a male heir. When the pope refused, Henry appointed an English archbishop, who granted the annulment. In 1534, Henry broke completely with the Church by issuing the Act of Supremacy, which made him the leader of the Church of England (Anglican Church).

Between 1536 and 1541, a French lawyer named John Calvin organized Protestant churches in Switzerland. Although he shared many of Luther's ideas, he also had ideas of his own:

- God determines who will go to heaven even before birth, an idea called **predestination**.

- A Christian person, whether chosen for salvation or not, should live a moral, upright life.

- The good Christian life is one of hard work and prayer, with only the simplest of pleasures.

Calvin's followers in Holland established the Dutch Reformed Church. In Scotland, John Knox established the Presbyterian Church, based on Calvinist teachings.

There were French Calvinists called Huguenots and English Calvinists called Puritans. Both groups were persecuted; many eventually escaped to America.

B. Counter-Reformation

Challenged by Protestantism, Pope Paul III called Church officials to the Council of Trent to discuss reforms. They ended the sale of indulgences, made plans to improve the training of priests, and restated basic Roman Catholic beliefs.

Ignatius Loyola founded the Society of Jesus to promote Catholicism. Its members, called Jesuits, were teachers and missionaries such as Francis Xavier, who went to Japan in 1549. Jesuits often accompanied Spanish and French explorers to America.

Because of this **Counter-Reformation**, Protestantism became less popular in Poland, Hungary, and other Eastern European nations. In Italy, France, Spain, and Portugal, Catholicism continued to be the main faith. It also took firm root in South and Central America and parts of North America.

C. Religious and Political Conflicts

Political ambitions and religious differences led to wars in England, Spain, France, and Germany.

Philip II, the Catholic king of Spain, hoped to invade and defeat England, ruled by Protestant Queen Elizabeth I. His goal was to strengthen both Spain and the Catholic Church. He sent the Spanish Armada (fleet) against England in 1588. The English defeated the Armada, however, and England remained Protestant.

From 1562 to 1598, French Catholics and Huguenots fought a series of civil wars that began with the St. Bartholomew's Day Massacre, a Catholic attack on Protestants. Powerful families of both faiths wanted the crown. Finally, the victorious Huguenot leader, Henry of Navarre, became King Henry IV of France and converted to Catholicism to secure his crown. He then outlawed the persecution of Huguenots by the Edict of Nantes in 1598.

The Thirty Years' War between the Catholic and Protestant states of Germany lasted from 1618 to 1648. Almost every country in Europe joined in the struggle. It was officially ended by the Treaty of Westphalia. Germany remained a collection of independent Protestant and Catholic states.

Protestant and Catholic Europe, 1600

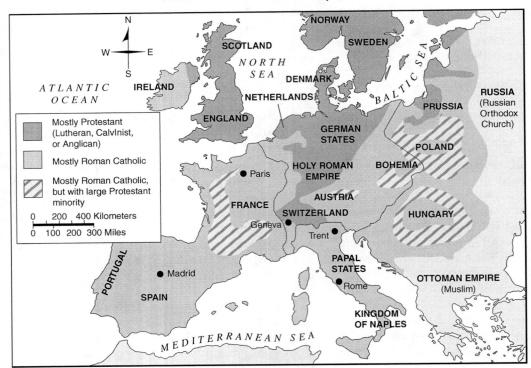

INFO CHECK

1. State the causes of the Protestant Reformation. What changes did it bring to Europe?

2. Summarize the role of each of the following in the Reformation: Martin Luther, Henry VIII, John Calvin, John Knox.

3. Explain how the Reformation led to the Counter-Reformation.

V. SOCIAL EFFECTS OF THE REFORMATION

A. Impact of Protestantism on Men and Women

Many wealthy Catholic women entered convents, where they developed talents for the arts, medicine, and administration. For Protestant women, marriage was the most important occupa-

Jewish father's plea for his daughter, accused of witchcraft

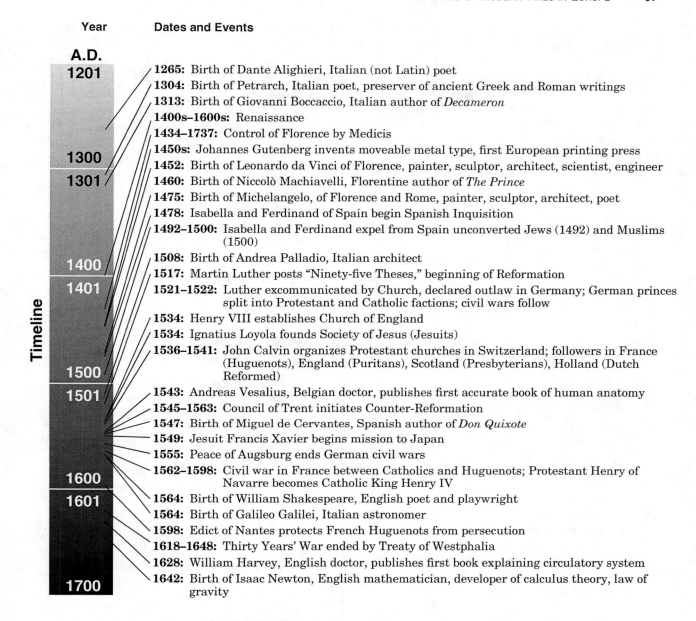

Year   Dates and Events

A.D.
1201

1265: Birth of Dante Alighieri, Italian (not Latin) poet
1304: Birth of Petrarch, Italian poet, preserver of ancient Greek and Roman writings
1313: Birth of Giovanni Boccaccio, Italian author of *Decameron*
1400s–1600s: Renaissance
1434–1737: Control of Florence by Medicis
1450s: Johannes Gutenberg invents moveable metal type, first European printing press
1452: Birth of Leonardo da Vinci of Florence, painter, sculptor, architect, scientist, engineer
1460: Birth of Niccolò Machiavelli, Florentine author of *The Prince*
1475: Birth of Michelangelo, of Florence and Rome, painter, sculptor, architect, poet
1478: Isabella and Ferdinand of Spain begin Spanish Inquisition
1492–1500: Isabella and Ferdinand expel from Spain unconverted Jews (1492) and Muslims (1500)
1508: Birth of Andrea Palladio, Italian architect
1517: Martin Luther posts "Ninety-five Theses," beginning of Reformation
1521–1522: Luther excommunicated by Church, declared outlaw in Germany; German princes split into Protestant and Catholic factions; civil wars follow
1534: Henry VIII establishes Church of England
1534: Ignatius Loyola founds Society of Jesus (Jesuits)
1536–1541: John Calvin organizes Protestant churches in Switzerland; followers in France (Huguenots), England (Puritans), Scotland (Presbyterians), Holland (Dutch Reformed)
1543: Andreas Vesalius, Belgian doctor, publishes first accurate book of human anatomy
1545–1563: Council of Trent initiates Counter-Reformation
1547: Birth of Miguel de Cervantes, Spanish author of *Don Quixote*
1549: Jesuit Francis Xavier begins mission to Japan
1555: Peace of Augsburg ends German civil wars
1562–1598: Civil war in France between Catholics and Huguenots; Protestant Henry of Navarre becomes Catholic King Henry IV
1564: Birth of William Shakespeare, English poet and playwright
1564: Birth of Galileo Galilei, Italian astronomer
1598: Edict of Nantes protects French Huguenots from persecution
1618–1648: Thirty Years' War ended by Treaty of Westphalia
1628: William Harvey, English doctor, publishes first book explaining circulatory system
1642: Birth of Isaac Newton, English mathematician, developer of calculus theory, law of gravity

Timeline: 1300, 1301, 1400, 1401, 1500, 1501, 1600, 1601, 1700

tion. Poor Protestants of both sexes benefited from the belief that each person should interpret the Bible personally; to do so, they had to learn to read.

Catholics did not believe in divorce. Protestants, on the other hand, viewed marriage as a contract that could be broken by either partner under certain circumstances.

According to Reformation marriage manuals, the husband was to support his family while the wife cared for the house and children and obeyed her husband. Both partners were expected to be faithful.

B. The Great Witch-Hunt

From the 15th through the 18th century, a great witch-hunt took place in Europe. It stemmed, in part from widespread insecurities following the Reformation's challenges to traditional religious ideas. People suspected that **heretics** (Catholics who rejected Church teachings) wanted to snare souls for the devil.

Another reason was the common belief that some illnesses had supernatural causes. More women than men were accused of witchcraft, probably because women frequently concocted medicines from herbs and other strange ingredients. When a woman tended a patient who died, she was sometimes accused of causing the death.

C. Status of Jews

In the early Middle Ages, Jews were well integrated into the European economy. Most were goldsmiths, physicians, traders, and moneylenders. They were protected against persecution by Catholic doctrine.

In 1215, Church leaders at the Fourth Lateran Council made a law requiring all Jews to wear a sign distinguishing them from Christians. People who held suspicions about religious groups could now target Jews. Such people, for instance, accused Jews of starting the plague.

In the 12th and 13th centuries, kings unified their realms by imposing religious and national uniformity. In 1290, King Edward exiled all the Jews from England. In the late 1400s, Queen Isabella and King Ferdinand made Catholicism the only religion in Spain by forcing Muslims and Jews to convert to Christianity or leave the country.

In 1478, Ferdinand and Isabella established the **Spanish Inquisition**. This court examined converted Jews and Muslims to determine if they were secretly practicing their former religions. Court officials often tortured suspects until they confessed to things that they had not done.

INFO CHECK

1. Explain why you AGREE or DISAGREE with each statement.
   • The lives of European women were improved by the Reformation.

   • The treatment of European Jews during the Reformation was an example of religious toleration.

2. Why did the rulers of Spain establish the Inquisition?

CHAPTER REVIEW

Multiple Choice

1. The shift from manor to city took place because

   1. serfs and peasants sought better lives
   2. fewer people died from the plague in cities
   3. lords wanted their serfs to leave the manor
   4. nomadic invaders threatened people's safety.

2. Why did cities contribute more than manors to European economic growth?

   1. Manors were overcrowded.
   2. City status denoted nobility.
   3. Cities served as ports where goods were received and as manufacturing centers.
   4. Cities were important places in which to practice religion.

3. European nobles began freeing their serfs because they

   1. realized serfdom was morally wrong
   2. needed soldiers to fight the king's armies
   3. wanted to collect rents from their lands, which serfs did not pay
   4. hoped to earn salvation for good deeds.

4. In the struggle for political power between nobles and the king, cities usually supported the

   1. king, because he led the nation
   2. king, who supported public works such as road building
   3. nobles, who allowed them to develop overseas trade
   4. nobles, to whom they felt allegiance.

5. Regulation of business, merchandise, and sales was done by the

   1. city charter
   2. guilds
   3. lord of the manor
   4. bishop of the Church.

6. Independent merchants, who were not part of the guilds, were called

   1. thieves
   2. vassals
   3. capitalists
   4. nomads.

7. European capitalists borrowed a method developed by the Muslims to raise large amounts of money. It was called a

   1. joint-stock company
   2. two-field system
   3. domestic system
   4. none of the above.

8. The rise of overseas colonies was directly related to

   1. the domestic system
   2. the manorial system
   3. feudalism
   4. mercantilism.

9. The Middle Ages was to Church-dominated religious themes as the

   1. Renaissance was to secular, worldly concerns
   2. Renaissance was to economic monetary organizations

3. Renaissance was to commercial banking syndicates
4. all of the above.

10. The Reformation and Counter-Reformation highlight the

1. political struggle between the pope and Holy Roman Emperor
2. political struggle between the pope and the German princes.
3. religious and political struggle between Protestants and Catholics
4. religious struggle between the Catholic Church and the Jesuits.

11. According to the illustration on page 94, which statement about printing in the 15th and 16th centuries is correct?

1. Printing was done entirely by hand.
2. Only one or two workers were required in a printing shop.
3. Workers were trained to operate printing presses.
4. Efforts to produce books more cheaply and in greater numbers failed.

12. According to the map on pages 90–91, the most powerful trading empires of the 16th and 17th centuries were

1. Spain and Portugal
2. China and Japan
3. Arabia and India
4. England and Australia.

Thematic Essays

1. *Task:* Using specific examples, discuss how the worldly, secular concerns of the Renaissance clashed with the religious concerns of the Roman Catholic Church. Consider in your answer world view, art, and science.

2. The Middle Ages was a period during which social and economic practices changed. *Task:* Using specific examples, explain why economic changes led to social changes.

Document-Based Questions

Use the documents and your knowledge of Global History and Geography to answer the questions.

1. Study the illustration on the bottom of page 94. How does the artist show that he sides with Luther against the Catholic Church?

2. Study the illustration on page 96. Why were Jews persecuted?

3. Tetzel said the following in a sermon on indulgences:

"You may obtain letters of safe conduct from the vicar of our lord Jesus Christ, . . . and convey it from all pains of purgatory, into the happy kingdom . . . with these confessional letters you will be able at any time in life to obtain full indulgence for all penalties imposed upon you. . . . "

What is Tetzel offering? Why is he doing this? Why did Luther object to this?

4. Luther wrote the following:

". . . by faith alone in Christ without works, are we declared just and saved . . . they cannot produce a letter to prove that the interpretation of Scripture . . . belongs to the Pope alone. . . . But we are all priests before God if we are Christians. . . . "

State the three issues Luther is presenting.

Document-Based Essay

Luther was able to spread his doctrines, while others who disagreed with the Church perished as heretics in the Inquisition. *Task:* Explain the reasons for Luther's success.

C H A P T E R
10

European Nation-States

I. DECLINE OF FEUDALISM AND RISE OF ABSOLUTE MONARCHY

As European kings gained power during the Middle Ages and the Renaissance, an important source of that power was middle-class support and financial backing. The middle class had grown wealthy from trade.

Between the mid-1500s and the late 1600s, European nations fought many wars. Middle-class wealth alone could not pay for these wars. Therefore, kings demanded money from landowners and peasants. Unable to meet the royal demands, both groups often rebelled.

A. Divine Right

Seventeenth-century rulers claimed a **divine right** (given by God) to rule. They believed that they represented God's will, which entitled them to absolute power.

B. Centralized Government

A government controlled by an absolute monarchy is centralized. Centralized governments in Europe developed into nation-states with strict boundaries, unified rule, and permanent armies. The citizens of such countries spoke the same language, shared cultural traits, felt national loyalty, and, in some cases, practiced the same religion.

II. EUROPEAN DYNASTIES

Some absolute monarchs established dynasties that controlled the country's government for several generations.

INFO CHECK

1. Explain why the growth of the middle class was so important to the rise of European nation-states.

2. Why do you think absolutism and the divine right of kings would not be popular today?

3. Can a nation-state exist without a centralized government? Explain your answer.

A. Tudors of England

Beginning with the reign of William the Conqueror (1066–1087), England had a strong central monarchy. William had come from Normandy and owned a large part of western France. English kings fought many wars with France to keep their hold on this land. One off-and-on armed conflict lasted from 1337 to 1453 and is known as the Hundred Years' War. In the end, England lost all its French lands.

In 1455, the Lancaster and York families fought for the English throne. The Lancasters' emblem was a red rose, and the Yorks' a white rose, so their conflict became known as the War of the Roses. After 30 years, Henry Tudor of the Lancaster family defeated Richard III of York. As Henry VII, he ruled from 1485 to 1509.

HENRY VII. To safeguard his rule, Henry imposed heavy fines on nobles who kept private armies. He courted the loyalty of other subjects by opening his advisory council to the middle class, the clergy, and low-level nobles. He made tax collections efficient and kept a private account, fed by fees and fines. Thus, he kept himself independent of Parliament when he was in need of funds.

Henry made trade agreements with the Netherlands, Spain, Florence, and Denmark, and supported the exploratory voyages of John Cabot. He also kept England out of foreign wars.

HENRY VIII. King Henry VII's son, Henry VIII (ruled 1509–1547), continued to strengthen the monarchy. He appointed ministers who supported him against Parliament and dismissed those who did not. After writing a book critical of Martin

Luther, the Roman Catholic Church gave Henry the title Defensor Fidelis (Defender of the Faith).

Unlike his father, Henry VIII was not careful with money. He spent a great deal on lavish entertainment and pursued unsuccessful wars of conquest.

When Henry set up the Anglican Church, or Church of England, in place of the Roman Catholic Church, he made himself its head.

ELIZABETH I. Henry's daughter Elizabeth I (ruled 1558–1603) was the last of the Tudors. Like her father, she appointed ministers who helped her get what she wanted from Parliament.

During Elizabeth's 45-year rule, she strengthened the Anglican Church and encouraged trade. In 1588, her navy decisively defeated the invading Spanish Armada. Although Sir Walter Raleigh failed to establish an English colony in North America, his attempt paved the way for successful future colonies. Like Henry VIII, Elizabeth was a patron of writers, painters, and playwrights.

INFO CHECK

1. Summarize the role of the Hundred Years' War and the War of the Roses in England's development as a nation-state.

2. Which of the Tudor monarchs do you find most impressive? Explain your answer.

B. Bourbons of France

HENRY IV. After Henry of Navarre ended the civil wars between Catholics and Huguenots, he became Henry IV of France, its first Bourbon king. He reduced the power of the nobility, prevented landlords from abusing peasants, and lowered peasants' taxes. His policies increased textile production, promoted trade, and restored war-damaged roads and bridges. Tax collection became more efficient too.

During Henry's reign, Samuel de Champlain founded a permanent settlement at what is present-day Quebec City in Canada.

LOUIS XIII. When Henry died, his son, Louis XIII, was still a child. Louis's mother, Marie de Médici, and her chief minister, Cardinal Richelieu, ruled until Louis became a man.

Richelieu set up a strong administrative system. The ruler appointed representatives to govern each district in France. These **intendants** established armies, supervised tax collections, regulated businesses, and monitored the nobility for signs of rebellion.

Richelieu promoted the textile industry and shipbuilding and encouraged private trading companies to colonize Canada and the West Indies.

Richelieu withdrew privileges from the Huguenots. On the other hand, he influenced Louis XIII to aid German Protestant princes during the Thirty Years' War, which kept the Catholic Holy Roman Emperor from being too powerful in Germany and threatening France.

LOUIS XIV. During Louis XIV's reign, France became the greatest power in Europe. Louis XIV became known as the "Sun King." To enhance his prestige, he built the magnificent palace of Versailles.

By keeping important nobles at Versailles, Louis prevented them from organizing against him. He entertained them lavishly and rewarded the most loyal with honors and high offices.

France became such a center of learning and the arts that all educated people in Europe spoke French and adopted French ways.

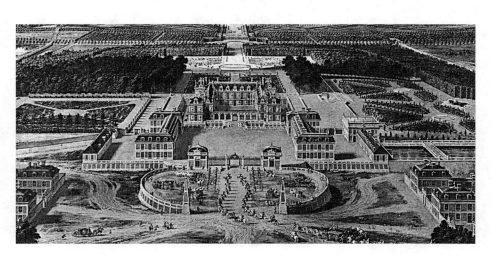

Louis XIV's Palace of Versailles and surrounding park, 1668. The Bourbon Rule was 1589–1792.

Louis ruled through the administrative system set up by Richelieu. The intendants put down all opposition to the king. Huguenots were persecuted, and many left to settle in North America.

One of Louis's ministers, Jean Baptiste Colbert, promoted mercantilism and encouraged the colonization of Canada.

Although industry prospered, constant wars in Europe and North America drained the royal treasury. Louis's successors inherited huge debts. Their efforts to raise money through heavy taxation finally caused the French people to turn against the monarchy.

INFO CHECK

1. Describe the efforts of Cardinal Richelieu to strengthen Bourbon rule of France.

2. What mistakes did the Bourbon kings make?

C. Habsburgs of Germany, Spain, and Central Europe

Members of the Habsburg family sat on the thrones of various countries from the 1200s to the early 1900s. The Holy Roman Emperors were all Habsburgs. In 1526, the dynasty split into two branches—one in Spain and one in Austria.

CHARLES V. Charles V inherited the Spanish throne in 1516 and became Holy Roman Emperor in 1519. During his reign, Spain gained a huge and profitable empire in both the Caribbean and Latin America. Charles outlawed Martin Luther and fought the Protestant princes in Germany. He strongly supported efforts to reform the Catholic Church.

Charles fought the French over territory in Italy. His forces also turned back attacks by Ottoman Turks in eastern Europe and around the Mediterranean.

In 1556, Charles gave up his throne to become a monk. His brother, Ferdinand I, became the Holy Roman Emperor (ruled 1558–1564).

PHILIP II. Charles' son, Philip II, became king of Spain (ruled 1556–1598). Hoping to restore Catholicism to England and gain more territory for Spain, Philip married Henry VIII's daughter, Queen Mary I. Since Mary died childless, the English crown went to Elizabeth I.

Philip instructed his administrators to write reports on all aspects of government. He consulted these reports before making decisions.

Wealth from Spain's Latin American colonies helped Philip build up his army and navy. Assisted by Italian forces, Spain turned back an Ottoman

Europe, 1648

Portrait of Empress Maria Theresa and her family in Schönbrunn Palace, Vienna

naval invasion of the western Mediterranean in 1571. Philip's unsuccessful use of the Spanish Armada in 1588 was an attempt to restore Catholicism in England.

MARIA THERESA. Maria Theresa ruled Austria-Hungary from 1740 to 1780. (Her husband, Francis I, was Holy Roman Emperor, because women could not hold that title.) Her reforms included the education of young children and attempts to limit the power of the great landlords over their peasants.

In 1772, Maria Theresa joined Russia and Prussia in partitioning (dividing) Poland, part of which became Austrian. The Habsburgs ruled Austria-Hungary until 1918.

INFO CHECK

1. Why did the Habsburg family have such a strong influence on European history?

2. What important role did Philip II play in the history of Spain and England?

D. Romanovs of Russia

After Russian rulers had pushed the Mongols out of Russia in 1480, the Russian kings Ivan III and Ivan IV ("the Terrible") took the title of **czar** (caesar). The early czars used extremely harsh methods to expand and unify Russia and strengthen the monarchy.

When Ivan IV died in 1584, no leader was powerful enough to take over the throne. In 1613, a group of clergy, nobles, and wealthy merchants chose a Romanov as czar. This family ruled Russia until the revolution of 1917.

PETER THE GREAT. Peter I (ruled 1682–1725) wanted to westernize Russia. In 1697, he went to the Netherlands and England disguised as a carpenter. He became familiar with their technological advances and returned to Russia with teachers, engineers, and craftspeople to teach the Russians new skills. He then set up schools and centers for scientific research. He brutally punished those who opposed the new ways.

Peter reduced the nobles' power and took control of the Russian Orthodox Church. He won territory along the Baltic Sea in a series of wars with Sweden. The Baltic ports increased Russian trade with Western Europe.

CATHERINE THE GREAT. Catherine II (ruled 1762–1796) continued to westernize Russia. She also encouraged Russian writers and artists, instituted reforms in education (and extended it to some women), and improved health care.

When Russia, Austria, and Prussia partitioned Poland in 1772, Catherine also acquired territory along the Black Sea, which gave Russia a seaport that was ice-free in winter.

At first, Catherine let large landholders control local governments while she protected peasants and serfs from abuse. After a large peasant uprising, however, she gave landlords more power than ever.

INFO CHECK

1. Why did the Romanovs think it was important to westernize Russia?

2. What did Russia gain in 1772?

III. EARLY LIMITS ON ABSOLUTE MONARCHY

During the Renaissance, common people came to believe that they had basic rights that their rulers had withheld from them. Political struggles developed between rulers and the ruled that sometimes led to **revolution** (the use or threat of violence to bring about basic changes in government).

A. Common Law and the Magna Carta

After William of Normandy conquered England in 1066, he ruled the whole country. His government collected taxes and decided important court cases. Nobles supported the king because he consulted them on important matters.

Henry II (ruled 1154–1189) appointed judges to travel around the country deciding cases. Their decisions, recorded and used as guides in future cases, formed the basis of **common law**; such law applied to everyone.

Kings in need of money often broke their own laws. When John became king in 1199, war costs had strained the national economy. John raised taxes and applied pressure in other ways to fill the treasury. He forced noble widows into unwelcome marriages. He married orphaned daughters of the nobility to anyone paying the highest price. He extorted money from towns and cities by threatening to cancel their charters.

John's barons and bishops rebelled by forcing him, in 1215, to sign the *Magna Carta*. This "great charter" stated the rights of the barons, which, in time, became the rights of common people too. No one, for example, could be sent to prison without receiving a jury trial. The Magna Carta showed that the king's power is limited by law. Many of its ideas are basic to the justice systems of Great Britain and the United States.

B. Parliament

The English developed other checks on absolute monarchy. Edward I (ruled 1272–1307) was the first king to ask townspeople, knights, clergy, and nobles to advise him. In 1295, these representatives met in the first **Parliament** to enact laws.

This "Model Parliament" was divided into the House of Lords and House of Commons. The Lords included nobles and church leaders, who inherited their seats in Parliament. The Commons was made up of wealthy merchants, elected or appointed.

Edward I felt that the new middle classes would be more willing to pay taxes if they helped make the laws. Placing their representatives in Parliament won him their support.

The Commons was less powerful than the Lords until the 20th century. Today, Parliament, rather than the monarch, governs the United Kingdom (Great Britain and Northern Ireland).

INFO CHECK

1. State the importance of the Magna Carta in both British and U.S. history.

2. Did the Model Parliament in 1295 strengthen or weaken absolutism in England? Explain your answer.

IV. REVOLUTIONS IN 17TH-CENTURY ENGLAND

A. Puritan Revolt

Queen Elizabeth I died in 1603 without children. A cousin, James I (ruled 1603–1625), succeeded her. He was a Stuart, the family that had ruled Scotland.

JAMES I. Parliament resented James for several reasons:

- He was a foreigner.
- He constantly requested money.
- He tried to impose taxes without Parliament's consent.
- He wanted an alliance with Catholic Spain.

CHARLES I. Charles I (ruled 1625–1649) was dedicated to absolute monarchy and the divine right of kings. When Parliament refused to grant him money, he forced loans from his knights and nobles.

Petition of Right. In 1628, Parliament agreed to give Charles money if he signed the *Petition of Right,* which prohibited the ruler from imposing taxes without Parliament's consent. It also stated that no one could be sent to prison unless the charges were made public.

Charles pretended to grant the petition but later raised taxes without asking Parliament. He had critics arrested and secretly tried in a special court, the Star Chamber. Charles dismissed Parliament and ruled alone until 1640.

Charles did not assemble Parliament again until he had no other way to raise money. When he tried to arrest members of Parliament opposed to his policies, a civil war broke out.

Civil War. The nobles, supporters of the Anglican Church, and many Catholics supported the king. They were called Royalists or Cavaliers. Supporters of Parliament were known as Roundheads (their hair was cut short and bowl-shaped). Many Roundheads were Puritans, whom Charles I had persecuted for criticizing the Church of England. The Puritans, backed by small farmers and merchants, controlled Parliament.

After 1643, Oliver Cromwell, a Puritan, led the Roundheads. His victory over the Royalists in 1648 put Parliament and the Puritans in control of England. In 1649, Charles I was convicted of treason and beheaded.

Eyewitness depiction of the execution of Charles I of England, 1649

B. Commonwealth and Protectorate

Cromwell made England into a republic called the **Commonwealth**. At first, Cromwell and Parliament shared power. After 1654, however, Cromwell took the title of Lord Protector of England and ruled as a dictator.

During the Commonwealth and Protectorate, England had its first, and only, written constitution, called the Instrument of Government. Found unacceptable by many, it was abandoned in 1657.

Cromwell, himself a Puritan, allowed other Christians, except Catholics, to follow their own beliefs. He encouraged Jews, exiled by Edward I, to return to England. He also improved trade by winning a short war with England's chief competitors, the Dutch, and by enforcing trade laws.

Between 1649 and 1651, Cromwell brutally put down Royalist uprisings in Ireland and Scotland.

At home, he offended the public by closing theaters and other public amusements and by banning newspaper articles critical of his government.

C. Restoration

After Cromwell's death in 1658, most of the English wanted a king once more. In 1660, Parliament invited Charles I's oldest son to return from exile. (Although a Protestant, Charles II had fought the Puritans on behalf of his father.) The rule of Charles II (1660–1685) is called the **Restoration**. The king and Parliament shared power, and Charles reopened the theaters and other places of amusement.

In 1679, Parliament passed the *Habeas Corpus Act*. It gave an arrested person the right to appear before a judge within a certain period. The judge would then decide on trial or release. Habeas corpus (Latin for "you should have the body") is an important part of the U.S. justice system.

Political parties began to develop during the Restoration. The Tories supported the king. The Whigs wanted a powerful Parliament.

D. Glorious Revolution

Charles' brother, James II, became king in 1685. He was a Roman Catholic and a believer in absolute monarchy. Since his daughters were married to Protestant princes, Parliament felt secure that England would remain Protestant. James's wife gave birth to a son in 1688, however. A son, whatever his age, inherited the throne before a daughter, and Parliament feared that James's son would reinstate Catholicism in England.

Parliament invited James's daughter Mary and her husband William to rule England. James fled to France. This **Glorious Revolution** brought to England rule by the House of Orange.

In 1689, the English *Bill of Rights* made it clear that Parliament would have more power than the monarch:

- No taxes could be imposed without Parliament's consent.

- No monarch could suspend laws made by Parliament.

- English courts could not impose cruel punishments.

- Parliament was to meet frequently, and all members were entitled to freedom of speech.

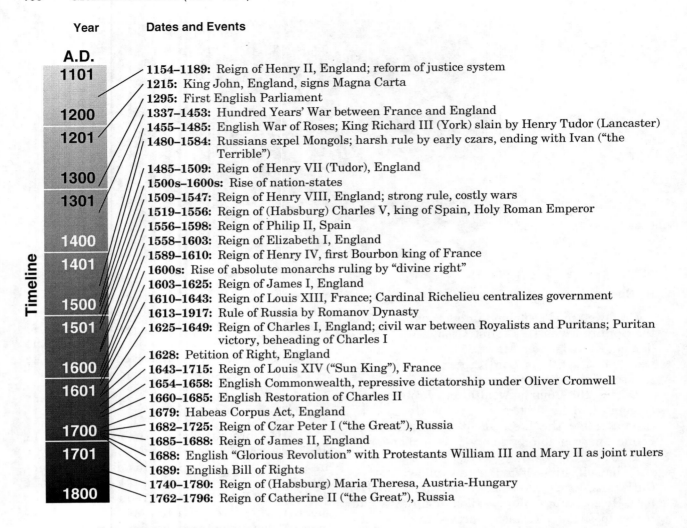

Year	Dates and Events

A.D.

1101

1154–1189: Reign of Henry II, England; reform of justice system

1215: King John, England, signs Magna Carta

1295: First English Parliament

1200

1337–1453: Hundred Years' War between France and England

1201

1455–1485: English War of Roses; King Richard III (York) slain by Henry Tudor (Lancaster)

1480–1584: Russians expel Mongols; harsh rule by early czars, ending with Ivan ("the Terrible")

1300

1485–1509: Reign of Henry VII (Tudor), England

1500s–1600s: Rise of nation-states

1301

1509–1547: Reign of Henry VIII, England; strong rule, costly wars

1519–1556: Reign of (Habsburg) Charles V, king of Spain, Holy Roman Emperor

1556–1598: Reign of Philip II, Spain

1400

1558–1603: Reign of Elizabeth I, England

1401

1589–1610: Reign of Henry IV, first Bourbon king of France

1600s: Rise of absolute monarchs ruling by "divine right"

1603–1625: Reign of James I, England

1500

1610–1643: Reign of Louis XIII, France; Cardinal Richelieu centralizes government

1613–1917: Rule of Russia by Romanov Dynasty

1501

1625–1649: Reign of Charles I, England; civil war between Royalists and Puritans; Puritan victory, beheading of Charles I

1628: Petition of Right, England

1600

1643–1715: Reign of Louis XIV ("Sun King"), France

1601

1654–1658: English Commonwealth, repressive dictatorship under Oliver Cromwell

1660–1685: English Restoration of Charles II

1679: Habeas Corpus Act, England

1700

1682–1725: Reign of Czar Peter I ("the Great"), Russia

1685–1688: Reign of James II, England

1701

1688: English "Glorious Revolution" with Protestants William III and Mary II as joint rulers

1689: English Bill of Rights

1740–1780: Reign of (Habsburg) Maria Theresa, Austria-Hungary

1800

1762–1796: Reign of Catherine II ("the Great"), Russia

Timeline

INFO CHECK

1. State one cause and two results of the Puritan Revolt.
2. PROVE or DISPROVE the following statements:

- The English had more rights under the Commonwealth than they did after the Restoration.
- The Glorious Revolution did nothing to increase democratic government in England.

CHAPTER REVIEW

Multiple Choice

1. The monarchs of the 17th century justified their attempts to gain absolute power by claiming that

   1. they had a divine right to rule
   2. the Mongols threatened an invasion
   3. the Holy Roman Emperor was all-powerful
   4. merchants were becoming too powerful.

2. Unlike an empire, a nation-state has

   1. people with different cultures speaking one language
   2. people with a shared culture and common language

   3. people with distinct customs, religions, and languages
   4. many groups of people, each seeking a national identity.

3. Henry VIII was declared Defender of the Faith because he

   1. criticized the ideas of Martin Luther
   2. wanted to replace Roman Catholicism with the Church of England
   3. admired the lifestyles of Catholic bishops
   4. sought the support of the Holy Roman Emperor against the King of Spain.

4. Elizabeth I can be characterized as a leader who

1. frequently engaged in offensive wars
2. was a weak ruler resented by the people
3. provoked religious conflict
4. supported trade, exploration, and the arts and sciences.

5. English common law was the result of the

1. Twelve Tables of Roman Law
2. writing down of Henry II's judges' decisions
3. translation of Hammurabi's Code
4. Puritan Revolt.

6. The significance of the Magna Carta was that it limited the power of

1. English kings
2. English nobles
3. Catholic clergy
4. English merchants.

7. Two causes of the English civil war of 1642 were

1. religion and foreign invasion
2. Charles I's favoritism to nobles and his plan to invade Spain
3. Charles I's use of the Star Chamber and attempted arrests of members of Parliament
4. fear of Parliament passing new tax laws and imprisoning nobles.

8. The only time when England did not have a king but had a written constitution was during the

1. Commonwealth
2. Glorious Revolution
3. War of the Roses
4. Restoration.

9. In France, Cardinal Richelieu

1. placed the Huguenots in power
2. set up an effective administrative system for France
3. extended French control over England, Scotland, and Wales
4. put Marie de Médici on the French throne.

10. The map on page 102 shows that

1. city-states existed in Europe as late as 1648
2. the Habsburgs ruled a number of different European nations
3. Europeans were beginning to unite into a single nation
4. the Holy Roman Empire comprised most of Europe's territory.

11. According to the timeline on page 106, between 1101 and 1800

1. freedom and democracy developed in most of the nations of Europe
2. dictators ruled with unlimited power and authority

3. most of Europe's royal families lost their thrones as a result of revolutions
4. monarchs ruled most nations in Europe while some democratic foundations were being put in place in England.

Thematic Essays

1. *Task:* Compare the rule of the Tudors in England with the rule of the Bourbons in France.

2. How did the Puritan Revolt increase the rights of the English people? *Task:* Consider religious and legislative issues in your answer.

Document-Based Questions

Use the documents and your knowledge of Global History and Geography to answer the questions:

1. From writings by Frederick II:

"I repeat, then, the sovereign represents the state; he and his people form one single body which can only be happy in so far as it is harmoniously united. The prince stands in relation to the society over which he rules as the head stands to the body."

Explain the author's view of the relationship between the people and the ruler.

2. From a book about the reigns of Elizabeth I and James I:

"The state of monarchy is the supremest thing upon earth: for kings are not only God's lieutenants upon earth and sit upon God's throne, but even by God himself they are called gods. . . . In the scriptures kings are called gods and so their power [is] compared to the Divine power . . . "

Identify and explain the theory of government that is being defended here.

3. From the Magna Carta:

"39. No freeman shall be taken, or imprisoned, or disseized, or outlawed, or exiled, or in any way harmed—nor will we go upon or send upon him— save by the lawful judgment of his peers or by the law of the land."

Whose rights were protected in this document? Who was threatening these rights?

4. From Two Treatises on Government by John Locke:

"There is . . . another way whereby governments are dissolved and that is when the legislature or the prince, either of them acts contrary to the trust. . . . The end of government is the good of mankind. And which is best for mankind: that the people should be always exposed to the boundless will of tyranny, or that the rulers should be sometimes liable to be opposed when they grow exorbitant in the use of their power, and employ it for the destruction, and not the preservation of the properties of their people?"

How does Locke's view of government differ from the views in the previous selections? What course of action is Locke attempting to justify?

Document-Based Essay

Task: Using specific examples from earlier readings and the chapter, describe how these documents mirror the political events that occurred in England.

UNIT REVIEW

Thematic Essays

1. Compare and contrast a day in the life of feudal England and feudal Japan. *Task:* Consider and cite political, social, and economic conditions in your answer.

2. Capitalism and the market economy arose out of the loss of life during the Crusades and the horrors of the Black Death. *Task:* AGREE or DISAGREE with this statement. Consider trade and the rise of merchants and a middle class in developing your answer.

Document-Based Questions

Use the documents and your knowledge of Global History and Geography to answer the questions.

1. From the writings of Erasmus, a Renaissance philosopher:

   "The world is waking out of a long deep sleep. The old ignorance is still defended with tooth and claw, but we have kings and nobles now on our side. . . . Time was when learning was only found in the religious orders. . . ."

What struggle is being referred to, and which sides are the kings and nobles supporting?

2. From the writings of Copernicus:

   "I too began to reflect the earth's capacity for movement . . . that the earth turns from west to

east, then, so far as pertains to the apparent rising and setting of the sun, moon, and stars. . . ."

What revolutionary scientific theory is described in this reading?

3. From the writings of Martin Luther:

   "[Copernicus is the] new astronomer who wants to prove that the earth goes round, and not the heavens, the sun, and the moon. . . . But as the Holy Writ declares, it was the sun and not the earth that Joshua bade stand still."

Describe Luther's theory about the heavens, and explain the reason he uses to support his views.

4. From a book about Galileo:

   "I Galileo . . . kneeling before you Most Eminent and reverent Lord Cardinals, Inquisitors General . . . swear that I must abandon the false opinion that the Sun is the center of the world, and immovable and that the earth is not the center of the world and moves and that I must not hold defend or teach . . . the said false doctrine."

Why would Galileo, a Renaissance man, give up his scientifically reached beliefs?

Document-Based Essay

Task: Describe the reasons for the conflict between Galileo and the Catholic Church. Include the scientific theory and opposing religious doctrine to support your answer.

UNIT IV

First Global Age (1450–1770)

Year A.D.	Dates and Events
1400	**1492:** Columbus discovers Americas for Spain
	1493–1528: Askia Muhammad rules Songhai Empire; Timbuktu becomes preeminent cultural center
	1494: Line of Demarcation gives Western Hemisphere to Spain except for Portuguese Brazil
	1497–1509: Portuguese expand trade from India to China, Japan, Southeast Asia
	1500s: Europeans introduce sheep, cattle, horses to Americas Spanish build forts in American Southwest, convert and dispossess Pueblos
1499	
1500	**1509:** Portuguese control Indian Ocean trade routes
	1519–1521: Magellan's Spanish expedition circumnavigates globe Cortés invades Mexico, defeats Aztecs, destroys Tenochtitlán
	1531–1533: Pizarro conquers Inca Empire, kills emperor
	1542: Spanish king bans enslavement of natives in New Spain; importation of African slaves increased
	1598–1640: Dutch build trading post on African Gold Coast, oust Portuguese, control European trade
1599	
1600	**1600s:** Native Americans tame wild horses for hunting, abandon farming culture
	1600s–1700s: Dutch in New Netherland, Indonesia, Sri Lanka, Caribbean, South Africa, South America
	1600s–1800s: Transport by Europeans of African slaves to Americas Slavery begins in Virginia, pervades South as cotton becomes major crop West Africa grows dependent on European goods, accepts European political control
1699	**1607:** Jamestown, Virginia, first permanent European (English) settlement in North America
1700	**1688:** French arrive in Cape Town; with Dutch, develop culture of Afrikaners
	1700s: France in eastern Canada, Mississippi Valley, Caribbean, India American, English, Dutch triangular slave trade—New York–Boston, West Africa, West Indies
	1756–1763: Seven Years' War involves most of Europe; Britain gains colonies in North America, India
1799	**1775–1783:** Iroquois-British alliance during American Revolution fatally weakens Iroquois League

C H A P T E R
11

Empires in the Americas Before 1500

I. MIGRATION TO THE AMERICAS

The first immigrants to the Americas were hunter-gatherers who crossed the Bering Strait from Asia to Alaska. The first groups probably arrived during an Ice Age about 40,000 years ago. The Bering Strait was frozen, and a land bridge lay between Siberia and Alaska. Other groups from Siberia probably came to North America during later periods of the Ice Age.

**Migration Routes From
Asia Into the Americas**

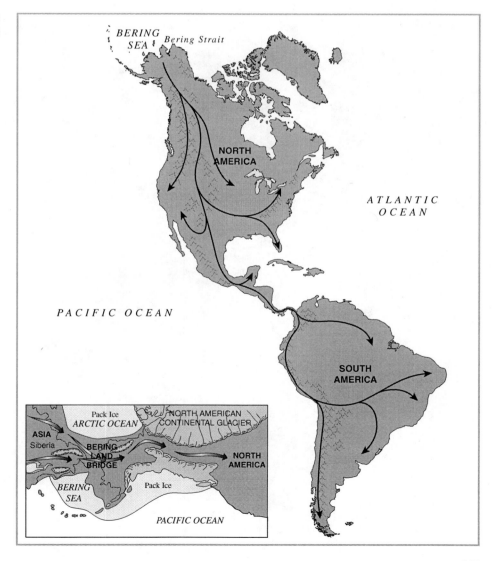

Evidence of the earliest permanent settlements in North America was found near Clovis, New Mexico, and dates from around 11,200 years ago. Remains of an earlier settlement—about 12,500 years ago—was found in southern Chile in South America.

A. Geography of the Americas

There is great diversity in the geography of North and South America. In northernmost North America is the **tundra**, a frozen plain. Present-day Canada and the United States were once mainly forests. Central North America consists of prairie and desert. A long mountain range extends from Alaska through North and Central America to the southern tip of South America; it is known as the Rocky Mountains in North America and the Andes in South America.

South America also has rain forests, areas of tropical scrub, and grassy plains. A desert strip stretches between its western mountains and the coast, and a larger desert is found in the southern region.

North and South America: Physical Map

INFO CHECK

1. Describe how the first immigrants arrived in the Americas.

2. Describe the diversity of climate in the Americas by region.

II. ADVANCED CULTURES OF MESOAMERICA

Mesoamerica consists of southern Mexico, Guatemala, Belize, and Honduras. Advanced cultures existed there as early as 1100 B.C.

Many features of early Mesoamerican culture—writing and number systems, calendars, pyramids—were like those of early cultures in Asia, Europe, and Africa. Mesoamericans, however, did not use the wheel for transportation, did not produce iron, and did not farm with plows.

A. Olmecs

The Olmec civilization originated on Mexico's Caribbean coast and flourished from about 1200 to 400 B.C. Scholars do not know why a civilization began in such a hot, swampy area.

SOCIETY. A central government ruled the Olmec state. Priest-kings headed the rigid class system. An elite group of warriors, administrators, and engineers were state managers. The lower classes consisted of farmers and artisans. At the bottom were slaves and serfs, who did heavy labor.

POPULATION CENTERS. The three main Olmec centers were San Lorenzo, La Venta, and Tres Zapotes (all Spanish names for the original unknown ones). The centers contained palaces, religious buildings, and marketplaces. The temples for religious ceremonies were large earthen mounds with flat tops.

ACCOMPLISHMENTS. The Olmecs had a writing system, a number system, and a calendar. Their **glyph writing** is made up of symbols and pictures of objects. The Olmecs made mirrors of the metal magnetite, which they probably used to reflect the sun's rays onto flammable materials and thus make fire.

Olmec artists carved massive heads from stone, some standing nine feet high and weighing 18 to 20 tons. **Anthropologists** (scientists who study past and present societies) believe that they represent priest-kings. The Olmecs also sculpted plumed serpents and creatures that were half jaguar and half human.

INFLUENCE. These god figures of the Olmecs appear in later Mesoamerican religions as well. In fact, so many features of Olmec civilization recur in later cultures that it is called the "mother" civilization of Mesoamerica. The Olmecs also had a strong influence on other contemporary societies.

TRADE. The Olmecs established trade networks involving many groups. These networks facilitated **cultural diffusion** as traders exchanged ideas and customs as well as goods.

Mesoamerican Civilizations

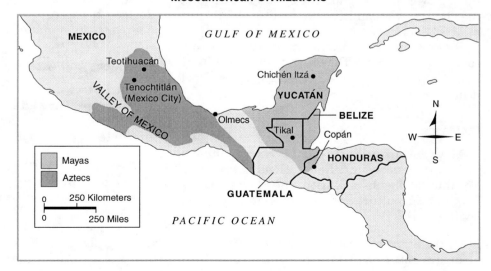

COLLAPSE. Around 900 B.C., some unknown group destroyed San Lorenzo. Soon, other centers declined too. The Olmec state collapsed in 600 B.C., but its culture continued elsewhere in new forms.

B. People of Teotihuacán

In about A.D. 300, a city called Teotihuacán arose northeast of what is present-day Mexico City. It shared many elements of Olmec culture:

- A social scale ranging from priest-kings and their administrators through craftspeople and farmers down to slaves and serfs

- Pyramids and the worship of the plumed serpent

- Calendars, a number system, and a writing system

CITY. Teotihuacán's streets were laid out in a **grid** (system of criss-crossed straight lines). The city contained two large pyramids—the Pyramid of the Sun and the Pyramid of the Moon.

Craftspeople and artisans lived in apartment-like buildings. Wealthy people lived in spacious, airy houses, with walls painted with murals. There were workshops for tanning leather, making pottery, and carving obsidian (hardened lava) into weapons and tools.

Teotihuacán was larger than most European or Asian cities of the time. At its height, 100,000 to 200,000 people lived there.

EMPIRE. The people of Teotihuacán established an empire by trade rather than conquest. They owned, for example, the sources of obsidian. Controlling the main supply of such necessities gave them power over neighboring societies. They, like the Olmecs, were an important cultural influence in Mesoamerica.

For unknown reasons, the great city was burned sometime between A.D. 600 and 650. Its culture, however, passed on to other peoples, who developed it further.

C. Mayas

Maya culture began in what is now Guatemala and later branched into Belize, Honduras, and the Yucatán Peninsula of Mexico. The Mayas adopted Teotihuacán culture and developed it into a great civilization.

CLASS STRUCTURE AND RELIGION. Maya class structure reflected that of the Olmec and Teotihuacán. The people worshiped nature gods, including the jaguar and plumed serpent. They honored their gods with human sacrifices.

AGRICULTURE. Maya civilization was based on agriculture. Farmers cleared plots in the rain forest and planted corn, beans, peppers, tomatoes, tobacco, cotton, fruits, and cacao.

TRADE. The Mayas traded with other Central American people, exchanging cloth and craft items for obsidian, jade, and the feathers of exotic birds.

BUILDING. The period between A.D. 250 and 900 is known as the Mayas' Classic Period. They built many ceremonial centers, such as Tikal in Guatemala and Copán in Honduras. Only priests and royalty lived there. The common people had small farms in surrounding areas.

Maya temples were tall, flat-topped pyramids. In some, religious ceremonies were held. In others, priests studied the stars and the movements of the planets. Thus, they were able to predict eclipses of the sun and moon and plan the agricultural cycle of planting and harvesting.

CULTURAL ACHIEVEMENTS. The Mayas knew the concept of zero and created a number system based on 20. They had an accurate 365-day calendar. Their writing system consisted of hieroglyphics representing ideas, dates, numbers, and sounds. It is not yet completely understood.

Craftspeople made beautiful pottery and jade jewelry. Artists painted murals, sculpted stone statues, and modeled clay figurines.

DECLINE. In the 800s, the Mayas, for unknown reasons, began to leave their cities and move to the Yucatán. There, they created great cities. About 1200, invaders from other parts of Mesoamerica destroyed these cities. Spanish explorers conquered the remaining Mayas in the early 1500s.

D. Toltecs and Aztecs

The Toltecs were more warlike than earlier cultural groups. They intermarried with inhabitants of Teotihuacán and adopted their customs. Soon, the Toltecs dominated the Valley of Mexico.

RISE OF THE AZTECS. In the 1200s, the Aztecs were a poor, weak people who had recently moved to marshy islands in Lake Texcoco, near present-day Mexico City.

They learned fighting skills from the Toltecs and adapted features of Teotihuacán culture. Within 200 years, the Aztecs had conquered most of central Mexico. Their empire reached its peak in the 1400s.

A GREAT CITY. In 1325, the Aztecs built the capital city of Tenochtitlán on an island in Lake Texcoco. Bridges connected it to the mainland. The city's food supply was grown on nearby islands, made by piling up mud from the lake bottom.

Aztec craftspeople worked in gold, silver, and precious stones. They wove fine cotton cloth. Their writing system resembled that of the Maya.

RELIGION. Among the Aztecs' many gods was Quetzalcoatl, the feathered serpent of the Olmecs. They believed that their nature gods required human blood to keep the world alive. The Aztecs, therefore, constantly fought their neighbors to obtain slaves and sacrificial victims.

SOCIETY. The Aztecs' social structure also consisted of nobles and priests, commoners, serfs, and slaves. The commoners were farmers and craftsworkers. The serfs, like those in medieval Europe, remained with the land as it passed from owner to owner. Slaves were eventually sacrificed to the gods. The emperor was considered a god, but he relied on a council of nobles to help him make decisions. Boys over ten went to school. Girls learned household skills at home.

SPANISH INVADERS. In 1519, a small band of Spanish soldiers led by Hernando Cortés arrived in Mexico looking for gold. With the help of the Aztecs' rebellious subjects, the Spaniards conquered the Aztec Empire. By 1522, the Spaniards had destroyed Tenochtitlán and built Mexico City on its ruins.

III. INCAS

From about 1250, the Incas built an empire in an area of the Andes Mountains that now includes parts of Ecuador, Peru, Bolivia, Chile, and Argentina. (See the map below.) People of the empire

South America: Inca Empire

Ruins of Machu Picchu, Inca city high in Peru's Andes Mountains

comprised 100 different cultural groups speaking 20 different languages.

WAY OF LIFE. The Inca emperor represented the sun god. He had total power over everyone and everything. The government owned all land and most businesses. Men farmed, served in the army, worked on construction projects, or mined for gold and silver. Some young women were trained to take part in religious ceremonies.

Farmers had to work temple and government land before they could work their own. Women had to weave set quotas of cloth for the government. The government stored food for times of need.

IMPERIAL RULE. The Inca Empire was ruled more successfully than that of the Aztecs. The government sent colonists into conquered lands so that they could teach the inhabitants the Inca language and way of life.

To prevent conquered rulers from rebelling, the Incas kept their sons as hostages in the Inca capital of Cuzco. After being educated by Inca teachers, these sons returned home to rule their people. Government officials watched conquered peoples closely. Those who did not pay their taxes or showed other signs of disloyalty were punished.

AGRICULTURE. To make use of the mountainous terrain, farmers planted crops, particularly potatoes, on terraces, flat areas dug into the mountainside and held in place by stonework. Because the climate was cold and very dry, farmers developed an efficient irrigation system.

SKILLS. The Incas had no written language. To aid communication, they built a vast road network connecting all parts of the empire. Messengers and armies moved quickly over these roads.

Inca doctors developed advanced medical treatments. They opened the skull to treat growths on the brain. They also discovered quinine, a medicine for malaria.

Inca craftsworkers were expert workers in gold and silver and skilled weavers. Stonemasons built structures so precisely that they needed no mortar to hold them together.

SPANISH INVADERS. In 1532, about 170 Spanish soldiers led by Francisco Pizarro invaded the Inca Empire. They seized and killed the emperor. By 1572, they had completed their conquest.

INFO CHECK

1. Define the term Mesoamerica.

2. List the advanced cultures of Mesoamerica and the dates during which each flourished.

3. What did these cultures have in common with Egypt and Mesopotamia?

4. Why did the Spanish want to conquer Mesoamerican cultures? How might the Americas be different today if the Spanish had never arrived?

IV. NORTH AMERICAN CULTURES

Native American peoples developed a wide variety of cultures in five main regions in what are today Canada and the United States— the Eastern Woodlands, Southwest, Plains, Northwest Coast, and Far North.

A. Iroquois (Eastern Woodlands)

The forests of the Eastern Woodlands are rich in game animals. The soil is fertile, and the climate is moist and mild. Native Americans of the Eastern Woodlands were hunters, farmers, and traders.

They used trees as building materials. They fashioned tools, weapons, and ornaments from stone, bone, and wood. A network of rivers enabled them to travel to other regions, where they traded their craftwork.

One of the largest groups in the Eastern Woodlands was the Iroquois. The Iroquois League of Five Nations was made up of the Seneca, Cayuga, Mohawk, Onondaga, and Oneida, later joined by the Tuscaroras from present-day North Carolina. They united to keep peace and defend one another from hostile outsiders.

GOVERNMENT. The Iroquois practiced a form of representative democracy. The leading women chose a chief, who was called a **sachem**. Each sachem represented his tribe at the Council of the League, the governing body of the Five (later Six) Nations.

Any Iroquois could attend a council meeting and present a proposal. After much discussion, the sachems would rule on each proposal.

North American Indian Cultures

A woman headed each **clan**, or group of related families. She owned all of the family's goods. No one could inherit anything except from his or her mother. Mothers arranged all marriages.

SOCIETY. A married man lived with his wife's clan while remaining a member of his mother's clan. His wife's brother raised and taught his children. When men got old, they returned to their mother's clan.

Several closely related Iroquois families shared a longhouse made of bark attached to wooden pole frames. A longhouse normally measured about 60 feet long, 18 feet wide, and 18 feet high. Longhouse villages were surrounded by stockades (high poled fences). Women raised corn, squash, and beans in fields outside the village. Men hunted, fished, and sometimes raided the villages of other tribes.

During the American Revolution, some Iroquois sided with the British. After the war, the Americans sent troops to punish them and permanently weakened the Iroquois League.

B. Anasazi (Southwest)

Many remains of Anasazi people have been found in an area called the Four Corners, where the borders of Colorado, New Mexico, Arizona, and Utah meet. Anthropologists believe that they were the ancestors of the Pueblo and Hopi who now live in the Southwest.

WAY OF LIFE. Originally hunter-gatherers, the Anasazi began to cultivate corn about A.D. 100. Lacking trees, they built multistoried houses from adobe (earthen bricks). Natural water was scarce, so the Anasazi built simple irrigation systems.

Skilled craftspeople, the Anasazi made beautiful pottery and fabrics, wove baskets so tightly that they held water and could be cooked in, and made special nets for snaring animals.

RELIGION. Anasazi ruins contain structures called **kivas**. On the walls of some of these underground rooms, pictures show supernatural figures bestowing rain, seeds, fish, and other good things on the earth. Kivas also contain altars and firepits where priests may once have performed sacred rites.

ABANDONMENT OF THE AREA. For unknown reasons, the Anasazi began deserting their cities in the late 1200s.

C. Pueblo (Southwest)

The Pueblo lifestyle was very similar to that of the Anasazi, who were probably their ancestors. The Pueblo lived in multistoried adobe houses. (When Spanish explorers found a cluster of these houses, they called it a "pueblo," the Spanish word for "town.")

WAY OF LIFE. The Pueblo were peaceful farmers. The men grew corn, beans, squash, and cotton.

Cliff dwelling from the 1200s, Mesa Verde National Park, Colorado

The women cooked, wove cloth, made pottery, and helped build their dwellings.

A council of religious leaders and clan chiefs governed each town. Community members were cooperative with one another, and little law enforcement was necessary. Troublemakers were shamed into good behavior.

RELIGION. Each Pueblo community had a kiva to serve as a religious center and meeting place for men. The Pueblo held many ceremonies to bring rain and other kinds of good fortune. They believed in spirits called **kachinas**, messengers from the gods who spent six months with the Pueblo and six months with the gods.

D. Apaches and Navajo (Southwest)

Sometime after A.D. 1000, the peaceful existence of the Pueblo was threatened by the Apaches and Navajo. These invaders were armed with more powerful bows and arrows than the Pueblo possessed.

WAYS OF LIFE. The Apaches remained hunters and raiders. The Navajo, however, gradually adopted more peaceful ways. Navajo men learned from the Mexicans the art of silversmithing. Men and women learned how to weave from the Pueblo. Today, the Navajo make up the largest Native American group in the United States.

GOVERNMENTS. A chief headed a group of Apache families but could not force a decision on them. Some chiefs inherited the role; others were chosen for their abilities.

Navajo family groups chose a leader to give advice. Policy decisions were made in public meetings in which both men and women took part. Only unanimous decisions were adopted.

ARRIVAL OF THE SPANISH. When the Spanish came to the Southwest in the mid-1500s, each group of Native Americans reacted characteristically. The Pueblo, at first, tried to live peacefully with them and even submitted when the Spanish forced them to convert to Christianity and work at missions and forts. In 1680, however, after repeated harsh treatment, the Pueblo rebelled. Although they remained under Spanish rule, they won the right to live and work in their own communities and practice their own religion.

The Navajo had few resources, and the Spanish left them alone. Nevertheless, the Navajo adopted many Spanish ways, such as raising sheep for wool, milk, and meat.

The Apaches successfully resisted the new invaders. Neither Spanish nor U.S. military forces were able to defeat them. They eventually agreed to a peace treaty with the U.S. government.

E. Peoples of the Great Plains

Among the best-known Native American peoples of the Plains were the Sioux, Cheyenne, and Comanche.

WAY OF LIFE. Before the arrival of Europeans, Native Americans of the Plains spent part of the year hunting buffalo and the remainder farming. The buffalo was vital to their existence. It provided meat and skins for clothes and tepees (cone-shaped tents in which the people camped while hunting). Buffalo bones were made into tools and weapons. Their droppings were burned as fuel.

Plains people chose a hunting leader for his courage and wisdom. He advised a council of male warriors. The council acted only on unanimous decisions.

The religion of Plains people was simple, with only a few great ceremonies. Each person looked for individual guidance from a spirit power.

EFFECT OF HORSES. Before the late 1600s, Plains people hunted on foot. Then, the Spanish brought horses with them. When some escaped and formed wild herds, Plains people learned to tame and ride them. On horseback, hunters could easily run down buffalo herds. Once they had tamed horses, the people devoted all their time to hunting and gave up farming.

WARRIORS. The use of horses improved the fighting skills of Plains people. They fought to avenge wrongs or acquire more horses. A warrior won great honor by touching an enemy in battle or stealing enemy horses. Such acts were called "counting coup."

SETTLERS AND CHANGE. After the mid-1800s, farmers, miners, and cattle ranchers pushed the Plains people out of their hunting grounds. These new invaders hunted buffalo not for food but for sport and soon killed most of them. With the disappearance of the buffalo, Plains people lost their most important resource. Then, the U.S. Army forced the tribes onto **reservations** (land set aside for them).

F. Northwest Coast Peoples

The Northwest Coast has a mild, wet climate and abundant resources. Native Americans who

Ornately carved totem pole of the Northwest Coast people, British Columbia, Canada

inhabited present-day British Columbia, Washington, and Oregon lived well. Among the most prosperous of them were the Tlingit and the Haida.

WAY OF LIFE. Northwest Coast villages were on the seashore or near a bay or river. A typical village had eight or more large wooden houses, each holding 30 to 40 related people including its chief. One of the house chiefs also served as village chief, a position passed on from one male relative to another.

The people were skillful woodworkers. They made handsome houses and carved elaborate **totem poles**. The carvings represented brave deeds of dead chiefs or denoted a family's special standing or privileges.

TRADE. Northwest Coast people grew only tobacco, which they used for trade. They also exchanged their craftwork for farm products.

FISHING. The people got most of their food from the sea and rivers. They hunted whales, seals, sea otters, and fish with harpoons and other fishing tools made of wood, bones, and shell. They used traps to catch salmon and other river fish.

CONFLICTS AND SOCIAL CLASSES. Northwest Coast tribes fought to settle conflicting claims to village sites and fishing places, to capture slaves for work and sacrifice, and to avenge a murder.

Most groups were divided into four social classes: chiefs, nobles, commoners, and slaves. Each person could advance to a higher class by showing skills and acquiring wealth. The most important demonstration of wealth was the **potlatch**, in which important community members gave away their belongings. Potlatches were also held to legalize a change in rank, a marriage, or the inheritance of a title.

ASSIMILATION. Northwest Coast peoples, like Native Americans elsewhere, lost their way of life with the arrival of Europeans. Many of them then assimilated (took to the new ways) by learning to sell their fish catches commercially, work in canneries, and raise potatoes. Less adaptable survivors were sent to U.S. reservations.

G. The Inuit (Far North)

Outsiders called the people of northernmost North America Eskimos, but they called themselves the Inuit ("the people"). They probably came from northern Asia, crossing into North America long after Native Americans had settled to the south.

WAY OF LIFE. The Arctic environment cannot support large numbers of people in one place, so the Inuit lived in small, scattered family groups. They traveled from place to place, hunting and fishing. The Inuit became highly skilled at living with extreme cold, snow, and ice.

They hunted caribou (North American reindeer), polar bears, whales, seals, and smaller game and fish. On hunting trips, they built **igloos** (shelters made of snow). Their village houses were made of sod and wood, built partially underground for warmth.

Overland, the Inuit traveled in sleds pulled by dogs. To hunt sea animals, they used **kayaks** (small one- or two-person boats made of waterproof skins stretched over wooden frames). They also built large open boats called **umiaks**.

RELIGION. The Inuit worshiped nature spirits, who could be influenced by special elders called **shamans**. Shamans, it was thought, had special

Year   Dates and Events

38,000 B.C.: Arrival of first Asian nomads into North America
10,000 B.C.: Artifacts of human settlement in Chile
9000 B.C.: Artifacts of human settlement at Clovis, New Mexico
1800 B.C.: Earliest migrations of Inuit from Asia to Arctic North America, Greenland
1200 B.C.: Earliest advanced cultures in Mesoamerica
1200–600 B.C.: Olmec civilization flourishes near Mexico's Caribbean coast
900 B.C.: Destruction by unknown forces of Olmec center, San Lorenzo

A.D.

101

500

501

900

901

1300

1301

1700

Timeline

A.D. 100: Anasazi of Southwest cultivate corn, settle in permanent villages
A.D. 250–900: Highest development of Maya civilization in Central America, Yucatán Peninsula
A.D. 300: Rise of city and civilization of Teotihuacán
A.D. 600–650: Teotihuacán destroyed by fire
A.D. 1000: Navajo and Apaches invade Pueblo settlements in Southwest
A.D. 1000–1500: Inuit absorb Viking settlers on Greenland
A.D. 1200–1400: Aztec move into Valley of Mexico, subdue Toltecs, build empire with huge capital at Tenochtitlán
A.D. 1200–1500s: Breakup of Maya civilization, first by Mesoamerican invaders, then by Spanish explorers
A.D. 1250–1400s: Incas build and rule huge empire along Andes Mountains, South America
A.D. 1500s: Europeans bring sheep, cattle, horses to Americas
A.D. 1500s: Spaniards reach Southwest
A.D. 1519–1522: Cortés and small Spanish force invade, conquer Aztec Empire
A.D. 1532–1572: Pizarro's Spanish force invades, conquers Inca Empire
A.D. 1600s: Wild horses reach Great Plains, Native Americans tame them, use them in buffalo hunts, give up farming culture; Iroquois League of Nations formed
A.D. 1680: Pueblo rebellion against harsh treatment by Spanish

magic to heal sick people and lure animals to be killed by hunters.

CONTACT WITH EUROPEANS. The Inuit met the Vikings who settled in western Greenland in 1500. Perhaps the two groups intermarried.

Vast numbers of Inuit died from diseases brought by Europeans. They also lost their survival skills as they became dependent on guns, metal knives, and tools.

INFO CHECK

1. Identify an interesting or important feature of each of the following cultures: Iroquois, Anasazi, Apaches, Plains tribes, Northwest Coast peoples, Inuit.

2. Which European groups most affected North American cultures? Was contact with Europeans helpful or harmful to Native Americans? Support your answer with examples from the chapter.

CHAPTER REVIEW

Multiple Choice

1. The first humans to come to America were probably

   1. nomadic warriors seeking riches
   2. sheepherders looking for pastureland
   3. hunter-gatherers seeking food
   4. European sailors seeking a short route to India.

2. Some of the major cultural differences between societies of the Western and Eastern hemispheres were caused by the

   1. different religious practices
   2. different geographic environments
   3. arrival of the last Ice Age
   4. different patterns of war and conquest.

3. The Olmecs were similar to the Mesopotamians and Egyptians in that they had

   1. a writing system
   2. a numbering system
   3. a calendar
   4 all of the above.

4. Which listing gives the correct chronological development of the civilizations named?

 1. Olmec, Inca, Maya
 2. Inca, Teotihuacán, Aztec
 3. Olmec, Teotihuacán, Aztec
 4. Aztec, Maya, Inca

5. Significant Mayan accomplishments are:

 1. great buildings and art, an accurate calendar, and a complex writing system
 2. a number system based on ten, an educational system, and a complex transportation system
 3. a large empire
 4. great buildings, terraced farms, and an island city.

6. The aim of Inca rule was to

 1. allow each conquered group to keep its own way of life
 2. control most aspects of everyone's life and make all groups follow one culture
 3. make everyone a skilled road builder and potato grower
 4. develop representative government in which conquered kings would take part.

7. Among the Iroquois, inheritance, family property, and clan leadership were decided by

 1. women
 2. warriors
 3. village elders
 4. sachems.

8. Pueblo ancestors belonged to the

 1. Iroquois
 2. Comanche
 3. Anasazi
 4. Inuit.

9. Survival of the Great Plains Indians was dependent on

 1. adequate rainfall to nourish crops
 2. fresh fish to supply protein and bones for needles
 3. tobacco to exchange for food and needed clothing
 4. buffalo herds for food, clothing, and bones for needles.

10. The Haida and Tlingit of the Northwest adapted to their environment by

 1. becoming nomadic warriors
 2. becoming sheep and cattle herders
 3. growing tobacco and fishing
 4. carving wood and farming vegetables.

11. The map on page 117 shows that

 1. few tribes settled in the Eastern Woodlands
 2. civilizations existed in many parts of North America

 3. Native American tribes consisted of a single cultural group
 4. Most North American tribes were located in California.

12. According to the timeline on page 121,

 1. the earliest peoples to populate North America were migratory
 2. North America was populated before 38,000 B.C.
 3. Europeans were among the first peoples to arrive in the Americas
 4. the Olmec civilization developed after that of the Incas.

Thematic Essays

1. Olmec civilization has been called the "mother civilization of Mesoamerica." *Task:* Using specific examples from their culture, describe how the Olmecs affected future civilizations in the region.

2. *Task:* Explain why the period of time from A.D. 250 to 900 is known as the Mayas' Classic Period.

Document-Based Questions

Use illustrations, documents, and your knowledge of Global History and Geography to answer the questions.

1. According to the map on page 115, Inca civilization extended through which countries and what major geographic feature?

2. What is geographically significant about Machu Picchu?

3. From an account of the Spanish conquest of Mexico:

"Here we had a clear prospect [view] of the three causeways by which Mexico communicated with the land, and of the aqueduct . . . which supplied the city with the finest water. . . . The noise and bustle of the market-place below us could be heard almost a league off, and those who had been at Rome and Constantinople said, that for convenience, regularity, and population they had never seen the like. . . ."

 What city is the writer describing? To what Mesoamerican culture does it belong? Why is the 16th-century Spanish writer impressed by this city?

4. What does the photograph on page 118 tell you about Native American life in the Southwest? How is this lifestyle different from or similar to your own?

Document-Based Essay

Compare and contrast one Mesoamerican empire with any European or Asian society that you have studied. *Task:* In your answer, cite examples from their cultures and governing practices that describe how they controlled their empires.

C H A P T E R
12

Rise and Fall of African Civilizations

I. GEOGRAPHICAL SETTING

The geography of Sub-Saharan Africa (south of the Sahara) includes rain forests, deserts, great rivers, **savannas** (grassy plains), mountains, basins, and deep valleys. Rain forests, deserts, and mountains make overland travel especially difficult, and powerful rapids and steep waterfalls discourage water travel. Because of this diversity of environments and natural barriers, sub-Saharan cultures have always differed widely.

Africa: Physical Map

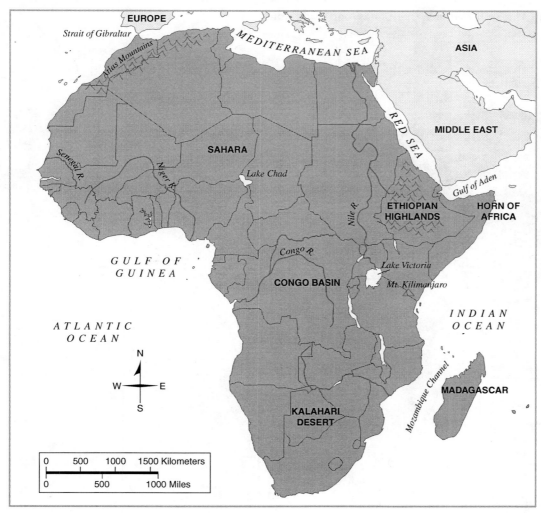

INFO CHECK

1. What major bodies of water are near Africa?

2. How did the geography of Africa affect the cultures of the sub-Saharan area?

II. EMPIRES OF WEST AFRICA

A. Ghana

The earliest empire in West Africa was Ghana, which was north and east of the Senegal River. (Present-day Ghana is elsewhere in West Africa.) By A.D. 300, the people of Ghana had learned to make iron. They also traded with the Romans.

In the 10th century, the Ghanaians conquered the town of Audagost and gained control of an important caravan route. The money brought in by new trade enabled the Ghanaians to expand their empire. By A.D. 1000, it was about the size of Texas.

RICHES. Parts of the empire were rich in gold mines. The Muslims traded salt, cloth, tools, and copper from North Africa for Ghanaian gold, ivory, and slaves. Salt was especially prized as a food preservative and essential nutrient. (People in a hot climate such as Ghana's lose large amounts of salt as they sweat.) Commerce with the Muslims made the kings of Ghana very rich.

GOVERNMENT. Kumbi-Saleh was the capital of the Ghana Empire. The king and his nobles headed a strong centralized government. A powerful army enforced their rule.

In the mid-11th century, North African Berber warriors, called Almoravids, conquered Ghana and most of West Africa. Under their rule, many members of Ghana's royal family became Muslim. In 1076, the Almoravids destroyed Kumbi-Saleh and weakened the power of the kings. As the Ghana Empire broke up, the Mali Empire absorbed it.

Early African Kingdoms, City-States, and Trade Routes

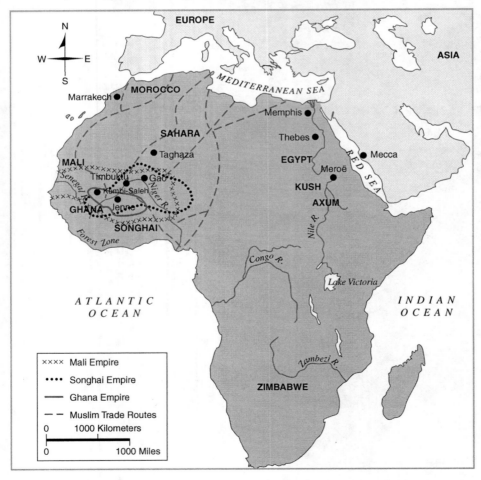

B. Mali

In 1235, a warrior-chief named Sundiata conquered a large territory along the Niger River. This land had been the part of the Ghanaian Empire containing gold mines. It laid the foundation for the empire ruled by Mali kings.

Before Europeans reached America, much of Europe's gold came from Mali. Ivory, cotton, and herds of cattle also made the empire rich. By the 14th century, Mali was twice as large as Ghana had been at its peak.

MANSA MUSA. Mansa Musa ruled Mali from 1312 to 1337. A Muslim, he helped spread Islam throughout his empire.

In 1324, Mansa Musa made a pilgrimage to Mecca (a Muslim religious obligation). During the trip, he spent and gave away so much gold that he caused **inflation** (a rise in prices) wherever he visited. The inflation lasted ten years.

Returning from Mecca, Mansa Musa brought many talented people to Timbuktu, Mali's capital city. These scholars, artists, engineers, and architects made Timbuktu's university a famous center for learning and the arts.

WAY OF LIFE. Timbuktu was a hub of commerce. Its laws were fair and its citizens law-abiding. Unlike women in other Muslim lands, Mali women took an active part in social and cultural life.

When Mansa Musa died, the power of Mali declined.

C. Songhai Empire

Songhai replaced Mali as the most powerful empire in West Africa. By the end of the 15th century, the Songhai king Sunni Ali had conquered a large territory along the Niger River. In 1468, he also captured Timbuktu from its desert tribal rulers. Sunni Ali ruled from 1464 to 1492.

CENTER OF LEARNING. Askia Muhammad, a nephew of Sunni Ali, ruled from 1493 to 1528. A devout Muslim, he based his laws on the teachings of the Quran, set up a fair tax system, and encouraged the establishment of Muslim schools.

Under Askia's rule, philosophers and scholars revived Timbuktu's reputation as a center of learning. Another Songhai city, Jenne, became famous for the skill of its doctors. Surgeons learned to operate on the human eye. Medical researchers discovered that mosquitoes carry malaria.

Songhai was not as accomplished in war craft. Under Askia's successors, soldiers armed with bows and spears could not withstand invaders who fought with guns. The sultan of Morocco conquered the Songhai Empire in 1591.

INFO CHECK

1. Explain the importance of the gold trade to the empires of West Africa.

2. Identify each of the following: Kumbi-Saleh, Sundiata, Mansa Musa, Timbuktu, Askia Muhammad, Jenne.

III. CITY-STATES OF EAST AFRICA

A. Trading Cities

In East Africa, Mogadishu, Malindi, Mombasa, and Kilwa developed into coastal city-states. Each one had its own ruler, made its own laws, had a small army, and controlled land outside its walls. The rulers obtained money by taxing traded goods.

These city-states traded with Indian, Chinese, and Muslim merchants by exchanging ivory, iron, and gold for cotton, glass beads, and porcelain. Control of the gold trade made Kilwa rich. In the 13th and 14th centuries, its rulers built fine stone palaces and homes. Mosques, parks, and fountains added to the city's beauty.

Ruins of the great mosque on the island city-state of Kilwa, present-day Tanzania

SWAHILI CULTURE. Over time, the different peoples of the coastal city-states adopted one another's languages and customs. This blending produced a culture called Swahili.

Most East Africans spoke the Swahili language. As they carried on foreign trade, they added words from Arabic and Asian languages to Swahili. They learned Arabic script.

Many Swahili people became Muslims, while others kept to the old African religions. Artists, craftsworkers, and storytellers created an advanced culture, with a comfortable lifestyle.

When Portuguese traders came to East Africa, the Swahili refused to grant them trading rights. The Portuguese attacked the city-states and destroyed them. The Portuguese and the Arabs then took over East African trade.

B. Great Zimbabwe

The ruins of Great Zimbabwe are located in southeastern South Africa. This great city and fort arose in the 11th century. The original inhabitants were cattle herders and farmers. To grow food for the increasing population, farmers expanded their plots by digging stone-supported terraces into the hillsides.

The area around Zimbabwe was rich in gold. In the 10th century, Zimbabwe's leaders began to trade with the Swahili. Eventually, they exchanged gold with China, Persia, and India for cotton, porcelain, and other Eastern goods. The wealth from this trade produced the city of Great Zimbabwe.

WAY OF LIFE. Many of Zimbabwe's people worked as gold miners. Others hunted elephants for their ivory tusks. The people believed that their king was a god and their prosperity depended on his good health. A sickly king was expected to make way for a healthy successor by killing himself.

Zimbabwe's ruler lived in splendid isolation. Only his wives and advisers were allowed to see him. Common people, such as farmers and soldiers, lived in small houses outside the city wall.

CHANGE AND DECLINE. No European ever saw Zimbabwe. The Portuguese tried unsuccessfully to seize goldfields outside the city. Although the destruction of the coastal city-states disrupted their trade with Zimbabwe, the city lasted until the 19th century. By that time, its trade had seriously declined, and conflict had weakened the ruling families. In 1830, migrating Zulu tribes invaded Great Zimbabwe and put its inhabitants to flight.

1. Describe the relationship between Swahili culture and the coastal cities of East Africa.

2. How did Great Zimbabwe become wealthy? What caused the kingdom's decline?

IV. ARRIVAL OF EUROPEANS: PORTUGUESE, DUTCH, AND FRENCH

A. The Portuguese

As Portuguese explorers sailed along West Africa in the 1400s, they stopped at its seaports to stock up on supplies. Thus, they discovered that the region was rich in gold and ivory.

TRADE. In 1472, the Portuguese began to trade with people in what is present-day Ghana. Because this area, midway along the West African coast, is rich in gold it came to be called the Gold Coast. The Portuguese protected their trade from European rivals by building a series of forts. They also made contact with the Congo Empire farther south. By converting its ruler to Christianity, they made him an ally and trade partner.

The Portuguese who followed the trailblazers Bartolomeu Dias (who sailed to the southern tip of Africa) and Vasco da Gama (who sailed around Africa to India) set up trading posts all along the African coasts. (See the map on page 127.)

B. The Dutch and French

THE DUTCH. In the late 1500s and early 1600s, Portugal was under Spanish control. Spain was so busy fighting France and putting down internal revolts that it did not have forces to counter opposition elsewhere. The Dutch were therefore able to gain control of most Portuguese territory in West Africa.

The Dutch began to colonize Africa in 1652. The Dutch East India Company, a government-backed private company, established a settlement called Cape Town. In 1688, Huguenots from France arrived there and gradually intermarried with the Dutch. These people, who called themselves Afrikaners, prospered as farmers and merchants. The few Africans of the area were friendly. Even had they been hostile, it would have mattered little. European diseases had killed many and weakened the rest.

Voyages of Dias and Da Gama Around Africa

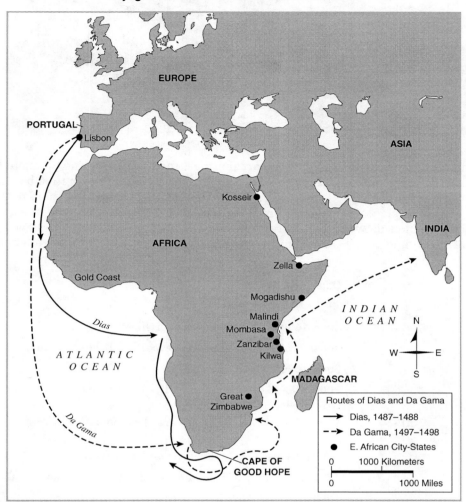

THE FRENCH. In 1658, the French built a settlement called St. Louis at the mouth of the Senegal River. They then built trading posts along the river and began a conquest of the entire Senegal region. In 1643, the French settled on Madagascar, an island off the east coast of Africa.

Europeans did not move into the interior of the continent. Its strong African rulers, hot, humid climate, and deadly diseases kept most Europeans along the coastal areas. The real European conquest of Africa would take place in the 19th century.

INFO CHECK

1. How did the Portuguese pursue their interests in Africa?

2. Why did early European explorers of Africa keep to the coastal regions?

V. RISE OF THE SLAVE TRADE

A. Slavery in Africa

As in civilizations elsewhere, African governments enslaved criminals, debtors, and prisoners of war.

Occasionally, the families adopted their slaves and gave them the opportunity to earn their freedom. Freed slaves had the same social status as everyone else. The children of free men and slave women were born free.

Many African slaves were sold to Arab traders who resold them in Asian markets. Berber traders of North Africa sold African slaves to Spain and Portugal.

B. Europeans and the Slave Trade

In the 17th century, the slave trade changed drastically. Europeans had established plantations

Nineteenth-century engraving of African slaves being marched to coastal market

in the Americas for growing sugarcane, rice, tobacco, and cotton—all crops requiring many workers.

At first, plantation owners forced Native Americans to do this work, but there were not enough of them, and many died from mistreatment and disease. The Spanish, Portuguese, British, Dutch, and French then bought slaves in West Africa and transported them to their American colonies.

African leaders raided villages and kidnapped people to sell to slave traders. From the 17th to the 19th century, traders sold as many as 10 million

Year	Dates and Events
A.D.	
301	**300s–1050s:** Ghana Empire flourishes
	700s: Arab traders establish seaports in East Africa to trade with India, China, Middle East
	800s–1000s: Rise of African city-state of Zimbabwe
600	**900s:** Ghana conquers Audagost, controls important caravan route, increases trade with Muslims
601	**1075:** Destruction of Ghana capital Kumbi-Saleh by Almoravids (Berbers); decline of Ghana Empire
	1200s–1300s: City-state of Kilwa (East Africa) grows rich by controlling gold trade
	1235–1255: Rule of Sundiata, foundation of Mali Empire, absorption of Ghana Empire
900	**1300s:** Peak of Mali Empire, center of prosperous gold mining
901	**1300s–1400s:** Portuguese explorers and traders arrive in East Africa, destroy Swahili city-states, take over (with Arabs) Swahili trade
	1312–1337: Reign of Mali king Mansa Musa; makes capital Timbuktu center of learning and arts; makes pilgrimage to Mecca (1324), spreads Islam throughout empire
1200	**1493–1528:** Reign of Askia Muhammad, greatest king of Songhai Empire, which replaces Mali
1201	**1500s:** Zimbabwe trade disrupted by Portuguese destruction of Swahili city-states; Portuguese fail to control Zimbabwe
	1509: Portuguese control Indian Ocean trade routes
	1591: Songhai Empire conquered by sultan of Morocco
1500	**1598–1640:** Dutch build trading post on Africa's Gold Coast, oust Portuguese, control its European trade
1501	**1600s–1800s:** Duration of African slave trade by which Spanish, Portuguese, Dutch, British, French transport West Africans to Americas
	1643: French build first settlement on Madagascar
1800	**1652:** Dutch East India Company establishes Cape Town in southern Africa
1801	**1658:** French establish St. Louis at mouth of Senegal River (West Africa)
	1688: French Huguenots arrive in Cape Town; with Dutch, develop new South African culture of Afrikaners
2000	**1830s:** Zulus attack weakened Zimbabwe; inhabitants abandon city

Timeline

Africans—mainly men. The Portuguese were the first Europeans to buy slaves in large numbers; they sent the slaves to their plantations in Brazil. By the 1650s, the Dutch, British, and French controlled slave-trading areas along the coast of West Africa. Arabs, and later Americans, also took an active part in the slave trade.

The voyage across the Atlantic Ocean killed many Africans. They were chained below deck in spaces too small to stand up in. Many starved or died from diseases. Some jumped overboard and drowned to escape a life of slavery.

C. Evils of the Slave Trade

The slave trade was rife with **racism**. European and American slave owners regarded Africans and Native Americans as inferiors because their skin was dark and they were not Christians. Moreover, because they came from cultures that were often simpler than European cultures, traders justified their treatment of slaves by arguing that they were less than human.

Profit was more important than humane considerations. European and American laws did not protect Africans and Native Americans. Therefore, traders could treat slaves like property. Members of the same family were often sold to different owners.

To prevent enslaved Africans from joining in revolt, traders separated members of the same tribe or village. Slaves on a plantation were usually strangers with different languages and beliefs. Therefore, they had to learn the language and culture of the plantation owner. Many thus lost their African heritage.

The slave trade damaged the people and cultures of West Africa as well. It robbed West African communities of young men and women who might have contributed to their tribes' welfare. The West Africans' growing dependency on European tools and weapons put them under European control. Moreover, the introduction of firearms made intertribal war more deadly.

INFO CHECK

1. Explain why you would AGREE or DISAGREE with the following statements:
   - The slave trade was a global business.
   - People of many nationalities profited from the slave trade.

2. Which of the evils of the slave trade do you consider the most damaging or destructive to Africans? Give reasons for your answer.

CHAPTER REVIEW

Multiple Choice

1. A result of the diversity of environments in sub-Saharan Africa is

   1. uniform cultures and lifestyles
   2. a variety of cultures
   3. frequent merging of tribes and kingdoms
   4. limited military and political conflict.

2. Ghana, Mali, and Songhai all grew wealthy and powerful because of their

   1. military technology and use of steel
   2. control of the caravan routes and goldmines
   3. religious conquests that spread Islam throughout West Africa
   4. sale of fellow Africans to Arab and European slave traders.

3. The Malian king Mansa Musa made a pilgrimage to Mecca in 1324. His trip was recorded and he was honored everywhere he traveled because

   1. he was a fierce warrior
   2. he was deeply religious
   3. he impressed leaders with his wealth

   4. the Holy Roman Emperor wanted him as an ally against the Muslims.

4. Select the best example of cultural diffusion in Africa.

   1. archaeologist finding ruins of a Portuguese fort
   2. European trading posts preserved as museums
   3. South African whites attending Calvinist church services
   4. the Swahili language containing Asian and Arabic words

5. In both the Kingdom of Zimbabwe and Japan, the ruler

   1. had limited powers
   2. shared power with his nobles
   3. was viewed as a god
   4. was selected by God.

6. The first European power to explore the coast of West Africa was

   1. Portugal
   2. England
   3. Holland
   4. France.

7. Intermarriage of French Huguenots and Dutch Protestants formed the basis of the new South African culture of the

   1. Afrikaners
   2. Senegali
   3. Gold Coasters
   4. Biafrans.

8. African kingdoms sold slaves to traders, who sold them to Spanish and Portuguese buyers. The slaves were needed because

   1. cotton plantations in both nations needed farmhands
   2. African slaves were valued as warriors
   3. African slaves were skilled metal workers
   4. plantations in the Americas needed many new workers.

9. The African region where most slaves were taken to and transported from was

   1. East Africa
   2. West Africa
   3. North Africa
   4. sub-Saharan Africa.

10. The map on page 124 illustrates that

    1. Timbuktu, Memphis, and Thebes were important cities located along Muslim trade routes
    2. Muslim trade routes were located primarily on the Atlantic and Mediterranean coasts
    3. the Nile River was an important means of transportation for the Muslim traders
    4. Europeans played a major role in early African trade.

11. The map on page 127 shows that both Dias and Da Gama

    1. reached the southern tip of Africa
    2. successfully sailed around Africa to India
    3. sailed from east to west
    4. began their voyages on the Gold Coast.

12. According to the timeline on page 128,

    1. the slave trade from West Africa to America took place between the 1600s and 1800s
    2. a number of great empires and civilizations existed from 300 to the 1500s
    3. African contact with the Portuguese took place prior to African contact with the British, French, or Dutch
    4. all of the above are true.

Thematic Essays

1. *Task:* Compare and contrast the reasons for the rise and fall of any two of the three African empires of Ghana, Mali, and Songhai. Consider in your answer such factors as religion, geography, natural resources, and family or governmental organization.

2. *Task:* Using historical examples from Mali, Songhai, or Ghana, discuss whether there was a relationship between trade and the spread of religion.

Document-Based Questions

Use your knowledge of Global History and Geography and the documents to answer the questions.

1. Using specific examples from the map on page 123, explain how the geographic environment of Africa divided the continent and hindered early exploration.

2. From a history of sub-Saharan Africa:

   "Muhammad bin Ebrahim al-Fazari, an eighth-century Arab astronomer, provides the first written mention of Ghana—what he calls the land of gold."

   What information does this reading provide in addition to Ghana being called a "land of gold"?

3. From the writings of al-Omari, one of the Egyptian sultan's officials:

   "This man Mansa Musa spread upon Cairo the flood of his generosity: there was no person, officer of the court, or holder of any office of the Sultanate who did not receive a sum of gold from him. . . . So much gold was current in Cairo that it ruined the value of money. . . . Let me add that gold in Egypt had enjoyed a high rate of exchange up to the moment of his arrival."

   What does al-Omari's report tell us about the economic effects of Mansa Musa's visit to Egypt?

Document-Based Essay

Early European historians believed Africans to be uncivilized barbarians. *Task:* Support or refute this view, citing specific historical and cultural evidence.

CHAPTER
13

Asians, Native Americans, and Africans Encounter Europeans

I. AGE OF EXPLORATION AND DISCOVERY

In the 15th century, Portugal, Spain, England, the Netherlands, and France sent expeditions in search of new trade routes.

A. National Explorations

PORTUGAL. Prince Henry sponsored expeditions to find a sea route to India by exploring the coast of West Africa. They led to a thriving Portuguese trade in African gold, slaves, and Indian spices and silks.

SPAIN. In 1492, Christopher Columbus made the first of his westward voyages for Spain. Landing in the Americas, Columbus believed that he had reached Asia, or the "Indies," and called the people "Indians."

King Charles V sent Ferdinand Magellan in search of a way around the Americas and on to Asian markets. The expedition lasted from 1519 to 1521 and was a success, although Magellan was killed en route.

ENGLAND. An Italian named John Cabot explored parts of Canada in 1497 and 1498, claiming Nova Scotia and Newfoundland for England. In 1576, Martin Frobisher explored the Labrador coast. Both explorers were looking for a Northwest Passage to take them around or through North America to Asia. The English established the first permanent European settlement in North America at Jamestown, Virginia, in 1607.

THE NETHERLANDS. In 1609, an Englishman named Henry Hudson explored North America for the Netherlands. At first, he searched for a Northwest Passage through the Arctic Ocean. Then, he explored the eastern part of the present-day United States. He claimed the area surrounding the Hudson River Valley for the Netherlands.

FRANCE. Between 1534 and 1541, Jacques Cartier explored the St. Lawrence River and eastern Canada. Another Frenchman, Samuel de Champlain, explored the St. Lawrence region in 1603. In 1608, Champlain established Quebec as the first permanent French settlement in North America.

French explorers were looking for gold and markets for French goods. Like other explorers of this period, they tried and failed to find a Northwest Passage.

B. Columbian Exchange

With the voyages of Columbus, people, animals, plants, and ideas began moving eastward and westward across the Atlantic in what became known as the **Columbian Exchange**.

Columbus brought horses, cattle, sheep, sugarcane, and the seeds of wheat, onions, and other plants to the Americas. He returned to Spain with turkeys, corn, potatoes, tomatoes, chili peppers, pumpkins, beans, peanuts, avocados, pineapples, and tobacco. Europeans subsequently brought their languages, religion, and cultures to the Western Hemisphere, as well as more animals and plants. Among the plants were those native to Africa, such as coffee, sweet potatoes, and bananas.

There were also bloody conflicts between the peoples of Europe and the Americas. Moreover, Native Americans died from smallpox, measles, and influenza, to which they had no resistance. In 1650, the Native American population of Latin America was about one-tenth of what it had been in 1500.

American gold and silver brought new wealth to Europe. Its trade expanded and its cities grew

Voyages of Exploration to North and South America

prosperous. Corn, beans, and potatoes improved the European diet and thus increased population. Poor Europeans tried to better their lives by settling land in the colonies.

II. RISE OF EMPIRES

A. Colonization

Exploration and discovery were followed by colonization and empire building.

SPAIN. By the end of the 16th century, New Spain included Mexico, Central America, most of South America, much of what is now the western United States, Florida, and a number of Caribbean islands. Spain also colonized the Philippine Islands in the Pacific Ocean.

FRANCE. France took control of New France—eastern Canada and the Mississippi Valley. It also established trading colonies in the Caribbean and India.

THE NETHERLANDS. The Dutch empire included New Netherland in the Hudson River Valley, a few Caribbean islands, and parts of South America and South Africa. It also claimed present-day Indonesia and Sri Lanka off the Asian coast.

PORTUGAL. Portugal's richest colony was Brazil in South America. Portugal also controlled trading areas on the coasts of Africa, India, and China.

GREAT BRITAIN. By 1750, Great Britain had 13 colonies on the Atlantic coast of North America. After fighting a series of wars against the Netherlands, Spain, and France, Great Britain also won control of Canada, India, New Netherland, and several Caribbean islands.

B. Competition

SPAIN VERSUS PORTUGAL. In 1494, Spain and Portugal settled a dispute over colonies in the Americas; they asked the pope to draw an imaginary line around the world from north to south. This *Line of Demarcation* ran through the eastern part of South America. Spain claimed the land west of the line, and Portugal claimed land east of the line. A similar agreement in 1529 gave Spain the Philippine Islands in the Pacific region.

SEVEN YEARS' WAR. Other nations fought wars over their rights to colonies. The most widespread was the Seven Years' War (1756–1763), fought in the Americas, Europe, and India. In the American colonies, the conflict was called the French and Indian War. Elsewhere, Britain, aided by Prussia,

European Land Claims in the Americas, 1700

fought France, Austria, and Russia, and gained large amounts of territory.

C. Dutch in East Indies

The Dutch East India Company, formed in 1602, dominated the trade of the "Spice Islands"—Sumatra, Borneo, Java, Celebes, and New Guinea. The company forced East Indian rulers to accept Dutch trading terms.

In 1641, the Dutch East India Company captured the Malayan city of Malacca from the Portuguese. It confined British trade to a small section of Sumatra. It forced local rulers to do business only with the company, and it told farmers what spices to raise. In spite of its power, the com-

pany went out of business in 1799 when the government of the Netherlands took over the East Indies.

By the 19th century, the Dutch controlled all of the East Indies. East Indians put up resistance to the colonial government, but Dutch military forces kept rebellions from spreading. Dutch rule continued until the 20th century, when the islands became independent Indonesia.

INFO CHECK

1. Explain the connection between European trade with Asia and voyages of exploration and discovery of the 15th to 17th centuries.

2. Define the terms Northwest Passage and Columbian Exchange.

3. Why did empire building by the Atlantic nations lead to more conflict than cooperation?

III. ENCOUNTER IN SOUTH AMERICA

A. Sword and Cross

Spanish military leaders who came to the Americas were called **conquistadors**. They respected only Spanish Catholics and believed that God wanted them to convert the Native Americans.

The conquistadors also searched for treasure. They killed, robbed, tortured, and enslaved Native Americans who got in their way and justified their actions by claiming to save the souls of people who worshiped false gods.

B. Conquest of Mexico

The 19-year-old Hernando Cortés (1485–1547) went from Spain to Hispaniola in the Caribbean (now the Dominican Republic and Haiti). For his help in subduing natives there, the colonial government gave him a plantation. Cortés hoped to grow richer by leading an expedition against the Aztecs in Mexico. By 1521, Cortés and only 600 soldiers defeated the Aztecs' army and destroyed Tenochtitlán, their capital.

REASONS FOR VICTORY. Cortés and his soldiers had guns, steel swords, and metal armor. The Aztecs had only spears, swords with obsidian blades, and armor of padded cloth.

At the time of Cortés's arrival, the Aztecs were anticipating the appearance of their god Quetzalcoatl as a pale, bearded man. Because Cortés fit

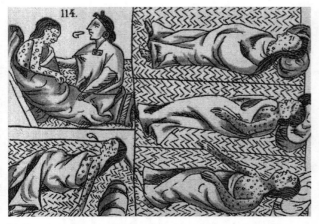

Native American suffering the stages of smallpox (from a Florentine codex)

this description, the Aztec emperor invited Cortés into Tenochtitlán.

Cortés made allies of the Aztecs' neighbors, many of whom had been enslaved or sacrificed by the Aztecs. A captive woman (Doña Malinda to the Spanish and Malinche to the Aztecs) translated Cortés's speeches asking the non-Aztecs to fight with him.

DESTRUCTION OF AZTEC CULTURE. The Spaniards shattered Aztec temples and statues and burned Aztec books. Determined to reshape Mexican culture, the conquistadors built Mexico City on the ruins of Tenochtitlán. Missionaries soon arrived to Christianize the Aztecs.

C. Overcoming the Mayas

About five years after destroying the Aztec Empire, the Spaniards marched against the already weakened Mayas in the Yucatán and present-day Guatemala. The Mayas hid in forests and fought back. It took the Spaniards about 20 years to defeat them. More missionaries then arrived to convert the native people.

D. Fall of the Incas

In 1531, Francisco Pizarro began a campaign against the Incas. Their empire was already weakened by a civil war between the emperor, Atahualpa, and his brother. Stealth and superior weapons helped the Spaniards. They captured Atahualpa, demanded and got a ransom for his life, and then killed him. By 1533, the entire empire became part of New Spain.

E. New Spain

In order to run the mines and plantations of New Spain at a profit, Spanish settlers needed cheap labor. They solved this problem by adapting the home country's **encomienda system** (estate management). A landlord in Spain could tax peasants living on his land. Landlords in New Spain began to force Native Americans on their estates to work without wages, that is, they enslaved them.

Cruel treatment and diseases rapidly decreased the native population. From about 25 million in 1519, it fell to about 1 million in 1605.

The missionary Bartolomé de Las Casas became known as the "Protector of the Indians." He asked the encomienda owners to treat their workers better. When they ignored him, Las Casas complained to the Spanish government. In 1542, the king banned slavery in New Spain. The landowners ignored the new law, and the encomienda system lasted until the late 1700s. Las Casas also encouraged the importation of Africans as replacements for Native Americans. Unfortunately, in this case, the landowners listened to him.

F. Portuguese in Brazil

In the 1530s, Portugal granted nobles huge tracts of land in Brazil. At first, the colony's main resource was the brazilwood tree, which yielded a red dye. The tree gave the colony its name. Later, the colonists began to grow sugarcane and mine gold and diamonds. Like the Spaniards, the Portuguese began to force natives to work their plantations and mines. It was difficult, however, to capture enough workers, and many Indians died from exhaustion and European diseases. Others fled to the forests. Plantation owners soon bought captive Africans to replace them.

As in New Spain, missionaries worked to convert the Indians and, sometimes, improve their conditions. The plight of African slaves, however, did not receive much attention.

INFO CHECK

1. Describe one noble and one selfish motivation of the Spanish conquistadors.

2. Should Hernando Cortés and Francisco Pizarro be regarded as military heroes? Why or why not?

3. What was the *encomienda* system? What was right or wrong about it?

IV. ENCOUNTER IN NORTH AMERICA

A. The English

In 1585, English settlers sponsored by Sir Walter Raleigh tried and failed to establish a colony on Roanoke Island off the coast of present-day North Carolina. At first, the Indians in the region helped the colonists survive in the new land. When one colonist killed the Indian chief, all aid ceased, and the English had to leave. A second attempt to settle Roanoke Island also failed.

In 1607, a group of settlers led by John Smith established a successful settlement, Jamestown. The English proceeded to found 13 colonies along the east coast of North America. Because their farms were smaller than the plantations of Latin America, there was little need for forced labor by Native Americans. The English did try to convert the Indians, but without force.

At first, relations between the English settlers and the Indians were friendly. Eventually, however, the settlers took too much of their land, and the Indians tried to drive them away.

B. The French

France's first settlement, Quebec, was mainly a trading post. Settlers and Indians were not rivals for land but were trading partners. The Indians exchanged furs for French knives, tools, and guns. They taught the French how to trap animals and survive in the forest. Many colonists married Indian women and joined their wives' communities. Catholic missionaries who came to convert the Indians lived in Indian villages and adopted some of their ways.

However, relations between the French and the Indians were not always good. The Iroquois were hostile to the French, who had made allies of their enemies, the Algonquians. In conflicts between the French and the English in North America, the Algonquians and Hurons sided with the French. The Iroquois fought for the English.

C. The Dutch

In 1624, the Dutch West India Company, hoping for huge profits from the fur trade, financed an expedition to set up colonies in New Netherland. Three trading settlements were founded— on the Hudson, Delaware, and Connecticut rivers. The trading post on the Hudson later became the city of Albany. In 1625, another group founded a settlement on Manhattan Island called New Amsterdam. It eventually became New York City.

THE DUTCH AND NATIVE AMERICANS. Dutch fur traders had good relations with the Iroquois. Dutch farmers, however, clashed with the Algonquians, who were suspicious of the Dutch-Iroquois friendship.

The Algonquians also resented the Dutch for turning their hunting grounds into farms. The Dutch had paid the Algonquians for the land and claimed ownership. The Indians, however, thought that the Dutch had given them presents for sharing their land. Other cultural differences also caused tension. When more colonists came and claimed more land, the Algonquians began to raid Dutch farms.

Then, some Algonquians came to a Dutch village seeking refuge from an enemy tribe. The Dutch leader ordered them killed, and open warfare erupted. The Netherlands government then recalled the Dutch leader and acknowledged the wrong done to the Algonquians. In 1645, a peace agreement was made that lasted for 10 years. A new war broke out in 1655, and in 1663, the Algonquians were decisively defeated.

THE DUTCH AND ENGLISH. The English and Dutch were trading rivals. In 1664, King Charles II sent English warships to New Amsterdam. They carried a claim that New Netherland belonged to England because of John Cabot's earlier explorations. Dutch merchants persuaded their leader, Peter Stuyvesant, to surrender to the English without a fight.

INFO CHECK

1. Compare English, French, and Dutch interactions with Indian tribes of North America. What was similar? What was different?

2. How did rivalries between the European colonizers affect the Indians?

V. SLAVERY AND THE SLAVE TRADE

A. Triangular Trade

During the 1700s, slave ships traveled a triangular route:

- Ships loaded with rum, iron goods, and guns left Boston or New York for West Africa, where captains traded their cargoes for gold, ivory, and slaves.

- Ships carried enslaved Africans on the so-called Middle Passage to Caribbean islands (the West Indies) and British North America and exchanged them for molasses.

- Ships carried molasses to Boston and New York to be made into rum.

The businesspeople of Boston and New York grew rich on this trade. So did the Dutch and English.

B. Slavery in the West Indies

Africans who survived the Middle Passage worked on sugar plantations in the West Indies. Conditions were so harsh that only the strongest and healthiest survived.

In the 1700s, a religious group called the Quakers asked the British government to outlaw slavery. In 1789, a freed African slave named Olaudoh Equiano wrote about the horrors of the Middle Passage and caused many to join the Quaker cause.

Slave-Trade Routes in the Western Hemisphere

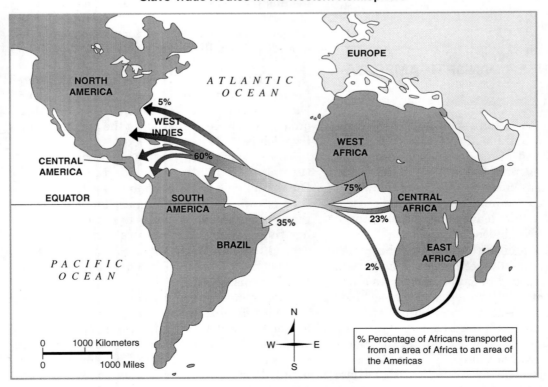

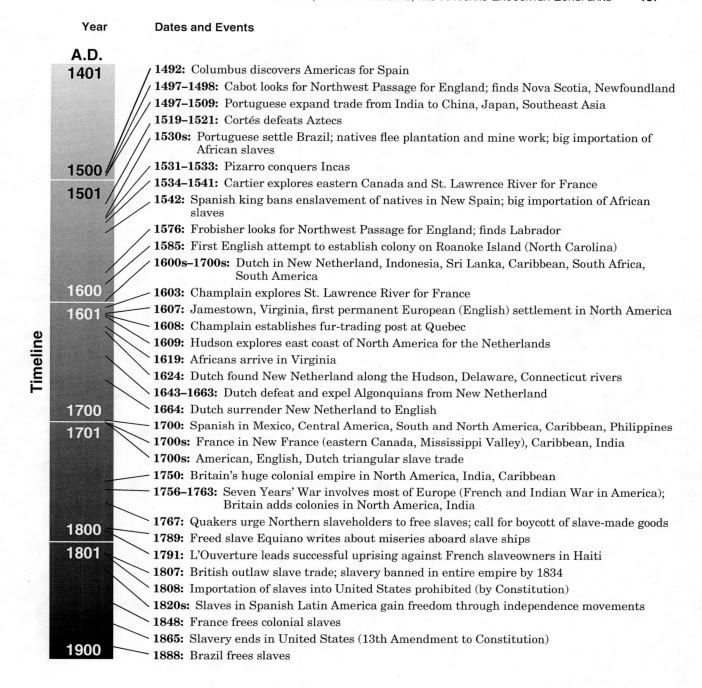

Year   Dates and Events

A.D.

1401

1492: Columbus discovers Americas for Spain

1497–1498: Cabot looks for Northwest Passage for England; finds Nova Scotia, Newfoundland

1497–1509: Portuguese expand trade from India to China, Japan, Southeast Asia

1519–1521: Cortés defeats Aztecs

1530s: Portuguese settle Brazil; natives flee plantation and mine work; big importation of African slaves

1500

1501

1531–1533: Pizarro conquers Incas

1534–1541: Cartier explores eastern Canada and St. Lawrence River for France

1542: Spanish king bans enslavement of natives in New Spain; big importation of African slaves

1576: Frobisher looks for Northwest Passage for England; finds Labrador

1585: First English attempt to establish colony on Roanoke Island (North Carolina)

1600s–1700s: Dutch in New Netherland, Indonesia, Sri Lanka, Caribbean, South Africa, South America

1600

1603: Champlain explores St. Lawrence River for France

1601

1607: Jamestown, Virginia, first permanent European (English) settlement in North America

1608: Champlain establishes fur-trading post at Quebec

1609: Hudson explores east coast of North America for the Netherlands

1619: Africans arrive in Virginia

1624: Dutch found New Netherland along the Hudson, Delaware, Connecticut rivers

1643–1663: Dutch defeat and expel Algonquians from New Netherland

1700

1664: Dutch surrender New Netherland to English

1701

1700: Spanish in Mexico, Central America, South and North America, Caribbean, Philippines

1700s: France in New France (eastern Canada, Mississippi Valley), Caribbean, India

1700s: American, English, Dutch triangular slave trade

1750: Britain's huge colonial empire in North America, India, Caribbean

1756–1763: Seven Years' War involves most of Europe (French and Indian War in America); Britain adds colonies in North America, India

1800

1767: Quakers urge Northern slaveholders to free slaves; call for boycott of slave-made goods

1801

1789: Freed slave Equiano writes about miseries aboard slave ships

1791: L'Ouverture leads successful uprising against French slaveowners in Haiti

1807: British outlaw slave trade; slavery banned in entire empire by 1834

1808: Importation of slaves into United States prohibited (by Constitution)

1820s: Slaves in Spanish Latin America gain freedom through independence movements

1848: France frees colonial slaves

1865: Slavery ends in United States (13th Amendment to Constitution)

1900

1888: Brazil frees slaves

Timeline

One event caused the British government to hesitate. In 1791, a freed slave named Toussaint L'Ouverture led a successful uprising against French slave owners in Haiti. Fearing that Africans on British islands in the West Indies might also rebel, Britain decided to ignore the rising protests. In 1807, however, it outlawed the slave trade. In 1834, it outlawed slavery throughout the British Empire.

France freed slaves in its colonies in 1848. Slaves in Latin America became free when countries there gained independence from Spain in the 1820s. Slaves in Spanish Puerto Rico and Cuba had to wait until 1873 and 1886, respectively, to be freed. Brazil freed its slaves only in 1888.

C. Slavery in North America

Africans arrived in North America in 1619. They were brought as slaves to work on rice, tobacco, and sugarcane plantations. When cotton became a major crop in the early 1800s, the South's economy

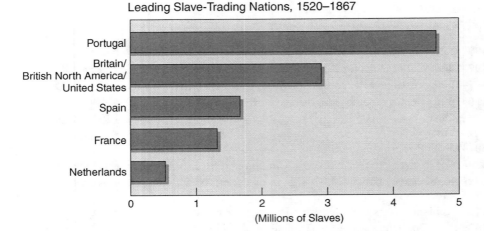

Leading Slave-Trading Nations, 1520–1867

(Millions of Slaves)

became more dependent than ever on cheap slave labor.

Small Northern farms did not require many workers. Northern slaves tended to do domestic and factory work. Most Southern slaves were field laborers; some were craftspeople.

Fear of slave revolts caused white Southerners to pass "slave codes." They prohibited slaves from owning weapons, learning to read, meeting in groups, and going from place to place without permission.

From the 1790s on, more and more U.S. citizens criticized the slave system. The Constitution pro-hibited the importation of slaves after 1808. Slavery ended, however, only in 1865, when the North won the Civil War and the U.S. Congress enacted the 13th Amendment to the Constitution.

INFO CHECK

- For each date, state an event or development related to the slave trade: 1619, 1789, 1791, 1807, 1808, 1834, 1848, 1865, 1873, 1888.

CHAPTER REVIEW

Multiple Choice

1. An item that Europeans purchased from Asia for health reasons was

   1. silk
   2. spices
   3. natural or carved precious stones
   4. porcelain and jade.

2. Two nations that searched for an all-water route to Asia and India were

   1. Portugal and the Netherlands
   2. France and Spain
   3. England and the Netherlands
   4. all of the above.

3. Voyages around the Cape of Good Hope proved that

   1. the world is flat
   2. a ship could sail around the southern tip of Africa

   3. a sea route to the Indian Ocean and India did not exist
   4. an all-water route to North America could not be found.

4. The Columbian Exchange refers to the movement across the Atlantic Ocean of

   1. people, animals, plants, and ideas
   2. precious minerals and slaves
   3. gold and feathers
   4. all of the above.

5. Cortés and Pizarro were able to defeat the Aztecs and Incas because of steel weapons, guns, Indian allies, and

   1. the corruption and cowardice of the Indian governments
   2. Indian warriors' surprise at Spanish tactics
   3. superstition and/or disunity among the Aztecs and Incas
   4. stolen maps of Indian strongholds.

6. The *encomienda* system in New Spain allowed landholders to

1. tax Indians living on their lands
2. force Indians to leave their lands
3. make Indians work without wages
4. none of the above.

7. New France's colonists had better relations with Indians than the Dutch or English did because the French

1. were not interested in acquiring land but in trading or trapping for furs
2. did not try to convert the Indians to Catholicism
3. refused to marry Indian women
4. were Huguenots fleeing religious abuse and determined to treat the Indians fairly.

8. Select the example that best illustrates cultural misunderstandings and anger between the Dutch and Algonquians.

1. The Algonquians had no beliefs, while the Dutch were deeply religious.
2. The Algonquians resented the Dutch for turning hunting grounds into farms, while the Dutch felt that they owned the land they had given the Algonquians money for.
3. The Algonquians valued their land and thought the Dutch foolish for selling off shares of theirs.
4. The Dutch wanted to buy furs, but the Algonquians sold only to French traders.

9. The worldwide struggle that left England the greatest colonial power was the

1. Hundred Years' War
2. Mayan 20-year struggle
3. Crusades
4. Seven Years' War.

10. The chart on page 138 shows that

1. Spain engaged in a smaller slave trade than the Netherlands
2. France and the Netherlands traded a larger combined total of slaves than Portugal
3. all European nations were involved in the African slave trade
4. nearly 3 million slaves were traded by Britain, British North America, and the United States.

11. According to the timeline on page 137,

1. the French were the first Europeans to outlaw slavery
2. Brazil freed its slaves after slavery ended in the United States

3. the British were the last Europeans to outlaw slavery
4. American slavery began in 1492.

Thematic Essays

1. *Task:* Select one area and discuss who benefited the most and who the least from initial encounters between Europeans and the people of Africa, Asia, or the Americas. Include specific historical examples to support your answer. Benefits may include natural resources, location, land, and markets.

2. *Task:* Compare and contrast the rise and fall of Dutch settlements in the Americas and in Asia. Factors to consider in your answer include: political and social organization, location, and geography.

Document-Based Questions

1. Study the illustration on page 134. Why were European diseases so deadly to Native Americans?

2. Study the map on page 133. Which nations gained immediate wealth from their colonies, and at whose expense?

3. From the writings of Bartolomé de Las Casas:

"That which led the Spaniards to these [terrible deeds] was the desire of gold, to make themselves suddenly rich . . . for the Spaniards so little regarded the health of their souls that they [allowed] this great [number] to die without the least light of religion. . . . The Indians never gave them the least cause to offer them violence. . . ."

Whose souls is Las Casas concerned about, and why?

4. From the writings of John Winthrop:

"It will be a service to the Church of great consequence to carry the Gospell into those parts of the world. . . . This land grows weary of her inhabitants . . . all towns complain of the burden of their poore. . . ."

Explain the two reasons Winthrop gives for leaving his homeland.

Document-Based Essay

Using specific social and economic examples from encounters between Europeans and Mesoamerican or African cultures, AGREE or DISAGREE with the statement: "What is beneficial to one person or culture, another finds harmful and destructive."

Thematic Essays

1. Prior to European discovery, the peoples of Mesoamerica had developed advanced societies. *Task:* Using social, economic, and governmental examples, compare and contrast the Mesoamerican societies with any African, Asian, or North American civilization.

2. "Technology enabled the Europeans to overcome geographic barriers and establish trading relations with China and Africa. Later, European technology was used to dominate those African and Chinese peoples." *Task:* Comment on the accuracy of this statement, using specific historical and geographic examples to explain the changing nature of encounters between Europeans, Africans, and Asians.

Document-Based Questions

Use your knowledge of Global History and Geography and the documents to answer the questions.

1. From a letter by King Louis XIV about France's commercial policy:

   "All merchants and traders by sea who buy ships or build new ones for trade or commerce will receive subsidies from us to help them. . . . Those who undertake long voyages will receive from us . . . subsidies for each ton of merchandise that they carry or bring back from the voyage. . . ."

   How and why is Louis XIV encouraging overseas trade?

2. An account of Vasco da Gama's meeting with the king of Calcutta in India:

   "Vasco da Gama said to the King: 'Sire, you are powerful and very great, above all the kings and rulers of India. The great King of Portugal, my sovereign, having heard of your grandeur . . . had a great longing . . . to send his ships with much merchandise to trade and buy your merchandise, and above all pepper and spices, of which there are none in Portugal. . . .' "

   Describe who is more powerful in this meeting, Da Gama or the king of Calcutta, and tell why you think so.

3. A letter from the Chinese emperor to King George III of England:

   "You, O King, live beyond the confines of many seas. Nevertheless, impelled by your humble desire to partake of the benefits of our civilization, you have dispatched a mission respectfully bearing your memorial. . . . Our dynasty's majestic virtue has penetrated into every country under heaven . . . we possess all things. I see no value on objects strange or ingenious and have no use for your countries' manufactures."

   What is the Chinese emperor's message to the king of England?

4. Antonio de Montesinos preached this sermon to Spanish colonists on the island of Hispaniola in 1511:

   "Why do you keep them [Native Indians] so oppressed and fatigued, neither giving them enough to eat nor taking care of them in their illness, for with the . . . work you demand of them they become ill and die, or rather you kill them with your desire to extract gold every day. . . . Be certain that, in the state in which you are, you can no more be saved than the Moors or Turks who lack and do not believe in the Christian faith."

   How would you have reacted to what Father Montesinos was saying? In your answer, consider the history of the period.

5. Study the illustration on page 134. How does it depict what occurred when Africans and Mesoamericans encountered European societies?

Document-Based Essay

Task: Use economic, scientific, and cultural examples either to AGREE or DISAGREE with this statement: "Non-Western societies gave much to the Europeans and received little in return."

UNIT V

Age of Revolution (1750–1914)

Year	Dates and Events

A.D.

1700

1762–1796: Catherine the Great of Russia exercises absolute power over peasants and serfs

1774–1792: Reign of Louis XVI; National Assembly limits king's power, widens commoners' rights

1775–1783: American Revolution—colonists win independence from Britain

1789–1799: French Revolution—end of absolute monarchy; Napoleon ends Directory, takes control of French government

1791–1804: L'Ouverture leads Haitian slave uprising; Dessaline wins independence from France

1810–1841: Many Latin American colonies win independence from Spain, Portugal, France

1814: Congress of Vienna sets up balance of power among European monarchies; suppresses nationalism

1799

1800

1825–1855: Nicholas I of Russia crushes liberal movement

1830: Belgians oust Dutch, set up constitutional monarchy

1830–1848: French oust Charles X in favor of Louis Philippe; rise of French middle class

1848: French oust Louis Philippe, set up Second Republic under Louis Napoleon

1848: Unsuccessful revolutions in Germany, Austria, Hungary, Italy; peasants gain basic rights

1848: Marx and Engels publish *Communist Manifesto*—class struggle, coming revolution

1852: Beginning of risorgimento; Cavour tries to unite northern Italian states against Austria

1852–1870: Louis Napoleon as Emperor Napoleon III sets up Second Empire

1899

1855–1881: Alexander II of Russia frees serfs, institutes social and legal reforms

1900

1857–1859: Sepoy Mutiny; British government rules India directly as colony

1861: Victor Emmanuel II named king of unified Italy

1881–1894: Assassination of Alexander II by Russian terrorists; Alexander III suppresses all opposition

1897: First Zionist congress meets in Switzerland to promote Jewish state in Palestine

1899: Boers revolt against British rule in South Africa

1908: Belgian government takes control of Congo from King Leopold

1910–1914: Madero, Villa, Zapata force dictator Díaz to flee Mexico; Huerta takes over government; revolutionists, with U.S. aid, force Huerta to resign

1911: Revolution led by Sun Yixian overthrows Manchus, declares China a republic

1999

1917–1922: Russian Revolution brings Communist leaders to power; Soviet Union created

CHAPTER

14

Revolutions in Science and Philosophy

I. SCIENTIFIC REVOLUTION

The **scientific method** arose during the Renaissance. It consisted of the study of physical reality by observation, experimentation, and drawing conclusions. Statements (observations) were accepted as truths only after they had been put to tests (experiments). Tests and results (conclusions) were written down so that other scientists could repeat them. This method led to so many advances in understanding nature that it caused a **scientific revolution**.

A. Renaissance Scientists

Medieval religious leaders taught that Earth and human beings were the focus of God's attention. Therefore, medieval scientists described a **geocentric solar system** in which the sun and planets revolve around the Earth. Renaissance scientists used the scientific method to disprove this theory.

COPERNICUS. Nicolaus Copernicus (1473–1543) was an astronomer and clergyman. He read the theories of Ptolemy, a renowned astronomer of the 2nd century A.D. Ptolemy had used the geocentric model of the solar system to develop rules that would help other astronomers follow the paths of planets around Earth. Copernicus found Ptolemy's rules inaccurate.

Copernicus turned to a model of the solar system proposed by Aristarchus, a Greek astronomer who lived in the 200s B.C. His model was **heliocentric**, demonstrating that Earth and the other planets revolve around the sun. Copernicus's book *On the Revolution of Heavenly Bodies* supported Aristarchus's ideas. Copernicus died the year his book was published.

Diagram of the pre-Copernican, Earth-centered universe, 1539

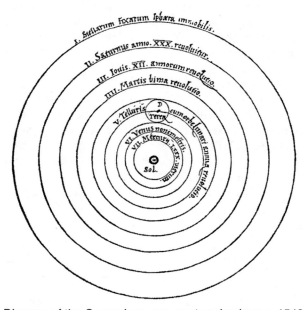

Diagram of the Copernican, sun-centered universe, 1543

Religious leaders condemned the book for contradicting their teachings. Most scientists also felt that the theory was wrong. If Earth revolved around the sun, they argued, everything on it would spin off into space.

KEPLER. In the early 1600s, Copernicus's theory gained support from Johannes Kepler of Germany. Kepler based his arguments on data collected by a Danish astronomer, Tycho Brahe. (Brahe had observed the heavens without a telescope, which had not yet been invented.) Kepler found that Brahe's data made sense only in a heliocentric solar system. Kepler then formulated three important laws:

- Planets follow oval-shaped paths around the sun.

- Planets revolve at different speeds from one another.

- The speed of each planet's revolution around the sun depends on its distance from the sun.

GALILEO. Galileo Galilei (1564–1642) was an Italian mathematician and astronomer. He realized that only the heliocentric model explained why planets appear to be different distances from Earth at different times of the year.

Fortunately, Galileo could use the just-invented telescope. He made one so powerful that he could observe distant heavenly bodies through it. He saw moons revolving around Jupiter—clear proof that all heavenly bodies do not revolve around Earth. In 1610, Galileo published his findings.

Galileo's persistence in defending Copernicus's heliocentric theory led Church officials to order him before the Inquisition. In 1633, when inquisitors threatened to burn Galileo at the stake for heresy, he recanted (took back) his claim that Earth moves around the sun.

Galileo's theories, however, were based on solid reasoning, careful analysis of recorded data, and visual evidence. Scientists could not dismiss them.

Galileo was famous for other experiments and conclusions as well. His law of inertia states that an object in motion tends to keep moving unless stopped by an outside force. He also found that falling objects fall at the same rate of speed regardless of mass.

VESALIUS. Andreas Vesalius (1514–1564) was a Flemish (Belgian) physician who used the scientific method by daring to dissect human bodies in public. His findings were collected in his book *On the Structure of the Human Body.*

Galileo's experiment on the Leaning Tower of Pisa, proving that objects of different mass fall at the same rate

Vesalius's views and methods came under severe attack by the Catholic Church, other physicians, and society at large. He was so angered by the criticism that he burned his notes and ceased to perform dissections for 20 years. Instead, he became court physician to Charles V and Philip II of Spain.

Eventually, however, Vesalius resumed his investigations. The science of anatomy, which he pioneered, is one of the great achievements of the scientific revolution.

BACON. Sir Francis Bacon (1561–1626) was an English philosopher, writer, and public official. In his book *The Advancement of Learning,* Bacon described how scientists use the scientific method to study the natural world. He argued in favor of **inductive reasoning,** by which a thinker develops general ideas after making specific observations about one or two events or things. Such reasoning suggests conclusions that may or may not be true.

DESCARTES. René Descartes (1596–1650) was a French mathematician, scientist, and philosopher. He felt that **deductive reasoning** was the most effective method of establishing natural laws. Deductive reasoning starts from a general principle obtained by inductive reasoning. From there, predictions about particular cases are made and then tested by observation and experimentation.

Descartes knew that if generalizations were false, they could not lead to true conclusions. (That is what happened when scientists had tried to explain the movement of heavenly bodies in a geocentric solar system.) Descartes stressed the importance of questioning all established ideas. Only the most self-evident principles, such as those used in geometry, should serve as the starting point for deductive reasoning.

NEWTON. Isaac Newton (1642–1727) was an English mathematician. He created the mathematical system called calculus. He also explained that the force of gravity keeps objects from flying off Earth and other planets and keeps planets in orbit around the sun.

Newton's identification of laws governing natural forces led to a **mechanistic worldview**. That is, since the universe obeys consistent laws, it can be viewed as a great machine.

LEEUWENHOEK. A Dutch scientist named Anton van Leeuwenhoek (1632–1723) helped to develop the microscope. He used it to study creatures too small to be seen by the unaided eye, such as bacteria and protozoa.

Leeuwenhoek's work disproved the theory of **spontaneous generation**—that tiny living things (lice, fleas) come from nonliving matter. They actually come from eggs.

B. Influence of the Scientific Revolution

After scientists had disproved ancient theories, historians no longer considered classical Greek and Roman culture as supreme. Future thinkers would make additional scientific advances, and this realization led to the concept of progress.

Political thinkers and economists began to feel that **rationality** (use of reason) could solve social problems. When rulers and the rich oppressed the poor, they were being irrational. Proper education could train both political leaders and common people to act humanely. Thus, people grew more concerned about the education of children. The 17th- and 18th-century belief that rationality could do away with superstition, poverty, and oppression gave this period the names of the **Enlightenment** and **Age of Reason**.

INFO CHECK

1. Define: scientific method, scientific revolution.

2. Explain the connection between the Renaissance and the scientific revolution. How did the work of Galileo illustrate this connection?

3. Why did the discoveries of Isaac Newton result in a mechanistic worldview?

4. Why were the 17th and 18th centuries known as the Enlightenment, or Age of Reason?

II. THE ENLIGHTENMENT IN EUROPE

In the late Renaissance, scientists realized how important it was to communicate with one another. Intellectuals soon formed an international community. New ideas about power, authority, and law spread quickly throughout Europe.

A. Political Thinkers

HOBBES. Thomas Hobbes (1588–1679) was an English political philosopher whose book *Leviathan* argued that government must be all-powerful.

Hobbes believed that people are constantly in conflict and lead difficult, dangerous lives. Insecurity causes them to submit to a ruler. The most efficient ruler is the absolute monarch. Thus, people enter into a **social contract**, exchanging freedom for security. Once people enter into such a contract, they have no right to change the ruler's policies.

Although Hobbes supported absolute monarchy, he claimed that power comes from the people. This challenge to the divine right of kings infuriated the Stuarts in England and Scotland. Hobbes also irritated church officials by stating that civil authority is superior to religious authority. Of course, his belief in an all-powerful government made democratic thinkers dislike him too.

LOCKE. The English philosopher John Locke (1632–1704) had influential theories about how institutions shape human personality. In *An Essay Concerning Human Understanding,* Locke stated that individuals are born without ideas or personality. A baby's mind is a **tabula rasa** (blank tablet). Family and school form the child's personality. Political freedom is also an important factor in shaping a good, productive person.

Locke felt that human nature, like the universe, is governed by natural laws—the pursuit of good and avoidance of pain. According to Locke, even babies have the power to reason, and institutions must help develop this power so that people can identify true goodness.

Moreover, humans must exercise certain natural rights—to life, liberty, and property. In *Two Treatises of Government,* Locke argued that a government must protect these rights; otherwise, its citizens have the natural right to change it. The American colonists who rebelled against England were inspired by Locke's political philosophy.

MONTESQUIEU. The Baron de Montesquieu (1689–1755) admired the English method of dividing political power among monarch, Parliament, and courts. He suggested that all governments mandate separation of powers among the executive, legislative, and judicial branches. The U.S. founders included his ideas about checks and balances of power in the Constitution.

VOLTAIRE. Under the pen name Voltaire, François Marie Arouet (1694–1778) wrote about government, religion, and philosophy. He supported Locke's idea of natural rights but felt that few people were capable of governing themselves. The best government was one headed by a good king. Voltaire criticized governmental persecution of people for their religious beliefs.

Voltaire was a **deist**. He believed that the universe had a planned order discoverable by reason. God was likened to a divine clockmaker, who, after creating the universe, wound it up and let it operate on its own.

ROUSSEAU. Jean-Jacques Rousseau (1712–1778) was a political philosopher who felt that reason and civilization destroyed the best in human nature. Precivilized people, or "noble savages," living in a state of nature were generous, free, spontaneous, and sincere.

In his book *The Social Contract* (1762), Rousseau admitted that modern society cannot function without some government. Therefore, people should make a contract, giving up some freedom in the interest of all members of their society. Rousseau warned, however, that the general will is not always that of the majority. Sometimes, a minority has a better sense of the common good. Those who disagree with the general will must nevertheless obey it.

Pro-democracy people liked Rousseau's idea that society should be ruled by a social contract rather than a monarch. They also agreed that political decisions should reflect the general will. Ab-

solute monarchs agreed with Rousseau that the majority is not always right; someone trained to rule should decide what is best for the nation.

B. Physiocrats

French economists of the Enlightenment, known as **physiocrats**, believed that a nation's wealth was based on agriculture rather than manufacturing and trade. Its economy should not be regulated but left to follow natural laws. The physiocrats opposed the mercantile system and limits on trade. Farmers should sell their goods at the best prices so that trade would increase and the entire nation become richer. Freedom from government regulation was referred to as **laissez-faire** ("leave it alone").

C. Enlightened Rulers

Some monarchs realized that reforms would strengthen their states. Therefore, they sought the advice of new political thinkers.

FREDERICK THE GREAT OF PRUSSIA. Frederick II (ruled 1740–1786) made reforms that reflected Enlightenment ideals. He adopted Voltaire's principle of tolerance and allowed his subjects freedom

Frederick the Great of Prussia astride his horse, in a contemporary engraving

of worship. He also improved Prussian schools, made the legal system fairer and clearer, and outlawed torture.

CATHERINE THE GREAT OF RUSSIA. Also influenced by Voltaire, Catherine the Great (ruled 1762–1796) made Russia's legal system more just and merciful, banned torture and religious persecution, and improved Russian schools. Nevertheless, Catherine had second thoughts about freeing the serfs after they engaged in a violent uprising. Deciding that they were dangerous, she gave the landlords absolute power over them.

MARIA THERESA AND JOSEPH II OF AUSTRIA. Maria Theresa (ruled 1740–1780) and her son Joseph II (ruled 1780–1790) made more sweeping reforms than Frederick or Catherine. Maria Theresa weakened the Church's control over her subjects, made Austria's tax system fairer, and gave some freedoms to the serfs.

Joseph bestowed civil rights on Jews and Protestants and passed laws against their persecution. He abolished serfdom. He also tried to make landlords pay their peasants in cash; the effort failed, since peasants used the barter system, and money was useless to them. Joseph's successor, Leopold II

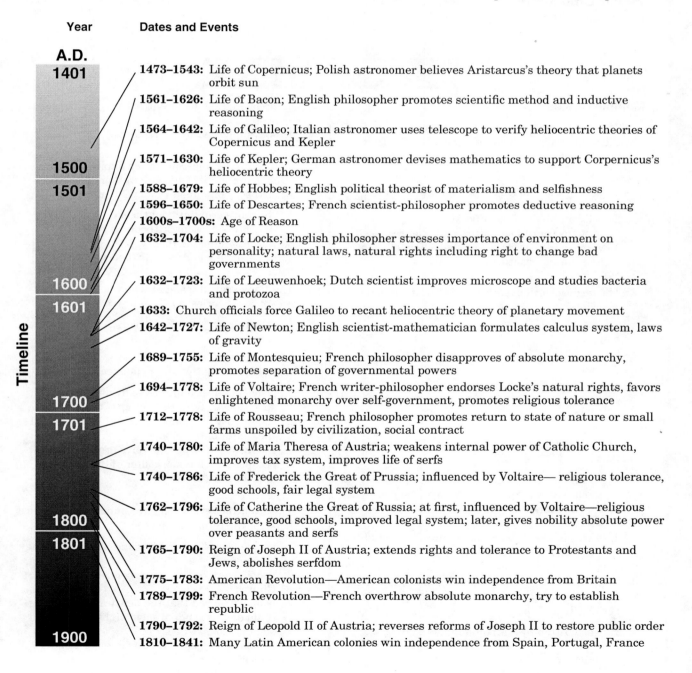

Year	Dates and Events
A.D. 1401	**1473–1543:** Life of Copernicus; Polish astronomer believes Aristarcus's theory that planets orbit sun
	1561–1626: Life of Bacon; English philosopher promotes scientific method and inductive reasoning
	1564–1642: Life of Galileo; Italian astronomer uses telescope to verify heliocentric theories of Copernicus and Kepler
1500	**1571–1630:** Life of Kepler; German astronomer devises mathematics to support Corpernicus's heliocentric theory
1501	**1588–1679:** Life of Hobbes; English political theorist of materialism and selfishness
	1596–1650: Life of Descartes; French scientist-philosopher promotes deductive reasoning
	1600s–1700s: Age of Reason
	1632–1704: Life of Locke; English philosopher stresses importance of environment on personality; natural laws, natural rights including right to change bad governments
1600	**1632–1723:** Life of Leeuwenhoek; Dutch scientist improves microscope and studies bacteria and protozoa
1601	**1633:** Church officials force Galileo to recant heliocentric theory of planetary movement
	1642–1727: Life of Newton; English scientist-mathematician formulates calculus system, laws of gravity
	1689–1755: Life of Montesquieu; French philosopher disapproves of absolute monarchy, promotes separation of governmental powers
1700	**1694–1778:** Life of Voltaire; French writer-philosopher endorses Locke's natural rights, favors enlightened monarchy over self-government, promotes religious tolerance
1701	**1712–1778:** Life of Rousseau; French philosopher promotes return to state of nature or small farms unspoiled by civilization, social contract
	1740–1780: Life of Maria Theresa of Austria; weakens internal power of Catholic Church, improves tax system, improves life of serfs
	1740–1786: Life of Frederick the Great of Prussia; influenced by Voltaire— religious tolerance, good schools, fair legal system
1800	**1762–1796:** Life of Catherine the Great of Russia; at first, influenced by Voltaire—religious tolerance, good schools, improved legal system; later, gives nobility absolute power over peasants and serfs
1801	**1765–1790:** Reign of Joseph II of Austria; extends rights and tolerance to Protestants and Jews, abolishes serfdom
	1775–1783: American Revolution—American colonists win independence from Britain
	1789–1799: French Revolution—French overthrow absolute monarchy, try to establish republic
	1790–1792: Reign of Leopold II of Austria; reverses reforms of Joseph II to restore public order
1900	**1810–1841:** Many Latin American colonies win independence from Spain, Portugal, France

Timeline

(ruled 1790–1792), reversed this and other reforms to restore social order. Once more, landlords could force their peasants to work for them.

D. Nationalism and Democracy

Feelings of cultural pride, loyalty, and patriotism are called **nationalism**. During the Enlightenment, many people expressed their nationalism by envisioning a great and just government for their nation. Patriots in some countries resisted absolute monarchy and foreign tyranny. Revolutionists in Britain's 13 American colonies and Spain's various Latin American colonies succeeded in replacing monarchy with democracy.

INFO CHECK

1. Select the Enlightenment political philosopher whose ideas you believe have had the greatest influence on government and society today. Give reasons for your choice.
2. Which Enlightenment philosopher do you DISAGREE with? Why?
3. Why have so many political leaders found Rousseau's ideas attractive?
4. How did Enlightenment ideas stimulate nationalism and democracy?

CHAPTER REVIEW

Multiple Choice

1. The Renaissance brought renewed confidence in the intellectual abilities of human beings. This meant that

    1. Church teachings on scientific theories and nature were no longer accepted without question
    2. religion was no longer accepted by most people
    3. humans controlled nature and science
    4. witches were accepted as controllers of nature and the supernatural.

2. The term scientific method refers to the practice of scientists

    1. accepting as fact theories that justified a person's actions
    2. observing, experimenting, and drawing conclusions
    3. accepting Church doctrines
    4. accepting nothing as fact unless it was self-evident.

3. The geocentric theory, endorsed by Ptolemy, stated that

    1. astronomers can predict planetary motions
    2. the heavens were created from a frozen ice mass
    3. Earth revolves around the sun like the rest of the planets
    4. Earth is the center of the solar system, and the sun and planets revolve around it.

4. Copernicus's book *On the Revolutions of Heavenly Bodies* was not acceptable to the Catholic Church because it

    1. was written by a Muslim infidel
    2. stated that the Greek god of war ruled the universe

    3. presented the heliocentric theory of the solar system
    4. was supported by Protestants.

5. Galileo used a telescope to see Jupiter's moons circling around it. This observation disproved what theory of planetary movement?

    1. Newton's gravitational theory
    2. Aristotle's geocentric theory
    3. Bacon's induction theory
    4. Copernicus's heliocentric theory

6. The Renaissance scientist who was forced to recant his theories was

    1. Copernicus   2. Kepler
    3. Galileo   4. Newton.

7. One of Newton's theories explained that

    1. gravity causes all items to fly off at different speeds away from the center of the planet
    2. the gravity of a planet pulls all items toward the center of the planet
    3. the moons of Jupiter revolve around Earth because Earth is the center of the universe
    4. none of the above.

8. The scientific revolution gave human society great hope for the future because

    1. people were living longer and had more money to spend
    2. people were freed from dependence on the Church
    3. people believed that the new way of thinking could enable them to solve problems and end superstitious beliefs
    4. people no longer relied on Greek or Roman philosophies.

9. During the American Revolution, political thinkers got the idea for a division of powers to prevent one branch of government from overpowering the others from

1. Descartes
2. Locke
3. Cartier
4. Montesquieu.

10. The French physiocrats believed in economic development through

1. manufacturing and trade
2. mercantilism
3. laissez-faire
4. price regulation.

11. Which conclusion can be reached after studying the two diagrams on page 143?

1. In 1539, many scientists believed that the planets revolve around the sun.
2. After Copernicus published his findings, everyone agreed that Earth revolves around the sun.
3. There was disagreement about the structure of the solar system during the middle 1500s.
4. An accurate explanation of the phases of the moon was discovered between 1539 and 1543.

12. According to the timeline on page 147,

1. the French Revolution took place about six years after the end of the American Revolution
2. revolution in Russia began between 1825 and 1855
3. all revolutions that took place between 1750 and 1914 were successful
4. Communists took control of Russia immediately after Marx and Engels published the *Communist Manifesto*.

Thematic Essays

1. Francis Bacon and René Descartes used different scientific methods. *Task:* Contrast these methods. With whose method do you agree? Why?

2. Identify any of the Enlightenment rulers. *Task:* Discuss whether the ruler was able to rule his or her subjects using the beliefs of the Enlightenment. Describe specific Enlightenment

social or political theories to support your position.

Document-Based Questions

Use the documents and your knowledge of Global History and Geography to answer the questions.

1. Study the text on page 145–146. Explain the difference between Hobbes's, Locke's, and Rousseau's views of the "state of nature."

2. Use facts from the text to describe what type of government each of the above writers would support.

3. The German philosopher Immanuel Kant wrote about the Enlightenment:

"What is Enlightenment . . . Dare to know! Have the courage to use your own intelligence! [This is] the motto of the Enlightenment. . . . Which restriction is hampering Enlightenment and which does not, or even promote it? I answer: the *public use* of a man's reason must be free at all times, and this alone can bring Enlightenment among men."

If you were an absolute monarch, how would you view the meaning and intent of this writing?

4. The Italian writer Niccolò Machiavelli wrote *The Prince* as a guide for rulers on how to maintain their powers:

"And in the actions of men, and especially princes from which there is no appeal, the end justifies the means. Let a prince aim at conquering and maintaining the state, and the means will always be judged honorable and praised by everyone. . . . A certain prince of the present time, . . . preach[es] peace and good faith, but he is really a great enemy to both, and either of them, had he observed them, would have cost him his state or reputation on more than one occasion."

Explain what Machiavelli is telling the prince to do in order to maintain power.

Document-Based Essay

Using specific examples, explain why the ideas of the Enlightenment were used both to support absolute monarchy and to challenge it.

CHAPTER
15

Political Revolutions

I. AMERICAN REVOLUTION

The Puritan Revolt and the Glorious Revolution prepared ground for the American Revolution in several ways:

- They caused the balance of power in England to shift from the monarch to Parliament.
- They encouraged the idea that the government should serve the interests of the governed rather than the ruler.

A. Conditions in the American Colonies

By 1750, growing populations and prosperous economies marked Britain's 13 American colonies. (In 1707, England and Scotland merged to become Great Britain.) Land was abundant. Protected by the British army and navy, the colonists felt secure.

White male Protestants with property had more rights than others, such as women, Catholics, and Jews. Slaves and Native Americans had no rights at all.

Under mercantilism, colonists traded legally only with Britain. Colonial manufacturing was discouraged.

GOVERNMENT. In the mid-1700s, either the king or a private developer appointed a colony's governor. White males with a certain amount of property were elected to legislatures, or assemblies. The governor held most of the power, but since elected members voted on taxes and expenditures, they could influence the governor's decisions.

RIGHTS. Most colonists considered themselves British and, therefore, entitled to the rights in the Bill of Rights of 1689.

Day-to-day regulation by the British government was difficult. Ships took two or more months to travel back and forth between Britain and the colonies. Until 1763, the colonies were almost self-governing.

B. Road to War

From the late 1600s through the mid-1700s, England and France fought wars to compete for world power and colonial control. One such conflict was known in Europe as the Seven Years' War and in North America as the French and Indian War. It lasted from 1756 to 1763. Great Britain won and gained much new territory. To pay war debts and future expenses for colonial protection, King George III (ruled 1760–1820) decided to tax the American colonists more heavily.

UNPOPULAR TAXES. One very unpopular tax was levied by the Stamp Act (1765). It taxed newspapers, pamphlets, legal documents, playing cards, and other items. (A stamp on an item showed that the tax had been paid.) Americans felt that Parliament had no right to tax them because they had no representatives there. "Taxation without representation is tyranny" became the rallying cry.

The Americans **boycotted** (stopped buying) British products and called a **congress** (meeting) to protest the Stamp Act. Since British merchants were hurt by the boycott, Parliament persuaded the king to repeal the Stamp Act.

In 1767, Britain passed the Townshend Acts. Again, colonial protests and a boycott forced a repeal. By 1770, all taxes except the one on tea had been lifted.

Colonial Response. Colonial leaders such as Samuel Adams and Patrick Henry wanted self-government for the colonies. When Parliament raised the tax on tea in 1773, more and more colonists supported these leaders. In 1773, a British ship carrying tea arrived in Boston. A group of disguised Americans dumped the tea into the harbor. This set off similar actions elsewhere.

English Colonies in North America, 1750

The king then closed Boston Harbor, suspended the government of Massachusetts, and moved British troops into Boston. The colonists called these the Intolerable Acts.

Leaders in Virginia called a meeting of delegates from each colony. This First Continental Congress, meeting in Philadelphia in 1774, called for a new boycott and urged Parliament and king to cease their acts against Boston and recognize basic colonial rights. After an unsatisfactory British response, the Americans began to train military groups called Minutemen and stockpile weapons.

In April 1775, British troops marched toward Lexington and Concord to arrest rebel leaders and seize weapons. Colonial forces drove the British back at Lexington and Concord. These battles began the American Revolution.

C. Beginning of a New Nation

At the Second Continental Congress, in May 1775, colonial leaders discussed how to conduct the war. On July 4, 1776, they approved the Declaration of Independence, which explained their withdrawal from the British Empire.

In the Declaration, Thomas Jefferson wrote, "We hold these truths to be self-evident, that all men are created equal, that they are endowed by their

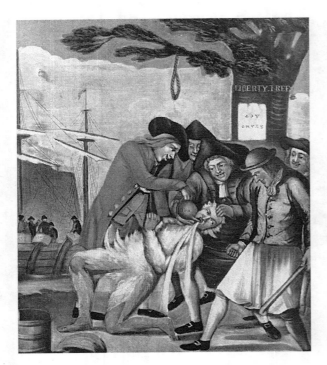

Bostonians paying the British tax collector—with tar, feathers, and scalding hot tea

Creator with certain unalienable rights, that among these are life, liberty, and the pursuit of happiness." These principles and the idea that governments that take away such rights should be replaced are based on John Locke's political philosophy.

Helped by Britain's enemy France, the Americans won the war after eight years. In 1783, the Peace of Paris recognized an independent United States of America extending from the Atlantic Ocean to the Mississippi River and from Canada to Florida.

The U.S. Constitution was adopted in 1788. It divided the government into legislative, executive, and judicial branches, an idea that came from Montesquieu. So did the idea that each branch should have powers to check the others. The list of individual rights and limits on governmental power came from Locke, the Magna Carta, and the English Bill of Rights.

INFO CHECK

1. Explain why you AGREE or DISAGREE with the argument that the American Revolution was a direct result of the Puritan Revolt and Glorious Revolution.

2. Were the American colonists justified in refusing to pay British taxes. Why or why not?

3. How did the Declaration of Independence and the Constitution reflect ideas of the Enlightenment?

II. FRENCH REVOLUTION AND NAPOLEONIC ERA

A. Background

INEQUALITY. French society was divided into three **estates**. High-ranking clergy and nobles made up the First and Second Estates. The Third Estate (97 percent of the French population) comprised professionals, peasants, and laborers. This group bore a heavy tax burden and did work that enabled the other Estates to live well. The lawmaking body, the Estates General, represented all three groups; however, since it met rarely, the majority of French people had little voice in government.

ECONOMY. France's economy was very shaky. The country had lost a war and colonies to England. It had then contributed large amounts of money to the American revolutionary government. Yet, the nobles and clergy refused to pay higher taxes.

UNJUST LEGAL SYSTEM. France had no court system and body of laws that applied to everyone. The king could imprison anyone for any reason for any length of time.

B. Beginning

In 1789, King Louis XVI (ruled 1774–1792) called the Estates General to discuss a new tax on landed property. The Estates disagreed about how its votes were to be distributed. The Third Estate had 600 representatives; the Second, 300; and the First, 300. Nevertheless, each Estate cast only one vote. Thus, the Third Estate, representing most of the French people, could be outvoted two-to-one by the other two estates.

NATIONAL ASSEMBLY. The Third Estate wanted one vote per representative. When the other two estates disagreed, the Third Estate withdrew and formed the National Assembly. Its members vowed to draft a constitution limiting the king's power and giving the common people more rights. Marquis de Lafayette, who had encouraged France to aid the American revolutionists, supported the National Assembly.

Threats by the king to arrest Assembly leaders caused riots all over France. On July 14, 1789, an angry crowd in Paris captured the Bastille, a fortress and political prison, seized arms, and freed prisoners. Leaders of the movement set up a government, the first step in the French revolt against absolute monarchy.

In the countryside, peasants burned manor houses and destroyed records of how much money or grain they owed the Church or landowners. People stopped paying taxes, royal officials fled France, and the king had to accept the National Assembly's government.

New Rights and a Constitution. In August 1789, the Assembly adopted the Declaration of the Rights of Man and of the Citizen. Influenced by the American Declaration of Independence, it declared that "all men are born free and equal in rights." It provided for freedom of speech, religion, and the press, and it guaranteed the people's right to participate in the government.

There were reforms of the legal system too—provisions for elected judges, trial by jury, and an end to brutal punishments. Nobles could no longer buy judicial and high military positions.

The Constitution of 1791 established a limited monarchy in which the king's powers could be checked by the legislature. Church land came under the control of the national government. After Louis XVI had accepted the constitution, the National Assembly was dissolved, and the people elected the Legislative Assembly to make laws for France.

C. Republic

In 1792, Prussia and Austria went to war with France to aid the royal family. (The French queen, Marie Antoinette, was the daughter of Maria Theresa of Austria.) They were later joined by Britain, Spain, and the Netherlands.

JACOBINS. A powerful extremist group, the Jacobins, convinced the French that King Louis XVI had plotted with Austria and Prussia to restore his rule. The Assembly then arrested the king and queen. The execution of the monarchs and many others was a "Reign of Terror," which ended with the fall from power of the Jacobin leaders. The Assembly also called for new elections of representatives for a National Convention. (Most males over 21 were allowed to vote.) The convention drew up a new constitution and created the First French Republic.

Patriotism. Although the Jacobin dictatorship fostered fear among the people, its ideals stimulated patriotism. "The Marseillaise" became the French national anthem. The phrase "liberty, equality, and fraternity" was a popular rallying cry. The French were united against their country's enemies. By 1795, the French army had successfully defended the nation and conquered parts of the Netherlands, Belgium, and Germany.

DIRECTORY. In 1795, the Directory, a five-member committee, took control of France. It was too corrupt to solve France's financial problems. In 1798, Britain persuaded other European powers to join the fight against France. By 1799, French armies had lost battles in Italy, Switzerland, and the Netherlands.

D. Napoleonic Era

BACKGROUND. Napoleon Bonaparte, born into poverty on the Mediterranean island of Corsica, was destined to occupy the French throne. After 1789, France chose leaders for their talent and energy rather than their noble birth. Napoleon won the respect of the French by a series of victories against rioters and invaders in France and national enemies abroad.

In 1799, he returned from foreign campaigns and moved quickly to replace the corrupt and inefficient Directory. The French people approved a new constitution giving Napoleon ruling power as first consul. By 1804, France was a republic no longer, but rather an empire ruled by Emperor Napoleon I.

CHANGES. Between 1802 and 1805, Napoleon instituted the Code Napoleon. It made all citizens equal before the law and remains the basis of the French legal system. The code has also served as a model for the legal systems of several European and Latin American countries.

Napoleon organized a public school system run by a committee called the University of France. He

General Bonaparte crossing the Alps to victory over Austria, while the Directory in France grows powerless

Napoleon's Empire, 1812

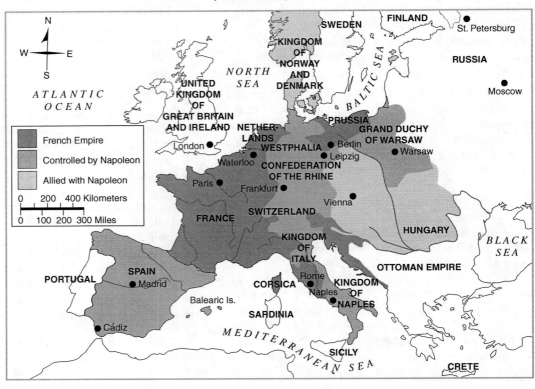

established the Legion of Honor, a society for people who had performed important services for France.

Napoleon developed a fairer taxation system and set up the Bank of France. Besides coining money and stabilizing the currency, the bank fostered economic conditions favorable to business.

NAPOLEONIC WARS. Shortly after Napoleon gained power, he defeated Austria and made temporary peace with Britain. But in 1803, Britain persuaded Austria, Russia, Sweden, and Naples to renew the fight. The Napoleonic Wars lasted from 1805 to 1815. By 1807, with Napoleon in control of most of Europe, only Britain and its powerful navy stood against him.

Actions Against Britain. Through laws called the **Continental System**, Napoleon banned all European trade with Britain and even tried to stop British colonial trade with the home country. When Russia and Portugal, among other countries, refused to follow orders, the emperor took action. France occupied parts of Portugal and invaded Spain. Napoleon's brother Joseph became king of Spain. In 1808, the Spanish and Portuguese retaliated by starting the Peninsular War. By 1813, Spain, Portugal, and Britain had pushed Napoleon's forces back into France.

Invasion of Russia. Napoleon invaded Russia in 1812 with some 600,000 troops and occupied Moscow in September. He found no reliable source of supplies at hand. In October, the Russians counterattacked and forced the French to retreat just as winter began. Only about 100,000 French soldiers survived.

In 1813, Prussia, Austria, and Russia defeated Napoleon at Leipzig, Germany, in the Battle of Nations. Early in 1814, the French people turned against their emperor, captured him, and exiled him to the Mediterranean island of Elba.

Final Defeat. In March 1815, Napoleon escaped and marched through France, where loyal soldiers joined his cause. Led by the British Duke of Wellington, Napoleon's enemies defeated him in June 1815 at Waterloo, Belgium. Napoleon died in exile on the South Atlantic island of St. Helena in 1821.

INFO CHECK

1. Identify the causes of the French Revolution. Which cause made life most difficult for 18th-century French people to endure?

2. How did the Declaration of the Rights of Man and Constitution of 1791 respond to the causes of the French Revolution?

3. Did the Jacobin government put into practice the ideals of liberty, equality, and fraternity? Explain your answer.

4. If you had lived in France in the early 19th century, would you have regarded Napoleon Bonaparte as an admirable leader? Why or why not?

III. LATIN AMERICAN REVOLUTIONS

A. Causes of Discontent

Under the Spanish government's mercantilism, Latin American colonists had to buy manufactured goods only from Spain and sell their products only to Spain. This policy enriched the home country at the expense of its colonies.

Spain also set up a colonial social system in which wealth and power were unequally distributed. Important political and military jobs went only to **peninsulares**, or colonists born in Spain. **Creoles**, colonists born in Latin America to Spanish parents, were usually wealthy and well educated; they resented the power of the peninsulares. **Mestizos**, born of Spanish and Indian parents, tended to work as clerks or estate overseers; they,

too, wanted more political power. **Peons** were Indians, Africans, and people of mixed heritage. They were laborers who lived in extreme poverty, with little hope of achieving wealth or power.

B. Beginnings

The successful revolutions in North America and France inspired Latin Americans to rebel against Spanish control. They also took hope from a successful rebellion in Saint Domingue.

In 1791, Toussaint L'Ouverture, a freed slave, led a slave uprising against the French colonists of Saint Domingue, the western part of the island of Hispaniola. Napoleon then sent an army to retake the island, and in 1802, Toussaint was captured and later died in a French prison. His successor, Jean-Jacques Dessalines, drove off the French. In 1804, Saint Domingue became independent and was renamed Haiti.

The Creoles were the strongest force for revolution. When Napoleon conquered Spain and put his brother Joseph on the Spanish throne in 1808, several Latin American colonies revolted against French rule. Even after the Spanish king was restored in 1814, the revolutions continued.

Latin America: Dates of Colonial Independence

C. Great Liberators

A number of gifted military and political leaders organized revolutions in Latin America.

HIDALGO. In 1810, a Mexican priest named Miguel Hidalgo led Indian followers in an uprising against Spanish rule. Hidalgo's army won a few battles but was stopped by Spanish forces at Mexico City. Hidalgo was captured and executed in 1811.

ITURBIDE. Agustín de Iturbide, a Creole, finally won freedom for Mexico. Soon after his victory, however, he proclaimed himself emperor. He was soon overthrown, and Mexico became a republic in 1824.

MIRANDA AND BOLÍVAR. Francisco de Miranda and Simon Bolívar began the struggle to free Venezuela in 1808. In 1812, a year after Venezuela won independence, Spain retook the country. Bolívar escaped to Colombia. Miranda died in prison.

Bolívar gathered enough support to drive the Spaniards from Colombia. After "The Liberator," as he was called, became president, he helped Venezuela regain its independence. He also aided the successful struggle against Spanish rule in Ecuador. Ecuador, Venezuela, and Colombia united as Gran Colombia under Bolívar's leadership. He hoped eventually to liberate and unite all of Latin America. In 1830, however, Gran Colombia broke up into its original three components.

SAN MARTÍN. José de San Martín helped Argentina win its independence. He also fought successfully to free Chile and northern Peru.

San Martín and Bolívar disagreed about how best to free southern Peru. When San Martín withdrew, Bolívar took northern Peru and sent forces to drive the Spaniards from the south. After southern Peru became independent, it was renamed Bolivia in honor of Bolívar.

PEDRO I. When Napoleon's soldiers invaded Portugal in 1807, King John VI fled to Brazil. His presence made the colony of Brazil a kingdom. When John returned to Portugal as a constitutional monarch in 1820, his son, Pedro, took over the Brazilian government.

The Portuguese legislature then tried to make Brazil into a colony once more. Brazilian Creoles, however, persuaded Pedro to become ruler of an independent Brazil, with the title Pedro I. Portugal recognized Brazil's independence. In 1889, the Brazilians overthrew Pedro's successor and made their country a republic.

D. Achievements and Problems

With independence, the Creoles gained political power and freedom from Spanish economic control. However, nationalism, ambitious regional leaders, and rugged terrain all worked against Bolívar's dream of a united Latin America. So did the Creole leaders' inability to win the loyalty of all citizens. New revolutions became common. Often the military would take over an unpopular government, and the military leader would govern as a **caudillo**, or dictator. Today, however, almost all Latin American governments are popularly elected democracies.

Independence did not help the peons. They often turned to violence to bring about meaningful change. They mainly wanted a fairer distribution of land.

Many Latin Americans wanted a government takeover of Church lands and their redistribution to the poor. Landowners and military leaders resisted this plan and maintained a rigid social control by class in most Latin American nations.

E. Role of the United States

The United States supported the movements for independence in Latin America. In 1822, the United States and Britain had cause to fear that European nations might try to win back their colonies. Latin America had become a profitable trading market, and Britain and the United States did not want that market shut off.

In December 1823, President James Monroe issued the *Monroe Doctrine*. It stated that the Americas were no longer open for colonization and that any attempt by the European powers to interfere in the affairs of the Americas would be considered "as dangerous to our peace and safety." Monroe made his move, confident that Britain's naval power would enforce his decisions.

INFO CHECK

1. What did Toussaint L'Ouverture and Jean-Jacques Dessalines contribute to the birth of Haiti?

2. Define: peninsulares, Creoles, mestizos, and peons. How did the interaction of these groups lead to revolutions in Latin America?

3. Which of the great liberators do you most admire? Give reasons for your selection.

4. Is it correct to argue that the revolutions in Latin American countries brought independence but not democracy? Why or why not?

Year	Dates and Events

A.D.

1601

1600s–1763: "Salutary neglect" of American colonies by Britain; increased self-government

1688: Glorious Revolution ends absolute monarchy in England; joint rule by William III, Mary II

1756–1763: Seven Years' War (French and Indian War in Americas) increased British debt; 13 colonies more highly taxed

1765: Stamp Act causes American boycott of British goods; act repealed

1767: Townshend Acts (new taxes) cause American boycott of British goods; repealed except for tea

1773: Boston Tea Party (dumping of tea); British close Boston Harbor, send troops

1774: First Continental Congress, Philadelphia

1774–1792: Reign of Louis XVI; National Assembly limits king's power, widens commoners' rights

1700

1701

1775: American Revolution begins at Lexington and Concord

1775: Second Continental Congress; Declaration of Independence

1783: Peace of Paris ends American Revolution, recognizes independent United States

1787: U.S. Constitution—separation of powers, checks and balances, individual rights

1789: Storming of Bastille; French Revolution; Declaration of Rights of Man

1791: First French constitution; limits powers of monarchy, Catholic Church; election of lawmakers

1791–1804: L'Ouverture leads Haitian slave uprising; Dessaline wins independence from France

1793: Louis XVI beheaded; Robespierre heads Reign of Terror

1794: Robespierre beheaded; Reign of Terror ends

1795: New French constitution creates corrupt and inefficient Directory

1798–1799: European powers defeat French in Italy, Switzerland, Netherlands

1799: Napoleon Bonaparte ends Directory, takes control of French government

1802–1805: New Napoleonic law code

1800

1805–1814: Most of Europe at war with France; trade blockades, invasion of Russia (French disaster)

1801

1813–1814: France defeated at Leipzig; Napoleon exiled to Elba

1815: Napoleon escapes Elba; rallies French; defeated at Waterloo by British; exiled to St. Helena

1816–1821: San Martín wins independence from Spain for Argentina (1816), Chile (1818), Peru (1821)

1819: Bolívar ("The Liberator") drives Spain from Colombia

1821: Iturbide wins Mexico independence from Spain; Bolívar wins independence for Venezuela

1822: Ecuador wins independence from Spain

1822: Pedro I becomes king of Brazilian monarchy, independent from Portugal

1823: Monroe Doctrine declares that Americas no longer open for colonization

1825: Independent Bolivia created

1900

1889: Brazil becomes republic

Timeline

CHAPTER REVIEW

Multiple Choice

1. John Locke wrote that the purpose of government is to protect its

1. citizens' religious and political freedoms
2. citizens' life, liberty, and property
3. citizens from abuse by the peasants
4. citizens from tyranny of the Church.

2. Thomas Jefferson and the other American political leaders were influenced by the

1. French Revolution and writings of Montesquieu

2. English Bill of Rights and writings of Locke
3. Directory and the Code Napoleon
4. 95 theses and other writings of Luther.

3. Prior to the French Revolution, French society was divided into three estates. The Third Estate complained that

1. peasants were lazy and not tending the fields
2. the Church was supporting the merchants against the nobility

3. lawyers and other professionals were not paying their fair share of taxes
4. they paid the most in taxes and had almost no say in government.

4. The king called the Estates General into session because he

   1. was an enlightened despot
   2. wanted all classes to be involved in governmental decision making
   3. was out of money and wanted the legislature to approve a tax on property
   4. needed approval to call out the army to deal with a military crisis.

5. The French supported Napoleon because

   1. he restored order and granted some of the equality promised in the revolution
   2. they liked a dictatorship in which they did not have to make any political decisions
   3. he defeated their worst enemy, the English
   4. he ruled by fear and terror with the help of the courts and guillotine.

6. Spanish colonial society was organized into four social classes: (a) creoles, (b) peons, (c) mestizos, and (d) peninsulares. Select the answer that places the classes in the correct social order from top to bottom.

   1. (a), (c), (d), (b)   2. (c), (a), (d), (b)
   3. (d), (a), (c), (b)   4. (b), (d), (a), (c)

7. Simon Bolívar's dream of a unified Latin America never happened because

   1. of power-hungry local rulers, nationalism, and rugged terrain
   2. Spain, France, and England developed colonies in Latin America
   3. the United States intervened, using the Monroe Doctrine
   4. Bolívar lost power and was captured and imprisoned by the Spanish.

8. The United States issued the Monroe Doctrine, but the British navy enforced it. The real reason behind the American and British actions was

   1. conflict over who would control Latin America
   2. that British and American merchants had found a rich market in Latin America
   3. that Britain and the United States were against the Spanish king
   4. that Britain and the United States wanted their own colonies in Latin America.

9. The Code Napoleon is important because it

   1. made all citizens equal before the law
   2. provided for trial by jury
   3. is the basis for the French legal system
   4. all of the above.

10. The map on page 151 shows that

    1. South Carolina was the most populous of the 13 American colonies
    2. by 1750, Massachusetts had laid claim to Maine
    3. the Great Lakes were vital transportation links for the American colonists
    4. all 13 American colonies had coastlines on the Pacific Ocean.

11. The illustration on page 152 shows that

    1. agents of the British crown were greatly feared in the 13 American colonies
    2. boycotts were the only effective means for colonials to protest taxation
    3. anger over British taxation sometimes led to violence
    4. American colonists did not like to drink tea.

12. Which statement is supported by the timeline on page 157?

    1. Napoleon dominated France and Europe from 1799 through 1825.
    2. Haitian slaves revolted and won their independence in the period 1791–1804.
    3. Napoleon ruled France prior to the French Revolution.
    4. The Monroe Doctrine encouraged San Martín and Bolívar to fight for the independence of various Latin American nations.

Thematic Essays

1. Events such as the Crusades and the Industrial Revolution changed the social structure of European society. *Task:* Assess the amount of political and social change brought to the Americas by the revolutions of the 18th and 19th centuries. Which groups of people benefited? Which did not?

2. *Task:* Assess the role of Napoleon as a "son of the Revolution." To what extent did he increase or decrease the rights of French citizens?

Document-Based Questions

Use the documents and your knowledge of Global History and Geography to answer the questions.

1. Study the map on page 154. Identify any nations that were not allied with, or part of, Napoleon's empire. How did geography limit Napoleon's conquests?

2. From a selection by the German poet Ernst Moritz Arndt:

   "Fired with enthusiasm the people rose with God for King and Fatherland . . . to save the

Fatherland and free Germany. The Prussians wanted war; war and death they wanted; peace they feared because they could hope for no honorable peace from Napoleon. . . . The most beautiful thing . . . was that all differences of position, class, and age were forgotten . . . that the one great feeling for the Fatherland, its freedom, its honor, swallowed all other feeling. . . . "

What emotion is the poet describing, and why is it happening?

3. From the decree of *levée en masse* (nation in arms), August 23, 1793:

"1. From this moment until that in which the enemy shall have been driven from the soil of the republic, all Frenchmen are [required] for the service of the armies.

The young men shall go to battle; the married men shall forge arms and transport provisions; the women shall make tents and clothing and serve in the hospitals; the children shall turn old linen into lint; the aged shall betake themselves to the public place in order to arouse the courage of the warriors and preach the hatred of kings and the unity of the Republic."

Who is involved in defending France and the Republic against its enemies? How is this different from what happened in the past?

4. Study the map on page 155. Explain why so many of the nations shown achieved their independence within a few years of one another?

Document-Based Essay

"Napoleon's armies overthrew the old ruling monarchies of Europe. His armies spread the ideals of liberty and equality. Yet his empire was destroyed by his actions and the ideals that his armies spread." *Task:* Using specific historical examples, explain this statement.

CHAPTER
16

Reaction to Revolutionary Ideas

I. EUROPE AFTER NAPOLEON

After the defeat of Napoleon, struggles between absolute monarchs and revolutionaries continued.

A. Three Different Viewpoints

Conservatives were privileged people, such as aristocrats. They wanted to preserve traditional forms of government and society.

Liberals were usually professionals and businesspeople. They wanted increased political power and rights.

Movements for more extreme political and social change developed later in the 1800s. Their members, called **radicals**, were usually workers and other disadvantaged people organized by intellectual leaders. They wanted a new system of government called **socialism**. A socialist society would be cooperative rather than competitive. Its government would bring about a more even distribution of wealth. Private property would be curtailed or abolished.

B. Congress of Vienna

Europe's conservative leaders met at the Congress of Vienna in 1814 to discuss how to prevent more political and social unrest in Europe. Great Britain, Russia, Prussia, and Austria made most of the decisions. This Quadruple Alliance had won the wars with Napoleon.

AIMS. The chief delegates wanted to establish a **balance of power** so that no nation would become militarily stronger than the others. The general agreement on aims reached during the congress is known as the Concert of Europe.

The leaders considered absolute monarchy the most stable form of government and supported the principle of **legitimacy** (inherited right to rule). Power was restored to royal families that had ruled France, Austria, Prussia, Spain, and the Italian states before the French Revolution and the Napoleonic Era.

The leaders of the congress also wanted to compensate with land and colonies those nations that had lost the most by war and had done the most to defeat Napoleon.

REPRESSION OF NATIONALISM. Powerful neighbors had divided the homelands of Poles, Belgians, and others. The congress was determined to keep these national groups from achieving self-government.

Prince Klemens von Metternich dominated the conference. Representing the culturally diverse Austrian Empire, he feared nationalism. If nationalist groups were allowed to form small independent countries, they would be in danger of attack by stronger expansionist powers. In spite of the congress's policy of repressing nationalism, however, it grew more powerful and led to violence throughout Europe.

EFFECT ON FRANCE. The congress did not impose harsh terms on France, in part to encourage it to accept Louis XVIII as king. Its boundaries remained the same as in 1792, and it was allowed to keep its overseas possessions. Nevertheless, France had to pay war damages to other nations and support troops stationed along its borders by the victorious nations.

Soon, demands for political change arose in France, as they did elsewhere.

INFO CHECK

1. Define: liberals, radicals, and conservatives. Which group dominated the Congress of Vienna? Why?

2. Explain how the desire for a balance of power and legitimacy influenced decisions reached by the Congress of Vienna.

Europe After the Congress of Vienna, 1815

3. Why did Metternich oppose the nationalism of less powerful ethnic groups?

II. FIGHT FOR DEMOCRACY AND NATIONALISM

Embodied in nationalism was the fervent belief that each ethnic group is best qualified to shape its own destiny.

A. Revolutions of 1830

Louis XVIII's Constitutional Charter of 1814 granted the French people many rights they had gained during the revolution and under Napoleon.

Not so, however, of his successor. In 1830, Charles X issued the July Ordinances, which dismissed the elected legislature and prevented most eligible French citizens from voting. The press also came under government control.

The people of Paris arose, and after three days, Charles's government collapsed. A committee of liberals then chose Louis Philippe, Duke of Orleans, as the new king. A new constitution limited his power and gave the vote to wealthy members of the middle class.

In 1830, the Belgians won independence from the Dutch and set up a constitutional monarchy.

The Poles fought in vain for freedom from Russia. An Italian revolt against Austrian rule also failed.

B. Revolutions of 1848

FRANCE. Economic setbacks and reports of government corruption endangered Louis Philippe's government. Moreover, liberals wanted the vote for most professional members of the middle class.

In February 1848, when the government banned a reformist political meeting, riots broke out. Unwilling to restore order by force, Louis Philippe resigned.

Revolutionaries set up the Second Republic, with an elected president and legislature. In December 1848, Louis Napoleon, Napoleon Bonaparte's nephew, was elected president. In 1852, he turned the Second Republic into the Second Empire and ruled as Emperor Napoleon III.

GERMANY, ITALY, AND AUSTRIA. Revolutions also took place in Germany, Italy, and Austria. Germans called for constitutions guaranteeing more political rights and for the unification of the German states into one nation. They offered to make the Prussian king, Frederick William IV, emperor. He refused on the grounds that, if elected, he could not be king by "divine right." The German revolution then collapsed.

Conservative forces in the Austrian Empire defeated attempts to establish republics in Italy and Hungary. Russia helped crush Hungarian uprisings. Conservatives also defeated demands by Austrian citizens for democracy. The unpopular Prince Metternich was forced to flee Austria.

During this period, peasants in western Europe gained some rights; they could own land and no longer owed labor to landlords.

C. Reforms in Britain

British liberals and conservatives brought about reforms without revolution. Conservatives accepted them so that change in Britain would be peaceful. The Reform Bill of 1832 doubled the number of voters (most from the middle class) by lowering property requirements. In 1867, another bill extended the vote to working-class men. Women still could not vote.

British slavery also ended. In 1807, William Wilberforce and Thomas Clark persuaded Parliament to outlaw the slave trade. In 1834, Parliament ended slavery in the British empire.

D. Absolutism and Reform in Russia

The Russian czars were absolute monarchs. Landowning nobles had almost complete power over their serfs, who made up more than 75 percent of the population.

ALEXANDER I. Alexander I (ruled 1801–1825) wanted gradual and moderate change. His main accomplishment was to staff the bureaucracy with better-trained officials.

On Alexander's death in 1825, a group called the Decembrists tried unsuccessfully to bring about more reforms. The new czar, Nicholas I (ruled 1825–1855), then suppressed all liberal movements.

ALEXANDER II. Alexander II (ruled 1855–1881) freed the serfs in 1861. They could now own land but had to pay high prices for it. The serfs' villages guaranteed the payments and, in effect, owned the land. Consequently, the serfs could not move about in search of better opportunities.

In 1864, Alexander II established **zemstvos**. These local elected bodies managed a district's education, health, and welfare. However, since local landowners controlled zemstvos, the serfs' benefits were limited.

Alexander also gave up personal control of the legal system. The accused were now tried by jury, with independent judges and lawyers. The czar still judged political cases.

Reaction to Reforms. Dissatisfied student groups spread socialist ideas among the poor. When the government intervened, the radicals turned to terrorism. Alexander II was assassinated on March 13, 1881. The new czar, Alexander III (ruled 1881–1894), ruled repressively.

E. Russian Expansionism and Nationalism

Russian nationalism in the 1800s took several forms.

IMPERIALISM. Imperialism sprang from the desire to make the country powerful enough to control other nations. Nicholas I waged war to win the

Peasant faces reflecting hardships of rural life in Russia in the late 1800s

Growth of Russia to 1900

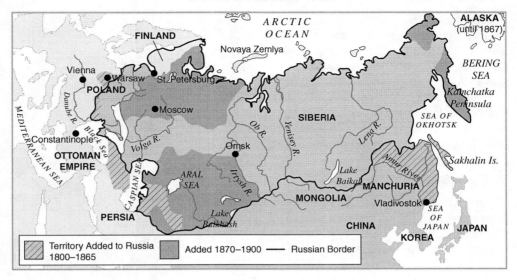

Caucasus, the area between the Black and Caspian seas. During Alexander II's reign, Russia took control of Muslim areas in Central Asia and a part of China along the Amur River.

Crimean War. Russia also wanted to control the Dardanelles and the Bosporus—straits connecting the Black and Mediterranean seas. In 1852, Russia sent troops into the Crimean Peninsula on the Black Sea's northern coast. Seeing this threat to the Ottoman (Turkish) Empire and the straits it controlled, Britain and France came to the aid of the Turkish forces and helped defeat the poorly equipped Russian army.

PAN-SLAVISM. Another expression of nationalism is a feeling of common identity by members of an ethnic group. Russian leaders claimed the right to protect all Slavic peoples in Europe. (Slavs are people in Eastern Europe and Russia speaking related languages.) This movement toward Slavic unity was called **Pan-Slavism**.

When Slavs in Montenegro and Serbia revolted against the Ottoman Turks in 1875, Russia helped them win independence. Russia also gained access to Bulgaria's seaport on the Aegean Sea. At the 1878 Congress of Berlin, European countries threatened by this expansion took away Russia's right to use the Bulgarian seaport.

DISCRIMINATION. Influenced by Pan-Slavism, the czars tried to force non-Russians in the Russian Empire to give up their cultures. They forbade Ukrainians to speak or write their language. When the Poles revolted in 1863, Russia banned public expression of Polish culture.

In the 1890s, Russia reinforced laws limiting where Jews could live, took away their right to attend school, and compelled them to serve long periods in the army. Jews were also left unprotected against **pogroms** (violent attacks on their communities).

INFO CHECK

1. List the causes and results of the revolutions of 1830 and 1848. Which revolution accomplished more? Explain your answer.

2. In 1848, revolutions occurred in nearly every European country except Britain and Russia. Why?

3. How did the struggle between liberalism and conservatism affect events in 19th-century Russia?

4. Explain how Pan-Slavism and persecution of Jews were related to Russian nationalism.

III. SOUTH AMERICA AFTER THE WARS OF INDEPENDENCE

A. Nonunification

South America's new republics failed to unite under one democratic government. One factor was geography. High mountains, dense rain forests, and a lack of natural harbors made travel difficult. Isolated peoples developed their own ways of life. Moreover, local leaders discouraged unification by appealing to nationalistic pride.

Some postwar leaders kept their armies and used them to win local support. A few of these military leaders became dictators.

B. Religion and Politics

Many revolutionists felt that the Catholic Church took money that could have helped the poor. To weaken the Church, these leaders did not allow it to collect tithes (taxes paid by a congregation to maintain their church).

Political factions disagreed about whether the Church or the state should appoint religious officials. Thus, many Church offices remained unfilled, and the Church lost some of its political power.

C. Class System

After the revolutions, the Creoles took political power. Peons and slaves remained impoverished and oppressed.

Some of the disadvantaged were able to move up in society. Free Africans in Latin America had more social mobility than free Africans in the United States. Revolutionary leaders freed slaves who had helped in the fight for independence, and those who had distinguished themselves in battle were rewarded with land and political power.

In general, however, it was more difficult to improve one's social position in Latin America than in the United States. The ruling classes passed repressive laws against peons who protested against poverty. Such laws provoked more unrest.

D. Economics

Most Latin American wealth came from big plantations and mines. After the revolutions, they still remained in the control of only a few people. Little better off than slaves, poor laborers survived by banding together to rob travelers.

With so many poor people, there were few local buyers for the products of the mines and plantations. Owners had to sell their goods to foreign markets. Consequently, each country became dependent on a few sources of wealth: Bolivia on tin, Chile on copper. Similarly, plantations produced only one or two major **cash crops** (those raised for sale rather than private use). Brazil, for example, exported sugar and coffee; when the demand for these goods decreased, the national economy suffered.

E. Mexican Revolution

Some Latin American leaders sought foreign investment in their economies. Political and social instability, however, often made investment in Latin America too risky. Mexico, for example, was rich in oil and minerals but so politically unstable

Agrarian Leader Zapata: Mexican revolutionary Emiliano Zapata, in a 1931 fresco by Diego Rivera

that foreign investors were reluctant to develop these resources.

DÍAZ. Porfirio Díaz became dictator of Mexico in 1876. He had his political opponents killed and sent police to clear the countryside of bandits. Díaz kept to the forms of constitutional government but made all decisions himself.

Once Mexico had a law-and-order regime, foreigners began to invest in its businesses. Unfortunately, the rich did not share their new wealth; wages remained low and land expensive. Several thousand families acquired half of Mexico's land. Very few farmers had land of their own.

Widespread protests arose against Díaz's repressive government and the foreigners who had too much control over Mexico's economy, government, and social structure.

MADERO. Francisco Madero began a movement to replace the Díaz dictatorship. In November 1910, small groups of poor farmers rebelled. Some of them, notably Francisco "Pancho" Villa and Emiliano Zapata, became successful leaders. In 1911, Díaz fled to France. By establishing a democracy, Madero hoped to end the revolution. But the farmers continued to fight for land reform.

HUERTA. General Victoriano Huerta sided with the landowners. In 1913, he had Madero killed and took over the government. When U.S. President Woodrow Wilson sent American troops to aid the revolutionaries in 1914, Huerta was forced to resign.

In 1917, a constitution for a new democratic government was drawn up, and Mexicans regained significant control of their own resources. The government divided plantations and mines among the poor and developed a plan for free public education.

ELUSIVE DEMOCRACY. Other Latin American countries fared less well. Large gaps between rich and poor remained. Leaders supported policies that brought in foreign wealth rather than those that could help the people.

INFO CHECK

1. Explain how each of the following prevented the unification of Latin America in the 19th century: geography, local leaders, and the class system.

2. Who were Pancho Villa and Emiliano Zapata? Why were they heroes to some Mexicans but not to others?

3. Why was democracy so difficult to achieve in 19th-century Latin America?

Year	Dates and Events

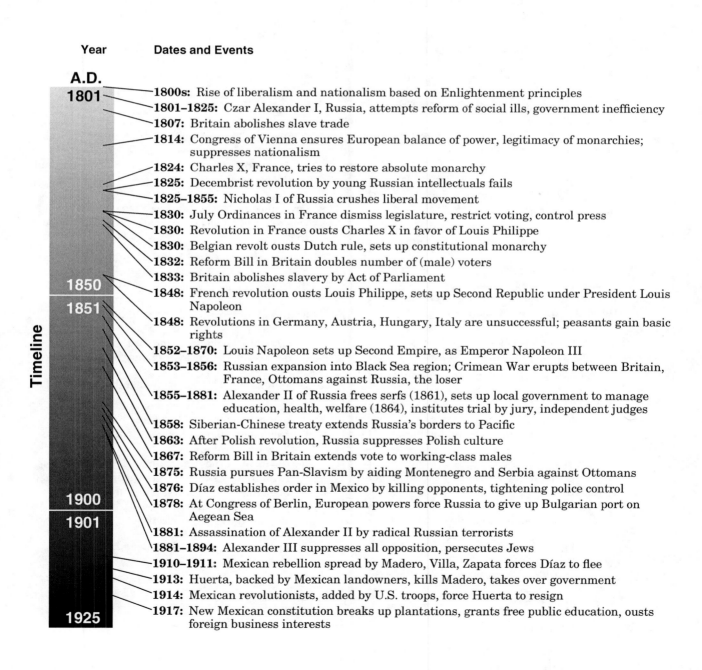

A.D.

1801

1800s: Rise of liberalism and nationalism based on Enlightenment principles

1801–1825: Czar Alexander I, Russia, attempts reform of social ills, government inefficiency

1807: Britain abolishes slave trade

1814: Congress of Vienna ensures European balance of power, legitimacy of monarchies; suppresses nationalism

1824: Charles X, France, tries to restore absolute monarchy

1825: Decembrist revolution by young Russian intellectuals fails

1825–1855: Nicholas I of Russia crushes liberal movement

1830: July Ordinances in France dismiss legislature, restrict voting, control press

1830: Revolution in France ousts Charles X in favor of Louis Philippe

1830: Belgian revolt ousts Dutch rule, sets up constitutional monarchy

1832: Reform Bill in Britain doubles number of (male) voters

1833: Britain abolishes slavery by Act of Parliament

1850

1851

1848: French revolution ousts Louis Philippe, sets up Second Republic under President Louis Napoleon

1848: Revolutions in Germany, Austria, Hungary, Italy are unsuccessful; peasants gain basic rights

1852–1870: Louis Napoleon sets up Second Empire, as Emperor Napoleon III

1853–1856: Russian expansion into Black Sea region; Crimean War erupts between Britain, France, Ottomans against Russia, the loser

1855–1881: Alexander II of Russia frees serfs (1861), sets up local government to manage education, health, welfare (1864), institutes trial by jury, independent judges

1858: Siberian-Chinese treaty extends Russia's borders to Pacific

1863: After Polish revolution, Russia suppresses Polish culture

1867: Reform Bill in Britain extends vote to working-class males

1875: Russia pursues Pan-Slavism by aiding Montenegro and Serbia against Ottomans

1876: Díaz establishes order in Mexico by killing opponents, tightening police control

1900

1901

1878: At Congress of Berlin, European powers force Russia to give up Bulgarian port on Aegean Sea

1881: Assassination of Alexander II by radical Russian terrorists

1881–1894: Alexander III suppresses all opposition, persecutes Jews

1910–1911: Mexican rebellion spread by Madero, Villa, Zapata forces Díaz to flee

1913: Huerta, backed by Mexican landowners, kills Madero, takes over government

1914: Mexican revolutionists, added by U.S. troops, force Huerta to resign

1925

1917: New Mexican constitution breaks up plantations, grants free public education, ousts foreign business interests

Timeline

CHAPTER REVIEW

Multiple Choice

1. The revolutions in Europe during the 19th century arose from the ideas and actions of the

   1. Renaissance and the Protestant and Catholic reformations
   2. Middle Ages, the Crusades, and international trade
   3. reconquest of Spain and the expulsion of Muslims and Jews
   4. Enlightenment and the American and French revolutions.

2. Select the choice that correctly links the group's social class with their political view.

   1. Workers and other lower-class people usually favored a radical or socialist form of government.
   2. Upper-class aristocrats usually favored a republican form of government.
   3. Middle-class businesspeople usually favored a conservative dictatorship.
   4. Clergy and religious persons usually favored a liberal democratic form of government.

3. The aim of the Congress of Vienna was to

   1. create an economic union that would rebuild the war-torn European states
   2. restore European monarchies that Napoleon had overthrown and establish a balance of power
   3. assist the nationalistic desires of people to establish their own countries
   4. prevent former monarchs from retaking their thrones and overseas colonies.

4. Identify the political philosophy and goal of Metternich at the Congress of Vienna.

   1. liberal—wanted governments to regulate the economy and end business competition
   2. socialist—wanted governments to regulate the economy and end business competition
   3. conservative—wanted to preserve the Austrian Empire by preventing the spread of nationalism
   4. radical—wanted to overthrow old monarchies and put Napoleon back on the throne.

5. Based on the 1830 July Ordinances, Charles X wanted to be

   1. a president
   2. an absolute monarch
   3. a limited monarch
   4. a Holy Roman emperor.

6. Britain did not suffer any revolutions in the 1800s because

   1. the king granted freedom to all serfs
   2. Parliament passed two voting reform bills
   3. Britain was not influenced by the Enlightenment
   4. Britain was ruled by an absolute monarch who used the army and secret police to prevent revolutions.

7. When nationalism results in one nation dominating another it is called

   1. mercantilism
   2. socialism
   3. capitalism
   4. imperialism.

8. The Russian government supported the Balkan states against the Ottoman Turks because of

   1. concern over the treatment of fellow Slavic rulers
   2. financial investments in Rumania and Serbia
   3. Pan-Slavic belief that Russia was the protector of all Slavic peoples in Europe
   4. the opportunity to control the Dardanelles and Bosporus.

9. One cause for Latin America's economic problems was reliance on one or two cash crops. This meant that

   1. the economy relied on the world market to sell its goods at fair market value
   2. the exchange of money for goods occurred at inflationary rates
   3. Brazil exchanged oil and gold for beef and vegetables
   4. when worldwide demand for the cash crops decreased, the entire economy was in trouble.

10. Studying the photograph on page 162 reveals that

    1. the lives of Russian peasants improved as a result of reforms of the czars
    2. technology had been recently introduced into Russia's rural areas
    3. the ideas of the American and French revolutions as well as the Englightenment had little impact on rural life in Russia
    4. peasants and serfs had reason to hope for improved living conditions.

11. The painting on page 164 depicts Emiliano Zapata as

    1. a tyrant
    2. a monarch
    3. a hero
    4. a frustrated loser.

Thematic Essays

1. Democratic beliefs and ideals shook the old ruling classes of Western Europe. However, the peoples of Russia and Latin America were less successful in establishing democratic governments. *Task:* Analyze the reasons for authoritarianism in Russia and Latin America. Consider geographic, economic, and social factors.

2. Metternich and the Congress of Vienna attempted to turn the clock back and restore deposed monarchs to their thrones. *Task:* Identify and explain two reasons why these efforts failed. Include specific examples from at least one nation in Europe.

Document-Based Questions

1. Study the map on page 163. Identify the geographic factors that would hinder the spread of information to the Russian people about the American and French revolutions and the ideas of the Enlightenment.

2. It was not until 1861 that Russian serfs were emancipated [freed]. This is a description of a Russian village community:

   " . . . the villages are bound together by ties quite unknown to the rural English population. . . . they cannot begin to mow or plow the fallow [unplanted] field until the village assembly has passed a resolution on the subject. . . . No peasant can permanently leave the village without the consent of the community, and this consent will not be granted until the applicant gives satisfactory security for his actual and future liabilities [taxes]."

   How did Russian society bind the peasant to the village and prevent individual action?

3. A young idealist wrote about village life in Russia:

   "Everyone who settles there, whether as artisan, or as communal teacher, or clerk is immediately under the eye of all. He is observed and his every movement is watched as though he was a bird in a glass cage. . . . The peasant is absolutely incapable of keeping secret the propaganda in his midst. . . . Thus, whenever a propagandist visits any of his friends, the news immediately spreads throughout the village."

   Why was it easy for the government to identify the propagandist, and difficult for the propagandist to hide among the people?

4. Russian revolutionaries wrote a letter to the new czar after the assassination of his father:

   "For this reason, your majesty: that a just government, in the true sense of the word, does not exist among us. A government should, in conformity with its essential principle of its existence, be the expression of the aspirations [goals] of the people, [it] should carry out only the will of the people."

   What are the justifications used by the revolutionaries for their actions? What are the sources of their political ideas?

Document-Based Essay

Task: Discuss why the peasants and serfs of Latin America and Russia were so slow to react to the ideas of the Enlightenment and the revolutions in America and France.

CHAPTER
17

Global Nationalism

I. WESTERN NATIONALISM

A. Unification of Germany

Before 1848, Germany was a confederation of 38 states, of which Prussia was the largest and most powerful. During the Napoleonic Wars, 16 states united as the Confederation of the Rhine, or German Confederation as it became known at the Congress of Vienna. It never developed a central government.

In 1848, the Frankfurt Assembly tried to unify Germany with King Frederick William IV of Prussia as emperor. He refused because he did not want to accept a crown offered by revolutionaries and liberals.

BLOOD AND IRON. Frederick William did, however, hope to become the absolute monarch of a Germany united under Prussia. In 1862, his successor Wilhelm I appointed Otto von Bismarck as his chief minister. Bismarck's policy, called "blood and iron," was to use war as the means of unifying Germany.

He faced serious obstacles. Austria and France opposed having a strong, unified Germany on their borders. And the princes ruling the separate German states did not want to lose power to a central government.

Schleswig-Holstein. In 1864, Danish forces took over Schleswig, a region between Denmark and Prussia. Citing the presence of many Germans in Schleswig, Prussia and Austria seized it, as well as the nearby province of Holstein (Prussia governed Schleswig, and Austria Holstein).

In 1866, the two powers' quarrel about administering the provinces erupted into the Austro-Prussian War, or Seven Weeks' War. Prussia was the victor.

North German Confederation. Bismarck organized the North German Confederation in 1867, with Prussia as the leader of many small northern German states. Four major states in southern Germany refused to join. Mainly Roman Catholic, they feared domination by the Protestant north Germans. They also feared provoking France.

Franco-Prussian War. To spur on the southern states to join his confederation, Bismarck provoked a war with France.

Emperor Napoleon III of France, for his part, wanted to curb Prussia's power and gain popularity at home by doing so.

A dispute between France and Prussia about whether a Prussian prince would rule Spain set off the war. Napoleon III did not want a Prussian to be king of Spain and sent an ambassador to King Wilhelm I. The king refused to announce publicly that no Prussian prince would become king of Spain and sent a telegram to Bismarck reporting the conversation. Bismarck changed the telegram, making it seem that the king had insulted the French ambassador, and made it public.

France declared war in July 1870. The south German states joined the North German Confederation so that the Franco-Prussian War was between France and a united Germany. Germany won a quick and decisive victory.

UNIFICATION. The Treaty of Frankfurt (May 1871) ended the war. France gave Germany Alsace Province and part of Lorraine, both of which were rich in coal and iron.

Then, the south German states joined the North German Confederation to form the German Empire (Reich). King Wilhelm I became the kaiser (emperor), and Bismarck was named the chancellor (prime minister). A new constitution created a two-house legislature consisting of the Bundesrat and Reichstag. All men over 25 could vote for members of the Reichstag.

B. Unification of Italy

Since the Middle Ages, Italy had been a collection of provinces, small kingdoms, and city-states.

Unification of Germany, 1871

From the early to the mid-1800s, Austria ruled much of Italy, with the pope controlling the central region around Rome.

MAZZINI. In the 1830s, Giuseppe Mazzini founded Young Italy, a secret society for the unification of a democratic Italy. He stirred up unsuccessful revolts and then fled abroad, where he continued to promote unification.

GARIBALDI. Giuseppe Garibaldi worked with Mazzini in the 1830s. He, too, fled abroad but returned to Italy in 1848 to lead troops in northern Italy in an unsuccessful revolt against Austria. He also worked to replace the pope's rule over Rome with a more liberal government. This effort also failed, and he was once again forced into exile.

CAVOUR. In 1852, unification gained new life as the **risorgimento**, or reawakening. The name was borrowed from a newspaper founded by Camillo di Cavour. Cavour used the paper to stir up the northern Italian states against Austrian rule. In 1852, King Victor Emmanuel II of Sardinia and Piedmont made Cavour his prime minister. Cavour believed in constitutional monarchy. By building up Piedmont's commerce and industry, he hoped to win Italian territory from Austria.

OVERCOMING OBSTACLES. Austria intended to keep firm control of northern Italy. Moreover, the pope opposed a strong national government that might threaten Church ownership of the Papal States in central Italy.

Cavour made a secret alliance with France and then provoked a war with Austria. When Austrian troops invaded Piedmont, the French aided the Italians. Thus, Piedmont gained Lombardy, a state previously controlled by Austria.

Austrian-controlled Tuscany, Parma, and Modena demanded unification with Piedmont. Because of the French-Italian alliance, Austria agreed. By 1860, Piedmont controlled all of Italy except the Kingdom of the Two Sicilies in the south, the Papal States in the center, and Venetia in the northeast.

RETURN OF GARIBALDI. In May 1860, Garibaldi landed in Sicily with an army of about 1000 soldiers. These "Red Shirts" won the Kingdom of the Two Sicilies and, with aid sent by Cavour, captured the Papal States, except for Rome. Victor Emmanuel II became king of Italy in March 1861.

Italy aided Prussia during the Seven Weeks' War against Austria. After the Prussian victory, Italy took over Austrian-ruled Venetia (1866). During the Franco-Prussian War, the Italian troops occupied Rome, which became the capital of the Kingdom of Italy in 1871.

C. Germany and Italy After Unification

GERMANY. Bismarck increased German military and naval power. Natural resources such as coal and iron aided the growth of German industries. The people lived well, and literacy was widespread.

Unification of Italy, 1859–1870

The kaiser reigned supreme. Bismarck weakened labor unions by giving workers old-age pensions and compensation for illness. (Germany was the first country to enact such social insurance.)

ITALY. Italy had few natural resources, and its industry and economy developed slowly. Many Italians were poor and illiterate.

The Italian constitution limited the king's power and provided for a parliament of elected lawmakers. At first, only a few wealthy males could vote, but by 1912, all Italian men could. Unfortunately, many poor Italians sold their votes, and the government became corrupt. Until 1904, the Catholic Church, which resented seizure of the Papal States, forbade Catholics to vote or hold office.

COLONIAL IMPERIALISM. Italy acquired Eritrea and Somalia in eastern Africa and Libya in North Africa. Germany took over the present-day African countries of The Gambia, Togo, Cameroon, Namibia, and Tanzania. It also controlled a few South Pacific islands.

<hr>

INFO CHECK

1. Describe Otto von Bismarck's policy of "blood and iron." Did the formation of the Reich

in 1871 signify the success or failure of this policy.

2. Which leader best fits each of the following descriptions?
   • the soul of Italian unification
   • the sword of Italian unification
   • the mind of Italian unification

3. After German unification, what steps did Bismarck take to limit the power of labor unions? Did these measures make Germany more democratic? Explain.

II. U.S. SECTIONALISM VERSUS NATIONALISM

In the 19th century, Americans believed in nationalism and Manifest Destiny—the right to settle the continent from the Atlantic to the Pacific and from Canada to the Gulf of Mexico. There was general support for the Mexican War (1846–1848), in which the United States took over a large section of Mexican land north of the Rio Grande.

A. Rise of Sectionalism

By mid-century, **sectionalism**—conflicting interests of the North, South, and West— began to replace U.S. nationalism. Industries had grown up mainly in the Northeast. The South and West were agricultural. Small Western farms needed only a few laborers, while large Southern plantations depended on the cheap labor of slaves.

THE NORTH AND SLAVERY. Northerners especially disapproved of the slave system. A group called **abolitionists** demanded an immediate end to it. Many Northerners were not abolitionists, but most believed, at the very least, that slavery should be confined to the South.

TARIFFS. Northern businesspeople favored high **tariffs** (taxes on imported goods). Southerners opposed high tariffs, which increased the cost of imports. The South traded its cotton, tobacco, and other agricultural products for goods manufactured in Britain and Europe rather than in the North.

INCREASED TENSION. Between 1850 and 1861, hostility grew between the proslavery, low-tariff Southern Democrats and the antislavery, high-tariff Northern Republicans. Southerners felt more loyalty to the South than to the country as a whole.

B. Civil War

In November 1860, Abraham Lincoln, a pro-Union, antislavery Republican, became president. Southerners feared that he would end slavery and destroy their economy. Within three months, South Carolina, Mississippi, Louisiana, Florida, Alabama, and Georgia seceded (withdrew) from the Union, as the United States was now called. The South renamed itself the Confederate States of America. By 1861, Texas, North Carolina, Virginia, Tennessee, and Arkansas had joined the Confederacy. On April 12, 1861, the Civil War broke out.

The war was marked by great bloodshed, with most of the fighting and the greatest destruction occurring in the South. The Northern victory in April 1865 forced the Southern states to rejoin the Union and ended slavery.

INFO CHECK

1. Explain the difference between nationalism and sectionalism in 19th-century America.

2. Complete the following sentences:
   • The two great sectional issues that divided 19th-century Americans were_____.
   • In 1860, many Southerners wished to secede from the United States because_____.
   • The Northern victory in the Civil War resulted in_____.

III. NATIONALISM IN INDIA

A. British Rule

From the 1600s to the 1900s, Britain ruled India but showed little respect for Indian religions or culture. The British built telegraph, railroad, and irrigation systems and created new industries. Industrial progress mainly helped the British; the Indians' living standards remained low.

The British governmental and legal systems were more powerful than those of individual Indian states. While attending college in England, many well-to-do Indians learned about civil rights and democracy; they felt that Indians should rule India.

SEPOY MUTINY. The Sepoy Mutiny set off Indian resistance to British rule. Until the mid-1800s, the East India Company acted as the British colonial government in India. **Sepoys** (Indian soldiers hired by the East India Company) were commanded by British officers and fought the French and local princes for trading rights and territory.

Mahatma Gandhi (right), advocate of nonviolence, with Jawaharlal Nehru, 1946.

Hindu sepoys could not touch beef, and Muslim sepoys could not eat pork. In 1857, however, the British army issued cartridges greased with beef and port fat. Since the end of each cartridge had to be bitten off before being inserted into the rifle, the sepoys refused to use the equipment.

When officers tried to force the sepoys to use the cartridges, they rebelled. Thousands of Indians joined their revolt. The rebels were put down in 1859, and the British government took over administration from the East India Company. Britain also promised not to interfere again with local religious practices.

Nationalist Reaction. Some Indians wanted to encourage the nationalistic feelings that had been unleashed, but they were slow to organize. Middle-class Hindus founded the Indian National Congress in 1885. Muslims set up the Muslim League in 1906. Although the main demand of these nationalists was for self-rule, they had differing ideas about political reform.

CONTINUED CLASHES. The British gradually allowed limited Indian participation in government, but they still looked down on Indians and did not encourage public education. Indian opposition to British rule increased.

Indian troops fought for the British in World War I (1914–1918). After the war, however, feeling against British rule became widespread. Authorities tried to contain the protests without violence.

In 1919, British officers grew suspicious of a peaceful festival in Amritsar. They ordered their soldiers to fire into a crowd of men, women, and children, killing 400 civilians and wounding 1200.

GANDHI. After Amritsar, demands for self-rule became intense. A lawyer named Mohandas K. Gandhi (1869–1948) became head of the Indian National Congress. He persuaded many Indians to turn from violence to **passive resistance**—boycotting British goods and refusing to serve in the armed forces, pay taxes, or obey British law.

Called "Mahatma" (the great one) by his followers, Gandhi and they were frequently jailed for their resistance. Gandhi also fasted (refused to eat) until his demands were met.

JINNAH. As president of the Muslim League, Muhammad Ali Jinnah (1876–1948) sometimes cooperated with the Indian National Congress. But he also sought British protection of Muslims from the Hindu majority.

NEHRU. Jawaharlal Nehru (1889–1964) became a strong Hindu nationalist leader in the 1930s. He, too, was jailed for his struggles on behalf of Indian independence.

B. Two Independent Nations

World War II (1939–1945) increased the desire for Indian independence. Then, too, the Hindus led by Gandhi and Nehru and the Muslims under Jinnah disagreed on how to govern India. In 1947, when bloody riots broke out throughout India, the British and the Indians agreed to carve from Indian territory the independent Muslim nation of

India and Pakistan

Pakistan. The greater part of the subcontinent became the independent Republic of India.

In 1948, Nehru became the first prime minister of India. Jinnah headed Pakistan. In 1948, Gandhi was assassinated by a Hindu extremist who objected to his call for fair treatment of Muslims.

IV. NATIONALISM IN THE MIDDLE EAST

From the 1500s until the 1920s, the Ottoman (Turkish) Empire united an area that included Turkey, parts of the Balkan states, the eastern Mediterranean, and parts of North Africa. As the central government grew weak, however, it lost the loyalty of various ethnic and national groups.

In answer to calls for reform, a new constitution was created in 1876. The **sultan** (ruler), however, dissolved the new lawmaking body.

In 1908, army officers called the Young Turks forced the sultan to restore the constitution. Reformers sought Westernized industrialization. Nationalists called for a Turkish republic.

After World War I, the victors divided the Ottoman Empire, Germany's ally, among themselves. France gained Lebanon and Syria. Britain, seeking to protect its access to India and its Middle East petroleum interests, took Iraq, Jordan, and the Holy Land (present-day Israel, then called Palestine).

During the war, Britain had encouraged Arabia to revolt against the Ottoman Empire. The Kingdom of Saudi Arabia under Ibn Saud came into being in 1932.

A. Turkey: The Fall of the Ottoman Empire

When the victors also tried to take over Turkey, the Young Turks under General Mustafa Kemal

Middle East, 1919–1939

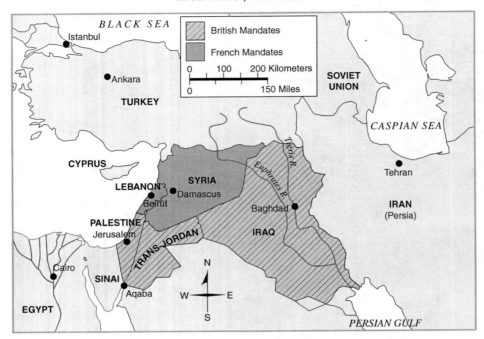

turned them back and captured Constantinople. In 1923, the Turks signed a treaty that gave them Asia Minor and a strip of European land between the Black and the Aegean seas. Kemal became president of the new government of Turkey.

B. Jewish Homeland

Jews have been persecuted throughout their history. In the late 1800s, an Austrian Jew named Theodor Herzl headed a movement called **Zionism** to establish a Jewish state in Palestine. (Zion is a biblical term for the ideal nation.) Russian persecution of Jews gave strength to the movement. In 1897, the Zionists held their first general meeting in Switzerland.

Zionists tried to persuade European leaders to support the Jewish claim. In 1917, Britain issued the Balfour Declaration, a promise to support a Jewish national homeland in Palestine. The Arabs felt betrayed by this plan to give land to non-Muslims, depite the presence of Jews in Palestine since Biblical times.

After 1933, the Nazis began a systematic policy to eliminate Jews from Germany. Many went to Palestine. In 1939, Britain, fearful of the Arab reaction, limited Jewish immigration to Palestine.

During World War II, the Nazis killed some six million Jews from Germany, Poland, and the other countries under their control. Postwar demands for a Jewish state in Palestine intensified. Jewish opposition to Britain's quota on Jewish immigration to Palestine caused the British to turn to the

United Nations. In 1947, the UN divided Palestine into a Jewish and an Arab state. The State of Israel was born in 1948.

Egypt, Syria, Lebanon, Iraq, and Jordan refused to recognize Israel. By 1949, after a year of fighting the Arabs, Israel had survived and gained new territory. It had not, however, gained peace.

INFO CHECK

1. How did British rule benefit India?

2. Why did Indian nationalists want independence from Britain?

3. Summarize the contributions to Indian independence of each of the following: Mohandas K. Gandhi, Jawaharlal Nehru, Muhammed Ali Jinnah.

4. Who were the Young Turks? What did they contribute to the formation of modern Turkey?

5. Define Zionism. Why has it been supported by Jews but opposed by Arab nationalists? How did this difference lead to conflict in the Middle East?

V. NATIONALISM IN CONTEMPORARY STRUGGLES

A. Bosnia

In 1990, as Communist control of Eastern Europe collapsed, Yugoslavia's parliament set about creating a multiparty system.

Yugoslavia was a union of six republics occupying part of the Balkan Peninsula. Once part of the Ottoman Empire, Yugoslavia had a population of mostly Eastern Orthodox Christians, with a large Muslim minority.

In 1991, Croatia and Slovenia declared independence. Serbia, largest of the republics, objected, and its leaders revived old hostilities between groups in the region. One cause of bitterness was Croatian cooperation with German invaders during World War II and Serb resistance. Fighting among Serbs, Croats, and other ethnic groups exploded into civil war.

In 1992, Bosnia-Herzegovina and Macedonia also declared independence. Yugoslavia now consisted of only Serbia and Montenegro.

Croats and Serbs fought each other, and both groups inflicted damage on Bosnia's Muslims. The Serbs adopted **ethnic cleansing**—a policy to wipe out the Muslim population. Although the UN failed to make peace, as 1994 ended, the Croats had agreed to stop fighting. Some NATO bombings of Bosnian Serb positions began to turn the tide. In November 1995, the presidents of Croatia, Bosnia, and Yugoslavia, on behalf of the Bosnian Serbs, signed a peace agreement after talks in Dayton, Ohio. U.S. and European troops worked with UN peacekeepers to maintain the shaky cease-fire. At the end of 1998, relations among ethnic groups were still strained and remained so into the 21st century.

B. Kosovo

The violence spread to Yugoslavia's Kosovo province. A large majority of the population, ethnic Albanians of the Muslim faith, was under the political control of the Serb Orthodox Christian minority. Muslim demands for self-rule provoked a Serb military crackdown. The Muslims formed a Kosovar Liberation Army (KLA), which fought for full independence and backed it up with **guerrilla warfare** (surprise raids by small bands of fighters).

In 1999, NATO and Russian leaders worked out a peace plan. Refusing to cooperate, the Serbs increased their attacks on the Muslims. Many Muslim Kosovars fled to Albania and Macedonia. NATO forces, acting in support of the KLA, bombed Serb troops and forced them out of the province. While an uneasy peace followed in Kosovo, violence erupted in Macedonia. The Macedonian government ordered its military and police to resist the tide of ethnic Albanians moving into their country. In 2001, the Albanians and the Macedonian government agreed to a NATO peace plan.

C. Northern Ireland

Southern Ireland (the Irish Free State)—from 1921, a self-governing country with ties to Britain—declared itself the independent Republic of Ireland in 1949. The population is mainly Roman Catholic. Northern Ireland (Ulster), which is mainly Protestant, chose to retain a close relationship with Britain.

The Catholics in Northern Ireland comprise a large minority, with strong ties to the Republic of Ireland. They never accepted the separation of the two Irelands. Protestants in Northern Ireland own most of its industries and have greater political control than Catholics do.

When Catholics began to hold civil rights demonstrations in 1969, Protestants attacked the demonstrators, and British troops were sent in to restore order.

IRISH REPUBLICAN ARMY VERSUS ULSTER DEFENSE ASSOCIATION. A private organization called the Irish Republican Army (IRA) had used violence against the British in the fight for independence in Southern Ireland. It now demanded that Britain allow Northern Ireland to join the Republic of Ireland.

The Ulster Defense Association (UDA), a Protestant group, terrorized Catholics with bombings and killings. In turn, the IRA bombed sites in England.

PEACE MOVE. The British and Irish governments and North Ireland's political parties negotiated the Multiparty Agreement of 1998. However, the IRA's refusal to give up its weapons endangered peaceful self-government under an elected assembly. This was unacceptable to political parties representing the Protestants. The collapse of the new government and the restoration of British rule were avoided in late 2001. Pressured by the U.S. government and others, the IRA agreed to disarm. In 2007, a new government based on power shared between Catholics and Protestants took office.

D. West Bank and Gaza

When, in 1949, the Jews and Arabs signed an armistice, they did not agree on Israel's boundaries. The Palestinians were angered by Israel's claim to much of Palestine and by the division of the city of Jerusalem into Arab and Jewish quarters.

PALESTINE LIBERATION ORGANIZATION. Displaced Palestinian Arabs sought refuge in Jordan, Syria, Lebanon, and Egypt. In 1964, they formed the Palestine Liberation Organization (PLO), which engaged in terrorism against Israel and

Year	Dates and Events
A.D.	
1801	**1830s:** Mazzini founds Young Italy to unify Italy under representative government
	1852: Beginning of risorgimento; Cavour tries to unite northern Italian states against Austria
	1857–1859: British army puts down Sepoy Mutiny; Britain takes control of Indian government
	1859: Franco-Italian war against Austria; Austrian Lombardy ceded to Piedmont
	1860: Piedmont controls all of Italy except for Two Sicilies, Papal States, Venetia
	1861: Garibaldi's Red Shirts and Piedmont army capture Two Sicilies, Papal States; Victor Emmanuel II named king of unified Italy
	1861: Southern U.S. states secede; Civil War erupts at Fort Sumter
	1864: Prussia wins Schleswig and Holstein from Denmark
	1866: Seven Weeks' War ends Austrian influence over Germany, gives Italy control of Venetia
	1867: Bismarck's North German Confederation extends Prussian authority to most of Germany
	1870–1871: Franco-Prussian War: Germany defeats France
	1871: German Reich proclaimed, with Wilhelm I, Prussia, as emperor, Bismarck as prime minister
	1871: Treaty of Frankfurt gives Alsace-Lorraine to Germany
	1897: First Zionist congress organized by Herzl, meets in Switzerland
	1906: Muslim League organized; political rival of Indian National Congress
	1908: Young Turks win sultan's recognition of 1876 constitution
	1917: Balfour Declaration
	1919: Treaty of Versailles gives Ottoman lands to France (Lebanon, Syria), Britain (Iraq, Jordan)
1900	**1921:** New Irish Free State in Roman Catholic Southern Ireland; Ulster remains united with Britain
1901	**1923:** Kemal becomes president of Turkey
	1932: Arabian tribes unite as Saudi Arabia under Ibn Saud
	1939–1945: World War II and Holocaust intensify Jewish demand for Palestinian homeland
	1947: UN divides Palestine into Jewish and Arab sectors
	1947: India becomes independent; creation of Muslim Pakistan
	1948: Jews declare State of Israel, initiating years of war with Egypt, Syria, Lebanon, Iraq, Jordan
	1949: Irish Free State becomes Republic of Ireland
	1964: Organization of PLO by displaced Palestinian Arabs
	1967: Israel wins war with Arabs, occupies Sinai, Golan Heights, West Bank
	1978: Camp David Accords; Israel evacuates Sinai, Egypt recognizes Israel
	1990s: PLO and Arafat renounce terrorism, recognize Israel, continue talks about independent Palestine
	1991–1992: Yugoslavian break-up; Croatia, Slovenia, Bosnia-Herzegovina, Macedonia delcare independence; Serbian objections lead to civil war and "ethnic cleansing" of Bosnian Muslims
	1993: Rabin promises future transfer of Gaza and West Bank to Palestinians
	1995: Dayton Accords; cease-fire in Bosnia
	1998: Peace agreement calls for Northern Ireland assembly, future vote by all Irish on union of Northern Ireland and Republic of Ireland
2000	**1998–1999:** War in Yugoslavia's Kosovo province; peace plan ousts Serbs, restores some self-rule to Kosovars
2001	**2001:** NATO troops prevent war between ethnic Albanians and Macedonian government forces
	2007: Power-sharing government established in Northern Ireland

(Left margin label: **Timeline**)

countries sympathetic to its position. The PLO and allied Arab countries launched two more unsuccessful wars against Israel, in 1967 and 1973. After winning the 1967 war, Israel occupied the Sinai Peninsula, the Golan Heights, and the West Bank.

PEACE INITIATIVES. In 1977, Egyptian president Anwar Sadat visited Israel. In 1978, U.S.

President Jimmy Carter brought Sadat and the Israeli leader, Menachem Begin, together to discuss differences. These talks led to the peace treaty of 1979, in which Israel agreed to evacuate the Sinai Peninsula. After the withdrawal in 1982, Egypt recognized Israel's right to exist.

Following a 1993 agreement, portions of the West Bank and Gaza were governed by a Palestin-

President Clinton fostering a diplomatic breakthrough between Yitzhak Rabin (left) and Yasir Arafat, Washington, D.C., 1993

ian Authority led by Yasir Arafat. Renewed violence ended the movement toward peace. Militant Palestinians, angered by the growth of Israeli settlements in the West Bank and Gaza, began an *intifada* (uprising). Terrorist attacks inside Israel resulted in the movement of Israeli military forces into Palestinian towns. In 2007, U.S. President George W. Bush persuaded Palestinian, Arab, and Israeli leaders to hold new peace talks in Annapolis, Maryland.

INFO CHECK

1. Identify the nationalist and ethnic groups that clashed in Kosovo province, and explain how the violence spread to Macedonia.

2. What issues have divided Catholics and Protestants in Northern Ireland? How did nationalism influence both groups?

3. How has nationalism divided Israelis and Palestinians in the 20th and 21st centuries?

CHAPTER REVIEW

Multiple Choice

1. The first attempt to unify the 38 German states failed because the

   1. Frankfurt Assembly voted to form a confederation
   2. Prussian king refused to accept power from liberals and revolutionaries
   3. rulers of the 38 German states refused to give up their powers
   4. German people felt loyalty to their local princes.

2. The person and policy that succeeded in unifying Germany were

   1. Frederick William IV of Prussia and his policy of "Divine Right"
   2. Emperor Napoleon III of France and his rebuilt Third Empire
   3. Otto von Bismarck and his policy of "blood and iron"
   4. Garibaldi and his "Red Shirt" policy.

3. As a result of the Franco-Prussian War, Bismarck achieved his goal to

   1. conquer France
   2. defeat Spain
   3. capture the British fleet
   4. unify German states under Prussia.

4. Austria and the pope opposed the unification of Italy because

   1. they both controlled lands that were part of the Italian peninsula
   2. the pope supported Prussia
   3. the leaders of Italian unification were enemies of the Church
   4. Austria refused to give up its claim to Rome.

5. The policy and practice that was adopted by many Indians to end British rule was

   1. boycott of British products
   2. refusal to serve in the British armed forces
   3. nonviolent, passive resistance
   4. all of the above.

6. Which did most to cause the collapse of the Ottoman Empire?

   1. birth of the State of Israel
   2. formation of the Arab League
   3. formation of Palestine under Arab and Jewish leadership
   4. revolt of the "Young Turks" under Kemal's leadership

7. The number of Jewish immigrants to Palestine in the 1930s increased because

   1. the government promised new settlers 40 acres of land and a mule for plowing
   2. anti-Semitism in Europe was increasing
   3. the British government needed settlers in the colony
   4. the discovery of oil brought immigrants seeking employment.

8. Northern Ireland, Bosnia, the West Bank, and Gaza have all been

   1. newly independent developing nations
   2. areas of United Nations peacekeeping efforts
   3. World Bank economic development zones
   4. sites of nationalistic conflicts.

9. Theodore Herzl and Mustafa Kemal were nationalistic leaders whose efforts resulted in the

   1. Franco-Prussian War
   2. founding of Israel and Turkey
   3. founding of Iran and Bangladesh
   4. Declaration of International Human Rights.

10. What was the reaction to the 1947 decision by the UN about Palestine?

    1. The British refused to enforce it.
    2. The Jewish inhabitants accepted it and the Arabs did not.
    3. The Arab inhabitants accepted it and the Jews did not.
    4. The neighboring Arab states offered to enforce it.

11. A comparison of the maps on pages 169 and 170 shows that

    1. both Germany and Italy had strong traditions of unity
    2. German and Italian unification were both accomplished by the early 1870s
    3. the Germans and Italians were once divided into a variety of states or kingdoms
    4. both statements 2 and 3 are accurate.

12. The photograph on page 172 shows that the two leaders appealed to Indian nationalism by promoting

    1. equality for untouchables
    2. voting rights for women
    3. traditional Indian culture and values
    4. separation of India into Muslim and Hindu states.

Thematic Essays

1. "Blood and iron," "passive resistance," "Young Turks," "IRA." "Zionism," and "PLO" all represent a policy or group related to nationalism. *Task:* Select *two*, each from a different region of the world, and compare and contrast their policies and the results they achieved.

2. Peoples, nations, and empires can be united or torn apart by nationalism. *Task:* Using historical examples, describe *one* situation that resulted in unification and *one* that ended in division.

Document-Based Questions

1. From "The Oath of Young Italy":

   "By the blush that rises to my brow when I stand before the citizens of other lands; to know that I have no rights of citizenship, no country, no flag. . . . By the memory of our former greatness . . . Convinced that God has ordained that a nation shall be. . . ."

   How did this oath appeal to Italians' pride and sense of nationalism?

2. From a speech by Otto von Bismarck:

   "The great questions of the time will not be decided by speeches and resolutions of majorities—that was the mistake of 1848 and 1849—but by iron and blood."

   Describe Bismarck's attitude toward the German parliament and its liberal democratic practices.

3. Study the photo on page 177. Explain the importance for the Middle East of the handshake between these men.

Document-Based Essay

Task: Using historical examples from the 19th, 20th and 21st centuries, answer the following question: Can nationalism be a force for peace?

CHAPTER
18

Economic and Social Revolutions

I. AGRARIAN REVOLUTION

A. Enclosure System

The **enclosure system** (fencing off a land-owner's field and planting it with cash crops) was first practiced in the Netherlands during the 1600s. Later, it spread to England and France.

OPEN-FIELD SYSTEM. Before the enclosure system, small farmers had been allowed to plant crops in a landowner's fields and graze their livestock on land not suitable for farming. Such jointly used pastures were called "commons."

SPECIALIZATION. The open-field system did not supply enough cash crops to meet the demands of Europe's expanding world trade. By enclosing their fields and planting them with cash crops, landowners could make bigger profits.

CROP ROTATION. Landowners also began to find out how to make their available land more productive and profitable.

The open-field system had given small farmers at least three fields in which to grow crops. They planted two of them each year and kept the third fallow (at rest) to restore its fertility. In the 1730s, Charles Townshend pointed out that a field did not have to be left fallow. It could be planted with turnips and clover—plants that return to the soil nutrients that such crops as wheat and barley take from it. Then, the turnips and clover could serve as animal feed during the winter. Thus, animals formerly slaughtered in the autumn could be kept to provide milk and wool all year.

Landowners using the enclosure system no longer grew a variety of crops to meet their workers' needs. They planted their fields with whatever crop brought in the most money.

B. Agrarian Inventions

Traditionally, farmers scattered seeds by hand across a field. In 1701, Jethro Tull invented a seed drill that planted seeds in a row. Farmers could now produce more crops with fewer seeds on the same amount of land. Tull also invented the horse-drawn hoe to break up the soil between the planted rows.

In the mid-1800s, the American inventor Cyrus McCormick devised a horse-drawn reaper. In one operation, it cut grain and separated seeds from stalks. Now, a few workers could tend large farms and produce more grain.

EFFECT ON SMALL FARMERS. The enclosure system and the new farming machines made it hard for small farmers to make a living from the land remaining to them. Many moved to towns and cities and took jobs in the new factories.

INFO CHECK

1. Describe the changes brought to European farming by the agrarian revolution of the 18th century.

2. If you were a small farmer in 18th-century western Europe, why might you object to the enclosure system?

II. INDUSTRIAL REVOLUTION

The Industrial Revolution began in Britain. Its government supported commercial interests. Its colonies supplied raw materials and served as markets for manufactures. British capitalists were eager to invest in inventions that would speed production in factories and mines. Moreover, agricultural advances had made it possible to grow more food for the swelling numbers of urban workers.

A. Textile Inventions

The production of textiles (cloth) was vital to Britain's economy in the 19th century. Manufacturers were eager to put to use faster weaving machines.

FLYING SHUTTLE. In 1733, John Kay invented the flying shuttle, which enabled only one person to operate a loom.

SPINNING JENNY AND POWER LOOM. As weaving cloth became speedier, more thread was needed. In 1764, James Hargreaves invented the spinning jenny, which spun thread eight times faster than the old spinning wheel. A water-powered spinning machine was developed in 1769.

Suddenly, looms could not weave fast enough to use all the available thread. In 1784, Edmund Cartwright invented a more effective power loom. The demand for raw cotton soared.

COTTON GIN. In 1793, American inventor Eli Whitney invented the cotton gin, which separated the seeds from cotton much faster than by hand. (As Southern plantations stepped up cotton production, more and more slave workers were needed as planters and pickers.)

B. From Home to Factory

Home manufacturing was called the **domestic (cottage) system**. Advanced weaving machines became too large and too expensive for use by the home weaver. Weavers increasingly worked in large factories instead.

POWER SOURCES. Early factories were built beside fast-running rivers or waterfalls, which powered their machines.

In the late 1700s, James Watt of Scotland improved the steam engine. His drew power from water heated over burning coals. Factories began to be built near towns close to coal mines, and coal mining became another important industry.

USE OF IRON. Iron parts were superior to wooden ones in the new machines. New processes produced better-quality iron for tools, machines, bridges, and other structures.

INDUSTRIALIZATION AND WEALTH. By the mid-1800s, Britain was an industrial nation. By the late 1800s, France, Germany, and the United States had also become industrialized.

Production by machine was fast, cheap, and efficient. As sales increased, factory owners grew rich. New methods of transportation opened up more markets, near and far. Traders and shippers also prospered. The new wealth went to build more factories, create more goods, and open up more markets.

C. Factory System

The factory system did not improve living standards for workers, however. Men, women, and children worked long hours, six days a week, for low wages. Employers spent no money on safety devices to protect workers. Ill or injured workers went unpaid.

INTERCHANGEABLE PARTS. Before the Industrial Revolution, weapon and tool parts were handmade and, therefore, varied in size and shape. When a gun trigger wore out, another one had to be specially made to fit that particular gun. In 1800, Eli Whitney invented a device that made triggers and other component parts the same size and shape. **Interchangeable parts** made the repair of weapons, tools, and machines cheap and fast.

MASS PRODUCTION. Machine-made parts led to the **mass-production system**, whereby each worker in a group made only one part for a multiple-part item. Workers who did a few simple tasks

Nineteenth-century mill workers in Lancashire, England

repeatedly became very fast. Factories with mass-production systems turned out large quantities of goods quickly and cheaply.

D. Economic Theory

ADAM SMITH. In 1776, Adam Smith published *An Inquiry into the Nature and Causes of the Wealth of Nations.* This book argued that the mercantile system of regulated economic activity should be replaced by free competition among businesses.

Supply and Demand. Demand for a popular product rises. If the supply is low, people will pay more for the item.

Manufacturers then produce more in hopes of making a larger profit. As the supply increases, however, manufacturers compete for customers by lowering prices or improving the product.

Competition and Laissez-Faire. Competition motivates people to be more efficient and turn out better products. **Free enterprise** (competitive capitalism) gives more businesspeople a chance to make more money while consumers (buyers) get better goods at the lowest possible prices. This theory became known as **laissez-faire** (French for "leave it alone"). Businesspeople liked the idea that government should allow them to compete freely with one another.

Smith warned that a manufacturer may try to eliminate competition by creating a **monopoly**, a business with sole control over the supply of a product. In such a case, the government should restore competition to the market.

E. Social Changes

MIDDLE-CLASS EMPOWERMENT. As the middle classes gained control over national economies, they became politically active. They also became more diversified. Whereas middle-class leaders had formerly been well-educated professionals or owners of long-established businesses, many of the new industrialists had begun as skilled workers. Others, such as Quakers and Jews, were members of minorities that had long been discriminated against.

ATTITUDES AND VALUES. Some new members of the middle class imitated the extravagant behavior of the aristocracy. Most, however, still honored such working-class values as self-discipline and thrift.

WHITE COLLAR WORKERS. Growing industries provided lower-middle-class people who could read, write, and do arithmetic with new job opportunities: schoolteachers, clerks, shopkeepers, traveling salespeople, bookkeepers, store managers, supervisors. These so-called **white-collar workers** owned no property and earned little more than factory and mine workers. But they took pride in their skills and significantly influenced the rise in literacy during the Industrial Revolution.

LABORERS. Before the Industrial Revolution, most laborers had been tenant farmers and peasants, along with a few carpenters, blacksmiths, bricklayers, or stonemasons. They lived in small farming communities, helping one another and relying on the local landowner. As they turned to factory work, they were on their own, without a community of neighbors.

EDUCATION. Factory workers put in long hours to earn just enough to survive. They were unable to attend school to improve their skills and position in society.

CHANGING HOUSEHOLD ROLES. In farm households, husbands and wives shared responsibility for the family. Women and girls milked the cows and spun thread. Men and boys farmed and wove cloth. Each of these jobs was equally important to the family economy.

In factory-tied families, however, men were given the better-paid, skilled work. Women did routine tasks for much less money. Even women with skilled jobs earned less than their male counterparts. Married women kept house and, if possible, did craftwork for extra income. (Housework usually took an entire day.)

Married women did not challenge the practice of giving the better jobs to men. A husband's wages were usually the sole source of family income. Moreover, rigid factory routines left little time for the care of infants and toddlers.

If a man did not earn enough to support his family, other members went to work. Even children put in full days at factories instead of school. Working-class children often grew up sickly, stunted, and illiterate.

FACTORY TOWNS. As factories sprang up, cities formed around them. Urban populations grew so rapidly that proper housing could not be built for the newcomers seeking jobs. Whole families lived in one or two tiny rooms. Multilevel **tenements** were built so closely together that the area quickly became a **slum**. Open sewers bordered streets. Factory smoke polluted the air. Epidemics of disease increased the already high death rate among slum dwellers.

F. Transportation and Communication

STEAMSHIPS. The American inventor Robert Fulton used steam to power boats. In 1807, his steamboat, the *Clermont,* traveled up the Hudson River from New York to Albany in 32 hours. (Sailboats took 96 hours.) Raw materials and finished goods could now be shipped to factories and to markets quickly.

By the mid-1800s, oceangoing steamships were replacing sailing ships. Because they used coal to make steam, steamships on long voyages had to stop periodically to take on more coal. The need for naval supply stations spurred the drive for colonies.

RAILROADS. In 1814, George Stephenson of England demonstrated the first successful steam-powered railroad locomotive. In 1825, he opened the first public railroad; it had 20 miles of track. Railroads soon crisscrossed Europe and the United States. The ease with which they transported heavy goods and large numbers of people quickly made them major businesses.

AUTOMOBILES. About 1885, Karl Benz of Germany created the first high-speed motor powered by internal combustion. At the same time, Gottlieb Daimler, another German, introduced the gasoline-powered engine. Their efforts gave birth to the automobile industry.

AIRPLANES. In 1903, two American brothers, Orville and Wilbur Wright, made the first successful flight in a heavier-than-air plane. Charles Lindbergh's 1927 nonstop solo flight from New York to Paris altered ideas about distances and travel.

TELEGRAPH. In the 1830s, Charles Wheatstone and William Cooke of Britain and Samuel F. B. Morse of the United States developed the telegraph. It used sound codes to send messages over electrical wires. In 1866, U.S. businessman Cyrus Field linked North America and Europe through a transatlantic cable.

TELEPHONE. Alexander Graham Bell of Canada and the United States developed a successful telephone in 1876. People could now communicate about business and private affairs over long distances almost instantly.

RADIO. Italian scientist Guglielmo Marconi sent a message across the Atlantic by radio waves in 1901.

Between 1904 and 1912, John Fleming of Britain and Lee De Forest of the United States developed the radio receiving set. Regular radio broadcasts began in 1920.

TELEVISION. In 1923, Vladimir Zworykin, a Russian-born American, invented tubes for broadcasting and receiving pictures through radio waves. Six years later, he demonstrated the first practical television system. However, the new medium was not available to the average household until the 1950s.

G. Power Sources

Natural gas was first used to provide early factories with light and heat. Later, it was piped into homes.

In 1859, Edwin Drake drilled the first oil well in western Pennsylvania. Petroleum soon became an important source of power and fuel.

In the late 1790s, Alessandro Volta, an Italian, created the first electric battery. The first electric generator began operating in 1832. In 1882, electric generators, developed by the American inventor Thomas Edison, began to light city streets in London and New York.

INFO CHECK

1. Define: Industrial Revolution, mass-production system, free enterprise, monopoly.

2. Describe the role of new inventions in 18th-century Britain. Why did so many relate to the production of cloth?

3. Explain why you would APPROVE or DISAPPROVE of Adam Smith's ideas if you were a businessperson during the Industrial Revolution.

4. Identify the social change that you believe did most to change lifestyles in Europe in the 1800s.

III. SCIENCE AND MEDICINE

A. Groundbreaking Scientists

DALTON. In 1803, British schoolteacher and chemist John Dalton theorized that atoms are the smallest parts of elements. The atoms of one element differ from the atoms of all other elements. Dalton devised a system of atomic weights based on the weight of hydrogen, the lightest element. While not entirely accurate, Dalton's theories were the basis of modern atomic theory.

FARADAY. In the early 1800s, Michael Faraday of England demonstrated that magnetism could produce electricity. His work made the electric generator possible.

ROENTGEN. Wilhelm Roentgen of Germany announced his discovery of X rays in 1895. They allowed doctors to examine the body's interior for broken bones or tumors.

CURIE. In 1898, Marie Curie, a Polish-born French woman, and her husband, Pierre, discovered the radioactive elements radium and polonium. Until the 1950s, radium was used to treat certain cancers. Polonium is still used in nuclear research.

DARWIN. According to Charles Darwin, a British naturalist, new forms of plants and animals developed from earlier forms over time in a process called **evolution**. Darwin's *On the Origin of Species by Means of Natural Selection* was published in 1859. He theorized that those animals and plants best suited to obtain food survive and reproduce. Others, less successful, die out. This idea has been called "the survival of the fittest."

MENDEL. An Austrian monk, Gregor Mendel, experimented with pea plants to see how they passed characteristics such as color on to new generations. His findings, published in 1866, influenced the development of modern genetics (the science of heredity).

B. Medical Pioneers

JENNER. In 1796, the British physician Edward Jenner introduced vaccination as a means to prevent smallpox. Smallpox was usually fatal and permanently scarred survivors.

PASTEUR. Louis Pasteur (1882–1895), a French scientist, proved that bacteria (germs) cause diseases. He also showed that a weak solution of disease-causing germs (a vaccine) injected into a person will produce antibodies that resist the germs. The antibodies remain in the system and protect the person whenever exposure to the germs occurs. Pasteur developed vaccines to treat rabies and anthrax.

Bacteria also cause milk to sour. Pasteur discovered that heating milk kills the bacteria. The process is called **pasteurization**.

KOCH. In 1882, the German physician Robert Koch isolated and grew (cultured) bacteria in order to study them. He identified the germ causing tuberculosis. Koch also found that bacteria in water and food transmit cholera, which can be prevented by keeping the food and water germ-free.

LISTER. In 1865, Joseph Lister, a British surgeon, first used strong chemicals (antiseptics) to kill bacteria in operating rooms. Patients were thus safeguarded from infections during and after surgery.

MORTON. In 1846, William T. G. Morton, an American dentist, used ether as an anesthetic (painkiller). He proved that reducing pain during surgery prevents shock and speeds recovery.

INFO CHECK

1. Why do you think the Industrial Revolution gave rise to so many scientific and medical advances?

2. Which 19th-century scientist best fits the following description? This person developed new ideas about the origins of plants and animals and is regarded as the founder of the study of evolution.

3. Identify the 19th-century scientists who discovered various connections between germs and disease.

IV. CULTURAL ADVANCES

The work of 19th-century painters, musicians, and writers reflected changed lifestyles and attitudes brought about by the social, political, and economic revolutions

For a summary of this artistic output, see the tables on page 185.

Marie Curie at work in her laboratory, 1905

Goya's *The 3rd of May,* showing Spanish patriots executed by Napoelon's troops

A. Painting

ROMANTICISM AND NATIONALISM. The painter Jean François Millet painted romantic scenes of peasant life, such as *The Angelus*. (The **romantic style** drew on emotion, drama, and, sometimes, fantasy, and was often associated with depictions of nationalism.)

One of the most striking nationalist paintings is Francisco Goya's *The 3rd of May,* which shows Napoleon's soldiers executing Spanish patriots.

REALISM. Realism replaced romanticism's idealized subjects by depicting scenes as people saw them. Gustave Courbet's matter-of-fact treatment of workers in *The Stone-Breakers* contrasts sharply with Millet's treatment of a similar theme.

Honoré Daumier showed the effects of the hard life of Parisian workers in his *Third Class Carriage*.

IMPRESSIONISM. Impressionism, developed during the 1860s and 1870s, was concerned with how the eye registers the play of light on objects. *The River* by Claude Monet shows how insubstantial objects reflected in water can look.

Working people of Paris, in Daumier's realistic *Third Class Carriage*

POSTIMPRESSIONISM. Postimpressionism was concerned with form and space rather than actual appearance. Paul Cézanne exemplified this style in his *Mont Sainte-Victoire,* which shows a landscape broken up into blocks of light and color.

B. Music

Romanticism and nationalism also affected music. Many of Ludwig van Beethoven's compositions are idealistic, emotional, and dramatic. His Third Symphony (*Eroica*) idealized Napoleon's conquests.

PAINTERS OF THE 19TH CENTURY

John Constable	England	1776–1837	Romanticism	*Stoke-by-Nayland*
J. M. W. Turner	England	1775–1851	Romanticism	*The Slave Ship*
Jean François Millet	France	1814–1875	Romanticism	*The Gleaners*
Francisco Goya	Spain	1746–1828	Romanticism	*The 3rd of May*
Eugène Delacroix	France	1798–1863	Romanticism	*Massacre at Chios*
Gustave Courbet	France	1819–1877	Romanticism	*The Woman With a Parrot*
Honoré Daumier	France	1808–1879	Realism	*The Washerwoman*
Édouard Manet	France	1832–1883	Realism	*Death of Maximilian*
Claude Monet	France	1840–1926	Impressionism	*Water Lilies*
Pierre-Auguste Renoir	France	1841–1919	Impressionism	*La Moulin de la Galette*
Edgar Degas	France	1834–1917	Impressionism	*Jockeys*
Paul Cézanne	France	1839–1906	Postimpressionism	*The Clockmaker*
Vincent van Gogh	Netherlands	1853–1890	Postimpressionism	*The Starry Night*
Paul Gauguin	France	1848–1903	Postimpressionism	*Two Tahitian Women*
Georges Seurat	France	1859–1891	Postimpressionism	*Sunday Afternoon on the Island of La Grande Jatte*

COMPOSERS OF THE 19TH CENTURY

Ludwig van Beethoven	Germany	1770–1827	Romanticism	The Ninth Symphony *(Choral)*
Richard Wagner	Germany	1813–1883	Romanticism	*Ring of the Nibelung*
Giuseppe Verdi	Italy	1813–1901	Romanticism	*Il Trovatore*
Peter Ilich Tchaikovsky	Russia	1840–1893	Romanticism	*1812 Overture*
Jean Sibelius	Finland	1865–1957	Romanticism	*Finlandia*
Edvard Grieg	Norway	1843–1907	Romanticism	*Peer Gynt Suite*
Claude Debussy	France	1862–1918	Impressionism	*La Mer*

WRITERS OF THE 19TH CENTURY

Percy Bysshe Shelley	England	1792–1822	Romanticism	*Adonais*
John Keats	England	1795–1821	Romanticism	"Ode on a Grecian Urn"
Samuel Taylor Coleridge	England	1772–1834	Romanticism	"The Rime of the Ancient Mariner"
William Wordsworth	England	1770–1850	Romanticism	*The Prelude*
Sir Walter Scott	Scotland	1771–1832	Romanticism	*Ivanhoe*
Alfred, Lord Tennyson	England	1809–1892	Romanticism	*Idylls of the King*
Alexandre Dumas	France	1802–1870	Romanticism	*The Three Musketeers*
James Fenimore Cooper	United States	1789–1851	Romanticism	*The Last of the Mohicans*
Honoré de Balzac	France	1799–1850	Realism	*Droll Stories*
Gustave Flaubert	France	1821–1880	Realism	*Madame Bovary*
Émile Zola	France	1840–1902	Realism	*Nana*
Charles Dickens	England	1812–1870	Realism	*David Copperfield*
Mary Ann Evans (George Eliot)	England	1819–1880	Realism	*Middlemarch: A Study of Provincial Life*
George Bernard Shaw	Ireland	1856–1950	Realism	*Arms and the Man*
Henrik Ibsen	Norway	1828–1906	Realism	*A Doll's House*
Leo Tolstoy	Russia	1828–1910	Realism	*Anna Karenina*
Samuel Clemens (Mark Twain)	United States	1835–1910	Realism	*Huckleberry Finn*

Giuseppe Verdi composed such great operas as *Rigoletto, Aida,* and *La Traviata.* A strong nationalist, he supported the Italian struggle for unification and often portrayed it in disguised form in his operas.

Toward the end of the century, some musicians, notably Claude Debussy, adopted the impressionistic style. They wanted their compositions to create poetic scenes and images.

C. Literature

ROMANTICISM. Romantic literature replaced the reason and balance of the Enlightenment with strong emotions, dreams, and fantasy. E. T. A. Hoffmann wrote bizarre tales involving figures from German folklore.

The young liberal poet Percy Bysshe Shelley celebrated the freedom of the human spirit in *Prometheus Unbound.* William Wordsworth wrote of simple people and natural beauty in a collection called *Lyrical Ballads.*

REALISM. Realistic writing began in France. Honoré de Balzac's series of novels, *The Human Comedy,* portrayed people savagely competing for wealth and power.

Science had shown realists that human life may be determined by outside forces. In his novel *War and Peace,* Leo Tolstoy traced the effects of Napoleon's Russian campaign on five families. At the same time, he demonstrated that great leaders are not really free but rather act according to "historical necessity."

The dramatist George Bernard Shaw criticized social attitudes and customs in such plays as *Major Barbara* and *Pygmalion.*

INFO CHECK

1. Explain the difference between romanticism and realism. How were they used to reflect political ideas and social conditions?

2. Would you describe Millet, Beethoven, and Hoffmann as romanticists or realists? Give reasons for your response.

V. INDUSTRIALISM

After the Industrial Revolution, extreme poverty became acute in the cities and countrysides of western Europe and the United States. People began to question traditional ideas about society, economics, and government.

A. Socialism

Socialists wanted factories, mines, and farms to be owned by the people in common. Necessities could then be produced at prices everyone could afford. Moreover, governments had an obligation to serve the needs of all people rather than an elite of wealthy landowners and industrialists.

UTOPIANISM. Some people, called **utopians,** believed that ideal societies were possible. A wealthy businessman, Robert Owen (1771–1858), bought a mill in Scotland and provided safe, healthful conditions for his employees. He also turned nearby New Lanark into a model community, with good schools and a high living standard.

Owen's other experimental communities, however, were less successful. Most people were unable to work sufficiently well together for the common good.

Exercise class in Robert Owen's model community at New Lanark, Scotland

BLANC. The French newspaperman Louis Blanc (1811–1882) attacked the government for favoring capitalists. Government should set up workshops employing all workers, he said, and, eventually, the workers would run the workshops. (National workshops were set up in 1846, but they failed.) Moreover, workers should produce according to their ability and be paid according to their needs.

In the 20th and 21st centuries, Britain, Germany, Norway, Sweden, Denmark, and France have sometimes elected Socialist-led governments.

B. Communist Movement

MARX AND ENGELS. In 1848, Karl Marx, a German living in London, and Friedrich Engels published the *Communist Manifesto*. This pamphlet outlined a belief that came to be known as scientific socialism, or **communism**.

Class Struggle. Marx blamed capitalism for the poverty of workers. Business owners put up the money (capital), brought workers, machines, and raw materials together, and produced goods. Workers earned small wages. Marx said that it was unfair for workers to receive less than capitalists; **proletarians** (workers) and the **bourgeoisie** (capitalists) were enemies in a "class struggle."

Revolution. Marx urged workers everywhere to rebel against capitalism and seize the sources of wealth. Everyone would then share equally, businesses would cooperate rather than compete, people would be free, and government would no longer be necessary.

Limited Acceptance. These theories appealed to those who had no other solution for poverty and unemployment. But the worldwide revolution never took place, partly because living standards for most Westerners began to rise.

Communism was more widely accepted where poverty was widespread. Russia and China, for example, adopted Communist governments, but the governments in both countries remained dictatorships.

C. Labor Union Movement

ORGANIZING. Workers in the same occupation formed organizations called **labor unions**, which could put united pressure on employers to raise wages and improve working conditions.

TACTICS. Union representatives presented their case to an employer in a process called **collective bargaining**. If an employer did nothing, the workers might strike (stop working). Sometimes, a union organized a boycott of the employer's product until an agreement was reached.

To stop a strike, an employer might hire strikebreakers (replacements) or call in the police or military troops. Some employers sent a **blacklist** of union activists to other employers, urging them not to hire the workers named.

HISTORY. British workers won the right to unionize in 1824. Until 1871, however, the government and factory owners forcefully discouraged unions.

Unions became strong in France in the 1880s and in Germany in the 1890s. In Russia, industrialization did not take hold until the late 1800s. As a result, unions became important only shortly before the 1917 revolution. By 1922, a Communist government would rule the newly organized Soviet Union.

In the United States, unions became legal in 1842. In 1869, workers formed the Knights of Labor, whose members included skilled and unskilled workers, women, and African Americans. The Knights of Labor demanded an eight-hour workday and the banning of child labor but declined before achieving these aims.

In 1886, the American Federation of Labor (AFL) was founded. It increased its already considerable power by joining with the Congress of Industrial Organizations (CIO) in 1955. Today, about 75 percent of all union members belong to the AFL-CIO.

POLITICAL INFLUENCE. In 1900, British liberals and trade unionists formed the Labour Party, which became a major force in British politics. Labor unions on the Continent also developed political parties whose candidates were elected to legislative bodies.

After the 1920s, unions and other reform groups influenced their governments to pass laws benefiting workers. Some protected children. Others set maximum work hours, minimum wages, and sanitary and safe factory conditions. Still others provided payments for on-the-job injuries, old-age pensions, and unemployment insurance.

D. Governmental Reforms

POLITICAL REFORMS IN BRITAIN. In Britain, the Reform Bill of 1832 gave **suffrage** (the right to vote) to all males with a certain amount of property. In 1885, Parliament gave working-class males the right to vote. Women won suffrage in 1918.

Now that the poor and uneducated could vote, reformers realized that they should be educated in order to make responsible political decisions. In 1880, the Elementary Education Act granted all children an elementary school education. Parliament also gave Catholics and non-Anglican Protestants the right to political activity.

LABOR REFORMS IN BRITAIN. In 1883, Parliament's Select Committee on Child Labor in Parliament limited the working day of children aged 9 to 12 to 8 hours and those 13 to 17 to 12 hours. There were so many child workers that, when they left for the day, mills and factories closed. Thus, the workday for adults was also shortened.

SUFFRAGE IN THE UNITED STATES. By 1850, most states had granted suffrage to all white men. In 1870, the 15th Amendment extended it to all men regardless of race or national origin. Women gained the vote in 1920.

U.S. PROGRESSIVES. American social reformers in the early 1900s were known as Progressives. So-called muckrakers wrote newspaper articles about unhealthful working conditions, slum life, and government corruption. The Progressives brought about reforms to protect child workers, establish social security benefits for all workers, and give voters the power to remove crooked politicians from office.

CHANGES IN FRANCE. Napoleon Bonaparte allowed the French people little or no political freedom but brought about many reforms: a new law code, a public school system, a fair taxation system, and peasant ownership of land.

Paris Commune. When Louis Napoleon's dictatorship ended, the National Assembly wanted to restore the monarchy. The workers of Paris rebelled and set up the Paris Commune in 1871. They demanded higher wages and a shorter workday. Although the rebellion failed, the government passed many reforms that the Communards had fought for.

E. Global Migrations

During the 19th century, many Europeans emigrated from their countries. Most went to the United States, in what is called the Atlantic Migration. Some were seeking work in U.S. cities, while others were escaping revolutions or religious persecution. Still others fled from famines.

GREAT FAMINE. In the mid-1800s, a great famine devastated Ireland, which was then part of Britain. Wealthy Protestant Irish families owned the great estates where poor Catholics worked. The landowners gave their tenant farmers only small plots on which to plant food.

The peasants raised potatoes, which are easy to plant and care for, take up little room, and thrive in moist climates like Ireland's.

From 1845 to 1851, a fungus originating in America destroyed the potato crops. Almost 25 percent of the Irish population starved or died from malnutrition.

At first, British charities opened soup kitchens in Ireland. When a banking crisis arose, however, all aid stopped, and British leaders turned the problem over to the Irish Poor Law system. It was authorized to set up workhouses but no facilities for the sick and dying who were too weak to work.

The British government did nothing to stop estate owners from evicting starving tenants unable to pay their rent. Indeed, they were often driven from their homes by troops.

F. Malthusian Economics

Thomas Malthus (1766–1834) and David Ricardo (1772–1823) were influential economic theorists. Malthus's *Essay on the Principle of Population* pointed out that human populations always increase faster than the amount of food they need. To prevent famine, people should have fewer children.

Based on Malthus's ideas, Ricardo's theory of "the iron rule of wages" stated that as the population increased, more people would need work. To compete for a limited number of jobs, they would accept very low wages. They would not starve, but they would have to work long and hard on whatever terms their employers set.

G. Social Darwinism

People who benefited from free competition accepted these theories while ignoring the possibility that large groups of people might not starve if the world's wealth were shared. The ideas of the English philosopher Herbert Spencer (1820–1903) encouraged such thinking.

Influenced by Darwin's theories about evolution, Spencer felt that societies, like animals, develop from primitive to more complex states. Economic competition stimulated progress by promoting the "survival of the fittest." (Applying the theory of nat-

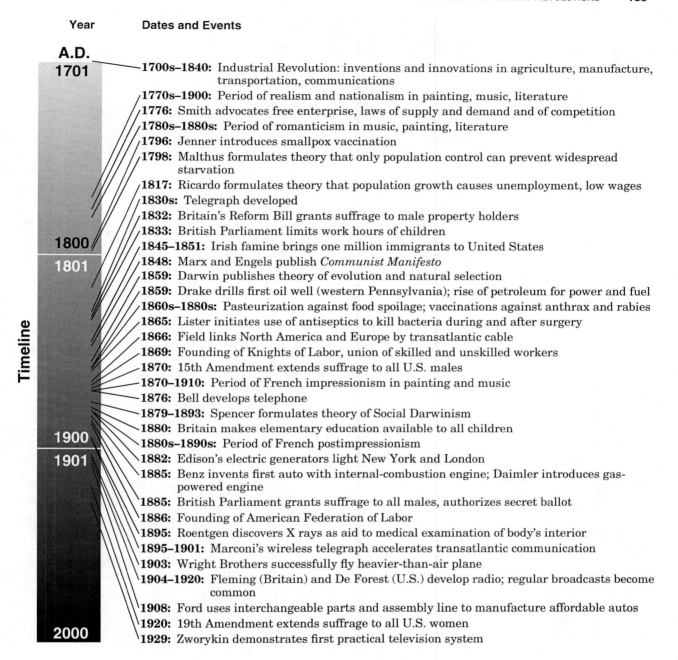

Year	Dates and Events

A.D.
1701

1800

1801

Timeline

1900

1901

2000

1700s–1840: Industrial Revolution: inventions and innovations in agriculture, manufacture, transportation, communications

1770s–1900: Period of realism and nationalism in painting, music, literature

1776: Smith advocates free enterprise, laws of supply and demand and of competition

1780s–1880s: Period of romanticism in music, painting, literature

1796: Jenner introduces smallpox vaccination

1798: Malthus formulates theory that only population control can prevent widespread starvation

1817: Ricardo formulates theory that population growth causes unemployment, low wages

1830s: Telegraph developed

1832: Britain's Reform Bill grants suffrage to male property holders

1833: British Parliament limits work hours of children

1845–1851: Irish famine brings one million immigrants to United States

1848: Marx and Engels publish *Communist Manifesto*

1859: Darwin publishes theory of evolution and natural selection

1859: Drake drills first oil well (western Pennsylvania); rise of petroleum for power and fuel

1860s–1880s: Pasteurization against food spoilage; vaccinations against anthrax and rabies

1865: Lister initiates use of antiseptics to kill bacteria during and after surgery

1866: Field links North America and Europe by transatlantic cable

1869: Founding of Knights of Labor, union of skilled and unskilled workers

1870: 15th Amendment extends suffrage to all U.S. males

1870–1910: Period of French impressionism in painting and music

1876: Bell develops telephone

1879–1893: Spencer formulates theory of Social Darwinism

1880: Britain makes elementary education available to all children

1880s–1890s: Period of French postimpressionism

1882: Edison's electric generators light New York and London

1885: Benz invents first auto with internal-combustion engine; Daimler introduces gas-powered engine

1885: British Parliament grants suffrage to all males, authorizes secret ballot

1886: Founding of American Federation of Labor

1895: Roentgen discovers X rays as aid to medical examination of body's interior

1895–1901: Marconi's wireless telegraph accelerates transatlantic communication

1903: Wright Brothers successfully fly heavier-than-air plane

1904–1920: Fleming (Britain) and De Forest (U.S.) develop radio; regular broadcasts become common

1908: Ford uses interchangeable parts and assembly line to manufacture affordable autos

1920: 19th Amendment extends suffrage to all U.S. women

1929: Zworykin demonstrates first practical television system

ural selection to human society is called **Social Darwinism**.) Eventually, society would consist of only the strongest and most productive people. Spencer's ideas particularly appealed to leaders who favored taking over weak countries and exploiting their resources.

INFO CHECK

1. How did socialism, communism, and the labor union movement respond to the problems arising from the Industrial Revolution? Why was communism regarded as the most revolutionary and potentially violent solution?

2. Why do you think the process of reform was less democratic in France than in Britain and the United States?

3. Explain why you AGREE or DISAGREE with the ideas of Thomas Malthus and David Ricardo.

4. How did the Industrial Revolution lead to the growth of a global economy?

CHAPTER REVIEW

Multiple Choice

1. With regard to agriculture, the beginning of which practice ended the other?

   1. technology—crop rotation
   2. open-field system—animal grazing
   3. enclosure movement—open-field system
   4. crop specialization—seed drill

2. The people who were negatively affected by the agricultural revolution were

   1. small farmers
   2. farmers having no land
   3. poor craftsman
   4. wealthy landowners.

3. In *An Inquiry Into the Nature and Causes of the Wealth of Nations,* Adam Smith presented the idea that government should

   1. not regulate or attempt to control business activity
   2. regulate or attempt to control business activity
   3. run all business
   4. run only "heavy-metal" industries.

4. Fulton is to steamboats as

   1. Benz is to airplanes
   2. Daimler is to steam engines
   3. Bell is to oil wells
   4. Morse is to the telegraph.

5. Charles Darwin's concept of evolution states that plants and animals that survive

   1. have naturally changed or adapted to their environment
   2. do so because the environment changes to suit their needs
   3. are developed by scientists to fit the environment
   4. evolve from lab tests.

6. Pasteur, Koch, and Lister all developed methods to use, prevent, or destroy

   1. the common cold
   2. bacteria
   3. diseases
   4. allergies.

7. The style of painting used by Goya and Delacroix in treating nationalistic themes was

   1. realism
   2. impressionism
   3. romanticism
   4. postimpressionism.

8. The economic theory that government should not regulate the marketplace or businesspersons is

   1. laissez-faire
   2. mercantilism
   3. capitalism
   4. socialism.

9. A person who believes that the people as a whole should own businesses and not produce for others' profit is a

   1. reactionary
   2. liberal
   3. radical
   4. socialist.

10. The photograph on page 180 illustrates that

    1. British children were given opportunity to work after school
    2. British factories during the 19th century were often cramped and unsafe
    3. more males than females worked in 19th-century British factories
    4. working conditions in British factories had improved by the 19th century.

11. The painting on the top of page 184 shows a style of art known as

    1. romantic
    2. abstract
    3. realistic
    4. impressionistic.

12. The painting on the bottom of page 184 strongly suggests that

    1. railroad travel in 19th-century France provided equal accommodations for everyone
    2. public transportation in 19th-century France was free but very crowded
    3. 19th-century French women using the railroads were required to nurse their babies in special cars separated from other passengers
    4. some artists used their work to protest abuses of the Industrial Revolution.

Thematic Essays

1. The Communists and the Utopians both developed plans to deal with social and economic problems of the working class. *Task:* Using historical examples, compare and contrast the methods proposed or adopted by each group to help workers. Include in your answer economic, social, and political examples.

2. In the 18th and 19th centuries, science and technology developed methods, materials, and inventions to make life and work easier, safer, and healthier for the common person. *Task:* Select and describe two examples that support this statement.

Document-Based Questions

Use the documents and your knowledge of Global History and Geography to answer the questions.

1. Study the painting on the bottom of page 184. The painting's title is *Third Class Carriage.* Describe the feelings of the people shown in this picture. Do you think they are happy or sad? Why?

2. Adam Smith wrote in the *Wealth of Nations:*

"By pursuing his own interest, he frequently promotes that of the society more effectually [better] that when he intends to promote it. I have never known much good done by those who affected to trade for the public good. . . . Every individual can in his local situation judge much better than any statesman or lawgiver can do for him."

Give two reasons, according to Adam Smith, why government should not regulate business and business activities.

3. From a report to the House of Commons:

"Were the children [beaten]?—Yes. With what?—A strap; . . . sometimes he got a chain and chained them, and strapped them all down the room. . . . Were the children excessively fatigued at the time?—Yes, it was in the afternoon . . . . You dragged the baskets?—Yes: down the rooms to where they worked. . . . It has had the effect of pulling your shoulders out?—Yes . . . . Were you heated with your employment . . . ?—No, it was not so very hot as in the summertime; in the wintertime they were obliged to have the windows open, it made no matter what the weather was, and sometimes we got very severe colds in frost and snow. . . . Suppose you had not been on time in the morning at these mills, what would have been the consequences?—We should have been quartered. What do you mean by that? If we were a quarter hour late, they would take off a half an hour. . . ."

Select and describe any *three* examples of how child workers were abused.

Document-Based Essay

Task: Using economic, political, and social examples, explain why workers were treated so poorly in early factories and mines.

19

Growth of Imperialism

I. MODERN IMPERIALISM

Imperialism is the policy of extending a nation's political and economic dominance over another territory or country. The Age of Imperialism lasted from the 1850s to about 1910.

Many nations, made wealthy by the Industrial Revolution, sought to ensure their prosperity by securing available raw materials for their factories and new markets for their products. Businesspeople wanted to invest their profits in new places. Colonies met all these needs.

Imperialism also increased a nation's military and political strength. Colonies could serve as supply bases and fortifications. Nationalistic countries competed with one another to acquire colonies as a source of strength, wealth, and prestige.

In addition, Westerners who believed in the superiority of their civilization regarded colonization as an opportunity to give non-Westerners the benefits of Western culture. It was also a chance to convert non-Christians.

INFO CHECK

1. Define imperialism.

2. State one economic and one political reason for imperialism.

3. Do you agree with the Western nations' justification for imperialism? Why or why not?

Colonial Empires, 1914

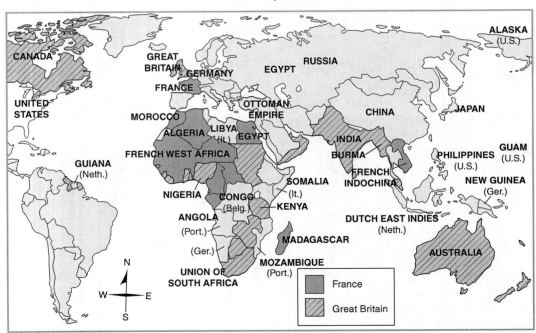

II. EMPIRE BUILDING

A. The British in India

BRITISH EAST INDIA COMPANY. The Seven Years' War (1756–1763) left Britain the major power in India. Princes who ruled portions not governed directly by Britain usually signed treaties placing their states under British protection.

With some restrictions, the East India Company ruled India until 1857. It exported Indian cotton, silk, and sugar. Within India, it built telegraph, railroad, and irrigation systems and set up a postal service and regional schools. It supervised the sepoy units defending India. British missionaries arrived to convert Hindus and Muslims.

STATUS OF INDIANS. The East India Company denied Indians equal rights and opportunities. Factory workers and servants earned low wages. Farmers got very little for their produce. Indians could not hold important government positions. Moreover, schools taught English and Western ideas while ignoring Indian history and advanced culture. After the Sepoy Mutiny of 1857, the British government took over the administration of India.

BRITISH RULE. The British government appointed a viceroy (governor) to head the Indian government. An Indian Civil Service (ICS) was created. Although the ICS employed Indians and Anglo-Indians in clerical and other positions, higher level administrators were British.

B. Imperialism in Africa

THE FRENCH. Claiming the need to stop pirating in the Mediterranean, the French colonized Algeria in 1830. In 1878, France gained control of Tunisia. A Franco-German dispute about Morocco

European Imperialism in Africa, 1914

ended in France's favor in 1911. France also acquired vast areas of West and Central Africa.

BRITISH HOLDINGS. Great Britain took over the largest portion of Africa, most of it in the eastern half. It also had scattered holdings in the west—Nigeria, the Gold Coast, Sierra Leone, and Gambia.

Suez Canal. In 1869, a French-Ottoman company built the Suez Canal in Egypt to link the Mediterranean and Red seas. It shortened the voyage of British ships to and from India. The Turkish ruler of Egypt owned the largest number of shares. When Britain bought those shares in 1875, it gained control of the canal. Because of its strategic location, Egypt was brought under British protection.

Central and East Africa. Britain gained control of British East Africa (now Kenya) in the 1880s and Uganda in the 1890s. In 1898, it also colonized Sudan, south of Egypt.

South Africa. In the early 1800s during the Napoleonic Wars, Britain took South Africa from the Dutch. The resentful Boers (Dutch farmers) in the area moved north and, in doing so, invaded an empire created by the Zulu leader, Shaka.

The Boers, aided by modern weapons and British support, defeated the Zulus. They then set up the independent Boer republics of the Transvaal and Orange Free State (now part of the Republic of South Africa).

In 1867 and 1868, rich diamond and gold deposits were found near the Boer territory. Cecil Rhodes, a diamond expert and promoter of British imperialism in Africa, then expanded British rule into what are now Zimbabwe and Zambia.

In 1899, the Boers rebelled against British rule. After three years, the British won but granted the Boers more political rights to prevent future unrest. In 1910, Boer and British areas were merged to form the Union of South Africa.

GERMANY AND ITALY. In the 1880s, Germany claimed German East Africa (now Tanzania) and acquired Togo and the Cameroons in West Africa. In 1895, Portugal, in payment for a loan, gave Germany the part of Angola now called Namibia.

Italy took over Libya in North Africa and part of Somalia in the northeast.

PORTUGAL AND SPAIN. Spain held several territories in the north and south of present-day Morocco.

Portugal's African colonies were Guinea-Bissau, Angola, and Mozambique.

BELGIUM. King Leopold of Belgium owned as his personal colony the large portion of central Africa known as the Congo. Mistreatment of inhabitants by the king's agents led the Belgian government to take over the colony in 1908.

INDEPENDENT COUNTRIES. Throughout Africa's colonial period, Ethiopia and Liberia remained independent. Liberia was founded in the 1820s by former U.S. slaves.

C. Berlin Conference

In 1884–1885, European imperialist powers, Turkey, and the United States held the Berlin Conference to set rules for dividing Africa (as well as regions in Asia and the Pacific). No Africans were present.

Before the conference, a nation might gain a colony by establishing a historical claim— for example, that its citizens had once inhabited and governed the area. After the conference, a nation merely had to make a formal announcement for its claim to a colony to be recognized.

The Berlin Conference recognized three kinds of imperial control:

- A nation could own and govern a colony directly.

- It could declare an area a **sphere of influence**, where it had sole investment and trading rights.

- It could make a weak country into a **protectorate**, which retained its ruler but observed policies set by the imperialist power.

Colonial boundaries rarely respected tribal locations or took local rivalries into account.

D. Spheres of Influence in China

China remained unindustrialized, partly owing to its **ethnocentrism**. That is, its emperors, the Manchus, were proud of their rich culture and looked down on Western technology. Lacking modern weapons, China could not resist the demands of Western imperialists who wanted more trading privileges there.

For Westerners, China was a market for European goods, and its huge population a potential source of cheap workers. European businesspeople also hoped to develop China's natural resources.

OPIUM WAR. Britain had an unfavorable **balance of trade** with China: it bought more than it

Spheres of Influence in 19th-Century China

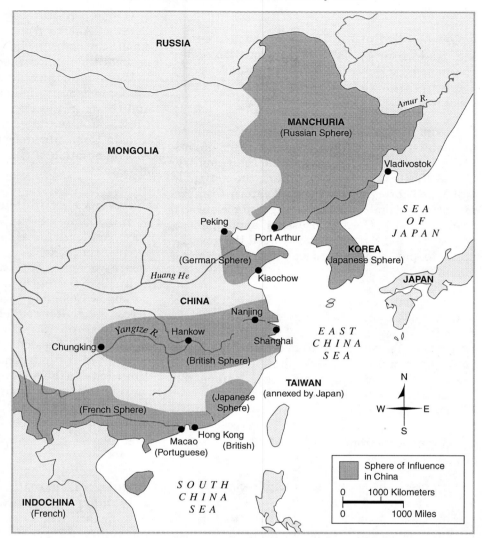

sold. Therefore, British traders began to sell opium to the Chinese, many of whom became addicted while the traders grew rich. When Chinese officials tried to end the opium trade in 1839, British ships invaded China. Unable to defend itself, China was forced to sign the Treaty of Nanjing in 1842.

Additional Rights. Traditionally, foreign traders had lived and worked only in the port of Canton. Under the treaty, China had to open five more ports and pay a large sum to Britain. China ceded the island of Hong Kong to Britain and reduced tariffs. It also granted foreigners **extraterritorial rights**, whereby those accused of crimes would be tried by their own courts and laws rather than those of China.

TAIPING REBELLION. In 1850, rebels disgusted with China's weakness tried to overthrow the Manchu Dynasty. The government asked the Western nations for help, but even with their aid, it took 14 years to crush the Taiping Rebellion.

In 1856, France and Britain, wanting more trading rights, attacked China and easily defeated it (China was still preoccupied with its rebels). Under the Treaty of Tiensin (1858), China opened 11 more ports and allowed foreign traders and Christian missionaries to move into the interior. The importation of opium was also made legal.

LOSS OF TERRITORY. Eventually, China lost its colonies too. Britain took Burma, France took Indochina (Cambodia, Laos, and Vietnam), and Russia gained territory in the north as well as the right to run a railroad through Manchuria.

In 1894, China and Japan fought the Sino-Japanese War over Korea. Japan won in 1895 and gained Taiwan and some islands near to home.

Korea remained independent, but Japan retained influence over it.

OPEN DOOR POLICY. To protect the prosperous U.S. trade with China, Secretary of State John Hay asked the European nations and Japan to respect one another's trading rights there. This proposal was called the Open Door Policy.

BOXER REBELLION. In 1900, a group of Chinese nationalists, the "Righteous and Harmonious Fists," tried to oust foreigners from their country. Called "Boxers" by the Westerners, the nationalists killed foreigners and pro-Western Chinese and attacked embassies in Bejing. A force of U.S., British, French, German, Russian, and Japanese troops crushed the rebels and forced the government to pay a huge **indemnity** (punishment money).

SUN YIXIAN. Chinese patriots wanted China to industrialize, eliminate foreign influences, and do more for its own people. In 1911, a revolution led by Dr. Sun Yixian (Yat-sen) overthrew the Manchus and made China a republic. The Western-educated Sun had sought support in Europe, the United States, and Japan.

Sun advocated "Three Principles of the People":

- Free China from foreign control.
- Establish a democracy.
- Improve the economy through socialism.

The Kuomintang (Nationalist party) tried to follow Sun's advice but had a difficult time doing so.

E. U.S. Imperialism

U.S. imperialism began in 1867 with the purchase of Alaska from Russia. Five years later, American planters in Hawaii led a revolt that brought the islands under U.S. control.

By winning the Spanish-American War (1898), the United States gained the Philippine Islands and Guam in the Pacific and Puerto Rico in the Caribbean. The United States had entered the war to help Cuba win independence from Spain, but U.S. domination of Cuban affairs continued long afterward.

PANAMA CANAL. After the Spanish-American War, the United States decided that a canal was necessary for national defense. Warships stationed in the Atlantic took too long to reach the Pacific, where the new U.S. territories were.

In 1903, Secretary of State John Hay failed to persuade Colombia to let a U.S. canal be built across its territory of Panama, the narrowest part of Central America. In November 1903, Panama revolted, and President Theodore Roosevelt quickly recognized its independence. Panama gave the United States the right to build and operate a canal and govern its surrounding area, the Panama Canal Zone. In return, the United States paid Panama an annual fee. The canal officially opened in 1920. On the last day of 1999, Panama took over its operation.

DOLLAR DIPLOMACY. The policy called **Dollar Diplomacy** encouraged U.S. businesses to build new factories in developing countries. If local instability became a threat to those business

Cartoon showing Western imperialists pulling at China from all directions—for China's own good!

Theodore Roosevelt, watchdog of economic welfare in the Americas—and debt collector

interests, the U.S. government would send in troops to protect American lives and property.

Between 1912 and 1934, Dollar Diplomacy became an excuse for U.S. interventions in Nicaragua, Haiti, the Dominican Republic, Mexico, and several other Latin American countries.

VIRGIN ISLANDS. In 1917, the United States acquired its last foreign territory when it bought the Virgin Islands from Denmark.

III. PERSPECTIVES ON IMPERIALISM

IMPOSING FOREIGN WAYS. As industrialization modernized, strengthened, and enriched colonized countries, it also disrupted their traditional ways of life. Before industrialization, native inhabitants lived in the same villages where they farmed and did craftwork. Suddenly, many of them had to learn new kinds of work and move away from their families to do it.

NEW GOVERNMENTS AND RELIGIONS. European officials replaced traditional rulers and introduced technology that made traditional methods seem worthless. Natives were taught that their country's welfare was less important than that of their new masters. Missionaries preached against local religions and stressed the importance of European clothes, languages, and behavior.

DISCRIMINATION AND RESENTMENT. Some natives lived better than they had before and eagerly adopted European ways. But the colonized people seldom competed successfully with Europeans in the quest for wealth and power. For the most part, Europeans regarded them as inferiors.

Eventually, most native people began to demand equal rights. Others, usually Western-educated, became openly nationalistic and clamored for renewed independence.

EFFECTS ON COLONIAL POWERS. Colonial resources and products brought great wealth to individuals in the home countries and to their national economies as well. Many Europeans built business or government careers in the colonies. Native music, art, and literature enriched Western culture, and evidence of ancient civilizations in Asia, Africa, and Latin America advanced Western learning.

Imperialism also altered relationships among the Western powers. Britain, preoccupied with governing its colonies, became less involved with its European neighbors. After unification, Germany had become strong. Its only rival on the Continent was France.

Russia occupied territory along its borders. The Western powers attempted to keep Russia from growing too powerful in South Asia.

TRIPLE ALLIANCE. To limit French power, Bismarck, Germany's chancellor, set up the Triple Alliance in 1882. This agreement among Germany,

Italy, and Austria was intended to isolate France from Europe's other major powers.

Aggression. When Wilhelm II became German kaiser in 1889, he dismissed Bismarck and began to make the Triple Alliance into an aggressive rather than restraining force. The buildup of the German navy alarmed Britain, which then began to build more ships itself.

Reaction. Feeling threatened by Germany's military buildup, France entered the arms race. Germany's smaller neighbors also began to feel unsafe.

INFO CHECK

1. Select one Western European nation that engaged in imperialism in the 19th and 20th centuries. Describe how it built an empire.

2. Define or identify: Sepoy Mutiny, Boer War, Opium War, Open Door Policy, Boxer Rebellion.

3. Explain the difference between a colony, a sphere of influence, and a protectorate.

4. Explain the role of Dollar Diplomacy in the building of the U.S. Empire.

IV. JAPAN AND WESTERN IMPERIALISM

After 1641, the Tokugawa Shogunate left only the port of Nagasaki open to foreign traders. Japan's isolation lasted more than 200 years, with only one Dutch trading ship arriving annually. From European books that the Dutch brought, Japanese scholars learned about Western ideas—particularly, geography, medicine, and military tactics.

A. Increased Trade

From the late 1700s on, Russian, British, French, and American officials tried and failed to establish relations with Japan. Then, in 1853, U.S. Commodore Matthew Perry sailed into Tokyo Bay with four ships. He presented Japanese officials with a

Japanese Imperialism, 1875–1910

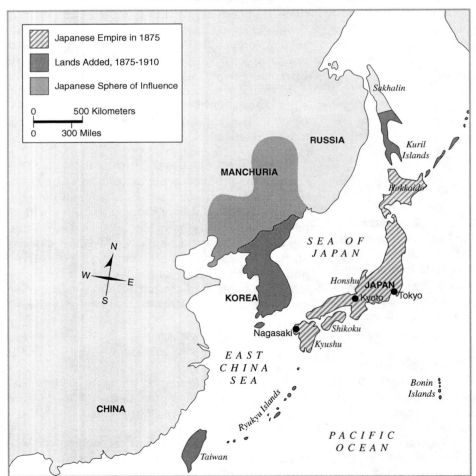

Year   **Dates and Events**

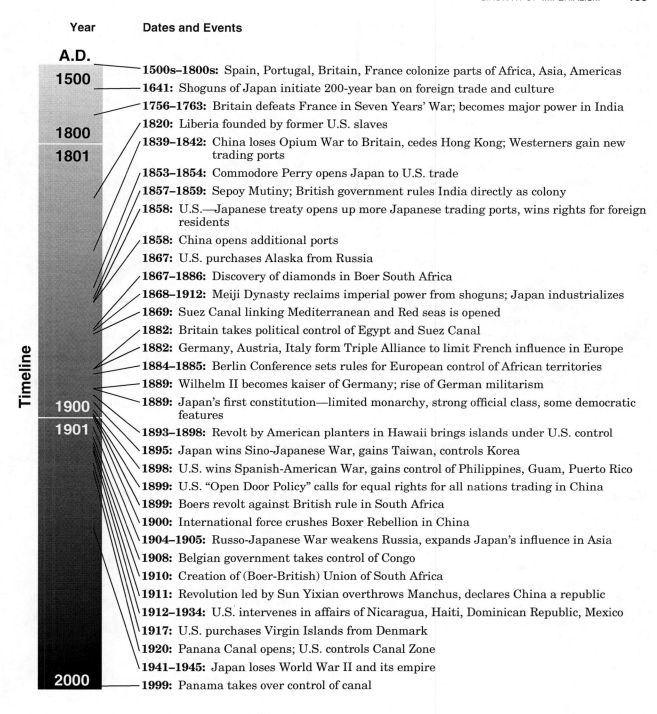

A.D.

1500

1800

1801

Timeline

1900

1901

2000

1500s–1800s: Spain, Portugal, Britain, France colonize parts of Africa, Asia, Americas

1641: Shoguns of Japan initiate 200-year ban on foreign trade and culture

1756–1763: Britain defeats France in Seven Years' War; becomes major power in India

1820: Liberia founded by former U.S. slaves

1839–1842: China loses Opium War to Britain, cedes Hong Kong; Westerners gain new trading ports

1853–1854: Commodore Perry opens Japan to U.S. trade

1857–1859: Sepoy Mutiny; British government rules India directly as colony

1858: U.S.—Japanese treaty opens up more Japanese trading ports, wins rights for foreign residents

1858: China opens additional ports

1867: U.S. purchases Alaska from Russia

1867–1886: Discovery of diamonds in Boer South Africa

1868–1912: Meiji Dynasty reclaims imperial power from shoguns; Japan industrializes

1869: Suez Canal linking Mediterranean and Red seas is opened

1882: Britain takes political control of Egypt and Suez Canal

1882: Germany, Austria, Italy form Triple Alliance to limit French influence in Europe

1884–1885: Berlin Conference sets rules for European control of African territories

1889: Wilhelm II becomes kaiser of Germany; rise of German militarism

1889: Japan's first constitution—limited monarchy, strong official class, some democratic features

1893–1898: Revolt by American planters in Hawaii brings islands under U.S. control

1895: Japan wins Sino-Japanese War, gains Taiwan, controls Korea

1898: U.S. wins Spanish-American War, gains control of Philippines, Guam, Puerto Rico

1899: U.S. "Open Door Policy" calls for equal rights for all nations trading in China

1899: Boers revolt against British rule in South Africa

1900: International force crushes Boxer Rebellion in China

1904–1905: Russo-Japanese War weakens Russia, expands Japan's influence in Asia

1908: Belgian government takes control of Congo

1910: Creation of (Boer-British) Union of South Africa

1911: Revolution led by Sun Yixian overthrows Manchus, declares China a republic

1912–1934: U.S. intervenes in affairs of Nicaragua, Haiti, Dominican Republic, Mexico

1917: U.S. purchases Virgin Islands from Denmark

1920: Panana Canal opens; U.S. controls Canal Zone

1941–1945: Japan loses World War II and its empire

1999: Panama takes over control of canal

letter from President Millard Fillmore asking for trading privileges. Perry returned the following year with more ships. Lacking modern weapons, the shogun was forced to sign a trade agreement with the United States.

American traders could now enter two Japanese ports. A resident U.S. consul served visiting American citizens and businesspeople. In 1858, a new treaty opened more ports to U.S. ships, set tariffs, and made Americans in Japan subject to U.S.

rather than Japanese laws. In return, the United States promised to help build up and modernize the Japanese army and navy. Japan made similar treaties with Britain, Russia, France, and the Netherlands.

B. Meiji Restoration

As increased contact with the West made the Japanese aware of the West's wealth and power, discontent with Tokugawa rule increased. In 1867, powerful nobles forced the shogun to resign. The following year, the emperor took power with the title of Meiji (enlightened rule). During his reign (1868–1912), Japan became strong and modernized: businesses imported new machinery, the government created a national army and navy, and new systems of communication were set up.

Japan's first constitution in 1889 created the **Diet** (parliament). The emperor, now viewed as a god, was given certain limited powers, while a small group of officials exercised real authority. Nevertheless, this strong central government permitted such democratic features as political parties.

C. Global Power

Lacking resources, Japan began colonizing nearby countries for raw materials and new markets. By winning the Sino-Japanese War, it gained control of Taiwan. Korea, officially independent, became a Japanese colony in 1910.

Russia and Japan fought the Russo-Japanese War (1904–1905) over interests in Korea and Manchuria. After Japan's victory, President Theodore Roosevelt helped negotiate the peace treaty. Japan won Russian-controlled territory in China, the southern half of Sakhalin Island, and the right to build a railroad in China. Russia recognized Japan's influence in Korea.

By participating in World War I (1914–1918), Japan gained German-owned islands in the Pacific.

During the 1930s and 1940s, Japan built the Greater East Asia Co-Prosperity Sphere as a means of uniting eastern Asia under Japanese control. Its military forces conquered much of China and Southeast Asia as well as many Pacific islands. After its defeat in World War II (1941–1945), Japan lost its empire.

INFO CHECK

1. How did Commodore Perry's visit to Japan in 1853 lead to the Meiji Restoration?

2. Explain the role of the Sino-Japanese War and the Russo-Japanese War in the rise of the Japanese Empire.

3. How was the Japanese Empire affected by World War I and World War II?

CHAPTER REVIEW

Multiple Choice

1. The Industrial Revolution encouraged imperialism because industrialized nations needed

   1. raw materials and markets
   2. investment opportunities
   3. military bases to expand their areas of conquest
   4. all of the above.

2. Until 1857, the private stock company that ruled India for profit was the

   1. Dutch West India Company
   2. Hanseatic League
   3. East India Company
   4. Merchants of Venice.

3. The Suez Canal was a vital waterway because it

   1. shortened the sailing distance between the east and west coasts of America
   2. controlled all sea travel between the Mediterranean Sea and Atlantic Ocean
   3. was the only ice-free waterway from Eastern Europe to the Atlantic Ocean
   4. shortened the sailing time from England to India.

4. South Africa was the location of many battles because

   1. imperialistic European powers sought control there
   2. European powers fought over natural resources
   3. native peoples, European immigrants, and imperialistic powers fought for control of the area and its natural resources
   4. its oil field were necessary for industrial growth.

5. The Berlin Conference illustrated that

   1. Germany dominated the Western European nations
   2. Africans' nationalistic desires were recognized by European nations
   3. the nations of the world were anxious to preserve world peace
   4. Africa was to be subject to European imperialism.

6. The superiority of Western military technology was demonstrated by the

   1. rapid defeat of the Chinese in the Opium War
   2. Taiping Rebellion

3. granting of extraterritorial rights only to European nations
4. privileges given to European merchants to trade in Canton.

7. Examples of Chinese nationalism would be

1. the Taiping Rebellion and Open Door Policy
2. the granting of extraterritorial rights and tariff reductions
3. formation of the Nationalist party and the Boxer Rebellion
4. none of the above.

8. Latin American nations were dominated by

1. Germany and its policy of expansionism
2. Russia and its policy of Pan-Slavism
3. America and its policy of Dollar Diplomacy
4. Britain and its policy of mercantilism.

9. Japanese nobles reacted to the growth of Western imperialism and the opening of China by

1. shutting out all foreign traders
2. supporting the shogun and his military advisers
3. forcing the Meiji Restoration
4. taking over Chinese and Korean territory.

10. Study the map on page 193 and choose the most accurate statement.

1. By 1914, colonies no longer existed in Africa.
2. The British and French had no colonies in 1914.
3. By 1914, imperialism had an impact on areas in both Asia and Europe.
4. France and England controlled much of Africa in 1914.

11. Which conclusion about spheres of influence in China can be reached by studying the map on page 195?

1. Industrial areas were usually included within spheres of influence.
2. Most spheres of influence were in southern China.
3. Spheres of influence tended to include coastal areas, rivers, and ports.
4. The government of China had lost control of none of its territory in the 19th century.

12. The artist who drew the cartoon on page 196 believed that

1. other nations were acting in China's best interests
2. the Chinese government was in complete control of its affairs
3. the nations of the world fought one another for preferential trade agreements

4. the way in which other nations pulled China apart and controlled it was not in China's best interests.

Thematic Essays

1. Ethnocentrism is an attitude common to all societies. *Task:* Describe how this attitude affected relations between the imperialistic nations of Europe and the peoples of China, Japan, and India. Take into consideration religious, social, and political factors.

2. Technology can have beneficial or harmful effects. *Task:* How did China and Japan view the value of Western technology?

Document-Based Questions

Use the documents and your knowledge of Global History and Geography to answer the questions.

1. Study the cartoon on page 197. Why is Theodore Roosevelt shown pulling ships and walking through oceans?

2. Japanese Prince Ito Hirobumi regarding the modernization of Japan:

" . . . We realized fully how necessary it was that the Japanese people should not only adopt Western methods but should also speedily become competent to do without the aid of foreign instruction and supervision. . . . I have always recognized the vital importance of a supremely efficient navy and army. . . ."

List the goals that the prince wants to pursue. Why is he urging this course of action?

3. From a Chinese leader's view of Japanese activities, December 10, 1874:

"Japan recently has changed to the practice of Western military methods, has imitated the West in building railways, setting up telegraph lines, opening coal and iron mines. . . . She has also sent many students to foreign countries to acquire learning and practice in the use of machinery and technology."

Describe two methods that this observer says Japan is using to modernize without being controlled by Europeans.

Document-Based Essay

Task: Using historical examples, explain why Japan, which is smaller than China, became an imperialistic nations while China remained dominated by imperialists.

Thematic Essays

1. Refer to the description of the Irish potato famine on page 188 and the following quote by Thomas Malthus to answer the question:

   "I say that the power of population is indefinitely greater than the power in the earth to produce subsistence for man. . . . Population, when unchecked, increases in a geometric ratio. Subsistence only increases in an arithmetic ratio."

   Task: In the case of the Irish potato famine, discuss whether Malthus's gloomy predictions were correct or whether other factors (social, political, economic, or cultural) contributed more to the famine.

2. Do you AGREE or DISAGREE that the majority of the world's people during the Industrial Age benefited from its new ideas, technologies, and inventions? *Task:* Include social and economic factors in your answer.

Document-Based Questions

1. Samuel Smiles in his book *Self-Help* (1859):

   "The spirit of self-help is the root of all genuine growth in the individual . . . it constitutes the true source of national vigor and strength."

   Why would this writer be opposed to labor unions?

2. Adam Smith in The Wealth of Nations:

   "Every man, as long as he does not violate the laws of justice, is left perfectly free to pursue his own interest his own way, and to bring both his industry [efforts] and capital [money] into competition with those of any other men or order of men."

   According to Smith, how will wealth be achieved? By whose efforts will wealth be achieved?

3. Adam Smith in The Division of Labour:

   "The greatest improvement in the productive powers of labour . . . seems to have been the effect of the division of labour. This great increase of the quantity of work is owing to three different circumstances . . . lastly to the invention of a great number of machines which facilitate [aid] labour and enable one man to do the work of many."

   Explain how Smith related technology to productivity.

4. Frederick Engels in Conditions of the Working Class in England (1844):

   "It is only when [a person] has visited the slums of this great city, that it dawns upon him that the inhabitants of modern London have had to sacrifice so much that is best in human nature in order to create those wonders of civilization with which their city teems. . . . Everyone exploits his neighbor with the result that the stronger tramples the weaker underfoot. The strongest of all, a tiny group of capitalists, monopolize everything while the weakest, who are in the vast majority, succumb [fall] to the most abject [deepest] poverty."

   What is the human cost of the advances of the Industrial Age and who is paying the price, according to Engels?

Document-Based Essay

Task: Using social and economic examples, explain why capitalists were able to control the lives of the majority of the people in England in the mid-1800s.

UNIT VI

Half-Century of Crisis and Achievement (1900–1945)

Year A.D.	Dates and Events
1900	**1905–1915:** Einstein's theories equating matter and energy—first step in development of nuclear power
	1914: Archduke Franz Ferdinand and wife assassinated; Central and Allied powers drawn into war
	1917: Germany renews U-boat raids on Allied (and U.S.) shipping; Zimmermann Note seeks Mexican-German alliance against U.S.; U.S. Congress declares war on Germany
1909	**1917–1922:** Russian Revolution; Communists in power; peace with Germany; creation of Soviet Union
1910	**1918:** Germans oust Kaiser Wilhem II, ask Allies for peace
	1919: Treaty of Versailles humiliates Germany; sets up new nations based on nationalism
	1919–1922: Mussolini founds Italy's Fascist party; becomes prime minister and absolute dictator
	1920s–1940s: Culture of anxiety, disillusionment ("Lost Generation," dada, cubism, surrealism)
1919	**1928:** Fleming discovers penicillin
1920	**1930s:** Great Depression causes worldwide economic disaster
	1931: Japan seizes Manchuria
	1933: As German chancellor, Hitler initiates systematic killing of Jews, other minorities, political enemies
	1934–1935: Chinese Communists' "Long March"
	1936: Formation of Rome-Berlin Axis
	1937–1945: Jian and Mao join forces to resist Japanese in China
1929	**1938:** At Munich, Britain and France appease Hitler by ceding Sudentenland to Germany
1930	**1939:** German invasion of Czechoslovakia; German-Soviet nonaggression pact; German blitzkrieg in Poland; Britain and France declare war on Germany
	1941: Japan bombs Pearl Harbor; U.S. declares war on Japan; Germany and Italy declare war on U.S.
	1942–1943: Soviets defeat Germans at Stalingrad; push them west toward Germany
	1944: D-Day; Allies invade Normandy, push Germans from France, Belgium, Netherlands
1939	**1945:** Mussolini executed; Italy signs armistice with Allies
1940	Russians enter Berlin, Hitler commits suicide, Germans surrender, war in Europe ends
	At Yalta Conference Allies plan German occupation, war crime trials, United Nations
	U.S. drops atomic bombs on Hiroshima, Nagasaki; Japan surrenders
	50 nations meet in San Francisco to organize UN; U.S. Senate approves U.S. membership
1949	**1945–1946:** Cold war begins

CHAPTER
20

Medicine, Science, and Technology in the Early 20th Century

I. MEDICAL ADVANCES

A. Infection Fighters: "Wonder Drugs"

PENICILLIN. In 1928, Scottish microbiologist Alexander Fleming discovered the infection-fighting drug penicillin. This rare mold had killed some disease bacteria that Fleming had been studying. He realized that it could also kill disease bacteria in humans but was unable to investigate further because penicillin was difficult to produce in large amounts.

In the late 1930s, several chemists at Oxford University produced enough pure penicillin to prove that it was a powerful **antibiotic**—a substance produced by one microorganism that can destroy another one.

Two of these chemists, Ernst Chain and Howard Florey, brought their techniques to the United States, where drug companies had the resources to produce large amounts of penicillin. By 1944, it was being widely used to fight infections in the wounded soldiers of World War II.

SULFA. In 1932, the German bacteriologist Gerhard Domagk discovered that a red dye, Prontosil, could cure infections in mice. Chemists soon developed a simpler form called **sulfanilamide**.

OVERUSE OF ANTIBIOTICS. The development of many "miracle drugs" followed the discovery of penicillin and sulfa. They have helped cure boils, wound infections, ear infections, tuberculosis, influenza, and bacterial meningitis.

Unfortunately, overuse of antibiotics has caused germs to build up resistance against them. Today, scientists are searching for new antibiotics that will fight drug-resistant infections.

B. Vaccines Against Disease

POLIO. Polio, or infantile paralysis, is caused by a virus that attacks the nervous system, paralyzing its victim. Children are especially susceptible to it.

In the 1950s, an American microbiologist named Jonas Salk developed a vaccine against polio. An oral vaccine produced by Albert Sabin in 1960 was even more effective. (In 1994, the nations of the Western Hemisphere were declared polio-free zones.)

OTHER DISEASES. Medical researchers produced vaccines against smallpox and such childhood diseases as measles and whooping cough. The *World Health Organization (WHO)* and the *United Nations Children's Fund (UNICEF)* set up programs to immunize children everywhere against diseases. By 1980, smallpox had been wiped out.

C. Advances in Surgery

By 1912, neurosurgery was being performed to repair damage to the nerves, brain, and spinal cord. During World War I, methods for treating wounds surgically, performing amputations, and correcting disfigurements were greatly improved. During the Spanish Civil War (1936–1939), new techniques of blood transfusion enabled surgeons to save even more lives.

The antibiotics newly available in the 1950s made surgery safer. Surgeons began to restore the functions of damaged body parts and to replace those that could not be repaired. In 1959, Dr. Åke Senning in Sweden implanted the first heart pacemaker. Dr. Christiaan Barnard of South Africa performed the first human heart transplant in 1967.

D. Mental Health

FREUD. Some physical symptoms, such as certain kinds of paralysis, seemed to have no medical causes. Patients with such symptoms were called **neurotics**. Dr. Josef Breuer showed that hypnotic suggestion could often relieve such symptoms.

Breuer's work influenced an Austrian neurologist named Sigmund Freud (1856–1939). At first, he tried various methods of hypnosis to treat neurotics. From these experiences, he developed the "talking cure," which developed into **psychoanalysis**.

In psychoanalysis, patients sit or lie down and free-associate. That is, they say whatever comes into their minds. Often, they recall their dreams.

Freud's work led him to form theories about human personality. One of the most important was that of the **unconscious**, the area of the mind that stores experiences too disturbing to think about. According to Freud, persons with such memories are often so filled with guilt that they become self-destructive or unethical. Education and punishment alone do not always result in productive and moral behavior. Freud hoped through psychoanalysis to free people from the grip of painful experiences so that they could make better use of their reasoning abilities.

Sigmund Freud, founder of psychoanalysis, 1921

JUNG. A Swiss doctor named Carl Gustav Jung (1875–1961) believed that the unconscious could have a creative and healing influence. Part of a person's unconscious is linked to the collective unconscious, which is a pool of **archetypes** (symbols and patterns common to the whole human race). For Jung, symbols and myths about rebirth and salvation show that the human mind tends naturally to heal itself. Jung's patients were encouraged to illustrate or write down their dreams so as to use the collective unconscious against mental illness.

ADLER. The Austrian Alfred Adler (1870–1937) used Freud's ideas to develop the theory of the **inferiority complex**: people with very poor opinions of themselves cannot adjust properly to society. Adler influenced mental health professionals dealing with criminals, drug addicts, and other ill-adjusted people.

VALUE OF THERAPY. The despair of many unhappy people has been relieved by various **psychotherapies** (methods of treating mental and emotional disorders). Theories about these treatments have resulted in important studies of human behavior. Psychology still helps social scientists develop methods of preventing crime and drug addiction. It has led to the establishment of local mental health agencies and such services as the National Institute of Mental Health in the United States, which trains psychologists and social workers and builds clinics and other facilities.

E. Lasting Results

Improved diet, drugs, medical techniques, and personal hygiene have extended the human life span throughout the world. Medical advances have reduced **infant mortality** (child deaths).

Public health officials are now on the alert for new viruses that threaten to cause widespread health problems. AIDS (Acquired Immune Deficiency Syndrome) has affected more than 30 million people, and scientists are still seeking ways to prevent and treat it. They are also trying to find the cause and cure of the Ebola virus.

INFO CHECK

1. Why were "wonder drugs" not made until the 20th century?

2. Define psychoanalysis and list its three pioneers. Whose theories make the most sense to you? Why?

3. Evaluate 20th century medical advances. To what extent have they helped people?

II. PURE SCIENCE AND TECHNOLOGY

A. Atomic Energy

THE CURIES. Until Marie and Pierre Curie discovered radium in 1899, physicists had thought that atoms were tiny, solid balls. The Curies observed that radium atoms do not have a constant atomic weight (the average mass of an atom in an element). Instead, they are always giving off particles of matter called electrons and protons.

PLANCK. In 1900, the German physicist Max Planck (1859–1947) discovered that atoms release their particles in uneven spurts, each of which he called a **quantum**. Planck's studies of subatomic energy (the energy of particles smaller than atoms) suggested that there is no sharp division between matter and energy.

EINSTEIN. Albert Einstein (1879–1955) developed the theory of relativity, which corrected Isaac Newton's concept that time and space are constant. In such a universe, speed and distance can be measured. Einstein pointed out that because everything is in motion, there is no fixed point at which to measure time and space; therefore, they are not constant. In other words, measurements of speed and distance are relative to the frame of reference (point) from which they are measured. The speed of light is an exception; from whatever frame of reference it is measured, it is constant.

Affirming Planck's theory, Einstein stated that matter and energy are basically the same thing. His equation $E = mc^2$, summarizing an atom's capability of releasing vast amounts of energy, was the first major step in developing atomic and nuclear weapons.

RUTHERFORD. A New Zealand physicist, Ernest Rutherford (1871–1937), described the structure of the atom in 1911. Units of electrical energy called protons orbit around a central particle, the nucleus. In 1917, Rutherford used artificial means to split the atom, which led to the development of atomic weapons and nuclear power plants.

MEITNER. In 1939, the Swedish-German physicist Lise Meitner (1878–1968) and the Austrian physicist Otto Frisch identified **nuclear fission**. This is the process by which a heavy nucleus combines with another particle and then divides into two lighter nuclei. Fission occurs in a chain reaction and releases an enormous amount of energy.

THE ATOMIC BOMB. World War II spurred efforts to produce superweapons utilizing nuclear fission. In 1940, Danish physicist Niels Bohr was at work on a theory of nuclear fission when the Germans invaded Denmark. Before the Germans could force him to produce an atomic bomb, he escaped to the United States in 1943. There, he worked with British and American scientists to produce the bomb.

The secret effort to develop an atomic bomb was called the *Manhattan Project*. Among the leading physicists involved were Enrico Fermi, J. Robert Oppenheimer, and Edward Teller.

Fermi had produced the first sustained nuclear reaction in 1943. Oppenheimer was director of the Manhattan District project that produced the bombs in 1945. When he opposed further development of nuclear weapons, Teller publicly criticized his judgment. Teller later formulated theories that led to the much more powerful thermonuclear (hydrogen) bomb.

Einstein baffles an audience of scientists with a chalk equation, 1931.

> ### INFO CHECK

1. Complete the following sentences:
- $E = mc^2$ is the formula that expresses Albert Einstein's _____ of _____.

- The development of atomic weapons and nuclear power plants was made possible when Ernest Rutherford _____.

- Niels Bohr worked on the theory of _____.

2. Explain why you AGREE or DISAGREE with J. Robert Oppenheimer's opposition to further development of nuclear weapons.

III. IMPROVED STANDARD OF LIVING

A. Electricity

As more homes became wired for electricity, the popularity of timesaving appliances such as refrigerators, washing machines, and vacuum cleaners soared. Elevators allowed architects to design skyscrapers.

Farmers especially benefited. Electrically powered machines made larger, more profitable farms possible. Some modern farms are so heavily automated that they resemble factories. Electricity powered factory machinery and office equipment. It made possible rapid means of communication other than the telephone.

Charlie Chaplin and four-year-old Jackie Coogan in the movie classic *The Kid,* 1920

B. Entertainment and Propaganda

MOVIES. In the 1890s, Thomas Edison created a device to show moving pictures. He then developed the early U.S. motion picture industry.

The first movie theaters opened in Los Angeles in 1902. Early films had no sound; dialogue was spelled out on the screen. Popular silent films included *The Great Train Robbery, Quo Vadis,* and *Birth of a Nation.* Some famous names from the 1920s film industry are Mack Sennett, creator of the Keystone Kops, Mary Pickford, Lillian Gish, Rudolph Valentino, and Charlie Chaplin.

By 1929, movies were widely equipped with sound tracks, just as Europe and the United States were in the grip of a severe financial depression. To help people escape their troubles, moviemakers turned out cheerful and romantic musical comedies.

Use as Propaganda. Movies were also used to spread **propaganda**—ideas that help a favored cause or damage an opposing one. In treating the Civil War and Reconstruction periods, the silent 1915 American film *Birth of a Nation* promoted the racist ideas of the Ku Klux Klan.

In Russia, the director Sergei Eisenstein's *Ten Days That Shook the World* treated early 20th century Russian history from the Communist point of view. In Germany, the Nazi dictator Adolf Hitler commissioned Leni Riefenstahl to make *The Triumph of the Will,* a documentary film glorifying the Nazi party.

RADIO. The first radio stations began broadcasting in the 1920s. American radio listeners could tune in to music, soap operas, news broadcasts, and ball games.

Politicians used radio to influence public opinion. Hitler and the Italian dictator Benito Mussolini banned all points of view but their own from national broadcasts. British Prime Minister Stanley Baldwin and U.S. President Franklin Roosevelt gave informal talks over the radio.

Commercials. In the United States, private companies owned radio networks. To pay for broadcasts, they sold airtime to advertisers, whose **commercials** used sales pitches and jingles to promote products.

The largest audiences tuned in to programs that made them feel good. Thus, advertisers seldom sponsored programs on controversial subjects. Some people complained that narrow commercial interests were shaping American thinking. Others feared that advertisers might control

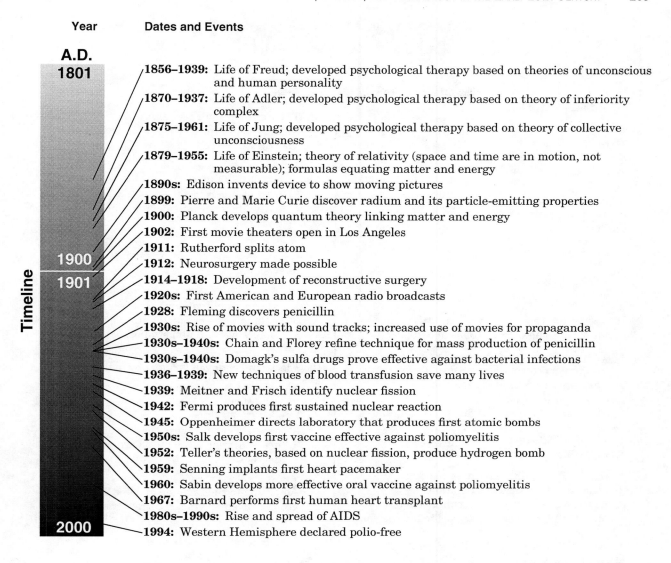

Year   Dates and Events

A.D.
1801

1856–1939: Life of Freud; developed psychological therapy based on theories of unconscious and human personality

1870–1937: Life of Adler; developed psychological therapy based on theory of inferiority complex

1875–1961: Life of Jung; developed psychological therapy based on theory of collective unconsciousness

1879–1955: Life of Einstein; theory of relativity (space and time are in motion, not measurable); formulas equating matter and energy

1890s: Edison invents device to show moving pictures

1899: Pierre and Marie Curie discover radium and its particle-emitting properties

1900: Planck develops quantum theory linking matter and energy

1902: First movie theaters open in Los Angeles

1900

1901

1911: Rutherford splits atom

1912: Neurosurgery made possible

1914–1918: Development of reconstructive surgery

1920s: First American and European radio broadcasts

1928: Fleming discovers penicillin

1930s: Rise of movies with sound tracks; increased use of movies for propaganda

1930s–1940s: Chain and Florey refine technique for mass production of penicillin

1930s–1940s: Domagk's sulfa drugs prove effective against bacterial infections

1936–1939: New techniques of blood transfusion save many lives

1939: Meitner and Frisch identify nuclear fission

1942: Fermi produces first sustained nuclear reaction

1945: Oppenheimer directs laboratory that produces first atomic bombs

1950s: Salk develops first vaccine effective against poliomyelitis

1952: Teller's theories, based on nuclear fission, produce hydrogen bomb

1959: Senning implants first heart pacemaker

1960: Sabin develops more effective oral vaccine against poliomyelitis

1967: Barnard performs first human heart transplant

1980s–1990s: Rise and spread of AIDS

2000

1994: Western Hemisphere declared polio-free

Timeline

the broadcasting of political opinions and news reports.

TELEVISION. Television as a mode of home entertainment eclipsed radio by the 1950s. Like the movies and radio, it was also largely controlled by commercial interests and proved an effective means of propaganda.

All three media, however, have made major contributions to modern society. They bring cultural events and information to a wide audience. They unite people in time of tragedy. On-the-spot pictures and news broadcasts showing the effects of war and disaster have often inspired viewers to send aid to the victims.

C. Contrasts in Living Standards

At the beginning of the 20th century, living standards in industrialized countries were much higher than in nonindustrialized countries. Most of the developing countries, whether colonized or newly independent, were in Asia, Africa, and Latin America. They relied heavily on traditional methods of farming. Their populations were divided into the very rich and the very poor. The poor seldom had access to benefits that people elsewhere took for granted—a good diet, health care, and education.

INFO CHECK

1. Which 20th-century invention do you think did most to improve the standard of living? Why?

2. How were new inventions used for purposes of political propaganda?

3. What great difference developed between industrialized and nonindustrialized countries in the 20th century?

CHAPTER REVIEW

Multiple Choice

1. In addition to new drugs, what other factors helped people live longer?

   1. improved diet and hygiene
   2. radio and television
   3. a longer workweek
   4. a change in climate.

2. An antibiotic is a microorganism that can kill another microorganism. An example of an antibiotic is

   1. penicillin
   2. salt cube
   3. sugar cube
   4. anthrax.

3. Why were the vaccines developed by Salk and Sabin so welcomed in the 1950s and 1960s?

   1. They made penicillin more effective.
   2. They gave protection against malaria.
   3. They protected children against the virus causing poliomyelitis.
   4. They protected people against mental illness.

4. The United Nations Children's Fund and the World Health Organization both

   1. protect the world's environment
   2. operate only in developed nations
   3. have programs to prevent childhood diseases
   4. have both been banned by Pacific Rim nations.

5. The major theories of Adler, Freud, and Jung attempted to prove that

   1. physical illness has nothing to do with one's self-image
   2. the mind and its memories can affect behavior
   3. hypnosis can assist in treating certain types of burns
   4. psychoanalysis is a waste of money.

6. Select the choice that correctly placed the events in their order of occurrence:

   1. atomic bomb—$E=mc^2$—Manhattan Project—study of subatomic energy
   2. study of subatomic energy—atomic bomb—$E=mc^2$—Manhattan Project
   3. $E=mc^2$—study of subatomic energy—atomic bomb—Manhattan Project
   4. study of subatomic energy—$E=mc^2$—Manhattan Project—atomic bomb

7. The "father of the hydrogen bomb" is

   1. Enrico Fermi
   2. Robert Oppenheimer
   3. Niels Bohr
   4. Edward Teller.

8. The German film *The Triumph of the Will* and the American film *Birth of a Nation* were similar in that they were both

   1. pieces of propaganda
   2. box office failures
   3. produced in color
   4. early films with music and dialog sound tracks.

9. Advertisers quickly saw the value of radio and television in

   1. influencing people's political ideas
   2. reaching a large number of people
   3. making large profits for station owners
   4. competing with film studios.

10. Electricity changed farming by making it

    1. harder to raise animals
    2. possible to run larger, more profitable operations
    3. necessary to decrease the size of farms
    4. necessary for farmers to earn college degrees.

11. According to the timeline on page 203, which group of events is in the correct chronological order?

    1. U.S. drops atomic bombs
       Russian Revolution
       Great Depression
       Hitler initiates systematic killing of Jews
    2. Great Depression
       Hitler initiates systematic killing of Jews
       U.S. drops atomic bombs
       Russian Revolution
    3. Hitler initiates systematic killing of Jews
       U.S. drops atomic bombs
       Great Depression
       Russian Revolution
    4. Russian Revolution
       Great Depression
       Hitler initiates systematic killing of Jews
       U.S. drops atomic bombs

12. Study the movie still on page 208, and select the statement that best decribes the situation depicted.

    1. I'm okay, you're okay.
    2. Want to hear another joke?
    3. It's you and me against the world.
    4. Happy New Year!

Thematic Essay

During the first half of the 21st century, advances in the treatment of physical and mental illness were made. *Task:* Describe any two such advances. Show how they improved the quality of life for millions of people.

Document-Based Questions

The scientific, medical, and technological advances of the period were to influence the lives of the world's people . Use the documents and your knowledge of Global History and Geography to answer the questions.

1. Review the timeline on page 209. Using specific examples, explain how such advances, made in the spirit of peace and progress, were put to effective use in times of war.

2. The following is from the letter of a German soldier, written in November of 1940 to his family in Germany:

   "The last words of the Fuhrer's radio address are over and a new strength streams through our veins. It is as if he spoke to each individually, to everyone of us, as if he wanted to give everyone new strength. With loyalty and a sense of duty, we must fight for our principles and endure to the end. . . ."

   Based on the reading, for what purpose was technology used, and was this purpose achieved?

3. Study the photo on page 207. In what scientific development did this scientist play a role? What positive and negative effects did that work have on society?

4. The atomic age began with the first successful test of an atomic bomb in the New Mexican desert on July 16, 1945. Here are the impressions of Brigadier General Thomas F. Farrell, who viewed the test from the test control center:

   " . . . Atomic fission would no longer be hidden in the cloisters [shelter] of the theoretical physicists' dream. . . . It was a great new force to be used for good or for evil. All seemed to feel that they had been present at the birth of a new age—the Age of Atomic Energy. . . . As to the present war . . . we now had the means to insure its speedy conclusion and save thousands of American lives. . . ."

   Describe what General Farrell's feelings were regarding the results of the test. What did he think should be a future use for the bomb?

5. In 1949, William Faulkner received the Nobel Prize for Literature. Here are a few lines from his acceptance speech:

   "Our tragedy is a general and universal physical fear so long sustained by now that we can hear it. There are no longer problems of the spirit. There is only the question of when will I be blown up? Because of this, the young man or woman writing today has forgotten the problems of the human heart in conflict with itself which alone can make good writing because only that is worth writing about. . . ."

   Discuss what Faulkner said people were thinking and writing about, as opposed to what be believed they should be writing about.

Document-Based Essay

"The century began with the belief that science and technology could heal the sick and improve the lives of the world's peoples. Unfortunately, those high hopes were to be lost in the hot and cold wars of the 20th and 21st centuries." *Task:* Write an essay that AGREES or DISAGREES with this statement. Include and describe specific examples of scientific and technological developments to support your essay.

CHAPTER
21

World War I

I. PHYSICAL SETTING

Various features of geography caused tension among Europe's nations. Friction is always likely when ambitious and powerful countries lie close to one another. Natural resources needed in industry and for the manufacture of weapons were unevenly distributed. So were natural barriers against invasion, such as mountains, oceans, and rivers.

After the Franco-Prussian War (1870–1871), Germany had annexed the bordering French province of Alsace and part of Lorraine. Both regions were rich in coal and iron.

The Atlantic Ocean and English Channel were natural defenses for Great Britain. Moreover, its navy, the greatest in the world, had helped it gain a vast empire. When Germany began expanding its own navy, British leaders feared that it might be used to cut off supplies of raw materials and thus ruin Britain's economy.

Lacking the natural resources necessary for industrialization, Italy looked longingly at Italian-speaking areas in Austria-Hungary.

Still in need of a warm-water port to expand its trade, Russia considered how to win the Turkish-controlled straits (Bosporus and Dardanelles) joining the Black and Mediterranean seas. Perhaps war would give it its best opportunity. Russia did not fear invasion; its troops had vast spaces in which to retreat from an advancing enemy.

INFO CHECK

1. PROVE or DISPROVE: Prior to World War I, European leaders were strongly concerned about their countries' geographic advantages and disadvantages.

2. State the geographic reason why Britain feared Germany's expansion of its navy before World War I.

II. CAUSES

A. Long-Term Causes

Long-term (underlying) **causes** of war develop over periods of time. Geography was only one factor contributing to long-standing causes of tension in Europe.

NATIONALISM. Nationalism helped give rise to imperialism. Various countries asserted their right to rule territory beyond their borders.

Nationalism also led to such movements as **Pan-Slavism** and **Pan-Germanism**. Russians and Germans felt a strong right and duty to protect people, no matter where, who shared their ethnic heritage. Thus, Russia supported Slavic Serbia against Germanic Austria-Hungary; Germany backed Germanic Austria-Hungary against Slavic Russia.

MILITARISM. Militarism is a national buildup of armies and navies. In Europe, such buildups created deep distrust. They also gave military leaders increasing influence over their nations' policies. Fear and distrust led to an **arms race**, with each country struggling to surpass the others in military might.

ENTANGLING ALLIANCES. By 1914, Pan-Germanism had led Germany to form the *Dual Alliance* with Austria-Hungary. When Italy joined, it became the *Triple Alliance*. Finally, the three countries allied with the Ottoman Empire and Bulgaria as the *Central Powers*.

In response to Germany's militarism, France and Great Britain had formed the *Entente Cordiale*. After Russia joined, it was called the *Triple Entente*. With the inclusion of Japan and other nations, the alliance's members were known as the *Allied Powers*.

These alliance systems did not increase security. Rather, they almost guaranteed that a clash between two nations would involve others as well.

European Political Alliances, 1914

Triple Alliance and Allies

Triple Entente and Allies

Neutral Nations

0   300   600 Kilometers

0   200   400 Miles

B. Immediate Causes

Immediate causes of war are contemporary events that trigger the fighting. They are usually closely related to long-term causes.

SERBIAN AIMS. Bosnia was an area within Austria-Hungary populated by South Slavs, who had cultural ties to the Serbs. Moreover, Serbia bordered South Slav lands and wanted to incorporate them into an enlarged Serbia. It would also gain a port on the Adriatic Sea. Serbian officials urged the South Slavs to revolt against Austria-Hungary.

ASSASSINATIONS. Archduke Franz Ferdinand was heir to the throne of the Austro-Hungarian Empire. When he and his wife visited the Bosnian capital, Sarajevo, in 1914, a Serbian nationalist shot and killed them. Austria-Hungary blamed Serbia for the murders and demanded the dismissal of Serbian officials opposed to Austria-Hungary. Serbia rejected the demands.

DECLARATION OF WAR. On July 28, 1914, Austria-Hungary declared war on Serbia, and the alliance systems came into play. Russia aided Serbia. Germany then declared war on Russia and France. When German forces moved through neutral Belgium toward France, Britain declared war

on Germany. Although a Triple Alliance member, Italy remained neutral until 1915. It then joined the Allied Powers in hopes of gaining Italian-speaking areas in Austria-Hungary.

INFO CHECK

1. List the long-term causes of World War I. Which of them made a conflict between any two nations the trigger for a larger war involving many nations? Why?

2. How are Pan-Slavism, Pan-Germanism, and nationalism related?

3. What role did Serbia play in the tense period before World War I?

III. GLOBAL CONFLICT AND CHANGE

World War I involved most major nations, lasted four years, and was waged in Europe, Africa, the Middle East, and on the Atlantic and Pacific oceans.

A. Western Front

The most important battles were fought in Europe. German armies crossed Belgium and invaded France. In 1914, a battle at the Marne River stopped the Germans from capturing Paris. From 1915 to 1917, the British and French fought the Germans, but little territory changed hands.

Soldiers on both sides took cover in filthy, damp, vermin-infested trenches and shot at one another across the "no-man's land" between. Enemy shells and poison gas took a huge toll of dead and wounded men.

B. Eastern Front

Austria-Hungary and Bulgaria defeated and occupied Serbia in 1915. In the same year, the Ottoman Turks stopped a British attempt to capture the Dardanelles.

German and Austrian armies invaded Russia in late 1914. The Russians suffered so much that they lost the will to fight. This desolation was to lead to a revolution and a Communist takeover of Russia's government.

In March 1918, the Russians signed the Treaty of Brest-Litovsk with Germany and withdrew from the war. Germany not only gained much Russian territory and valuable resources, it no longer had to fight on two fronts.

C. Africa and the Middle East

In 1914, the Allies occupied all of Germany's African colonies except German East Africa (present-day Tanzania).

Britain defended Egypt's Suez Canal from the Ottoman Turks but was unable to loosen their hold on Syria and Iraq. By 1917, however, Arab nationalists had helped the British take control of Jerusalem, Baghdad, and Damascus from the Ottomans.

D. War at Sea

To cripple the German economy, Britain seized all ships carrying goods to German ports. This caused a shortage of food in Germany.

Despite British control of the seas throughout the war, many German light cruisers and submarines (U-boats) slipped past the blockade and attacked Allied ships. By 1917, Britain was also suffering from food shortages.

E. U.S. Entry

The United States, sympathetic to the Allies but neutral in policy, traded with both Britain and Germany. As the war continued, however, many American lives were lost in German submarine attacks on U.S. ships. The attack on the British liner *Lusitania* in May 1915 killed 128 Americans. U.S. President Woodrow Wilson warned the Germans to stop unrestricted submarine warfare. At first they agreed, but in February 1917, they resumed all-out submarine activity. Americans grew increasingly anti-German.

In January 1917, the German foreign secretary, Arthur Zimmermann, sent a telegram called the Zimmermann Note to the Mexican government. In the event of a German-U.S. war, it said, Ger-

World War I: Battlefronts and Areas Controlled by Each Side

many would help Mexico regain Texas, Arizona, and New Mexico in exchange for Mexican support of Germany. When the British made this message public, Americans were outraged.

For many Americans, who viewed the Central Powers as undemocratic and militaristic, a Central Powers victory would spell the end of democracy in Europe. President Wilson, who was committed to making the world "safe for democracy," persuaded Congress to declare war on Germany on April 6, 1917.

F. End of the War

U.S., French, and British forces stopped the last great German offensive of the war. A few months later, U.S. troops ousted the Germans from St. Mihiel, which they had held since 1914.

The discouraged German people revolted, Kaiser Wilhelm II resigned, Germany became a republic, and its new leaders asked for peace. The **armistice** (agreement to stop fighting) was signed on November 11, 1918.

G. Peace Conference

LEADERS. The most important leaders at the peace conference, held at Versailles, were U.S. President Wilson, British Prime Minister Lloyd George, French Premier Georges Clemenceau, and Italian Premier Vittorio Orlando.

This occasion marked the debut of the United States as a world power. President Wilson wanted fair treatment for the Germans. His Fourteen Points asked for a "peace without victory." Wilson also wanted to end secret treaties, guarantee freedom of the seas, and reduce military weaponry. The other Allied leaders, however, wanted revenge on Germany and as much territory and wealth as they could force from it. In particular, the French were determined that Germany would never again invade France.

TERMS. The Treaty of Versailles, signed in June 1919, included a war guilt clause: Germany was held responsible for World War I. Historians consider this clause unfair since all the combatant nations had helped to start the war. Germany had to pay huge **reparations** (payments for war damages).

The Allies divided Germany's colonies among themselves. France took back Alsace and Lorraine. Poland received the Polish Corridor in northeast Germany. The Allies took control of important industrial areas and mineral resources in western Germany. Finally, German military forces were greatly reduced.

The terms of the Treaty of Versailles caused severe recession, inflation, and unemployment in Germany.

SIDE AGREEMENTS. Agreements with nationalists within the Central Powers broke up the empires of Germany, Austria-Hungary, and Russia. (Nationalist movements within colonies of the Allied nations began to grow at the same time.) Minority groups united to form Czechoslovakia. Bosnia, Herzegovina, and Montenegro joined Serbia as the new Yugoslavia. The new nations of Finland, Estonia, Latvia, and Lithuania were carved out of Russia.

Like several of the new countries, Germany became a republic—the Weimar Republic. Thus, the victorious Allies felt that democracy in Europe had been strengthened.

LEAGUE OF NATIONS. The Allied leaders accepted Wilson's proposal to establish a League of Nations dedicated to finding peaceful solutions to international problems. (Unfortunately, the League, as constituted, could not enforce its decisions.) The original member nations numbered 42.

The United States Senate, using its power to approve all treaties, rejected the Treaty of Versailles and the League of Nations. The dissenting senators feared that the United States might become too deeply involved in European problems.

OVERWEIGHTED.

PRESIDENT WILSON. "HERE'S YOUR OLIVE BRANCH. NOW GET BUSY."

Lampoon of Woodrow Wilson's over-optimistic view of the post-World War I world

Europe After the Treaty of Versailles

The Senate's decision weakened the power and prestige of the League.

INFO CHECK

1. If you had been a World War I soldier, why might you have preferred service on the Eastern Front or in Africa to trench warfare on the Western Front?

2. Why did Germany rely so heavily on U-boats during World War I?

3. Explain why you AGREE or DISAGREE: The entry of the United States into World War I ensured Allied victory.

4. World War I was regarded by many as the "war to end all wars." Why was this hope not fulfilled?

IV. COLLAPSE OF THE OTTOMAN EMPIRE

A. Empire Before World War I

The Ottoman Empire had started its decline in 1699, when Austria took away Hungary. In a series of wars in the 1700s, Russia won a large area north of the Black Sea. The Greeks broke free in 1829.

In the mid-1800s, Western European leaders feared that a breakdown of the Ottoman Empire would upset the balance of power. Therefore, they protected the Turks (and their own interests) when Russia tried to seize the straits between the Black and Mediterranean seas. They also sided with the Turks against Russia during the Crimean War (1854) and the Russo-Turkish War (1877–1878). Nevertheless, the Turks lost much territory to Russia, and Britain gained the island of Cyprus.

B. Arabs, Turks, and Jews

In honor of the British promise to help Hussein ibn-Ali found an independent Arab state, T. E. Lawrence, a British officer, led Arab guerrilla forces in a revolt against the Turks. By 1918, Arab and British troops had conquered Iraq and Syria. In the secret Sykes-Picot Agreement of 1916, however, Britain had claimed Palestine, Jordan, and Iraq, while France claimed Syria, Lebanon, and much of southern Turkey.

In the Balfour Declaration of 1917, Britain had made conflicting promises to the Arabs and the Jews. It subsequently kept its promise to support a Jewish homeland in Palestine but reneged on its commitment to also protect Arab rights in the region. The Arabs still resent this betrayal.

Defying these land grabs by the Allied Powers, the Young Turks led by General Mustafa Kemal captured Constantinople. In 1923, the Treaty of Lausanne recognized Turkey's independence. Kemal became president of the new government with the title of Atatürk (father of the Turks).

INFO CHECK

1. Summarize the role of each of the following in the fall of the Ottoman Empire: Russo-Turkish War, Arab Revolt, Sykes-Picot Agreement, Balfour Declaration.

2. What did the Young Turks and Mustafa Kemal do to hasten the founding of a modern Turkish nation?

V. SCIENTIFIC, LITERARY, ARTISTIC, AND CULTURAL CHANGE

A. Science and Technology

WEAPONS. The Maxim machine gun, used by both the Allies and Central Powers, killed so many so quickly that it made cavalry charges suicidal. Therefore, trench warfare was largely defensive. The prevailing strategy of trying to wear down the enemy helped to prolong the war.

Seeking to break the deadlock, inventors produced poison gas, flamethrowers, tanks, and airplanes, along with protective devices such as gas masks and barbed wire.

MEDICINE. A prime example of the reconstructive surgery developed during World War I was the grafting of healthy skin onto burned areas of the body. Blood transfusion procedures led to the establishment of blood and plasma banks.

PSYCHOLOGY. Psychotherapists became interested in a condition called shellshock. On returning home, soldiers often complained of nightmares, irritability, depression, and guilt. They relived war events through mental flashbacks.

Later known as battle fatigue, this condition, psychologists learned, can be caused by any stressful experience. It is now called **post-traumatic stress disorder (PTSD)**, and doctors treat it with drug therapy and psychotherapy.

B. Literature

HEMINGWAY. The American writer Ernest Hemingway (1899–1961) almost lost the use of his legs in World War I. He later moved to Paris, where many writers who had lost their old ideals were trying to create new artistic values. Hemingway adopted a code of personal courage and stoicism, demonstrated in such novels as *The Sun Also Rises* and *For Whom the Bell Tolls*. His short sentences and spare use of adjectives give his prose an immediate, energetic quality.

STEIN. Gertrude Stein (1874–1946) was another American writer in Paris. Her experimental style reflects a world that has lost clarity and order. Stein's repetition of simple words gives her writing an insistent, childlike quality.

Some of Stein's most famous works are *Three Lives, The Making of Americans,* and *The Autobiography of Alice B. Toklas.*

JOYCE. The Irishman James Joyce (1882–1941) was an experimental writer whose prose style, "stream of consciousness," embodied the technique of free association used in Freud's psychoanalysis. Joyce's dream imagery, slips of the tongue, and run-on thoughts reveal subconscious ideas and feelings. His work expresses dissatisfaction with Western culture, but, at the same time, its humor and liveliness show affection and hope for humanity. Joyce's most famous works are *A Portrait of the Artist as a Young Man, Ulysses,* and *Finnegans Wake.*

MALRAUX. The French writer André Malraux (1901–1976) treated 20th-century political problems. His novel *Man's Fate* is about the Chinese revolution of 1911.

BRECHT. The German writer Bertolt Brecht (1898–1956) wrote poems and plays exposing the greed and corruption pervading political and social systems. His musical play *The Threepenny Opera* is one of his best-known works.

C. Art

Many artists of the early 20th century tried to express how the technologies and horrors of World War I had made the world meaningless and absurd.

DUCHAMP. The French painter Marcel Duchamp (1887–1968) was prominent in **dadism** (*dada* means "hobbyhorse"). The message of this movement was that art no longer reflected beauty, truth, and order. To show how technology had

Marcel Duchamp's *Nude Descending a Staircase, No. 2:* motion shown as a series of movements in one painting

warped taste and artistic values, Duchamp exhibited such everyday things as a bicycle wheel as art objects.

Duchamp also painted cubist pictures. **Cubism** is a style of painting, influenced by motion pictures and African art, in which objects are broken down into their geometric components. A striking example is Duchamp's *Nude Descending a Staircase.*

DALI. The Spanish artist Salvador Dali (1904–1989) was one of the foremost practitioners of **surrealism**, which developed from dadism, with strong influences from psychoanalytic theory. Surrealistic images are typically dreamlike or hallucinogenic, and rendered with photographic clarity. One of Dali's best-known paintings, *The Persistence of Memory,* shows a watch melting on a tree branch in a barren landscape.

PICASSO. The Spanish painter Pablo Picasso (1881–1973) worked in many artistic styles. He is, however, best known for cubism. One of Picasso's cubist masterpieces is *Les Demoiselles d'Avignon.* In *Guernica,* Picasso used surrealist techniques to depict the horrors of war.

RIVERA AND OROZCO. Diego Rivera (1886–1957) and José Orozco (1883–1949) were two important Mexican mural painters. Using techniques and images from Maya and Aztec murals, they painted scenes from contemporary Mexican life and history.

D. Popular Culture

The end of the war brought prosperity to the victors. Americans, in particular, had money to spend on the movies and other entertainments made possible by advances in technology. Affordable cars gave them more freedom of movement.

WOMEN. During the war, when most young men were in the army, women filled their jobs at home. Doing men's work and earning good wages gave them self-confidence. They bobbed their hair (cut it short), wore shorter skirts, and behaved in ways that many considered shocking. Many women agitated for the right to vote.

AFRICAN AMERICANS. African Americans made great contributions to popular culture. The jazz music that they played became so popular that the 1920s became known as the Jazz Age. African Americans also invented exciting dance forms such as the Charleston and the Lindy Hop.

NEW CULTURAL LEADER. The United States suddenly became a world cultural as well as political leader. Movies and radio introduced American culture to Europe. Europeans were especially enthusiastic about African American entertainers such as cabaret singer Josephine Baker.

INFO CHECK

1. Identify the World War I-era medical advances that you regard as most beneficial. State your reasons.

2. Which of the post-World War I writers was most inspired by the teachings of Sigmund Freud? How did this writer's books differ from others of the 1920s and 1930s?

3. How did cubism differ from surrealism? For each, name an artist whose work reflected the style.

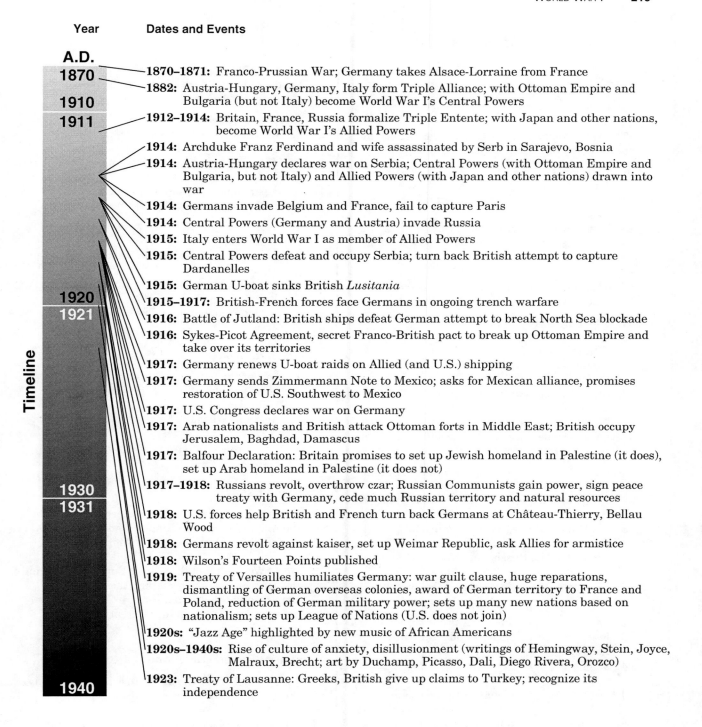

Year	Dates and Events

A.D.

1870 **1870–1871:** Franco-Prussian War; Germany takes Alsace-Lorraine from France

1910 **1882:** Austria-Hungary, Germany, Italy form Triple Alliance; with Ottoman Empire and Bulgaria (but not Italy) become World War I's Central Powers

1911 **1912–1914:** Britain, France, Russia formalize Triple Entente; with Japan and other nations, become World War I's Allied Powers

1914: Archduke Franz Ferdinand and wife assassinated by Serb in Sarajevo, Bosnia

1914: Austria-Hungary declares war on Serbia; Central Powers (with Ottoman Empire and Bulgaria, but not Italy) and Allied Powers (with Japan and other nations) drawn into war

1914: Germans invade Belgium and France, fail to capture Paris

1914: Central Powers (Germany and Austria) invade Russia

1915: Italy enters World War I as member of Allied Powers

1915: Central Powers defeat and occupy Serbia; turn back British attempt to capture Dardanelles

1915: German U-boat sinks British *Lusitania*

1915–1917: British-French forces face Germans in ongoing trench warfare

1920
1921
1916: Battle of Jutland: British ships defeat German attempt to break North Sea blockade

1916: Sykes-Picot Agreement, secret Franco-British pact to break up Ottoman Empire and take over its territories

1917: Germany renews U-boat raids on Allied (and U.S.) shipping

1917: Germany sends Zimmermann Note to Mexico; asks for Mexican alliance, promises restoration of U.S. Southwest to Mexico

1917: U.S. Congress declares war on Germany

1917: Arab nationalists and British attack Ottoman forts in Middle East; British occupy Jerusalem, Baghdad, Damascus

1917: Balfour Declaration: Britain promises to set up Jewish homeland in Palestine (it does), set up Arab homeland in Palestine (it does not)

1917–1918: Russians revolt, overthrow czar; Russian Communists gain power, sign peace treaty with Germany, cede much Russian territory and natural resources

1930
1931
1918: U.S. forces help British and French turn back Germans at Château-Thierry, Bellau Wood

1918: Germans revolt against kaiser, set up Weimar Republic, ask Allies for armistice

1918: Wilson's Fourteen Points published

1919: Treaty of Versailles humiliates Germany: war guilt clause, huge reparations, dismantling of German overseas colonies, award of German territory to France and Poland, reduction of German military power; sets up many new nations based on nationalism; sets up League of Nations (U.S. does not join)

1920s: "Jazz Age" highlighted by new music of African Americans

1920s–1940s: Rise of culture of anxiety, disillusionment (writings of Hemingway, Stein, Joyce, Malraux, Brecht; art by Duchamp, Picasso, Dali, Diego Rivera, Orozco)

1940 **1923:** Treaty of Lausanne: Greeks, British give up claims to Turkey; recognize its independence

Timeline (vertical label)

CHAPTER REVIEW

Multiple Choice

1. An immediate cause of World War I was the assassination of the Archduke Franz Ferdinand and his wife. A long-range cause was

  1. militarism   3. entangling alliances
  2. nationalism   4. all of the above.

2. Austria-Hungary, with German support, presented a series of demands to Serbia. The nation that, in the name of Pan-Slavism, supported Serbia in its refusal to meet those demands was

  1. Great Britain   3. France
  2. Italy   4. Russia.

3. A member of the Triple Alliance that remained neutral until 1915 and then joined the Allies was

   1. Japan
   2. Serbia
   3. Italy
   4. Russia.

4. The 1918 Treaty of Brest-Litovsk was important to Germany because

   1. Germany no longer had to fight a two-front war
   2. Germany gained military assistance from Russia
   3. Russia came under German rule
   4. Russia reentered the war based on a military assistance pact.

5. Two German actions that greatly angered President Wilson and the American people were

   1. attacking Italy and France
   2. unrestricted submarine warfare and the Zimmermann Note
   3. joining with Austria-Hungary and attacking Belgium
   4. spreading the German measles and sauerkraut.

6. The Allied leaders who met to decide on the terms of the peace treaty represented the nations of

   1. France, Russia, the United States, and Great Britain
   2. Italy, Serbia, the United States, and Great Britain
   3. the United States, Great Britain, Italy, and France
   4. Japan, Serbia, Russia, and Italy.

7. The Treaty of Versailles required Germany to

   1. accept responsibility for the war
   2. pay huge reparations for war damages
   3. lose all overseas colonies and Alsace and Lorraine
   4. all of the above.

8. After World War I, the map of Europe changed, as old empires disappeared and new nations formed. Select one former empire and a nation that arose out of its collapse:

   1. Russian Empire—Finland
   2. German Empire—Iran
   3. Ottoman Empire—Estonia
   4. Austro-Hungarian Empire—Turkey

9. The Sykes-Picot Agreement and the Balfour Declaration ignored the nationalistic feelings of

   1. Africans
   2. Arabs
   3. Italians
   4. Turks.

10. After World War I, artistic disillusionment with the old order and lack of faith in the future was clearly expressed by

    1. Picasso's *Guernica*
    2. Hemingway's *A Farewell to Arms*
    3. the dada movement
    4. African Americans' introduction of jazz.

11. A comparison of the maps on pages 213 and 216 shows that, as a result of World War I,

    1. the former Balkan states were unified as Yugoslavia
    2. Spain was punished for its membership in the Triple Alliance
    3. the border between Norway and Sweden was altered
    4. new independent nations were created in Africa.

12. The cartoon on page 215 refers to

    1. the warlike nature of Europeans
    2. the expected survival of colonialism after World War I
    3. President Wilson's efforts to restore the forests and wildlife of a devastated Europe
    4. the unrealistic proposal for a League of Nations.

Thematic Essays

1. If World War I had not occurred, is it likely that the Austro-Hungarian Empire would have lasted longer? *Task:* Give reasons for your answer.

2. World War I altered the map of Europe, destroying the Austro-Hungarian Empire, the German Empire, and the Russian Empire. *Task:* Discuss the role of nationalism in the creation of new nations in Europe.

Document-Based Questions

Use your knowledge of Global History and Geography and the documents to answer the questions.

1. Study the map on page 213. Identify the nations known as the Central Powers and explain how they received that name.

2. From a statement by a British official before the war:

   "It is clear that France and Russia are decided to accept the challenge thrown out to them. Whatever we may think of the merits of the Austrian charges against Serbia, France, and Russia, consider these are pretexts and that the bigger cause of Triple Alliance versus Triple Entente is definitely engaged. . . . Our interests are tied up with those of France and Russia in this struggle. . . . "

How does this reading reveal entangling alliances as a cause of World War I?

3. From an American newspaper reporter's account of the German army's destruction of Louvain, a town in Belgium:

"The Germans sentenced Louvain to become a wilderness. . . . Money can never restore Louvain. Great architects and artists, dead these six hundred years, made it beautiful, and their handiwork belonged to the world. At Louvain it was war upon the defenseless, war on churches, colleges, shops of milliners and lacemakers; war brought to the bedside and fireside; against women harvesting in the fields, against children in wooden shoes playing in the street. . . . "

Is the reporter stating fact, opinion, or both? Is he pro-German or anti-German? Give reasons for your answers.

4. From President Wilson's war message to Congress on April 2, 1917:

" . . . announcement of the Imperial German Government that on and after the first day of February it was its purpose to put aside all restraints [controls] of law and humanity and use its submarines to sink every vessel that sought to approach the ports of Great Britain. . . . I was for a little while unable to believe that such would in fact be done by any government that had hitherto [previously] subscribed [followed] the humane practices of civilized nations. . . . "

What actions of the German government is President Wilson referring to? How did he feel about the actions of the German government? Use the document to support your answer.

Document-Based Essay

Referring to World War I: Entangling alliances and modern technology resulted in a most expensive and deadly war. It killed millions of soldiers and civilians and altered the map of Europe. *Task:* Using historical information, PROVE or DISPROVE the accuracy of this statement.

CHAPTER
22

The Post–World War I Era

I. REVOLUTION AND CHANGE IN RUSSIA

As Russia was industrializing in the early 1900s, its leaders were trying to build an empire. They set up a sphere of influence in Chinese Manchuria and then sought to occupy northern Korea. Japan, with its own claims on northern Korea, declared war in 1904 and won the Russo-Japanese War in 1905.

A. Revolution of 1905

Defeat by Japan increased Russian resentment of Czar Nicholas II's autocratic government. The middle class pushed for political reforms. Factory workers unionized and supported Socialist reformers. Minority groups such as the Poles and Ukrainians agitated for independence.

The time was ripe for change. Part of the army had been weakened by the Russo-Japanese War, and the other part was protecting Russian interests in Manchuria.

Dissidents began with peaceful demonstrations. A workers' group led by a priest presented a petition to Nicholas at the Winter Palace in St. Petersburg. When palace guards fired on them, they were provoked to rage. Faced with a revolution, Nicholas let his subjects elect a **duma** (parliament) but kept its actions under tight control.

B. Effects of World War I

At first, World War I unified Russia. Expansionists saw an opportunity to gain Balkan territory. Liberals and Socialists hoped that an alliance with France and Britain would help democratize Russia. All Russians were passionate in defense of their country.

But defeats, casualties in the millions, and food shortages quickly disillusioned the people. Nicholas ignored demands to withdraw from the fighting and did nothing to ease the starvation and poverty.

RUSSIAN REVOLUTION. In March 1917, moderate leaders initiated the Russian Revolution by ousting Nicholas II and setting up a provisional government. They promised constitutional democracy but kept Russia in the war. In November 1917, Vladimir I. Lenin led a second revolution.

LENIN. A follower of Karl Marx, Lenin believed that socialism would replace capitalism through violence. According to Marx, the first Socialist revolution would occur in a more industrialized, less agricultural country than Russia. Lenin realized, however, that Russian peasants were ready to revolt; indeed, many had already seized estates of the nobility. Lenin promised that they could keep what they had taken if they followed him.

BOLSHEVIKS. Lenin's Bolshevik (later called Communist) party took over the government. It immediately withdrew Russia from the war, sacrificing its rights to neighboring land in Eastern Europe that held a third of the Russian population, a third of its agriculture, and half of its industry. Eventually, Russia regained much of this territory.

To defend their government, the Communists, or Reds, fought various groups of anti-Communists, or Whites. In need of resources for the civil war effort, Lenin imposed "war communism" on the government and economy. The government took over most industries, banks, and railroads and seized much of the peasants' crops.

NEW GOVERNMENT. Lenin allowed workers and peasants to elect representatives to the legislature, but he really ran it. As its official policy, the Communist government adopted **atheism** (the belief that God does not exist). It forbade Russians to make class distinctions.

ONE PARTY. The Communist party was the only legal one. Newspapers were censored. In 1918, the czar and his family were executed to prevent their rescue by the Whites. The new secret police, the Cheka, was authorized to kill opponents. By 1921, the Communists had defeated the Whites. In 1922, Russia became the Union of Soviet Socialist Republics (USSR)—the Soviet Union.

ECONOMIC CHANGES. Lenin then instituted the New Economic Policy (NEP), which made some compromises with Marxism. Peasants were allowed to sell surplus grain for profit. Although the government still owned major economic institutions, small manufacturers regained control of their businesses. NEP improved the Russian economy.

C. Stalin and the Modern Totalitarian State

After Lenin's death, Joseph Stalin controlled the Soviet Union from 1924 to 1953.

COMMAND ECONOMY. Stalin replaced NEP with a **command economy** (state control of industry, agriculture, production, quantities, and prices). He did so partly because NEP showed signs of a slowdown and partly because it allowed too many capitalistic practices.

FIRST FIVE-YEAR PLAN. To speed up Russian industrialization, Stalin initiated two *Five-Year plans*. The first called for industrial output to increase by 250 percent in five years, with increase of agricultural production set at 150 percent. The government took over all industries and peasant land. Some peasants were put to work on **collective farms**. Others labored in factories and mines and on construction sites.

COLLECTIVIZATION. Outraged at the loss of their land, many peasants burned their crops and killed their livestock. Those working on collective farms often did so halfheartedly. Consequently, grain production did not increase, and there was a famine between 1932 and 1933.

Nevertheless, collectivization went ahead. The government had taken away the peasant's political rights, and it could force them to produce food for industrial workers. At the end of the first five years, Stalin had set the basis for the Soviet planned economy.

SECOND FIVE-YEAR PLAN. The second Five-Year Plan began in 1933. To make the Soviet Union economically independent of the West, heavy industry such as steel production took precedence over consumer goods. In 1938, only Germany and the United States outranked the Soviet Union in industrial production.

EDUCATION. Soviet people received free public education. Thus, more of them were able to become

Soviet Union, 1917–1938

managers and professionals. For ordinary people, however, the living standard did not improve. Sales taxes were high. Money bought less than before the Five-Year plans. Also, with fewer consumer goods being produced, there was less to buy.

REPRESSION. Stalin ruled by terror. He first turned the secret police on peasants who resisted collectivization. Later, he set them on any opponents, real or potential. Torture to elicit confessions of political crimes was common. Trials were often rigged, the accused almost always found guilty, and most of them killed, imprisoned, or exiled to gulags (labor camps) in Siberia. In the purges of the 1930s, millions were arrested, imprisoned, and killed.

The Red army occupied the non-Russian republics of the Soviet Union. Their governments became replicas of the Soviet model.

Kemal Atatürk ("Father of the Turks"), introducing language reform

INFO CHECK

1. Explain the connection between World War I and the Russian Revolution of 1917.

2. Identify or define: Vladimir I. Lenin, Joseph Stalin, war communism, New Economic Policy, Five-Year plans.

3. Describe the most significant political changes brought to Russia and the non-Russian republics by the 1930s.

II. BETWEEN WORLD WARS (1919–1939)

A. League of Nations

The Allies had intended the League of Nations to be a neutral forum to hear countries' disputes. The opponents were supposed to abide by the League's decision. Nations that went to war were to be subjected to a trade ban by other League members.

The League, however, had no enforcement power. Japan and Italy, for example, violated its principles by aggression in Asia and Africa.

The League gave France and Great Britain **mandates** (authorities to rule) over Ottoman territories and German colonies. The mandate holders were supposed to help the inhabitants set up their own governments. But because the "protector" nations controlled the process, they had, in effect, been given the right to colonize territory.

B. Westernization of Turkey

ATATÜRK. After taking control of Turkey in 1923, Atatürk set up a one-party system and made

reforms without putting them to the vote. He refused to allow self-government to ethnic minorities such as the Kurds and Armenians.

New Government. Atatürk's reforms, however, established a framework for future democracy. The Turkish legal system was now based on European rather than Islamic law. School subjects reflected the European model. No longer restricted by Islamic law, women could vote. Men were permitted to have only one wife, and women could sue for divorce.

Cultural Changes. Turks were ordered to wear Western-style clothes and use the new Turkish alphabet based on Roman letters rather than Arabic script. Atatürk's government also fostered industrialization.

Opposition. Many Turkish Muslims wanted to retain Islamic tradition and law. They formed the Islamic party.

C. Women's Suffrage Movement

BEGINNINGS. In 1792, an Englishwoman, Mary Wollstonecraft, wrote *A Vindication of the Rights of Women.* She argued that if women were as well educated as men, they would be able to support themselves and make good political decisions.

BRITAIN. In 1867, the philosopher John Stuart Mill petitioned Parliament to give women the vote.

Mill, Emily Davies, an educator, and others founded the first women's **suffrage** (right to vote) society— The National Union of Women's Suffrage Societies. Emmeline Pankhurst founded the Women's Social and Political Union in 1903. Its members, called suffragettes, practiced civil disobedience. British women's contributions to the war effort during World War I helped them win the vote in 1918.

THE UNITED STATES. American abolitionists began the fight for women's suffrage by organizing the Seneca Falls Convention in 1848. When the 15th Amendment gave African Americans the right to vote in 1870, Susan B. Anthony and Elizabeth Cady Stanton demanded to know why it did not include women. Another group, headed by Lucy Stone and Julia Ward Howe, felt the 15th Amendment could only help women win their rights.

Anthony and Stanton's National Woman Suffrage Association worked to gain married women the right to own property. Stone's American Woman Suffrage Association worked for suffrage on the state level. In 1869, Wyoming gave women the right to vote. The two suffrage organizations united in 1890.

In the early 1900s, Alice Paul of the National Women's party organized mass marches and hunger strikes. During World War I, however, women concentrated their efforts on helping the war effort.

After the war, the demand for women's suffrage increased. Finally, in August 1920, the 19th Amendment gave American women the right to vote in national elections.

D. Rise of Fascism in Italy

Many Italians believed that they should have been awarded more territory for their help in winning World War I. During the 1920s, unemployment and high prices increased the unrest.

FASCIST PARTY. The Fascist party, founded by Benito Mussolini in 1919, comprised mainly unemployed veterans. **Fascism** championed nationalism and militarism and worked to replace democracy with a one-party dictatorship.

In October 1922, Mussolini and 10,000 armed Fascists marched on Rome. Fearing civil war, the king asked Mussolini to become prime minister.

DICTATORSHIP. Mussolini outlawed other political parties. The secret police arrested critics, and the government forbade strikes and regulated all economic activity. Newspapers and radio broadcasts were censored. Schoolchildren were taught that the individual existed to serve the state. Boys trained to be soldiers, and girls were expected to become mothers of large families.

Although Mussolini strengthened Italian industry and agriculture, wages fell, work hours increased, and taxes rose.

Dictator Benito Mussolini declaiming to Italian troops from atop a tank

INFO CHECK

1. State the reason for the establishment of the League of Nations. Why was it unsuccessful?

2. Why did some Turks regard Mustafa Kemal as a great leader while others did not?

3. Compare the women's suffrage movements in Britain and the United States. What were the most important similarities?

4. Define fascism. Why did so many Italians accept the leadership of Benito Mussolini in 1922?

III. WORLDWIDE DEPRESSION

A. U.S. Economy

In the United States, the booming stock market of the 1920s disguised many problems. Farmers got such low prices for crops that many could not repay their mortgages. Banks that relied on mortgage payments failed. Americans, who were buying a lot on credit, were often unable to pay off their debts, and many manufacturers were forced out of business.

The New York stock market crashed in October 1929. Many investors had bought stocks "on margin" by borrowing from their stockbrokers. Then, stock prices began to fall. Investors, fearing huge debts, rushed to sell their stocks. Other investors panicked and did the same.

B. Ripple Effect

American investors who had lent money to European businesses began to demand payment. Thus, capital was drawn from countries still struggling with World War I debts. Manufacturers tried to sell their goods in order to repay these loans. With too few people to buy their goods, world prices collapsed. The loss of markets also caused production to fall off.

LOSS OF JOBS AND HOPE. In 1932, about 17 percent of Britain's workforce was unemployed. In 1933 in the United States, the figure was almost 25 percent. Germany was the hardest hit of all. Unable to work and earn, people felt worthless and without hope.

REACTION IN THE UNITED STATES. President Franklin D. Roosevelt's New Deal policy tried to reduce unemployment by creating agencies to manage new public works projects (government-financed programs to benefit the public). The best known was the Works Progress Administration

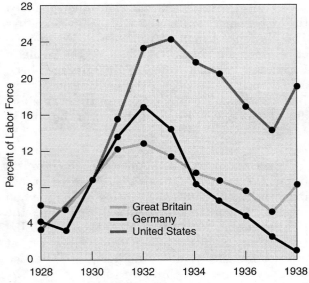

Unemployment During the Great Depression (1928–1938)

(WPA), which constructed bridges, highways, and public buildings. By utilizing the abilities of desperate people, the agency did much to prevent a revolution in the United States. Even so, serious unemployment remained a problem until the U.S. entry into World War II in 1941.

Roosevelt also initiated a national social security system and, by passing the National Labor Relations Act of 1935, legalized collective bargaining by unions.

BRITISH SOLUTIONS. British leaders practiced strict economy to balance the country's budget and gave subsistence welfare to the unemployed. After 1932, the economy recovered by itself.

FRENCH REACTION. French leaders were unable to solve the problems of the depression. Fascist organizations rioted and spread propaganda. Socialists, radicals, and communists united in the Popular Front party. Léon Blum, leader of the Popular Front, was elected premier (prime minister) in 1936. His attempts to pass reforms similar to those of Roosevelt, however, produced threats of revolution from conservatives and fascists. Blum resigned in June 1937.

INFO CHECK

1. How and when did the worldwide depression begin?

2. Which government do you believe responded most successfully to the problems caused by the worldwide depression? Explain.

IV. RISE OF TOTALITARIANISM

Totalitarianism is a form of political dictatorship that controls every aspect of its citizens' lives. In the period before World War II, such systems had a tight grip on both Germany and Japan.

A. Weimar Republic and the Rise of Nazism

Many Germans blamed the democratic Weimar Republic for agreeing to the terms of the Treaty of Versailles. High unemployment, soaring prices, and a huge war debt had made the people resentful. Just as the economy began to improve, the Great Depression of 1929 hit.

HITLER. Adolf Hitler, a World War I hero, personified German contempt for the Weimar Republic. A brilliant public speaker, he easily won support for his Nazi party. He said that Germans were a superior race, destined to rule the world. He claimed that communists, socialists, and democrats were to blame for Germany's defeat and economic problems. He singled out the Jews as his main target, inflaming anti-semitism as a means of gaining political support.

Nazi propaganda poster of Hitler receiving a pledge from the German people: Führer, we follow your lead!

In 1923, Hitler attempted, and failed, to seize the state of Bavaria. While in prison, he wrote *Mein Kampf* (My Struggle). It set forth his racist ideas and his plans for world domination.

THIRD REICH. During the early 1930s, the Nazis gained a large number of seats in the legislature. In January 1933, Hitler became chancellor of Germany and quickly turned Germany into a dictatorship known as the Third Reich. As Führer (leader), he controlled industrial and agricultural production, education, newspapers, and radio broadcasts. Children had to join the Hitler Youth organization to learn how to be "good Nazis."

The Nazis sent political enemies and millions of Jews and other minorities to **concentration camps** (prisons). There, prisoners were either murdered on arrival or worked, starved, or tortured to death.

B. Japanese Militarism and Expansion

Having few natural resources, Japan must import raw materials to run its industries. In the 1920s and 1930s, its leaders developed a long-range plan—the East Asia Co-Prosperity Sphere—to acquire raw materials by conquering East Asia. Control of China was the chief aim.

MANCHURIA. Japan seized Manchuria in northeast China in 1931, renamed it Manchukuo in 1932, and pretended to give it independence. In reality, Japan controlled the government and began to use its natural resources.

CHINA. In 1937, Japanese forces overran northern China, capturing the capital Nanjing (old spelling Nanking), and committing atrocities on its citizens. But General Jian Jieshi (old spelling Chiang Kai-shek), head of the Chinese government, moved the Nationalist government to western China and set up a new capital. Japan's war with China lasted from 1937 to 1945.

REACTION OF THE WEST. The League of Nations condemned Japan's aggression. The United States, the Soviet Union, and other countries also protested and gave aid to China. But no one was willing to fight Japan, and the Japanese pursued their conquests. In 1940, they moved into northern Indochina (present-day Vietnam).

C. China After World War I

In joining the Allies in World War I, China had expected to gain Russian territory. When peace negotiators ignored China's claim, nationalist student groups formed the May Fourth Movement and demonstrated against the West.

JIAN JIESHI AND MAO ZEDONG. Some Chinese became Communists, among them Mao Zedong, a supporter of the May Fourth Movement. The Communists opposed the Nationalist government set up by Dr. Sun Yixian.

Jian Jieshi took over from Sun in 1925 and attacked the Communists. In 1927, civil war broke out, and the Nationalists succeeded in driving the Communists into China's interior. From early 1934 to 1935, some 100,000 Communists made the "Long March" from the south to the northwest, at a cost of more than 50,000 lives.

When Japan invaded China in 1937, Jian and Mao temporarily united against the common enemy.

INFO CHECK

1. Define totalitarianism. Was the Third Reich a totalitarian state? Why or why not?

2. Why did Adolf Hitler and the Nazi party become popular with so many Germans in the 1930s? What do you find attractive or objectionable about Hitler's ideas?

3. Describe the impact of Japanese militarism on China. Why was the League of Nations unable to help China and other Asian nations?

V. NATIONALIST MOVEMENTS AGAINST IMPERIALISM

A. India

SUPPORT FOR BRITAIN. During World War I, about 1.2 million Indians served as soldiers and laborers in Europe, Africa, and the Middle East. The British repaid many of them with better government jobs. This helped a small group, but the long war brought real hardships to the native people.

ALL-INDIA NATIONALISM. Nationalist groups worked to improve the status of all Indians. Both the moderate and radical factions of the Indian National Congress united as the All-Indian Congress party. This party, however, had mainly Hindu leaders.

MUSLIM VIEW. Muslims founded the Muslim League. The Congress party persuaded the Muslim League to join in the Lucknow Pact of 1916, whereby Muslims and Hindus demanded that India become a self-governing dominion similar to Canada.

ROWLATT ACTS. Returning Indian soldiers were still not treated with respect, and jobs were scarce. After Indian demonstrations against British rule, the British forced passage of the Rowlatt Acts of 1919, which were designed to prevent conspiracies against the British government.

Nationalist Indian groups all over India rioted. In Amritsar, a peaceful gathering caused nervous British troops to kill and wound hundreds of people. This Amritsar Massacre turned even moderates against the British. Mohandas Gandhi urged civil disobedience, nonpayment of taxes, and a boycott of British goods.

THE INDIA ACT. The British hastily promised to help the Indians develop their own government. The India Act of 1919 stated that during transition from colony to independent state, India would be governed by both British and native officials. The British would handle taxes, police, and the courts, while the Indians would see to agriculture, health, and education. Millions of Indians gained suffrage to elect various levels of officials.

A NEW CONSTITUTION. In 1935, a new constitution gave Indians an even stronger voice in government. By 1947, they had gained complete control of the country. But fateful conflicts between Muslims and Hindus were just ahead.

B. Arab Nations

IRAQ. The British appointed Prince Faisal of Syria to be king of Iraq. In 1932, Faisal (ruled 1921–1933) persuaded Britain to give Iraq independence in exchange for Iraqi military support.

EGYPT. A surge of nationalism in Egypt after World War I convinced the British to leave. In 1922, Britain allowed Egypt to set up its own government, a constitutional monarchy, but continued its military occupation. In 1936, British troops were restricted to the Suez Canal Zone.

SYRIA AND LEBANON. The French kept their mandate in Syria and acquired Lebanon as well. Lebanon became a republic but remained under French protection. In 1943, it attained full independence. Syria became independent in 1946.

OIL AND POWER. Arab landowners and merchants gained financial benefits from supporting Britain and France. Arab armies could not face down Western armies; moreover, Western companies owned Arab oil fields. Arab rulers were content to receive huge amounts of money for allowing Western companies to explore and drill for oil.

C. Iran

INFLUENCE OF BRITAIN AND RUSSIA. During the 19th century, the shah of Iran kept his country independent by granting economic privileges to Britain and Russia. In 1906, nationalists forced the shah to set up an Islamic government under an Islamic constitution. Russia and Britain moved in and divided Iran: Britain took the oil-rich region around the Persian Gulf, and Russia took over northern Iran. By 1912, Russia virtually ruled Iran but lost all control during the Bolshevik Revolution. In 1919, a British attempt to take over the Iranian government failed.

REZA SHAH PAHLAVI. In 1925, Reza Khan overthrew the government and became the new shah, taking the name Reza Shah Pahlavi. Modeling himself on Atatürk, Reza Shah created a modern

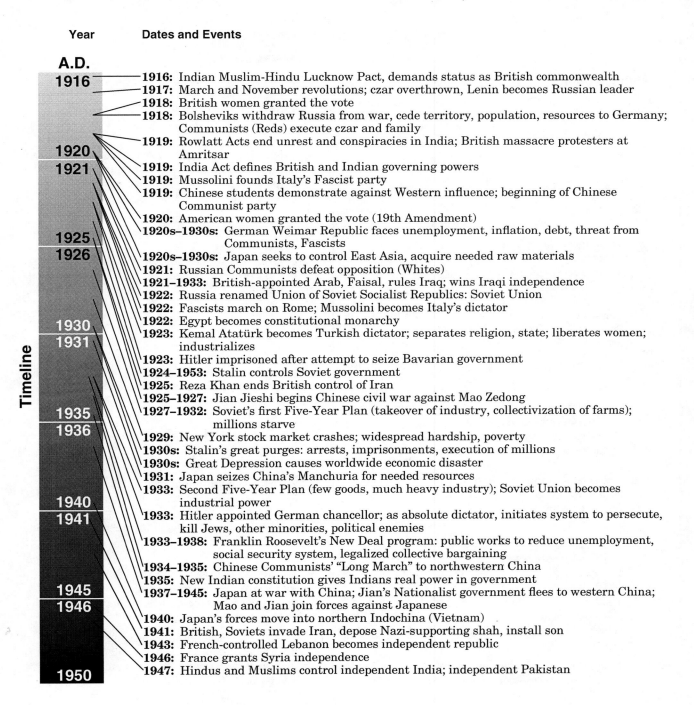

Timeline

Year	Dates and Events
A.D.	
1916	**1916:** Indian Muslim-Hindu Lucknow Pact, demands status as British commonwealth
	1917: March and November revolutions; czar overthrown, Lenin becomes Russian leader
	1918: British women granted the vote
	1918: Bolsheviks withdraw Russia from war, cede territory, population, resources to Germany; Communists (Reds) execute czar and family
1920	**1919:** Rowlatt Acts end unrest and conspiracies in India; British massacre protesters at Amritsar
1921	**1919:** India Act defines British and Indian governing powers
	1919: Mussolini founds Italy's Fascist party
	1919: Chinese students demonstrate against Western influence; beginning of Chinese Communist party
	1920: American women granted the vote (19th Amendment)
1925	**1920s–1930s:** German Weimar Republic faces unemployment, inflation, debt, threat from Communists, Fascists
1926	**1920s–1930s:** Japan seeks to control East Asia, acquire needed raw materials
	1921: Russian Communists defeat opposition (Whites)
	1921–1933: British-appointed Arab, Faisal, rules Iraq; wins Iraqi independence
	1922: Russia renamed Union of Soviet Socialist Republics: Soviet Union
	1922: Fascists march on Rome; Mussolini becomes Italy's dictator
	1922: Egypt becomes constitutional monarchy
1930	**1923:** Kemal Atatürk becomes Turkish dictator; separates religion, state; liberates women; industrializes
1931	**1923:** Hitler imprisoned after attempt to seize Bavarian government
	1924–1953: Stalin controls Soviet government
	1925: Reza Khan ends British control of Iran
	1925–1927: Jian Jieshi begins Chinese civil war against Mao Zedong
1935	**1927–1932:** Soviet's first Five-Year Plan (takeover of industry, collectivization of farms); millions starve
1936	**1929:** New York stock market crashes; widespread hardship, poverty
	1930s: Stalin's great purges: arrests, imprisonments, execution of millions
	1930s: Great Depression causes worldwide economic disaster
	1931: Japan seizes China's Manchuria for needed resources
	1933: Second Five-Year Plan (few goods, much heavy industry); Soviet Union becomes industrial power
1940	**1933:** Hitler appointed German chancellor; as absolute dictator, initiates system to persecute, kill Jews, other minorities, political enemies
1941	**1933–1938:** Franklin Roosevelt's New Deal program: public works to reduce unemployment, social security system, legalized collective bargaining
	1934–1935: Chinese Communists' "Long March" to northwestern China
	1935: New Indian constitution gives Indians real power in government
1945	**1937–1945:** Japan at war with China; Jian's Nationalist government flees to western China; Mao and Jian join forces against Japanese
1946	**1940:** Japan's forces move into northern Indochina (Vietnam)
	1941: British, Soviets invade Iran, depose Nazi-supporting shah, install son
	1943: French-controlled Lebanon becomes independent republic
	1946: France grants Syria independence
1950	**1947:** Hindus and Muslims control independent India; independent Pakistan

army, constructed railroads, and began to industrialize Iran. He granted more rights to women. To end foreign domination and to strengthen the economy, he raised taxes on foreign businesses, especially oil companies.

When Reza Shah tried to separate religion and state, he lost the support of Iran's powerful Muslim leaders. To maintain authority, Reza Shah became repressive and even supported Nazi Germany. British and Soviet troops invaded Iran in 1941 and forced him to abdicate in favor of his son Mohammad Reza.

INFO CHECK

1. List the colonized countries in which demands for independence grew stronger after World War I.

2. Identify each of the following: Mohandas Gandhi, King Faisal, Reza Shah Pahlavi.

3. Describe the roles of the Indian National Congress and the Muslim League in achieving independence for India by 1947.

4. How did Iran gain independence from Britain and Russia?

CHAPTER REVIEW

Multiple Choice

1. Czar Nicholas II allowed his subjects to elect a governing body called the

   1. Diet
   2. Congress
   3. Duma
   4. Reichstag.

2. Russia's participation in World War I hastened the fall of the czar because it resulted in

   1. high casualty rates
   2. military defeats
   3. massive food shortages
   4. all of the above.

3. Lenin's New Economic Policy was closer to Socialist than Communist economic practices because

   1. the government controlled all the business and agricultural decision making
   2. the economy had a mixture of government and private ownership of business and agriculture
   3. it was a command economy
   4. the government allowed private individuals to make all economic decisions for the state.

4. Under Stalin, the change from farming one's own land to forced labor on government-owned farms was known as

   1. blitzkrieg
   2. socialism
   3. collectivization
   4. capitalism.

5. The League of Nations was supposed to provide a place for nations to resolve differences peacefully. However, if the nations did go to war, then the League would

   1. stop trade with the warring countries
   2. send in a peacekeeping force

   3. dismiss the warring countries from membership
   4. use the massive military forces loaned to it by the United States.

6. Under the League of Nations, the former colonies of the Ottoman and German empires were to be assisted in forming their own governments. The result was to

   1. establish dictatorships
   2. put the former colonial peoples on the road to self-government
   3. prohibit the colonization of the territories
   4. take economic advantage of the former colonies.

7. After World War I, Turkey and Iran made efforts to achieve

   1. women's rights
   2. modernization
   3. popularly elected governments
   4. tribal loyalties.

8. The purpose of the suffrage movement was to

   1. help African Americans win the right to vote
   2. achieve voting rights for women
   3. protest the suffering of the migratory farm workers
   4. protest the suffering of the enslaved peoples of the world.

9. Worldwide depression and the failure of many Western European governments to achieve order and stability in their nations led to the

   1. spread of Communist governments
   2. spread of democratic governments
   3. rise of parliamentary governments
   4. rise of military dictatorships

10. Examine the map on page 223. Which is the most accurate conclusion about the Soviet Union between 1917 and 1938?

    1. Japan, China, and India joined the Soviet Union.
    2. The Soviet Union extended approximately 1,000 miles from east to west.
    3. The Soviet Union comprises a number of republics.
    4. The official title of the Soviet Union was Russia.

11. The most accurate conclusion to be drawn from the line graph on page 226 is that

    1. the Nazis in Germany had eliminated all unemployment by 1938
    2. during the worldwide depression, Britain had higher unemployment than Germany
    3. the worldwide depression had a less severe impact in the United States than in Britain or Germany
    4. Hitler probably owed much of his public support to his success in combating unemployment between 1933 and 1938.

12. The propaganda poster on page 227 was an attempt to convince people that

    1. Hitler was supported by the vast majority of the German people
    2. the Nazis could not govern without the public support of the German people
    3. Jews were fearful of Hitler's growing power in Germany
    4. most of the people of Europe were sympathetic to the Nazi cause.

Thematic Essays

1. The governmental and economic practices of Communist Russia, Fascist Italy, and Nazi Germany differed greatly from those of the democracies of Europe and the United States. *Task:* Using examples from the areas of economics and government, compare and contrast the practices of any two of the dictatorships with the practices of a democracy such as Great Britain or France.

2. The Treaty of Versailles was intended (a) to punish the German nation for causing World War I and (b) to prevent Germany from regaining its military power. The League of Nations was intended to preserve the peace of Europe. *Task:* Using specific historical examples, explain why none of these goals was achieved.

Document-Based Questions

Use the documents and your knowledge of Global History and Geography to answer the questions.

1. Study the photos on pages 225 and 227. What do they tell you about each leader?

2. From Benito Mussolini:

   " . . . The Fascist conception of life stresses the importance of the State. . . . The State became the conscience and will of the people. . . . Fascism is totalitarian. . . . It discards pacifism [anti-war beliefs]. . . . "

   How do you think Mussolini would react to demands for individual rights and freedoms?

3. Adolf Hitler, while in jail for attempting to overthrow the government, wrote in *Mein Kampf:*

   "There must be no majority decisions, but only responsible persons. . . . Surely every man will have his advisors by his side, but the decision will be made by one man . . . responsibility can and may be borne by only one man, and therefore only he alone may possess the authority and right to command. . . . "

   Discuss how this quote reflects the ideology of dictatorship. How did the Third Reich reflect this ideology?

4. A description of Kemal Atatürk:

   "When he came there was a dynasty, the Ottomans and he needed a nation, Turkey. . . . Mustafa Kemal knew . . . that you cannot have a strong nation composed of weak individuals, and that a country cannot be strong if it is ridden with disease, ignorance, and poverty. . . . The foe was the turban and the fez, the women's veil and the peasants' ignorance, the illiteracy of the shepherd and the people's indifference. . . . The nation was mightier than Allah. . . . The good Turk wore European dress and the fez belonged to a dead era. . . . The state was secularized and Turkey was no longer wedded to Islam."

   Who and what was Kemal attacking, and what did he wish to achieve?

5. Study the photo on page 224. Discuss what the photo tells about cultural changes in Turkey. Why do you think some Turks opposed these changes?

6. After Italy attacked Ethiopia, the League of Nations voted to use economic sanctions against Italy but was not supported by the non-League nations of the world. The emperor of Ethiopia appeared before the League of Nations and appealed for aid:

   "In October 1935 Italian troops invaded my territory. . . . I assert [state] that the problem . . . is much wider than merely a question of . . . Italian aggression, it is collective security, it is the very existence of the League. It is the value of promises to small states that their integrity and independence shall be respected and assured. . . . What undertakings can be of any value if the will to keep them is lacking?"

Discuss the emperor's sentiments toward the League. Why does he use the term "collective security" to describe the League?

Document-Based Essay

Leaders such as Stalin, Hitler, and Atatürk claimed to have the solutions to their nations' problems after World War I. They were willing to take drastic measures to change the conditions of their countries. *Task:* For any *two* such leaders, list the economic and political problems of their nations and then describe the effect their solutions had on those nations.

CHAPTER
23

World War II

I. THE NAZI STATE (1933–1945)

A. Taking Total Control

CULTURE. Adolf Hitler banned art, literature, and music that contradicted Nazi values. Nazi mobs burned the written works of renowned Jews such as Sigmund Freud and Albert Einstein.

ECONOMY. During his first year as chancellor, Hitler started public works programs. Defying the Treaty of Versailles, he rearmed Germany. These policies created jobs for the unemployed and increased industrial output.

NATIONAL PRIDE. The Treaty of Versailles had damaged German national pride. Hitler assured Germans that they were the master race; other races existed to serve them.

POWERFUL ORATIONS. At political rallies, Hitler made impassioned speeches denouncing Jews and Communists and urging German expansion into other countries for lebensraum (living space). The people's knowledge of public events was limited to what they learned from state-approved radio broadcasts, movies, and publications.

YOUTH. The Nazi party controlled all schools and universities. Children from the ages of 6 to 18 had to join groups that taught them Nazi ideals. If parents objected, the children might be taken from them.

At age six, boys began to train for the Hitler Youth by means of athletics, camping, and classes in history from the Nazi viewpoint. At ten, they joined the Jungvolk (Young Folk) and at 14 graduated to the Hitler Youth. At this point, military training was compulsory because boys entered the army at age 18.

Girls joined the League of German Girls. They were encouraged to exercise vigorously in order to grow into healthy mothers of soldiers.

SUPPRESSION. Germans who opposed Hitler were killed or imprisoned.

INFO CHECK

1. Give at least one reason for the acceptance of Hitler and nazism by each of these groups: workers, business leaders and industrialists, veterans, supernationalists and racists.

2. Evaluate the Nazi education program Do you APPROVE or DISAPPROVE of it? Why?

3. What happened to Germans who opposed nazism?

II. ROAD TO WAR

A. German Aggression in Europe

France and Britain were still weak economically and militarily from World War I. Neither wanted to go to war.

RHINELAND. After rearming Germany, Hitler sent troops into the Rhineland, between France and Germany, an area that was to be kept free of armed forces. German commanders were under orders to withdraw if the French showed signs of opposition.

The French were unable to take a stand without British support, which was not forthcoming. Thus, Hitler gained the Rhineland and its reserves of coal and iron.

AUSTRIA. In 1938, Hitler increased Germany's size and power by annexing Austria, a union prohibited by the Treaty of Versailles. Again, no one took any action.

CZECHOSLOVAKIA. More than three million Germans lived in the Sudetenland in western Czechoslovakia. In the 1930s, Nazi agents there stirred up antigovernment riots. In 1938, Hitler, on threat

Europe: Axis Aggression, 1930–1940

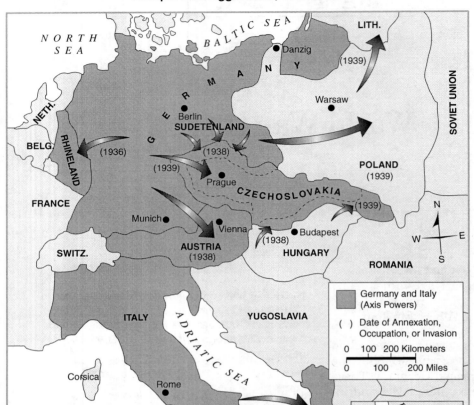

of invasion, demanded that Sudetenlanders vote on whether to unite with Germany.

Appeasement. During the 1930s, the British and French policy was **appeasement**—to maintain peace by giving in to Hitler and Mussolini. In September 1938, British Prime Minister Neville Chamberlain and French Premier Edouard Daladier met with Hitler and Mussolini in Munich to discuss the Sudetenland situation. (No Czech delegates were invited.) The participants decided that Germany could take the Sudetenland in exchange for Hitler's promise to end further Nazi aggression in Europe.

B. Italian Aggression in Africa

In October 1935, Mussolini invaded Ethiopia, which bordered Italian Somaliland in eastern Africa. Its army could not defend itself against the well-equipped Italian forces.

The Ethiopian emperor Haile Selassie pleaded with the League of Nations for help. The League asked its members to ban sales of food and war materials to Italy until it withdrew. Unfortunately, many members ignored the request, and in May 1936, Italy annexed Ethiopia.

C. Spanish Civil War

In 1936, General Francisco Franco, a Spanish military officer, led a revolt against Spain's democratic government. The Loyalists, who supported the government, received some Soviet, European, and U.S. aid. Fascist Italy and Nazi Germany gave Franco strong support. After three years of great suffering, the Spanish Loyalists finally lost the war. In 1939, Franco established a Fascist dictatorship in Spain.

INFO CHECK

1. List Hitler's violations of the Treaty of Versailles. Why did the United States and other nations fail to stop these actions?

2. Name the leaders who attended the Munich Conference of 1938. How did the decisions reached reflect the policy of appeasement?

3. How did the Italian invasion of Ethiopia and the Spanish Civil War bring the world closer to World War II?

III. GLOBAL CONFLICT

In March 1939, Hitler defied the Munich Conference and took over the rest of Czechoslovakia. Britain and France vowed to resist further Nazi aggression.

A. Outbreak of War

NONAGGRESSION PACT. In 1936, Hitler and Mussolini formed the Rome-Berlin Axis and made an informal agreement with Japan. The Rome-Berlin-Tokyo Axis was created in 1940.

In 1939, Hitler and Stalin signed a **nonaggression pact** (pledge not to attack each other). Temporarily secure from attack from the east, Hitler was free to plan new aggression.

INVASION OF POLAND. On September 1, 1939, German forces struck Poland with great speed and mobility. Germans called this tactic **blitzkrieg** (lightning war).

Britain and Poland had a mutual assistance treaty. Joined by France, Britain demanded an end to the attack. When Hitler refused, France and Britain declared war on Germany. Meanwhile, the Soviet Union attacked Poland from the east. In less than a month, Germany and the Soviet Union divided Poland between them.

Russia also seized Latvia, Lithuania, and Estonia on the Baltic Sea and made them part of the Soviet Union. It then advanced on Finland in the "Winter War" of 1939–1941, in which Finland lost territory to the Soviet Union.

MOVEMENT NORTH AND WEST. In April 1940, German forces took over Norway and Denmark and then conquered Belgium and Holland. France fell to a German invasion in June 1940. At this point, Italy entered the war.

OCCUPYING FRANCE. The Germans divided France into Occupied France in the north, under German control, and Vichy France in the south, administered by pro-German French officials.

Most of the French regarded those who cooperated with Vichy as traitors. Some leaders escaped to North Africa and Britain. General Charles de Gaulle organized the French in Britain into the "Free French."

BATTLE OF BRITAIN. Britain stood alone against the dictators. The technically neutral United States, Britain's colonies, and some of its former colonies sent aid.

Winston Churchill, the new prime minister, made speeches to bolster British courage. In August 1940, the German air force started the Battle of Britain—the unrelenting bombing of British cities, industrial areas, seaports, and military installations. The Royal Air Force, however, destroyed large numbers of German planes.

By June 1941, the air raids eased, and Britain seemed safe from a land invasion. Churchill praised the Royal Air Force: "Never in the field of human conflict was so much owed by so many to so few."

EASTERN EUROPE. Italian forces conquered Albania in 1939. Hungary and Romania joined the

American cartoon depicting the Nazi menace, 1940

Berlin-Rome-Tokyo Axis in late 1940. Bulgaria followed in 1941. By May 1941, Fascist forces had crushed Yugoslavia and Greece and thus gained control of the Balkans.

INVADING THE SOVIET UNION. In June 1941, Hitler broke the nonaggression pact with Stalin and invaded the Soviet Union to gain its oil-rich and grain-producing areas. Britain and the United States sent arms and food to the Soviets. After the Soviets counterattacked in December 1941, a

harsh winter stopped the Germans from advancing on Moscow.

B. Holocaust

Hitler set up a "New Order" in Europe. Germans colonized Eastern Europe. Deserving members of the "master race" were rewarded with farms, factories, and businesses, with the original owners serving as their employees. Millions of European prisoners of all nationalities and culture

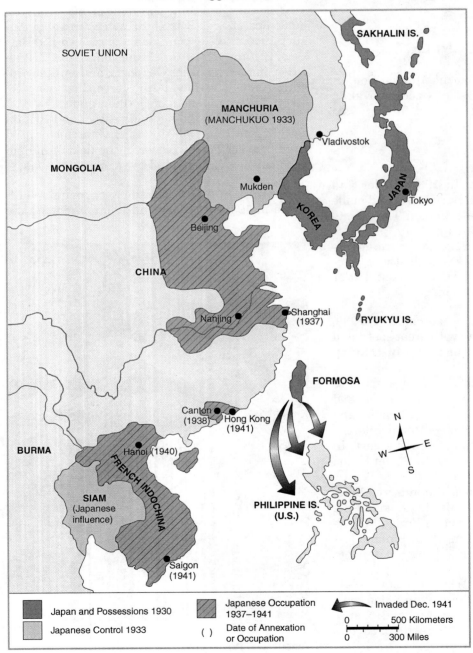

Asia: Axis Aggression, 1930–1940

groups—Jews, Gypsies, Russians, Poles, homosexuals, the disabled—slaved in factories built within the concentration camps. Hitler had marked most of them for elimination.

ANTI-SEMITISM. The 1935 Nuremberg Laws nullified citizenship for German Jews. During Kristallnacht (Night of Broken Glass) on November 9–10, 1938, Nazis attacked Jews and looted their homes, synagogues, and businesses.

Many Jews fled to other parts of Europe, Britain, and North and South America. Most countries, however, including the United States, limited the number of Jews who could enter.

The Nazis called their continued presence in Europe "the Jewish problem." In January 1942, the Wannsee Conference was called to plan a "final solution"—the elimination by extermination of all Jews in death camps. This Nazi plan is an example of **genocide**, the deliberate mass killing of an entire national, ethnic, or religious group.

Death Camps. One of the largest death camps was Auschwitz in Poland, where some three million Jews were murdered. In all, the Nazis killed at least six million Jews and an equal number of Poles, Russians, Gypsies, homosexuals, and others.

The Nazis' attempted genocide of Jews is now known as the **Holocaust**.

C. Shaky U.S. Neutrality

AID TO BRITAIN. In March 1941, in spite of U.S. neutrality, President Franklin Roosevelt persuaded Congress to pass the Lend-Lease Act. It authorized the United States to sell, lend, or lease military equipment to the Allies. Britain could also buy U.S. arms if it paid cash and carried them in its own ships. After the Germans attacked the Soviet Union, it also received U.S. aid.

D. Japanese in Asia

After Japan began its takeover of French and Dutch colonies in Indochina and the Dutch East Indies (now Indonesia), President Roosevelt banned the export of petroleum, petroleum products, and scrap metal—all vital to Japanese industry. Japan was unable to persuade the United States to change its policy.

E. U.S. Declaration of War

On December 7, 1941, Japan bombed the U.S. naval base at Pearl Harbor, Hawaii. Most of the planes and ships of the Pacific fleet were destroyed.

Thus, the Japanese were free to take over East Asia and key Pacific islands. They also attacked the Philippines, Hong Kong, and Thailand, and pushed on to the Netherlands East Indies with its oil resources.

On December 8, the United States declared war on Japan. Three days later, Germany and Italy declared war on the United States.

INFO CHECK

1. Identify or define: Rome-Berlin-Tokyo Axis, blitzkrieg, Winter War, Occupied France, Vichy France, Winston Churchill.

2. Explain the importance of the Battle of Britain. What was the United States doing at this time?

3. How did Hitler change German policy toward Russia in June 1941? Why?

4. Define the term "New Order." What was the role of the Holocaust in the New Order? Why was the Holocaust a policy of genocide?

5. How did Japanese actions in Asia bring the United States into World War II?

IV. FIGHTING WORLD WAR II

In January 1942, the United States, Britain, the Soviet Union, and 23 other nations signed the Declaration of the United Nations. The Allies pledged a united effort to defeat the Axis. Their first aim was to win the war in Europe, while channeling enough supplies and soldiers to the Pacific to contain further Japanese aggression.

A. Allied Strategy in Europe

By winning the Battle of El Alamein in Egypt in November 1942, the British kept the Italians and Germans from taking the Suez Canal. Allied forces then landed in Algeria and Morocco. By May 1943, they controlled all of North Africa.

STALINGRAD. In February 1943, the Germans suffered a major defeat at Stalingrad (present-day Volgograd) but held on in the western Soviet Union until fall. Then, the Soviets advanced west toward Germany and south into the Balkans. They reached Berlin in April 1945.

The Allies invaded Italy in July 1943. Mussolini was ousted, imprisoned, and later executed by anti-Fascists. The new Italian government signed an **armistice** (temporary halt in fighting) in September, and Rome fell to the Allies in June 1944. Germany occupied northern Italy until May 1945.

World War II in Europe, 1943–1945

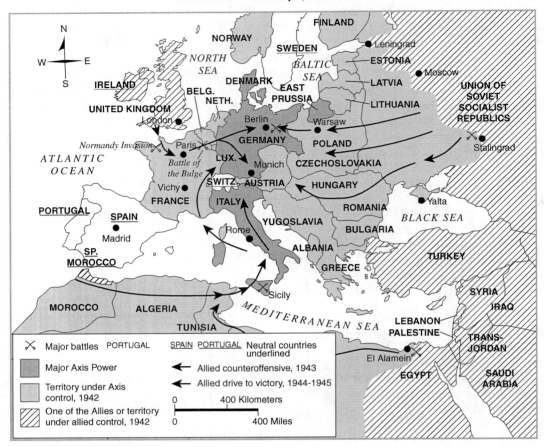

D-DAY. On June 6, 1944 (D-Day), U.S. General Dwight D. Eisenhower led Allied troops across the English Channel to Normandy, France. They pushed the German forces out of France, Belgium, and Holland. In December 1944, the Germans attacked in Belgium (Battle of the Bulge), but the Allies made a successful counterattack.

V-E DAY. As the Allies moved into Germany, Hitler committed suicide. Shortly afterward, Germany surrendered. The war in Europe was officially over on May 8, 1945 (V-E Day).

B. Allied Strategy in the Pacific

BATAAN DEATH MARCH. In the battle for the Philippines, U.S. and Filipino troops retreated from Manila to the Bataan Peninsula, where they surrendered on April 9, 1942. The Japanese force-marched their starving captives to a distant prison camp, shooting about 10,000 who could not keep up.

SEA BATTLES. In May 1942, the Allies won the Battle of the Coral Sea, which prevented the

Japanese from invading Australia. A second naval victory in 1942, the Battle of Midway, stopped Japan's eastward advance.

ISLAND HOPPING. The Allied strategy in the Pacific was called "island hopping." They attacked key Japanese-held islands and used the ones they won as bases to invade other islands. The Japanese on bypassed islands were cut off from supplies and support. Some key islands where battles were fought were Guadalcanal, Tarawa, Kwajalein, and Iwo Jima.

In the fall of 1944, General Douglas MacArthur landed in the Philippines. The U.S. Navy then destroyed most of the Japanese Navy in the Battle of Leyte Gulf.

CHINA AND INDIA. Chinese forces kept the Japanese from overrunning all of China. British and Indian troops pushed the Japanese out of eastern India and Burma.

CLOSING IN ON JAPAN. In early 1945, U.S. bombers rained great destruction on major Japan-

World War II in the Pacific, 1941–1945

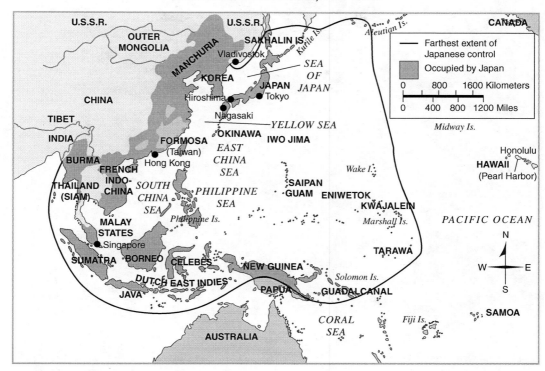

ese cities. In April, U.S. troops landed on the island of Okinawa, 350 miles south of Japan.

Atomic Bomb. When Japanese leaders refused to surrender, as the United States urged, it dropped an atomic bomb on Hiroshima on August 6, 1945. Between four and five square miles of the city were leveled and more than 80,000 people killed. Two days later, the Soviet Union declared war on Japan. With the Japanese still refusing to surrender, the United States dropped an atomic bomb on Nagasaki on August 9. Japan officially surrendered on September 2, 1945 (V-J Day).

C. New Technology

The atomic bomb was only one of the technological advances that played a role in World War II. Even conventional bombs caused far greater destruction than those of World War I.

Giant aircraft carriers brought fighter planes close to their targets and were vital to the success of the war in the Pacific. The United States had no land bases between Hawaii and Australia, and the Japanese controlled the islands in between.

Radar enabled soldiers to detect approaching enemies and pinpoint targets. Armored tanks

bulldozed their way into cities and across enemy lines.

INFO CHECK

1. Who were the Allied Powers?
2. How did each of the following lead to Allied victory in World War II? El Alamein, Stalingrad, D-Day, V-E Day.
3. Explain how island hopping and the atomic bomb led to Allied victory in the Pacific.

V. PLANNING THE POSTWAR WORLD

A. Yalta

In February 1945, Stalin, Churchill, and Roosevelt met at Yalta on the Black Sea to discuss peace terms for Germany. They agreed that the Soviets, British, French, and Americans would each occupy a zone in Germany, essentially dividing Germany into eastern and western parts. Germany was disarmed and its war criminals punished. The Soviets were allowed to keep control of several Eastern European countries.

The Yalta conferees also agreed to replace the League of Nations with a new peace organization, the United Nations.

"The Big Three"—Churchill, Roosevelt, and Stalin— meeting at Yalta, 1945

B. United Nations

In April 1945, delegates from 50 nations organized the *United Nations (UN)*. The U.S. Senate approved U.S. membership.

The UN works to keep the world at peace and to improve the lives of its people. It has six major components:

- The *General Assembly* oversees UN operations and discusses questions posed by members. All independent countries are eligible. Each member has one vote.

- The *Security Council* is charged with keeping world peace. It has ten rotating and five permanent members—the United States, Russia, Great Britain, China, and France. Each of the five can veto any proposed actions.

- The *Secretariat* manages the day-to-day operations of the UN. Its head, the *Secretary General,* is the UN's spokesperson and helps settle disputes among nations.

- The *Economic and Social Council* undertakes projects to improve living standards and health conditions throughout the world and to promote human rights and educational and cultural cooperation.

- The *International Court of Justice* hears disputes between countries that agree to abide by its decision.

- The *Trustee Council* helped the colonies and territories of Japan, Germany, and Italy to develop self-government. Now that these territories are independent, the council's status is inactive.

C. Early Postwar Developments

U.S. troops under General MacArthur occupied postwar Japan. A new constitution made it a democracy and ended the emperor's godlike status. Japan was allowed to have only a defensive military force. Japanese war criminals were tried and punished.

At Nuremberg, Germany, an International Military Tribunal met in 1945 and 1946 to try 22 Nazi leaders charged with crimes against humanity, violations of international law, and the waging of aggressive warfare. Nineteen were found guilty.

Many war criminals who escaped to other countries were tracked down by organizations in the United States, Israel, and elsewhere. The most infamous was Adolf Eichmann, who had planned the arrest and deportation to death camps of millions of Jews. Found living in Argentina, Eichmann was captured by Israeli commandos in 1960, tried in Jerusalem, and executed.

The Soviet Union occupied most of the Eastern European countries that it had liberated from Nazi rule. They became known as **satellites** because of their dependence on Soviet leadership for economic and political policy decisions. Winston Churchill said that Eastern Europe was cut off from Western influence by "an iron curtain."

The Soviet Union and the United States had the largest military forces left in the world. The United States had the strongest economy.

INFO CHECK

1. Explain why you AGREE or DISAGREE with this statement: The Yalta Conference had little influence on postwar Germany.

2. How does the UN General Assembly differ in composition and duties from the Security Council?

3. Define: satellite (nation), iron curtain. What do they indicate about Eastern Europe after World War II?

VI. LITERATURE AND ART

A. Literature

GERMAN WRITERS. Thomas Mann wrote such famous novels as *Buddenbrooks, Death in Venice, The Magic Mountain,* and *Doctor Faustus.* In *Doctor Faustus,* the tragic vision of a solitary composer is set against the rise of nazism in Germany. Because of his severe criticism of the Nazis and his marriage to a Jewish woman, Mann was forced to flee Germany in 1933.

The Nazis also persecuted Erich Maria Remarque, who had written about World War I in his novel *All Quiet on the Western Front.* Remarque took refuge in the United States.

FRENCH WRITERS. The early novels of Louis-Ferdinand Céline reflected the pessimism and anxiety caused by World War I. Two of his most famous are *Journey to the End of Night* and *Death on the Installment Plan.* His work became increasingly full of rage. Accused in 1944 of collaborating with the Nazis, Céline fled to Denmark, where he was imprisoned.

Jean-Paul Sartre was a philosopher of **existentialism**, which is concerned with the plight of persons who take responsibility for their acts without knowing what is good or evil. Most people find this freedom too frightening to accept. The hero of Sartre's play *Dirty Hands* struggles to accept his freedom to make decisions. In the end, he refuses to be used by a corrupt political group even though his decision leads to his death.

Existentialists like Sartre formed part of the resistance movement against Nazi occupation of France.

ENGLISH WRITERS. World War I, the Great Depression, and Fascist aggression had a great impact on British intellectuals. It is exemplified in the works of three English poets, W. H. Auden, Cecil Day-Lewis, and Stephen Spender.

Auden experimented with many poetic forms and published numerous volumes of poetry. His poem *The Age of Anxiety* expressed the confusion and aimlessness felt by people during World War II.

The Room and Other Poems and *Whispering Roots* are among the collections of poems that Day-Lewis published after World War II. In 1968, he became poet laureate of England.

Spender also published several collections of poetry. His autobiography *World Within World* traces the important intellectual trends of the 1930s and 1940s.

U.S. WRITERS. In his novel *Dragon's Teeth,* Upton Sinclair chronicled Hitler's rise to power.

Sinclair Lewis's novels exposed the mediocrity of middle-class America. In *It Can't Happen Here,* he depicted the kinds of moral weaknesses that might make Americans fall prey to a fascist dictator.

B. Art

The Nazis banned the more experimental forms of modern art. So many artists took refuge in the United States that the center of artistic activity shifted from Europe to New York.

KANDINSKY AND EXPRESSIONISM. The Russian painter Wassily Kandinsky originated **expressionism** in the early 1900s. Kandinsky felt that even though paintings are inspired by personal feelings and experiences, they can arouse a universal response. He pointed out that music, which relies on mathematics, can transform a subjective feeling into something that everyone can experience. Therefore, his paintings, like music, were abstract and used line and color with mathematical precision.

Kandinsky's influence continued after his death in 1944. Many painters who fled Europe— Max Ernst (German), Fernand Léger (French) André Masson (French), Piet Mondrian (Dutch)—brought Kandinsky's ideas with them.

ABSTRACT EXPRESSIONISM. In the United States, expressionism, as practiced by some notable painters, became known as **abstract expressionism**:

- Willem de Kooning, originally from the Netherlands, was best known for abstract pictures of women.

Timeline

Year	Dates and Events

A.D.

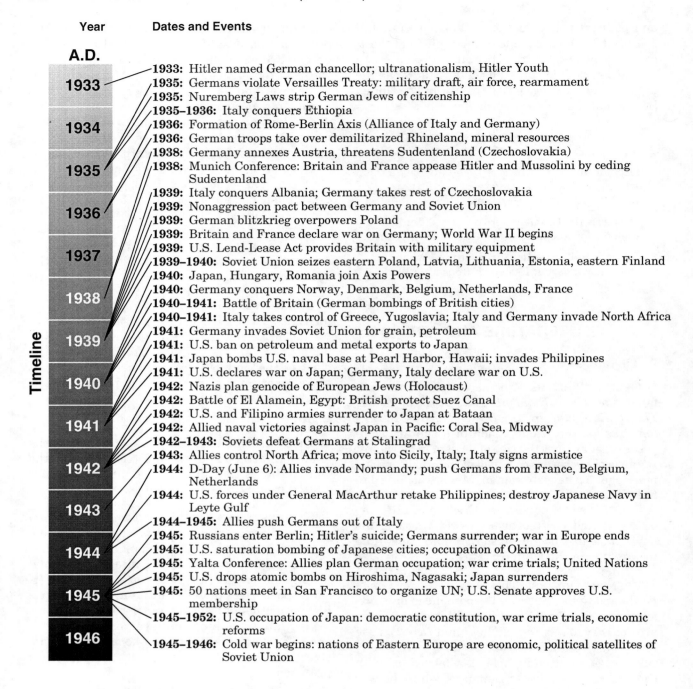

1933: Hitler named German chancellor; ultranationalism, Hitler Youth
1935: Germans violate Versailles Treaty: military draft, air force, rearmament
1935: Nuremberg Laws strip German Jews of citizenship
1935–1936: Italy conquers Ethiopia
1936: Formation of Rome-Berlin Axis (Alliance of Italy and Germany)
1936: German troops take over demilitarized Rhineland, mineral resources
1938: Germany annexes Austria, threatens Sudentenland (Czechoslovakia)
1938: Munich Conference: Britain and France appease Hitler and Mussolini by ceding Sudentenland
1939: Italy conquers Albania; Germany takes rest of Czechoslovakia
1939: Nonaggression pact between Germany and Soviet Union
1939: German blitzkrieg overpowers Poland
1939: Britain and France declare war on Germany; World War II begins
1939: U.S. Lend-Lease Act provides Britain with military equipment
1939–1940: Soviet Union seizes eastern Poland, Latvia, Lithuania, Estonia, eastern Finland
1940: Japan, Hungary, Romania join Axis Powers
1940: Germany conquers Norway, Denmark, Belgium, Netherlands, France
1940–1941: Battle of Britain (German bombings of British cities)
1940–1941: Italy takes control of Greece, Yugoslavia; Italy and Germany invade North Africa
1941: Germany invades Soviet Union for grain, petroleum
1941: U.S. ban on petroleum and metal exports to Japan
1941: Japan bombs U.S. naval base at Pearl Harbor, Hawaii; invades Philippines
1941: U.S. declares war on Japan; Germany, Italy declare war on U.S.
1942: Nazis plan genocide of European Jews (Holocaust)
1942: Battle of El Alamein, Egypt: British protect Suez Canal
1942: U.S. and Filipino armies surrender to Japan at Bataan
1942: Allied naval victories against Japan in Pacific: Coral Sea, Midway
1942–1943: Soviets defeat Germans at Stalingrad
1943: Allies control North Africa; move into Sicily, Italy; Italy signs armistice
1944: D-Day (June 6): Allies invade Normandy; push Germans from France, Belgium, Netherlands
1944: U.S. forces under General MacArthur retake Philippines; destroy Japanese Navy in Leyte Gulf
1944–1945: Allies push Germans out of Italy
1945: Russians enter Berlin; Hitler's suicide; Germans surrender; war in Europe ends
1945: U.S. saturation bombing of Japanese cities; occupation of Okinawa
1945: Yalta Conference: Allies plan German occupation; war crime trials; United Nations
1945: U.S. drops atomic bombs on Hiroshima, Nagasaki; Japan surrenders
1945: 50 nations meet in San Francisco to organize UN; U.S. Senate approves U.S. membership
1945–1952: U.S. occupation of Japan: democratic constitution, war crime trials, economic reforms
1945–1946: Cold war begins: nations of Eastern Europe are economic, political satellites of Soviet Union

- Robert Motherwell expressed his horror of fascism in pictures inspired by the Spanish Civil War.

- Clyfford Still, under the influence of abstract expressionism, painted upright, jagged shapes against dark backgrounds.

- Mark Rothko created compositions of colored rectangles against glowing backgrounds.

- Jackson Pollock felt that art was made by the unconscious mind. He hurled or dripped paint onto canvases and called this technique "action painting."

INFO CHECK

1. Select one writer and one artist of the World War II era and describe the work of each.

2. Define: existentialism, expressionism. How do they differ?

CHAPTER REVIEW

Multiple Choice

1. The Young Folk and Hitler Youth movements in Germany were organized for

1. teaching Nazi ideology
2. sports training
3. military basic training
4. all of the above.

2. Increasing the size of the German army, organizing an air force, and reoccupying the Rhineland are all examples of Hitler's

1. violation of the Treaty of Versailles
2. policy of nonalignment
3. demilitarized policy
4. pacifist policy.

3. The agreement of the British and French governments to turn over the Sudetenland to Hitler's Germany is an example of

1. neutrality
2. nonalignment
3. appeasement
4. blitzkrieg.

4. The treaty that paved the way for the German invasion of Poland and support of Hitler's future war plans was the

1. Berlin Conference
2. Rome-Berlin-Tokyo Axis
3. Kellogg-Briand Pact
4. Treaty of Portsmouth.

5. Before the establishment of concentration camps, the Nazis showed their anti-Semitic beliefs by

1. attempting to control German churches
2. passing the Nuremberg Laws
3. drafting Jewish youths into work battalions
4. removing travel restrictions for Jews.

6. The World War II term that refers to the planned destruction of a culture or religious group is

1. anti-Semitism
2. Kristallnacht
3. serial murder
4. genocide.

7. The Lend-Lease Act enabled the United States to

1. sell munitions to either Germany or the Allies
2. allow the purchase of war materials by any combatants
3. sell, loan, or lease war materials to the Allies
4. sell, loan, or lease war materials to the Axis.

8. The technological development that ended World War II and dominated postwar foreign policy was the development of

1. atomic weapons
2. radar
3. jet airplanes
4. attack-class submarines.

9. The Yalta Conference was important because

1. President Roosevelt did not attend
2. the terms for peace and the division of Germany into four zones was agreed to
3. Stalin and Churchill lost elections and were replaced by other leaders
4. German representatives signed the agreement ending the war.

10. The UN was formed to

1. separate Germany from the rest of the world
2. raise money for countries in need of assistance
3. form a military stronghold against Hitler
4. work for world peace and security.

11. The maps on pages 238 and 239 show that

1. Germany, Italy, and Japan were unsuccessful at keeping peace with their neighbors
2. Germany, Italy, and Japan invaded, attacked, or occupied many neighboring nations
3. Japan was less aggressive against its neighbors than were Italy and Germany
4. Italy and Germany invaded nations to their west while Japan invaded its eastern neighbors.

12. The photograph on page 240 shows that

1. there was little concern about the world's future after the defeat of the Axis Powers
2. the Allied leaders met for the purpose of structuring the postwar world
3. there were few disagreements between Stalin, Churchill, and Roosevelt
4. plans for creating the UN were made at Yalta.

Thematic Essays

1. *Task:* Explain how nationalism and propaganda aided Hitler's domination of Germany and set off World War II.

2. Many Germans willingly followed nazism. *Task:* Name a Nazi practice that would appeal to each of the following: a business owner, a factory worker, a teenager. Explain how these practices would cause such people to support nazism.

Document-Based Questions

Use the documents and your knowledge of Global History and Geography to answer the questions.

1. Study the map on page 238. Explain whether Germany's position in Europe was an advantage or disadvantage in a general war. Use information on the map to support your answer.

2. After Prime Minister Chamberlain agreed to Hitler's demand for the Sudetenland, he returned from Munich and defended his actions in the House of Commons:

   "Ever since I assumed my present office my main purpose has been to work for the pacification of Europe. . . . The path that leads to appeasement is long and bristles with obstacles. The question of Czechoslovakia is the latest and perhaps the most dangerous. Now that we have moved past it, I feel that it may be possible to make further progress along the road to sanity. In our relations with other countries everything depends upon there being sincerity and good will on both sides. I believe that there are sincerity and good will on both sides of this declaration."

   What policy is Chamberlain following and what has he received from Hitler in return for signing away a piece of Czechoslovakia?

3. Prime Minister Chamberlain explained his views on war and the Sudetenland:

   "However much we may sympathize with a small nation confronted by a big and powerful neighbor, we cannot in all circumstances undertake to involve the whole British Empire simply on her account. If we have to fight, it must be on large issues that. . . . I am myself a man of peace to the very depths of my soul. Armed conflict between nations is a nightmare to me. . . . "

What is Chamberlain's attitude to giving small nations help when they are threatened? Do you AGREE or DISAGREE with his views?

4. On May 11, 1940, Chamberlain resigned and Winston Churchill took office. Here are Churchill's responses in the House of Commons to questions about what his government's policy and aim would be:

   "You ask, what is our policy? I will say it is to wage war, by sea, land, and air, with all our might and with all the strength that God can give us. . . . You ask what is our aim? I can answer in one word: It is victory, victory at all costs, victory in spite of all terror, victory however long and hard the way may be. . . . "

Compare Churchill's policy with Chamberlain's.

5. A few days before the surrender of France in June 1940 and the defeat and forced evacuation of British troops at Dunkirk, Prime Minister Churchill addressed the House of Commons:

   "Even though large tracts of Europe and many old and famous states have fallen or may fall . . . we shall fight on the seas and oceans. . . .

   "We shall defend our Island, whatever the cost may be, we shall fight on the beaches, we shall fight on the landing grounds, we shall fight in the fields and in the streets, we shall fight in the hills; we shall never surrender. . . . "

If you were a British citizen at this time, how would you react to this speech? If you were a German general, why would you be discouraged by this speech?

Document-Based Essay

Task: Compare and contrast the attitudes and actions of the two British prime ministers and discuss the value of Winston Churchill's wartime leadership to Great Britain.

UNIT REVIEW

Thematic Essays

1. How did technology affect the lives of people and politics of nations in the 20th century? *Task:* Include in your answer military and industrial advances as well as communication and transportation advances.

2. At the beginning of World War II, the dictatorships and military aggressions of Italy, Germany, and Japan seemed unstoppable. Why were they initially so successful and democratic

responses so weak? *Task:* Consider in your answer the types of governments, world economic conditions, experiences in World War I, and people's attitudes.

Document-Based Questions

Use your reading of the chapters and the documents to answer the questions that follow.

1. In 1792, two years after the French issued their revolutionary "Declaration of the Rights of Man,"

Mary Wollstonecraft published this statement entitled "Vindication of the Rights of Woman":

" . . . Contending for the rights of woman, my main argument is built on the simple principle that if she is not prepared by education to become the companion of man, she will stop the progress of knowledge and virtue. . . . Let woman share the rights, and she will emulate [copy] the virtues of man; for she must grow more perfect when emancipated [freed]. . . . "

What does Wollstonecraft want for women and why?

2. John Stuart Mill, English philosopher and member of Parliament, in 1869 argued for women's rights in his work "The Subjection of Women":

" . . . To have a voice in choosing those by whom one is to be governed, is a means of self-protection due to everyone. . . . The majority of the women of any class are not likely to differ in political opinion from the majority of men of the same class, unless the question be one in which the interests of women, as such, are in some way involved; and if they are so, women require the suffrage as a guarantee of just and equal consideration. . . . "

Identify three reasons Mill gives for granting suffrage to women.

3. In 1883, Susan B. Anthony spoke about the right to vote in the United States:

"It was we the people; not we, the white male citizens; nor yet we, the male citizens; but we, the whole people, who formed the union. And we formed it, not to give the blessings of liberty, but to secure them; not to the half of ourselves and the half of posterity, but to the whole people— women as well as men."

How and in what ways do Anthony's views AGREE or DISAGREE with arguments presented in the previous documents?

4. From a speech given by Emmeline Pankhurst in 1913:

"I want to say here and now that the only justification for violence, the only justification for damage to property, the only justification for risk to comfort of other human beings is the fact that you have tried all other available means and failed to secure justice. . . . Our marriage and divorce laws are a disgrace to civilization. . . . After she has risked her life to bring a child into the world [a woman] has absolutely no parental rights over the future of that child. . . . [A man can] bring his mistress into the house to live and she can not get legal relief from such a marriage. . . . Take the industrial side of the question; have men's wages for a hard day's work ever been so low and inadequate as are women's wages today . . . ?"

What sort of actions is Pankhurst willing to take for her cause, and how does she justify them?

5. How does the poster show the changing role of women brought about by factory work and the world wars?

UNIT VII

The World Since 1945

Year	Dates and Events
A.D.	
1940	**1945:** Potsdam Conference: Allied leaders recognize Soviet control of Eastern Europe
	1948–1952: Marshall Plan: U.S. economic aid to European nations recovering from war
	1949: Organization of NATO, defense pact of Western nations
1949	**1950–1953:** Korean War: South (with U.S. aid) against North (with Chinese aid)
	1959: Castro leads Cuban revolt; sets up Communist state allied to Soviets
1950	**1960:** Iran, Kuwait, Saudi Arabia, Venezuela organize OPEC to regulate production and price of oil
	1961: East Germans build Berlin Wall
	1962: Cuban Missile Crisis: Soviets remove missiles, U.S. pledges nonintervention in Cuba
1959	**1966–1968:** "Great Cultural Revolution," in China
1960	**1967:** Six-Day War: Israel occupies East Jerusalem, parts of Syria, Jordan, Egypt
	1971–1973: East Pakistan rebels against West Pakistan; becomes nation of Bangladesh
	1973–1975: U.S.–North Vietnam peace; North Vietnam defeats the South
1969	**1977:** U.S. and Communist China establish diplomatic relations
	1985: Gorbachev becomes Soviet leader; perestroika (economic reforms), glasnost (openness)
1970	**1989–1991:** Poland, Hungary, Czechoslovakia, Albania, Bulgaria, East Germany hold free elections, turn out Communists
1979	**1990:** Reunification of East and West Germany
	1991: Operation Desert Storm drives Iraq from Kuwait
1980	**1991:** Collapse of Soviet Union and end of cold war; Soviet republics form CIS
	1994: Multiracial government rules South Africa for first time, with Mandela as president
1989	**1997:** Britain returns Hong Kong to China
	1999: Czech Republic, Hungary, Poland become members of NATO
1990	**2000:** First crew goes aboard International Space Station
	2001: Al Qaeda terrorists destroy World Trade Center in New York City and damage Pentagon in Washington, D.C. U.S. President George W. Bush declares war on global terrorism
1999	**2002:** U.S. and British forces remove Taliban government and destroy Al Qaeda bases in Afghanistan
2000	**2003:** U.S. and British forces invade Iraq and end regime of Saddam Hussein
	2005: Palestinian elections place Hamas in control of their government
2009	**2006:** Mideast tensions increase as Iraq moves toward civil war; Israel fights Hamas in Gaza and Hezbollah in Lebanon

CHAPTER
24

Cold War

I. COMPETITION FOR WORLD LEADERSHIP

After World War II, the United States and the Soviet Union emerged as **superpowers** with exceptionally powerful military forces. They began to compete for world leadership. Competition developed into hostility, which deepened into the so-called **cold war** (1945–1990). At first, however, only the United States had nuclear weapons.

A. Soviet Control of Eastern Europe

TEHERAN. At the 1943 conference in Teheran, Iran, the Allies accepted Stalin's final assault plan on Germany. The Americans and British attacked from France, while the Soviets struck from the east. As the Soviets drove the Axis forces from Poland, Bulgaria, Romania, Hungary, parts of Yugoslavia, and much of Czechoslovakia, they occupied those regions themselves.

YALTA. At the 1945 Yalta meeting, Stalin tried to make Soviet control of Eastern Europe official. Churchill and Roosevelt insisted that each country choose its own government. In a compromise, the Eastern European countries were to have free elections, but their policies had to be friendly to the Soviet Union.

POTSDAM. Stalin wanted a buffer zone of Communist allies between Germany and the Soviet Union. In July 1945, at the conference in Potsdam, Germany, Stalin noted that no Eastern European country would elect a Soviet-friendly government. To avoid unpleasant conflict on the issue, Britain and the United States assented to Soviet control of the countries in question.

At Potsdam, Clement Attlee had replaced Churchill as British prime minister, and Harry Truman had replaced Franklin Roosevelt as U.S. president.

B. Soviet Expansion and U.S. Response

TRUMAN DOCTRINE. In postwar Greece, **guerrillas** (rebels specializing in surprise attacks) wanted a Communist government. Soviet satellites sent them aid.

At the same time, the Soviets were pressuring Turkey and Iran to give up territory bordering the Dardanelles between the Black and Mediterranean seas.

In March 1947, President Truman sent Greece, Iran, and Turkey aid in their fight against Communist forces. This program, the *Truman Doctrine,* stated that the United States would "support free peoples" resisting takeover by outside forces.

MARSHALL PLAN. To prevent the spread of Communist political parties in Europe, U.S. Secretary of State George C. Marshall introduced the *Marshall Plan* in 1947. It asked all European nations, including the Soviet Union, to participate in an economic recovery plan, which the United States would fund. The Communist countries refused.

Between 1948 and 1952, $12 billion in U.S. aid went to 16 West European countries. Thus, the region remained democratic and achieved greater prosperity than ever.

CONTAINMENT. President Truman established the Point Four Program to give technical assistance to developing nations in Africa, Asia, and Latin America.

Together, the Truman Doctrine, Marshall Plan, and Point Four Program made up the policy of **containment**. Its aim was to block Soviet expansion into areas that had been free of communism in 1945.

BERLIN BLOCKADE. To test the will of the West, Soviet troops helped Czech Communists turn out their elected government in February 1948.

Berlin, in East Germany, was divided into Soviet East Berlin and West Berlin, controlled by Britain,

Berlin children greeting a
U.S. plane flying in food over
the Soviet blockade

France, and the United States. The Soviets tried to take over all Berlin by closing highways and railroad lines that brought supplies from West Germany to West Berlin. To avoid sending in troops and possibly starting a war, the United States and its allies airlifted supplies to Berlin.

Planes brought in more than 7,000 tons of food, fuel, and machinery every day. After 11 months, the Soviets reopened the land routes across East Germany.

C. Military Alliances

NATO. In 1949, twelve Western nations formed the *North Atlantic Treaty Organization (NATO)* against Soviet aggression. They stated that an at-

Europe After World War II

The Cold War: Opposing European Alliances

NATO (1949–)		Warsaw Pact (1955–1990)
Belgium (1949)	Lithuania (2004)	Albania (1955; withdrew 1968)
Britain (1949)	Luxembourg (1949)	Bulgaria (1955)
Bulgaria (2004)	The Netherlands (1949)	Czechoslovakia (1955)
Canada (1949)	Norway (1949)	East Germany (1955)
Denmark (1949)	Poland (1999)	Hungary (1955)
Estonia (2004)	Portugal (1949)	Poland (1955)
France (1949)	Romania (2004)	Romania (1955)
Germany (reunited) (1990)	Slovakia (2004)	Soviet Union (1955)
Greece (1951)	Slovenia (2004)	
Hungary (1999)	Spain (1982)	
Iceland (1949)	Turkey (1951)	
Italy (1949)	United States (1949)	
Latvia (2004)	West Germany (1954)	

tack on one member was an attack on all. Later, Greece, Turkey, West Germany, and Spain also joined NATO. U.S. troops under NATO command were stationed in Europe, especially in West Germany.

WARSAW PACT. In 1955, the Soviet Union and its satellites organized the *Warsaw Pact* against NATO aggression. In 1968, Albania forged ties with Communist China and resigned from the pact. Yugoslavia's leader, Josip Broz, called Tito, preferred to remain independent of the Soviet Union. The Warsaw Pact ended in 1991, after the collapse of the Soviet Union. NATO still exists.

D. Nuclear Weapons and the Space Race

The superpowers competed to develop the deadliest weapons. In 1949, the Soviet Union produced its first atomic bomb. In the early 1950s, both the United States and the Soviet Union developed the more powerful hydrogen bomb.

Once the superpowers were more or less equal in nuclear power, the space race began; the aim was to build Earth-orbiting satellites that could detect where the other side had stockpiled its bombs.

In 1957, the Soviets launched *Sputnik 1,* the first Earth-orbiting satellite. The U.S. satellite *Explorer I* was put into orbit in 1958. In 1961, Soviet cosmonaut Yuri Gagarin became the first person to orbit Earth. In 1969, the United States landed two men on the moon.

INFO CHECK

1. Explain how superpower competition after World War II led to the cold war.

2. Define containment. List the steps taken by the United States to implement this policy.

3. Name the two great alliance systems of the cold war. How did they change in the early 1990s?

4. How did the space race begin? List space race achievements of the United States and the Soviet Union.

II. CONTROL OF DEVELOPING COUNTRIES

After the war, most colonized countries became independent. At first politically and economically weak, they relied on stronger countries for aid and advice. In return, their helpers expected trade advantages and political alliances.

When Nikita Khrushchev succeeded Stalin in 1953, he extended "friendship treaties" to developing countries in Asia, Africa, and Latin America. He also offered military advice and support to colonized peoples who were not yet independent.

A. North Africa and the Middle East

EGYPT. In 1955, the Soviet Union and Egypt, under Gamal Abdel Nasser, made an arms agreement, and the Soviets promised to help Egypt against Israel. To lure Egypt away from Soviet ties, the United States offered Nasser funds to build the Aswan Dam on the Nile River. Nasser, however, continued to favor the Soviets. In 1956, Nasser took the Suez Canal from France and Britain, planning to apply the tolls paid by ships using the canal to the Aswan Dam project. Britain, France, and Israel invaded Egypt.

Israel seized the Gaza Strip along the Mediterranean coast from Egypt. As Israel prepared to invade the Sinai Peninsula, and France and Britain moved to seize the Suez Canal, the Soviet Union threatened to drive all three from Egypt.

The United States joined the Soviet Union in protesting the invasion. Fearing a third world war, UN peacekeeping troops occupied the area around the canal and opened it to all ships except those from Israel. The Soviet Union then gave Egypt money and technical aid for constructing the Aswan Dam.

IRAQ. In July 1958, General Abdul Karim Kassem, a radical nationalist, led a revolt against pro-Western Iraq and set up a pro-Communist republic there. After Kassem was assassinated in 1963, three regimes followed, the last of which brought Saddam Hussein to power. In

The Middle East

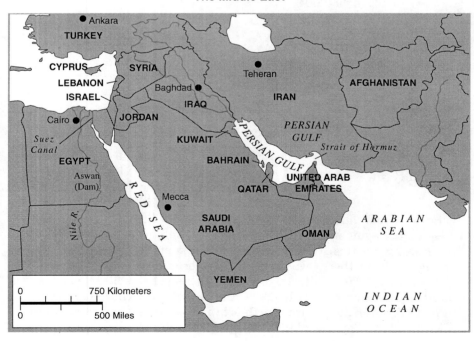

1972, Iraq and the Soviet Union signed a formal alliance.

B. AFRICA

REPUBLIC OF THE CONGO. After the Congo declared independence from France in 1960, different Congolese groups struggled for power. With Soviet support, the Congo became a Communist state in 1964 but kept economic ties to several Western nations. Strikes and other problems plagued the country. In 1990, the Congo set up a multiparty political system and abandoned Marxist ideology.

ANGOLA. After Portugal freed Angola in 1975, civil war broke out. The Soviet Union backed the *Popular Movement for the Liberation of Angola (MPLA),* and Cuba sent in troop support. The United States and South Africa allied with the *National Union for the Total Independence of Angola (UNITA).*

In 1976, MPLA formed a Marxist government, which UNITA refused to recognize, and the violence continued. In 1991, Angola, Cuba, and South Africa signed a peace treaty, all political parties were legalized, and UNITA, refusing to accept the results of the 1992 elections, continued to oppose MPLA. A cease-fire agreement was reached in 2006.

C. Latin America

CUBA. The unequal distribution of wealth in Cuba caused social unrest. In 1959, Fidel Castro led a successful Communist revolution, and Cuba became a close ally of the Soviet Union. American leaders were disturbed because of Cuba's proximity to the U.S. mainland.

CHILE. In Chile, U.S. corporations controlled the copper industry, inflation was high, and a few landowners held most of the country's wealth. In 1970, Salvador Allende, a Marxist, was elected president. He nationalized the copper companies and banks and speeded up a program to equalize land distribution.

The U.S. *Central Intelligence Agency (CIA)* aided anti-Allende forces, and in 1973, his government was overturned. A right-wing **junta** (postrevolutionary governing group) under General Augusto Pinochet took control and returned businesses and land to private owners. Pinochet then imposed harsh military rule and censorship, which were strongly condemned by international human rights groups.

The Chilean economy thrived. In 1988, Pinochet lifted military restraints. However, Chileans rebelled when he tried to force his own election as president for an additional eight years. In 1989, they elected a more democratic president.

GUATEMALA. In 1951, Guatemala's president started a farm reform program. He took land held by the American-owned United Fruit Company. In 1954, the country's military, with U.S. support, took over the government.

Leftist guerrillas struggled against the repressive regime and its "death squads," organized to crush resistance in Indian villages. Even foreign diplomats were murdered.

In the mid-1980s, moderate leaders came into power but were unable to stop the political murders, even with the support of *Amnesty International* and the UN Commission for Human Rights. Finally, people suspected of "death squad" activity were arrested. In 1993, Guatemalans elected a pro-human rights president, and three years later, the civil war ended.

INFO CHECK

1. How did the conflicts between Israel and its Arab neighbors affect cold war competition in the Middle East?

2. Why do historians regard Angola's long civil war as an outgrowth of the cold war?

3. How did U.S.-Soviet competition affect events in Cuba and Chile?

III. COLD WAR ESCALATION

A. Korean War

In 1945, U.S. troops took over southern Korea from Japan, and Soviet troops occupied North Korea. The dividing line was the 38th parallel (line of latitude). The South's anti-Communist, representative government soon became a dictatorship. The North became Communist. U.S. troops left South Korea in 1949.

ATTACK. In June 1950, North Korean troops invaded South Korea. President Truman urged the UN to intervene, and a favorable vote was taken in the Security Council in the absence of the Soviet Union. The UN then asked members to organize a fighting force. The United States and 15 other members sent fighting units under the command of U.S. General MacArthur.

Korean War

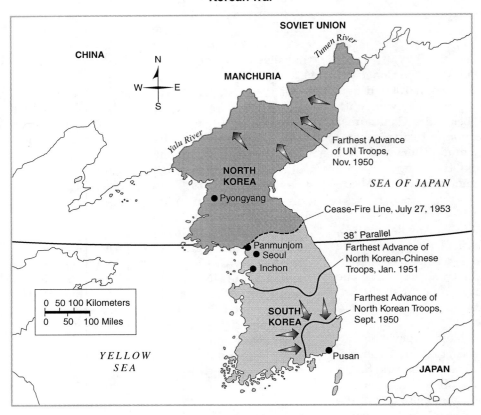

CHINA

SOVIET UNION

Tumen River

MANCHURIA

Yalu River

NORTH KOREA

● Pyongyang

Farthest Advance of UN Troops, Nov. 1950

SEA OF JAPAN

Cease-Fire Line, July 27, 1953

38° Parallel

● Panmunjom
● Seoul
● Inchon

Farthest Advance of North Korean-Chinese Troops, Jan. 1951

Farthest Advance of North Korean Troops, Sept. 1950

0 50 100 Kilometers
0   50   100 Miles

SOUTH KOREA

● Pusan

JAPAN

YELLOW SEA

FIGHTING. The South Korean and the UN troops nearly pushed the Communists out of Korea. In November 1950, Chinese soldiers joined the North Korean Communists. The fighting was then centered on the 38th parallel. In July 1953, an armistice was signed, but North and South Korea formally ended the war only in 1996.

POSTWAR KOREA. South Korea has prospered and become more democratic; a U.S. force remains there. North Korea is still a Communist dictatorship.

B. Vietnam

After World War II, France wanted to resume control of its colonies in Indochina. A Communist-nationalist group led by Ho Chi Minh fought to free Vietnam. The Soviet Union aided the Vietnamese, and the United States backed the French. In 1954, the Vietnamese won an overwhelming victory at Dien Bien Phu.

In June 1954, peace agreements at Geneva, Switzerland, made Laos and Cambodia independent and divided Vietnam at the 17th parallel, with Communists in control of North Vietnam and anti-Communists in South Vietnam. Elections were planned for 1956 to choose one government for all

Vietnam. The United States and South Vietnam considered the agreements unfair and did not sign. The elections were never held; South Vietnam claimed that election results in the North would be falsified, and many Vietnamese distrusted the dictator who ruled South Vietnam as president.

From 1965 to 1973 U.S. and South Vietnamese forces battled North Vietnamese and Communist Viet Cong troops. Withdrawal of U.S. forces in 1973 led to the unification of Vietnam under Communist rule in 1975.

C. Eastern Europe

HUNGARY. In October 1956, Hungarian students and workers successfully worked for the election of a liberal Communist leader. The new government promised to hold free elections and end Hungary's military alliance with the Soviet Union. Fearing that other countries would follow Hungary's lead, Nikita Khrushchev put down the new government by force.

CZECHOSLOVAKIA. In 1968, when Leonid Brezhnev succeeded Khrushchev, the Czechs also tried to liberalize their government by replacing the Soviet-backed leader with the reformer Alexander Dubcek. Dubcek lifted censorship and put trade

Southeast Asia

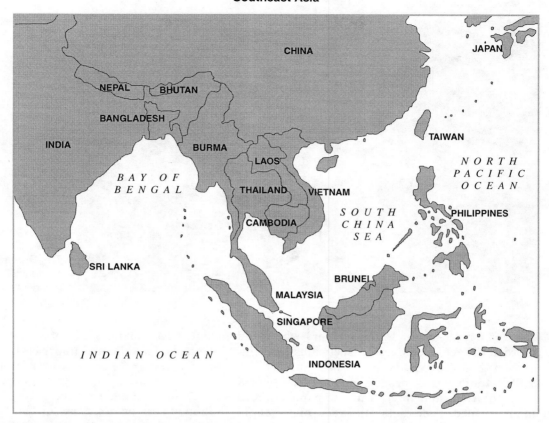

unions, managers, and consumers in charge of economic planning. There was no move to end the military alliance with the Soviets, but Brezhnev did not want the germ of self-government to spread. In August 1968, he sent 500,000 soldiers to occupy Czechoslovakia, which surrendered and canceled the reforms.

INFO CHECK

1. Compare the causes of the Korean War with the beginnings of the Vietnam War. What were the similarities and differences?

2. Describe developments in Hungary and Czechoslovakia in the 1950s and 1960s. Why do you think Western democracies took no action to aid the revolts?

IV. ECONOMIC ISSUES

Nearly all the postwar democracies had capitalistic economies, while the Communist countries had command economies. Offered the choice between communism and democracy, the leaders of developing countries tried to decide which kind of economic system would help them industrialize and create jobs.

A. Free-Market Versus Command Economy

The Soviet Union began to lose the cold war in the late 1980s, largely because of its command economy. One reason why the Soviet Union and its satellites grew poorer was their refusal to produce enough consumer goods, as in the West. For Eastern Europeans, even food and clothing were scarce because industries produced mainly military weapons and the technology needed for the space race.

Meanwhile, U.S. President Ronald Reagan (in office 1981–1989) increased military spending. The Soviet economy could not compete, especially after its expensive and prolonged war in Afghanistan began in 1979. (It had invaded that country to aid the pro-Communist government.) By 1991, the Soviet Union had collapsed and the cold war ended.

B. Economic Progress in India

India's efforts to industrialize were largely successful. Besides textiles, it produced automobiles, airplanes, satellites, computers, and nuclear reactors.

The Green Revolution was created by scientists who developed seeds that thrive in tropical climates, better fertilizers and insecticides, and more

The Green Revolution yields a bountiful wheat harvest in India.

efficient irrigation. In India, farmers who could afford fertilizer, seeds, and insecticides have increased their crop yield.

Still, India cannot produce enough food to feed its population, and many Indians cannot afford imported food. Poor diets, illiteracy, and a rapid population growth keep India poor.

India's advances in high-tech industries promise to further improve its economy. By the 21st century, firms from western countries were investing in India's high-tech industries and exporting thousands of jobs to India. It was uncertain, however, that this success would spread through the rest of the Indian population.

C. Economic Progress in Latin America

INDUSTRIALIZATION. Postwar Brazil and Mexico built factories and produced goods to export, but they could not build up domestic markets. Many Latin Americans could not afford to buy their products.

EXPLOITATION. Foreign investors, to whom Latin American industrialists turned for help, often grew rich on the local resources and gave little in return. Many were from the United States, and the resulting distrust of Americans caused several Latin American countries to adopt Socialist governments.

UNREST. Successful industrialization often brought unrest. Urban industrial workers demanded social change and tended to vote for So-

cialist reformers. Fearing the loss of their privileges, the middle and upper classes strengthened their support for conservative leaders.

AGRICULTURE. In much of Latin America, a few landowners owned most of the best land. They grew cash crops such as bananas and coffee rather than foods needed by the population. The wealthy bought imported food, which the poor could not afford.

Land Distribution. To ensure profits, planters grew cash crops on large plantations, a system that became the backbone of many national economies. Left-wing governments, however, divided large plantations among poor farmers, which angered landlords and the American companies that did business with them. The U.S. government helped landlords overthrow reform governments in Chile and Guatemala.

D. Economic Progress in Africa

Many African nations sought to modernize by nationalizing their industries. Unfortunately, during their colonial status, they had not been properly educated by their imperial masters. The newly formed companies lacked trained managers and skilled workers. Poor decision making, low-quality products, and changing world markets caused many businesses to fail.

FOOD PRODUCTION. African leaders, determined to industrialize, often ignored agricultural improvements. Old techniques could not produce enough food to feed Africa's expanding populations. And traditional farming caused erosion and exhausted the soil.

During droughts, more and more farmland dried out in a process known as **desertification**. This problem is particularly acute in West Africa, which has been struck by devastating famines. Hunger and disease have fanned political rivalries and caused many bloody conflicts.

E. Economic Recovery in Europe and Japan

GERMANY. The Allies transferred a large portion of postwar eastern Germany to Poland. Consequently, millions of displaced Germans were relocated to Soviet-occupied East Germany. There, the scarcity of housing and food and the Soviet takeover of German industries slowed economic recovery.

Under the Marshall Plan and a free-market economy, West Germany became a leading industrial power in the 1950s.

COMMON MARKET. The Marshall Plan strengthened ties among Western European countries. In 1957, six of them formed the *European Economic Community (EEC)* to follow common policies and increase mutual trade. Later, six more countries joined this so-called *Common Market,* which aimed to create a single currency and banking system. In 1991, the EEC and another group of European countries began to merge and became the *European Economic Area.* In 1994, it was renamed the *European Union (EU).* Membership increased to 27 nations in 2007.

COMECON. In 1949, the Soviet Union and its satellites formed the *Council for Mutual Economic Assistance (COMECON)* to encourage trade among members. In 1991, COMECON disbanded.

JAPAN. In 1947, the new Japanese constitution established a democratically elected legislature (the Diet). A prime minister was to head the government.

Japan and the Allies signed an official peace treaty in 1951, which stripped Japan of its colonies. (Japan regained several of them in 1972.) The mutual defense pact of 1952 allowed U.S. troops to stay in Japan for an indefinite time. Japan and the Soviet Union signed a separate agreement in 1956.

With U.S. aid, Japanese industry, especially the automobile and electronics industries, grew rapidly after the 1950s. Its economy became the second largest in the world, and by the 1990s, Japanese products dominated markets around the world.

F. Pacific Rim Economies

Because of their strong economies, South Korea, Taiwan, Hong Kong, and Singapore have been called the "four tigers" of East Asia.

At first, these Pacific Rim countries imported most manufactured goods and gradually improved their economies by developing strong domestic markets. Once their people's needs were satisfied, they began to manufacture and export radios, televisions, computers, and other electronic devices.

In the mid-1990s, inefficient banking practices and corrupt financial deals caused an economic crisis in East Asia. It soon spread to Europe, Latin America, and the United States. Most Pacific Rim nations then undertook reforms of their banking practices and put in place safeguards against crooked financing.

G. OPEC and an Oil Crisis

In 1960, Iran, Kuwait, Saudi Arabia, and Venezuela formed the *Organization of Petroleum Exporting Countries (OPEC).* In the next ten years, eight other nations joined. OPEC members were able to regulate the production and price of oil. The Arab members thus gained a powerful weapon against Israel and its supporters.

In the Six-Day War of 1967, Israel took Egypt's Sinai Peninsula, Syria's Golan Heights, Jordan's West Bank, and the Jordanian half of Jerusalem. The Arabs refused Israel's offer to return these territories in exchange for formal Arab recognition of Israel's right to exist.

During the 1973 war between Arabs and Israelis, OPEC raised the price of oil and reduced shipments of oil to Israel's supporters.

Increasing hostility between some Middle Eastern countries and the West also interfered with the flow of oil from the Mideast to the West. In 2003, the U.S. and Britain invaded Iraq. The instability that followed severely reduced production of Iraqi oil.

In 2006, the U.S. and other nations tried to stop Iran from a suspected attempt to develop nuclear weapons. Iran retaliated by threatening to withdraw its oil from the global market, thus causing a further rise in oil prices. That same year, they rose even higher when Israel invaded southern Lebanon. To prevent a global economic crisis, OPEC members tried to reduce prices by increasing oil production. As a result, prices fell slightly.

INFO CHECK

1. Explain the difference between free-market economies and command economies. Which type

did the Soviet Union have? What problems did this cause for the Soviet Union?

2. PROVE or DISPROVE: Too much reliance on cash crops and foreign investment caused widespread poverty in Latin America.

3. Explain why economic recovery from World War II in Germany and Japan was faster and better than in other countries.

4. Define: Pacific Rim, four tigers. How did these countries develop strong economies after World War II?

5. What is the connection between Western nations' dependence on oil and their desire for peace in the Middle East?

V. CHINESE COMMUNIST REVOLUTION

A. Communist Takeover

In 1937, Nationalist Jiang Jieshi and Communist Mao Zedong had joined forces against the Japanese invading China. At the end of World War II, they resumed fighting each other.

Many Chinese considered the Nationalist government corrupt and dictatorial. It favored landlords and factory owners over peasants and

Mao Zedong overlooking Tiananmen Square, Beijing

workers. Thus, the Communists, led by Mao Zedong and Zhou Enlai, won wide support by executing landowners and distributing their property among peasant farmers. In 1949, the Communists won the civil war, and the Nationalist government fled to Taiwan, an island off the China coast.

B. Mao Zedong's Leadership

Mao's government, the People's Republic of China, was a dictatorship. Zhou served as premier. Existing industries were nationalized and new ones put under government control. Mao's "Great Leap Forward," begun in 1958, was meant to increase agricultural production; peasant farms were combined into agricultural communes. As the peasants resisted, however, output decreased.

RED GUARDS. To quiet critics, Mao launched the "Great Cultural Revolution" in 1966. He closed schools and universities and organized student groups, called Red Guards, to force people into obedience as members of a classless society. Some peasants and army units fought the Red Guards until Mao called a halt to the movement in 1968.

MAO VERSUS CONFUCIUS. Under communism, the Confucian principle of loyalty to family was replaced by loyalty to the state. Mao's teaching became the main guide for Chinese thought and behavior.

RELATIONS WITH THE SOVIET UNION. The Soviet Union helped Mao set up a Communist government. At first, the two countries were united against Western democracies. In the late 1950s, however, China began to disagree with Soviet aims and resented Soviet efforts to cooperate with the United States. Armed clashes over Soviet-Chinese border territories occurred. In 1963, Communist China broke off relations with the Soviets.

CHINA AND THE WEST. Most Western powers established diplomatic relations with Communist China. The United States regarded Nationalist China in Taiwan as the legitimate government.

In the early 1970s, this attitude changed. In 1971, Communist China took over the UN seat of Nationalist China and became one of the permanent members of the Security Council. In 1972, Richard Nixon became the first U.S. president to visit the People's Republic of China. In 1977, the United States and China established full diplomatic relations.

At the same time, U.S.-Taiwan relations remained friendly. The Nationalists continued to receive U.S. military aid and favorable trading terms.

C. Deng Xiaoping and Jiang Zemin

In 1976, a more moderate leader, Deng Xiaoping, succeeded Mao Zedong. Deng initiated the "Four Modernizations," a program that advanced science and technology, agriculture, industry, and national defense.

AGRICULTURE. Under Deng's program, peasants could once again farm in small family units and decide which crops to grow. In six years, food production increased by more than 50 percent.

INDUSTRY. Deng permitted Western manufacturers to open factories in China. Since goods produced in China were cheaper than imports, Chinese consumerism increased. Citizens began to set up businesses. Foreign investment was encouraged. By 2007, China had the fastest economic growth rate in the world.

TIANANMEN SQUARE MASSACRE. In April 1989, university students demonstrated against government restrictions and corruption. On May 17, more than a million citizens of all ages gathered in Tiananmen Square in Beijing. When the government sent in soldiers and tanks, unarmed people blocked their entrance.

On June 4, 1989, after a two-week standoff, the army pushed its way into the square. Hundreds of students were killed or imprisoned.

REFORMS. To reconcile the Chinese to these violations of human rights, Deng claimed that the demonstrators had plotted to disrupt national unity. As a further appeasement, he resumed his economic reforms, which led to increased prosperity. At the same time, he tightened restrictions on political expression and continued to mistreat political prisoners.

Democratic nations spoke out against Deng's treatment of his opponents. The United States threatened to revoke China's special trading privileges unless Deng showed respect for human rights. This threat, however, had little, if any, effect on the Deng regime. Even after Deng's death in 1997, the two countries continued to disagree on this issue. In 2006, President Hu Jintao ordered the building of a "harmonious socialist society."

FOREIGN RELATIONS. A continuing buildup of Chinese military forces worried U.S. and Asian leaders. However, the tension somewhat eased when China joined in condemnation of global terrorism after the September 11, 2001, attacks on the United States.

HONG KONG. The island of Hong Kong was a British colony from 1898 to 1997, when it reverted to China. China promised not to interfere with Hong Kong's free-market economy or democratic government for 50 years. Nonetheless, a legislature appointed by China has set limits on the activities of parties that oppose the Communist government. China has also reduced the number of people who can vote in legislative elections. In 2006, the police gained authority to wiretap telephones, monitor e-mails, and place listening devices in homes and offices. So far, however, the people of Hong Kong have many of the freedoms that they enjoyed under British rule.

D. Women in Communist China

Traditionally, Chinese women were seldom educated. Parents arranged marriages. Wives were their husbands' property. Men could have more than one wife.

Under the Nationalists, women could choose their own husbands. Many went to school, owned property, and entered the business world. Poor and rural women, however, remained restricted.

Under communism, Chinese women are equal to men. Arranged marriages have been discouraged, and **polygam**y (having more than one spouse) outlawed. Women can become government officials and enter the professions.

The lives of both men and women, however, are subject to control. The Chinese do not have freedom of speech. Students cannot choose subjects for study. Married couples are allowed only one child.

Nevertheless, China's movement toward a free-market economy have created opportunities to earn more money and enjoy a higher living standard. However, rural poverty and increasing pollution remain 21st century problems.

INFO CHECK

1. Identify: Jiang Jieshi, Mao Zedong, Zhou Enlai, Deng Xiaoping, Hu Jintao.

2. Explain why you AGREE or DISAGREE with these statements:

   • The long struggle between Communists and Nationalists had little effect on China's political and economic development after World War II.

   • By the 1990s, China developed a free-market economy while remaining a political dictatorship.

3. Describe the changing role of women in China.

Year	Dates and Events

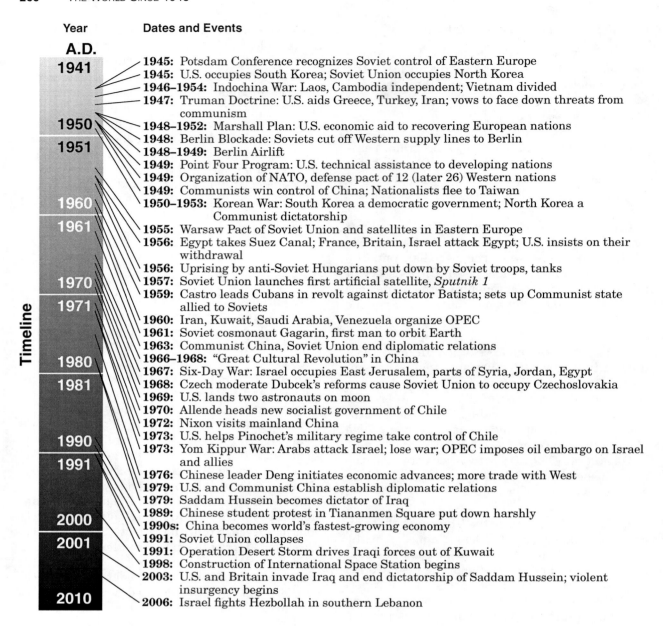

A.D.

1941

1945: Potsdam Conference recognizes Soviet control of Eastern Europe
1945: U.S. occupies South Korea; Soviet Union occupies North Korea
1946–1954: Indochina War: Laos, Cambodia independent; Vietnam divided
1947: Truman Doctrine: U.S. aids Greece, Turkey, Iran; vows to face down threats from communism

1950

1948–1952: Marshall Plan: U.S. economic aid to recovering European nations

1951

1948: Berlin Blockade: Soviets cut off Western supply lines to Berlin
1948–1949: Berlin Airlift
1949: Point Four Program: U.S. technical assistance to developing nations
1949: Organization of NATO, defense pact of 12 (later 26) Western nations
1949: Communists win control of China; Nationalists flee to Taiwan

1960

1950–1953: Korean War: South Korea a democratic government; North Korea a Communist dictatorship

1961

1955: Warsaw Pact of Soviet Union and satellites in Eastern Europe
1956: Egypt takes Suez Canal; France, Britain, Israel attack Egypt; U.S. insists on their withdrawal
1956: Uprising by anti-Soviet Hungarians put down by Soviet troops, tanks

1970

1957: Soviet Union launches first artificial satellite, *Sputnik 1*
1959: Castro leads Cubans in revolt against dictator Batista; sets up Communist state allied to Soviets

1971

1960: Iran, Kuwait, Saudi Arabia, Venezuela organize OPEC
1961: Soviet cosmonaut Gagarin, first man to orbit Earth
1963: Communist China, Soviet Union end diplomatic relations
1966–1968: "Great Cultural Revolution" in China

1980

1967: Six-Day War: Israel occupies East Jerusalem, parts of Syria, Jordan, Egypt
1968: Czech moderate Dubcek's reforms cause Soviet Union to occupy Czechoslovakia

1981

1969: U.S. lands two astronauts on moon
1970: Allende heads new socialist government of Chile
1972: Nixon visits mainland China
1973: U.S. helps Pinochet's military regime take control of Chile

1990

1973: Yom Kippur War: Arabs attack Israel; lose war; OPEC imposes oil embargo on Israel and allies

1991

1976: Chinese leader Deng initiates economic advances; more trade with West
1979: U.S. and Communist China establish diplomatic relations
1979: Saddam Hussein becomes dictator of Iraq
1989: Chinese student protest in Tiananmen Square put down harshly

2000

1990s: China becomes world's fastest-growing economy
1991: Soviet Union collapses

2001

1991: Operation Desert Storm drives Iraqi forces out of Kuwait
1998: Construction of International Space Station begins
2003: U.S. and Britain invade Iraq and end dictatorship of Saddam Hussein; violent insurgency begins

2010

2006: Israel fights Hezbollah in southern Lebanon

Timeline (vertical label)

CHAPTER REVIEW

1. To aid the economic recovery of postwar Europe, the U.S. secretary of state introduced

1. containment
2. Dollar Diplomacy
3. the Marshall Plan
4. the Roosevelt Corollary.

2. Immediately after World War I, the United States refused to join the League of Nations and followed a policy of isolationism. After World War II, it joined the UN and followed a policy of

1. neutrality
2. containment
3. aggression
4. isolationism.

3. The importance of the Berlin Airlift was that it

1. moved men and machines to the battle zone
2. demonstrated Allied determination to prevent a Soviet takeover of West Berlin
3. showed the military value of airpower
4. provided cheap plane tickets for tourists to West Berlin.

4. Prior to World War II, the major powers formed alliances that were called the Triple Entente and Triple Alliance. After World War II, they were called the

1. Communist League and Alliance for Progress
2. Warsaw Pact and NATO
3. Arab League and American League
4. ZYO and PLO.

5. The Middle East was valued by both the Soviet Union and the Western democracies because of

1. the Panama Canal and uranium deposits
2. naval coaling stations and military airports
3. the Suez Canal and oil deposits
4. military alliances and rich diamond reserves.

6. In Latin America, military dictators often ruled with support from the

1. military, wealthy landowners, and foreign investors
2. League of Nations and foreign capitalists
3. peasants and the Catholic Church
4. UN and Amnesty International.

7. The nations of Western Europe formed the Common Market. The Soviet Union and its Eastern European satellites formed the COMECON. These organizations were formed to create

1. military alliances
2. soccer leagues
3. consumer research companies
4. trade and economic cooperation.

8. In order to create heavy industries in the Soviet Union, Stalin had his Five-Year plans. To develop heavy industry in China, Mao had his

1. Great Cultural Revolution
2. Red Guards
3. reeducation policy
4. Great Leap Forward.

9. The map on page 251 suggests that

1. NATO and Warsaw Pact nations had equal military power
2. the world was dominated by two opposing European alliances
3. the nations of Africa formed a third alliance.
4. the Soviet Union had greater power and influence than the United States.

10. Use the chart on page 251 and the timeline on page 260 to select the most accurate statement.

1. The reunification of Germany occurred after the collapse of the Soviet Union.
2. Both NATO and the Warsaw Pact were created in the same year.

3. The Soviet Union collapsed after many nations of Eastern Europe held free elections in which the Communist party was defeated.
4. The cold war ended when Gorbachev became Soviet leader.

Thematic Essays

1. China has undergone many changes. Discuss the differences and similarities in the economic and governmental policies and practices of Mao Zedong and Deng Xiaoping. *Task:* Include the Great Leap Forward, Red Guards, Four Modernizations, and Tiananmen Square.

2. Compare and contrast free-market and command economies. *Task:* Explain the role of government in each type of economic organization. Give examples of countries that have practiced one or the other of these systems. State the importance of this issue in the cold war and post–cold war eras.

Document-Based Questions

Use your knowledge of Global History and Geography and the documents to assist you in answering the questions.

1. Study the photo on page 258.

Give reasons why such a large picture of Mao would appear in this busy capital city square.

2. Mao Zedong wrote in 1952:

"... the present rulers of Great Britain and the United States are still imperialists. Internationally we belong to the side of the anti-imperialist front, headed by the Soviet Union.... Who are the people? They are the working class, the peasantry and ... the bourgeoisie.... Under the leadership of the working class and the Communist Party these classes unite to create their own state ... so as to enforce the dictatorship over the henchmen of the imperialist—the landlord class and the bureaucratic capitalist class...."

3. Study the photo on page 250.

How does this photo illustrate the cold war that matched the Soviet Union and its Communist allies against the United States and its allies?

Identify the operation in progress. Explain why it was a political and technological victory for the West.

4. President Truman speaking before the first session of the 80th Congress in 1947:

"... The very existence of the Greek State is today threatened by the terrorist activities of several thousand armed men, led by

Communists. . . . the United States must supply this assistance. . . . No other nation is willing and able to provide the necessary support for a democratic Greek Government. . . . Greece's neighbor, Turkey, also deserves our attention . . . one of the primary objectives of the foreign policy of the United States is the creation of conditions in which we and other nations will be able to work out a way of life free from *coercion* [pressure]. . . . At the present moment in world history, nearly every nation must choose between alternative ways of life. The choice is too often not a free one. . . . I believe we must assist free peoples to work out their [futures] in their own ways."

What conflict is being discussed here, and what role does Truman plan for the United States?

Document-Based Essay

Task: Explain why the former World War II allies—the Soviet Union and the United States—became postwar adversaries. Include in your essay: political power and economic competition.

CHAPTER
25

Postwar Africa, Asia, and Middle East

During the cold war, Western capitalist countries and Japan became known as the **first world**, Communist countries as the **second world**, and **developing nations**—those in various stages of industrialization—as the **third world**.

I. COLLAPSE OF BRITISH IMPERIALISM ON THE SUBCONTINENT

The biggest blow to British imperialism was the formation of the independent nations of the subcontinent—India, Pakistan, and Bangladesh. They and other former British colonies joined the *Commonwealth,* an association for discussing economic, scientific, educational, and other issues of common interest. Started in the early 1900s, the Commonwealth eventually numbered 53 members.

A. Bangladesh

In 1947, the new nation of Pakistan comprised a western and an eastern province. The separated peoples shared the Muslim religion but little else. Although West Pakistan was less populous, it was better represented in the government. When East Pakistan demanded independence in the late 1960s, the West Pakistan government put it under martial law. Helped by India, East Pakistan fought for independence and became the nation of Bangladesh in 1973.

B. India After Independence

DEMOCRATIC SOCIALISM. As prime minister, Jawaharlal Nehru adopted **democratic socialism**. This system is a combination free-market and command economy. The government owns and operates such industries as railroads, automobiles, and banking. Consumer goods and agriculture are in private hands.

KASHMIR. In 1947, India and Pakistan fought over the northern province of Kashmir. The UN arranged a cease-fire in 1949. The territory is still in dispute, however, and occasional fighting breaks out.

MEMBERS OF THE COMMONWEALTH

Antigua and Barbuda	Great Britain	Namibia	Sri Lanka
Australia	Grenada	Nauru	Swaziland
Bahamas	Guyana	New Zealand	Tanzania
Bangladesh	India	Nigeria (suspended 1995)	Tonga
Barbados	Jamaica	Pakistan	Trinidad and Tobago
Belize	Kenya	Papua New Guinea	Tuvalu
Botswana	Kiribati	St. Kitts and Nevis	Uganda
Brunei	Lesotho	St. Lucia	Vanuatu
Cameroon	Malawi	St. Vincent and the Grenadines	Western Samoa
Canada	Malaysia	Seychelles	Zambia
Cyprus	Maldives	Sierra Leone	Zimbabwe
(The) Dominica	Malta	Singapore	
Gambia	Mauritius	Solomon Islands	
Ghana	Mozambique	South Africa	

Asia After World War II

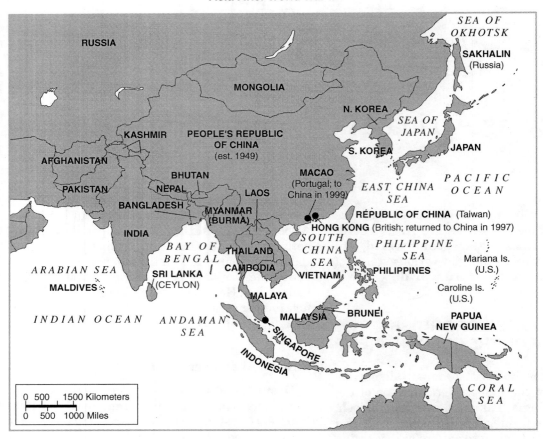

NEWLY INDEPENDENT NATIONS OF ASIA, POST–WORLD WAR II

Nation	Date of Independence	Former Ruler
Brunei	1984	Great Britain
Cambodia	1953	France
India	1947	Great Britain
Indonesia	1949	The Netherlands
Laos	1949	France
Malaya	1957	Great Britain
Malaysia	1963: union of Malaya, Singapore, Sarawak-Sabah; Singapore withdrew in 1965	Great Britain
Maldives	1965	Great Britain
Myanmar (Burma)	1948	Great Britain
North Korea	1948	Soviet Union (occupation)
Pakistan	1947	Great Britain
Papua New Guinea	1975	Australia
Philippines	1946	United States
Singapore	1965	Malaysia
South Korea	1948	United States (occupation)
Sri Lanka (Ceylon)	1948	Great Britain
Vietnam	1954	France

INDIRA GANDHI. Indira Gandhi (Nehru's daughter, unrelated to Mohandas Gandhi) became prime minister in 1966. She attempted to institute birth control and tried to fight government corruption. Meeting resistance, Gandhi proclaimed a state of emergency in 1975, assumed temporary dictatorial powers, and prosecuted dishonest officials, tax evaders, and black marketeers. She also tried to force poor farmers to observe state-endorsed methods of birth control.

The Indians then voted her out of office. Her successors, however, could not achieve cooperation, and Gandhi was reelected prime minister in 1980.

Gandhi now had to deal with new nationalist groups. One of them, the Sikhs, wanted more independence for their state, the Punjab. In 1984, Gandhi sent an army there to control violence. After her soldiers stormed the Sikh's Golden Temple at Amritsar, radical Sikhs ordered Sikh members of Gandhi's bodyguard to assassinate her. Outraged Hindus then began a random slaughter of Sikhs.

RAJIV GANDHI. Rajiv Gandhi succeeded his mother as prime minister. He calmed the violence but could not solve the problem of extreme nationalism. India's large population slowed economic growth, government corruption continued, and more nationalist groups demanded independence. Gandhi resigned in 1989. While campaigning for reelection in 1991, he was killed by Tamil nationalists.

RAO. Narasimha Rao became prime minister in 1991. The corruption and incompetence of the Congress party during his term of office caused demands for his resignation.

VAJPAYEE. The Hindu Nationalist party, led by Atal Behari Vajpayee, took control of the government in 1997. By 2001, he had made little progress in improving India's economy. Nor had he resolved the conflict with Pakistan over the mainly Muslim province of Kashmir.

SINGH. The Congress Party regained control of the government in 2004. Manmohan Singh became prime minister.

INFO CHECK

1. Why do you think so many colonies of European nations and the United States gained their independence after, rather than before, World War II?

2. Identify two countries in which ethnic or religious conflicts led to violence after independence had been won. Select one of these countries and explain how the problem developed.

II. AFRICAN INDEPENDENCE MOVEMENTS

A. From Colonialism to Independence

GHANA. By 1948, Britain wanted Ghana to undergo gradual transition to self-rule. Kwame Nkrumah of the Convention People's party rejected the proposal and incited Ghanaians to riot and strike. Although jailed by the British, Nkrumah won the national elections of 1951. In the free elections that followed the departure of Britain in 1957, he defeated his rivals.

EASTERN AND SOUTHERN AFRICA. Rhodesia had a large population of white settlers who were determined to keep the country under British control. The whites in Northern Rhodesia (now Zambia) were too few to postpone decolonization for long. The whites in Southern Rhodesia, however, successfully opposed African nationalists. After a guerrilla war, the nationalists defeated the whites in 1980. They named their new country Zimbabwe.

WESTERN AFRICA. In the late 1950s, President Charles de Gaulle decided to free French possessions in Africa. To ensure the future cooperation of French Equatorial Africa and West Africa, he divided them into 13 separate territories. In each one, elections were held to decide whether ties with France would continue after independence. A territory voting no would lose all further support from France.

Guinea voted against a continued relationship. Its example of complete self-government led the other territories to seek greater self-rule as well.

CENTRAL AFRICA. Belgium, which had kept the Congolese poor, uneducated, and subservient, faced hard fighting by nationalists. The Belgians left in 1959, and tribal conflict, civil war, and foreign interference soon overwhelmed the new state of Congo-Kinshasa, later renamed Zaire. (Its first name distinguished it from its neighbor Congo-Brazzaville, which gained independence from France in the same year, 1960.)

Colonial Independence in Africa and the Middle East

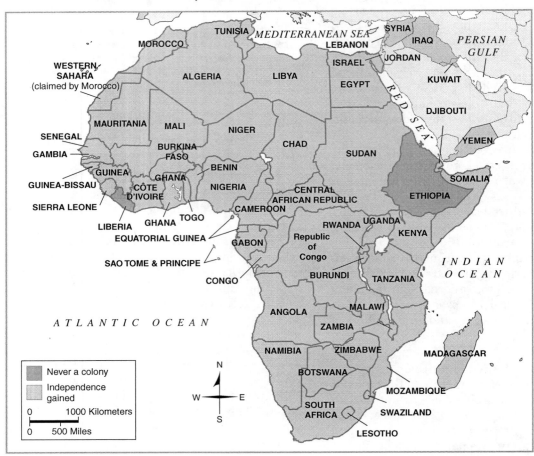

NEWLY INDEPENDENT NATIONS OF AFRICA AND MIDDLE EAST, POST–WORLD WAR II

Nation	Date	Former Ruler(s)
Algeria	1962	France
Angola	1975	Portugal
Benin	1960	France
Botswana	1966	Great Britain
Burkina Faso	1960	France
Burundi	1962	Belgium
Cameroon	1961	France, Great Britain
Central African Republic	1960	France
Chad	1960	France
Congo	1960	France
Côte d'Ivoire	1960	France
Djibouti	1977	France
Egypt*	1922	Great Britain
Equatorial Guinea	1968	Spain
Gabon	1960	France
(The) Gambia	1965	Great Britain
Ghana	1957	Great Britain
Guinea	1958	France
Guinea-Bissau	1974	Portugal
Iraq*	1932	Great Britain
Israel	1948	Great Britain
Jordan	1946	Great Britain

(continued)

NEWLY INDEPENDENT NATIONS OF AFRICA AND MIDDLE EAST, POST–WORLD WAR II (*continued*)

Nation	Date	Former Ruler(s)
Kenya	1963	Great Britain
Kuwait	1961	Great Britain
Lebanon	1943	France
Lesotho	1966	Great Britain
Libya	1952	France, Great Britain
Madagascar	1960	France
Malawi	1964	Great Britain
Mali	1960	France
Mauritania	1960	France
Morocco	1956	France, Spain
Mozambique	1975	Portugal
Namibia	1990	South Africa
Niger	1960	France
Nigeria	1960	Great Britain
Rwanda	1962	Belgium
São Tomé and Príncipe	1975	Portugal
Senegal	1960	France
Sierra Leone	1961	Great Britain
Somalia	1960	Britain, UN as trustee
South Africa*	1931	Great Britain
South Yemen	1967	Great Britain
Sudan	1956	Egypt
Swaziland	1968	Great Britain
Syria	1946	France
Tanzania	1961	Great Britain
Togo	1960	France
Tunisia	1956	France
Uganda	1962	Great Britain
Zaire	1960	Belgium
Zambia	1964	Great Britain
Zimbabwe	1980	Great Britain

* The asterisked nations achieved independence before World War II.

B. Tribalism Versus Nationalism in Nigeria

In 1954, Nigerian nationalists accepted the British proposal for a gradual transition to self-rule. In 1960, Nigeria achieved independence. In spite of their preparation, Nigerians had a difficult time building their state.

ETHNIC RIVALRIES. There were many competing ethnic groups: the feared Yoruba warriors of the southwest, the Ibo businesspeople in the southeast, the powerful Hausa and Fulani in the north. These groups compromised on sharing political power, and Nigeria became a federation of states. The national government in the southern capital of Lagos shared power with state governments in the north, west, and east. Each region's most powerful tribe led its political party. The rights of minorities, however, were protected by law.

TRIBAL WARS. Nevertheless, the Yoruba tried to dominate the minorities in the Western Region, who moved to form their own region in the mid-west. When the Yoruba stopped them by force, tribal wars broke out.

DICTATORS. During this turmoil, a military group took over the Lagos government and executed the leading politicians. To stop the fighting in the Western Region, regional governments were eliminated and the entire country put under martial law.

At first, the military dictators seemed preferable to the former government, which had been corrupt and too Westernized. The Hausa and Fulani, however, distrusted the Ibo officers who had led the coup. When the military council declared the dictatorship, the Hausa and Fulani rebelled, slaughtered thousands of Ibos, and took over the government.

BIAFRA. The Ibos then seceded and set up the independent state of Biafra in the Eastern Region.

The resulting war lasted three years. The Nigerian forces cut off all supplies to Biafra until the starving Ibos surrendered.

Peace followed, and Nigeria prospered from oil exports. After 13 years, the dictatorship returned political power to a civilian regime. As world oil prices fell, Nigeria was plunged into poverty. In 1983, the military retook the government. In 1998, Nigeria tried to establish a democratically elected government. By 2002, about one third of Nigeria's 36 states had adopted sharia, the Islamic legal code. In 2007, the People's Democratic Party (PDP) won Nigeria's presidential elections. Human rights groups believe that the PDP won by fraud and voter intimidation. Nigeria remains one of the world's poorest countries.

C. Tribalism in Kenya and Rwanda

KENYA. The British minority in Kenya were in firm control. During the 1940s, a Kikuyu tribal leader, Jomo Kenyatta, challenged them, and a terrorist group called the Mau Mau raided European-owned farms and murdered the inhabitants. The British unjustly accused Kenyatta of ordering the Mau Mau raids and jailed him.

When the terrorism continued, the British realized that they had lost control. Power shifted gradually, and in 1963, Kenyans chose Kenyatta as their first prime minister.

His successor, Daniel arap Moi, is a member of the Kalenjin tribe. Larger tribes—the Kikuyu, Luo, and Luyha—want more political influence. Still, even though other parties became legal, Moi's party suppressed opposition. New hope came in 2002 when Mwai Kibaki, an economist, was elected president. Extreme violence accompanied his re-election in 2007.

RWANDA. While still a Belgian colony, Rwanda was controlled by the Tutsis, even though the Hutus made up the majority. When the Tutsis pressed for independence, the Belgians helped the Hutus rebel. Hutus slaughtered Tutsis, who fled to Zaire and other neighbors.

When Rwanda gained independence in 1962, Tutsi guerrillas formed the *Rwandan Patriotic Front (RPF)*. In 1993, it forced the government to sign a cease-fire. UN peacekeeping troops helped restore calm.

Ethnic Warfare. When Rwanda's president was killed in a plane crash in 1994, some blamed the Tutsis. Others suspected extremist Hutus who wanted to ruin chances for a permanent peace with Tutsis. Hutu extremists once more began to kill Tutsis and moderate Hutus, who crowded into refugee camps, where they died of cholera and other diseases.

The RPF then seized the capital of Kigali and set up a coalition government of Tutsis and Hutus. At the same time, the two rival groups continued to fight. The Tutsis gained strength. In 1996, UN troops left. General Paul Kagame, the RPF leader, became Rwanda's first Tutsi president in April 2000. Kagame was relected in 2003.

D. South Africa

APARTHEID. The white minority in South Africa instituted a policy of **apartheid** (Afrikaans for "apartness"). The races were strictly separated, and blacks could not vote, had to carry passes, and were subject to arrest at any time. The Asian population also suffered forms of discrimination.

In the 1980s, moderate groups used peaceful means to work for full black participation in the government. Protest demonstrations in black areas increased, many of them led by Desmond Tutu, a black Anglican archbishop. Tutu, who urged his followers to use the nonviolent tactics of Mohandas Gandhi, won the 1984 Nobel Peace Prize.

SANCTIONS. The white government treated black resistance harshly. South Africa then became the target of several countries' **sanction**s (bans on trading with a country that violates international law). As poverty in South Africa increased, so did violence between blacks and whites. Foreign companies withdrew their investments.

By 1990, a more moderate leadership had reduced the level of discrimination. In 1992, a majority of white South Africans voted to end apartheid and minority rule. A new constitution was written, and multiracial elections were held in April 1994.

THE ANC. The *African National Congress (ANC)* had led the fight for equality and political power. In 1990, President F. W. de Klerk recognized the ANC and freed its leader, Nelson Mandela, who had been imprisoned for sabotage since 1962. Nevertheless, clashes between rival black groups and attacks on blacks by white extremists made reform difficult.

MANDELA. In 1994, Mandela became president, with de Klerk as one of two vice presidents. The multiracial government took steps to improve the lives of blacks without alienating others. Mandela promised to keep the free enterprise system, trade with other African nations resumed, and the economy improved. Black unemployment remained high, however. Housing was inadequate. Crime was common.

Mandela is accompanied by his former wife Winnie, moments afer his release from prison February 11, 1990 after serving 27 years in jail.

In June 1999, ANC leader Thabo Mbeki was elected to be Mandela's successor as president. Among the many hard-to-solve problems faced by his government was the growing AIDS threat. As many as seven million people may die of AIDS by 2010. Other problems are a high crime rate and unemployment.

E. Pan-Africanism

In May 1963, 32 African countries established the *Organization of African Unity (OAU)*—now known as the *African Union (AU)*. Today, the AU's 53 members meet annually in Addis Ababa, Ethiopia.

The AU has been effective in maintaining peace in Africa. During the 1960s, it successfully mediated disputes between Algeria and Morocco and in Zaire and Nigeria. It helped the ANC end white minority rule in South Africa and the Southwest African People's organization to win Namibia's independence. In 2005, the AU sent troops to Darfur, a province of Sudan, to reduce ethnic violence there.

INFO CHECK

1. Describe the roles played in African independence movements by each of the following: Kwame Nkrumah, Jomo Kenyatta.

2. Explain why you AGREE or DISAGREE with the following: Tribalism has been more of a problem in Kenya than it has been in Nigeria and Rwanda.

3. Why do many students of African history regard Nelson Mandela and F. W. de Klerk as heroes?

III. NATIONALISM AND COMMUNISM IN SOUTHEAST ASIA

A. Vietnam War

In 1957, the North Vietnam leader, Ho Chi Minh, encouraged South Vietnamese Communists, known as the Vietcong, to begin guerrilla warfare against the U.S.-backed South Vietnamese government. The Vietcong hoped to unite Vietnam under Communist rule.

U.S. President Dwight Eisenhower sent a few hundred nonfighting advisers to South Vietnam. By 1962, President John Kennedy had increased the number of advisers to several thousand.

U.S. leaders feared (1) that Communist China might take over Vietnam and (2) that the Soviet Union would influence Ho Chi Minh. According to their "Domino Theory," if Vietnam fell to the Communists, the rest of Southeast Asia would go down also. This policy influenced U.S. decisions throughout the 1960s.

In 1964, U.S. destroyers in the Tonkin Gulf off North Vietnam reported inaccurately that they had been fired on. Believing the report, President Lyndon Johnson obtained extensive war powers from Congress in the Gulf of Tonkin Resolutions— a near declaration of war against North Vietnam. Johnson ordered the bombing of North Vietnam. Eventually, some 536,000 U.S. troops fought the Vietcong and North Vietnamese forces.

END OF THE WAR

The loss of many soldiers without a victory upset many Americans, who demanded peace and criticized U.S. involvement in a foreign civil war. President Richard Nixon gradually turned the fighting over to the South Vietnamese. In January 1973, a peace agreement was signed. All U.S. troops left Vietnam by April 1973.

The South Vietnamese lost the war in 1975. Vietnam became a unified Communist country. Communists also took over Cambodia and Laos, but not all of Southeast Asia.

AFTER THE WAR

To relieve poverty, Vietnam encouraged free enterprise. *Doi moi,* the privatization of farms, increased food production. New businesses arose.

During the late 20th and early 21st centuries, a new generation of Vietnamese leaders attempted to improve relations with the United States and other Western nations. In 1994, U.S.-Vietnam trade resumed, ending a 19-year embargo. Diplomatic relations between the two countries began in 1995. Vietnam and the United States signed a full trade agreement in July 2000.

Vietnam, Laos, and Cambodia, 1954–1965

By 2006, the United States had become Vietnam's largest export market. Vietnam's movement toward a market economy has attracted foreign investment. It became a member of the World Trade Organization in 2006.

B. Cambodia

In 1975, Communist leader Pol Pot led a group called the *Khmer Rouge* in the takeover of Cambodia. They persecuted anti-Communists, closed schools, sent thousands of people to slave labor camps, and killed about one million. After Vietnamese forces invaded Cambodia in 1979, the brutality stopped.

The Vietnamese withdrew in 1989. In 1991, rivalry among four political groups, including the Khmer Rouge, led to civil war. The Khmer Rouge opposed UN peace efforts and tried to seize more territory.

Nevertheless, UN-sponsored elections were held in May 1993. The national assembly adopted a constitution providing for a coalition government under a monarchy. Prince Norodom Sihanouk became king, and his son, Prince Ranariddh, became prime minister. In 1997, Deputy Prime Minister Hun Sen drove out Ranariddh and took control.

The UN discouraged the new government's efforts to share power with Pol Pot's Khmer Rouge rebels. They continued to attack the government from camps set up along the Thailand border.

In 1997, one Khmer Rouge faction persuaded the government to give it a voice in Cambodian affairs. Another faction put Pol Pot on trial for the murders of rival officials. Sentenced to house arrest for life, he died in 1998. By the mid-1990s, private businesspeople controlled a majority of Cambodia's economic resources, and the government set about improving education.

In 2005, Prime Minister Hun Sen began to arrest critics of his policies. Many feared that he was beginning to set up a one-party dictatorship.

INFO CHECK

1. Should the United States have become involved in Vietnam's civil war? Why or why not?

2. Explain why Cambodia has had so many problems since 1975.

IV. CONFLICTS AND CHANGE IN THE MIDDLE EAST

The Middle East includes a part of North Africa and southwest Asia, which share Arab traditions and the Islamic religion.

A. Lebanon

Lebanon's population is Muslim and Christian. In 1943, the two groups agreed to share government power, and the cooperation lasted until the 1970s. As Palestinian refugees from the Arab-Israeli wars streamed into Lebanon, however, Muslims came to outnumber Christians. The Palestinians were more militant than the Lebanese Muslims.

As the *Palestine Liberation Organization (PLO)* launched raids on Israel from Lebanon, Israel counterattacked. In the mid-1970s, internal conflict broke out between Lebanese Christians, who opposed attacks on Israel, and Lebanese Muslims, who favored them. In 1976, Syria, backed by the Soviet Union, sent in troops to stop the civil war.

In June 1982, Israel, aiming to destroy the PLO, invaded Lebanon. PLO leader Yasir Arafat escaped to Tunisia. When a right-wing Christian militia group massacred civilian refugees, an international peacekeeping force arrived in Lebanon. Suspecting that the force had come to support the Christians, Muslim terrorists killed 241 U.S. and 58 French soldiers. The force was removed in 1984.

In 1991, the Syrian-backed Lebanese Army disarmed various private militias. Lebanese Prime Minister Rafiq al-Hariri, elected in 1993, began to rebuild the economy and restore law and order. Hariri was assassinated in 2005. Many Lebanese blamed Syria for this and demanded the withdrawal of Syrian troops from Lebanon. In mid-2006, the Hezbollah, a Lebanon-based terrorist organization, kidnapped an Israeli soldier. This set off hostilities between Israel and Hezbollah. An Israeli invasion of Lebanon was halted by a UN cease-fire resolution.

B. Iranian Revolution

Under Iran's Shah Mohammad Reza Pahlavi (ruled 1941–1979), women gained the vote, and the economy profited from oil production and new industries. Some Iranians complained that the new wealth benefited only an elite class. Devout Muslims wanted a return to Islamic tradition. In 1979, Muslim revolutionaries led by Ruhollah Khomeini ousted the shah.

Khomeini, a high Muslim official, took the religious title *ayatollah* and became head of the strict religious government. His followers hated the United States for its support of the shah while ruler and in exile. In 1979, militants attacked the U.S. embassy and held 53 American occupants hostage for 444 days.

Meanwhile, border disputes, religious differences, and other antagonisms between Iran and Iraq resulted in war when Iraqi leader Saddam Hussein invaded Iran in September 1980. Iran has supplied Hezbollah with weapons against Israel. Until 2007, the United States suspected that Iran was developing nuclear weapons. In spite of Western protests, President Mahmoud Ahmadinejad

Iranian woman standing before a poster of Ayatollah Khomeini, Teheran, 1993

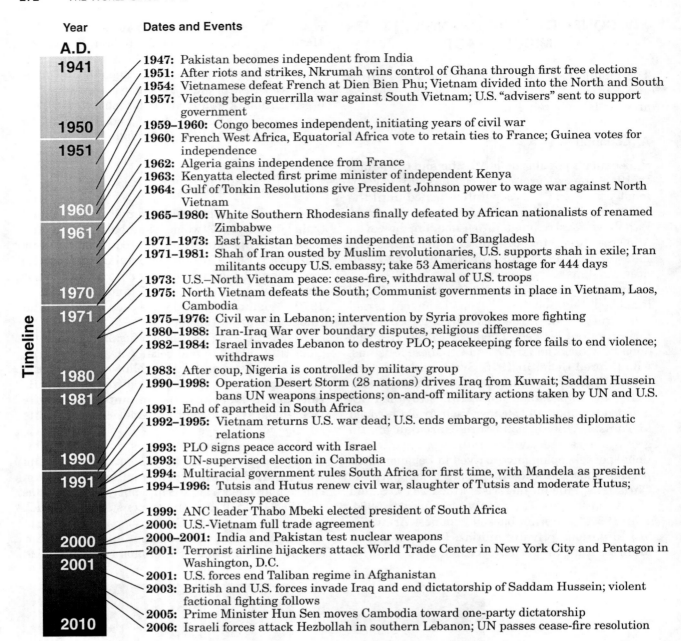

Year	Dates and Events
A.D.	
1941	**1947:** Pakistan becomes independent from India
	1951: After riots and strikes, Nkrumah wins control of Ghana through first free elections
	1954: Vietnamese defeat French at Dien Bien Phu; Vietnam divided into the North and South
1950	**1957:** Vietcong begin guerrilla war against South Vietnam; U.S. "advisers" sent to support government
	1959–1960: Congo becomes independent, initiating years of civil war
1951	**1960:** French West Africa, Equatorial Africa vote to retain ties to France; Guinea votes for independence
	1962: Algeria gains independence from France
	1963: Kenyatta elected first prime minister of independent Kenya
	1964: Gulf of Tonkin Resolutions give President Johnson power to wage war against North Vietnam
1960	**1965–1980:** White Southern Rhodesians finally defeated by African nationalists of renamed Zimbabwe
1961	**1971–1973:** East Pakistan becomes independent nation of Bangladesh
	1971–1981: Shah of Iran ousted by Muslim revolutionaries, U.S. supports shah in exile; Iran militants occupy U.S. embassy; take 53 Americans hostage for 444 days
1970	**1973:** U.S.–North Vietnam peace: cease-fire, withdrawal of U.S. troops
1971	**1975:** North Vietnam defeats the South; Communist governments in place in Vietnam, Laos, Cambodia
	1975–1976: Civil war in Lebanon; intervention by Syria provokes more fighting
	1980–1988: Iran-Iraq War over boundary disputes, religious differences
	1982–1984: Israel invades Lebanon to destroy PLO; peacekeeping force fails to end violence; withdraws
1980	**1983:** After coup, Nigeria is controlled by military group
1981	**1990–1998:** Operation Desert Storm (28 nations) drives Iraq from Kuwait; Saddam Hussein bans UN weapons inspections; on-and-off military actions taken by UN and U.S.
	1991: End of apartheid in South Africa
	1992–1995: Vietnam returns U.S. war dead; U.S. ends embargo, reestablishes diplomatic relations
	1993: PLO signs peace accord with Israel
1990	**1993:** UN-supervised election in Cambodia
1991	**1994:** Multiracial government rules South Africa for first time, with Mandela as president
	1994–1996: Tutsis and Hutus renew civil war, slaughter of Tutsis and moderate Hutus; uneasy peace
	1999: ANC leader Thabo Mbeki elected president of South Africa
	2000: U.S.-Vietnam full trade agreement
	2000–2001: India and Pakistan test nuclear weapons
2000	**2001:** Terrorist airline hijackers attack World Trade Center in New York City and Pentagon in Washington, D.C.
2001	**2001:** U.S. forces end Taliban regime in Afghanistan
	2003: British and U.S. forces invade Iraq and end dictatorship of Saddam Hussein; violent factional fighting follows
2010	**2005:** Prime Minister Hun Sen moves Cambodia toward one-party dictatorship
	2006: Israeli forces attack Hezbollah in southern Lebanon; UN passes cease-fire resolution

(label at left: Timeline)

has stated that he will continue to develop nuclear energy for peaceful purposes. In 2006, the dispute was taken before the UN Security Council. Ahmadinejad has also defied warnings against interfering in Iraq. In 2007, he announced plans to expand ties with that country.

C. Persian Gulf War

In August 1990, Saddam Hussein invaded neighboring Kuwait, which Iraq had long claimed. After seizing oil fields and a Persian Gulf seaport, Hussein's forces moved to the Saudi Arabian border.

U.S. President George Bush sent forces to protect Saudi Arabia. The UN demanded Iraq's withdrawal from Kuwait by January 15, 1991, on threat of military force. Iraq stayed put, and Operation Desert Storm began on January 17, 1991. A UN coalition of 28 nations drove Iraq out of Kuwait.

Victory did not end Saddam Hussein's rule or bring peace. UN forces had to protect an Iraqi minority, the Kurds, from Hussein's troops. UN inspection teams tried to make sure that Iraq was not building nuclear, chemical, and biological weapons. Despite repeated bombings of Iraqi military sites by the United States and Britain, Saddam Hussein rebuilt his armed forces by 2001. In March 2003, U.S. and British troops invaded Iraq and ended Saddam Hussein's dictatorship. Despite the election of a new government, violent conflict between Shiite and Sunni militias caused continuing death and destruction.

D. Extremism and Terrorism

Throughout the late 20th and early 21st centuries, extremist Muslim groups have engaged in acts of terrorism against Israel and its Western supporters. One of these is the Islamic Jihad, which means Islamic Holy War. Iran and Syria are suspected of sponsoring this group. Libya and Syria are also suspected of backing similar groups.

The PLO, led by Yasir Arafat, began as a collection of groups determined to destroy Israel. In 1993, after years of conflict, the PLO signed a peace agreement with Israel. Among the terrorist groups that refused to accept the peace accord was *Hamas,* a militant branch of the Muslim Brotherhood.

Starting in 1998, Hamas led an *intifada* (uprising) of Palestinians against Israeli authority in the West Bank and Gaza territories. A wave of Palestinian-sponsored suicide bombings and assassinations killed many in Israel. The Israeli government responded with military attacks on Hamas leaders and Palestinian towns. In 2006, a Hamas victory in Palestinian elections cast doubt on the Palestinians' desire for peace with Israel.

By 2007, Hamas controlled Gaza while the Palestinian Authority, led by Mahmoud Abbas, governed the West Bank.

Islamic fundamentalist violence increased in Egypt in the late 20th century. They made unsuccessful attempts to murder President Hosni Mubarak in 1995 and 1999. Muslim extremists attacked and killed foreign tourists frequently in 1997 and 1998.

Al Qaeda, led by Osama bin Laden, is a terrorist network operating in the Middle East and elsewhere. Al Qaeda's goals have been to destroy Israel and drive U.S. troops out of Saudi Arabia. It was responsible for the September 11, 2001, attacks on New York City and Washington, D.C. The U.S. military campaign in Afghanistan, in 2001, was directed at the destruction of Al Qaeda and the Taliban government that supported it. However, Taliban and Al Qaeda insurgents continued to fight NATO forces and the elected government of President Hamid Karzai.

INFO CHECK

1. Identify the countries that have been involved in Lebanon's civil war. Which of these countries do you think did the most to bring peace to Lebanon? Why?

2. Why did Iran not come to the aid of Iraq during the Persian Gulf War?

3. Identify Al Qaeda and Hamas, and explain what they have in common.

CHAPTER REVIEW

Multiple Choice

1. After World War II, European imperialism on the continents of Asia and Africa began to end because

   1. European nations realized the need to treat former colonial people as equals
   2. native peoples turned to imperialism
   3. exhausted by the war, European nations could not spare the money or military forces to overcome nationalistic demands
   4. the UN ordered them to give up their colonial empires.

2. Disputes between India and Pakistan are of concern to the rest of the world because both

   1. have nuclear weapons
   2. have larger armed forces than the major powers
   3. are highly industrialized
   4. supply a major portion of the world's rice.

3. Periods of genocide occurred in

   1. South Africa and Kenya
   2. Rwanda and Cambodia
   3. Vietnam and Kenya
   4. India and Bangladesh.

4. Apartheid was ended in South Africa because of

   1. economic sanctions and withdrawal of foreign investments
   2. the activities of Desmond Tutu and the ANC
   3. the courage of moderate white leaders to take actions unpopular with the white minority in general
   4. all of the above.

5. Although India's constitution outlawed discrimination based on caste and granted full citizenship and equality to women, the problems of caste and women's rights still exist because

1. not all Indian parties signed the constitution
2. conservative women's groups protested against the changes
3. traditional beliefs and practices are hard to end by legislation
4. India's rapid growth made the laws unenforceable.

6. The development of the newly independent African nations was hampered by

    1. European imperialism
    2. tribalism
    3. Pan-Africanism
    4. communism.

7. A successful, nonviolent tactic used by the world community to force the South African government to change its apartheid policy was

    1. economic sanctions
    2. letters of protest
    3. guerrilla movements
    4. UN inspections.

8. Lenin's NEP policy and Vietnam's economic policy of *doi moi* were similar in that they

    1. mandated strictly command economies
    2. relied on barter for exchange of goods and services
    3. encouraged free enterprise, particularly in farming
    4. were based on five-year plans.

9. The clash of traditional religious beliefs with the needs of a secular state occurred in

    1. Israel and England
    2. Japan and China
    3. Egypt and Lebanon
    4. Turkey and Iran.

10. The map and chart on pages 266 show that

    1. many African nations achieved independence during the 1960s
    2. Ethiopia never achieved full independence
    3. the nations of the Middle East all achieved independence by 1948
    4. by 1970, imperialism no longer existed in Africa.

11. Use the timeline on page 272 to identify the correct chronological order for the following events:

    1. Mandela elected president of South Africa
       Pakistan independence from India
       Gulf of Tonkin Resolutions
       Operation Desert Storm
    2. Operation Desert Storm
       Gulf of Tonkin Resolutions
       Mandela elected president of South Africa
       Pakistan independence from India
    3. Pakistan independence from India
       Gulf of Tonkin Resolutions
       Operation Desert Storm
       Mandela elected president of South Africa
    4. Gulf of Tonkin Resolutions
       Operation Desert Storm
       Mandela elected president of South Africa
       Pakistan independence from India

Thematic Essays

1. Gandhi's policy of nonviolence, together with the strain of World War II, succeeded in ending British rule in India. Since independence, India's political and social history has been filled with violence. *Task:* Explain the reasons for the violence. Consider the religious, political, and nationalistic causes for the violence.

2. African nationalism often relied on the ability of one man to unify the peoples of his nation. *Task:* Select any two African leaders and describe their policies as well as the forces they had to overcome to unify their nations. Consider economics, tribalism, imperialism, superpower rivalry, racism, and individual leadership qualities.

Document-Based Questions

Use your knowledge of Global History and Geography and the documents to answer the questions.

1. Gamal Abdel Nasser discusses the strength of the Arab peoples:

    " . . . there are three main sources that should be taken into account. The first . . . is that we are a community of neighboring peoples . . . and a civilization which has given rise to three holy religions. . . . As for the second source of strength it is our land itself and its position on the map— that important strategic position which embraces the crossroads of the world, and thoroughfare of its traders. . . . There remains the third source: oil. . . . "

    Of the three sources of strength Nasser refers to, which has been the one that the Arab nations have used against their enemies? Describe how it was used and whom it was used against.

2. From the Proclamation of Independence of the State of Israel:

    "The land of Israel was the birthplace of the Jewish people. Here their spiritual, religious and national identity was formed . . . here they wrote and gave the Bible to the world . . . the Balfour Declaration reaffirmed . . . the historic connection of the Jewish people with Palestine and their right to reconstitute their National Homeland. The recent holocaust, which engulfed millions of Jews in Europe, proved anew the need to solve the problem of the homelessness and lack of independence of the Jewish people by means of reestablishing of the Jewish State. . . ."

What are some of the cultural, political, and social justifications given for the Israeli Proclamation of Independence?

3. From the Palestinian Declaration of Independence of November 15, 1988:

" . . . Palestine, the land of three monotheistic faiths, is where the Palestinian Arab people was born, on which it grew, developed and excelled. The Palestinian people was never separated from or diminished in its . . . bonds with Palestine . . . the Palestinian Arab people never faltered and never abandoned its conviction in its rights of return and independence. . . . It calls upon Arab compatriots [fellow Arabs] . . . to intensify efforts whose goal is to end Israeli occupation. . . . "

Compare the continued needs stated in this declaration with those in the Israeli declaration. Do you think there will be continuing conflict between the Israelis and Palestinians? Why?

4. Study the photo on page 271. The violent Iran-Iraq War lasted eight years, and the only result was the deaths of hundreds of thousands. Explain the factors that caused two neighboring Islamic nations to engage in combat. Identify the leader of Iraq during the Iran-Iraq War. How were he and the Ayatollah Khomeini similar in their attitudes toward the United States?

5. Study the cartoon. Who or what does the figure on the rope represent? Identify a Middle East crisis during the 21st century.

Document-Based Essay

Did the cold-war superpower rivalry start the conflict in the Middle East or simply add fuel to a fire that already existed? *Task:* Explain the roles of conflicting nationalistic and religious beliefs, strategic location, and natural resources.

CHAPTER
26

Europe Facing a New Century

I. END OF THE COLD WAR

A. Soviet Actions

The Soviet Union's postwar control of Eastern Europe was rigid. In 1953, Soviet tanks ended protests by East Berlin workers. In 1961, East Germany built the Berlin Wall to prevent the flight of its inhabitants to West Berlin.

In 1962, Soviet leader Nikita Khrushchev refused U.S. President John F. Kennedy's request to remove Soviet missiles siloed in Cuba. After a U.S. naval blockade of Cuba, Khrushchev agreed to remove the missiles. Kennedy, in turn, promised not to invade Cuba and to remove U.S. missiles in Turkey.

The next Soviet leader, Leonid Brezhnev, initiated **détente** (relaxation of tensions between East and West). In 1972, President Richard Nixon visited Moscow. He and Brezhnev agreed to cooperate in science and technology, space exploration, and trade.

Earlier, the two leaders had begun *Strategic Arms Limitation Talks (SALT),* which led to a reduction in the number of certain nuclear weapons.

In 1979, President Jimmy Carter and Brezhnev prepared a SALT II treaty to limit the number of long-range bombers and missiles. The United States, however, had doubts that the Soviets really wanted peace. These suspicions seemed confirmed when Soviet troops invaded Afghanistan in 1979. The United States then refused to sign SALT II.

B. Gorbachev in Power (1985–1991)

The United States felt more confidence in the next Soviet leader, Mikhail Gorbachev. One of his two new programs, **perestroika** (restructuring), aimed to vitalize the Soviet economy by allowing private businesses. The other program, **glasnost** (openness), granted citizens increased freedom of speech and the press.

In 1987 and 1991, two major U.S.-Soviet treaties to reduce nuclear arms were signed. Gorbachev also ended the Afghanistan war in 1989 and cut off support to Marxist governments and movements around the world.

In August 1991, Communist officials critical of Gorbachev's reforms led an unsuccessful coup. To further sap their power, Gorbachev resigned from the Communist party. The Soviet government then suspended all party activities. The Communist party no longer controlled the government, the economy, or the military.

In spite of these reforms, Russia, Ukraine, and the 13 other republics of the Soviet Union declared

"Let's Get A Lock For This Thing"

–from *Straight Herblock* (Simon & Schuster, 1964)

John F. Kennedy and Nikita Khrushchev uniting against the nuclear menace, inspired by the Cuban Missile Crisis. (from *Straight Herblock* [Simon & Schuster, 1964])

independence. In 1991, Gorbachev resigned as Soviet president. Most of the republics then formed the *Commonwealth of Independent States (CIS),* with Russia the dominant state. The collapse of the Soviet Union ended the cold war. To encourage democracy and free-market economies in the new republics, Western nations sent financial aid and advisers.

Boris Yeltsin had been elected president of Russia in 1990. In October 1993, Communists and ultranationalists tried to oust him, but he won the national elections held in December. A new constitution was approved. Reelected in 1998, Yeltsin continued to move toward capitalism and good relations with the West. Severe economic problems, however, hampered his efforts.

C. Fall of Communism in Eastern Europe (1989–1990)

SOLIDARITY. In 1980, Lech Walesa, a worker from Gdansk, Poland, became head of the trade union Solidarity. It demanded that all unions be freed of Communist control and that the Polish-Soviet alliance be reexamined. When the government agreed to some changes, the workers demanded more, until Solidarity was outlawed in 1981. Walesa was arrested and military rule imposed. After Western protests, Walesa was released in 1982, and martial law lifted in 1983.

Economic problems fueled more protests. The Communist party allowed free elections in 1989.

Solidarity members won and formed the first non-Communist government in a former Soviet satellite. In 1990, Walesa was elected president.

Soviet Reaction. Gorbachev had abandoned the Brezhnev Doctrine that Soviets had the right to protect communism in any satellite. Changes in Poland proceeded undisturbed.

Reactions Elsewhere. Between 1989 and 1991, Hungary, Czechoslovakia, Albania, and Bulgaria held peaceful free elections. Romanians overthrew and executed their brutal president, Nicolae Ceausescu, who had refused to allow free elections.

EAST GERMANY. In 1989, East Germans tore down the Berlin Wall. In 1990, free elections led to the fall of the Communist party and reunification of East and West Germany.

INFO CHECK

1. What was the great worldwide fear during the cold war? What steps did the United States and the Soviet Union take to make the world safer?

2. List the succession of events that ended the cold war in 1991.

3. Who do you think did more to cause the fall of the Soviet Union—Mikhail Gorbachev or Boris Yeltsin? Give reasons for your choice.

4. How did Soviet abandonment of Brezhnev's policies lead to change in Eastern Europe?

Germans from East and West Berlin taking over the hated wall, 1989

II. POST-SOVIET REPUBLICS

A. Commonwealth of Independent States (CIS)

Minsk, the capital of Belarus, became the headquarters of the Commonwealth of Independent States (CIS). The Russian ruble became the standard currency. The CIS agreed to work for nuclear disarmament. Each republic was to have its own military forces.

Western nations opened diplomatic relations with the post-Soviet republics and sent them substantial economic and humanitarian aid.

B. Yeltsin in Power (1990–1999)

Yeltsin initiated the **privatization** of Russian industries. Shares of stock were sold or given to private individuals. Each Russian received a certificate authorizing trade in stocks. The government also gave managers and workers free shares in their companies. In line with communism's theory that the people own everything, the people received the proceeds from the sale of businesses.

OPPOSITION. Russians who had prospered and held power under communism feared a loss of privilege. Workers had enjoyed job security whether they were productive or not. The free market, however, requires optimal business efficiency. Workers now worried about layoffs and large cutbacks in social services.

HARDSHIP. The reforms caused a drop in production. As food and consumer goods became scarce, prices rose, and millions lost their jobs. As crime and government corruption increased, many Russians lost faith in democracy, private enterprise, and Yeltsin himself.

C. Developing a Democratic Russia

By late 1992, old-style bureaucrats, former Communist bosses, and ultranationalists in the government wanted to slow privatization and undermine Yeltsin's power. When Yeltsin asked for greater economic control, the parliament reduced his powers.

CRISIS. In March 1993, Yeltsin tried to take emergency powers and govern by decree (legal order). His opponents called for his impeachment and removal from office. Russia's Constitutional Court agreed that Yeltsin had violated the constitution but did not remove him from office.

A **referendum** (popular vote) clearly supported Yeltsin. He proposed a new constitution to strengthen the presidency and limit the parliament's powers. Before the constitution could be adopted, Yeltsin suspended his vice president, dissolved the parliament, and called for new legislative elections. Parliament claimed that these actions were illegal and voted to replace Yeltsin with the vice president. Yeltsin refused to yield.

Commonwealth of Independent States

REVOLT. As government leaders held round-the-clock sessions in their headquarters, Yeltsin surrounded them with soldiers and police. On October 3, 1993, civilians who supported the parliament charged Yeltsin's force with weapons. After 26 hours, the government troops broke into the parliament and arrested the chairman, the vice president, and dozens of supporters.

PROBLEMS. In December 1993, voters approved the new constitution. Yeltsin's opponents, however, won many seats in the State Duma (parliament's new lower house). Clashes between Yeltsin and the parliament continued. Prices rose. Economic officials slowed down privatization, printed more money, and tried to increase production.

D. War With Chechnya

Russia has ruled Chechnya, a small region in the south, since the 1860s. Chechnya's largely non-Russian population is mainly Muslim.

In 1994, Chechnya declared independence. Within eight months, the Russian army devastated the capital, Grozny, and wiped out much of its industry. A 1995 peace settlement gave Chechnya a large degree of self-rule but not independence.

In 1999, hostilities erupted once more. Russia's renewed assault on Chechnya continued into the 21st century.

E. Western Reaction to Yeltsin

Although Western leaders expressed alarm at the war in Chechnya, they generally sided with Yeltsin in his political struggles. In January 1993, Yeltsin and U.S. President George Bush signed a new arms-reduction treaty, *START II,* to eliminate land-based missiles with multiple warheads. Two-thirds of each side's nuclear warheads were to be destroyed by the year 2007.

F. New Elections

Yeltsin lost ground in the 1995 parliamentary elections. The opposition party slipped even more. A revived Communist party won nearly one-third of the seats.

Nonetheless, Yeltsin won the 1996 presidential election. He changed cabinet ministers several times, but massive aid from the West failed to prop up the economy. By 1999, many businesses were not paying taxes. To prevent total economic collapse, the *International Monetary Fund (IMF)* committed even more money to Russia. But confidence in Yeltsin declined.

On December 31, 1999, Yeltsin resigned and Vladimir Putin became president. Putin proved to be a strong and able leader. He improved the Russian economy by increasing oil production. Putin negotiated friendship and trade agreements with China and North Korea in 2001. He opposed a missile defense plan proposed by U.S. President George W. Bush.

Putin supported the U.S.-led war on global terrorism that began in 2001. In 2003, however, he opposed the Anglo-American invasion of Iraq.

President Putin was becoming increasingly authoritarian. When, in 2005, Mikhail Khodorkovsky, head of the Yukos oil company, funded political parties opposed to Putin, Putin imprisoned him. The president also began to appoint provincial governors, who had formerly been elected. In spite of these political regressions, Russia's market econ-

Chechen women hold portraits of missing relatives during a demonstration in Grozny February 23, 2006.

omy has continued to grow, partly because demand for Russian oil is high.

INFO CHECK

1. Describe the problems of Russia in the 1990s. If you were a Russian citizen at this time, would you oppose or support Boris Yeltsin? Give reasons for your answer.

2. Why do you think the leaders of the United States and other Western nations supported Yeltsin?

3. Why do the people of Chechnya want independence from Russia? Why do you think the Russian government has refused to give Chechnya its independence?

III. BEYOND RUSSIA: NATIONALISM AND ECONOMIC REFORM

A. Ukraine

Ukrainians had resented Russian rule since czarist times. In a 1991 referendum, 90 percent of Ukraine's 52 million people chose independence. Ukraine and Russia then quarreled over how to divide a former Soviet fleet in the Black Sea. Russia got most of the ships and, in return, canceled Ukraine's debt for natural gas purchases.

In 1954, Khrushchev had given Crimea, once part of Russia, to Ukraine as a gesture of friendship. After 1991, Russian nationalists there demanded its self-rule or return to Russia. Russia's government would not interfere.

Russia and Ukraine have remained mutually dependent. Most of Ukraine's oil and gas comes from Russia, and much of Russia's food comes from Ukraine. Moreover, Ukraine is a large market for Russian goods.

Some Ukrainians wanted to keep Soviet nuclear missiles siloed in Ukraine. In the end, Ukraine, Belarus, and Kazakhstan destroyed their nuclear weapons. Of the former Soviet republics, only Russia retained nuclear weapons.

Ukraine's free-market reforms caused sharp internal economic shocks. Western nations offered to make large loans. They also offered to install a safer nuclear power plant at Chernobyl, where a 1986 nuclear accident had spewed radiation over the area and across Europe.

Elected in 2004, President Viktor Yushchenko has pursued pro-western policies.

B. Kazakhstan

Russia had ruled Kazakhstan in Central Asia since the 1700s. Its main ethnic groups are Kazakhs and Russians. Kazakhs speak a Turkic language and are Sunni Muslims. Ethnic Russians dominate the urban industries, which have gradually been privatized.

The country produces vast amounts of cotton and grain and has such mineral resources as oil, gas, iron, gold, silver, copper, and chromium. It also has a space-launching facility at Baikonar, whose lease to Russia provides additional income. Kazakhstan's potential for economic growth has attracted Western investors. Kazakhstan, Belarus, and Russia form a free-trade zone.

C. Azerbaijan and Armenia

Armenia and Azerbaijan became Soviet republics after the Russian Revolution. Turkey, Iran, and Russia had long competed for them because of their natural resources and proximity to southeastern Europe. The Azeris are Shiite Muslims and have historical and cultural ties to Turkey. The Armenians are mainly Christian. Many Armenians live within Azerbaijan.

The Armenians in Azerbaijan wanted to unite their sector with a willing Armenia. Mass demonstrations first caused riots between ethnic Armenians and Azeris and then war. A cease-fire was announced in 1991, with Armenian forces in control of the disputed region of Nagorno Karabakh. Led by Russian, French, and U.S. negotiators, efforts to end the conflict peacefully continued into the early 21st century.

D. Belarus

Belarus is a parliamentary republic with close economic ties to Russia. The Belarussians are Slavs akin to Russians and Ukrainians. They follow the Eastern Orthodox religion.

Elected in 1994 and reelected in 2006, President Aleksander Lukashenko has imprisoned his opponents. The U.S. and the E.U. have banned several Belarusian government officials from entering their countries.

E. Eastern Europe

CZECH REPUBLIC AND SLOVAKIA. In 1918, Czech and Slovak lands were united as Czechoslovakia. In 1989, it again became an independent country, with Vaclav Havel as president.

Traditionally, Czechs have been influenced by the West, while Slovaks have looked to Hungary and Russia for trade and support. In 1993, the Slovaks set up Slovakia as a nation independent of the Czech Republic. In 2004, the Czech Republic

Polish President Lech Kaczynski and his wife Maria exchange flowers with Czech President Vaclav Klaus and his wife Livia upon their arrival at presidential residence at Lany Castle near Prague.

and Slovakia joined the European Union and Slovakia became a NATO member.

POLAND. To solve its economic problems, Polish leaders tried "shock therapy." They introduced free-market capitalism all at once rather than gradually, as in other Eastern European countries.

The strategy brought a rush of Western consumer goods and a sharp rise in foreign trade. Polish businesses could not compete, industrial production fell, wages dropped, and unemployment soared. Lech Walesa, who had spearheaded the changes, lost popularity.

In the 1990s, advances in private enterprise and an increase in foreign investment led to economic growth in Poland. By mid-2006, its growth rate was over 5 percent and inflation was the lowest in the EU. Poland became a member of NATO in 1999 and of the European Union in 2004.

Lech Kaczynski became president in 2005 and his brother Jaroslaw Kaczynski was appointed prime minister in 2006 but lost an election to Donald Tusk in 2007. These leaders have succeeded in making Poland more democratic. Their government has reduced the number of parliamentary seats held by former Communists. A new anticorruption agency screens officers of the military intelligence service for criminal behavior.

HUNGARY. Hungary followed Poland and Czechoslovakia in separating from the Soviet Union. At first, it established close ties to these countries. After Czechoslovakia's split, Hungary became concerned for the Hungarian minority in Slovakia.

Hungary's change to a free-market economy was difficult. The economy soon recovered through privatization and foreign investment.

F. NATO and Eastern Europe

Many former satellites sought membership in NATO as protection against Russia. But NATO members were not ready to fight in their defense. They were asked to work toward full membership by joining a "Partnership for Peace."

In 1997, Yeltsin signed an agreement to ease the way for Eastern European nations to join NATO.

The Czech Republic, Hungary, and Poland joined NATO in 1999. Bulgaria, Latvia, Estonia, Lithuania, Romania, Slovakia, and Slovenia joined NATO in 2004. Serbia, Bosnia, and Montenegro were offered Partnerships for Peace in 2007.

INFO CHECK

1. Why does Kazakhstan have a better economic future than most of the other republics of the CIS?

2. Identify the two major goals of the Eastern European nations after the cold war. What was the role of Poland during this period?

IV. WESTERN EUROPE

A. Germany

EFFECTS OF REUNIFICATION. Eastern Germany was far less developed economically than western Germany. Its former Soviet markets were gone. German Chancellor Helmut Kohl offered long-term assistance—from business subsidies to welfare payments.

Germans were taxed to help finance this aid. Some western Germans thought eastern Germans were "freeloaders," which many eastern Germans resented. A 1992–1993 recession made tensions worse. Although the economy improved, unemployment in eastern Germany remained high. In 2005 Angela Merkel, a Christian Democrat, became Chancellor and formed a government by creating a "grand alliance" with the Social Democrats.

NATIONALISM. During the 1970s and 1980s, expanding West German industries had hired many "guest workers" from Turkey and other countries. Many others sought refuge from crises in the Middle East and elsewhere. The recession and continuing unemployment fueled resentment of these foreigners. Neo-Nazis adopting the "Germany-for-Germans" policies of Hitler's time became active. Kohl's government had to curb extremist violence by law. Meanwhile, Germany limited the number of immigrants seeking jobs.

B. France

DE GAULLE. In 1958, General Charles de Gaulle became premier and then president of France, with expanded powers. He encouraged economic and technological advances and supported European unity. De Gaulle resigned in 1969 after losing a referendum on constitutional changes that would have strengthened his powers even more.

Under de Gaulle, cities were rebuilt, consumer goods became more available, and more students went to universities. He ended France's colonialism in Asia and Africa and negotiated independence for Algeria in 1962. He also tried to increase trade with the rest of Europe.

SOCIALISTS. The next two presidents, Georges Pompidou and Valéry Giscard D'Estaing, both supported Gaullist policies. In 1981, the global oil crisis and the economic problems it brought resulted in a Socialist victory. François Mitterrand became president and remained in office until 1995.

The Socialists increased tax-supported public services and utilities. They gave workers and unions more power and increased social welfare benefits. In 1984, however, a faltering economy necessitated sharp tax cuts and a reduction in government spending.

CONSERVATIVES. Ongoing economic problems caused voters to elect more conservative leaders, who were strengthened by a growing resentment of foreign workers, especially from former French colonies in North Africa. Right- and left-wing governments alternated in power throughout the 1990s.

Jacques Chirac, the conservative mayor of Paris, became president in 1995 but lost support by raising taxes and reducing spending on education. Left-wing parties won important government seats in the 2004 election. In 2005, French voters defeated a proposed EU constitution. President Chirac's opposition to the Iraq War created tension between his government and U.S. President George W. Bush's administration.

In November 2005, riots broke out across France. These were led mainly by second- or third-generation African Muslims and showed the government's inability to integrate immigrants into French society and to deal with high unemployment.

A Conservative, Nicolas Sarkozy, became president in 2007. He promised to reduce unemployment, cut taxes, increase workers' productivity, shrink government bureaucracy, and other reforms. Many in the immigrant community distrusted Sarkozy's goodwill toward them.

C. Great Britain

After World War II, the Labour party led Great Britain. It instituted the National Health Service, a system of socialized medicine, and nationalized economic enterprises, such as the Bank of England, coal, and steel.

PROBLEMS. During the 1960s and 1970s, Britain's loss of its colonial markets and lag in manufacturing productivity injured its economy. In 1973, hoping to find new markets, it joined the *European Economic Community (EEC).*

Many of Britain's white majority resented the influx of nonwhite immigrants. In the 1960s, the government restricted immigration from Commonwealth countries.

Meanwhile, the struggle between Protestants and Catholics over Northern Ireland led to increasing political terrorism in British cities.

THATCHER. In the 1980s, a Conservative government led by Margaret Thatcher returned nationalized industries to private ownership and reduced government spending. It also reduced the power of labor unions.

Under Thatcher, Britain went to war with Argentina over the Falkland Islands. Thatcher supported Gorbachev's policies of glasnost and perestroika. She joined U.S. President Ronald Reagan in opposing the spread of communism and in limiting nuclear arms.

When Parliament passed the unpopular poll tax that Thatcher favored, she lost support. Challenged by other party leaders for opposing closer ties with Europe, she resigned in 1990.

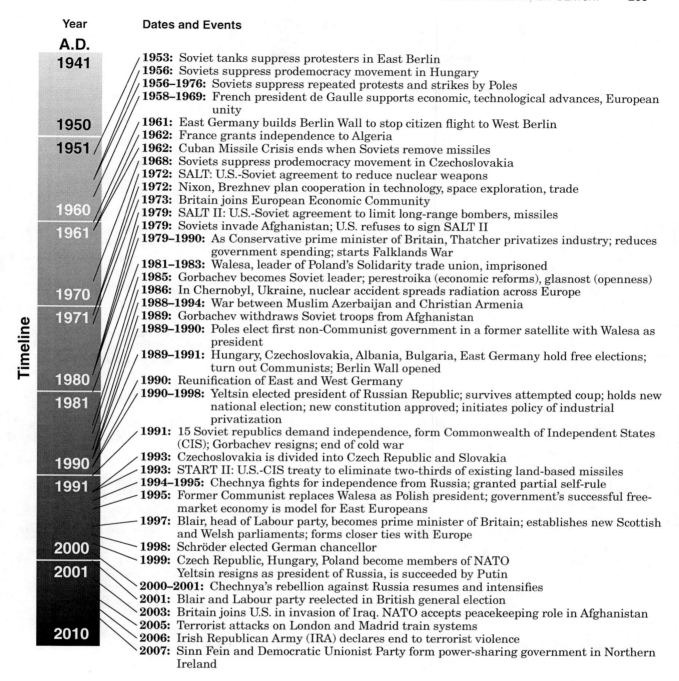

Year

A.D.

Dates and Events

1941

1950

1951

1960

1961

1970

1971

1980

1981

1990

1991

2000

2001

2010

Timeline

1953: Soviet tanks suppress protesters in East Berlin

1956: Soviets suppress prodemocracy movement in Hungary

1956–1976: Soviets suppress repeated protests and strikes by Poles

1958–1969: French president de Gaulle supports economic, technological advances, European unity

1961: East Germany builds Berlin Wall to stop citizen flight to West Berlin

1962: France grants independence to Algeria

1962: Cuban Missile Crisis ends when Soviets remove missiles

1968: Soviets suppress prodemocracy movement in Czechoslovakia

1972: SALT: U.S.-Soviet agreement to reduce nuclear weapons

1972: Nixon, Brezhnev plan cooperation in technology, space exploration, trade

1973: Britain joins European Economic Community

1979: SALT II: U.S.-Soviet agreement to limit long-range bombers, missiles

1979: Soviets invade Afghanistan; U.S. refuses to sign SALT II

1979–1990: As Conservative prime minister of Britain, Thatcher privatizes industry; reduces government spending; starts Falklands War

1981–1983: Walesa, leader of Poland's Solidarity trade union, imprisoned

1985: Gorbachev becomes Soviet leader; perestroika (economic reforms), glasnost (openness)

1986: In Chernobyl, Ukraine, nuclear accident spreads radiation across Europe

1988–1994: War between Muslim Azerbaijan and Christian Armenia

1989: Gorbachev withdraws Soviet troops from Afghanistan

1989–1990: Poles elect first non-Communist government in a former satellite with Walesa as president

1989–1991: Hungary, Czechoslovakia, Albania, Bulgaria, East Germany hold free elections; turn out Communists; Berlin Wall opened

1990: Reunification of East and West Germany

1990–1998: Yeltsin elected president of Russian Republic; survives attempted coup; holds new national election; new constitution approved; initiates policy of industrial privatization

1991: 15 Soviet republics demand independence, form Commonwealth of Independent States (CIS); Gorbachev resigns; end of cold war

1993: Czechoslovakia is divided into Czech Republic and Slovakia

1993: START II: U.S.-CIS treaty to eliminate two-thirds of existing land-based missiles

1994–1995: Chechnya fights for independence from Russia; granted partial self-rule

1995: Former Communist replaces Walesa as Polish president; government's successful free-market economy is model for East Europeans

1997: Blair, head of Labour party, becomes prime minister of Britain; establishes new Scottish and Welsh parliaments; forms closer ties with Europe

1998: Schröder elected German chancellor

1999: Czech Republic, Hungary, Poland become members of NATO
Yeltsin resigns as president of Russia, is succeeded by Putin

2000–2001: Chechnya's rebellion against Russia resumes and intensifies

2001: Blair and Labour party reelected in British general election

2003: Britain joins U.S. in invasion of Iraq. NATO accepts peacekeeping role in Afghanistan

2005: Terrorist attacks on London and Madrid train systems

2006: Irish Republican Army (IRA) declares end to terrorist violence

2007: Sinn Fein and Democratic Unionist Party form power-sharing government in Northern Ireland

LABOUR PARTY. Led by Tony Blair, the Labour party won control of the government in 1997 and again in 2001. Blair established more self-government in Scotland and Wales and strove for a permanent peace in Northern Ireland. He deployed British forces to support the U.S. war on global terrorism in Afghanistan and joined the U.S. invasion of Iraq. Blair lost favor with many voters because he supported the Iraq War. Members of his own party forced Blair out of office in 2007. He was succeeded as Labour prime minister by Gordon Brown.

INFO CHECK

1. Explain why you AGREE or DISAGREE with the following: The reunification of Germany in 1990 gave rise to economic and social problems.

2. Why did riots break out in France in 2005? How did this issue contribute to the election of Conservative leaders?

3. Identify 20th century leaders of the Labour and Conservative parties in Britain. State two policies followed by Prime Minister Blair.

CHAPTER REVIEW

Multiple Choice

1. Leonid Brezhnev's policy of cooperation with the United States and Western Europe was called

   1. the Good Neighbor policy
   2. appeasement
   3. containment
   4. détente.

2. The purpose of the SALT I and II treaties was

   1. to spread the use of natural seasonings
   2. agreement by the superpowers to protect the seas and the environment
   3. agreement by the superpowers to limit the use and number of nuclear weapons
   4. agreement by the superpowers to support the UN.

3. Two exceptions to the Communist party's reliance on command economic principles took place at the beginning and the end of the Soviet Union. They were

   1. Lenin's NEP and Gorbachev's perestroika
   2. Stalin's collectivization and Five-Year plans
   3. Gorbachev's glasnost and Trotsky's Red Guards
   4. Czar Alexander's serf emancipation and Czar Peter's westernization.

4. In the 20th century, the major power in Eastern Europe changed its name several times. It was first called Russia, next

   1. the USSR, and today the Russian Federation
   2. the USSR, and today the Soviet Union
   3. Soviet Russia, and today the USSR
   4. the Peoples' Republic, and today the Commonwealth of Nations.

5. Yeltsin's attempt to move Russia from a command economy to individual ownership of businesses, factories, and farms is known as

   1. collectivization
   2. the Great Leap Forward
   3. privatization
   4. the Five-Year plans.

6. The Soviet leader who did most to end the cold war was

   1. Joseph Stalin
   2. Nikita Krushchev
   3. Leonid Brezhnev
   4. Mikhail Gorbachev.

7. Economic growth of the reunified Germany has

   1. sped up after its two economically powerful sections rejoined

2. ceased, as each section fights for military control of the other
   3. moved ahead, as East and West Germany have joined economic forces to control the world computer market
   4. had problems because of East Germany's high poverty and unemployment levels.

8. When the Soviet Union collapsed, the non-Communist nations of the world were very concerned about

   1. immigration of Communists into their nations
   2. invasion of the former Soviet Union
   3. the many nuclear weapons of the former Soviet Union
   4. payment of debts owed to them by the former Soviet Union.

9. Political and economic changes in Eastern Europe, the collapse of the Soviet Union, and economic problems in the West have resulted in

   1. a worldwide depression
   2. an increase in military dictatorships
   3. more military alliances
   4. the realization by the world's nations that events anywhere in the world can affect their economies.

10. Use the information contained in the map on page 278 and your knowledge of Global History and Geography to select the most accurate statement:

   1. Georgia, Belarus, Ukraine, and Russia are now independent nations.
   2. The Soviet Union continues to exist.
   3. Russia has colonized Estonia and Latvia.
   4. Mongolia, China, Sweden, and Denmark have joined in a military alliance with the former Soviet Union.

11. The photographs on pages 279 and 281 show that

   1. Communists continue to hold and control former Soviet satellites
   2. people in areas formerly controlled by Communists now may feel a greater freedom to assemble and speak their minds
   3. women continue to be oppressed in most nations of the former Communist bloc
   4. oppression, even by as strong an organization as the Communist party, cannot last long.

Thematic Essays

1. The Soviet leaders, Brezhnev and Gorbachev, tried to do three things: maintain Soviet power, improve the economy, and achieve better relations with the

West. *Task:* For each of the leaders, select one of the goals and describe the efforts made to reach it. Consider in your answer Salt I and II, the Afghanistan invasion, perestroika, glasnost, and the Commonwealth of Independent States.

2. The collapse of the Soviet Union allowed the reunification of the German nation. *Task:* Imagine that you are a reporter who, one year after the reunification, interviews factory workers from former East and West Germany. What positive and negative things would each tell you about reunified Germany? Consider political, social, and economic issues and concerns in your answer.

Document-Based Questions

1. Gorbachev explained the need for reform:

   "The Soviet Union, the world's biggest producer of steel, raw materials, fuel and energy, has shortfalls in them due to wasteful or inefficient use.... Our rockets can find Halley's comet and fly to Venus with amazing accuracy, but side-by-side with these scientific and technological triumphs is an obvious lack of efficiency in using scientific achievements for economic needs, and many Soviet household appliances are of poor quality ... the improvements in living standards was slowing down and there were difficulties in the supply of foodstuffs, housing, consumer goods and services...."

   Explain why the Soviet economy was a mixture of success and failure.

2. Milovan Djilas, a Yugoslavian and a former Communist, wrote a book titled *The New Class* in 1957. He stated:

   "The communist East European countries did not become satellites of the USSR because they benefited from it, but because they were too weak to prevent it. As soon as they become stronger, or as soon as favorable conditions are created, a yearning for independence and for protection of 'their own people' from Soviet hegemony [control] will rise among them...."

   Have the words of this man proved to be correct? Explain.

3. From a 1990 New Year's Day address to the Czechoslovakian people by President Vaclav Havel:

   " ... entire branches of industry are producing things for which there is no demand while we are short of the things we need. The state, which calls itself a state of workers, is humiliating and exploiting them instead. Our outmoded economy wastes energy, which we have in short supply.... We have spoiled our land, rivers and forests, inherited from our ancestors, and we have, today, the worst environment in the whole of Europe...."

   Is President Havel praising or condemning Czechoslovakia's command economy in 1990? Explain your answer.

4. Study the photo on page 279. What caused the fighting between the Russian and Chechen forces?

5. Study the cartoon. What events is the cartoonist trying to portray?

© 1989 by Herblock in *The Washington Post*

Document-Based Essay

Was the collapse of the Soviet Union caused by the efforts of the United States and its allies, or internal causes, or some combination of both? *Task:* Use the documents and your knowledge of Global History and Geography to present a factually supported answer. Explain why you AGREE or DISAGREE with the claim of some Americans that the United States won the cold war.

CHAPTER
27

The Developing World

I. POLITICAL UNREST IN LATIN AMERICA

A. Argentina

PERÓN. General Juan Perón was elected president of Argentina in 1946. Supported by the Catholic Church, industrial workers, and city residents, he became dictator by courting popular approval. His wife Evita instituted popular projects, while Perón played on the people's nationalism. He gave workers a stronger political voice and increased social benefits for the poor. He brought about rapid industrialization and reduced foreign economic influence. Those who opposed his policies were suppressed.

Argentina's economy depended on wheat and beef. When world prices for them dropped in the early 1950s, Perón froze wages and cut welfare programs. Civil dissatisfaction led to a military takeover in 1955.

For 18 years, a series of weak leaders ruled Argentina. Perón, who remained influential, became president again in 1973. But dissension among his followers, his failing health, and a high rate of inflation weakened the regime.

AFTER PERÓN. After 1976, a series of corrupt generals controlled Argentina. Their secret "death squads" killed opponents, and political dissidents, many of them young, simply disappeared. The "Mothers of the Plaza de Mayo" gathered in the square in Buenos Aires where the presidential palace stands and displayed pictures of their missing sons and daughters. By thus attracting the support of international human rights groups and the foreign press, the mothers helped weaken the military regime. In 2005, the Supreme Court revoked amnesty laws barring prosecution for human rights crimes committed under military rule.

FALKLAND ISLANDS WAR. In 1982, the tyranny was ended by a war between Britain and Argentina over the Falkland (Malvinas) Islands. The British victory led to the disgrace and resignation of the ruling general in mid-1982. The suspension of military rule allowed the Argentine people to reestablish civilian rule in 1983.

In 1989, Carlos Saúl Menem became president. Economic reforms and increased economic growth led to his reelection in 1995. By 2002, however, President Eduardo Duhalde, elected in 2001, was struggling with a long recession. He negotiated with the International Monetary Fund (IMF) for a large rescue loan, which rescued Argentina from economic collapse.

ECONOMIC DEVELOPMENT. During the administration of Néstor Kirchner, elected president in 2003, the rising prices for farm exports helped the economy improve. Although by mid-2004 unemployment had fallen around 15 percent, problems nonetheless continued. Electric power shortages slowed recovery, and Argentina's failure to pay some of its debts discouraged foreign investment. More than half of all Argentinians remained below the poverty line. In 2005, Kirchner stated that Argentina had paid its debt to the IMF.

B. Cuba

The 1991 collapse of the Soviet Union ended aid to Cuba. A drop in trade with Eastern Europe further damaged its economy. Fuel shortages limited industrial production.

In 1993 and 1994, President Fidel Castro introduced limited free-market reforms: private ownership of small businesses, use of foreign currency, and agricultural cooperatives. The reforms, however, were not immediately effective.

BOAT PEOPLE. In August 1994, some 35,000 Cubans crowded into boats and sailed for the United States. Their government did nothing to stop them. In May 1995, President Bill Clinton

Rafters row out of the Bay of Cojimar, outside Havana, in route to the U.S. in this August 29, 1994 photo.

announced an end to the 35-year-old policy of granting Cuban refugees free entry to the United States. After Cuba downed two planes owned by U.S. citizens in 1996, the long-standing U.S. embargo on Cuban trade was also tightened.

In 1999, the United States eased the embargo. Because of continuing political and economic challenges, Cuba's future remains uncertain.

In 2002, the United States began to use its naval base at Guantánamo Bay as a prison for Taliban and Al Qaeda enemy combatants.

The Organization of American States (OAS) has unsuccessfully urged the United States to end its trade embargo on Cuba. In 2004, President George W. Bush sought to hasten the end of the Castro government with travel restrictions. Failing health caused Fidal Castro to turn over much of his authority to his brother Raoul Castro, in 2006.

C. Haiti

In 1986, twenty-eight years of dictatorship by the Duvalier family over Haiti came to an end. Four years of military rule followed.

ARISTIDE. In 1990, Haitians elected Jean-Bertrand Aristide, a left-wing Catholic priest, as president. The military and a group of wealthy people that it protected felt threatened by Aristide's proposed reforms. In September 1991, the military ousted Aristide and took power.

EMBARGO. The United States and the *Organization of American States (OAS),* a cooperative association of Western Hemisphere nations, demanded that Aristide be restored to power. They also placed an embargo on Haiti in October 1991, which seriously damaged the economy. In June 1993, a new UN embargo on oil and arms to Haiti made things worse.

Most Haitians had always lived in poverty with an upper class of less than 5 percent of the population controlling the limited wealth. The embargoes only intensified unemployment and starvation among the poor. Nevertheless, Haitians supported the sanctions in the hope that they would bring back Aristide.

REFUGEES. Fearing rebellion, the army terrorized the Haitians, who tried to flee to the United States by boat. In the view of Presidents Bush and Clinton, the boat people were seeking economic gain rather than fleeing political oppression. The U.S. Coast Guard returned many refugees to Haiti and transferred others to "safe havens" in Latin America. Critics blasted this policy as racist.

NEGOTIATIONS. The UN was unable to negotiate Aristide's return. In May 1994, UN sanctions were tightened.

The United States threatened invasion. Some of Aristide's supporters feared that a U.S. invasion would lead to occupation, as it had from 1915 to 1934. Others felt that there was no other way.

In July 1994, the UN Security Council authorized the use of force against Haiti. On the eve of a U.S. invasion, U.S. negotiators persuaded the military to let the troops land peacefully. General Raoul Cedras, the dictator, agreed to leave Haiti.

RETURN OF ARISTIDE. On October 15, 1994, President Aristide returned to Haiti. He urged his supporters to seek no revenge against the military.

REBUILDING. UN peacekeepers replaced most of the U.S. soldiers. A new parliament was elected in 1995. Six months later, René Préval, a close associate of Aristide's, was elected president. (By law, Aristide could not succeed himself.) Haiti was still in poverty and unstable when UN troops left in 1997. That same year, Aristide formed a new political party and reentered Haitian politics. He was elected president again in 2000, but was forced to resign in 2004. Much of the country is controlled by gangs and privately armed militias.

D. Venezuela

Venezuela, a democracy since 1958, has the largest oil reserves outside the Mideast. In 1998, Hugo Chávez became president of Venezuela. He angered the U.S. government by making friendly overtures to Fidel Castro, lobbying other oil-rich South American countries to raise oil prices, recognizing guerrilla movements in nearby countries, and denouncing U.S. involvement in Colombia's drug war.

Chávez has improved public services for Venezuela's poor. At the same time, he has used the popularity won by these improvements to increase presidential power. His power-grabbing measures include a new constitution eliminating an important legislative body and increasing the presidential term to six years. When he merged all Venezuelan labor unions into one body, the International Labor Organization and the United Nation's high commissioner for human rights expressed concern over his growing power. Business leaders in every city of Venezuela held strikes protesting Chávez's new laws in 2001.

By 2006, Chávez and President George W. Bush were rivals for influence in Latin America. Many people both in Venezuela and abroad admire his social service programs but feel that he may be using the army to crush dissent. Chavez' attempt to again increase presidential powers in 2007 was defeated by popular vote.

E. Mexico

In 1993, Mexico joined the *North American Free Trade Agreement (NAFTA)* with Canada and the United States in spite of tension between the U.S.

Drug Enforcement Agency (DEA) and Mexican security forces. U.S. officials, trying to stop the flow of drugs across the Mexican border, identified Mexican *traficantes* (drug dealers) living in open luxury in Mexico.

Carlos Salinas de Gortari, Mexico's president from 1988 to 1994, cooperated with the DEA by creating military and police organizations against drug operations. Mexican agents destroyed marijuana and opium poppies and intercepted drugs moving into the United States through Mexico. Some Mexicans objected to U.S. involvement in their domestic affairs. Others feared that the anti-drug campaign would strengthen the military.

Soon after Ernesto Zedillo became president in 1994, the Mexican economy nearly collapsed. In 1995, President Clinton sought to assure Zedillo's cooperation in the drug war with a multi-billion-dollar rescue package from the United States.

In Chiapas, Mexico's poorest state, an armed uprising by the Zapatista Revolutionary party began in 1994. Guerrilla attacks on government targets and battles between the army and the rebels caused the PRI, the ruling political party since 1929, to lose the 2000 elections. Opposition candidate Vincente Fox Quesada became president. By 2001, government talks with the Zapatistas had accomplished little. Felipe Calderón became president in 2006.

INFO CHECK

1. Identify the Latin American country led by each of the following: Fidel Castro, Jean-Bertrand Aristide, Hugo Chávez, Felipe Calderón.

2. Which of the above leaders do you regard as most admirable? Which do you regard as least admirable? Give reasons for your choices.

3. Name two Latin American countries that experienced revolutionary movements in the 1990s. Which revolution was more successful in achieving its goals? Why?

II. POST-COLD WAR "HOT SPOTS"

A. North Korea

The Democratic People's Republic of Korea remains committed to the Communist struggle against capitalism and uses its economic resources for military production. In the 1990s, a fuel shortage reduced industrial and agricultural output and caused a serious food shortage. In the late

1990s, drought and other weather problems made the shortage worse.

Communist party leader Kim Il Sung had controlled North Korea for its first 46 years. When he died in July 1994, his son Kim Jong Il, commander of military forces, succeeded him.

NUCLEAR PROGRAM. In 1993, North Korea refused to allow international inspections by the *International Atomic Energy Agency (IAEA)* of its nuclear power facilities. It also announced its intention to withdraw from the 1968 Nuclear Nonproliferation Treaty, the first nation to make this threat.

In October 1994, after U.S. warnings against its withdrawal, North Korea promised to freeze nuclear weapons development and then end it. In return, the United States promised to arrange for $4 billion in energy assistance from Japan and South Korea, including two light-water nuclear reactors for producing electricity. Their by-products are hard to use for nuclear weapons.

The development and testing of missiles by North Korea has been regarded as a threat to the security of other nations, especially Japan and the United States. In August 2001, North Korean leader Kim Jong Il promised to suspend ballistic missile launches until 2003.

In 2003, North Korea announced that it was capable of building nuclear weapons. China arranged for the United States, South Korea, Japan, Russia, and China to hold talks with North Korea in an effort to persuade it to give up its nuclear program in exchange for economic assistance. After some difficulty, Kim Jong Il agreed in 2007 to close its main nuclear reactor in exchange for aid.

B. South Korea

After the Korean War, a military group ruled South Korea. In 1987, citizens demanded the right to elect a president. Since 1990, South Korea has forged a relatively stable two-party political system.

ECONOMIC BOOM AND BUST. Since World War II, *chaebol* (large, powerful family-run businesses) have controlled the economy. Some 97 percent of the labor force works in manufacturing and service industries. The major industries are textiles and automobiles.

In October 1997, the financial crisis that had earlier hit Southeast Asia adversely affected South Korea's economic prosperity. Corporations began to fail, and the won (the national currency) fell sharply in value. South Korea requested emergency economic aid from the International Monetary Fund (IMF). In 1997, South Koreans elected Kim Dae Jung as president. A former dissident and political prisoner, he began the task of restoring international confidence in the South Korean economy.

REUNIFICATION ON HOLD. In 1972, South and North Korea agreed to work toward reunification. In 1985, they discussed economic issues; they opened trade relations, and South Korea began investing in North Korea. In 1991, the two nations formally ended the Korean War. In June 2000, North Korea's Kim Jong Il and President Kim Dae Jung held a first-ever summit conference. Relations between the two countries showed some improvement. Roh Moo-Hyun was elected president in 2002.

C. Sudan

Sudan is a large, arid country with a population that exceeds 32 million. Religious differences split its population. The Arab northerners are mostly Muslims and the black African southerners are either Christians or animists (people who believe that all of nature is suffused by spirits).

After gaining independence from Britain and Egypt in 1956, Sudan chose a parliamentary coalition government. A military group deposed this government in 1958 and banned all political parties. Riots in 1964 brought about a brief period of civilian rule, which ended in another military coup in 1968.

In 1971, Jaafar Mohammed al Nemery became president. When, in 1983, Nemery imposed Islamic law on civil courts throughout the country, a civil war broke out between north and south. In the mid-1980s and the late 1990s, severe droughts added to the economic hardships caused by political instability. From 1985 to 1989, a succession of three governments ruled Sudan.

At the beginning of the 21st century, war and famine had killed almost two million Sudanese. In 2004, Sudan's government and the southern Sudanese agreed to share the nation's wealth, most of which came from the oil-producing south. The United States and other Western nations hoped that peace between the north and south of Sudan would give their oil companies access to the oil fields. They also hoped that political stability would prevent terrorists from forming bases in Sudan.

In 2004, however, fighting resumed. Local Muslim militias killed over 200,000 non-Muslim people in the western Darfur region. Despite diplomatic efforts by the African Union and by various

A Rwandan refugee is helped out of a railway wagon by an unidentified aid worker in Kisangani. Thousands of Rwandan refugees are being airlifted by the UN to Rwanda where they fled the 1994 genocide.

Western nations, the fighting worsened. In 2006, a faction of the Sudanese Liberation Army, formed to liberate the non-Muslims of Darfur, began battling its former Sudanese Liberation Army allies in order to gain more territory. They also began to attack the non-Muslim civilians they had joined forces to protect. Thousands of civilians fled to makeshift camps with scant water, food, or health services.

The situation grew into what the United Nations called the "world's worst humanitarian crisis." Local and international aid organizations attempted to care for the 2.5 million refugees but were rendered almost powerless by lack of funds, restrictions imposed by the Sudanese government, and attacks made on them by combatants. In 2007, the Sudanese government agreed to allow UN and African Union peacekeeping troops into Darfur.

D. Somalia

The British- and Italian-held portions of Somalia gained independence in 1960 and united to form one country. During the cold war, the United States and the Soviet Union competed for influence in the region. With the aid of Soviet-equipped troops, Ethiopia defeated Somalia after 11 years of war.

When the cold war ended, local clan leaders attacked the Somali government. By late 1992, the Somali government had been destroyed. Drought and famine led to the deaths of several hundred thousand people. Due to attacks by clan militias, missions conducted by UN and humanitarian organizations ended in 1995.

In 2004, peace talks between clan members led to the establishment of a transitional government, which the UN supported. Fighting between militias continued, however.

By 2006, Islamist militias with links to Al Qaeda controlled much of Somalia. Rich Somali businesspeople, preferring the order brought by the Islamists to the anarchy of clan warfare, at first accepted Islamic rule. In 2006, however, the businesspeople began to resent the strict Islamic regime. When later in 2006, Ethiopia again attacked Somalia, the Islamic forces retreated to Mogadishu. Ethiopia supported the forces loyal to Somalia's President Abdullah Yasuf Ahmed as they fought against the Islamists.

E. China

CONTINUED REPRESSION. After the 1989 massacre in Tiananmen Square, Deng Xiaoping discouraged further moves toward democracy. Political suspects were tortured. Deng clearly felt that the Chinese would continue to accept Communist rule as long as their standard of living kept rising.

MFN STATUS. Since the 1970s, China has enjoyed most favored nation (MFN) status, which allows it to export products to the United States at the lowest tariff rate. MFN status must be renewed annually. In May 1993, President Clinton warned China that renewal depended on an improvement in its human rights record. In particular, the use of Chinese prison laborers to make goods for export to the United States should stop. Moreover, China should allow certain opposition leaders and their families to leave the country.

Some U.S. leaders wanted the president to stand firm in his demands. Others argued that unrestricted trade with China created thousands of American jobs and billions of dollars in contracts. They believed that trade would open up Chinese society and promote the rule of law in due course. Moreover, ongoing trade would encourage China to allow its citizens to buy products such as satellite dishes that would put them in touch with the West. In May 1994, President Clinton renewed China's MFN status.

TRADE AND HUMAN RIGHTS. With a growth rate exceeding 10 percent, China has become the fourth-largest economy after the U.S., Japan, and Germany. Increased domestic spending and rising exports have caused this expansion.

China's trade surplus with the rest of the world has led to global friction. Most of China's exports go to the U.S. and Europe, causing fears of job losses in these regions. American and European Union officials have pressured China to allow its currency, the yuan, to increase in value. This would make Chinese exports less attractive abroad and make foreign imports more competitive with Chinese domestic goods. In 2006, teams in China and the United States began to conduct "strategic economic dialogues" about trade, currency values, and piracy of movies and software.

China is a powerful member of the Association of Southeast Asian Nations (ASEAN). Through this organization, China has invested in Indonesian oil and natural gas fields. It has caused an economic boom in Australia by buying Australian iron ore, aluminum, and uranium. China has made large loans to Cambodia, Laos, Myanmar, and other poor Asian countries.

In the early 21st century, there was little evidence that economic growth in China had resulted in advances in human rights there. President Hu Jintao, in office since 2003, has jailed critics and closed newspapers. In 2006, his government began to limit free speech on the Internet. Human rights groups criticized the U.S. search engine companies, Yahoo and Google, for helping the Chinese government to use the Internet to track dissidents. Government troops have fired on people taking part in public demonstrations.

MILITARY STRENGTH. As China expanded its military forces, U.S. strategists saw the buildup as a challenge to U.S. and Japanese interests in East Asia. Many nations joined the United States in protesting Chinese underground nuclear testing in the mid-1990s.

POPULATION CURBS. China has the world's largest population. The government strongly encourages couples to have only one child. The United States, however, denounced China's chosen methods of birth control, which include compulsory sterilization, forced abortions, and fines for unauthorized pregnancies.

Local officials are charged with seeing that people in their districts meet family planning targets. As a result, a lower birthrate than had been planned for the year 2010 has already been achieved.

HONG KONG. Britain returned Hong Kong to Chinese rule on July 1, 1997. China promised that Hong Kong would remain a free-market economy for 50 years.

Raising of the Chinese flag in Hong Kong, 1997

China replaced Hong Kong's Legislative Council with the Provincial Legislature. This body has placed limits on opposition to government policies and reduced the number of candidates in elections.

TAIWAN. In 2000, the Taiwanese people defied China by choosing as their president Chen Shui-bian, whose Democratic Progressive Party advocated independence from China. China had threatened war if the Taiwanese elected Chen. After the election, however, Chen talked less about independence, and China's threats subsided.

INFO CHECK

1. Explain why you AGREE or DISAGREE with the following: The United States should not have interfered with North Korea's nuclear development program.

2. Why are U.S. leaders concerned about China's human rights and military policies? How has China's improved economy affected human rights for the Chinese?

3. If you were a citizen of Hong Kong, would you APPROVE or DISAPPROVE of the transfer from British to Chinese rule in July 1997? Give reasons for your answer.

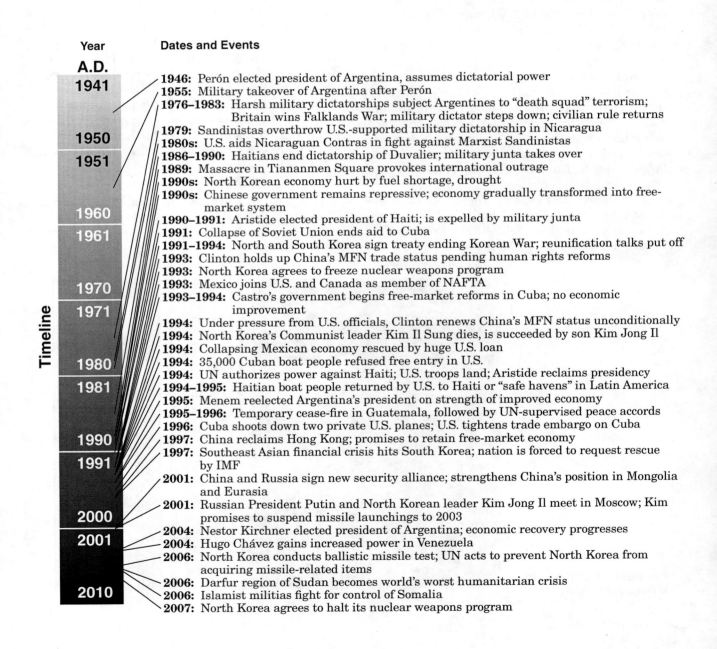

Timeline

Year A.D.	Dates and Events
1941	**1946:** Perón elected president of Argentina, assumes dictatorial power
	1955: Military takeover of Argentina after Perón
	1976–1983: Harsh military dictatorships subject Argentines to "death squad" terrorism; Britain wins Falklands War; military dictator steps down; civilian rule returns
1950	**1979:** Sandinistas overthrow U.S.-supported military dictatorship in Nicaragua
	1980s: U.S. aids Nicaraguan Contras in fight against Marxist Sandinistas
1951	**1986–1990:** Haitians end dictatorship of Duvalier; military junta takes over
	1989: Massacre in Tiananmen Square provokes international outrage
	1990s: North Korean economy hurt by fuel shortage, drought
	1990s: Chinese government remains repressive; economy gradually transformed into free-market system
1960	**1990–1991:** Aristide elected president of Haiti; is expelled by military junta
1961	**1991:** Collapse of Soviet Union ends aid to Cuba
	1991–1994: North and South Korea sign treaty ending Korean War; reunification talks put off
	1993: Clinton holds up China's MFN trade status pending human rights reforms
	1993: North Korea agrees to freeze nuclear weapons program
1970	**1993:** Mexico joins U.S. and Canada as member of NAFTA
1971	**1993–1994:** Castro's government begins free-market reforms in Cuba; no economic improvement
	1994: Under pressure from U.S. officials, Clinton renews China's MFN status unconditionally
	1994: North Korea's Communist leader Kim Il Sung dies, is succeeded by son Kim Jong Il
	1994: Collapsing Mexican economy rescued by huge U.S. loan
1980	**1994:** 35,000 Cuban boat people refused free entry in U.S.
1981	**1994:** UN authorizes power against Haiti; U.S. troops land; Aristide reclaims presidency
	1994–1995: Haitian boat people returned by U.S. to Haiti or "safe havens" in Latin America
	1995: Menem reelected Argentina's president on strength of improved economy
	1995–1996: Temporary cease-fire in Guatemala, followed by UN-supervised peace accords
1990	**1996:** Cuba shoots down two private U.S. planes; U.S. tightens trade embargo on Cuba
	1997: China reclaims Hong Kong; promises to retain free-market economy
1991	**1997:** Southeast Asian financial crisis hits South Korea; nation is forced to request rescue by IMF
	2001: China and Russia sign new security alliance; strengthens China's position in Mongolia and Eurasia
	2001: Russian President Putin and North Korean leader Kim Jong Il meet in Moscow; Kim promises to suspend missile launchings to 2003
2000	**2004:** Nestor Kirchner elected president of Argentina; economic recovery progresses
2001	**2004:** Hugo Chávez gains increased power in Venezuela
	2006: North Korea conducts ballistic missile test; UN acts to prevent North Korea from acquiring missile-related items
	2006: Darfur region of Sudan becomes world's worst humanitarian crisis
2010	**2006:** Islamist militias fight for control of Somalia
	2007: North Korea agrees to halt its nuclear weapons program

CHAPTER REVIEW

Multiple Choice

1. Latin America's economic problems were often caused by

    1. too much dependence on one or two cash crops
    2. bad weather conditions
    3. worldwide depression
    4. high import tariffs on its products.

2. Many Latin Americans of Indian descent do not benefit from their nations' wealth because

    1. their nations are all very poor and lack natural resources
    2. the Indians do not care to live in Western-style houses
    3. wealth and political power are limited to the military and the descendants of the Spanish
    4. Indians live so far from the capital that their governments cannot easily communicate with them.

3. Latin Americans still resent or are fearful of the U.S. government and its actions because

    1. Americans polluted the Amazon River
    2. former U.S. governments intervened in the running of many Latin American countries
    3. U.S. businesspeople are still being given unfair trading advantages in Latin America
    4. American missionaries are transported in U.S. military airplanes.

4. The Plaza de Mayo in Argentina and Tiananmen Square in China are famous because they are places where

    1. tourists get information
    2. famous churches are found
    3. fast-food restaurants are located
    4. human rights demonstrations were held.

5. Military rule in Argentina ended in 1982, after the defeat of the military in the brief, but costly, war they fought with Great Britain over control of

    1. the Panama Canal
    2. the Falkland (Malvinas) Islands
    3. Easter Island
    4. Jamaica.

6. The United States has supported military dictatorships in Latin America because they

    1. were anti-Communist governments
    2. sent troops to fight in the Persian Gulf War
    3. built advanced military equipment for the United States
    4. loaned the United States money to pay off foreign debts.

7. North Korea is a "hot spot" because of

    1. the unrest of its people
    2. its wish to reunite with South Korea
    3. its development of nuclear weapons
    4. its self-imposed isolation.

8. Which problem contributed most to the humanitarian crisis in Sudan?

    1. recurring droughts
    2. U.S. desire for access to Sudan oil fields
    3. ethnic and religious differences within the population
    4. interference in Sudanese affairs by the African Union

9. Restoring Aristide as president of Haiti was important in order to show

    1. Cuba's power in the Caribbean
    2. that democratically elected officials should be allowed to hold office
    3. the weakness of the OAS
    4. that Haiti was a major Caribbean country.

10. The Chinese allowed the people of Hong Kong to keep their

    1. own government for 50 years
    2. free-market economy for 50 years
    3. British governor for 50 years
    4. tax-free status for 50 years.

11. Which of the following is the best generalization to be made about events on the time line on page 292?

    1. Efforts at democratic reform have collapsed in Latin America but show signs of progress in Asia.
    2. The global economy has steadily declined since 1946.
    3. The period represented has seen a range of events that include conflict, cooperation, democracy, and repression.
    4. The United States has played a diminished role in global affairs.

12. The photograph of Cuban boat people on page 287 shows us that

    1. most Cubans are dissatisfied with Fidel Castro and Communist rule
    2. some Cubans are desperate enough to attempt a difficult and hazardous journey to the United States
    3. Cubans attempting to reach the United States generally deal with calm and stable ocean currents
    4. Cuban refugees are welcomed into the United States.

Thematic Essays

1. The cold war affected almost all parts of the world. *Task:* Describe how the rivalry between the United States and the Soviet Union affected Central American countries. Consider social, political, economic, and military policies in your answer.

2. Do you AGREE or DISAGREE that the Korean Peninsula continues to be a focus of world concern. *Task:* State economic and strategic reasons in your answer.

Document-Based Questions

Use your knowledge of Global History and Geography and the documents to answer the questions.

1. Former Prime Minister Nehru of India explaining his nation's foreign policy in 1955:

   " . . . As we all know, Asia is no longer passive today; it was passive enough in the past. It is no longer a submissive Asia; it has tolerated submissiveness too long. The Asia of today is dynamic. . . . "

   What do you think is meant by the repeated reference to Asia no longer "being submissive"?

2. From a 1963 report by A. M. Rosenthal, a reporter from *The New York Times,* regarding the changing role of the Japanese emperor and Japan:

   "Japan set about recasting the image of the emperor to fit her new needs. A nation that had died economically now ranks as the fourth industrial power in the world. . . . Japan, the defeated enemy, is eagerly called one of the three pillars of the free world. . . . There is a part of Japan that reaches out to the emperor in memory of what he used to be. . . . "

   Why are the Japanese proud of the post-World War II development of their country?

3. Study the photo on page 291. Why is the flag ceremony a sign of changing relations between China and the West?

Document-Based Essay

Great changes have occurred in the developing world. *Task:* List three developing nations. For each, identify a political or economic change that occurred in the late 20th or early 21st century.

UNIT REVIEW

Thematic Essays

1. After winning their struggle against European imperialism, many former colonies continued to have widespread fighting in their homelands. *Task:* Select two nations, each from a different region treated in this unit. Discuss the reasons peace and governmental stability have not occurred in each country. Consider in your answer religious, tribal, racial, or political factors.

2. Economics played a major role in 20th century politics. The rise of Nazi and Fascist dictators and the fall of communism all can be traced to economic causes. *Task:* Identify and explain those economic factors in a well-thought-out essay. Consider inflation, depression, command economies, heavy industry, and consumer goods.

Document-Based Questions

Use readings from the chapters and your knowledge of Global History and Geography to answer the questions.

1. Study the cartoon on page 276. Why were the countries of the world so afraid of nuclear weapons?

2. Study a map of North America and the Caribbean. Why would the United States be afraid of Soviet missiles in Cuba?

3. Winston Churchill, in a speech given at Westminster College in Fulton, Missouri, in March 1946, said:

   " . . . From Stettin in the Baltic to Trieste in the Adriatic, an iron curtain has descended across the Continent. Behind that line lie all the capitals of the ancient states of Central and Eastern Europe . . . all those famous cities and their populations lie in what I must call the Soviet sphere. . . . "

   What was happening in Eastern and Central Europe behind the iron curtain?

4. Ayatollah Ruhollah Khomeini gave a speech titled *Message to the Pilgrims* on September 13, 1980, in Teheran, Iran. In it, he said:

   " . . . Muslims who are now sitting next to the House of God, engaged in prayer! Pray for those who are resisting America and other superpowers, and understand that we are not fighting against Iraq. The people of Iraq support our Islamic revolution; our quarrel is with America, and it is America whose hand can be seen emerging from the sleeve of the Iraqi government.

According to the Ayatollah, who are the Iranians fighting? Why are the Iraqis and Iranians fighting if the Iraqi people support the Islamic revolution?

Document-Based Essay

Identify two nonmilitary 20th- or 21st-century occurrences that you believe were turning points in global history. *Task:* Discuss these changes. Consider for inclusion religion, nationalism, colonialism, economics, technology, and the competition between different political systems.

UNIT VIII

Global Connections and Interactions

CHAPTER
28

Global Economic Trends

I. NEW ECONOMIC ORDER

When third world countries in Asia, Latin America, and Africa decided to industrialize, some of their leaders decided to adopt command economies in the hope of speeding up the process. The Soviet Union responded by buying their goods and giving them financial and military aid. A new economic order took shape, however, as the Soviet Union and the nations of Eastern Europe abandoned communism for free-market economies. They then cut off aid to developing countries, which soon adopted the free-market system too.

A. Integration of Developing Nations

In the early 1990s, some industrialized nations experienced a decrease in the growth rates of their economies. France and Japan suffered the most.

The developing nations then began to compete with the more prosperous industrialized ones. The *Chinese Economic Area (CEA)*—China, Hong Kong, and Taiwan—became the fourth-ranking center of economic growth in the global market.

Some Eastern European countries became big exporters to the West.

In 1992, Poland, Hungary, the Czech Republic, and Slovakia signed trade agreements with the European Union (EU). Originally a group of Western European nations, the EU had a membership of 27 nations in 2007. These included several Eastern European nations and the islands of Malta and Cyprus. These countries have removed barriers to the free movement across their borders of people, goods, and services. Many use a single European currency—the euro. A European Parliament makes laws and a European Commission coordinates policies and economic and political integration. A European central bank sets a common monetary policy.

The EU has focused on competing successfully with Japan and the United States. Fear of losing jobs to Eastern European immigrants led to the defeat of a proposed EU constitution in 2005.

B. Competition for Investment

Investments began to shift from the industrialized to developing countries. Regions such as Southeast Asia had lower labor costs, greater productivity, and more rapidly growing markets than the West did. Many Eastern European and Latin American countries sold government-owned businesses to foreign as well as domestic investors. As developing nations attracted more investors, they sent more goods and people to the West. Many Western businesses **downsized**; they cut expenses by eliminating jobs and asking older employees to retire early.

Some companies built factories in developing countries to save money on wages. Brazilian and Mexican workers, for example, earned one-tenth of what industrialized workers did. When South Korea, Taiwan, Hong Kong, and Singapore—Asia's four tigers—created high-tech industries, multinational corporations built factories there. Investors then poured billions of dollars into the stock markets of India, Mexico, and other third world nations.

INFO CHECK

1. Define: third world, command economy, free-market economy, Chinese Economic Area (CEA), European Union (EU).

2. Why do you think many of the developing nations began to build free-market economies in the 1980s and 1990s?

3. Describe the competition between developing and industrialized nations. How did this cause problems for businesspeople and their employees in the industrialized nations?

4. Identify the four tigers of Asia. How did they attract investment by multinational corporations?

II. DECISION MAKING IN DEVELOPING COUNTRIES

A. India

When India gained independence, it needed to industrialize quickly. The government adopted **democratic socialism**, whereby it owned large industries while private individuals owned consumer and agricultural industries.

Thus, India began to modernize but did not grow prosperous. In the early 1990s, the government privatized the large industries and wooed more foreign investors. By the mid-1990s, India was exporting high-tech goods. U.S. investments in India grew to more than $1.14 billion.

B. Argentina and Brazil

In the early 1990s, some Latin American countries aimed for low inflation, balanced budgets, smaller bureaucracies, deregulation of industry, and lower tariff barriers.

Argentina launched such free-market reforms in 1991. By 1994, its inflation rate had dropped from 1344 percent to less than 5 percent. Its debt dropped to 25 percent of its **gross domestic product (GDP)**—the total value of goods and services a country produces in a year. Lowered tariffs brought in foreign investment and goods. The government sold almost all state-owned businesses. Tax collections rose sharply. In the first half of the 1990s, Argentina's rate of economic growth topped 6 percent for four years in a row, among the best in the world. Unfortunately, an economic crisis followed.

By the start of the 21st century, Argentina could not pay its debts. Loans from the IMF helped stabilize the economy in 2004.

Elected president in 2003 and again in 2006, Néstor Kirchner led Argentina's economic recovery. Rising prices for farm exports helped put the economic growth rate at 11 percent by mid-2004. In 2005, Argentina had paid its debt to the IMF. Unemployment has declined, but more than half of all Argentineans still remain below the poverty line.

Brazil introduced free-market measures in the 1990s. A recession occurred, however, that caused Brazil to seek help from the IMF. Although this loan bolstered its economy, by 2004, Brazil urgently needed foreign investment. Brazil began to focus on its growing trade with China.

C. Egypt

The Egyptian government nationalized banking, insurance, mining, power production, and transportation in 1961. The economy faltered, however, after the 1967 war with Israel. In 1970, Egypt shifted to private enterprise and looked to the West for increased trade.

In 1972, Egypt dismissed its Soviet advisers and lost Soviet aid. In 1979, it signed a peace treaty with Israel and lost Arab aid. Nevertheless, with financial help from the West, the economy expanded.

President Hosni Mubarak faced political problems that hurt the Egyptian economy. A fundamentalist organization, the *Islamic Group,* attempted to ruin Egypt's tourist industry by attacking foreign visitors. It also tried, but failed, to assassinate Mubarak. The unrest discouraged foreign investment.

D. Chad: A New Petrostate

Chad gained independence from France in 1960. Its Christian government, however, continued to need French assistance against Muslim rebels and bordering Libya.

During its first multiparty election, held in 1996, Chad elected Idress Déby as president. Chadians reelected him in 2001 and in 2006. Déby is a military leader whose government is known for its corruption.

Although Chad is one of the poorest countries in the world, it is rich in oil. In the early 2000s, it began to take steps to become a *petrostate.* Supervised by the World Bank, a group of American, Canadian, and Asian oil companies built an underground pipeline to bring crude oil from Chad through neighboring Cameroon to the Atlantic coast. In 2004, the contract that the Chadian government signed with the oil companies enlarged its treasury by about 40 percent.

The World Bank has insisted that the new oil money be used to benefit the people of Chad. Parliament passed a law requiring that 85.6 percent of the *petrodollars* be spent on education, health programs, water management, and rural development. A 2006 agreement between the World Bank and the Chadian government, however, gave the government the freedom to spend more money on military supplies. Oil has not yet improved the lives of most Chadians. Oil companies in the United States and Canada, however, are training Chadians to take key oil industry positions.

E. Africa and the United States

The United States imported 17 percent of its oil from sub-Saharan Africa in 2004. It was estimated that this would increase to 25 percent by 2014, with Nigeria, Angola, Gabon, the Congo Republic, Cameroon, and Chad as the chief exporters.

F. Asian Economic Crisis

With the world's economies so interdependent, economic decision making is now an international affair, as a 1997 economic crisis in Asia demonstrated.

In 1997, Thailand owed more than its treasury held. Its currency, the baht, lost value worldwide. The Bank of Thailand could not protect it, and the baht and the stock market fell.

The crisis then hit Malaysia, Indonesia, and the Philippines. When Hong Kong's stock market dropped, so did markets all over the world. Although Western stock markets recovered, financial experts predicted very slow economic growth in Asia for years to come.

INFO CHECK

1. If you were a citizen of Argentina or Brazil, would you APPROVE or DISAPPROVE of the economic reforms practiced by your leaders? Give reasons for your answer.

2. How did the 1997 Asian economic crisis begin? How and why were the economies of the Western nations affected?

III. GLOBAL AND REGIONAL ECONOMIC ORGANIZATIONS

A. Group of Eight

The *Group of Eight (G-8)* consists of Britain, Canada, France, Germany, Italy, Japan, Russia and the United States. They have met annually since 1975 in an attempt to keep the global economy healthy. Russia joined more recently.

DANGERS IN THE GLOBAL MARKET. One of G-8's main concerns is the speed of international monetary transactions, thanks to computers and other high-tech devices. A crisis such as the one in Southeast Asia can almost immediately affect other stock markets. Every 24 hours, $1 trillion is exchanged on the world's currency markets. When such sums move too fast at the wrong time, a small crisis can quickly become a catastrophe.

GOALS. At the 1995 summit, G-8 leaders stated the need for an improved early warning system to minimize harm from economic shocks. They also

proposed creating an emergency fund to help countries in financial crisis.

Other economic aims include stimulating world trade by lowering tariffs, preventing or containing recessions, and reducing chronic unemployment. Political aims are to promote human rights, limit nuclear proliferation, and solve political crises. During the early 1990s, the G-8 contributed billions of dollars to help Russia develop a free-market economy.

The G-8 members are advised against acting unwisely. Japan was pressured to buy more from Europe and North America and thus restore the balance of trade. When the United States was spending more than it was collecting in tax revenues, it was urged to balance its budget.

B. World Bank

Created after World War II, the *World Bank* is the largest lender to developing countries. Most of its loans go to developing countries prosperous enough to pay the money back. G-8 nations, with 45 percent of the shares, control the bank; the U.S. president selects the bank president. No major bank programs have proceeded without U.S. approval.

A NEW TREND. President George W. Bush nominated Paul Wolfowitz as head of the World Bank in 2005. Wolfowitz drew international criticism by using World Bank money to fight graft and corruption. Critics claimed that he lent money to those countries that followed policies favored by the World Bank instead of to help people in developing countries live better lives. Wolfowitz was replaced in 2007 by Robert B. Zoellick.

C. International Monetary Fund

The *International Monetary Fund (IMF)* is closely associated with the World Bank. Established in 1944, the IMF ensures orderly payment between industrial nations. When no other source is available, it lends money to rich and poor nations. Wealthy nations such as the United States, France, Britain, Germany, and Saudi Arabia control and finance the IMF.

The IMF's primary mission is to help developing nations with troubled economies. But first, it requires them to develop free-market economies and cut **budget deficit**s (gaps between government income and spending). According to critics, IMF policies expose developing nations to the greed of international corporations, corruption, social unrest, and political instability. Supporters argue that competition will make the economies of developing nations healthier.

ACTIVITIES. In the 1990s, The IMF helped the former Soviet republics and Eastern European nations change from Communist command economies to free-market economies.

In the 2000s, countries such as Argentina and Brazil began to repay their loans to the IMF. They wanted to save money by eliminating future IMF interest costs and to free themselves from IMF economic control.

Managing Director Rodrigo Rato announced a two-year reform program to restructure the IMF. He wanted to reflect the shifting balance of power in the global economy by increasing the voting rights of developing countries.

During the Asian economic crisis of 1997 and 1998, the IMF helped reduce inflation and stimulate the economies of many struggling countries.

D. World Trade Organization

ORIGINS. In the 1990s, the *World Trade Organization (WTO)* grew out of the *General Agreement on Tariffs and Trade (GATT)*. This group had aimed to expand world trade by reducing tariffs.

The WTO fosters trade in services as well as goods. With a membership of 150 countries, it is a specialized agency of the UN.

GOALS. To make global trade freer for all, the WTO requires members to treat one another as equals—the most-favored-nation clause. Any member that grants a trade benefit to another member must also extend that benefit to all other members. The WTO also fosters the economies of developing countries by keeping tariffs low and promoting fair competition.

However, talks held from 2000 to 2006 failed when the United States refused to reduce subsidies to farmers unless the developing nations provided more market access for American agricultural products.

E. European Union

ORIGIN. The *European Union (EU)* grew out of the European Community (EC). In 1992, EC members signed a treaty in the Dutch city of Maastricht. It became the EU and removed most barriers within Western Europe to the movement of people, goods, and services. Members were committed to a single European currency, the euro, by the year 2002 and to pooling foreign and defense policies. In 2002, 12 EU members replaced their national cur-

rencies with the euro. Britain, Denmark, and Sweden, however, preferred to delay this step.

PROS AND CONS. Many people viewed the EU as an important step toward Europe's political unification. The British and others, however, feared that a strong EU would threaten the independence of individual nations.

MEMBERSHIP. Many nations applied to join the EU. Norway was one of the few that have rejected membership. Turkey and several other countries are waiting to join. It was felt that Turkey was neither economically strong nor democratic enough. In 1995, EU leaders allowed free trade between its members and Turkey. This step brought Turkey closer to full membership. Some members, threatened by competition from lower-priced Eastern European steel, textiles, and farm products, disliked the EU's plan to expand its membership. Most agreed, however, that the EU had to grow if it wanted to compete successfully with the United States and Japan.

ORGANIZATION OF THE EU. The European Parliament, the legislative body of the EU, meets in Strasbourg, France. The 567 members of the parliament are elected every five years. The number elected from each country depends on its population. Members are seated by party, not by nationality. The parliament approves or rejects candidates nominated by the council as members of the European Commission. It must also approve the appointment of the commission's president. Its main function is to control the budget of the EU. It can pass laws that apply to all EU nations. A council of ministers represents the governments of the member nations. It must approve all laws and budgetary decisions. The European Commission is responsible for executing the laws and decisions of the council and the parliament.

F. Organization of Petroleum Exporting Countries

Rapid price increases in oil during and after 1974 led to higher profits for OPEC nations and advanced their development of new sources. The resulting increase in supply, however, drove down prices in the early 1980s. Since then, OPEC has used production quotas to limit supply and stabilize prices.

In the early 21st century, tensions in the Middle East and a severe hurricane season in the Gulf of Mexico helped to triple oil prices. In July 2006, hostility between Israel and Lebanon caused oil

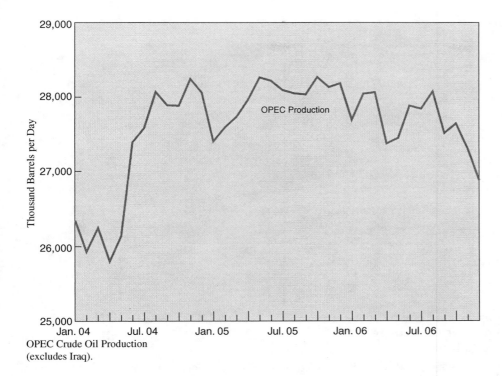

OPEC Crude Oil Production
(excludes Iraq).

prices to shoot up to $77.03 a barrel. OPEC increased production. When prices dropped to $65.61 a barrel, OPEC members began to consider cutting oil production again. In 2007, however, the price of oil soared to $100.00 barrel.

The United States was humbled by OPEC's control of oil production and pricing in the 1970s. (From *Herblock on all Fronts* [New American Library, 1980])

G. North American Free Trade Agreement

In 1991, Canada, the United States, and Mexico negotiated the *North American Free Trade Agreement* (**NAFTA**). It aims to eliminate tariffs and other trade barriers within 15 years and eventually create a single market of 380 million people.

Presidents George Bush and Bill Clinton believed that NAFTA would help North America compete with such economic blocs as the EU. Expanded markets would help North America's most competitive industries grow, increase U.S. high-tech jobs and exports, spur democratic reform in Mexico, and reduce illegal immigration from Mexico to the United States.

Leaders in Canada and Mexico were divided. Critics feared the growing political power of U.S. multinational companies in their countries. Supporters claimed that only NAFTA will allow North American countries to compete with Europe, Japan, and the developing nations.

In 1994, Mexico faced an economic crisis that obscured the effects of NAFTA. Over a six-week period, the peso fell sharply in value, buying far fewer imported goods than before. Earlier in 1994, U.S. exports to Mexico had pulled ahead of imports. During most of 1995, the situation was reversed.

H. CAFTA

In 2005, U.S. President George W. Bush signed the Central American Free Trade Agreement

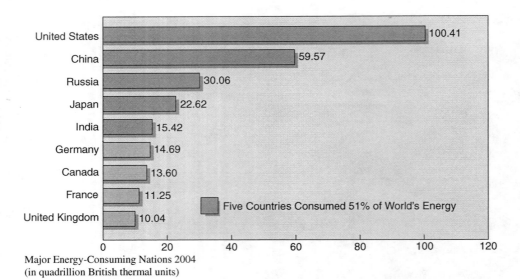

Major Energy-Consuming Nations 2004
(in quadrillion British thermal units)

(CAFTA) into law. Labor unions and environmentalists opposed the agreement. It allowed greater access for U.S. products in El Salvador, Guatemala, Honduras, Costa Rica, the Dominican Republic, and Nicaragua. It made large percentages of U.S. manufactured products and farm products tariff free and eliminated or reduced barriers to telecommunications, insurance, and financial services.

I. Commonwealth of Nations

Commonwealth members have cooperative trade relations. Britain once lowered tariffs for Commonwealth goods imported into the British market. When it joined the EU in 1973, however, this preferential treatment ceased. Nonetheless, Britain's EU membership makes it a better market for Commonwealth goods. Moreover, Britain's membership makes it easier for Commonwealth countries to enter trade agreements with the EU.

INFO CHECK

1. Summarize the functions of each of the following: G-8, World Bank. How does the United States exercise influence in these organizations? Is this good or bad for the global economy?

2. Briefly explain the role of each in regulating the global economy: IMF, WTO, EU, OPEC, NAFTA, CAFTA, Commonwealth of Nations.

3. Why would developing nations with troubled economies be more dependent on the IMF than upon any other economic organizations listed above?

4. Why might it be argued that NAFTA was established to accomplish in the Americas what the EU is accomplishing in Europe?

IV. MODERNIZATION VERSUS TRADITION

With very little preparation, the peoples of Africa, Asia, and Latin America have had to adapt to new working methods, technologies, and social relationships.

A. China

Some Western experts say that a free-market economy would make China more democratic. To increase production, businesspeople will have to give workers the freedom to plan. Once they are used to on-the-job decision making, they may also demand the right to make political decisions.

In the early 21st century, there were few signs that economic progress had led to political freedom or better social conditions. The urban middle class had greater economic and educational opportunities, but rural villagers remained poor. An environment contaminated with industrial waste threatened their health. The Chinese Communist government continued to curb dissent. In 2006, however, President Hu Jintao declared that social improvements were as important as economic growth.

B. Japan

Until recently, Japan has maintained a blend of Western business techniques and traditional culture. Corporate leaders and workers felt a mutual loyalty comparable to that between feudal lords and samurai warriors. Feeling their connection to powerful and protective institutions, employees eagerly worked long hours for moderate pay.

In the late 1990s, this "samurai work ethic" began to weaken. Many workers wanted more leisure, larger homes, and higher pay. At the same time, as the economy underwent recession, the tradition of lifetime employment ended. Many Japanese lost their jobs.

C. India

Traditionally, many Indians worked in **cottage industries**; small groups made craft items in their own homes. Gandhi and other leaders hoped that a new economic system would accommodate cottage industries. In that way, traditional crafts would keep people mindful of traditional values.

In the 21st century, however, India's most important industries have been the manufacture of high-tech products. In 1998, the government began testing nuclear weapons. This has also increased tension between India and Pakistan, also a nuclear power.

D. Egypt and Algeria

In Egypt and Algeria, economic problems have left many young people unemployed. In search of a sense of purpose, many join fundamentalist Islamic movements that engage in terrorism as a means to improve society. Western advisers have counseled President Hosni Mubarak of Egypt to supplement police action with the creation of jobs.

E. Changing Roles of Women

SAUDI ARABIA. In most Muslim countries, women are not equal to men. They cannot easily get a divorce, travel without written permission from a male relative, appear in public without covering themselves with a long garment and veil, and often not even walk in the street without a male escort.

In Saudi Arabia, however, women can work, though only in jobs alongside other women. Women teachers and doctors, for instance, must associate only with women students and patients.

When the demand for Middle East oil fell, the Saudi economy suffered. Many families needed two salaries, and men began encouraging their wives to work. Liberals hoped that women would become so necessary to the economy that they would earn better pay, be integrated with workers of both sexes, and enter fields formerly open only to men. Even with existing restrictions, Saudi women have made a difference to their country's economy. By 1996, women owned at least 40 percent of Saudi Arabia's private wealth.

AFGHANISTAN. From 1996 to 2001, Afghanistan was ruled by fundamentalist Islamics, the **Taliban**. They arrested and executed all who did not conform to their strict interpretation of Islamic law. Men had to be bearded and dressed in traditional robes. Women could not work or leave home without a male escort. Those without male relatives faced misery and starvation. In public, women had to be covered from head to foot. Some of them were permitted to work for the *World Food Program* in 2001.

The Taliban let Osama bin Laden, Saudi-born leader of the Al Qaeda, use Afghanistan as a base. Al Qaeda terrorists from many countries were taught methods of destruction there.

After the September 11, 2001, terrorist attacks on New York City and Washington, D.C., a U.S. war on global terrorism began. U.S. forces helped anti-Taliban Afghans, especially the *Northern Alliance,* end Taliban rule. By early 2002, thousands of Taliban/Al Qaeda fighters had been captured—some imprisoned at a U.S. military base at Guantanamo Bay, Cuba. Osama bin Laden disappeared. Some thought that he had died or escaped to Iran with other Al Qaeda survivors. Hamid Karzai, Northern Alliance leader, became president of Afghanistan in the country's first election.

The United States and other nations pledged aid to establish a stable Afghan government. Fighting between N.A.T.O. troops and Taliban and Al Qaeda militants continued.

INFO CHECK

1. Compare economic and cultural change in China and Japan in the late 20th and 21st centuries. How has the process of change been similar in these countries? How has it been different?

2. Explain why you AGREE or DISAGREE:
   - Economic change must always cause cultural and political change.
   - The economic changes of the 1990s resulted in more rights and political and economic power for women in developing nations.

V. SOCIAL PROBLEMS AND CRISES

In many countries, improved conditions have enriched only a small elite. Economists measure a nation's wealth by how well all its people live.

A. World Hunger

A large and growing population can strain a country's food supply and increase food prices. In

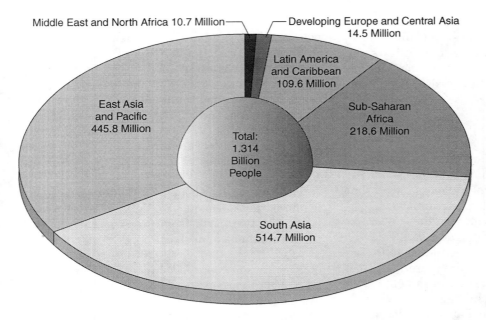

Middle East and North Africa 10.7 Million — — Developing Europe and Central Asia 14.5 Million

Latin America and Caribbean 109.6 Million

East Asia and Pacific 445.8 Million

Sub-Saharan Africa 218.6 Million

Total: 1.314 Billion People

South Asia 514.7 Million

Extreme Poverty (people living on less than 1$ U.S. a day), by Region, 1993
Note: By 2000, most poverty had declined. Exceptions: (1) Developing Europe and Central Asia, where transition from communistic command economies to free-market economies was slow; (2) Sub-Saharan Africa, where civil wars, low economic growth, and the spread of AIDS kept millions at the brink of survival.

the 1940s, scientists initiated the **Green Revolution**; its aim was to develop more productive strains of corn, rice, and other grains so that populous developing countries could grow more food. Moreover, individual governments have tried to limit high birthrates.

Unfortunately, political instability also affects a country's living standard. When rival leaders contend for control of a region, their fight usually inflicts deliberate suffering on innocent inhabitants.

SOMALIA. When British Somaliland gained independence in 1960, it joined Italian Somaliland to form Somalia. Somalia later laid claim to Ogaden in Ethiopia, where many Somalis lived. The Soviet Union sent Cuban troops to help Ethiopia, and the United States sent weapons to the Somalis. In the war that followed (1977–1988), the Cubans defeated Somali forces.

Internal Conflict. Within Somalia, rival leaders battled for control. By late 1992, when the government had been destroyed, drought and famine brought disease and starvation. The International Red Cross and the UN brought in food, fuel, and medicine, but rival warlords attacked the relief workers and took the supplies.

UN Intervention. In 1993, the UN sent U.S. and other military forces to Somalia to protect relief workers and stop the fighting among warlords. The strongest of them, General Muhammad Farah Aydid, resisted UN suggestions to try political rather than military competition with other factions. In a U.S-UN attempt to capture Aydid, 18 U.S. soldiers died. U.S. forces withdrew by March 1994. The following year, the UN also pulled out.

The Somali factions fought on. By 2007, the country was a battleground between Islamist and government troops supported by Ethiopian forces.

B. Urbanization

After World War II, cities of many developing nations expanded more than threefold. Cities in industrialized North America and Europe have also grown much larger since 1945. Western cities, however, already had such infrastructures as sewage systems and power sources, as well as social welfare institutions. Most developing countries had no such resources.

The population explosion and industrialization have contributed to urban growth. So has the move of rural people to cities in search of work no longer available back home.

C. Cities of the Developing World

In developing nations, one "supercity" often boasts most of the country's industries, hospitals, and schools. It is, therefore, a magnet for vast numbers of people. Large squatter settlements mushroom on the outskirts, where the city's limited plumbing and lighting systems, schools, and hospitals cannot serve them.

In a 2001 report, the UN Food and Agriculture Organization (FAO) criticized the governments of the developing world and their city planners for not paying enough attention to increasing malnutrition and the lack of safe and regular food supplies for the poor. Calcutta, in India, and São Paulo, in Brazil, were cited, along with most African cities, as places where 50–70 percent of the population live in poverty.

D. International Drug Trade

CONTROLLING ILLEGAL DRUGS. Political corruption complicates the fight against drug trafficking. Drug lords use world financial markets to "launder" (camouflage) the source of their profits. High-tech equipment for sending messages in unbreakable codes make long distance drug deals easy and safe. When the **cartel**s (price-fixing drug monopolies) cannot bribe the antidrug officials, they threaten them and their families.

U.S. WAR ON DRUGS. Latin American leaders have tried to control drug trafficking without directly confronting the cartel members. In 2003, chemical spraying from aircraft reduced Colombia's coca crop by 32 percent. Economic problems inhibit the crackdown on drug production however. For impoverished Bolivian peasants, for example, the sale of coca leaves can help whole farm communities survive.

The *United Nations Drug Control Program (UNDCP)* has tried to subsidize a switch from coca crops to legal ones. It has given farmers tools and training, funded new farm-to-market roads, and set up rural hospitals and basic medical services.

U.S. officials believe that alternative crop development must be combined with tough policing. A U.S.-trained Bolivian police force has raided coca farms, factories, and illegal airstrips, and arrested drug traffickers. Recently, officers of the *Drug Enforcement Agency (DEA),* working with Latin American security services, have also tried to reduce the flow of illegal drugs into North America.

Latin American Objections. Some Latin Americans think that the United States should reduce the demand for cocaine at home before policing Latin America. U.S. officials, they feel, do not fully understand the economic and political situation. Many drug traders have no other source of income. As taxpayers and voters, they bolster their country's stability. Leaders of drug-producing countries need the cartel's military resources to combat political terrorism, and they often prefer to negotiate with drug lords rather than fight them.

Following the fall of the Taliban regime, poppy, from which opium is produced, became Afghanistan's major crop. In 2006 and 2007, drug traffickers flooded the global drug market with opium from Afghanistan.

INFO CHECK

1. Why is Somalia regarded as an example of the difficulties of dealing with hunger in the third world?

2. Define urbanization. Why has it been more of a problem in developing nations than in industrialized nations?

3. What suggestions would you make to leaders in the United States and Latin America for dealing with the international drug trade?

CHAPTER REVIEW

Multiple Choice

1. Nations that used the Soviet-style command economy tended to place the majority of their natural, monetary, and labor resources into the areas of

   1. consumer and civilian industries and products
   2. heavy industries and military products
   3. educational and housing developments
   4. civilian-oriented, technological, and communication industries.

2. In the 1990s, developing nations and Pacific Rim countries received investment monies because

   1. the developed nations needed places to safeguard their excess funds
   2. the developed nations wanted to assist the poorer nations in improving their standards of living

   3. Western and Communist nations were competing for allies in the third world and Pacific Rim
   4. they had lower labor costs, greater productivity, and growing markets for sales.

3. An economic system that combines elements of private and government ownership of business is known as

   1. a command economy
   2. capitalism
   3. democratic socialism
   4. privatization.

4. Economic problems in one area of the world affect other parts of the world because

   1. all nations borrow money from one another
   2. having less money to spend reduces trade with other nations

3. some nations only sell finished goods
4. some nations have nothing of value to sell.

5. The EU, OPEC, G-8, and IMF are all examples of

   1. military alliances
   2. political parties
   3. global or regional communication companies
   4. regional or global economic organizations.

6. If you represented a developing nation and needed economic advice or a loan, you could turn to the

   1. Warsaw Pact
   2. Truman Plan
   3. World Bank
   4. Federal Credit Union.

7. The WTO, EU, and NAFTA all seek to

   1. encourage trade and reduce tariff barriers
   2. promote development of the former republics of the Soviet Union
   3. promote development of the nations of Latin America
   4. develop military technology in the area of space travel.

8. Examples of problems that still exist in developing nations are

   1. overspending on consumer and luxury goods
   2. famine and fighting between local warlords or militias
   3. natural disasters destroying the economy
   4. how to safely destroy their stockpiles of atomic weapons.

9. The governments of some developing nations have been criticized by the UN's Food and Agriculture Organization because

   1. their leaders devote too few resources to recreational facilities
   2. many city dwellers live in poverty and suffer from malnutrition and other ills
   3. government posts are closed to women
   4. slum dwellers are forced to move to the countryside.

10. The graph that appears on page 304 shows that

    1. the industrial nations need little petroleum.
    2. Japan is a major consumer of energy
    3. China, Russia, and the United States consume the most energy
    4. India consumes more energy than the U.S.

11. The cartoon on page 303 shows that during the 1970s

    1. the United States dominated the Arab nations
    2. the United States was dependent on imported oil

3. OPEC was controlled by the United States
4. the nations of the West turned to the production of synthetic oil.

Thematic Essays

1. The economic system in the newly independent states of the former Soviet Union brought good news and bad news for the people. The good news was that consumer goods were being produced and people could open their own businesses. But the bad news was that wages and job security were not guaranteed in a free-market economy. *Task:* Explain how these countries were helped.

2. Economic competition among nations, regions, and Communist and Western nations has slowly given way in the face of global interdependence. *Task:* Identify and describe any two examples of economic activities that would support that statement. Consider for inclusion in your essay regional or worldwide economic unions, world banking, or economic regulatory agencies.

Document-Based Questions

Use the documents and your reading of the chapter to answer the questions.

1. From a discussion including Drs. Athayde and Facio and former U.S. Senator Morse dealing with change in Latin America:

   Dr. Athayde: " . . . we feel that it is necessary to establish an effective system of economic cooperation among all the nations. . . . "

   Dr. Facio: " . . . a greater effort toward an economic development that will permit an increase in the wealth in order that it may be more widely distributed. Economic progress and social justice must go hand in hand. . . . "

   Senator Morse: " . . . I think land reform is probably the first step that needs to be taken. . . . In many parts of Latin America there is not a fair tax system . . . a narrowing of the economic gap, the gap between the great masses of poverty-stricken people and the small number of very, very rich people. . . . The rich people have also got to show confidence in Latin America. They've got to get their money out of New York and Swiss banks and back into Latin America, and invest their money in the future of Latin America. . . . "

   ("Today's Revolution," from *Americas* magazine.)

   What actions do the three speakers claim are necessary for economic change in Latin America?

2. From a book about Soviet communism by Louis Fisher:

" . . . The twentieth century's biggest problem is the control of personal, group and national power. My acceptance of Soviet Russia was, I suspect, a by-product of my protest against the power over human beings which accumulated wealth and property have given to their owners. . . . Then Soviet Russia emerged, promising to break forever the power of landlords, trusts, big business exploiters and private capital generally. . . . I now realize that Bolshevism is not the way out because it is itself the world's biggest [massing together of] power over man. . . . The Kremlin [dominates] its citizens not only by the police and prison power but also by the greater power [natural to] the ownership and operation of every economic enterprise in the nation. . . . "

Why did Fisher first accept but later reject the Communist economic system?

3. Study the pie chart on page 306.

Identify the world region in which poverty affects the most people. Would you describe the nations of this region as developing or industrialized? Which global economic organization might help them reduce poverty? What actions might this organization take?

4. Look at the cartoon on page 303.

How does the cartoon show the power of a group to cripple the economies of the world's most developed nations? In your answer, describe the factors that make it possible.

Document-Based Essay

In the late 20th century, many developing nations altered their economic systems. *Task:* For each of two developing nations, describe a change in the economic system and the problems or benefits that resulted.

29

Search for Global Security

I. STRUGGLE FOR GLOBAL PEACE

A. UN Peacekeeping Role

UN peacekeepers try to end wars so as to save lives, end destruction, and allow economic rebuilding to begin. The UN has sent troops into many areas, including those where domestic conflicts persist—Somalia, Bosnia, and Haiti. Some UN missions have involved civil wars.

REASONS FOR FAILURE. Ideally, UN forces move into the troubled areas only after opposed factions stop fighting. They make sure that all sides observe the cease-fire. They run free elections and bring supplies to civilians. In places such as Rwanda, Somalia, and Bosnia, however, UN peacekeepers found themselves in the midst of ongoing wars.

At the end of the 20th century, the number of UN peacekeeping operations at first increased dramatically, but soon decreased just as dramatically. Whereas there were 28 such missions in 1993, only 18 were operational in 2006—in Africa, the Middle East, southern Europe, and East Asia.

COMPOSITION OF FORCES. From a peak of 78,000 in 1993, the number of UN troops declined to approximately 74,561 by 2006. Member nations supplied the soldiers, who were usually only lightly armed and instructed to return fire only under attack. (The soldiers did not always follow these orders.)

Lack of Cooperation. The cost of UN peacekeeping operations was $4.75 billion by 2006. Member nations were supposed to cover the expenses. Many nations—including the United States—however, felt that their shares were too large and refused to pay. The United States was the UN's biggest debtor, but it demanded that its share be cut before it paid up. In 2001, a

UN peacekeeping forces in the Balkans

U.S. payment of $582 million in back dues was approved.

B. UN Decision Making

UN membership grew from 53 countries in 1945 to 192 in 2006. Only the 15-member Security Council, however, made most peacekeeping decisions, with the permanent members—the United States, Russia, Britain, France, and China—exercising veto power. The Security Council has ten nonpermanent members. In 2005, the African Union, the Group of Four (Brazil, Germany, India, and Japan), and other nations proposed that the Security Council membership be increased to 25.

C. Social and Economic Programs

The rise of nazism after World War I showed that dangerous movements often grow out of poor economic and social conditions. Therefore, the UN founders set up the *Economic and Social Council (ECOSOC)*.

ECOSOC studies and recommends ways of improving economic and social cooperation among nations and in global regions. It also fosters human rights, the improved status of women, and control of illegal drugs. ECOSOC supervises the *United Nations Children's Fund (UNICEF)*.

PEOPLE-CENTERED WORLD ORDER. In 1990, ECOSOC launched the United Nations Development Program for "people-centered world order." In such an order, private citizens as well as leaders will benefit from a nation's economic development.

Experts in the program work on the principle that money should not be saved at the expense of the general welfare. For example, instead of shutting down unnecessary industries, governments should find new uses for them. They should also invest more in education and aid small businesses.

HUMAN DEVELOPMENT SCALE. The United Nations Development Program rates nations on such criteria as average life expectancy, educational standards, and per capita (each person's) income.

Several developing countries scored higher on the human development scale than more industrialized ones. The United States, for example, was in sixth place; there is a broad gap between living standards of white Americans and those of other races. The poorest African nations, where only a small elite enjoys the national wealth, rated the lowest human development scores.

The program rated countries where people live longer, are better educated, and enjoy better sanitation above countries where people earn high salaries.

The United Nations Development Program noted that, in most nations, women have fewer job opportunities and lower earnings than men. In developing nations, women also face inferior health care, nutrition, and education.

D. North Atlantic Treaty Organization

NEW STRATEGIES AND ORGANIZATION. In 1991, NATO leaders met in Rome to reorganize military forces. New problems in Eastern Europe, the Balkans, and the Middle East necessitated new strategies.

- Eastern European countries wanted to join NATO for protection from Russia.

- Political and ethnic conflicts in the former Yugoslavia seemed likely to spread.

- Iraqi dictator Saddam Hussein threatened Middle Eastern security.

- Iran was supporting terrorist organizations.

- Tension between Israel and its neighbors continued.

It was especially important to control hostilities in the Middle East where vast oil supplies were located.

Traditionally, NATO had massed its forces in Germany to meet threats from Eastern Europe and the Soviet Union. To prepare for conflicts in southern areas, NATO divided its forces into smaller units, backed by highly mobile reserves.

U.S. soldiers would have to intervene in any war in the Middle East. They could best do so from bases in Germany. In 1998, President Clinton said that he would maintain 100,000 troops in Europe.

EXPANSION OF NATO. To enable the nonmember nations of Eastern Europe to cooperate militarily and politically with NATO, NATO leaders established the *Partnership for Peace*. In 1995, Russia became one of the 27 countries that joined the Partnership for Peace. In 1999, Poland, Hungary, and the Czech Republic became full members of NATO.

Bulgaria, Estonia, Latvia, Lithuania, Romania, Slovakia, and Slovenia were invited to join NATO in 2004. To qualify for NATO membership, the seven invited nations had to commit themselves to make internal political and military reforms. In its turn, NATO promised to assist the nations to do so and to guide them as they assimilated to the Western member nations.

NATO IN THE 21ST CENTURY. In the early 2000s, NATO members were planning a NATO Rapid Response Force to respond to terrorist threats. In 2002, they were discussing the NATO-Russia Council and military action beyond Europe.

France and Germany opposed the 2003 U.S.-British invasion of Iraq, while Britain, Italy, Spain, and the Eastern European nations supported it.

NATO's first peacekeeping mission beyond Europe was in Afghanistan in 2003. Afghanistan's Taliban regime had sheltered Al Qaeda leadership, responsible for the 2001 terrorist attacks in the United States. Although defeated by the U.S. and Afghan opposition forces, Taliban fighters continued to resist the NATO forces. By late 2006, NATO commanded 33,000 soldiers from 37 countries in Afghanistan.

INFO CHECK

1. List the kinds of difficulties encountered by UN peacekeepers.

2. How would you respond to the argument that UN military forces should not be involved in dangerous peacekeeping missions?

3. Explain the Human Development Scale of the United Nations Development Program. Why did several nations receive higher ratings than the United States?

4. How has NATO changed in mission and composition since the end of the cold war?

II. LIMITING NUCLEAR PROLIFERATION

A. Cold War Strategies

By the late 1960s, the United States and the Soviet Union were roughly equal in nuclear strength. This led to the belief that *mutual assured destruction (MAD)* would prevent a nuclear holocaust. Neither power would bomb the other and risk its own destruction. World safety depended on equal stockpiles of deadly weapons.

The **superpower**s tried to keep this balance of power. From 1963 until the collapse of the Soviet Union in 1991, they negotiated arms control agreements.

B. Nuclear Arms Control

Eighty-one percent of U.S. citizens polled in April 1982 voted in favor of banning nuclear weapons. U.S. peace groups reached out to similar groups in Western Europe, Eastern Europe, and the Soviet Union. These movements declined after Ronald Reagan became president in 1984.

C. Antinuclear Agencies and Treaties

The *International Atomic Energy Agency (IAEA),* an independent UN agency, was founded in 1957. Its 122 members encourage peaceful uses of atomic energy.

In 1968, more than 175 nations signed the *Nuclear Nonproliferation Treaty (NNT)* to halt the spread of nuclear weapons. The signers agreed that officials of the International Atomic Energy Agency could inspect their nuclear facilities.

The *London Suppliers Agreement* was founded in 1976 to stop the spread of nuclear materials and technology to nations with no nuclear weapons.

EURATOM is an authority that controls nuclear proliferation in Western Europe. It can bring a nation that changes nuclear material into nuclear weapons before the European Court of Justice. Unfortunately, nuclear proliferation continues.

D. Spread of Nuclear Arsenals

In 2005, seven nations—the United States, Russia, China, France, Britain, India, and Pakistan—were known to have nuclear weapons. Israel was believed to have a nuclear stockpile of 172 warheads. In spite of strong international opposition, North Korea and Iran were in the process of developing nuclear programs. North Korea admitted to planning for nuclear weapons. Iran said it did not intend to produce weapons.

The use of nuclear weapons to settle political differences began to seem more likely. Some world leaders had no scruples against using lethal weapons against civilians, and terrorists had increasing access to nuclear technology.

The attack on the United States in 2001 increased the fear of a nuclear strike. Terrorists had hijacked commercial airplanes and crashed them into the World Trade Center in New York City and the Pentagon in Washington, D.C.

Critics used this event to argue against President George W. Bush's missile defense plan, which called for the placement of a high-tech system in outer space to track and destroy missiles fired by hostile nations. Pointing out that the 2001 attack proved that missiles were not the only threats, they called for efforts to stop the spread of all weapons of mass destruction. Government agencies in several countries set up broad security measures to guard against chemical, biological, and nuclear weapons.

INFO CHECK

1. Explain how each of the following protects the world from nuclear war: IAEA, NNT, London Suppliers Agreement, EURATOM.

2. Why do you think preventing the spread of nuclear arsenals has been so difficult? What might be a solution?

III. CRISES IN NUCLEAR CONTROL

A. Ukraine

When newly independent, Ukraine sought to keep as protection against Russia the 1800 nuclear warheads that the Soviets had stationed there.

The United States, Russia, and Britain promised to support Ukraine's independence and give it economic aid if, in return, it gave up its nuclear weapons and signed START I and the Nuclear Nonproliferation Treaty. The Ukrainian president accepted the bargain. In November 1994, Ukraine's parliament ratified the Nuclear Nonproliferation Treaty.

B. North Korea

After North Korea's refusal to allow international inspectors to examine its civilian nuclear power program, it threatened to withdraw from the Nuclear Nonproliferation Treaty when the inspectors continued to insist. In 1994, the Western powers, Japan, and South Korea offered North Korea $4 billion in energy assistance if it would freeze and then end its nuclear weapons development. North Korea agreed to this exchange.

In 2003, however, North Korea announced that it possessed weapons-grade plutonium and would develop nuclear weapons. To deal with this new crisis, China organized a series of talks involving itself, North Korea, Japan, the U.S., Russia, and South Korea. In early 2007, North Korea agreed to close its plutonium-processing facility in return for fuel oil shipments.

Prior to this agreement, in 2006, North Korea had held two nuclear tests. In response to these tests, the UN Security Council barred nations from selling or transferring to North Korea material that could be used to make nuclear, biological, and chemical weapons, and ballistic missiles. It also forbade international travel by people associated with North Korea's nuclear program.

C. Monitoring Iraq and Iran

IRAQ. After the 1991 Persian Gulf War, UN inspectors discovered that Iraq was building nuclear

Saddam Hussein protesting his innocence while stockpiling chemical weapons. (AUTH ©*The Philadelphia Inquirer*. Reprinted with permission of UNIVERSAL PRESS SYNDICATE. All rights reserved.)

weapons, using precision equipment and technology supplied by British and German companies.

From 1998 to 2001, British and American planes bombed Iraqi military targets. This was the allies' response to Saddam Hussein's repeated refusal to allow UN inspectors access to sites they wished to monitor.

U.S. and British forces invaded Iraq in 2003. After they had deposed Saddam Hussein, they found no weapons of mass destruction.

IRAN. World leaders were more concerned about Iran's nuclear program than about North Korea's. Iran had a revolutionary Islamic government, supported terrorist groups, and aspired to dominate the Middle East. The West also feared that if Iran had nuclear weapons, Saudi Arabia, Egypt, and other nations would also want them.

Europeans, Americans, Russians, and Chinese offered Iran a package of incentives if it did not develop nuclear weapons and threatened it with tougher economic sanctions if it did. Iranian leaders argued that, like India, they had a right to nuclear weapons. However, a 2007 U.S. intelligence report stated that Iran had abandoned its effort to develop nuclear weapons.

D. Efforts to End Nuclear Testing

The Nuclear Nonproliferation Treaty came up for renewal in 1995. The major nuclear powers wanted to extend it indefinitely. Many smaller nations proposed an extension of 25 years; they would agree to indefinite extension only if the nuclear powers promised to give up their own arsenals. The nuclear powers won the indefinite extension by repeating old promises to comply and by promising to conclude a comprehensive ban on nuclear testing by the end of 1996.

Aboveground nuclear tests release harmful radiation into the atmosphere. In 1963, the United States, Britain, and the Soviet Union signed the Limited Nuclear Test-Ban Treaty, which banned testing in the atmosphere, underwater, or in space. It allowed underground tests, however. In recent years, China and France have observed the same restriction. India and Pakistan conducted underground nuclear tests in 1998.

E. Comprehensive Test-Ban Treaty

In October 1992, the United States, Russia, France, and Britain declared a moratorium (temporary halt) on nuclear weapons testing. Meanwhile, a 38-nation conference in Geneva, Switzerland, discussed a comprehensive treaty to ban all testing, including underground.

The United States and Russia said that very limited underground testing was necessary to check the reliability of their weapons. Nonnuclear states were opposed. In August 1995, President Clinton promised to conduct no tests, which put pressure on Russia to follow suit.

China and France were widely condemned for conducting nuclear tests while the ban was being discussed. Both nations said that only limited testing would take place until the end of 1996, when they would sign the treaty.

By 2006, more than 177 nations had signed the treaty, but only 137, including Russia, had ratified it. Although the United States had signed the treaty in October 1999, the U.S. Senate voted against ratification.

INFO CHECK

1. How did the United States and other nations respond to nuclear weapons crises in Ukraine and North Korea? How successful were these efforts?

2. Why did the United States and Britain bomb Iraq between 1998 and 2001? Explain why you AGREE or DISAGREE with these actions.

3. How does the Comprehensive Test-Ban Treaty differ from the Nuclear Nonproliferation Treaty?

IV. INTERNATIONAL WEAPONS TRADE

World leaders often denounce the arms trade and, at the same time, encourage it. Many nations export arms. China leads in the production of light arms such as rifles and also sells missiles. Sweden sells everything from fighter planes to submarines. The United States outsells almost everyone else.

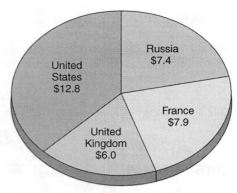

Major Arms-Selling Nations 2005 (value of sales in U.S, billion $)

After the cold war, the U.S. government cut back purchases from U.S. arms manufacturers. With the arms industry on the verge of collapse, the government stepped up promotion of exports.

A. Attempts to Limit Arms Sales

The United States, Canada, Britain, France, Germany, Italy, and Japan started the *Missile Technology Control Regime (MTCR)* in 1987. It limits exports of all but the shortest-range ballistic and cruise missiles. A separate agreement restricts sales of arms and military technology to such "troublesome" states as Iraq, Iran, North Korea, and Libya.

In 1993, the Clinton administration tried to stop Russian sales of missile technology to India and of dangerous chemicals to Libya. Americans could not trade with Russian companies that violated international limits on missile exports. Moreover, the U.S. government refused to cooperate on the construction of a U.S.-Russian space station unless Russia kept within the limits.

China did not sign the MTCR but agreed to observe the controls. Nevertheless, it sold missile

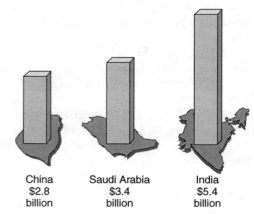

Major Arms-Buying Nations 2005 (value of purchases in U.S. $)

technology to Pakistan and purchased military technology from Israel. U.S. exports to China of high-tech American goods were then cut off.

From a peak of $61 billion in 1988, arms sales dropped to around $25 billion a year by the end of the 20th century. In 2005, Russia surpassed the U.S. as the major supplier of weapons to developing nations.

B. Arms Buildup in Asia

Weapons suppliers in the United States, Russia, France, and Germany compete for business in Asia. Starting in 1988, China bought more and more Russian military supplies. Neighboring Japan and Taiwan fear that a strongly armed China might attack them.

In the late 20th and early 21st centuries, North Korea became a serious threat to peace. Hostile to the United States and Japan, it stationed 65 percent of its one million troops near the demilitarized border with South Korea. Potential missile sales to Asian and Middle Eastern nations were also worrisome.

By 2001, North Korea's missiles were capable of reaching Alaska and Hawaii. North Korea has also sold missiles to developing nations in the Middle East and Asia.

INFO CHECK

1. Explain why you AGREE or DISAGREE with the following: "The United States is opposed to the international trade in weapons, but also participates in it!"

2. In the early 21st century, China and North Korea continued to increase their military forces. Which country do you think presents the greater threat to world peace? Why?

V. HUMAN RIGHTS

In June 1993, in Vienna, the UN hosted a World Conference on Human Rights. Delegates from 160 countries and 1000 nongovernmental organizations attended. They discussed the rights of women, minorities, native peoples, migrant workers, the handicapped, and other groups.

A. Debating the Issue

Believing that no government should withhold human rights from its citizens for any reason, the Western nations wanted to strengthen the UN's authority to defend human rights. Several developing nations wished to keep Westerners out of their internal affairs; they did not think that democratic government was a human right.

The delegates adopted an agenda. The United States proposed that a UN High Commissioner for Human Rights be appointed. *Amnesty International,* a nongovernmental human rights organization, protested that the conference had added nothing to earlier UN human rights declarations.

B. International Concern

The 1945 UN Charter stated that the organization should promote "universal respect for . . . fundamental freedoms for all without distinction as to race, sex, language, or religion." In 1948, the General Assembly unanimously adopted the *Universal Declaration of Human Rights*.

The world's nations have made a number of international agreements on human rights: the *International Covenant of Civil and Political Rights* (1966), the *American Convention on Human Rights* (1969), the *Helsinki Accords* (1975), and the *African Charter on People's and Human Rights* (1981). Nongovernmental organizations supported those agreements, educated people about human rights abuses, and spoke out against abusive nations.

C. Protecting Human Rights

During the 1980s, several governments joined to promote human rights in other countries. The Scandinavian countries and the Netherlands reported on denying economic aid to countries in violation. The European Community based its international trade on human rights practices. Canada and Australia announced that human rights issues would affect their participation in international projects. The Council of Europe denied membership to Turkey until it improved its human rights practices. During the 1980s, the United States began to oppose anti-Communist dictators it had once supported.

Fearful of losing Western economic aid, Argentina and Uruguay installed democratic governments. International concern for human rights encouraged Filipinos and Haitians to revolt against oppression. The South Korean military regime permitted democratic elections.

World attention has been focused on China's persecution of the Falun Gong, a popular religious sect combining Buddhism, Taoism, ritual exercise, and meditation. It was banned by the government in 1999. Imprisonment of its members continued into the 21st century.

D. Human Rights in the 21st Century

Terrorist attacks in the United States, Britain, Spain, and other countries led to limits on basic democratic freedoms. Following the 2003 invasion of Iraq by U.S. and British forces, human rights groups condemned abuse of Muslim prisoners at the American detention center in Guantánamo Bay, Cuba, and at the Abu Ghraib prison in Iraq. They accused the Central Intelligence Agency (CIA) of keeping terrorist suspects in secret prisons in Eastern Europe, where they could be questioned without trial and possibly tortured.

Both U.S. President George W. Bush and British Prime Minister Tony Blair tried to expand police power to tap citizens' telephones without warrants and to arrest and detain suspects without charging them with crimes.

E. Immigrants and Aliens in Europe

In 1992, Western Europe's population of legal immigrants soared to nearly 20 million. The estimated number of illegal immigrants was 2 million. Later on, there was an easing of the flow of **alien**s (people without citizenship in their resident country).

Most new arrivals required economic aid. At the time, however, Western Europe was experiencing bad economic times. Moreover, UN funding for refugee assistance was tight.

The newcomers were poor, lacking in job skills, and different in culture and race. Approximately half the immigrants to Western Europe in the 1990s were Muslims, most from North Africa but also from Bosnia, Turkey, Pakistan, and Somalia.

The local people resented competing with new arrivals for scarce jobs and shelter. In Belgium, Austria, and Italy, anti-immigrant political parties gained new supporters. In Spain, nationalist groups called for the expulsion of Arabs and Africans.

F. German Reaction to Immigrants

In Germany, the percentage of foreigners in the population was higher than in any other Western European country. Economic and social problems had followed the unification of East and West Germany in 1991. Some Germans felt that the immigrants had added to these problems. Ultranationalist groups attacked the foreigners. Most Germans condemned these attacks.

By 2006, significantly fewer immigrants were entering Germany, while the number of Germans leaving the country for better opportunities elsewhere had increased. A high unemployment rate and slow economic growth led to the emigration of doctors, engineers and other professionals. German universities and local authorities created "welcome centers" to help skilled foreigners get resident permits, find homes, and enroll in language classes.

G. Immigration in Britain

In 2004, Britain, Ireland, and Sweden were the only European countries to grant Eastern European immigrants unlimited access to their job markets. Hundreds of thousands of people from nations that had been newly admitted to the EU went to Britain for work. Although the new arrivals filled the need for lower-skilled workers, many Britons were hostile toward them. They claimed that the immigrants strained medical and educational resources. Consequently, the British government announced in 2006 that it would let in only skilled workers from Bulgaria and Romania, which became EU members in 2007.

H. Integration Problems in France

In 2005 and 2006, people in the poor neighborhoods of France rioted for three weeks. They were mainly immigrants and the children of immigrants from Africa. They protested against unemployment and lack of social mobility. France has always tried to mold immigrants into French citizens but did not succeed in doing so with these new immigrants. Discrimination against the African newcomers produced a large jobless underclass. The violence this discrimination produced led native French citizens to choose more conservative leaders. In August 2006, Foreign Minister Nicolas Sarkozy ordered the deportation of illegal immigrants. Sarkozy became President of France in 2007.

I. Immigrants and Aliens in America

Although it is a nation founded and populated by immigrants, the United States has in the past put quotas, or limits, on the number of people who could be accepted from each country. During the early 20th century, these quotas favored people from Western Europe. In 1965, applicants from all nations were given a chance to become U.S. citizens. In the 1990s, quotas on immigrants were resumed.

In the early 2000s, Asians, Africans, and Latin Americans outnumbered Europeans. People who resented immigrants claimed that their use of social services increased taxes and that they took jobs from native citizens. Often, though, immigrants filled jobs that no one else wanted.

Concerns about illegal immigration and border security led to the construction of 700 miles of additional fencing along the U.S.-Mexican border and more vehicular barriers, checkpoints, and detection technology. Mexican President Felipe Calderón claimed that these measures would not stop illegal immigrants. Although U.S. President George W. Bush opposed amnesty for illegal immigrants, he felt that it was necessary to deal with those already in the United States. Therefore, he proposed allowing them to have temporary jobs. In 2007, this proposal gave illegal immigrants new hope for amnesty.

J. Dutch Encourage Immigration

During the late 20th century, economic growth in the Netherlands increased. A labor shortage ensued. To fill the need for both blue-collar and white-collar workers, Dutch business leaders and government officials recruited immigrants from other European countries, Africa, Asia, and the United States. To encourage immigrants to the Netherlands, employment agencies have offered free housing, transportation, and instruction in the Dutch language. A few years later, the Netherlands had nearly two million immigrants. In response to anti-Islamic feeling that began to arise in 2006, the Dutch government limited new immigration.

K. African Migrations: Hutu and Tutsi

Conflict between the Hutus and the Tutsis resumed in 1994. It was triggered by the assassination of the Hutu president. Blaming the Tutsis, Rwandan government soldiers and Hutu militia slaughtered Tutsis and moderate Hutus. To escape the killing, people poured into Tanzania and Zaire (now the Democratic Republic of the Congo).

One million refugees returned to Rwanda in 1996. When the conflict ended in 1998, the Rwanda government and a UN-sponsored tribunal tried and convicted many accused of genocide. In 2000, General Paul Kagame became Rwanda's first Tutsi president. After reelecting him in 2003, Rwandans approved a new constitution and elected a new parliament. In 2004, village tribunals began trials of genocide suspects.

INFO CHECK

1. Define human rights.

2. Identify three international agreements to protect human rights.

3. Explain why each of the following has become a matter of concern to the UN and other human rights organizations: political dissidents, refugees and aliens, ethnic minorities.

VI. TERRORISM AND ULTRANATIONALISM

A. Threat to Global Security

TERRORISM (systematic use of violence to achieve political goals) is widespread. Ultranationalists who want a particular national or ethnic group to dominate their country attack people of other cultures in what amounts to racism. Such right-wing extremists threaten both domestic and global peace.

B. Recent Terrorist Acts

On September 11, 2001, terrorists hijacked four passenger planes. Two destroyed the World Trade Center in New York City, a third damaged the Pentagon in Washington, D.C., and a fourth crashed in Pennsylvania. Thousands were killed, and American economic and social life was disrupted. The disaster was attributed to Al Qaeda terrorists based in Afghanistan and led by Osama bin Laden, a multimillionaire from Saudi Arabia. He had funded many terrorist groups and seemed to be building an international terrorist network.

President Bush placed the U.S. military on alert and asked America's allies to join in a war on global terrorism. It began by destroying Al Qaeda bases in Afghanistan and removing its Taliban regime, which had sheltered bin Laden's organization. By early 2002, the allies controlled most of Afghanistan. Bush also created an Office of Homeland Security.

Subsequent terrorist acts included letters to U.S. government officials and media personalities that carried anthrax spores. Federal and state officials put in place new security to counter the threat of chemical and biological attacks.

There were two previous terrorist attacks in the United States. In 1993, a car bomb exploded in the World Trade Center, killing six. In 1995, a truck bomb demolished the Alfred P. Murrah Federal Building in Oklahoma City, killing 168.

C. Terrorism in Other Areas

Terrorist campaigns against legitimate governments have broken out and continued for years in many areas of the world.

During the 1960s, an organization known as ETA began terrorist operations in Spain. For more than two decades, the Abu Sayyaf Muslims have committed terrorist acts in the southern Philippine Islands. In 1995, Islamic opponents of the Algerian government, angry that the French had cooperated

Alleged Group	Probable Motivation	Target(s)	Date(s)
ETA	Independence for the Basque provinces	Spain	1960s–2000s
Muslim Moro Front	Independence from the Philippines	Philippines	1980s–2000s
Ultranationalist Balkan groups	Destruction of other Yugoslavian groups	Other Balkan groups	1990s
Drug gangs, leftist guerrillas	Government crackdown on drug trafficking	Festival in Bogotá, Columbia	1993
Hamas	Opposition to peace talks between Palestine and Israel	Israel	early 2000s
Radical Islamic Groups	General opposition to Western governments	London subway system	2005
Lashkar e-Taiba	Damage to India's economy	Mumbai, India	2006
Al Qaeda	General opposition to Western governments	American airplanes in British air terminal	2006
Hezbollah	Destruction of Israel	Israel	2006–

with Algerian leaders, set off bombs in subway cars and garbage cans in French cities.

By 2003, acts of terrorism in the Middle East had halted peace talks between Israel and the PLO. The suicide bombings by the Palestinian terrorist group Hamas led Israel to step up its military attacks against Palestinian extremists. In 2006, Hezbollah, the Lebanese-based terrorist militia, began firing rockets into Israel. The rockets were made by Iran and supplied to Hezbollah by Syria.

Terrorist bombs exploded in a commuter train in Mumbai, India's financial and film capital in July 2006. Aimed at wealthy businesspeople, the attack was meant to damage India's economy. A similar attack targeted the London subway system in 2005. Carried out by British citizens of Pakistani descent, the attack showed the success of radical groups in recruiting young British Muslims. In 2006, British police prevented an attack on American airplanes flying between Britain and the United States by a group that also included British-born Muslims.

D. Ultranationalist Violence

Ultranationalist violence is usually directed against ethnic or religious groups but may also be aimed at governments opposed to ultranationalist goals. The neo-Nazis, for example, arose in Germany and other countries to revive Hitler's drastic methods against minorities and foreigners. Skinheads follow neo-Nazi ideas.

BALKANS. Wars in Bosnia, Kosovo, and Macedonia after the 1991 breakup of Yugoslavia saw large-scale violence between Serbs, Croats, and ethnic Albanians, made worse by Christian-Muslim hatreds. In 2001, two Serb commanders of a prison camp pleaded guilty before the UN War Crimes Tribunal of persecuting Muslims and Croats. Three Bosnian Muslim army officers were tried for atrocities against Croats and Serbs. Slobodan Milosevic, former Serbian president, was tried for genocide and war crimes in Bosnia, Kosovo, and Croatia.

UNITED STATES. In the United States, such neo-Nazi groups as the *Aryan Brotherhood* and the *Nation* have vandalized synagogues and attacked and killed members of other minorities.

E. Controlling Terrorism and Ultranationalism

In January 1997, the UN General Assembly adopted a resolution to unite its members against international terrorism. It encouraged nations to share information, conduct joint investigations, and improve detection methods.

After the attack on New York City in 2001, the justice and interior ministers of 15 European Union member nations agreed on a common definition of a terrorist crime, with heavier penalties. To do away with time-consuming extradition processes, they approved the creation of arrest warrants enforceable in all 15 countries.

INFO CHECK

1. Explain why you APPROVE or DISAPPROVE of the methods used by terrorists and ultranationalists to achieve political change.

2. PROVE or DISPROVE:
   - Terrorism came to the United States.
   - Terrorism and ultranationalism are global problems.
   - Terrorists and ultranationalists are often racists.

3. Describe the methods used in the 1990s and thereafter to combat terrorism and ultranationalism.

CHAPTER REVIEW

Multiple Choice

1. Although UN peacekeeping efforts succeeded in Haiti, El Salvador, and Cambodia, they failed in Bosnia, Rwanda, and Somalia because UN forces there

   1. took sides in the conflict
   2. were placed in the midst of ongoing wars
   3. left because they ran out of money
   4. were militarily unprepared for war.

2. Recently, the UN has had difficulty maintaining a peacekeeping force because

   1. Soviet and U.S. conflict prevented forming such a force
   2. the smaller, less powerful nations did not want to participate in peacekeeping efforts
   3. many nations did not want to pay the high costs needed to support the peacekeeping force
   4. the United States did not want to send its forces in support of a UN peacekeeping effort.

3. The United Nations Development Program rates a nation's ability to improve its citizens' living standards. It uses such criteria as

   1. life expectancy, education, and quality of life
   2. per capita income, male-to-female births, and size of families
   3. type of government and whether the economy is agricultural or industrial
   4. government stability, number of people receiving welfare, and food stamps.

4. The reorganization of NATO in the 1990s provided for the

   1. defense of Western Europe
   2. ability to respond to Middle Eastern crises
   3. stabilization of Eastern Europe
   4. all of the above.

5. The nuclear balance of power between the Soviet Union and the United States resulted in

   1. the destruction of the environment
   2. both sides cooperating in arms negotiations and limitation agreements
   3. both sides assisting their allies in building atomic weapons
   4. the nonaligned nations becoming allies of either the Soviet Union or the United States.

6. The nations of the world were concerned about the military and nuclear weapons of the former Soviet Union because

   1. many nuclear weapons needed to be safeguarded or destroyed
   2. its generals and soldiers were hiring out as mercenary armies
   3. threats of nuclear war were made against the West by those who did not want the breakup of the Soviet Union
   4. the Soviet military might destroy the oil supplies needed for world industries and commerce.

7. Along with conventional and nuclear weapons, another major issue for the world community has been

   1. a ban on smoking
   2. a ban on violence in movies
   3. human rights abuses
   4. women demanding the right to vote.

8. Recently, in Europe, immigrants and aliens were not always accepted because

   1. they were smarter than the local people and got the best jobs
   2. they brought with them strange languages and beliefs
   3. local people feared they would cause revolutions and political unrest
   4. many came needing assistance, and economic hard times placed them in competition with citizens for jobs and housing.

9. Africa has seen a continuing flood of refugees and violence because

   1. imperialist nations were forcing out the native peoples
   2. UN forces were fighting against apartheid
   3. Nigerian government forces were seeking to end the Biafran separatist movement
   4. fighting continued in Somalia, Sudan (Darfur), Congo and other countries.

10. One of the most persistent obstacles to world peace has been the use of terror tactics. Terrorists are

    1. all located in the Middle East and are religious fanatics
    2. all located in Eastern Europe and are religious fanatics
    3. to be found worldwide and have religious as well as nationalistic goals
    4. radicals who have grudges against a few people, governments, or companies.

11. Among the difficulties faced by the UN in peacekeeping operations are

    1. the refusal of member nations to contribute military forces
    2. disagreements between the Security Council and the General Assembly

3. substandard weapons and equipment
4. a lack of experienced officers.

12. A conclusion suggested by the charts that appear on page 314 is that

1. major arms-buying nations purchase weapons from each other
2. the United States is the leading exporter of arms while India is the leading buyer
3. Asians have purchased most of the arms on the world market
4. Europeans sell weapons exclusively to nations of the Middle East.

Thematic Essays

1. During the cold war, the world was afraid that conflict between the two superpowers would lead to nuclear destruction. *Task:* Explain why that did not occur and describe the efforts of the two superpowers and the UN to prevent nuclear destruction. Consider for inclusion in your answer, balance of power, MAD, IAEA, and NNT.

2. The UN has met with limited success in trying to achieve world peace. *Task:* Using specific historical examples, identify and explain reasons for peacekeeping success or failure.

Document-Based Questions

1. In 1963, a nuclear test ban treaty was drafted and signed by the United States, Great Britain, and the Soviet Union. It stated:

" . . . as their principal aim the speediest possible achievement of an agreement on general and complete disarmament under strict international control . . . which would put an end to the armament race. . . . Each of the parties to this treaty undertakes to prohibit, to prevent, and not to carry out any nuclear weapon test or explosion. . . . "

What was the goal of the three nations that signed this treaty, and why do you think other nations have failed to follow their lead?

2. Selections from the United Nations Charter:

" . . . to unite our strength to maintain international peace and security, . . . to employ international machinery for the promotion of the economic and social advancement of all people . . . to take effective and collective measures for the prevention and removal of threats to the peace and for suppression of acts of aggression or other breaches of the peace."

Describe the main purpose of the UN and how it appears to be different from the League of Nations.

3. Look at the cartoon of Saddam Hussein on page 313. Identify the symbols on the containers and over Hussein's head. Explain why the cartoonist used them in the picture. Why was the accuracy of this cartoon questioned?

4. From an article by Michael T. Klare on global security:

" . . . it is apparent that the problem of preventing and controlling local, ethnic, and regional conflict has become the premier world security concern of the post-cold war era. Because such conflicts are likely to [grow] in the years ahead, and because no single group is willing or able to guarantee global peace and stability, United States and world leaders will be forced to [enlarge] existing peacekeeping instruments and to develop new techniques. . . . "

Describe the writer's view of the future and the suggestion he makes for future peace.

Document-Based Essay

Task: Identify any two major causes of world conflict. Describe what actions individual nations and peacekeeping organizations have taken to resolve the two problems you identified.

CHAPTER
30

Global Trends and Issues

I. SCIENCE AND TECHNOLOGY

Developed in the 1940s, the compact electronic computer processes and stores information rapidly. In 1970, scientists introduced the silicon microchip, which can store thousands of **transistors** (devices that conduct electrical signals). The microchip allows computers to operate at lightning speed and store huge amounts of information. A microchip is so tiny that computers can be built in compact sizes.

A. Information Superhighway

With computers, vast amounts of information can be sent long distances almost instantaneously. They have speeded up communication between businesses and clients and transformed the global economy.

The computerized flow of information is called the **information superhighway**. By 1990, the production and sale of information accounted for 50 percent of the U.S. gross national product.

INTERNET. The **Internet** is the part of the information superhighway that links far-flung computers into a giant network called the *World Wide Web*. People can reach the Internet in their homes or cars by means of telephone signals. By 2003, many Internet users were changing from dial-up modem technology—in which a modem converts digital computer signals into sounds that telephones can process—to high-speed access technologies, such as cable modem, satellite, and Digital Subscriber Line (DSL). People exchange messages (electronic mail, or E-mail), share the information stored in computers, and search for new information over the Internet.

Businesses have been competing so frantically to offer services over the World Wide Web that it became the fastest-growing segment of the Internet. It delivers print, sound, still pictures, and

Electronic Numerical Integrator and Computer (ENIAC), introduced in 1946

Thumbnail-sized microchip, designed to handle all of ENIAC's functions

moving video images. Many businesspeople seek to turn the World Wide Web into a global shopping mall by making transactions with electronic cash and on-line credit cards. Unfortunately, other people have learned to counterfeit the cash and steal the credit card numbers.

B. Satellite Technology

Artificial satellites that orbit Earth can be used for military surveillance; that is how the Pentagon first knew of Soviet missiles in Cuba. Satellites equipped with infrared detectors that sense heat can detect missiles as they are launched, giving defensive weapons time to intercept in midair.

Satellites transmit distant TV and radio programs by relaying electronic beams. They tell scientists about changes in the upper atmosphere and detect and identify particles and forces around Earth. They make long-range weather predictions possible. As astronomical observatories, they are placed so far above Earth that stars can be seen without atmospheric distortion. They serve as laboratories for biological experiments.

In 2006, the National Aeronautics and Space Administration (NASA) launched two satellites on a four-year mission to gather three-dimensional views of the sun. The satellites will help scientists predict the billion-ton eruptions of electrified gas and deadly particles that disrupt power grids on Earth and cause electrical damage to spacecraft in orbit.

Together, computers and satellites produce complex maps—vegetation, three-dimensional topography, and bird habitat maps. The two technologies can be combined to give scientists a clear picture of how Earth's land, oceans, and atmosphere interact.

C. Global Communications

An explosive growth in the field of wireless communication has taken place in the 21st century.

Wireless communications include cellular telephones, two-way paging devices, handheld computers, and mobile fax machines. All use radio waves to send and receive information.

"Smart phones" provide Internet access, text messaging, and e-mail in addition to wireless telephone service. Headsets can be attached to smart phones and other electronic devices to free the user's hands. Global Positioning System additions can be connected to many smart phones. A keyboard, which communicates wirelessly with the smart phone, can also be added. The I-Tech Virtual Laser Keyboard paints a keyboard in laser light on any surface.

Many U.S. banks urge customers to bank online from home. Not only could they transact business at their own convenience; banks could save money by closing some branches.

Other 21st-century developments include a global tracking service by ORBCOMM, a U.S. space-technology company. Through its network of 35 lightweight, low-Earth-orbit satellites, an "on call" rescue system would let motorists obtain help when their cars break down.

D. Space Exploration

In 1957, the Soviets launched *Sputnik,* an orbiting space satellite. Advances in satellite technology have led to improved television, radio, and telephone communications; more accurate weather forecasting; and important information about other planets. In 1989, the information received from U.S. *Voyager 2* as it passed Neptune enhanced the value of unmanned missions.

In the 1980s, the main emphasis of space exploration was to construct large orbiting space stations where astronaut-scientists could conduct experiments in a gravity-free environment. The stations were reached by reusable space shuttles that are a blend of space capsule and airplane.

MARS. In 1997, the *National Aeronautics and Space Administration (NASA)* placed *Pathfinder* on the surface of Mars. The vehicle sent out the tiny *Sojourner* to rove the Martian surface, take pictures, and scoop up soil samples. *Pathfinder* sent back valuable data on Martian geology.

JUPITER. In 1994, cameras aboard *Galileo,* a U.S. spacecraft launched in cooperation with Germany, recorded a spectacular collision between Jupiter and a flurry of comet fragments. *Galileo* later orbited Jupiter to study the dense clouds in its atmosphere and its many moons.

SPACE STATION. In the 1990s, construction of an international space station began. It is the largest cooperative scientific project in history. Besides Russia and the United States, 14 other nations are participating. Laboratory and crew facilities have been designed for long-term occupation. The first crew of the station went aboard in November 2000.

Space shuttle flights, such as those of the *Discovery* and the *Atlantis* in 2006, were made in order to continue work on the International Space Station. President George W. Bush has ordered the shuttle program to be shut down in 2010 in favor of sending a new generation of space vehicles to the moon.

One of the project's most important experiments has been a study of the effect of low gravity on the human body. Research on long-term changes in Earth's environment is also planned.

***COLUMBIA* DISASTER.** In February 2003, an undetected structural flaw caused the space shuttle *Columbia* to explode as it reentered Earth's atmosphere. All seven astronauts died.

CHINA IN SPACE. In October 2003, China made its first foray into space. A Chinese astronaut aboard *Shenzhou 5* orbited Earth several times before landing safely in the Gobi Desert.

E. Health and Medical Technology

AIDS. HIV, the virus causing AIDS, can hide in blood cells a long time. It is hard to detect early when treatment is most effective. Eighteen antibody drugs combat AIDS. British AZT does little for those with HIV but it has helped those with full-blown AIDS. Researchers are studying HIV immunity, hoping to duplicate its biochemical process in the infected.

ALZHEIMER'S. This disease causes severe memory loss. American scientists have developed a rice-grain-sized capsule to be inserted into the brain. It contains thousands of cells that make the brain hormone **nerve growth factor (NGF)**, lack of which may cause Alzheimer's.

The capsule's plastic membrane shields its cells from attack by the human immune system while letting NGF escape.

ALA. ALA is a natural acid that briefly sensitizes cancer cells to light. A low-powered laser and ALA can destroy surface cancers without causing prolonged sensitivity to sunlight. ALA dosages and laser intensities are being tested.

LASERS. Precisely focused laser beams can detect a problem and remove or repair it with little damage to nearby tissue. Invaluable in eye surgery, lasers may also unclog blocked arteries.

LUNG CANCER. Lung cancers should be found while small and localized. Photosensitive drugs that make tumors glow under ultraviolet (UV) light do this. LIFE (lung-imaging fluorescent endoscope) machines are now in production.

GENES. Cystic fibrosis attacks the lungs. A U.S. researcher has engineered a gene that enables lungs to make a protein to fight the disease. The search for genetic treatments of such diseases as cancer and diabetes is underway. Genes may soon be used as drugs.

Such **genetic engineering** is the manipulation of **DNA** in order to change traits or produce organisms. DNA is the genetic code to how an organism is made and operates.

Mutations (errors in gene coding) cause 3000 to 4000 hereditary diseases. In 1990, the *Human Genome Project* began decoding all genetic information found in DNA. The **genome** (genetic script) is the basis for physical life in humans, including causes and treatment of diseases.

Cloning. **Cloning** is the process by which an organism is reproduced from one parent, without fertilization. A clone's genetic structure matches its parent's. In 1997, Scottish scientists created the first clone of an adult animal, a sheep named Dolly. By 2006, regenerative medicine, a practice that aims to replace or rebuild diseased or damaged tissue using the body's own healthy cells, had made progress.

INFO CHECK

1. Describe the computer revolution of the late 20th century. How has it changed the ways in which we live and work?

2. Define: information superhighway, Internet.

3. Explain the relationship linking the microchip, the modem, and the flow of information and ideas.

4. List some of the uses of satellite technology.

5. Identify a significant development in each of the following areas: telecommunications, space exploration, health and medical technology.

II. ENVIRONMENT

A. Environmental Destruction

Chemicals in fertilizers, factory solvents, lead batteries, and paper pollute soil and water. Burning of carbon fuels for heat and energy has poisoned air and elevated temperatures. Scientists predict that such warming will melt polar ice caps and cause coastal flooding.

NUCLEAR SAFETY. Safe storage of radioactive by-products from nuclear plants is difficult. Leaks contaminate crops and water.

In March 1979, the reactor in Three Mile Island, Pennsylvania, spilled radioactive material by accident; very little escaped from the containment building. The 1986 nuclear accident in Chernobyl, Ukraine, spread radiation locally and across Europe. In 2002, Austria and the Czech Republic agreed on safety improvements at a Czech nuclear power plant near Austria's border. In nuclear-free Austria, some political groups demanded that the plant be closed.

ACID RAIN AND DEFORESTATION. Deforestation is worldwide. **Acid rain**, the combination of moisture and airborne chemicals from factories and cars, has damaged the forests of industrialized nations.

Harvesting lumber or clearing forests for other land uses has caused even more harm, particularly in the Amazon rain forest, the largest one in the world. Although such forests cover only 7 percent of Earth's land surface, they contain 50 percent of its plants and animals. Thousands of species face extinction each year through deforestation. (Every hour, 4500 acres of trees are being felled.)

DESERTIFICATION. Desertification of farmland and grassland is caused by drought, overgrazing of animals, and felling too many trees. The roots of trees and bushes prevent topsoil from being blown away. In Africa, the Sahara is taking over the Sahel grassland on its southern border at an alarming rate.

B. International Efforts for Environmentalism

RIO CONFERENCE. In 1992, delegates from 178 countries attended the *United Nations Conference on Environment and Development (UNCED)* in Rio de Janeiro. They drew up a list of environmental policies that included:

- the Rio Declaration, a list of environmental and economic development concerns
- statements about preventing global climate changes and protecting threatened forests

KYOTO CONVENTION. In December 1997, delegates from more than 150 nations attended the UN's *Third Conference of the Parties (COP-3)* in Kyoto. They met to draw up the first international treaty on reducing carbon dioxide emissions into the atmosphere.

When coal, gasoline, and wood are burned, carbon dioxide is released and mixes with water vapor in the atmosphere The result is a dangerous increase in the **greenhouse effect** and a predicted rise in the world's temperature. Global warming threatens to destroy our environment.

The delegates discussed a two-year negotiation process that followed the Rio Conference. The final treaty, the *Kyoto Protocol,* limited the amount of greenhouse gases for industrialized nations and allowed developing nations to set their own limits. Industrialized nations were advised to plant and protect forests, which absorb carbon dioxide. American opponents argued that cutting the use of carbon fuels to the required extent would damage the U.S. economy. The Kyoto Protocol was signed by 178 nations in 2001. The United States, however, rejected it.

C. Air Pollution Controls

The *1990 Clean Air Act* stiffened antipollution laws for motor vehicles in the United States. Models sold in the mid-1990s emitted only 1 percent as much as those 20 years older. California and 12

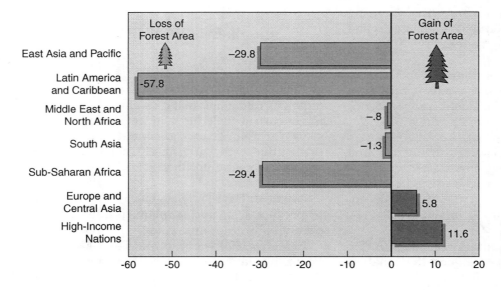

Annual Loss or Gain of Forest Areas (thousands of square kilometers), by Region, 1990–1995

other states introduced even tougher standards in the late 1990s.

The Environmental Protection Agency (EPA) further limited auto emissions affecting ozone concentration levels in 1997. In 2006, California added to its tough air pollution standards an Emissions Trading Scheme with other states. The European Union had introduced an Emissions Trading Scheme in 2005. Such programs set targets for emissions and give emission allowances to industry. If companies wish to emit more than their allowances, they must buy extra allowances from other industries, states, or countries.

AUTO EMISSIONS. A high-performance zero-emission car would offer the convenience of any other car but give off no pollutants. In Sweden, Volvo has developed an Environmental Concept Car (ECC), which operates on batteries, making it a zero-emission vehicle when used in congested cities. In other conditions, the driver can switch to a gas turbine engine that drives an ultra-efficient, high-speed generator. Even in this mode, the car emits low levels of pollution.

One carmaker has displayed an electric race car. It combines a turbine and flywheel, providing 500 horsepower for quick acceleration. Automakers are also finding new ways to cut polluting emissions from gasoline-powered engines. Diesel fuel, for example, has just 3 percent of the sulfur content of older fuels. It was available in late 2006 for use in trucks and buses. Ethanol, a much cleaner fuel than gasoline, has been produced from corn.

Biotechnology companies are also researching ways to genetically alter soybeans, beans, and prairie switchgrass to produce clean biofuels. In 2007, a New Zealand company began efforts to produce ethanol from carbon monoxide.

D. Recycling

Several major U.S. companies have joined with the *Environmental Defense Fund (EDF)* to reduce the use of landfills (legal garbage dumps). Paper products make up one-third of municipal trash.

To improve the quality of paper made from recycled trash and increase its use, scientists are trying to make it brighter and stronger—for example, by adding discarded wood fiber.

E. New Signs of Global Warming

In September 2006, NASA scientists reported new evidence that greenhouse gases were changing the climate of the Arctic region. Since satellite observation of the region began in 1978, the amount of sea ice around the Arctic Ocean has steadily shrunk.

A 2006 British government report called for more research into low-carbon technologies. The report warned that unless action was taken to reduce carbon emissions, coastal flooding in Europe and America, drought in Africa, stronger hurricanes, and rising sea levels around the world could turn 200 million people into refugees.

The most promising technologies for slowing global warming are solar and wind power, farm-produced fuels, energy-efficient buildings, and environmentally friendly automobiles. Unfortunately, U.S. federal spending on energy research and development fell to half what it was in 1979. Internationally, government energy research has also declined. Only Japan has increased research spending in recent decades. The Japanese focus has been on fuel efficiency and solar technology.

INFO CHECK

1. Why are environmentalists today more concerned about the future of our planet than they were in earlier decades? Do you AGREE or DISAGREE with their concern? Explain.

2. Why were global warming and the greenhouse effect major concerns at the Kyoto Convention of 1997? What did the delegates decide to do about this problem?

3. How are improvements in automobile design related to the effort to reduce air pollution?

III. POPULATION PRESSURES AND POVERTY

A. Family Planning

Developing countries are trying to establish family-planning programs, but people who observe traditional cultures and religions resist birth control. Still, more people are beginning to cooperate with government birth control policies. In Africa, where such policies are least successful, the average woman had between five and seven children in 2005, as opposed to an average of eight a few years earlier.

Experts predict a peak in world population at about 9 billion people by 2050. It is expected to decline to about 8.4 billion by 2100. It is hoped that advances in technology will cope with limited resources. Although small and densely populated, Belgium and Holland have social and economic programs which enable a high standard of living; these may be models for the rest of the world.

B. Policies and Programs

In 1994, representatives from 179 nations attended the *International Conference on Population and Development (ICPD)* in Cairo, Egypt.

A key issue was family planning. Governments were urged to educate their people, especially women, to make their own reproductive choices, including the decision to prevent unwanted pregnancies. These efforts will require affordable, high-quality health facilities and educational and counseling services to coordinate family-planning programs.

The *Population Information Network (POPIN)* is a group of international, regional, and national population institutions. Founded in May 1979, it is funded mainly by the UN and its *Department of Economic and Social Affairs (DESA)*.

POPIN distributes information on population issues, such as migration and population control, and helps regions and nations coordinate activities dealing with these issues. It is a community where developed and developing nations can meet and share information.

INFO CHECK

1. Explain the relationship between rapid population growth and poverty, especially in the third world's developing nations.

2. List the measures to maintain standards of living recommended to world governments at the International Conference on Population and Development in 1994. Which measures do you think will be most effective?

IV. WOMEN'S RIGHTS

A. Women's Conference in Beijing

In 1995, the *Fourth World Conference on Women* was held in Beijing. Nongovernmental organizations held a separate conference nearby. The Beijing delegates assessed women's progress in human rights. Advances include greater female literacy and increased governmental recognition of women's rights. But abuses continue. During the wars in Bosnia and Rwanda, women were systematically raped. Almost everywhere, women experience social, economic, and legal discrimination.

Women hold candles for world peace during the International Women's Conference 2005 in Bangalore.

The delegates expressed different goals. In some developing countries, key issues include selling women as slaves and ritual mutilation of girls. In the United States, the focus is on reproductive rights and sex equality, including employment and promotion opportunities, salary differences, and sexual harassment. Common issues were sex discrimination and domestic violence (physical abuse within a family).

A 2006 report on Syria by the UN Development Fund for women concluded that nearly 25 percent of married Syrian women have been beaten. That year, the president of Iran lifted a ban on the attendance of women at sporting events. The U.S. National Academy of Sciences reported that bias hinders women from entering or advancing in scientific fields.

Gang rapes of thousands of women in Sudan's Darfur province occurred in the early 2000s. The rapes were a deliberate Sudanese government policy to demoralize several African tribes.

B. World Leaders

Women's rights groups have been encouraged by women gaining leadership positions in several nations.

SELECTED WOMEN WORLD LEADERS

Country	Name	Office	Date Elected
Bangladesh	Khaleda Zia	Prime minister	1991
China	Dr. Margaret F. C. Chan	Director-General of the World Health Organization	2006
Germany	Angela Merkel	Chancellor (head of government)	2005
Indonesia	Megawati Sukarnoputri	President	2001
Liberia	Ellen Johnson-Sirleaf	President	2005
Republic of Ireland	Mary Robinson	UN high commissioner for human rights	1997
United States	Nancy Pelosi	Speaker of the House	2006
United States	Condoleezza Rice	Secretary of state	2005

INFO CHECK

1. Explain why you AGREE or DISAGREE with the following statement: Women's rights issues are mostly confined to developing countries.

2. State the differences in goals between women's groups in the United States and those in developing nations.

CHAPTER REVIEW

Multiple Choice

1. The modern computer operates quickly and can store vast amounts of information in small spaces because of

   1. the information superhighway
   2. satellites
   3. corporate downsizing
   4. silicon chips called microchips.

2. Examples of how science and technology have benefited individual lives include

   1. laser-guided surgery
   2. personal computers
   3. electronic mail
   4. all of the above.

3. The international space station, NASA, and space shuttles are all related to

   1. cold war spy technology
   2. joint scientific study and space-exploration efforts
   3. U.S. efforts to build antimissile defenses
   4. joint Canadian, French, and Japanese military programs.

4. Technology can be harmful to the environment and humans if not carefully supervised. Examples of such dangers are

   1. typhoid and AIDS
   2. Chernobyl and Three Mile Island
   3. desertification and deforestation
   4. Alzheimer's disease and laser technology.

5. The greenhouse effect refers to the environmental situation caused by the

   1. growing of onions indoors during the winter months
   2. growing of flowers throughout the year
   3. warming of Earth's atmosphere caused by carbon dioxide gas
   4. loss of water in Earth's atmosphere when the moon rises in the midnight sky.

6. Japan and the United States have many differences with regard to trade and economic concerns. An area where they both agree is

   1. the need to find usable, environmentally safe nonfossil fuels
   2. the number of automobiles produced and traded in each other's country
   3. the number of items imported into each other's country
   4. the need to develop and test nuclear weapons.

7. After observing the recent famines caused by overpopulation, Thomas Malthus would probably have

   1. suggested the use of family-planning clinics
   2. agreed with the population-control programs established by the Chinese government
   3. said he knew that a country's food supply does not keep pace with increases in population
   4. all of the above.

8. The late 20th-century inequality between developed and developing nations caused the rise of

   1. the cold war and nuclear arms races
   2. radical nationalistic and religious fundamentalist movements
   3. imperialism and colonial empires
   4. international peacekeeping organizations.

9. The fact that economic crises, drug trafficking, and environmental concerns can affect all regions of the world highlights the

   1. power of the Internet
   2. power of worldwide communication
   3. global economic and social interactions of today's world
   4. need for a return to family values.

10. The bar graph on page 324 illustrates

    1. that most of the world's nations are facing the problem of deforestation
    2. that high-income nations and the nations of Europe and Central Asia are adding more woodland than they are losing
    3. that nations of the third world suffer the most loss of forest areas
    4. all of the above.

11. The photograph on page 326 illustrates that

    1. women's issues now receive an international focus
    2. women from the United States and Western Europe no longer participate in international women's conferences
    3. third world nations have little interest in the women's movement
    4. women from traditional societies are less likely to be affected by the women's movement than those in industrialized nations.

Thematic Essay

The regions of the world have become more directly affected by one another. *Task:* Identify and describe one positive and one negative consequence of that fact and explain what the world community is doing to either continue the positive or eliminate the negative situation. Consider regional associations, world bodies, and scientific inventions, technology, and communication developments in your answer.

Document-Based Questions

1. Look at the illustration of an early computer and a modern microchip on page 321. Compare and contrast the two pictures. What scientific and technological implications for humankind can you draw from the two pictures?

2. Professor Abelardo Villegas, referring to the work of the Alliance for Progress in Latin America:

   "No radical transformation of Latin American society can be expected in so short a time as 20 years. Many South American countries have not changed substantially since colonial days and it is futile to hope that they will do so by 1984."

   Why do you think Professor Villegas was pessimistic about the progress of the Latin American people toward freedom and a higher standard of living? Consider geography, societal classes, and types of government.

3. From the historian Hans Kohn:

   " . . . interest in the classics is growing; hundreds of thousands of copies of books about ancient Greece and Rome are sold in paperback editions. . . . Records and FM radio make available the finest music of all periods to a much wider public than ever before. While the West studies Oriental [Asian] and African music and sculpture, the East learns to master Western techniques in all arts. . . . Is it too much to hope that the new spirit developing out of the world revolution of our time will produce more lasting results that will benefit mankind?"

   How has 21st-century technology increased cultural diffusion?

Document-Based Essay

Science and technology have the potential to improve human life or create horrible weapons of mass destruction. *Task:* How have science and technology been used to improve human life and preserve the global environment?

UNIT REVIEW

Thematic Essays

1. The 1997 economic problems of Pacific Rim nations such as Japan and Korea and the former nations of the Soviet Union affected the stock markets and economies of the entire global community. *Task:* Identify and briefly discuss two reasons why this has occurred and explain two actions that world bodies or regional associations took to deal with these crises. Factors to consider include technology, communications, global investments, the World Bank, and the IMF.

2. Developing nations often experience many societal and cultural conflicts as they seek to modernize their economies and ways of life. The influence of religion, women's rights and roles, family size, and traditional customs are some of the issues they must confront. *Task:* Select two developing nations and identify a problem of modernization and the programs or policies developed to deal with that issue. Include in your essay whether the nations have succeeded in overcoming the conflicts or, if not, why they are having continued difficulty with them.

Document-Based Questions

1. Public Announcement, U.S. Department of State, Office of the Spokesman, Bangladesh, September 11, 1998:

"Bangladesh is experiencing the most devastating flooding in its history. Approximately seventy percent of the country is under water, and many areas are inaccessible. Many people have drowned, and hundreds of thousands are suffering from flood-related diseases. U.S. citizens should consider deferring nonessential travel to Bangladesh because of the severity and the extent of the flooding, the deteriorating health conditions, and the breakdown of essential services."

Public Announcement, U.S. Department of State, Office of the Spokesman, China, August 18, 1998:

"Serious flooding of the Yangtze River continues in the Wuhan region of China. U.S. citizens contemplating travel on the Yangtze River should consider this information until flooding subsides."

In what region of the world are these events occurring? Who is issuing the warning? What is the cause of the problem?

2. *Worldwide Caution,* September 24, 1998:

"In light of the August 7 bombings of the U.S. embassies in Nairobi, Kenya, and Dar es Salaam, Tanzania, the August 20 U.S. air strikes in Afghanistan and Sudan, and the apprehension of persons believed to have been involved in the U.S. embassy bombings, the potential for retaliatory acts against Americans and American interests overseas continues to exist. In addition, terrorists . . . continue their threats against the United States and have not distinguished between military and civilian targets."

Identify the reasons for the worldwide caution and explain why it involves citizens of other nations.

3. October 1998:

(a) Top Story: *Conflict / Yugoslavia: U.S. warns of looming NATO attack.*

"Western diplomats said Thursday an attack on Yugoslavia by North Atlantic Treaty Organization forces appeared imminent, unless Yugoslav security forces withdraw from Kosovo."

(b) *Human Right / Bolivia: 3,000 peasants demand title deeds.*

"Three thousand peasant farmers from various regions of Bolivia began a march "For Water, Land, and Life" Thursday in the capital La Paz, demanding title deeds to their land and protesting a draft law which they say will force them to pay fees for the use of water."

Identify the world problems and proposed solutions that each of these articles describes.

4. Look at the cartoon.

Who are the "kids" in front of the store and why are their toys so dangerous?

Document-Based Essay

The global community is confronted by both man-made and natural dangers. *Task:* Identify any two of those dangers, explaining why so many nations are affected and what the global community is trying to do to control or end those threats.

STUDENT'S STUDY GUIDE

Global History and Geography is a two-year, four-semester course. Therefore, it is important to develop a strategy for remembering key topics and details. In that way, you will minimize difficulties in taking the Regents examination that concludes the second year.

I. BASIC STRATEGIES FOR STUDY

A. Review Frequently

Review daily or several times each week the material covered in class, and do all your homework assignments. Such periodic review will help you understand the connections between different parts of the world and various eras of history without the need for cramming the day before a test.

B. Write Identifications, Not Definitions

Be sure you can explain the significance or historical importance of terms, names, and phrases that you encounter in the course. This is called *identification*. If your teacher asks you to keep an identification list, limit each identification to three or fewer sentences.

C. Identify Recurring Vocabulary Terms

Terms such as **cultural diffusion, democracy, totalitarianism, culture, civilization, revolution, nationalism**, and **imperialism** come up again and again in Global History and Geography. Identify them as they are repeated throughout the course.

D. Create Broad Questions That Focus on Key Themes

By recasting the material under study into questions or problems, you will create an outline for study and understanding. Here are several examples from Unit I, Ancient World (4000 B.C.–A.D. 500):

- How did early river civilizations change the nature of human life?
- What did ancient Greece and Rome contribute to modern society?
- How did trade connect the cultures of Rome and China?
- How do belief systems or religions influence the way people live?

Learning to write such probing questions will teach you to arrange the material into smaller units of study and help you anticipate possible test questions.

E. Review Graphics Provided in Class and Your Textbook

Illustrations will be included in the Regents examination. Familiarity with graphs, maps, tables, charts, drawings, paintings, cartoons, and photographs will help you interpret and analyze them. (Specific suggestions for developing skill with graphics are given in Section II.)

F. Review Info Check and End-of-Chapter Questions

Info Check questions reinforce your understanding of key topics, section by section. Chapter and Unit reviews simulate questions on the Regents examination. As you answer them, you will become familiar with the Regents format.

G. Determine Cause-and-Effect Relationships

When you understand chronology—the order of historical events—you will better understand why events have taken place. This is called the *cause-and-effect relationship*.
Consider the following statements:

- World War II was the *cause* of the founding of the United Nations because the world's nations realized that a third world war would be a catastrophe.

- The creation of the United Nations was one of the *effects* of World War II.

You should also understand that the cause of one event may be the effect of another:

- The rise of Napoleon as emperor of France was an *effect* of the French Revolution.

- Napoleon's rule was the *cause* of wars in Europe.

Ask yourself (a) what past events caused the event you are studying to take place and (b) what the later effects of that event were. Thus, you will realize that history appears to flow from one topic to another, and that no event occurs in isolation.

II. REGENTS EXAMINATION, PART I: MULTIPLE CHOICE

The Regents examination is a three-hour test consisting of three parts: 50 multiple-choice questions, worth 55 percent of the score; one thematic essay, worth 15 percent; and one document-based question and essay (DBQ), worth 30 percent.

STANDARD MULTIPLE CHOICE. Most multiple-choice questions are like those you have regularly answered in high school. A question or statement requires completion. There are four possible choices. Here are strategies for answering standard multiple-choice questions:

- Read all the choices. There are often one or more "decoy" choices. That is, they look as if they might be correct but, in fact are not. Decoys often precede the correct answer, and the careless student will be tempted to choose incorrectly.

- Note such words as "all," "none," "always," and "never," which often signal an incorrect choice. Such words allow for no exceptions.

- Note key terms that often point to the correct answer.

- Weed out incorrect choices by the process of elimination.

- Do not get stalled by a particular question. First answer the questions you know. Then attack questions that you can narrow down to two choices. Tackle the rest of the questions last.

Now put these strategies to work by answering the following multiple-choice questions from past Regents examinations:

Question 1
Which statement best reflects the effect of mercantilism on the colonies in Latin America?

1. Markets in the colonies were closed to manufactured goods from the home country.

2. Land was distributed equally between the social classes.

3. Industries in the colonies manufactured the majority of finished goods for the home country.

4. The wealth of the colonial power increased at the expense of the colony.

If you know that mercantilism means that colonies existed for the benefit of the home country, you will eliminate choices 1 and 2.

If you understand that colonies were sought for natural resources and markets, you will realize that the home country did not want colonies to develop competitive factory systems, and you will eliminate choice 3.

Choice 4 is the best answer because it most closely describes the goals of mercantilism and its effect on colonies.

Question 2

During India's independence movement, Mohandas Gandhi's boycott of British-made products was effective because the British considered India a major

1. shipping center

2. industrial center

3. market for manufactured goods

4. source of mineral resources.

You need to know that "boycott" means consumers' refusal to use or buy a product. Choice 2—that India is an industrial center—is unlikely because the British wanted to sell manufactured goods in India.

Note that in choice 4, "mineral resources" is another term for "raw materials." They are needed to manufacture consumer products but do not directly affect the buying or selling of a product; therefore, choice 4 cannot be the correct answer.

Choices 1 and 3 both concern the distribution or selling of British goods. Which of the two is most directly related to selling products to consumers? Choice 1 uses the word "shipping," which involves the movement of goods but has little to do with a boycott. Choice 3 uses the word "market," which concerns the buying and selling of goods, which would be directly affected by a boycott. Therefore, choice 3 is the better choice.

MULTIPLE CHOICE AND INTERPRETING GRAPHICS. Some multiple-choice questions ask you to interpret an illustration, a graph, or a chart. This requires the development of special skills, such as identifying the meaning of symbols, the artist's point of view, and the underlying significance of figures in a scene. The following cartoon and questions are from the August 1998 Regents examination:

Question 3

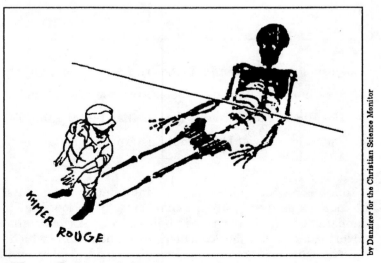

by Danziger for the Christian Science Monitor

The main idea of the cartoon is that the Khmer Rouge

1. is responsible for the genocide practiced in Cambodia in the past

2. is most responsible for the problem of overpopulation in Cambodia today

3. continued to force an agrarian economy on Cambodia

4. has widespread popular support.

The purpose of the question is to determine if you understand the cartoonist's idea, not to see if you know in detail about the Khmer Rouge in Cambodia. The cartoon contains the following components:

(a) a soldier turning to look at his shadow; (b) the label "Khmer Rouge" near the soldier; (c) a shadow looking like a skeleton. (You should recognize that the skeleton probably symbolizes death.)

Reread the four choices. The process of elimination should lead you to several conclusions.

There is no obvious relationship between symbols in the cartoon and overpopulation (choice 2).

The sinister nature of the cartoon suggests that the Khmer Rouge has little support from the people (choice 4).

The remaining choices test your understanding of key vocabulary words—"genocide" (choice 1) and "agrarian" (choice 3). "Agrarian," which relates to agriculture, has no obvious connection with the cartoon. But if you know that "genocide" means the deliberate destruction of a group of people by those in power, you will make a connection between such a policy and the skeleton in the cartoon. Thus, choice 1 is the most logical answer.

Now consider the following chart and questions, also from the August 1998 Regents:

Question 4

Which conclusion about world oil reserves can best be drawn from the information in the chart?

World Oil Reserves by Region and Availability		
Region	**Oil Reserves** (billion barrels)	**Availability** (number of years)
Middle East	660	110
Latin America	125	51
Former Soviet Union & Eastern Europe	60	13
Africa	59	28
Asia, Australia, & New Zealand	47	20
North America	42	10
Western Europe	18	13
World	1,011	44

Source: *State of the World 1991*, W. W. Norton

1. Most of the people in Latin America are employed by the oil industry.

2. Searching for alternative fuel sources is no longer necessary.

3. The Middle East accounts for less than half the world's oil reserves.

4. The former Soviet Union and Eastern Europe have fewer years of oil reserves available than Africa does.

To interpret the chart, study the information it presents. Note the title, column heads, and date in the source line. specifically, the chart lists: (a) various regions of the world and the world as a whole; (b) number of barrels in reserve (in billions) for each; (c) availability of the reserves in years for each.

Next examine the four conclusions and determine which one best answers the question.

Conclusion 1: There is no information about employment in the chart.

Conclusion 2: This must be untrue because the chart shows that oil reserves are limited.

Conclusion 3: This must be untrue because the chart shows that the Middle East has 660 billion barrels in reserve, more than half of the world's reserves of 1,011 billion barrels.

Conclusion 4: The chart shows that the former Soviet Union and Eastern Europe have only 13 years of oil availability left, whereas Africa has 28 years. Therefore, conclusion 4 is true.

Here is a map question from the January 1999 Regents examination:

Question 5

Which conclusion is valid, based on the information shown on the map?

European Imperialism in Africa, 1914

1. All of North Africa was controlled by France.

2. Belgium was the last country to establish colonies in Africa

3. The Union of South Africa was settled by the Spanish in the early 20th century.

4. Great Britain and France controlled most of Africa.

Conclusion 1: The words *all* and *never* usually disqualify an answer. For example, although France controlled much of northwestern Africa, other nations also controlled parts of northern Africa.

Conclusion 2: There are no dates for colonization on the map, which disqualifies this answer.

Conclusion 3: The map shows that Great Britain controlled South Africa in the early 20th century, which disqualifies this answer.

Conclusion 4: A view of the entire map and key shows that this is the valid conclusion to be drawn from information on the map and, therefore, the correct answer.

III. REGENTS EXAMINATION, PART II: THEMATIC ESSAY

The thematic essay focuses on a theme spanning several periods or linking several events in Global History and Geography. It asks you to show how well you understand the theme's importance and its role in the course. Examples of themes include nationalism, imperialism, social mobility, diversity, geography, technology, ethnocentrism,, cultural diffusion, warfare, and peacekeeping.

The following thematic essay, for example, might appear on the Regents examination:

Theme
Nationalism. Throughout Global History and Geography, nationalism has had positive and negative effects.

Task
Define "nationalism." Select *one* country studied and give specific historical examples of nationalism within that country. Describe a situation where nationalism was *either* a positive *or* a negative force in the country's history.

Suggestions: You may use any nation studied in Global History and Geography except the United States. Consider Venezuela (19th century), Germany (19th and 20th centuries), China (early 20th century), India (20th century), Kenya (post–World War II), and the Balkans (late 20th century). You are *not* limited to these suggestions.

Key words and phrases in the task directions are: define, select *one* country, give specific historical examples, describe a positive *or* negative situation. By jotting them down, you create a checklist for organizing the thematic essay.

Write the thematic essay as you would write any essay in class or for homework. Observe the following guidelines:

A. Analyze the Question

Be sure you understand the theme and directions by reviewing key words and phrases.

B. Organize the Information

Add the general information you plan to write about to your checklist to create an "instant outline." For the sample thematic essay, you might include:

- definition of nationalism: love of country, desire to see one's country powerful and successful, patriotism

- one country: Germany

- specific historical examples: Bismarck and unification (blood and iron), Adolf Hitler and nazism

- positive *or* negative situation: nazism led to World War II and the Holocaust, division of Germany.

Notice how you have expanded your checklist with ideas to flesh out your essay. The outline should take only about five minute.

C. Develop the Thesis

Use the theme or task of the thematic essay to create an original thesis, such as the following thought-provoking one: "Although nationalism may have both positive and negative effects on a nation, in Germany the effect was so negative that it resulted in World War II, the Holocaust, and, finally, the division of Germany itself."

D. Write the Introductory Paragraph

The introductory paragraph should include the thesis statement and background of your essay. Introduce examples taken from the instant outline and to be used in the essay. Include the definition of nationalism and two examples to be discussed: Bismarck's policy of blood and iron and Hitler's nazism.

E. Write the Supporting Paragraphs

These paragraphs *explain* your answer with facts, details, and examples. Elaborate on the facts from your instant outline. Be as specific as possible. *Do not* use meaningless facts or information unrelated to your theme.

F. Write the Concluding Paragraph

The concluding paragraph should restate the thesis in a fresh, interesting manner and briefly summarize the essay. A good concluding paragraph to the sample thematic essay would be: "German nationalism was based on warfare. This nationalism, which started with Bismarck's policy of blood and iron, ultimately led to Hitler's nazism, the Holocaust, World War II, and the division of Germany from the mid-1940s until the early 1990s."

G. Check the Essay

If time permits, reread your essay to correct grammar, spelling, punctuation, sentence structure, and errors in fact. Does your essay read clearly and make sense? Rereading the essay can improve your grade for the thematic essay portion of the Regents examination.

GENERIC THEMATIC ESSAY RUBRIC.   Those who score your thematic essay will use the following guidelines, or scoring scale:

5   Shows clear and deep understanding of theme.
Addresses all aspects of task.
Shows ability to analyze, compare, and contrast issues and events.
Writes cohesive [unified], cogent [convincing] essay that uses rich array of detail.
Summarizes key arguments and points made in essay.
Includes strong introduction and conclusion.

4   Understands theme and defines it.
Discusses most aspects of task.
Theme is supported with accurate facts, examples, and details, but is somewhat uneven in
    treatment.
Analyzes issues and events.
Writes well-developed essay that includes many details.
Includes good introduction and conclusion.

3   Defines theme acceptably.
Fails to address all aspects of task.
Minimal factual errors are present.
Analyzes issues and events, but not in depth.
Writes coherent essay with some detail.
Restates theme in introduction and concludes with simple restatement of task.

2   Attempts to address theme, but uses vague and/or inaccurate information.
Develops faulty analysis of theme. Narrative goes off on tangents; essay lacks focus.
Introduction and/or conclusion is vague or missing.

1   Shows limited understanding of theme and omits concrete examples; details are weak or missing.
Lacks analysis of issues and events beyond stating vague and/or inaccurate facts.
Strings random facts together in weak narrative that lacks focus.
Has no introduction or conclusion.

0   Fails to address theme.
Includes so many indecipherable [unreadable] words that response makes no sense.
Blank paper.

IV. REGENTS EXAMINATION, PART III: DOCUMENT-BASED QUESTIONS AND ESSAY (DBQ)

This essay calls for you to answer a general question after interpreting a variety of documents about the topic (maps, pictures, cartoons, graphs, charts). A specific question on each document tests your understanding of it. Here is a sample DBQ:

PART A: DOCUMENT-BASED QUESTION. The following documents relate to the positive and negative effects of imperialism. Examine each document carefully and then answer the question that follows it.

Document 1

"Modern progressive nations lying in the temperate zone seek to control 'garden spots' in the tropics [mainly in Africa, Latin America, and Asia]. Under [the progressive nations'] direction these places can yield tropical produce. In return, the progressive nations bring to the people of those garden spots the foodstuffs and manufactures they need. [Progressive nations] develop the territory by building roads, canals, railways, and telegraph. They can establish schools and newspapers for the colonies [and] give these people the benefit of other blessings of civilization which they have not the means of creating themselves."

—O. P. Austin, "Does Colonization Pay?" *The Forum*

1. According to the author, what benefits did the colonies receive from the "modern progressive nations"?

Document 2

"Learning civilized ways is hard work."

2. What did colonization mean for the people of a region that was a colony?

Document 3

"To begin with, there are the exporters and manufacturers of certain goods used in the colonies. The makers of cotton and iron goods have been very much interested in imperialism. Their business interests demand that colonial markets should be opened and developed and that foreign competitors should be shut out. Such aims require political control and imperialism.

"Finally, the most powerful of all business groups are the bankers. Banks make loans to colonies and backward countries for building railways and steamship lines. They also make loans to colonial plantation owners, importers, and exporters.

"The imperialist business interests have powerful allies. Military and naval leaders believe strongly in extending the white man's rule over the 'inferior races.' To this company may be added another element—the missionary. Missionaries went forth to preach a kingdom beyond this world. But they often found themselves the builders of very earthly empires. . . . Last, but by no means least, let us add politicians to our list of empire builders."

—*Imperialism and World Politics,* Parker T. Moore, 1926

3. Who are the empire builders described in this passage?

Document 4

"When the whites came to our country, we had the land and they had the Bible. Now we have the Bible and they have the land."

—African proverb

4. How did the Africans feel about the missionaries?

Document 5

The White Man killed my father,
My father was proud.
The White Man seduced my mother,
My mother was beautiful.
The White Man burnt my brother beneath the noonday sun,
My brother was strong.
His hands red with black blood
The White Man turned to me;
And in the Conqueror's voice said,
"Boy! a chair, a napkin, a drink."

—*An Anthology of West African Verse,* David Diop, 1957

5. What were some negative affects on Africa of imperialism?

Document 6

"Colonialism's greatest misdeed was to have tried to strip us of our responsibility in conducting our own affairs and convince us that our civilization was nothing less than savagery, thus giving us complexes which led to our being branded as irresponsible and lacking in self-confidence. . . . "The colonial powers had assimilated each of their colonies into their own economy. "Our continent possesses tremendous reserves of raw material and they, together with its potential sources of power, give it excellent conditions for industrialization. . . . "

—Sekou Toure, West African nationalist, 1962

6. In 1962, what was the response of this West African nationalist to years of colonialism?

Document 7

This German cartoon, published in the early 20th century, is entitled "Thus colonize the English."

7. What is the point of view of this cartoonist about European imperialism?

PART B: ESSAY. Evaluate *both* the positive and negative effects of imperialism.

Organize your essay. An introductory paragraph should state your position The next paragraphs should develop your position and lead to a conclusion. Include specific historical details and refer to the documents you analyzed in Part A. You may include additional information from your knowledge of Global History and Geography.

Approach the DBQ as you would any other essay question. Use the same guidelines as for the thematic essay, with one addition: Add references from *most* of the documents.

Look again at the seven documents in the sample DBQ. (Most DBQs have between six and nine documents.) Notice that there are two cartoons. The DBQ usually includes two graphic documents—cartoons, tables, charts, graphs, or pictures. Note that the documents contain a variety of ideas and perspectives on the topic—in this case, imperialism. Some documents may be contradictory. This is not done to confuse you but to assess how well you analyze different points of view. (When you prepare your essay response, you will need to account for some of the differences of opinion.)

Now look at the questions following the documents. They test your understanding of the main idea of each document. All questions must be answered. Your answers may help you organize your essay response.

GENERIC DOCUMENT-BASED QUESTION RUBRIC. Those who score your document-based questions and essay will use the following guidelines, or scoring scale:

5 Thoroughly addresses all aspects of task by accurately interpreting most documents while incorporating related outside information.

Discusses all aspects of task and richly supports discussion with accurate facts, examples, and details.

Weighs importance, reliability, and validity of evidence.

Analyzes conflicting perspectives in documents. Weaves documents into body of essay.

Includes strong introduction and conclusion.

4 Addresses most aspects of task by utilizing most documents and incorporating limited outside information that is somewhat uneven in treatement.

Discusses most aspects of task and supports thesis with accurate facts, examples, and details.

Recognizes that all evidence is not equally reliable and valid.

Reflects conflicting perspectives and complexity of task. Discussion of documents is somewhat descriptive and analytical.

Includes good introduction and conclusion.

3 Addresses some aspects of task by utilizing some documents but incorporating little or no outside information.

Attempts to discuss some aspects of task, supporting discussion with some facts and examples.

Minimal factual errors are present.

Does not always recognize difference in reliability and vailidity of evidence.

Acknowledges conflicting perspectives. Discussion of documents is more descriptive than analytical.

Paraphrasing of documents is apparent.

Restates theme in introduction and concludes with simple restatement of task.

2 Attempts to address task with limited use of documents. No outside information apparent.

Shows little recognition of different aspects of task, with little discussion or use of factual knowledge.

Does not recognize differences in reliability and validity of evidence.

Reiterates [repeats] contents of documents. Only one perspective is acknowledged.

Has vague or no introduction and/or conclusion.

1 Demonstrates very limited understanding of task.

Shows little or no recognition of different aspects of task. Contains factual errors.

Fails to use or vaguely refers to documents.

Has no introduction or conclusion.

0 Fails to address the question.
No response.
Blank paper.

Note the requirements for category **5.** All aspects of the task must be addressed, the documents must be accurately interpreted, and "outside information" (information in addition to the documents) must be included. Details must be given and explained and evidence weighed. In other words, you must "read between the lines" of the document. Ask yourself how the writer or cartoonist feels. Is there a personal opinion or bias evident, or is the writer or cartoonist being fair? Finally, a strong thesis and conclusion are musts.

V. PRACTICAL PLAN FOR SUCCESS ON THE REGENTS EXAMINATION

A. Initial Preparation

There is no substitute for adequate, regular preparation. Your teacher will probably review highlights of the past two years of Global History and Geography. But this is not enough. In-class review merely suggests what you need to study and know.

Allow yourself four to six weeks of study time. It is better to study half an hour daily over this period than to cram for many hours several days before the examination. To review effectively, try the following suggestions:

- Separate your studying into separate historical sections or periods. On average, two to four days should be spent on each one.

- Plan a daily study schedule. This will help you adequately cover the entire Global History and Geography course.

- Spend a short time reviewing the previous day's work to reinforce what you have already covered.

- Study when you are alert rather than after exercise or a big meal.

- Avoid distractions (television, radio, telephone, the Internet).

- Take a five-minute break each study hour to help you stay fresh and retain what you have learned.

B. Knowing How and What to Study

Take a practice Regents examination before you begin your course of study. This will help you identify areas of study that need special attention. After reviewing for several weeks, take a different Regents examination. How far have you progressed, and what material still needs more review? (Your teacher should be able to supply you with past Regents examinations.)

C. Knowing the Examination Format

Use the practice Regents examinations to familiarize yourself with how each part of the test is structured. Understanding the form of each group of questions and how best to answer each one will help you maximize your score.

D. Knowing Important Vocabulary Terms and Names

You will not remember every term and name discussed over the past two years, but you should be familiar with important terms that apply to all periods of Global History and Geography, as well as terms and names related to particular historical eras. As you proceed through your course of study, make a list of these terms and names for periodic review.

Here are some tips for identifying such terms and names:

- **Check off familiar terms.** The number of them that you already know will boost your confidence.

- **Review eras for which you know the fewest terms.** Your check-off will identify areas in which you need more help. The text glossary will give you basic definitions.

- **Make appropriate connections.** Linking related words, names, and terms is an effective way to reinforce the details in a large amount of material.

- **Do not try to learn every term.** Trying to memorize everything is frustrating and practically impossible. Build a list designed to reacquaint you with key terms in Global History and Geography. The concepts they represent will be likely test subjects.

- **Identifications are more important than definitions.** A definition gives you only the meaning of a term. An identification of a term's historical significance is a building block that will help you link one important concept with another.

E. Final Preparation

You have done everything possible to prepare for the Regents examination. Now get a good night's sleep. Arriving well rested at the testing room is the best preparation at this point. Last-minute cramming will be of little or no help and will prove harmful if it makes you too tired to perform well.

GLOSSARY

abacus first adding machine, invented by Sung Dynasty mathematicians

abolitionist in United States, pre–Civil War reformer opposed to slavery

abstract expressionism style of painting attempting to cause emotional responses by nontraditional, nonrepresentational means

acid rain pollution caused when industrial and exhaust fumes in air dissolve in water vapor and fall as precipitation

Age of Reason European period (1600s–1700s) when scholars believed that all human problems could be cured by reason; Enlightenment

agriculture farming

alien person without citizenship in country of residence

alliance agreement between two or more nations to aid one another in wartime

analysis separating facts and ideas to understand issue or problem

animism religious belief in which humans try to make environment safe and productive by pleasing spirits in nature

annulment authorized dissolution of marriage by Roman Catholic Church

anthropologist scientist who studies past and present human societies

anti-Semitism hostility to Jews and discrimination against them

antibiotic substance produced by one microorganism that can destroy another one

apartheid policy of strict racial segregation formerly enforced by white minority government of South Africa against blacks and other racial groups

apostle one of 12 men who traveled with Jesus and helped in his teachings

appeasement policy of making concessions to aggressors to maintain peace

apprentice young person learning trade and paying for training by shop labor

archetype in psychoanalysis, unconscious pool of symbols and patterns common to all humans

archipelago group of many islands

aristocracy rule by nobles

armistice temporary agreement to stop fighting

arms race struggle by rival nations to surpass each other in military might; specifically, Soviet-U.S. competition to build more nuclear weapons with greater destructive power

artifact physical remains of culture, such as tools, clothes, money, or food

assimilation gradual process by which minorities and immigrant adopt majority's culture

astrolabe navigational instrument used to determine latitude and time of day

atheism belief that God does not exist

automatic teller machine (ATM) computerized machine to perform basic banking functions and facilitate on-line banking at home

bakuhan Japanese system of government devised by Tokugawa shoguns to limit power of daimyos

balance of power political strategy of preventing one nation from becoming stronger than any other

balance of trade difference between nation's exports and imports

barter trading goods and services one has for those one wants

Bedouin member of nomadic people of Arabian desert

bill of exchange document authorizing foreign banker to pay money to local business agents of distant Muslim merchant

blacklisting employer tactic of weakening union by circulating names of "undesirable" employees

blitzkrieg lightning war; specifically, violent, surprise German offensive during World War II, characterized by speed and mobility

bourgeoisie business, or middle, class

boycott refusal to buy product in order to force change in policy

Brahmin priest of ancient Aryan civilization in India who shared power with king; member of highest Hindu caste

bubonic plague pandemic, deadly disease of 14th century, spread from Asia to Europe by ships carrying flea-infested rats; Black Death

budget deficit gap existing when government spending exceeds income

bureaucracy large group working directly for government

Bushido in feudal Japan, code of chivalry for samurai

caliph descendant of Muhammad and local ruler within Muslim Empire; also, Muhammad's fatherin-law and successor Abu Bakr

caliphate central government of Muslim Empire consisting of caliph and subordinate officers

capital money used for investment

capitalism economic system in which means of production are privately owned and businesses compete for profits; free enterprise

capitalist investor in business

caravel triangular-sailed, three-masted ship of 16th and 17th centuries, capable of great speed against wind

cartel price-fixing drug monopoly

cartography mapmaking

cash crop crop grown for sale rather than private use

caudillo Latin American military dictator

chivalry in feudal system, code requiring knight to be loyal, brave, courteous, merciful, generous, and charitable

city charter document recognizing a city's independence of manorial system and right to self-government

city-state independently governed city and surrounding farms and villages

civilization large group of cultures with high degree of social and technological development

clan group of related families

cloning process by which organism is reproduced from only one parent without fertilization

cold war period of Soviet-U.S. rivalry and suspicion (1945–1991), marked by spying, hostile propaganda, arms race, and race in space

collective bargaining negotiations between labor and management

collectivization Soviet takeover and consolidation of farmland and use of forced peasant labor

Columbian Exchange global interchange of people, animals, plants, ideas, and diseases that began after European discovery and conquest of Americas

command economy system in which government controls industry and agriculture by deciding on producers, products, quantities, and prices

commercial paid radio or television advertisement to promote product or service

Commercial Revolution change from feudalism and manorial system to unregulated business and trade

common law English legal code based on written decisions of traveling judges in 12th century

Commonwealth English republic under Oliver Cromwell

communism political system in which government controls all economic activity and often incites revolution elsewhere to extend its sway

compass navigational instrument with magnetic needle pointing north, used to determine directions on Earth's surface

concentration camp isolated area of confinement for victims of racism, refugees, political prisoners, and prisoners or war

Confucianism philosophy of Confucius, based on respect for parents, ancestors, teachers, and rulers

congress formal meeting of delegates to discuss and act on some question

conquistador Spanish military leader in conquest of Americas

conservative person supporting tradition, social stability, and lesser role for government

constitution written plan of government

consul one of two highest elected officials in Roman Republic, who enforced laws, supervised administration, and commanded wartime army

consumer one buying goods and services

containment U.S. cold-war policy of preventing Soviet power and influence from spreading to non-Communist nations

Continental System Napoleon's banning of trade with Britain by other nations

cottage industry manufacture of craft items at home

creole Latin American colonist born to Spanish parents

critical-thinking skills methods by which historians use evidence to reach conclusions: analysis, inference, judgment, hypothesis, generalization, prediction

Cro-Magnon early human linking Neanderthals to modern humans

Crusades religious wars of 11th to 13th century, fought by Europeans seeking to regain Holy Land from Turks

cubism style of painting that breaks an object into geometric components so that it seems to be seen from several angles

cultural diffusion one culture's borrowing of another culture's useful or attractive elements

culture group's essential way of life—technology, beliefs, economy, government

culture of cities historical belief that cities are prime characteristic of civilization

cuneiform Sumerian writing system of wedge-shaped marks pressed into wet clay with pointed stick

currency something used as medium of exchange, such as money

czar absolute monarch ("caesar") of Russia

dadism French artistic movement that ridiculed traditional ideas of beauty, truth, and order

daimyo in feudal Japan, large landholder in control of local affairs

deductive reasoning generalization by inductive reasoning, followed by predictions about particular cases, tested by observation and experiment

deforestation clearing of forests, as by lumbering, in order to use land in other ways

deism belief that God planned orderly universe and left it to run on its own, and that human reason is path to all truth

demand quantity of goods or services wanted at fair prices

democracy government in which people rule directly or through elected representatives

democratic socialism system in which free-market and command economies are combined

desertification process by which once-fertile land becomes desert

détente Brezhnev's policy of relaxing tensions between United States and Soviet Union

Diet Japanese parliament

divine right belief by 17th-century European monarchs that God had appointed them to rule their subjects

DNA genetic code to how an organism is made and operates

document written record, such as book, report, letter, or government paper

domestic system manufacture of goods at home, whereby capitalist pays for raw materials and labor and sells products for profit

downsizing elimination of jobs and increase in retirements in order to lower business expenses

Druid priest or learned man of Ancient Celts

duma Russian parliament

dynasty succession of rulers belonging to same family

$E = mc^2$ Einstein's formula summarizing atom's capability of releasing enormous energy

Eastern civilization inclusive cultures of Asia and islands of Pacific Ocean

emir territorial governor within Muslim Empire responsible for maintaining army and collecting taxes

empire many different lands and cultures under one government

enclosure system 18th-century agricultural system in which large landowners excluded small farmers from their fields in order to grow crops for profit

encomienda system forced labor inflicted on Native Americans by landlords in New Spain

Enlightenment European period (1600s–1700s) when scholars believed that all human problems could be cured by reason; Age of Reason

ephor one of five elected Spartan officials who weighed king's actions and controlled education and slave system

epic long poem about legendary or historical hero, originally passed down orally

epigraph inscription on monument or building

escalation continuing increase in number of troops engaged in war

estate one of three political division in 18th-century France: clergy; nobles; professional people, peasants, and laborers

ethnic cleansing Serbian policy to eliminate Muslim populations of Bosnia and Kosovo

ethnocentrism culture that feels superior and refuses to allow foreign influences

Eurasia Europe and Asia considered as one landmass

evolution natural process by which new forms of plants and animals come into being

excommunication legal authority of pope to prevent person from attending church, confessing sins, or receiving communion

existentialism philosophy concerned with plight of individuals who take responsibility for their acts without knowing what is good and evil

expressionism style of painting depicting subjective emotions and reactions aroused by objects and events

extraterritorial rights agreement that foreign residents in country will be tried in their own courts by their own laws

fascism government characterized by militarism, extreme nationalism, and one-party dictatorship

Fertile Crescent land curving from eastern Mediterranean to Persian Gulf and watered by Tigris and Euphrates rivers

feudalism medieval system of government based on pledges of loyalty by less powerful in return for land and protection by more powerful

first world during cold war, Western capitalist countries and Japan

flagellant 14th-century Roman Catholic zealot who inflicted self-punishment by whipping, criticized Church, and often assumed unauthorized clerical role

free enterprise competitive capitalism

generalization making statement of opinion that is not particular or specific

genetic engineering manipulation of DNA to change traits or produce organisms

genocide mass killing of national, ethnic, or religious group

genome entire genetic material of organism; genetic script

geocentric theory belief that sun and planets revolve around Earth

glasnost Gorbachev's policy to grant Soviet citizens increased freedom of speech and press

Glorious Revolution establishment by British Parliament in 1689 of limited monarchy of William and Mary

glyphs writing system of several Mesoamerican cultures, consisting of symbols and pictures of objects

Gothic architectural style characterized by thin stone walls, high ceilings, large windows of stained glass, pointed arches, tall towers, and flying buttresses

graphics art, architecture, sculpture, jewelry, and interior decoration

Great Schism 11th-century split between Eastern and Western branches of Christian Church

Greco-Roman civilization blending of Greek and Roman cultures of Classical Age

Greek fire Byzantine weapon consisting of chemical mixture ignited and aimed at enemy targets

Green Revolution after 1940s, program aimed at developing more productive strains of corn, rice, and other grains in and for developing nations

greenhouse effect predicted change in world climate caused by excessive amounts of carbon dioxide building up in atmosphere

grid system of crisscrossed straight lines, as in city street plan

gross domestic product (GDP) annual market value of country's goods and services

guerrilla warfare surprise raids by small bands of fighters

guild medieval organization to protect businesspeople's interests and regulate business practices

haiku Japanese poem of 17 syllables divided into three lines

Hegira Muhammad's flight from Mecca to Medina

heliocentric theory belief that Earth and other planets revolve around sun

Hellenistic civilization Greek culture of Classical Age, enriched by contact with Egypt, Mesopotamia, Persia, and India

helot state slave in ancient Sparta

heresy rejection by baptized Roman Catholic of Church's revealed truth; proclamation of ideas not approved by Church

heretic baptized Roman Catholic who rejects Church's revealed truth

hierarchy system of ranking social, political, and religious officials

hieroglyphics ancient Egyptian writing system using pictures to represent sounds, words, and ideas

Holocaust systematic killing of Jews and other minorities by German officials during World War II

Homo sapiens early human who differed from modern humans; Neanderthal

Homo sapiens sapiens modern human or direct ancestor

humanism Renaissance movement to improve life through study of classical literature and personal experience

human rights right of people everywhere to fair treatment by governments and free expression of political opinion without fear of imprisonment, torture, or death

hypothesizing stating idea or theory and testing whether it is fact

icon religious image painted on wood and used in devotions

igloo Inuit shelter made of snow

immediate cause (of war) contemporary event that helps trigger warfare

imperialism policy of extending nation's political and economic dominance over foreign territory or country

impressionism style of painting that attempts to show effect of light on objects

indemnity fine paid as compensation for loss or damage

indentured servant person agreeing to work for certain number of years in exchange for passage to America

inductive reasoning generalization based on observing a few specific cases

indulgence purchased promise, authorized by Roman Catholic Church, that person's stay in purgatory will be limited

infant mortality death of children

inference noting facts or ideas to reach conclusion

inferiority complex psychoanalytic theory that people with poor opinions of themselves cannot adjust properly to society

inflation constant rise in prices

information superhighway multiple paths through which computerized information flows

intendant in 17th-century France, royal representative of monarch, with full power to control country district

interchangeable parts separate elements of manufactured product that are made exactly alike to facilitate assembly and repair

interdependence inevitable impact of one nation's financial and trading actions on those of other nations

interdiction legal authority of early popes to punish monarch by preventing any religious service in kingdom except baptism and last rights

Internet network of computers connected by modems and telephone lines to service providing information on almost any subject

joint-stock company organization in which merchants buy shares and resulting capital is invested in business projects

judgment weighing evidence to form opinion

junta postrevolutionary governing group

kabuki Japanese form of drama—ritual acting, dancing, music, and colorful costumes

kachina in Pueblo religion, spirit of god that lived with humans half the year

kayak one- or two-person Inuit boat

kiva underground room used by Anasazi for religious rituals

knight in feudal system, mounted nobleman achieving special military rank after service as page and squire

labor union organization of workers seeking to raise wages and improve working conditions

laissez-faire economic theory that business competition should not be regulated by governments

lay investiture appointment of bishop by nonmember of clergy, such as king

legitimacy recognition of hereditary monarchy's right to rule

liberal person supporting efforts to make government more democratic

limited resources natural sources of wealth

literature poetry, stories, and myths revealing human thoughts, beliefs, values, and religion

loess fertile yellow soil

long-term cause (of war) factor that develops over time and eventually leads to war

lunar calendar system for dividing year according to phases of moon

mandarin official of Tang Dynasty tested for talent and memory by difficult civil service examination

mandate authority to command or rule

manor in the feudal system, lord's house, land, and workers

manorial system in feudal system, economic arrangement by which peasants and serfs were bound to lord's land and required to work it

market economy system in which individuals and businesses decide what to produce and sell and for how much

martyr person put to death for religious beliefs

mass-production system manufacturing process in which each worker in group makes only one part for multiple-part item

matriarchy family in which descent is traced through females

mechanistic worldview belief that universe obeys consistent laws and humans are capable of discovering those laws

mercantilism economic theory that colonies exist to enrich home country: colonies supply raw materials, which home country uses to make goods to be sold in colonies for profit

messiah In Judaism, descendant of David who will be king and savior of Jews

mestizo Latin American colonist born of Spanish and Indian parents

microchip tiny bit of silicon containing complex of components for conducting electric signals

midwife woman trained to deliver babies

militarism policy glorifying nation's armed forces and aggressive spirit

moat water-filled ditch surrounding castle walls and serving as first line of defense

modem device allowing one computer to communicate with another over telephone line

monarchy rule by king or queen

monastery religious center where monks live, meditate, work, and teach

monopoly exclusive control over supply of product or service

monotheism belief in one god

mosaic Byzantine wall or floor decorations made of colorful inlaid stones

mujahadin Afghan guerrilla force; Islamic warriors

mummification process perfected in ancient Egypt by which corpse is preserved with herbs, oils, and linen wrappings

nationalism feelings of cultural pride in and loyalty and patriotism to one's native land

natural law Stoic idea that laws ruling humans should conform to nature and needs of humans

natural rights theory that people are born with certain rights, such as of liberty and property, and that governments are formed to protect those rights

nazism political and economic system of Germany under Hitler, characterized by totalitarianism, socialism, ethnocentrism, and absolute dictatorship

Neanderthal early human who differed from modern humans; Homo sapiens

Neolithic Revolution developing technology of New Stone Age (6000–3000 B.C.)

nerve growth factor (NGF) brain hormone

neurosis mental disturbance characterized by person's loss of contact with reality and concurrent awareness of disability

nomadic society culture group on the move in search of food and grazing

nonaggression pact pledge between nations not to attack each other

nuclear fission chain reaction in which heavy nucleus releases enormous energy

nunnery religious center where nuns live, meditate, work, and teach

oasis area of desert with fertile soil watered by underground streams

oligarchy rule by wealthy businesspeople

oral history saga or other form of history memorized and passed on by word of mouth

page in feudal system, young male servant in training for knighthood

Pan-Germanism movement in Germany to protect all German-speaking people in Europe

Pan-Slavism movement of ethnic identity and mutual protection by Russian and Eastern European Slavs

parliament assemblage of nobles, clergy, and elected commoners called together to make nation's laws; (*cap.*) two-house British legislative body

passive resistance nonviolent opposition to British rule in India, marked by refusal to buy Britain's goods, serve in its army, pay its taxes, or obey its laws

pasteurization process of heating food and beverages in order to kill dangerous bacteria

patriarchy family in which descent is through males and father heads household

patrician wealthy landowner in ancient Rome

patron wealthy person who hires professional services of artists and rewards them generously

Pax Mongolia period of prosperity and peace in Eurasia during reign of Kublai Khan

Pax Romana 200-year period beginning in 27 B.C. during which Roman Empire experienced peace, security, and cultural accomplishments

peninsulare person born in Spain and eligible for high position in its Latin American colonies

peon poor Latin American laborer of Indian, African, or mixed heritage

perestroika Gorbachev's policy to make Soviet economy more efficient

periodization method used by historians to study how various cultures of same period differed and interacted

pharaoh absolute ruler of ancient Egypt

pilgrimage holy journey

plebeian in ancient Rome, member of class of small farmers, tradespeople, craftsworkers, and debtors

pogrom organized massacre of helpless people, particularly Jews

polis (*pl.* **poleis**) independent city-state of ancient Greece

politics art or science of government

polygamy having more than one spouse

polytheism belief in many gods

post-traumatic stress disorder (PTSD) condition characterized by nightmares, irritability, depression, and guilt, caused by stressful experience; battle fatigue

postimpressionism style of painting emphasizing form, space, and color rather than actual appearance

potlatch ceremonial feast of Northwest Coast people in which host family sought honor by excessive generosity **predestination** teaching of John Calvin that soul's salvation and eternal life in heaven are determined by God even before birth

prediction using observation, experience, or reasoning to describe future event or result

price amount of money set by seller or offered by buyer as value of something

primacy issue among 4th-century Christians about whether leaders of Western (Roman) Church had more or less authority than emperor in Constantinople

privatization sale of government-owned businesses to independent investors

proletarian member of laboring class

propaganda ideas spread to benefit favored cause or damage opposing one

protectorate country whose ruler is supported by imperialistic power that sets government policy

Protestant any Christian during Renaissance or later who challenged beliefs and practices of Roman Catholic Church

psychoanalysis treatment of neurosis through discussion—free association, reliving of troubling experiences, recall of dreams; "talking cure"

psychotherapy method of treating mental or emotional disorder

purgatory in Roman Catholicism, place where souls of deceased who regret their sins are made worthy of heaven through suffering

quantum very small subdivision of many kinds of energy

racism prejudice and discrimination based on belief that certain races are superior to others

radical one supporting extreme changes in existing government

rationality use of reason

realism artistic expression that attempts to describe or portray life accurately

Reconquist‡ final expulsion in 1492 of Muslims from Spain

Reformation Renaissance-inspired movement demanding reform and change in Roman Catholic Church and leading to creation of Protestant congregations

reincarnation Hindu belief that humans are reborn in new bodies or different forms that indicate whether they led good or evil lives

reparations payments for war damages

republic government in which people elect officials to make and enforce laws

reservation land set aside for use of one or more Native American tribes

Restoration English monarchy under Charles II

resurrection Christian belief that Jesus rose from dead

revolution use or threat of violence to bring about basic changes in government

risorgimento 19th-century unification movement in Italy

Romanesque architectural style characterized by think stone walls, small windows, and rounded arches

romantic style artistic expression employing drama, high emotion, and often fantasy

rule of law responsibility of citizens to obey laws, pay taxes, and take part in civic affairs

sacrament religious ritual such as baptism or confession

saga long historical poem of Scandinavia, originally passed down orally

samurai Japanese knight

sanction ban on trade with country violating international law

satellite (*nation*) in post–World War II era, country dominated by Soviet Union

sati (*also* **suti** *and* **suttee**) in India, ritual suicide in which widow throws herself on husband's funeral pyre

savanna grassy plain

scarcity condition resulting when there is less of something than needed

scientific method Renaissance-inspired system of study—observation, experimentation, repetitive investigation, drawing of conclusions

scientific revolution 18th-century advances in science, mathematics, and medicine

second world during cold war, Communist countries

sectionalism strong attachment and loyalty to region within nation; in United States, regional rivalries leading to Civil War

secularism rejection of religious considerations in favor of day-to-day experience

sepoy native soldier of British-ruled India hired by East India Company

serf in feudal system, member of lowest class, usually bound for life to manor, unable to rise socially, and subject to lord's will

shaman Native American religious leader who spoke to spirits and cured illness with herbs, sweats, and spells on evil spirits

share certificate of part-ownership in company based on amount invested; stock

shari'a Islamic legal code based on legal interpretation of ulema

sheik elected leader of Arabian nomadic tribe

Shi'ite member of dissenting Muslim group believing that caliphs should be descended from Muhammad's blood relative Ali

shogun chief military general of feudal Japan

skald ancient Scandinavian poet-historian

slum rundown, polluted area of crowded tenements built closely together

social contract surrender by members of society of some freedoms in order to best serve interests of entire society

Social Darwinism theory that individuals, social groups, and businesses advance by means of free competition and that stronger will triumph over weaker

socialism form of government with state-regulated economy, restrictions on private property, and even distribution of wealth

solar system organization of heavenly bodies based on Galileo's theory that Earth and other planets move around sun

Spanish Inquisition 15th-century Spanish court that used torture and other severe means to determine whether subjects—in particular, converted Jews and Muslims—were good Roman Catholics

specialization division of economy into distinct kinds of work, such as farming, manufacturing, and trading

specific gravity relative density of object

sphere of influence area dominated by imperialistic foreign power

spontaneous generation disproved theory that living things come from nonliving matter

squire in feudal system, personal servant of knight

suffrage right to vote

sulfanilamide early infection-fighting drug

sultan ruler of Muslim state

Sunnite member of Muslim group believing that caliphs do not have to be blood descendants of Muhammad

superpower in cold-war era, Soviet Union or United States because of enormous military power of each; after cold war, United States

supply quantity of goods or services available at all prices

surplus amount remaining after what is needed has been used up

surrealism artistic movement strongly influenced by dadism and employing hallucinogenic and dreamlike images

tabula rasa in John Locke's philosophy, baby's mind as blank tablet on which rearing and education will record unique human personality

Taliban after 1995, Islamic fundamentalist government of Afghanistan

Taoism philosophy of Lao-tzu, based on living simply and in harmony with nature

tariff tax on imported goods

tenement multilevel dwelling divided into family units of several small rooms

terrorism systematic use of violence to achieve political goals

third world nations in various stages of industrialization; developing nations

tithe religious tax, usually tenth of earnings, collected by early popes from people living on Church land

totalitarianism political dictatorship that controls every aspect of citizens' lives

totem pole elaborately carved wooden post used by Northwest Coast people as memorial, bone depository, or symbol of family pride

traditional economy system that produces basic necessities by farming, herding, or fishing

transistor device that conducts electric signals

tribune in Roman Republic, one of ten officials elected to protect plebeian rights

tribute payment by one ruler or nation to another for protection or as sign of submission

tundra cold zone in high latitudes with no trees and limited vegetation

tyranny rule by single individual with absolute power

umiak Inuit boat capable of carrying load of goods or several people

urbanization rapid growth of country's cities

utopian 19th-century socialist who tried to set up ideal community in which members contributed to and shared in economic success equally

vassal in feudal system, person who pledged loyalty and service to lord or monarch

veto power of tribunes in Roman Republic to reject decisions of consuls and Senate

Western civilization inclusive cultures of Americas and Europe

white-collar worker middle-class wage earner who uses literary and mathematical skills, such as schoolteacher, clerk, or bookkeeper

zemstov in 19th-century Russia, local government elected to manage education, health, and welfare

Zionism movement to establish Jewish state in Palestine

INDEX

GLOBAL HISTORY AND GEOGRAPHY
JANUARY 2014

Part I

Answer all questions in this part.

Directions (1–50): For each statement or question, record on your separate answer sheet the *number* of the word or expression that, of those given, best completes the statement or answers the question.

1 **"Price of Oil Hits Record High"**
  "Tribes Fight Over Control of Natural Resources"
  "Government Rations Goods for Duration of War"

These headlines all relate to the economic concept of

(1) overproduction (3) entrepreneurship
(2) interdependence (4) scarcity

2 Which nation is located on a peninsula?

(1) Brazil (3) Saudi Arabia
(2) Philippines (4) Austria

3 The Indus, Ganges, and Brahmaputra were important to ancient India because they were

(1) high mountain ranges that protected India from invasion
(2) great rivers that flowed through India's fertile northern plain
(3) Aryan gods to whom the priests prayed for rain
(4) ruling dynasties that united the people of Harappa and Mohenjo-Daro

4 What was one of the most important contributions of the Greek city-state of Athens?

(1) development of direct democracy
(2) diffusion of a monotheistic belief system
(3) promotion of the equality of all humans
(4) creation of a writing system using hieroglyphics

5 Which belief system was the basis for the civil service exams given during the Han, Tang, and Song dynasties?

(1) legalism (3) Buddhism
(2) Daoism (4) Confucianism

Base your answer to question 6 on the map below and on your knowledge of social studies.

Source: *Guide to the Essentials*, Prentice Hall
(adapted)

6 Charlemagne's 9th century empire covered territory which today would include the countries of

(1) Poland and Russia
(2) Spain and Portugal
(3) France and Germany
(4) Ireland and the United Kingdom

7 Which statement about the Islamic Golden Age is a fact rather than an opinion?

(1) Islamic medicine was more advanced than Chinese medicine.

(2) Poetry and literature were more important fields of study for Muslims than was mathematics.

(3) Knowledge of astronomy was used by Muslims to fulfill religious obligations.

(4) Islamic philosophies relied less on Greek philosophical masters than on Indian philosophical masters.

8 The early eastern European Slavic civilization at Kiev adopted the Eastern Orthodox religion, the Cyrillic alphabet, and certain styles of art and architecture as a result of

(1) wars with Japan

(2) conquests by Mongol invaders

(3) visits to western European countries

(4) trade with the Byzantine Empire

9 China, Korea, and Japan share cultural similarities in part due to their

(1) clashes with Russian imperialists

(2) shared river systems

(3) contacts through trade

(4) unification under Mongol rule

10 The development of banking during the Commercial Revolution in western Europe was significant because it

(1) provided capital resources to merchants for investment

(2) allowed peasant farmers to finance the construction of new homes

(3) enabled the proletariat to challenge the bourgeoisie

(4) created pensions for retired workers

11 In general, in which direction did the Black Death spread during the 14th century?

(1) from Europe to the Americas

(2) from Africa to Southeast Asia

(3) from Asia to Europe

(4) from the Americas to Asia

12 One result of the Protestant Reformation was

(1) fewer challenges to Church authority

(2) a decline in religious unity in western Europe

(3) the disbanding of the Jesuit order

(4) a weakening of the Inquisition

13 For which achievement is Suleiman the Magnificent best known?

(1) building the Dome of the Rock in Jerusalem

(2) spreading Christianity into the Balkan Peninsula

(3) conquering the Russian capital of Moscow

(4) uniting the Ottoman Empire under an efficient government structure

Base your answer to question 14 on the passage below and on your knowledge of social studies.

… In the 1930s, Sylvanus G. Morley of Harvard, probably the most celebrated Mayanist of his day, espoused [argued for] what is still the best-known theory: The Maya collapsed because they overshot the carrying capacity of their environment. They exhausted their resource base, began to die of starvation and thirst, and fled their cities en masse, leaving them as silent warnings of the perils of ecological hubris [overconfidence]….

— Charles C. Mann, *1491: New Revelations of the Americas Before Columbus*

14 According to this passage, what was a major question Morley was trying to answer about the Mayas in the 1930s?

(1) Why did the Mayas abandon their cities?

(2) What was the structure of the Maya governments?

(3) How did religious beliefs affect the Maya economy?

(4) Which neighboring city-state conquered the Mayas?

15 Which technological development enabled European navigators to determine their location during the Age of Exploration?

(1) lateen sail   (3) cross bow

(2) astrolabe   (4) caravel

16 The Encounter occurred as a result of European explorers crossing the

(1) Atlantic Ocean
(2) Sahara Desert
(3) Andes Mountains
(4) Mediterranean Sea

17 In colonial Spanish America, which system was developed by the Spanish to support plantation agriculture?

(1) barter   (3) domestic
(2) encomienda   (4) guild

18 What happened in Russia as a result of actions taken by Peter the Great?

(1) Russia was weakened by French invasions.
(2) Catholicism was adopted as the state religion.
(3) The Duma was reformed and the serfs were freed.
(4) Russia borrowed Western ideas and expanded its territories.

19 Which heading best completes the partial outline on British history below?

I. _____
   A. Magna Carta
   B. Glorious Revolution
   C. Bill of Rights

(1) Rise of Absolutism
(2) Beginning of Socialism
(3) Challenges to Papal Power
(4) Evolution of Parliamentary Democracy

20 Why is the Enlightenment considered a turning point in world history?

(1) The factory system was used to mass-produce goods.
(2) Martin Luther broke away from the Roman Catholic Church.
(3) Europeans changed their thinking about the role of government.
(4) The Columbian exchange occurred.

21 One way in which Robespierre and Louis XVI of France are similar is that both

(1) were removed from power during the French Revolution
(2) adopted ideas of the Congress of Vienna
(3) implemented policies of religious tolerance
(4) decreased government control of the economy

22 One way in which Toussaint L'Ouverture, Simón Bolívar, and José de San Martín are similar is that they all were

(1) supporters of mercantile policies
(2) leaders of independence movements
(3) democratically elected leaders
(4) industrial labor reformers

23 Which geographic feature most aided England during the Industrial Revolution?

(1) desert climate
(2) natural harbors
(3) mountainous terrain
(4) monsoon winds

24 Mass starvation in Ireland in the 1840s led directly to the

(1) formation of communes
(2) granting of independence
(3) migration of people overseas
(4) usage of petrochemical fertilizers

25 One major reason European countries engaged in imperialism in the late 19th century was to

(1) gain a better understanding of unknown territories
(2) ease tensions with their rivals
(3) develop treatments for diseases
(4) obtain markets for their manufactured goods

26 One way in which Emperor Meiji of Japan and Kemal Atatürk of Turkey are similar is that they both

(1) crushed secessionist movements
(2) worked to modernize their nations
(3) conquered eastern neighboring territories
(4) protested against economic sanctions

Base your answer to question 27 on the poster below and on your knowledge of social studies.

Source: Poster by E. Kealy in Susan R. Grayzel, *Women and the First World War*, Pearson Education

27 This World War I poster is an example of

(1) diversity   (3) toleration
(2) dissent   (4) propaganda

28 Which development occurred in Germany as a result of the terms imposed by the Treaty of Versailles?

(1) Soviet occupation
(2) political instability
(3) overseas expansion
(4) economic prosperity

29 The original goal of Pan-Africanism was to

(1) demand democratic reforms
(2) encourage ethnic rivalry
(3) promote a united Africa
(4) divide Africa into separate countries

30 The establishment of the independent countries of Czechoslovakia, Hungary, and Yugoslavia was the result of

(1) the Franco-Prussian War
(2) the Berlin Conference
(3) World War I
(4) the Munich Pact

31 Which goal was most important to the Indian nationalist movement?

(1) independence from British rule
(2) establishing a laissez-faire economy
(3) forming a totalitarian state
(4) expansion of territory

32 Which geographic factor was most significant in helping the Soviet Union withstand German attacks in World War II?

(1) The Ural Mountains served as a barrier to advancing German armies.
(2) Distance and harsh winters disrupted German supply lines.
(3) Extensive food-producing areas kept the Soviet armies well fed.
(4) Numerous ports along the Arctic Sea allowed for the refueling of Soviet transport ships.

33 Which geographic region has the greatest number of members in the Organization of Petroleum Exporting Countries (OPEC)?

(1) South America   (3) Southeast Asia
(2) sub-Saharan Africa   (4) Middle East

34 The economic policies of Mikhail Gorbachev of the Soviet Union and of Deng Xiaoping of China included

(1) elements of capitalism
(2) boycotts on foreign products
(3) a one-child policy
(4) a reliance on agricultural self-sufficiency

35 What was the main reason refugees fled Rwanda in the 1990s?

(1) ethnic conflict
(2) expansion of the Sahel
(3) devastation from an earthquake
(4) Cold War tensions

Base your answer to question 36 on the diagram below and on your knowledge of social studies.

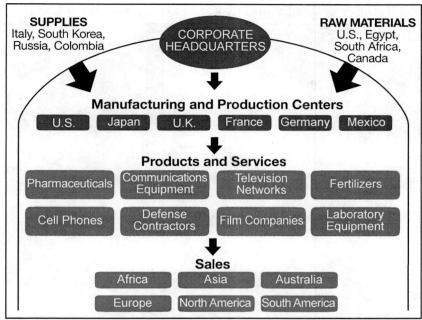

SUPPLIES
Italy, South Korea, Russia, Colombia

CORPORATE HEADQUARTERS

RAW MATERIALS
U.S., Egypt, South Africa, Canada

Manufacturing and Production Centers

| U.S. | Japan | U.K. | France | Germany | Mexico |

Products and Services

| Pharmaceuticals | Communications Equipment | Television Networks | Fertilizers |

| Cell Phones | Defense Contractors | Film Companies | Laboratory Equipment |

Sales

| Africa | Asia | Australia |

| Europe | North America | South America |

Source: Roger B. Beck et al., *World History: Patterns of Interaction*, McDougal Littell, 2005 (adapted)

36 Which concept is being shown by this 2005 diagram?

   (1) recession   · (3) socialism

   (2) urbanization   (4) globalization

37 What is one way the conflict between India and Pakistan over Kashmir and the conflict between the Palestinians and Israelis in the Middle East are similar?

   (1) Both conflicts concern territorial and religious issues.

   (2) Hostilities within these regions were provoked by the United Nations.

   (3) Both conflicts emerged as a result of the breakup of the Soviet Union.

   (4) Tensions in these regions were caused by efforts to remain nonaligned.

38 The creation of the European Union (EU) and of the North American Free Trade Agreement (NAFTA) were efforts to

   (1) attain economic benefits through regional organization

   (2) achieve world peace through military alliances

   (3) reduce resource depletion through economic planning

   (4) address environmental problems through coordinated research

Base your answer to question 39 on the map below and on your knowledge of social studies.

Estimated Number of Adults and Children Living with HIV/AIDS as of 2010

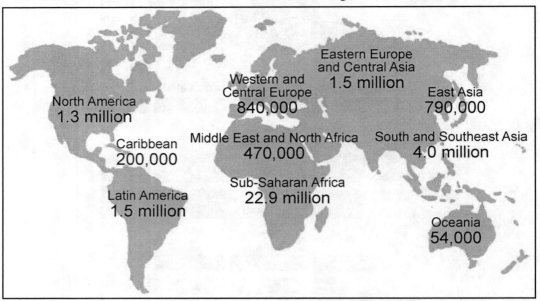

Source: UNAIDS: World AIDS Day Report 2011 (adapted)

39 The data on this map suggest that HIV/AIDS

(1) originated in South and Southeast Asia
(2) is declining in developing societies
(3) requires global cooperation to solve the problem
(4) has been restricted to temperate climates

40 Since 1999, what has been the primary role of the North Atlantic Treaty Organization (NATO) in world affairs?

(1) conducting war crimes trials
(2) protecting Western Europe from Soviet aggression
(3) lowering tariffs between member nations
(4) carrying out crisis management and peace enforcement tasks

41 Which current global problem was initiated with the development of atomic weapons?

(1) threats to world peace from unrestricted nuclear proliferation
(2) increased health risks for humans and animals from industrial pollution
(3) elevated carbon dioxide in the atmosphere due to the deforestation of the rainforests
(4) changes in world weather patterns and species habitats due to melting polar ice caps

42 The Neolithic Revolution is most closely associated with

(1) using child labor in factories
(2) domesticating plants and animals
(3) learning to control fire
(4) developing iron technology

43 Which sequence places these laws in the correct chronological order?

(1) Code of Hammurabi → Justinian Code → Napoleonic Code → Twelve Tables
(2) Justinian Code → Twelve Tables → Napoleonic Code → Code of Hammurabi
(3) Code of Hammurabi → Twelve Tables → Justinian Code → Napoleonic Code
(4) Twelve Tables → Napoleonic Code → Code of Hammurabi → Justinian Code

44 Which philosophy that was developed during the Renaissance is associated with a shift in focus away from religious subjects toward more secular subjects?

(1) humanism   (3) communism
(2) absolutism   (4) scholasticism

Base your answer to question 45 on the statement below and on your knowledge of social studies.

… I conclude, then, returning to being feared and loved, that since men love at their convenience and fear at the convenience of the prince, a wise prince should found himself on what is his, not on what is someone else's; he should only contrive to avoid hatred, as was said.

45 This statement is taken from the written work of

(1) John Locke   (3) Adam Smith
(2) Niccolò Machiavelli   (4) Ignatius Loyola

46 One similarity in the rule of Akbar the Great and the rule of Elizabeth I is that both leaders implemented policies that encouraged

(1) compulsory education
(2) military disarmament
(3) voter participation
(4) religious toleration

47 One way in which the caste system in traditional India and the Estates system of pre-revolutionary France are similar is that

(1) occupations were attained by merit
(2) social mobility was very limited
(3) status was determined by education
(4) impact on the daily lives of people was minimal

48 • Opium War (1839–1842)
  • Taiping Rebellion (1850–1864)
  • Boxer Rebellion (1898–1901)

This series of events is most closely associated with the

(1) spread of communism to China and Korea
(2) growing concerns about the influence of the West in China
(3) alliance formed between Vietnam and China
(4) increasing expansion of civil and political rights in China

49 Forced famine in Ukraine (1932–1933) was a direct result of

(1) Czar Nicholas's involvement in World War I
(2) Vladmir Lenin's New Economic Policy
(3) Joseph Stalin's collectivization
(4) Nikita Khrushchev's removal from power

50 "River of Sorrows Floods Again"
"Thousands Missing After Huang He Overflows"
"Over 10 Million Reported Homeless After 1931 Flooding"

These newspaper headlines describe the effects of geography on the people of

(1) China   (3) India
(2) Japan   (4) Vietnam

Answers to the essay questions are to be written in the separate essay booklet.

In developing your answer to Part II, be sure to keep these general definitions in mind:

(a) <u>describe</u> means "to illustrate something in words or tell about it"

(b) <u>discuss</u> means "to make observations about something using facts, reasoning, and argument; to present in some detail"

Part II

THEMATIC ESSAY QUESTION

Directions: Write a well-organized essay that includes an introduction, several paragraphs addressing the task below, and a conclusion.

Theme: Human Rights—Justice

> At different times in history, individuals have defended human rights using a variety of methods. Their efforts have met with varying degrees of success.

Task:

> Select *two* individuals and for *each*
> - Describe the historical circumstances that led the individual to defend human rights
> - Describe a method the individual used to defend human rights
> - Discuss the extent to which the individual's effort was successful

You may use any individual from your study of global history and geography. Some suggestions you might wish to consider include Bartolomé de las Casas, John Locke, Mary Wollstonecraft, Father Miguel Hidalgo, Emiliano Zapata, Mohandas Gandhi, Father Oscar Romero, Lech Walesa, Nelson Mandela, Aung San Suu Kyi, and the Dalai Lama.

You are *not* limited to these suggestions.

Do *not* select an individual from the United States.

Guidelines:

In your essay, be sure to
- Develop all aspects of the task
- Support the theme with relevant facts, examples, and details
- Use a logical and clear plan of organization, including an introduction and a conclusion that are beyond a restatement of the theme

Part III

DOCUMENT-BASED QUESTION

This question is based on the accompanying documents. The question is designed to test your ability to work with historical documents. Some of these documents have been edited for the purposes of this question. As you analyze the documents, take into account the source of each document and any point of view that may be presented in the document. Keep in mind that the language used in a document may reflect the historical context of the time in which it was written.

Historical Context:

> Throughout history, people have changed their environments to meet their needs. These changes have had both positive and negative effects on people, societies, and regions. Examples include the ***development of irrigation in ancient Egypt,*** the ***construction of chinampas by the Aztecs,*** and the ***mining of coal in Great Britain during the Industrial Revolution***.

Task: Using the information from the documents and your knowledge of global history, answer the questions that follow each document in Part A. Your answers to the questions will help you write the Part B essay in which you will be asked to

> Select ***two*** changes people have made to their environment mentioned in the historical context and for ***each***
> - Explain why this change to their environment was needed
> - Discuss how this change affected people, a society, and/or a region

In developing your answers to Part III, be sure to keep these general definitions in mind:

- (a) <u>explain</u> means "to make plain or understandable; to give reasons for or causes of; to show the logical development or relationships of"
- (b) <u>discuss</u> means "to make observations about something using facts, reasoning, and argument; to present in some detail"

Part A
Short-Answer Questions

Directions: Analyze the documents and answer the short-answer questions that follow each document in the space provided.

Document 1

> The first successful efforts to control the flow of water were made in Mesopotamia and Egypt, where the remains of the prehistoric irrigation works still exist. In ancient Egypt, the construction of canals was a major endeavor of the pharaohs and their servants, beginning in Scorpio's time. One of the first duties of provincial governors was the digging and repair of canals, which were used to flood large tracts of land while the Nile was flowing high. The land was checkerboarded with small basins, defined by a system of dikes. Problems regarding the uncertainty of the flow of the Nile were recognized. During very high flows, the dikes were washed away and villages flooded, drowning thousands. During low flows, the land did not receive water, and no crops could grow. In many places where fields were too high to receive water from the canals, water was drawn from the canals or the Nile directly by a swape or a shaduf. These consisted of a bucket on the end of a cord that hung from the long end of a pivoted boom, counterweighted at the short end. The building of canals continued in Egypt throughout the centuries....

Source: Larry W. Mays, "Irrigation Systems, Ancient," *Water Encyclopedia* online (adapted)

1 Based on this document, state **two** problems ancient Egyptians faced as a result of the uncertain flow of the Nile. [2]

(1)_____

_____

Score ▢

(2)_____

_____

Score ▢

Document 2a

This frieze, or architectural adornment, on an ancient temple portrays Egyptians using shadufs, devices that enabled them to transfer water from the Nile to their fields.

Source: James Barter, *The Nile*, Lucent Books

Document 2b

After the death of Alexander the Great, a series of three pharaohs named Ptolemy ruled Egypt. The culture of Egypt during that period was primarily Greek.

… In the Ptolemaic period, Greek temple records presented each region as an economic unit, and referred to the name of the canal which irrigates the region, the cultivated region which is located on the river's banks and is directly irrigated with its water, and the lands located on the region's border that could be reclaimed. The beds irrigation system allowed cultivating one winter crop; while in summer, the only lands that could be cultivated were the high lands away from the flood. Thus, when the Egyptians invented tools to lift water, such as the shaduf, they were able to cultivate two crops per year, which was considered a great advance in the field of irrigation. The shaduf was invented in the Amarna period and is a simple tool which needs two to four men to operate. The shaduf consists of a long, suspended pole weighted at one end and a bucket tied at the other end. It can lift about 100 cubic meters (100,000 liters) in 12 hours, which is enough for irrigating a little over a third of an acre.…

Source: Agriculture – Part I, Ancient Egypt History, EgyptHistory.com

2 Based on these documents, what was *one* effect the invention of the shaduf had on the Egyptians?   [1]

_____

_____

Score ☐

Document 3

… The water laws of ancient Egypt were primarily concerned with ensuring that each farmer along the river had fair access to the waters during the floods and that no farmers were denied their fair share of irrigated water. If a farmer, for example, farmed many miles from the river, those owning land close to the river had to allow him to have access to a water canal running through their land.

Water laws also prohibited the taking of water from canals by farmers not contributing to the labor of filling the canal with water. How much water one was entitled to take from a canal depended on how much time one spent filling that canal. If, for example, ten farmers contributed ten hours of labor filling irrigation canals with water, any one of them who took more than one hour's worth of water could be put to death….

Source: James Barter, *The Nile,* Lucent Books

3 According to James Barter, in what way did the government ensure that farmers had fair access to water? [1]

_____

_____

Score ☐

Document 4

Aztec Farming Method

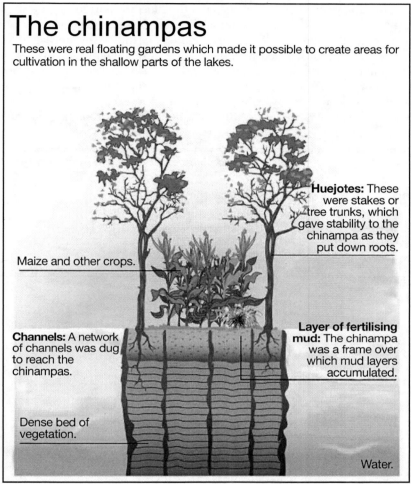

The chinampas

These were real floating gardens which made it possible to create areas for cultivation in the shallow parts of the lakes.

Huejotes: These were stakes or tree trunks, which gave stability to the chinampa as they put down roots.

Maize and other crops.

Channels: A network of channels was dug to reach the chinampas.

Layer of fertilising mud: The chinampa was a frame over which mud layers accumulated.

Dense bed of vegetation.

Water.

Source: www.icarito.cl (adapted)

4 Based on the information provided by this diagram, why did the Aztecs build chinampas?   [1]

_____

_____

Score ☐

Document 5

… Chinampas added both living and agricultural space to the island. Houses could be built on chinampas after they were firmly in place, and the plots were used to grow a great variety of products, from maize and beans to tomatoes and flowers. The Mexica [Aztec] built chinampas all around Tenochtitlan, like their neighbors in the freshwater lakes to the south. They were, however, constantly faced with the danger of flooding, which brought salty water across the chinampas and ruined the land and crops. Lake Texcoco accumulated minerals from the river water running into it, which caused the water to be brackish [mix of fresh and salt water]. In the mid-15th century, this problem was solved; a dike was built, separating the western section of the lake where Tenochtitlan was located and protecting the city from salty water and some flooding.…

Source: Frances F. Berdan, *The Aztecs,* Chelsea House Publishers

5a According to Frances F. Berdan, what was *one* way the chinampas benefited the Aztecs?   [1]

_____

_____

Score ☐

b According to Frances F. Berdan, what was *one* problem that farmers on the chinampas faced?   [1]

_____

_____

Score ☐

Document 6

… The capital city, which may have had a population as high as 200,000 to 300,000 in the early sixteenth century, was a superb example of planned growth. By building out into the lake, the Aztecs consolidated and enlarged the original two islands which in turn were linked to the mainland by three large causeways. Fresh water was brought to the city from the mainland by aqueduct.…

Source: Jeremy A. Sabloff, *The Cities of Ancient Mexico: Reconstructing a Lost World,* Thames and Hudson

6 According to Jeremy A. Sabloff, what was *one* way building out into the lake benefited the Aztec Empire and its capital city of Tenochtitlán?   [1]

_____

_____

Score ☐

Document 7a

> … The shortage of wood was very serious. Wood was the main fuel used for cooking. It was essential for ship-building, and charcoal was needed to smelt [process] iron ore. A new source of energy was urgently required. This was supplied by coal.
>
> Already coal had replaced wood for cooking and heating in any place that could be reached by sea or by navigable river. Iron was being imported, although there was plenty of iron ore in Britain. Coal was growing harder to mine, as seams near the surface were exhausted, and deeper seams needed pumps to drain them [water from the mines]….

Source: Diana Knox, *The Industrial Revolution,* Greenhaven Press

7a According to Diana Knox, why was coal needed?   [1]

_____

_____

Score ☐

Document 7b

> … At first, coal was dug from open pits, but gradually the mines had to go deeper. Shafts were sunk down, and galleries [underground rooms] were dug sideways into coal seams. As the shafts went lower, they began to fill with water. Some miners had to work all day with their legs in water. It was not until steam pumps were introduced in the early 1700s that the water could be drained….

Source: Andrew Langley, *The Industrial Revolution,* Viking

7b According to Andrew Langley, what was *one* way people modified the environment to obtain coal?   [1]

_____

_____

Score ☐

Document 8

Prior to the use of coal, water was the primary source of power for factories and machines in Great Britain. Water sources that could fuel these factories were limited. Therefore industries were not able to grow and factories were often remotely located.

> … With the shift to coal, the pattern was reversed, reflecting the difference in the power source. Coal spawned [generated] much larger and ever more mechanized factories because the power available from underground was so much greater than that supplied by a waterwheel. And, because its energy had already been handily condensed over millions of years, coal concentrated the factories and workforces in urban areas instead of dispersing them throughout the countryside. In short, coal allowed the industrialization of Britain to gain a momentum that was nothing short of revolutionary.…

Source: Barbara Freese, *Coal: A Human History,* Perseus Publishing

8 According to Barbara Freese, what was **one** effect the shift from water power to the use of coal as a source of power had on Great Britain?   [1]

_____

_____

Score [   ]

Document 9

A Rainton Mine Disaster in Durham, Great Britain on December 18, 1817

An explosion claimed twenty seven lives, eleven men and sixteen boys. The blast occurred before all the men had descended [into the mine]. Had it occurred later there would have been 160 men and boys in the pit. Early reports of the total number of lives lost amounted to twenty six, and those principally boys. The explosion took place at 3 o'clock in the morning, before the hewers [men who cut coal from the seam] had descended the pit and from this circumstance about 160 lives have been preserved. Every exertion was made to render assistance to those in the mine and two men fell having been suffocated by the impure state of the air. The viewers and agents were extremely active and had nearly shared the same fate. The pit in which this accident occurred, was always considered to be quite free from explosive matter and in consequence of this supposed security the safety lamps had never been introduced into it the miners continuing to work by the light of candles.

Source: The Coalmining History Resource Centre online, UK

9 According to this document, what were *two* dangers workers faced in the Rainton coal mine?   [2]

(1)_____

_____

Score ☐

(2)_____

_____

Score ☐

Part B
Essay

Directions: Write a well-organized essay that includes an introduction, several paragraphs, and a conclusion. Use evidence from *at least four* documents in your essay. Support your response with relevant facts, examples, and details. Include additional outside information.

Historical Context:

Throughout history, people have changed their environments to meet their needs. These changes have had both positive and negative effects on people, societies, and regions. Examples include the *development of irrigation in ancient Egypt,* the *construction of chinampas by the Aztecs,* and the *mining of coal in Great Britain during the Industrial Revolution.*

Task: Using the information from the documents and your knowledge of global history, write an essay in which you

> Select *two* changes people have made to their environment mentioned in the historical context and for *each*
> - Explain why this change to their environment was needed
> - Discuss how this change affected people, a society, and/or a region

Guidelines:

In your essay, be sure to
- Develop all aspects of the task
- Incorporate information from *at least four* documents
- Incorporate relevant outside information
- Support the theme with relevant facts, examples, and details
- Use a logical and clear plan of organization, including an introduction and a conclusion that are beyond a restatement of the theme

GLOBAL HISTORY AND GEOGRAPHY
JUNE 2014

Part I

Answer all questions in this part.

Directions (1–50): For each statement or question, record on your separate answer sheet the *number* of the word or expression that, of those given, best completes the statement or answers the question.

Base your answer to question 1 on the map below and on your knowledge of social studies.

Early Israelites: Abraham's Journey, ca. 2000 B.C.

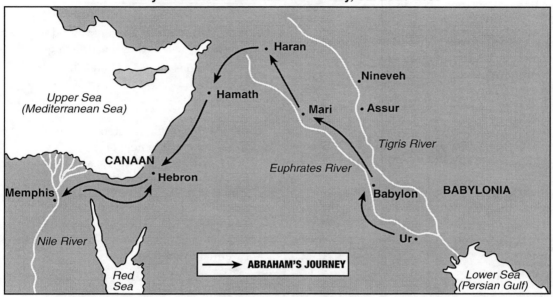

Source: Farah and Karls, *World History: The Human Experience*, Section Focus Transparencies, McGraw-Hill
(adapted)

1 Based on the information provided by this map, where did Abraham's journey originate?
   (1) Sahara Desert
   (2) Nile River valley
   (3) Mesopotamia
   (4) Mediterranean Sea

---

2 People do not often create records for the benefit of historians. They produce them for other reasons....

— Chris Hinton, 1998

Based on this statement, historical sources often contain
   (1) evidence that can be biased
   (2) facts that are completely balanced and reliable
   (3) accounts that represent all points of view
   (4) summaries that detail research about the distant past

3 Which concept is essential to the study of economic systems?
   (1) self-determination   (3) citizenship
   (2) factors of production   (4) human rights

4 Which major geographic feature has hindered cultural diffusion between India and China?
   (1) Himalaya Mountains   (3) Gobi Desert
   (2) Deccan Plateau   (4) Great Rift Valley

5 Which statement about the Bantu migration is an opinion rather than a fact?

(1) The migration occurred gradually over a long period of time.
(2) Language and knowledge spread from northwestern to southern and eastern Africa.
(3) The lack of primary documents makes it difficult to determine the exact cause of the migration.
(4) Bantu civilization was superior to those civilizations that it displaced.

6 Historically, the Huang He has also been known as the "River of Sorrows" because

(1) frozen ports have made trade difficult
(2) cataracts have made transportation impossible
(3) floods have destroyed crops and villages
(4) burials have taken place at the sacred waters

7 Both the Han dynasty and the Roman Empire were known for

(1) developing decentralized political structures
(2) having governments dominated by a merchant class
(3) using examinations to select officials
(4) having long periods of stable government

8 Which belief system is considered monotheistic?

(1) Judaism   (3) Confucianism
(2) Shinto   (4) animism

9 The Golden Age of India's Gupta Empire is known for its

(1) development of gunpowder
(2) sea trade routes to Europe
(3) acceptance of Christianity as an official religion
(4) advancements in mathematics and medicine

10 Which geographic factor enabled the cities of Nanjing and Mogadishu to develop into powerful trading centers?

(1) location on waterways
(2) abundance of natural resources
(3) predictable rainfall from the monsoon cycle
(4) access to mountain passes

Base your answer to question 11 on the chart below and on your knowledge of social studies.

Objects Discovered off the Java Coast in the 10th-Century Cirebon Shipwreck

- Emerald green Islamic glass
- Chinese porcelain decorated with dragons and birds
- Jeweled gold-plated Arabian ceremonial daggers
- Bronze religious objects with Hindu and Buddhist symbols

11 What does this archaeological find indicate about Southeast Asia during the 10th century?

(1) Religious objects from China were a major import.
(2) Precious gems and metals were exported to Africa.
(3) Europeans dominated East Asian and Middle Eastern trade networks.
(4) The region served as a crossroads between Arab and Chinese traders.

12 Development and expansion of banking, insurance companies, and stock exchanges were essential to the system of

(1) feudalism   (3) capitalism
(2) tribute   (4) bartering

13 A key feature of European Renaissance culture was

(1) an outlook emphasizing classicism, secularism, and individualism
(2) a reliance on the Pope and his knights to maintain political stability
(3) a shift in production from the domestic system to the factory system
(4) a way of thinking stressing humility and Christian faith

14 Martin Luther, John Calvin, and Henry VIII all played a key role in the

(1) attempts made to reclaim the Holy Land
(2) fall of the Ottoman Empire
(3) end of religious unity in Europe
(4) establishment of parliamentary democracy in Britain

15 The practice of Islam throughout much of West Africa is evidence that

(1) Islam spread beyond the borders of the Arabian peninsula
(2) Chinese trade carried Islamic beliefs to West Africa
(3) Islam originated in West Africa and spread to the Middle East
(4) Europeans encouraged Islamic beliefs during the colonial period

16 Which statement is consistent with the ideas of Niccolò Machiavelli?

(1) Democratic principles should be followed faithfully.
(2) The law should be subject to the will of the leader.
(3) Human rights should be respected in all countries.
(4) Markets should operate with little governmental interference.

17 What was a major cause for the shift in European trade from the Mediterranean Sea to the Atlantic Ocean during the late 1400s?

(1) Ottoman Turks seized control of Constantinople.
(2) The Ming dynasty authorized Zheng He to make long-distance voyages.
(3) The Tokugawa shogunate adopted an isolationist policy.
(4) Christian crusaders captured Jerusalem.

18 The location of the Inca civilization of South America demonstrates the

(1) importance of trade with western Europe
(2) ability of humans to adapt the environment
(3) influence of cultural diversity
(4) complexity of indigenous belief systems

19 Why is Ferdinand Magellan's voyage considered a turning point in world history?

(1) Portugal's claims to southern Africa were established.
(2) His ship was the first to land in the Americas.
(3) One of his ships was the first to circumnavigate Earth.
(4) Britain's control of the seas ended.

20 In the 17th and 18th centuries, the primary goal of mercantilism as practiced by European countries was to

(1) glorify the power and aggressiveness of the military
(2) create laws which guaranteed individual freedoms
(3) teach the natives Christianity and offer them protection in exchange for labor
(4) increase their supply of gold and silver through a favorable balance of trade

21 The impact of the printing press, astrolabe, and caravel on 16th-century Europe demonstrates the ability of technology to

(1) limit which ideas can be transmitted
(2) redefine human understanding of the world
(3) reinforce established traditional beliefs
(4) exploit new sources of energy

22 One way in which Peter the Great, Louis XIV, and Philip II are similar is that each

(1) supported missionary efforts of the Roman Catholic Church
(2) sought to centralize power by limiting the power of the nobility
(3) fought to block the establishment of British colonies in the Western Hemisphere
(4) challenged feudal practices by emancipating serfs

23 New scientific knowledge and understandings that developed during the Scientific Revolution were most often based on

(1) observation and experimentation
(2) church law and faith
(3) superstition and ancient practices
(4) geometric formulas and astrology

24 Which pair correctly links the region where Enlightenment ideas first developed to a region to which those ideas spread?

(1) Asia → eastern Europe
(2) Africa → southeastern Asia
(3) western Europe → the Americas
(4) eastern Africa → India

25 Baron de Montesquieu believed that a separation of powers would

(1) prevent tyranny by acting as a check on power
(2) restore authority to the Roman Catholic Church
(3) increase corruption of political authority
(4) decrease the power of the middle class

26 Which mountains were an obstacle to Simón Bolívar's efforts to unify Gran Colombia?

(1) Alps   (3) Zagros
(2) Andes   (4) Urals

27 • Abundant coal resources
   • Development of steam power
   • Building of an extensive canal system

In the late 1700s, these conditions allowed the Industrial Revolution to begin in

(1) Japan   (3) Russia
(2) Germany   (4) England

28 Laissez-faire practices are most closely associated with a

(1) traditional economy
(2) market economy
(3) command economy
(4) mixed economy

29 As a result of the Russo-Japanese War, Japan came to be seen by Europeans as

(1) a likely area for colonization
(2) the strongest of the imperialist countries
(3) a leader in the movement for nonalignment
(4) an emerging global threat

Base your answer to question 30 on the speakers' statements below and on your knowledge of social studies.

Speaker A: The British East India Company does not respect my beliefs. I cannot follow dharma and remain their soldier. I will return to my family in a Tamil village.

Speaker B: My rebellious countrymen cannot accept my new religion and so they hate me and my "foreign devil" friends. The missionaries leave Beijing tomorrow for England. I must join them before the church compound is surrounded.

Speaker C: The czar's soldiers came again today, looted our village, drove off our livestock, and trampled anyone in their way. They even burned our synagogue. Our way of life is gone. It is time to emigrate to Palestine.

30 What is the primary focus of these speakers?

(1) civil war
(2) economic reforms
(3) religious persecution
(4) colonial oppression

31 Which condition is most closely associated with Mexico between 1910 and 1930?

(1) revolutions and political instability
(2) establishment of a state religion
(3) rapid industrialization by locally owned corporations
(4) widespread support for foreign intervention

32 The difficult, year-long journey made by Mao Zedong and his Communist followers in 1934 through China's mountains, marshes, and rivers was called the

(1) Cultural Revolution   (3) Boxer Rebellion
(2) Great Leap Forward   (4) Long March

Base your answer to question 33 on the map below and on your knowledge of social studies.

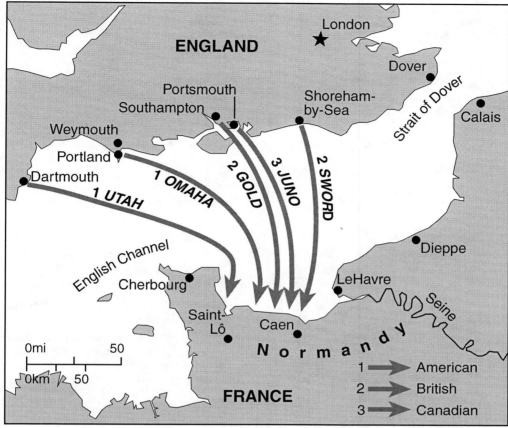

Source: National Geographic Magazine online, 2002 (adapted)

33 The World War II military action shown on this map was significant because it

    (1) took the pressure off the war in the Pacific

    (2) led directly to the war crimes trials in Nuremberg

    (3) caused Germany to resort to unrestricted submarine warfare

    (4) forced Germany to fight the Allies on eastern and western fronts

34 Which statement about the Soviet economy under Joseph Stalin is accurate?

    (1) The Soviet Union increased its power by developing heavy industry.

    (2) The government reduced its role in planning industrial production.

    (3) Farmers were encouraged to compete in a free market economy.

    (4) A large selection of consumer goods became available in the Soviet Union.

35 In the 1940s, the leadership of the Indian National Congress and the leadership of the Muslim League supported the goal of

    (1) helping the British fight World War II

    (2) removing British control from the subcontinent

    (3) abolishing caste distinctions and discrimination

    (4) establishing a unified government based on religious teachings

Base your answer to question 36 on the time line below and on your knowledge of social studies.

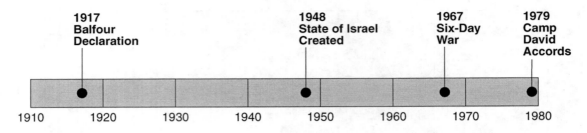

1917
Balfour
Declaration

1948
State of Israel
Created

1967
Six-Day
War

1979
Camp
David
Accords

1910   1920   1930   1940   1950   1960   1970   1980

36 Which region is directly associated with the events shown on this time line?

(1) Latin America   (3) Central Africa
(2) Middle East   (4) Southeast Asia

Base your answer to question 37 on the cartoon below and on your knowledge of social studies.

"It doesn't matter that you said nothing—I saw you *think* something!"

Source: Eric Godal, January 10, 1943 (adapted)

37 Which type of political system is being depicted in this 1943 cartoon?

(1) direct democracy   (3) theocratic republic
(2) monarchy   (4) totalitarian

38 Immediately after World War II, which country exerted political and economic control over Poland, Hungary, and Romania?

(1) France   (3) Soviet Union
(2) United States   (4) Great Britain

39 The main reason oil-producing states formed the Organization of Petroleum Exporting Countries (OPEC) was to

(1) promote foreign ownership of oil fields
(2) lift economic sanctions and establish free trade
(3) improve trade relations with the West
(4) influence the price of oil and set production levels

40 What was a goal of the student protestors in Tiananmen Square in 1989?

(1) independence for Taiwan
(2) removal of troops from South Korea
(3) access to foreign products
(4) democratic reforms

41 What is one way post–World War II North Korea and post–World War II East Germany are similar?

(1) Monarchies were reestablished in both countries.
(2) Democratic principles flourished in both countries.
(3) Both communist governments faced economic stagnation.
(4) Both countries threatened to use chemical weapons against China.

Base your answer to question 42 on the cartoon below and on your knowledge of social studies.

Source: Mike Keefe, *The Denver Post*, 1995

42 The cartoonist's point of view is best expressed in which statement about the United Nations?

(1) Its leadership celebrated its 50th successful military campaign.
(2) It engaged in acts of war as a method of peacekeeping.
(3) It succeeded in its diplomatic efforts.
(4) Its military forces received many awards for their actions.

43 • Tutsis and Hutus in Rwanda
 • Russians and Chechens in southwestern Russia
 • Tamils and Sinhalese in Sri Lanka

In the 1990s, which situation characterized the relationship of the peoples listed for each of these regions?

(1) cooperative political compromise
(2) development of a shared economy
(3) movement toward religious toleration
(4) brutal civil conflict

44 During the 20th century, in which area has deforestation been a significant environmental issue due to the expansion of industrial mining, the growth of corporate farms, and the development of new road networks?

(1) Sahara Desert
(2) Tibetan Plateau
(3) Amazon Basin
(4) Ukrainian Steppe

Base your answer to question 45 on the cartoon below and on your knowledge of social studies.

Source: Brian Barling, *Christian Science Monitor*, March 30, 2006

45 The policies of which 20th-century leader helped to create the situation shown in this 2006 cartoon?

(1) Deng Xiaoping   (3) Aung San Suu Kyi
(2) Kim Jong Il   (4) Ho Chi Minh

Base your answer to question 46 on the passage below and on your knowledge of social studies.

…The deposits of fine sediment left by natural floods sustain the fertility of floodplain soils. The 5,000-year history of agriculture in the Nile Valley and delta of Egypt depended on the annual Nile River flood that left a veneer of new silt over the valley floor each year. Modern dams on the Nile — particularly the Aswan High Dam, which can store the entire annual flood — have destroyed the natural system of fertilization, necessitating huge imports of artificial fertilizers.…

— Oberlander and Muller, *Essentials of Physical Geography Today, Second Edition*, Random House, 1987

46 Based on this passage, a valid conclusion would be that

(1) natural fertilizers are less effective than artificial fertilizers
(2) technological advances sometimes create unforeseen problems
(3) yearly flooding is harmful to Egyptian agriculture
(4) farmers in the Nile Valley operate at a subsistence level

Base your answer to question 47 on the passage below and on your knowledge of social studies.

… I, John of Toul, make known that I am the liege man of the lady Beatrice, countess of Troyes, and of her son, Theobald, count of Champagne, against every creature, living or dead, saving my allegiance to lord Enjorand of Coucy, lord John of Arcis, and the count of Grandpré. If it should happen that the count of Grandpré should be at war with the countess and count of Champagne on his own quarrel, I will aid the count of Grandpré in my own person, and will send to the count and the countess of Champagne the knights whose service I owe to them for the fief which I hold of them. But if the count of Grandpré shall make war on the countess and the count of Champagne on behalf of his friends and not in his own quarrel, I will aid in my own person the countess and count of Champagne, and will send one knight to the count of Grandpré for the service which I owe him for the fief which I hold of him, but I will not go myself into the territory of the count of Grandpré to make war on him.…

47 In which period of western European history was the relationship described in this passage most common?

(1) Neolithic   (3) Medieval
(2) Classical   (4) Napoleonic

48 During the feudal period of Japanese history, the emperor had mainly symbolic authority. Which statement best explains the reason for this situation?

(1) Power had been granted to shoguns and daimyos.
(2) Communist guerillas had destabilized domestic political institutions.
(3) A democratic constitution prevented the emperor from centralizing authority.
(4) American occupation forces had undermined the belief in the emperor's divinity.

Base your answers to questions 49 and 50 on the images below and on your knowledge of social studies.

Image A: Inca

Source: Felipe Guaman Poma de Ayala,
Nueva Coronica y Buen Gobierno,
Biblioteca Ayacucho

Image B: Ireland

Source: John Reader,
Potato: A History of the Propitious Esculent,
Yale University Press

49 Which generalization is best supported by these images?

(1) Potatoes have been a key source of food for diverse populations at various times.
(2) The Inca produced more potatoes than any other civilization in history.
(3) The only crop Irish women and children produced was potatoes.
(4) Potatoes could only be grown in mountainous regions.

50 Which historical event connects the activity shown in Image *A* to the activity shown in Image *B*?

(1) opening of the Silk Road trade
(2) Columbian exchange
(3) formation of the Hanseatic League
(4) establishment of trans-Saharan trade

Answers to the essay questions are to be written in the separate essay booklet.

In developing your answer to Part II, be sure to keep these general definitions in mind:

   (a) <u>describe</u> means "to illustrate something in words or tell about it"

   (b) <u>discuss</u> means "to make observations about something using facts, reasoning, and argument; to present in some detail"

Part II

THEMATIC ESSAY QUESTION

Directions: Write a well-organized essay that includes an introduction, several paragraphs addressing the task below, and a conclusion.

Theme: Change—Challenges to Tradition or Authority

> Throughout history, individuals have challenged established traditions and authorities. Their efforts have inspired or influenced change and have met with varying degrees of success.

Task:

> Select *two* individuals who have challenged tradition or authority and for *each*
> - Describe the established tradition or authority as it existed before it was challenged by the individual
> - Discuss how the individual challenged established tradition or authority
> - Discuss the extent to which change was achieved as a result of this challenge

You may use any individual from your study of global history and geography. Some suggestions you might wish to consider include Martin Luther, Galileo Galilei, Mary Wollstonecraft, Toussaint L'Ouverture, Charles Darwin, Vladimir Lenin, Emiliano Zapata, Mohandas Gandhi, Ho Chi Minh, Nelson Mandela, Mikhail Gorbachev, Aung San Suu Kyi, and Wangari Mathaai.

You are *not* limited to these suggestions.

**Do *not* choose an individual from the United States or
Gavrilo Princip from the Balkan States for your answer.**

Guidelines:

   In your essay, be sure to
   - Develop all aspects of the task
   - Support the theme with relevant facts, examples, and details
   - Use a logical and clear plan of organization, including an introduction and a conclusion that are beyond a restatement of the theme

Part III

DOCUMENT-BASED QUESTION

This question is based on the accompanying documents. The question is designed to test your ability to work with historical documents. Some of these documents have been edited for the purposes of this question. As you analyze the documents, take into account the source of each document and any point of view that may be presented in the document. Keep in mind that the language used in a document may reflect the historical context of the time in which it was written.

Historical Context:

Turning points are events that result in regional and worldwide change. Three turning points that transformed societies and regions were the ***outbreak of the bubonic plague,*** the ***signing of the Nanjing Treaty,*** and the ***assassination of Archduke Ferdinand.***

Task: Using the information from the documents and your knowledge of global history, answer the questions that follow each document in Part A. Your answers to the questions will help you write the Part B essay in which you will be asked to

---

Select ***two*** turning points mentioned in the historical context and for ***each***

- Describe the historical circumstances surrounding this turning point
- Discuss changes that occurred within a society and/or region as a result of this turning point

---

In developing your answers to Part III, be sure to keep these general definitions in mind:

(a) <u>describe</u> means "to illustrate something in words or tell about it"

(b) <u>discuss</u> means "to make observations about something using facts, reasoning, and argument; to present in some detail"

Part A
Short-Answer Questions

Directions: Analyze the documents and answer the short-answer questions that follow each document in the space provided.

Document 1

Origins and Spread of the Black Death in Asia

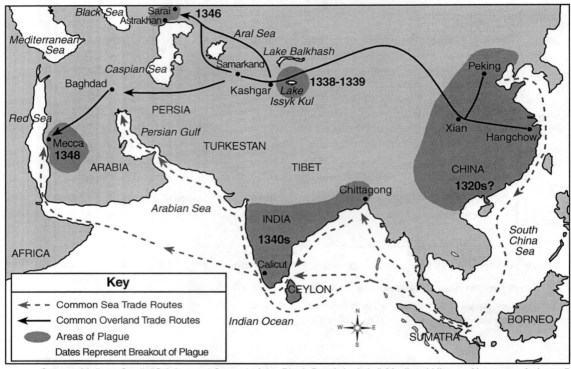

Source: Melissa Snell, "Origins and Spread of the Black Death in Asia," *Medieval History,* About.com (adapted)

1 Based on the information on this map, what activity contributed to the spread of the Black Death?   [1]

_____

_____

Score ☐

Document 2

In this excerpt, William H. McNeill discusses the interpretation of historical evidence to explain how the plague was spread. He suggests that available evidence makes it unlikely that the plague was found in China before 1331.

> …By contrast, after 1331, and more particularly after 1353, China entered upon a disastrous period of its history. Plague coincided with civil war as a native Chinese reaction against the Mongol domination gathered headway, climaxing in the overthrow of the alien rulers and the establishment of a new Ming Dynasty in 1368. The combination of war and pestilence [disease] wreaked havoc on China's population. The best estimates show a decrease from 123 million [in] about 1200 (before the Mongol invasions began) to a mere 65 million in 1393, a generation after the final expulsion of the Mongols from China. Even Mongol ferocity cannot account for such a drastic decrease. Disease assuredly played a big part in cutting Chinese numbers in half; and bubonic plague, recurring after its initial ravages at relatively frequent intervals, just as in Europe, is by all odds the most likely candidate for such a role….

Source: William H. McNeill, *Plagues and Peoples*, Quality Paperback Book Club (adapted)

2 According to William H. McNeill, what was *one* way the plague affected China after 1331?   [1]

_____

_____

Score ☐

Document 3

Social and Economic Effects of the Plague in Europe

> The plague had large scale social and economic effects, many of which are recorded in the introduction of the *Decameron*. People abandoned their friends and family, fled cities, and shut themselves off from the world. Funeral rites became perfunctory [superficial] or stopped altogether, and work ceased being done. Some felt that the wrath of God was descending upon man, and so fought the plague with prayer. Some felt that they should obey the maxim [saying], "Eat, drink, and be merry, for tomorrow you may die." The society experienced an upheaval to an extent usually only seen in controlled circumstances such as carnival [festival]. Faith in religion decreased after the plague, both because of the death of so many of the clergy and because of the failure of prayer to prevent sickness and death….

Source: "Plague," *Decameron Web,* Brown University (adapted)

3 According to this article, what was *one* effect of the plague on European society?   [1]

_____

_____

Score ☐

Document 4

...The Chinese had long been opposed to the opium trade. The drug had been introduced into China by Dutch traders during the seventeenth century. As early as 1729, there were imperial decrees forbidding the sale and smoking of this "destructive and ensnaring vice." In 1796, Jiaqing, the new emperor, placed a complete ban on its importation, but he was a weak administrator and soon pirates and opium merchants were bribing officials to look the other way. By 1816, the [British] East India Company had imported 3,000 chests of opium from its poppy fields in the north Indian state of Punjab. By 1820, this had risen to 5,000 and by 1825 to almost 10,000.

As more and more Chinese became addicts, and silver flowed out of the economy to British coffers, the Chinese government moved toward confrontation. The emperor Daoguang, who came to the throne in 1821 was a reformer, and, supported by his advisor Lin Zexu (1785–1850), the emperor banned opium in 1836 and ordered the decapitation of "foreign barbarians" who concealed and traded the drug....

Source: Perry M. Rogers, ed., *Aspects of World Civilization: Problems and Sources in History, Volume II,* Prentice Hall
(adapted)

4a According to Perry Rogers, what was **one** reason the Chinese were unsuccessful in halting the opium trade? [1]

_____

_____

Score [ ]

b According to Perry Rogers, what was **one** effort made by the Chinese to halt the European trade in opium? [1]

_____

_____

Score [ ]

Document 5

The Treaty of Nanjing was signed by Great Britain and China following the Opium War (1839–1842).

An Excerpt from the Treaty of Nanjing

ARTICLE III.

It being obviously necessary and desirable, that British Subjects should have some Port whereat they may careen and refit their Ships, when required, and keep Stores for that purpose, His Majesty the Emperor of China cedes [gives] to Her Majesty the Queen of Great Britain, etc., the Island of Hongkong, to be possessed in perpetuity [forever] by Her Britannic Majesty, Her Heirs and Successors, and to be governed by such Laws and Regulations as Her Majesty the Queen of Great Britain, etc., shall see fit to direct.

Source: "Treaty of Nanjing (Nanking), 1842," USC-UCLA Joint East Asian Studies Center

5 What did the British gain as a result of the Treaty of Nanjing?   [1]

_____

_____

Score [ ]

Document 6a

THE REAL TROUBLE WILL COME WITH THE "WAKE."

Source: Joseph Keppler, *Puck*, August 15, 1900 (adapted)

Document 6b

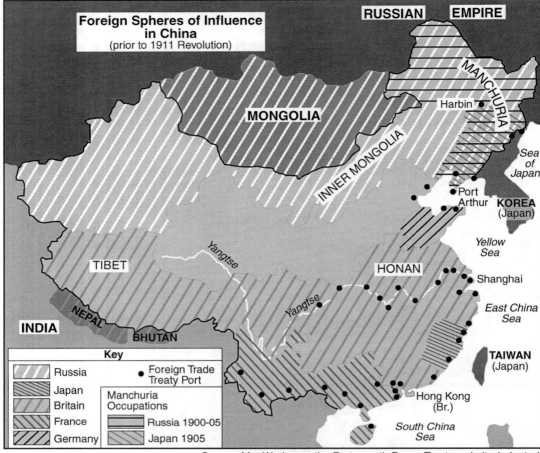

Foreign Spheres of Influence in China
(prior to 1911 Revolution)

RUSSIAN   EMPIRE

MANCHURIA

MONGOLIA

Harbin

INNER MONGOLIA

Sea of Japan

Port Arthur

KOREA (Japan)

Yellow Sea

TIBET

Yangtse

HONAN

Shanghai

East China Sea

Yangtse

INDIA

NEPAL

BHUTAN

TAIWAN (Japan)

Hong Kong (Br.)

South China Sea

Key

Russia	• Foreign Trade Treaty Port
Japan	Manchuria Occupations
Britain	
France	Russia 1900–05
Germany	Japan 1905

Source: MapWorks, on the Portsmouth Peace Treaty website (adapted)

6 Based on this 1900 Joseph Keppler cartoon and the information on this map, state **one** problem China faced after the Treaty of Nanjing took effect.   [1]

_____

_____

Score ☐

Document 7a

The Eastern Question and the Balkans

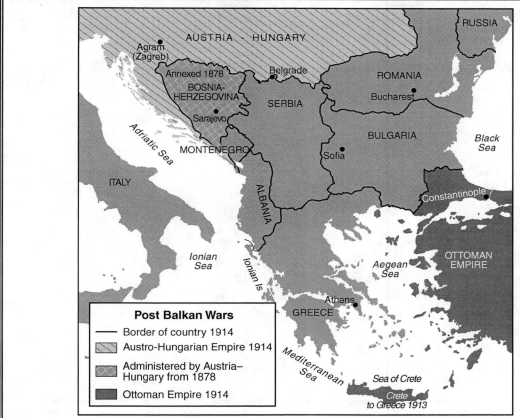

Source: Patrick K. O'Brien, ed., *Oxford Atlas of World History*, Oxford University Press
(adapted)

…As a result of the Balkan Wars (1912–1913) Serbia had doubled in size and there were growing demands for the union of south Slavs (Yugoslavism) under the leadership of Serbia. Austria had a large south Slav population in the provinces of Slovenia, Croatia, the Banat and Bosnia. Austria was very alarmed at the growing power of Serbia. She [Austria-Hungary] felt Serbia could weaken her [Austria-Hungary's] own Empire.

The Austrians decided that they would have to wage a preventative war against Serbia in order to destroy her growing power. They were waiting for the correct pretext (excuse). When Franz Ferdinand was shot, the Austrians saw this as the perfect opportunity to destroy Serbia. But when she [Austria-Hungary] attacked Serbia, Russia came to her [Serbia's] aid and the war spread.…

Source: Stephen Tonge, "Causes of the First World War," A Web of English History online (adapted)

7a According to Stephen Tonge, what was **one** cause for tension between Austria and Serbia? [1]

_____

_____

Score [ ]

Document 7b

This is an excerpt of the testimony given by Gavrilo Princip reprinted in *The Sarajevo Trial*. He was accused of assassinating Archduke Ferdinand of Austria-Hungary and his wife in July 1914.

The Hearing of Gavrilo Princip
12 October 1914
In the Afternoon

…Pr. [Prosecutor]: — Call Gavrilo Princip. (He is brought in.) Do you consider yourself guilty?

Acc. [Accused, Gavrilo Princip]: — I am not a criminal, because I destroyed that which was evil. I think that I am good.…

Pr.: — What kind of ideas did you have?

Acc.: — I am a Yugoslav nationalist and I believe in the unification of all South Slavs in whatever form of state and that it be free of Austria.

Pr.: — That was your aspiration. How did you think to realize [accomplish] it?

Acc.: — By means of terror.

Pr.: — What does that signify?

Acc.: — That means in general to destroy from above, to do away with those who obstruct and do evil, who stand in the way of the idea of unification.

Pr.: — How did you think that you might realize your objectives?

Acc.: — Still another principal motive was revenge for all torments which Austria imposed upon the people.…

Pr.: — What was the feeling about Austria in your circles?

Acc.: — It was the opinion that Austria behaved badly to our people, which is true, and certainly that she (Austria) is not necessary.…

Source: W. A. Dolph Owings et al., eds., *The Sarajevo Trial, Volume I,* Documentary Publications

7b Based on this excerpt from *The Sarajevo Trial*, what was **one** goal of Gavrilo Princip?   [1]

_____

_____

Score ☐

Document 8a

British Training Poster

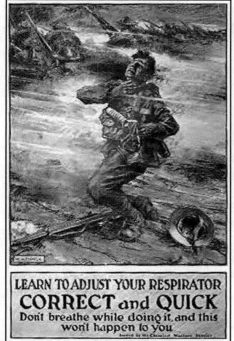

Source: W. G. Thayer, 1915,
Library of Congress,
Prints and Photographs online catalog

Document 8b

German Trenches, ca. June 16, 1916

Source: Library of Congress, Prints and Photographs online catalog

8 Using information from these images, state *one* impact Gavrilo Princip's assassination of Austria-Hungary's Archduke Ferdinand had on European countries.   [1]

_____

_____

Score ▢

Document 9

Europe, 1914

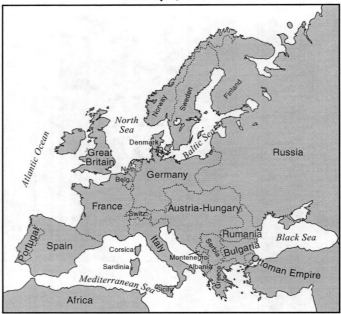

Europe, 1923

Source: Abraham and Pfeffer, *Enjoying World History*, AMSCO
(adapted)

9 Based on these maps, what was **one** change to the political boundaries of Europe that occurred after World War I? [1]

_____

_____

Score

Part B
Essay

Directions: Write a well-organized essay that includes an introduction, several paragraphs, and a conclusion. Use evidence from *at least four* documents in your essay. Support your response with relevant facts, examples, and details. Include additional outside information.

Historical Context:

Turning points are events that result in regional and worldwide change. Three turning points that transformed societies and regions were the **outbreak of the bubonic plague,** the **signing of the Nanjing Treaty,** and the **assassination of Archduke Ferdinand.**

Task: Using the information from the documents and your knowledge of global history, write an essay in which you

> Select *two* turning points mentioned in the historical context and for *each*
> - Describe the historical circumstances surrounding this turning point
> - Discuss changes that occurred within a society and/or region as a result of this turning point

Guidelines:

In your essay, be sure to

- Develop all aspects of the task
- Incorporate information from *at least four* documents
- Incorporate relevant outside information
- Support the theme with relevant facts, examples, and details
- Use a logical and clear plan of organization, including an introduction and a conclusion that are beyond a restatement of the theme

GLOBAL HISTORY AND GEOGRAPHY
AUGUST 2014

Part I

Answer all questions in this part.

Directions (1–50): For each statement or question, record on your separate answer sheet the *number* of the word or expression that, of those given, best completes the statement or answers the question.

1 Which feature is considered a natural barrier?

(1) Great Rift Valley
(2) Aswan Dam
(3) Panama Canal
(4) Great Wall of China

2 A library's holdings include the following title: *A Forgotten Kingdom, Being a Record of the results obtained from the excavation of two mounds, Atchana and Al Mina, in the Turkish Hatay.*

Which field of study would have been most responsible for conducting the excavation?

(1) economics
(2) sociology
(3) archaeology
(4) political science

3 Which practice is closely associated with most ancient river valley civilizations?

(1) recording events in cave paintings
(2) using irrigation systems
(3) developing democratic traditions
(4) spreading monotheistic religious customs

4 Which achievement played an important role in pre-Columbian Mesoamerican civilizations?

(1) use of gunpowder
(2) production of corn
(3) domestication of horses
(4) development of sugar plantations

5 One way in which filial piety in Confucian China and citizenship in ancient Athens are similar is that both

(1) emphasized duties and responsibilities in society
(2) encouraged the development of advanced technology
(3) promoted respect for the physical environment
(4) required that legalist principles be followed

Base your answers to questions 6 and 7 on the passage below and on your knowledge of social studies.

… It was during the Arab period, particularly under the Umayyads (756–1031), that Qurtubah [Cordova] enjoyed its prime and grandeur and took its place as the most civilized city in Western Europe. None of the other Spanish historic cities — Toledo, Seville, and Granada — approached it in material prosperity and intellectual attainments. When Christendom was deep in its Dark Ages, Moslem Cordova was rearing men, evolving ideas, writing books, erecting buildings, and producing works of art that constituted a unique civilization. In the West it had one peer in Constantinople and in the East another, Baghdad. At no time before or after did any Spanish city enjoy such distinction.…

— Philip K. Hitti, *Capital Cities of Arab Islam*

6 Based on this passage, what is a major criterion used to measure the distinctive civilization found in Cordova?

(1) unique religious beliefs
(2) distance from Baghdad
(3) intellectual achievements
(4) depth of the Dark Ages

7 Which term is best illustrated using this passage?

(1) golden age
(2) divine right
(3) spheres of influence
(4) global interdependence

8 Which group used the stirrup, skilled horsemanship, and siege warfare techniques to conquer much of Asia and part of Europe in the 12th and 13th centuries?

(1) Japanese
(2) Vikings
(3) Persians
(4) Mongols

Base your answer to question 9 on the map below and on your knowledge of social studies.

The Asian Migrations 800–600 BC

The Chinese Empire in 800 BC

Eurasian nomads, driven westwards by increasing Chinese pressure, 800–600 BC

The general direction of nomad migrations, 800–500 BC

Possible area of scattered Slav settlement by about 600 BC

Source: Martin Gilbert, *Atlas of Russian History*, Oxford University Press, 1993 (adapted)

9 Which conclusion can best be inferred from the information on this map?

(1) The peoples of Europe and Southwest Asia were influenced by Eurasian nomads.
(2) Significant amounts of trade took place between Asia and Europe.
(3) African culture was shaped by Asian migration.
(4) The peoples of Southeast Asia migrated to South Asia.

Base your answer to question 10 on the map below and on your knowledge of social studies.

Trade Routes in the Indian Ocean, ca. AD 500–1000

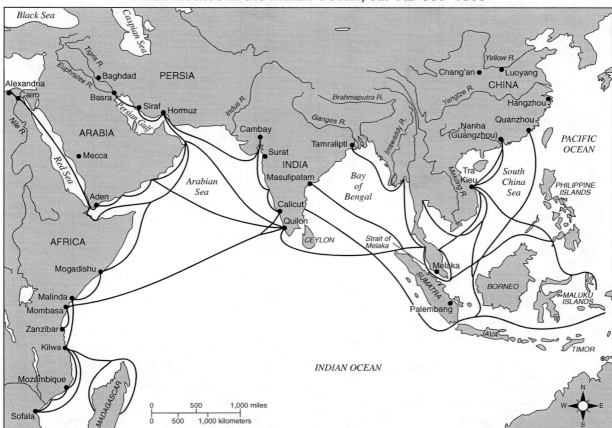

Source: Maps.com (adapted)

10 Based on the information on this map, which statement is a valid conclusion?

(1) Indian Ocean trade existed before the European Age of Exploration.
(2) African cities were isolated from overseas trade.
(3) The Indian Ocean trade network ended in A.D. 1000.
(4) These trade routes united the Western Hemisphere.

---

11 Which statement concerning the influence of geography on Japan is most accurate?

(1) Widespread mineral deposits led Japan to industrialize before England.
(2) The lack of natural barriers made it easy to conquer Japan.
(3) Large tracts of arable land made Japan a leading agricultural exporter.
(4) Japan's location allowed selective borrowing from China.

12 Mansa Musa's pilgrimage to Mecca demonstrates that he practiced

(1) animism   (3) Islam
(2) Sikhism   (4) Buddhism

13 Which geographic region made up much of the Ottoman Empire?

(1) Scandinavia
(2) Iberian Peninsula
(3) Indian Subcontinent
(4) eastern Mediterranean Basin

14 During the rise of capitalism in Europe, merchants and bankers began to establish

(1) systems based on bartering
(2) rules that forbid loans to the wealthy
(3) quotas to control production
(4) insurance companies and joint stock companies

15 • Johannes Gutenberg
   • King Henry VIII
   • John Calvin

Which event in European history was most directly influenced by these individuals?

(1) Reconquista
(2) Glorious Revolution
(3) Protestant Reformation
(4) trans-Atlantic slave trade

16 Which situation came *first*?

(1) Spain introduced the encomienda system.
(2) Portugal claimed Brazil.
(3) Spain and Portugal competed for colonies in the Americas.
(4) Columbus arrived in the Caribbean region.

17 The term *mercantilism* is best described as

(1) an economic policy in which a colonial power controls trade
(2) an international policy of laissez-faire economics
(3) a network linking industrialized nations
(4) an exchange of land between nobles

18 Which characteristic is associated with the rule of both Akbar the Great and Suleiman the Magnificent?

(1) promoting equal rights for women
(2) expanding the role of legislative bodies
(3) forcing the conversion of citizens to Christianity
(4) practicing religious tolerance toward members of society

19 Historians frequently portray Louis XIV's construction of the palace of Versailles and Peter the Great's building of the city of Saint Petersburg as

(1) shrines to religious beliefs
(2) monuments to personal rule
(3) examples of colonial architectural influences
(4) efforts to isolate and protect the ruler

20 One way in which the Scientific Revolution and the Enlightenment are similar is that both

(1) led to increased power for royal families in Europe
(2) sought to reconcile Christian beliefs and science
(3) questioned traditional values and past practices
(4) promoted nationalistic revolutions in eastern Europe

Base your answer to question 21 on the passage below and on your knowledge of social studies.

> … We must ask ourselves three questions.
> 1. What is the Third Estate? *Everything.*
> 2. What has it been until now in the political order? *Nothing.*
> 3. What does it want to be? *Something.* …
>
> — Abbé Sieyès, 1789 (adapted)

21 Based on this passage, what did the Third Estate want?

(1) independence from France
(2) more influence in the political system
(3) removal of the monarchy
(4) freedom of religion in France

22 Adam Smith's *Wealth of Nations* stressed the importance of

(1) tradition
(2) supply and demand
(3) large corporations
(4) government ownership

23 Which social change occurred during the Industrial Revolution?

(1) growth of the working class
(2) development of the extended family
(3) expansion of privileges for the landed nobility
(4) increased status for religious leaders

24 During the 1800s, many Latin American countries were characterized by a

(1) reliance on cash crops
(2) transition to command economies
(3) redistribution of land to the peasants
(4) withdrawal from the world market

Base your answer to question 25 on the poem below and on your knowledge of social studies.

Colonizer's Logic

These natives are unintelligent —
We can't understand their language.

Chinweizu (Nigeria)

— *Voices from Twentieth-Century Africa*:
Griots and Towncriers

25 The "logic" of the colonizers described in this Nigerian poem reflects their

(1) utopian plan
(2) educational goals
(3) militaristic behavior
(4) ethnocentric attitude

26 Which description of trade patterns best represents the relationship between Africa and Europe during the late 19th century?

(1) Trans-Saharan trade caravans led by Europeans were the most profitable.
(2) South Africa was of no interest to European traders.
(3) Raw materials were shipped from Africa to European industries.
(4) Rivers were the key highways connecting Europeans to much of the African interior.

Base your answer to question 27 on the cartoon below and on your knowledge of social studies.

Source: Abraham and Pfeffer, *Enjoying World History*, Amsco School Publications

27 This cartoon suggests that political power is often acquired through

(1) the inheritance of land
(2) market demands
(3) religious conversion
(4) the use of technology

28 One way in which the government under Czar Nicholas II of Russia and the government under Benito Mussolini of Italy are similar is that both governments

(1) liberated the serfs and industrial workers
(2) reformed the executive branch by incorporating theocratic principles
(3) established policies of censorship and repression
(4) used televised propaganda to rally the masses

29 The movement to establish a Jewish homeland in Palestine is best known as

(1) Zionism   (3) Marxism
(2) multi-culturalism   (4) militarism

Base your answer to question 30 on the cartoon below and on your knowledge of social studies.

THE BOILING POINT.

Source: Leonard Raven-Hill, *Punch*, October 2, 1912

30 This 1912 cartoon depicts
 (1) efforts to contain the Boxer Rebellion
 (2) tensions in pre–World War I Europe
 (3) reactions to the Bolshevik Revolution
 (4) responses to the rise of the Weimar Republic

31 A primary objective of the New Economic Policy (NEP) in the Soviet Union was to
 (1) promote private ownership of heavy industry
 (2) organize support for educational reforms to improve literacy
 (3) coordinate efforts to end World War I
 (4) gain stability by increasing production

32 Ho Chi Minh and Jomo Kenyatta were leaders of movements that were attempting to achieve
 (1) nuclear disarmament   (3) pan-Africanism
 (2) self-determination   (4) collective security

Base your answer to question 33 on the passage below and on your knowledge of social studies.

… Whatever we may wish or hope, and whatever course of action we may decide, whatever be the views held as to the legality, or the humanity, or the military wisdom and expediency [advisability] of such operations, there is not the slightest doubt that in the next war both sides will send their aircraft out without scruple [hesitation] to bomb those objectives which they consider the most suitable….
— H. Trenchard, Marshal of the Royal Air Force, 1928

33 This passage implies that the author is
 (1) grateful for the availability of new weapons
 (2) aware that new weapons have broadened the theater of war
 (3) certain that there will be no future wars
 (4) anxious about the legality of future military operations

Base your answer to question 34 on the excerpt below and on your knowledge of social studies.

… We have already said that there are only three ways left to Japan to escape from the pressure of surplus population. We are like a great crowd of people packed into a small and narrow room, and there are only three doors through which we might escape, namely, emigration, advance into world markets, and expansion of territory. The first door, emigration, has been barred to us by the anti-Japanese immigration policies of other countries. The second door, advance into world markets, is being pushed shut by tariff barriers and the abrogation [cancellation] of commercial treaties. What should Japan do when two of the three doors have been closed against her? It is quite natural that Japan should rush upon the last remaining door….
— Hashimoto Kingorō, 1939 Speech

34 The author of this excerpt is presenting an argument for Japan to follow a policy of
 (1) self-restraint
 (2) isolation
 (3) urbanization
 (4) economic imperialism

Base your answers to questions 35 and 36 on the cartoon below and on your knowledge of social studies.

**'By Government Decree Every Member of the
Commune Is Entitled to a Private Lot'**

Source: Edmund Valtman, *Hartford Times,* March 9, 1961 (adapted)

35 The main purpose of this 1961 cartoon is to

(1) criticize Chinese government policy   (3) reinforce Chinese government propaganda
(2) praise Chinese government leaders   (4) question Chinese government spending

36 The Chinese communes referred to in this 1961 cartoon are most closely associated with the

(1) Hundred Flowers Campaign   (3) Cultural Revolution
(2) Great Leap Forward   (4) Four Modernizations

37 Which event was the primary reason the United Nations called for a Convention on the Prevention and Punishment of Genocide in 1948?

(1) Bosnian massacres
(2) killing fields in Cambodia
(3) Holocaust
(4) Hutu-Tutsi conflict

38 In the post–World War II period, which issue is most closely associated with the boundaries created for newly independent African countries?

(1) expansion of urban centers
(2) ethnic tensions
(3) spread of AIDS
(4) drought-related famine

Base your answer to question 39 on the photograph below and on your knowledge of social studies.

Telephone Kiosk, South Africa

Source: Bentley and Ziegler, *Traditions & Encounters: A Global Perspective on the Past*, McGraw-Hill, 2003 (adapted)

39 Which policy is represented in this photograph?

(1) perestroika   (3) détente
(2) apartheid   (4) extraterritoriality

40 Geopolitics play an important role in the Middle East today because of its

(1) fertile soil and favorable climate for cash crops
(2) navigable rivers and diamond mines
(3) effective natural barriers and high altitude
(4) strategic location and oil resources

41 • Over farming and overgrazing on marginal lands
   • Extended droughts in the Sahel region
   • Wind erosion of topsoil

These situations have all contributed to

(1) population growth in Southwest Asia
(2) deforestation in South America
(3) desertification in sub-Saharan Africa
(4) increased reliance on fossil fuels in Asia

42 "Indira Gandhi Becomes Prime Minister of India" (1966)

"Corazon Aquino Becomes First Elected Leader of Philippines" (1986)

"Benazir Bhutto Becomes Prime Minister of Pakistan" (1988)

These headlines indicate that women as leaders

(1) have gained some political power in traditionally patriarchal societies
(2) have attained key positions in a wide variety of industries
(3) were banned from political roles during the 20th century
(4) were limited to one term in office

43 Which description best fits the Neolithic Revolution?

(1) moving from urban centers to rural centers
(2) using petrochemical fertilizers and pesticides to increase production
(3) replacing human laborers with machines
(4) shifting from hunting and gathering to farming as a way of life

44 What was an important strategy used by both the Romans and the Incas to unify their empires?

(1) building a large network of roads and bridges
(2) using powerful navies to protect sea trade routes
(3) supporting free-market economies by minting silver coins
(4) granting citizenship and voting rights to conquered peoples

Base your answer to question 45 on the graphic organizer below and on your knowledge of social studies.

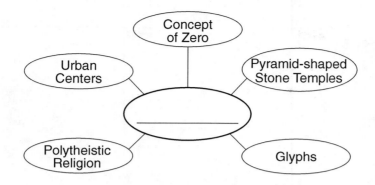

45 What is the best title for this graphic organizer?
   (1) Features of Hellenistic Culture
   (2) Achievements in Medieval Europe
   (3) Developments in Czarist Russia
   (4) Characteristics of Maya Civilization

46 A study of the Gupta Empire would include information about
   (1) Egyptian conquests
   (2) Muslim architectural influences
   (3) medical and mathematical achievements
   (4) the British East India Company's trading posts

47 • Zheng He's seven voyages are sponsored by the government.
   • Corn and peanuts are introduced into the people's diet.
   • The Forbidden City is built in Beijing.

   Which time period is associated with these statements?
   (1) Ming dynasty
   (2) Tokugawa shogunate
   (3) rule of Kublai Khan
   (4) Japanese annexation of Korea

48 The 1453 conquest of Constantinople is an important turning point in global history because it
   (1) ushered in Pax Romana
   (2) began the Middle Ages
   (3) contributed to the rise of the Ottoman Empire
   (4) signified the end of the Napoleonic Wars

49 One way in which Karl Marx, Vladimir Lenin, and Fidel Castro are similar is that each believed in
   (1) supporting a capitalist system
   (2) preserving a rigid social system
   (3) spreading the teachings of Christianity
   (4) achieving change through revolution

Base your answer to question 50 on the map below and on your knowledge of social studies.

The World in 1930

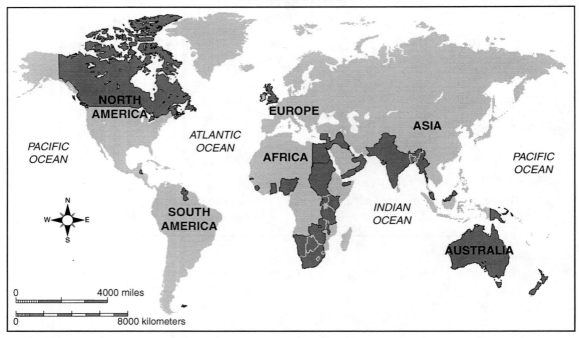

50 What do the *dark-gray* areas on this map represent?

   (1) the British Empire

   (2) countries attending the Congress of Vienna

   (3) newly independent French colonies

   (4) members of the Hanseatic League

Answers to the essay questions are to be written in the separate essay booklet.

In developing your answer to Part II, be sure to keep these general definitions in mind:

(a) **describe** means "to illustrate something in words or tell about it"

(b) **explain** means "to make plain or understandable; to give reasons for or causes of; to show the logical development or relationships of"

(c) **discuss** means "to make observations about something using facts, reasoning, and argument; to present in some detail"

Part II

THEMATIC ESSAY QUESTION

Directions: Write a well-organized essay that includes an introduction, several paragraphs addressing the task below, and a conclusion.

Theme: Change—Political Leaders

> Political leaders have come to power under a variety of circumstances. Once in power, these leaders implemented policies and practices that have affected people, societies, and regions in different ways.

Task:

> Select *two* political leaders and for *each*
> - Describe the historical circumstances that brought this political leader to power
> - Explain *one* policy or practice that was put into effect under this leader
> - Discuss how this policy or practice affected a specific group of people or society or region

You may use any political leader from your study of global history and geography. Some suggestions you may wish to consider include Shi Huangdi in China, William and Mary in England, Napoleon Bonaparte in France, Emperor Meiji in Japan, Vladimir Lenin in Russia, Jawaharlal Nehru in India, Fidel Castro in Cuba, Ayatollah Khomeini in Iran, and Nelson Mandela in South Africa.

You are *not* limited to these suggestions.

Do *not* use political leaders from the United States in your answer.

Guidelines:

> **In your essay, be sure to**
> - Develop all aspects of the task
> - Support the theme with relevant facts, examples, and details
> - Use a logical and clear plan of organization, including an introduction and a conclusion that are beyond a restatement of the theme

Part III

DOCUMENT-BASED QUESTION

This question is based on the accompanying documents. The question is designed to test your ability to work with historical documents. Some of these documents have been edited for the purposes of this question. As you analyze the documents, take into account the source of each document and any point of view that may be presented in the document. Keep in mind that the language used in a document may reflect the historical context of the time in which it was written.

Historical Context:

> *Armed conflict*, *disease*, and *child labor* have affected children throughout the world. Governments, groups, and individuals have attempted to reduce the effects of these global issues on children.

Task: Using the information from the documents and your knowledge of global history, answer the questions that follow each document in Part A. Your answers to the questions will help you write the Part B essay in which you will be asked to

---

Select *two* global issues mentioned in the historical context and for *each*
- Describe the effects of the global issue on children
- Discuss how governments, groups, and/or individuals have attempted to reduce the effects of this global issue on children

---

Do *not* make the United States the focus of your essay.

In developing your answers to Part III, be sure to keep these general definitions in mind:

(a) <u>describe</u> means "to illustrate something in words or tell about it"
(b) <u>discuss</u> means "to make observations about something using facts, reasoning, and argument; to present in some detail"

Part A
Short-Answer Questions

Directions: Analyze the documents and answer the short-answer questions that follow each document in the space provided.

Document 1

The Toll of War
(Child victims of armed conflicts, 1990s)

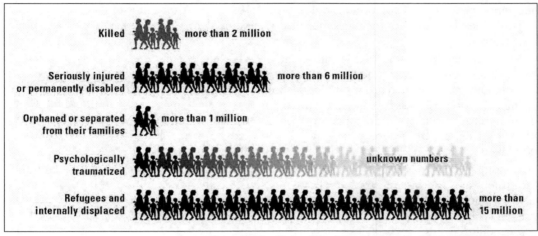

Source: *The State of the World's Children, 2000,* UNICEF (adapted)

1 Based on the information in this chart, state *one* way a child's life may be changed as a result of armed conflicts.   [1]

_____

_____

Score [ ]

Document 2

Child Soldiers

> To commemorate our 25th anniversary, The Advocates for Human Rights would like to dedicate this issue of Rights Sites News to the abolition of one of the worst forms of child labor, child soldiers. When armed conflict exists, children will almost inevitably become involved as soldiers. In over twenty countries around the world, children are direct participants in war. Denied a childhood and often subjected to horrific violence, an estimated 200,000 to 300,000 children are serving as soldiers for both rebel groups and government forces in current armed conflicts. These young combatants participate in all aspects of contemporary warfare. They wield AK-47s and M-16s on the front lines of combat, serve as human mine detectors, participate in suicide missions, carry supplies, and act as spies, messengers or lookouts.
>
> Physically vulnerable and easily intimidated, children typically make obedient soldiers. Many are abducted or recruited by force, and often compelled to follow orders under threat of death. Others join armed groups out of desperation. As society breaks down during conflict, leaving children no access to school, driving them from their homes, or separating them from family members, many children perceive armed groups as their best chance for survival. Others seek escape from poverty or join military forces to avenge family members who have been killed....
>
> Despite progress achieved over the last decade in the global campaign to end the recruitment and use of child soldiers, large numbers of children continue to be exploited in war and placed in the line of fire. The international treaty on child soldiers, the *Optional Protocol to the Convention on the Rights of the Child on the involvement of children in armed conflict*, entered into force on February 12, 2002. With over 100 countries signed on, this treaty is a milestone in the campaign, strengthening the legal protection of children and helping to prevent their use in armed conflict....

Source: "Child Soldiers Edition," *Rights Sites News*, The Advocates for Human Rights, Spring 2008

2a According to the Advocates for Human Rights, what is **one** problem faced by child soldiers? [1]

_____

_____

Score ☐

b According to the Advocates for Human Rights, what is **one** effort that has been made to keep children, or former child soldiers, from being used in armed conflict? [1]

_____

_____

Score ☐

Document 3

NEW YORK, 4 April 2006 — Ridding the world of landmines and other explosive remnants of war could be accomplished in years instead of decades, saving thousands of children from devastating injuries and death, UNICEF said today on the first International Day for Mine Awareness and Assistance in Mine Action....

Landmines are designed to disable, immobilize or kill people travelling by foot or in motor vehicles. Other explosive remnants of war include unexploded ordnance — weapons such as grenades and cluster bombs that did not explode on impact but can still detonate — and weapons that are discarded in civilian areas by combatants, known as abandoned ordnance. These munitions outlast the conflicts during which they were planted and become hazards for innocent civilians, particularly for unsuspecting children who often make the fatal mistake of playing with the unfamiliar objects....

Children suffer debilitating physical injuries from mine explosions, often losing fingers, toes and limbs. Some are left blind or deaf. An estimated 85 per cent of child victims die before they can get medical attention. Many disabled victims lose opportunities to go to school, and often cannot afford rehabilitative care. The persisting threat of mines takes its toll on entire societies, perpetuating poverty and underdevelopment....

More than three-quarters of the world's nations have ratified the Mine Ban Treaty since it came into force in 1999, outlawing the production, stockpiling and use of antipersonnel landmines. According to the International Campaign to Ban Landmines, the number of countries thought to be producing, stockpiling and using landmines has dropped significantly over the last decade....

UNICEF supports and implements mine action activities in over 30 countries, and believes that mine-risk education is key to preventing the death and disabling of children. Through programmes brought to their schools and communities, children are taught how to live safely in areas contaminated with landmines and other explosive remnants of war....

Source: "Saving Children from the Tragedy of Landmines," UNICEF Press Release, April 4, 2006

3a What is **one** problem land mines or unexploded ordnance cause for children, according to UNICEF?   [1]

_____

_____

Score ☐

b What is **one** effort being made to reduce the effects of land mines or unexploded ordnance, according to UNICEF? [1]

_____

_____

Score ☐

Document 4

Deaths to Children Under 5, by Cause, 2000–2003

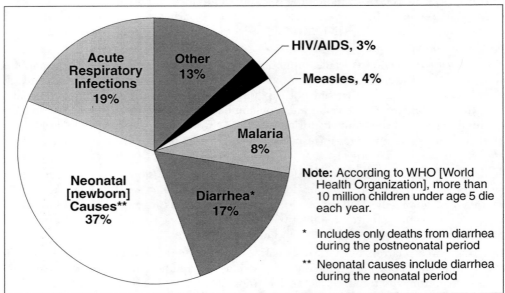

Source: *World Health Report*, World Health Organization, 2005 (adapted)

4 As shown in this World Health Organization chart of children who died under the age of five, identify **one** health issue that caused more than 15% of the deaths.   [1]

_____

_____

Score ☐

Document 5

… Millions of children in developing nations die from diseases like pneumonia, measles and diarrhea that claim twice as many lives each year as AIDS. Vaccines prevent these basic illnesses. Bill Gates pledges billions of dollars to vaccinate the world's children. Problem solved. But it's not that easy.

Money alone won't rid dirty water of parasites that can blind and cripple. It won't fix bad roads that keep people from getting care. It won't end the political corruption and violent unrest that erase health advances. It won't stop a population explosion that contributes to poor health. It can't even prevent a rat from gnawing through the power cord of a refrigerator used to store vaccines in a remote West African clinic.…

In late 1998, Gates donated $100 million to create a program dedicated to getting new and underused vaccines to children in the poorest countries. A year later, he gave a stunning $750 million to help launch a new superstructure for improving childhood vaccinations, the Global Alliance for Vaccines and Immunization (GAVI)—a coalition of international public health agencies, philanthropists and the pharmaceutical industry.…

Gates knows that vaccines can't do it all, not when a regional hospital in Nigeria draws its water from an open pit in the ground. Or where a 6-year-old Ivory Coast boy with a leg twisted by polio faces a life of begging because his mother couldn't afford a trip to a clinic for vaccines. Or where a broken board on a bridge can halt the shipment of medicine for days.…

Source: Tom Paulson, "Bill Gates' war on disease, poverty is an uphill battle,"
Seattle Post-Intelligencer, March 21, 2001

5a According to Tom Paulson, what is *one* situation that makes it difficult to reduce childhood diseases in developing nations? [1]

_____

_____

Score ☐

b According to Tom Paulson, what is *one* way money donated by Bill Gates has been used to help reduce childhood diseases in developing nations? [1]

_____

_____

Score ☐

Document 6

...Doctors Without Borders/Medecins Sans Frontieres (MSF) [a non-profit medical organization] has witnessed firsthand how a lack of medicine for treatable infectious disease destroys many lives in the developing world. In response, MSF has launched the Access to Essential Medicines Campaign. Introduced in November 1999, the MSF campaign has been working worldwide to find long-lasting solutions to this crisis. The campaign has four main goals: to increase access to certain medicines; to support high quality local manufacture and import of less expensive medicines; to implement and apply international trade rules regarding medicines; and to bring together governments, the pharmaceutical industry, and organizations to focus on investment in, research on, and development of essential medicines for neglected disease....

Source: Catherine Gevert, "A Lack of Medicine," *Faces*, March, 2005

6 What is **one** way Doctors Without Borders/MSF hopes to reduce the occurrence of infectious diseases in the developing world, according to Catherine Gevert? [1]

_____

_____

Score ☐

Document 7

... "Tens of thousands of refugees have fled to urban areas in Pakistan since September 11, [2001], but almost all international assistance and protection efforts are focused on refugees in camps, and the situation for young Afghans in the cities is deteriorating seriously," said Jane Lowicki, Senior Coordinator, Children and Adolescents Project, who visited Pakistan in January. "Many of these refugees and the communities that are struggling to support them are wondering why help promised by the U.S. and other countries has not reached them."

With few alternatives for earning a livelihood, many Afghan refugee parents in urban areas are forcing their children to work in high-risk industries to support the household. "Thousands are carpet weavers, others are street children working as garbage pickers, beggars, brick makers, house servants and, in some cases, drug sellers," Lowicki said. "These young workers are the poorest and most desperate among the Afghan community. Their work exposes them to disease, physical and sexual abuse, and few have access to health services, education or recreation. Their situation has become even more difficult since Sept. 11 because many new young refugees have entered the competition for work, and resources are scarce."

Afghan refugee adolescents and children, some as young as five years old, are working harder than ever for less money. The formerly lucrative carpet weaving industry, for example, which relies heavily on cheap Afghan child labor, bottomed out after Sept. 11; young refugees are now being paid less than half of what they were making to weave carpets for markets around the world.

In many cases, children and adolescents are the primary wage earners for their families, and all of the young Afghan refugees interviewed for the report said they urgently need food, shelter and medical care. They also eager for a chance to go to school and to learn skills and trades to support themselves through less hazardous work....

Source: "Afghan Refugee Children and Adolescents in Pakistan's Cities Receive Minimal International Assistance,"
Women's Commission for Refugee Women and Children Press Release, May 30, 2002

7 According to the Women's Commission for Refugee Women and Children, what is *one* problem Afghan refugee children face in Pakistan?   [1]

_____

_____

Score ☐

Document 8a

This is an excerpt from a Web-only interview conducted as part of *Enterprising Ideas*, a project of *NOW on PBS*.

RugMark USA

Ten years ago [in 1994], RugMark USA was established to eradicate child labor in the handwoven rug industry. Using a unique "certification" method, RugMark USA has created a model that generates income to finance its programs for children and raises awareness among consumers about the prevalence of child labor. Nina Smith, RugMark USA's executive director, believes the RugMark model could be applied to other industries, including Brazil's shoe industry, India's silk weaving and embroidery sectors and the cocoa industry in West Africa. We talked with Smith about why the RugMark model works and what big challenges the organization is facing....

NOW [host]: Describe RugMark's strategy to change the use of child labor in the industry.

Smith: Our goal is to change the market dynamics so that there is no longer a demand for child labor. If we can educate the marketplace—consumers, interior designers, architects, importers, retailers—about what they can do then ultimately the message is sent to the manufacturers that child labor won't be tolerated—in essence eliminating the demand.

The idea has three components: First, you have to raise awareness and educate people about the problem of child labor and to look for our independently certified child-labor-free rugs. On the ground in South Asia we have an inspection and monitoring system. Companies whose rugs receive the RugMark label agree to random, surprise inspections at their factories or village-based looms....

Source: "RugMark USA," *NOW on PBS: Enterprising Ideas,* July 26, 2007

8a According to Nina Smith, what is **one** way RugMark USA is attempting to end the use of and eliminate the demand for child labor?   [1]

_____

_____

Score ☐

Document 8b

This is an advertisement RugMark used in its campaign to raise awareness about carpets and rugs made with child labor.

THE SINGLE MOST BEAUTIFUL THING ABOUT AN IMPORTED RUG.

Nearly 300,000 children are exploited as child labor in the carpet industry. This has to end, and it will. RugMark is the international organization devoted to building the schools, programs and opportunities that give children back their childhood. It's working, from Pakistan to India to Nepal, and you can help. Look for the certified and numbered RugMark label on the back of an imported rug. It's your best assurance that no children were exploited in the manufacture of the carpet you're buying. Because an imported rug that was made using child labor is ugly no matter what it looks like.

Source: www.rugmark.org (adapted)

8b According to this advertisement, what is **one** action RugMark has taken to improve the lives of children? [1]

_____

_____

Score ☐

Document 9

Give a "Red Card* to Child Labour"
in celebration of the World Day Against Child Labour 2006!

… The day, which is observed worldwide on the 12th of June, is intended to serve as a catalyst for the growing worldwide movement against child labour, as reflected in the 160 ratifications of Convention No. 182 on the worst forms of child labour and the 144 ratifications of Convention No. 138 on the minimum age for employment. The event on 12 June will be celebrated with the presence of football [soccer] stars that will "kick the ball" against child labour, in a match with girls from the Geneva International School and the Signal de Bernex Football Club. The idea behind the game is that girls and boys should be given the time to study and play, and that child labour and its worst forms symbolically get a "red card". This action is linked to the "Red card to child labour" campaign which since its inception in 2002 has reached thousands of people in all continents. The idea is that the values in football, such as, team spirit, youth empowerment, solidarity among countries, non-discrimination regarding religion, gender and race, are also shared by the ILO [International Labour Organization]. Using the symbol of the Red Card at International football competitions offers the opportunity to spread one simple, universal message over time and benefits from media coverage. Building this kind of strategic alliance is a very good way to reinforce the global movement against child labour.

Source: "Celebration of the World Day Against Child Labour," The International Programme on the Elimination of Child Labour of the International Labour Organization, June 2006

* A red card is issued to remove a player from a game for committing a serious violation.

9 Based on this excerpt from a brochure, what are *two* actions that have been taken to aid in the elimination of child labor? [2]

(1)_____

_____

Score ☐

(2)_____

_____

Score ☐

Part B
Essay

Directions: Write a well-organized essay that includes an introduction, several paragraphs, and a conclusion. Use evidence from *at least four* documents in your essay. Support your response with relevant facts, examples, and details. Include additional outside information.

Historical Context:

> **Armed conflict**, **disease**, and **child labor** have affected children throughout the world. Governments, groups, and individuals have attempted to reduce the effects of these global issues on children.

Task: Using the information from the documents and your knowledge of global history, write an essay in which you

> Select *two* global issues mentioned in the historical context and for *each*
> - Describe the effects of the global issue on children
> - Discuss how governments, groups, and/or individuals have attempted to reduce the effects of this global issue on children

Do *not* make the United States the focus of your essay.

Guidelines:

In your essay, be sure to
- Develop all aspects of the task
- Incorporate information from *at least four* documents
- Incorporate relevant outside information
- Support the theme with relevant facts, examples, and details
- Use a logical and clear plan of organization, including an introduction and a conclusion that are beyond a restatement of the theme